Let My Children Go

E. Ray Moore, Jr., Th.M.

E. Ray Moore, Jr., has served 26 years in ministry as a pastor, as a Director of a Christian ministry, and as a U.S. Army Reserve Chaplain (Lt. Colonel.). He is a veteran of the Gulf War where he was awarded the Bronze Star Medal. He was placed on retired status with US Army Reserve in 1999.

He is a graduate of Grace Theological Seminary, Winona Lake, Indiana, having earned the Master of Divinity (cum laude) in 1974 and the Master of Theology in 1979.

He has been married to the former Gail Laurens Pinckney of Charleston, SC, for 33 years. They have four children and two grandchildren. Their family has participated in either home schooling or Christian schools for 25 years, and they were chosen South Carolina Parents of the Year in 2000.

Ray is Director of the Exodus Mandate Project.

Let My Children Go is his first book.

Let My Children Go

Copyright ©2002 by
E. Ray Moore, Jr.
Chaplain (Lt. Col.)
U.S. Army Reserve Ret.

Published by Gilead Media
Columbia, SC, U.S.A.

All Bible passages are from *The Holy Bible, New King James Version,* (Nashville, Tennessee: Thomas Nelson, Inc.) 1982. Used by permission.

Editorial Assistance:	Steven Yates, Ph.D., James Rizzuti
Proofread by:	Gail Moore, Leslie Rizzuti
Typeset & Designed by:	James Rizzuti
Cover by:	Jeff Evans

Library of Congress Cataloging-in-Publication Data
Moore, Jr., E. Ray
   Let My Children Go (352 pgs.)
   ISBN#1-931600-16-3
   1. Christian schools   2. Home schooling
   3. Public schools   4. Secular humanism

Printed in the United States of America

DEDICATION

In memory of David and Ann Drye, who died June 14, 1999. "Saul and Jonathan were beloved and pleasant in their lives, and in their death they were not divided: They were swifter than eagles, they were stronger than lions ... How the mighty have fallen in the midst of the battle" (2 Samuel 1:23, 25a).

PREFACE

This book is about hope. Both the nation and the Church are in a moral and spiritual free-fall. Some despair, while others labor on, pray and hope. In Biblical history there have been other dark moments. The family and children were under attack from the Old Testament Pharaoh. The Christian home and family are under attack today.

On March 28, 2002, Christian family leader, Dr. James Dobson, on his Focus on the Family radio broadcast, stated, "In the State of California, if I had a child there, I wouldn't put the youngster in a public school.... I think it's time to get our kids out...." We are grateful to Dr. Dobson for this bold stand and hope that it encourages others to take a similar position.

Let My Children Go begins as one family's journey into hope. As the result of providing for our children home schooling and Christian schools, my wife, Gail and I have experienced "...no greater joy than to hear that our children walk in truth" (3 John 4).

Writers and theologians have gone before and helped shape my worldview on education. Several served as intellectual mentors. I am grateful to many such as Samuel

Blumenfeld, Douglas Wilson, R.J. Rushdoony, John Taylor Gatto and Murray Rothbard.

Dr. Raymond and Dorothy Moore inspired my family in our early home-schooling days through their many books. Michael Farris and the staff at Home School Legal Defense Association gave early courage and fortitude to us and many others.

In the development of the Exodus Mandate Project since 1997, I am indebted to numerous friends and coworkers. Board members Richard Cooper, Dr. Henry Jordan, and Treasurer Robert Woodwyk make our continued service possible. Without their support, we couldn't go forward.

Other coworkers as Rev. and Mrs. (Becky) Joe Morecraft, III; Rev. and Mrs. (Judy) Wayne Rogers; Brig. General and Mrs. (Shady) T.C. Pinckney; and Bobbie Ames gave us early and ongoing encouragement that we were on track with this ministry.

Caryl and Pat Matrisciana produced the video, "Let My Children Go," and have provided constant inspiration. Marshall Fritz has provided counsel and support for the Exodus Mandate Project. He also made important editorial suggestions for this book. Dan Smithwick has also provided advice and research to confirm our central thesis. We thank attorney Bruce Shortt as representative of the many volunteers for Exodus Mandate.

Dr. Steven Yates provided valuable research and editorial assistance in the preparation of the final manuscript. James Rizzuti did the final editing and book design. Christian attorney Michael Peroutka provided financial support and counsel.

Finally, my partner, Gail Moore, was proofreader and supporter. She, with our four children, has given me a life message that makes this book more than theory.

E. Ray Moore, Jr.

Let My Children Go

"I would say to you, dear friends, it may require some sacrifice, but I urge you to send your children to godly schools... to Christian schools, that they might receive a godly Christian education. If you send them off to some public school, keep in mind that you're shooting dice with your children's eternal souls. It is a gamble no Christian should be willing to make. Don't send an eight-year-old out to take on a forty-year-old humanist.... I have never seen any people more unhappy than fathers or mothers who have come to me and said, 'Where did we go wrong? We gave him everything, and now he's turned his back completely on everything we believe.' Yes, they gave him everything but a Christian education."

Dr. D. James Kennedy
Coral Ridge Ministries

"I don't want my children fed or clothed by the state, but I would prefer that to their being educated by the state."

Max Victor Belz
Grain dealer, Grundy County, Iowa

"I am sure as I am of the fact of Christ's reign that a comprehensive and centralized system of national education separated from religion, as is now commonly proposed, will prove the most appalling engine for the propagation of anti-Christian and atheistic unbelief, social and political, which this sin-rent world has ever seen."

Professor A.A. Hodge
Princeton Theological Seminary, 1887

"For over one hundred years, Americans have been running a gigantic experiment in government schools, trying to find out what a society looks like without God. Now we know."

Douglas Wilson, Author
Recovering the Lost Tools of Learning

INTRODUCTION

PUBLIC SCHOOLS IN CRISIS

WORLDVIEWS

CHRISTIANS ARE NOT POWERLESS: THE CASE FOR A NEW PARADIGM IN CHRISTIAN EDUCATION

A terrible crisis has developed in the schools to which most Americans entrust their children. On April 20, 1999, two teenage boys walked into their high school bearing lethal weapons and calmly began shooting down their fellow students. Once they had shot and killed 15 people, including a teacher, and wounded several others, they turned their guns on themselves.

PUBLIC SCHOOLS IN CRISIS

The killings at Columbine High School in Littleton, Colorado, shocked the conscience of the nation. There were detailed investigations into the lives of the two shooters, Eric Harris and Dylan Klebold, and the so-called

"Trenchcoat Mafia" to which they belonged, a loose group of chronic misfits at Columbine.

An examination of their personal websites uncovered a preoccupation with Nazi and occult themes and with mass murder. The two youths had entertained fantasies that went much further than what actually happened. They wanted to blow up their school with everyone in it. Then they wanted—of all things!—to go to the Denver Airport, hijack a plane and fly it into the World Trade Center! In this, the last of their death wishes, they provided stunning prescience of the evil that would come to America's shores two and a half years later.

The Columbine killings had a clear and very ominous, religious dimension. Several of the survivors contended that Harris and Klebold had been *singling out* students known to be Christians.

Rachel Scott was one example, very likely singled out ahead of time. Another case, one that several survivors mentioned, was that of Cassie Bernall, who hadn't been a Christian very long. One of the killers asked her point blank, "Do you believe in God?" When she replied, "Yes," without hesitation, he shot her in the face. Christian students were shot down in cold blood for their beliefs. Up until that day, Columbine had seemed to be a model public school.

A STRING OF SHOOTINGS IN PUBLIC SCHOOLS

But Columbine was only the most dramatic of a string of shootings in public schools that occurred during the 1990's, a period during which the government and the mass media were assuring Americans that the economy was doing well and that the country was on the right course.

Previous shootings had occurred in Bethel, Alaska; Pearl, Mississippi; West Paducah, Kentucky; Jonesboro, Arkansas; Edinboro, Pennsylvania; Fayetteville, Tennessee; and

Springfield, Oregon. Many were killed, many were wounded.

The public schools to which today's parents send their children are clearly not the type of places they attended themselves. When the Baby Boomers were in high school, discipline problems existed, and students sometimes got caught with marijuana in their lockers. But the idea of a pair of students harboring such intense hatred that they would gun down their fellow classmates would never have occurred to anyone.

However, these shootings are extreme cases of a more general phenomenon: today's public schools have grown increasingly violent. Many, especially in large, urban areas, have metal detectors on all their entrances.

Gangs have proliferated with rival groups both having armed themselves with guns as well as knives and ready to fight each other on a moment's notice. Many public schools in the inner-cities have banned gang insignia in an effort to stem the warfare.

INTELLECTUAL DETERIORATION

There is plenty of less frightening testimony that a terrible crisis has developed in public schools. Abundant evidence, assembled from test scores and elsewhere, assures us that today's public school graduates do not have the mastery of basic subjects that earlier generations had.

Students are leaving public high schools in record numbers without having acquired basic writing skills, reading comprehension or mathematical ability. They know little or nothing of this country's founding or its history. They cannot place major historical figures or events in the right century. They cannot walk up to wall maps and point out significant foreign countries. This intellectual deterioration has spread into public colleges and universities that have admitted more and more unprepared students into college level work. Public universities have had to expand remedial programs that did not even exist 50 years ago. Many colleges have become degree mills, where many students graduate still lacking the basic knowledge needed for intelligent participation in representative government, much less the skills for today's work place.

A FLAWED PHILOSOPHY

Tragically, many of these impaired students have adopted a flawed philosophy: They believe themselves *entitled* to good grades in school and then to a well-paying job. They have little or no interest in matters of learning. And perhaps saddest of all, if they grew up attending church with their parents, they very often stopped church attendance during their college years.

As they enter adulthood, they proceed as if a connection to anything transcending their daily life is irrelevant. Their transcendant aim is obtaining that high-tech job and taking their place in the global economy, something that doesn't always happen if they haven't developed the necessary skills.

During the 1990's, much of the country seemed to have fallen under a kind of collective hypnosis. President Bill Clinton engaged in an extramarital affair with a woman not much older than his daughter, lied under oath to cover it up, and was credibly accused of a number of other sexual indiscretions involving women (one of them a sexual assault).

The majority response seemed to be that Bill Clinton was "personally flawed but politically effective."

Many people remained convinced that all was well because, again, the economy seemed to be doing well. With their 401k accounts surging, the majority wanted no presidential change.

SEPTEMBER 11, 2001

Of course, on September 11, 2001, we received the worst possible wake-up call when terrorists who had received their training in this country reduced the twin towers of the World Trade Center and a portion of the Pentagon to rubble, killing over 3,000 people. It was the worst carnage on U.S. soil since the Battle of Antietam.

Our nation's response to the crisis has been to call for unity and begin what could prove to be a very difficult and very long war against an international terrorist network that is extremely hostile to American values.

As the country has entered this crisis, however, have we thought about where we stand as a nation? We have seen an explosion of signs reading, "God Bless America." But *has* God blessed America? Does America deserve His blessings? What has moved us from the Columbine killings to the more recent crisis?

WORLDVIEWS

Everyone has a worldview. What is a worldview? It is a general perspective on the world around us, a kind of lens through which we see people and events around us whether we are aware of those views or not. It tells us what kind of world this is, who we are, what is of value in life, and what we may hope for. Animals, such as dogs and cats, can simply exist. They do not reflect on the meaning and nature of their existence. But humans cannot thrive without some sense that there is a purpose for their existence. They need "reference points" that place events, other human beings, and the world generally, into a comprehensive framework that shapes their values, especially their moral compass, and guides their beliefs and actions.

Professional philosophers have a wide variety of "–ism" names for a multitude of theories. However, there are really just two very basic kinds of worldviews. Worldviews will either be God-centered or man-centered. Christianity, of course, is the God-centered worldview most familiar in our culture.

According to Christianity, the God who revealed Himself to man in the Bible is at the center of creation, and stands prior to everything else: "In the beginning was the Word, and the Word was with God, and the Word was God... All things were made through Him, and without Him nothing was made that was made." (John 1:1,3).[1] According to Christianity, moreover, man-centered worldviews are futile because man is a fallen being with an innate sinful nature: "for all have sinned and fall short of the glory of God" (Romans 3:23). We cannot save ourselves from this sinful condition, and we cannot build up and maintain a functional social order or any part of it, such as an educational system, unless we acknowledge the centrality of God and His will for our lives.

Then we must personally accept that the only path to true salvation is through Jesus Christ, who paid for our sins on the cross: "For by grace you have been saved through faith, and that not of yourselves; it is the gift of God, not of works, lest anyone should boast" (Ephesians 2:8-9); "For the wages of sin is death, but the gift of God is eternal life in Christ Jesus our Lord." (Romans 6:23); "For God so loved the world that He gave His only begotten Son, that whoever believes in Him should not perish but have everlasting life." (John 3:16).

The Christian's life is defined by the supernatural, personal relationship the Christian develops with Jesus Christ: "... I have come that they may have life, and that they may have it more abundantly." (John 10:10).

Humanism (or *secular humanism*) is a generic term for any of a number of man-centered worldviews that try to replace God with Man. According to humanists, the universe is self-existing and uncreated; human beings are not the children of God but the product of a long, continuous and very natural, impersonal process.

THE RELIGION OF HUMANISM

Humanists completely reject the supernatural. They have convinced themselves that humanity can dispense with God and with any transcendent source for moral values. But while they have attempted to wrap themselves in the cloak of modern science (in a fashion that would have shocked the architects of the original scientific revolution, such as Isaac Newton, who was a Christian), humanists deceive themselves if they believe they have delivered to the world anything other than an alternative faith, one that is resolutely hostile to Christianity. Occasionally, humanists have offered entirely forthright statements of what they want to do, and where they want to do it. Consider:

> I am convinced that the battle for humankind's future [the mind] must be waged [and won] in the public school classrooms by teachers who correctly perceive their role as the proselytizers of a new faith: a religion of humanity that recognizes and respects the spark of what theologians call divinity in every human being. These teachers must embody the same selfless dedication as the most rabid fundamentalist preachers, for they will be ministers of another sort, utilizing a classroom instead of a pulpit to convey humanist values in whatever subject they teach, regardless of the education level: preschool day care or large state university.
>
> The classroom must and will become an arena of conflict between the old and the new—the rotting corpse of Christianity, together with all its adjacent evils and misery, and the new faith of humanism, resplendent in its promise of

a world in which the never-realized Christian ideal of "love thy neighbor" will finally be achieved....

It will undoubtedly be a long, arduous, painful struggle replete with much sorrow and many tears, but humanism will emerge triumphant. It must if the family of humanity is to survive.[2]

This statement in one of the leading humanist publications in the country, openly acknowledges that secular humanism is a faith, a "religion of humanity," not a science, and promoting a secular humanist invasion and takeover of public schools. Public schools, the author tells us very openly, are to become the battleground between Christianity and humanism.

Constructing and propagating worldviews is not an idle, intellectual pastime pursued by academics. Clearly, worldview is a foundation. It has an impact on your life. It helps you form the ultimate convictions that you should hold and upon which you should act.

If your worldview is Christian, it will—or should—have one set of consequences. If your worldview is humanist, then other consequences will follow. An entire culture can adopt Christianity as its guiding philosophy, and this will have consequences for everyone in it. Or it can embrace man-centered humanism, and different consequences will ensue.

Neither a person nor a culture can simply be "neutral" with regard to worldviews. Both will embrace and live out a God-centered worldview or a man-centered one. If you maintain neutrality, you have already rejected the God-centered worldview and by default have embraced a man-centered one.

The history of modern secular humanism is convoluted, and beyond the scope of this book, but it will be sufficient to say for now (we will expand on this in Chapter Two) that modern secular humanism grew out of the philosophy that originated during the 18th and 19th century Enlightenment. This philosophy either tried to cast doubt on the existence of God or render the whole issue of God's existence irrelevant to man's life here on Earth.

LINK BETWEEN HUMANISM AND EVOLUTION

Secular humanism's advocates had already begun to work under the assumption that the concept of sin was not valid and, instead, that problems stemmed from bad social arrangements. They felt that a different social order would produce a "new human being."

Later, they borrowed from the theory of evolution and its suggestion that living things were continuously improving themselves.

Secular humanists came to see human nature as infinitely improvable, even perfectible. Today they work piecemeal at reforming human institutions—government, corporations, and especially education—and have made far more progress institutionalizing their worldview than the average citizen realizes.

As the previous quote spells out plainly, one of the secular humanists' main instruments for spreading their philosophy was the schools. As we will show, humanist infections in the schools began in Europe and spread to America toward the middle of the 1800's. The main vehicle for the spread of humanism in America has indeed been the public school system, and began early in our nation's history.[3]

The consequences are evident for all to see. Secular humanism tries to replace Christianity, but it does not have a credible moral framework that gives meaning and direction to individual human lives. Of course, only a personal relationship with God through Jesus Christ can provide that.

We were not created to be entirely self-sufficient, inner-directed men and women. We were created to follow the one God who is larger than ourselves. This is clear from the fact that those without God invariably follow or serve or identify with something other than themselves—be it modern science, a political movement, or simply fame and celebrity in this life. The very fact of our inability to thrive without a worldview giving our lives a sense of direction points to this need for a larger framework. But no evidence exists that the secular-humanist vision for modern society is achievable.

The most prominent effort to build up an entire society on an explicitly atheistic foundation, the Marxist Soviet Union, was the most brutal dictatorship in history and a total failure in meeting human needs.

DETERIORATION OF CHRISTIAN VALUES

Secular humanists in America have adopted a piecemeal approach to advancing their cause, removing God from the public scene a little at a time. The consequences of our ceasing to be a Christian nation have been devastating, as they have led directly to *nihilism,* the idea that neither the universe nor our own personal lives have any moral absolutes. This leads to events like the Columbine killings, as well as to a generation of lost young people who fill the emptiness in their lives and hearts with drugs, meaningless and dangerous promiscuous sexual encounters, and mindless televised entertainment, much of it graphically violent.

Humanism can also lead to the idea that the government, or the state, can save us if only citizens give it sufficient power, and that a meaningful life can be secured by conforming to its dictates. Government has become, in the eyes of many secular humanists, a kind of secular god.

It began with the public schools, or as we shall shortly be calling them, state-sponsored or state-run schools.

It is clear to nearly everyone, no matter his or her world-view, that public schools are deteriorating. We have seen endless efforts to "reform" the public schools—ranging from large scale government social engineering programs like Goals 2000 to smaller ones such as tax-funded vouchers and charter schools.

We have seen efforts to "rediscover" morality through character education, a movement many Christians are supporting. While some of these efforts are better than others, all are merely detours on the way to failure. In contrast, our assertion in this book is much bolder than to advocate more "reform."

You'll receive a complete plan of action as this book progresses. Frankly, it's the only plan that has a chance of sustainable success. And it will result in a marvelous resurgence of Christian values and worldview that will benefit our culture dramatically.

CHRISTIANS ARE NOT POWERLESS: THE CASE FOR A NEW PARADIGM IN CHRISTIAN EDUCATION

The concern expressed by many about the loss of Christian principles in our public schools is commendable. But the Christian community as a whole, especially many pastors, is unsure about what to do.

Because of a string of Supreme Court decisions dating back to the 1940's, it seems clear that a curtain has dropped on any expression of the essence of Christianity—the birth, life, crucifixion and resurrection of Jesus Christ our Lord and Savior—in the public schools.[4]

Starting with *Everson v. Board of Education* in 1947, the first case to dismiss the Bible from American public schools, the Supreme Court has stripped Christian principles and expression of them from the public school system.

Over a dozen cases have been handed down, the most recent being the *Santa Fe* decision that restricts student prayers at athletic events. While many Christians question the interpretation of the Constitution behind these rulings, they must acknowledge their reality, and accept the fact that the public schools and society at large accept them as valid. Such rulings are now so embedded in Supreme Court jurisprudence as to be practically irreversible, at least in the near future. They have become the worldview and law of the land.

What is important to realize is that the Christian community is not powerless in the face of these rulings. It is one thing to protest, but protests are unlikely to achieve any helpful result. It is one thing to advocate reform in the public schools, but so far, all reforms have failed.

FORMULATING A PLAN OF ACTION

What is needed is a plan that can be translated into action on the part of Christian educators, Christian parents and their pastors.

This book's purpose is to present that plan. The time has come for Christian parents to abandon the state-sponsored public-school system in favor of home schooling and participation in the development of networks of private, Christian schools, many of them based out of churches. This alone can resurrect the God-centered worldview and place it at the center of the education of our children.

In other words, we want this book to inaugurate a new way for thinking about education in American society, and precipitate a paradigm shift in the thinking of Christians about how they educate their children. This concept, that of a paradigm, is important to understand. The term gained currency following Thomas S. Kuhn's use of it in one of the most important books of the past half-century, *The Structure of Scientific Revolutions.*[5] Paradigms are not worldviews; it is more accurate to say that paradigms presuppose worldviews. Paradigms have more to do with concrete problem-solving strategies, actual achievements and plans for action.

The current paradigm for thinking about education in American society, even among the majority of Christians, simply takes for granted the idea that "free" public schools are necessary, and that even if the public schools have some problems those problems can be fixed with the right reforms. There is no room in this paradigm for the possibility that the public schools simply cannot be fixed and ought to be abandoned. Yet this is exactly what we will maintain in this book.

Our current situation and adherence to Biblical principles both call for something much more radical than advocating reform. In the paradigm for Christian education we will develop in this book, public schools—state-sponsored schools—cannot be reformed and should be abandoned in favor of home schooling and private Christian schools where a God-centered worldview animates the entire curriculum. According to Scripture, God actually commands us to do this.

ACCESS TO THE MINDS OF THE YOUNG

Educating the next generation is of crucial importance. The secular humanists, as we will also see very shortly, realized very early in our country's history the importance of gaining control of the schools in order to gain access to the minds of the young. The creation of the state-sponsored school was central to this effort.

It will be important for Christians to realize that state-sponsored schools were never a component of this country's original heritage, as defined by the Founding Fathers. The U.S. Constitution never mentions education, and it never authorized the government to set up and run schools. The state-sponsored school system and the acceptance of it by Christian parents is a kind of hypnosis produced by the modern paradigm of education that takes public schools for granted. The time has come to reject this paradigm, reject the secular humanist worldview behind it, and take back our children.

OUR MISSION AS CHRISTIAN EDUCATORS

It is important to stress, then, that *we are not trying to reform the public schools. Nor are we trying, in any sense, to "take them over."* Our mission as Christian educators must be nothing less than complete independence from the state-sponsored educational system. We believe that carrying forth this mission could be an important strategy in reversing our present moral and cultural decline and restoring the moral foundation of this nation.

This is, of course, an ambitious order. It must be approached prayerfully, with God's Word, the Bible, firmly before us. Most Christians, like most Americans generally, are accustomed to public schools and just consider them part of the landscape of American life. This is because of the dominant paradigm, which takes state-sponsored education for granted as necessary.

Many Christians compartmentalize their faith; that is, they don't allow Scripture to address certain areas. Still, Scriptural Law is written to be obeyed. One area Christians have historically and tragically compartmentalized has been the education of their children, so we will take a look at specific Biblical instructions (in Deuteronomy, Matthew's Gospel and elsewhere) regarding the education of children.

What we will discover is that God assigned responsibility for education to the family, with assistance from the Church. When secular humanism came to be the dominant worldview among the educational intelligentsia of our society and when the necessity of state-sponsored education became the dominant paradigm, even among Christians, the government—federal, state and local—was able to usurp the responsibility of the family and the Church. The government, however, has no God-ordained role in education any more than it has a constitutional role.

ABANDONING GOVERNMENT SCHOOLS
We therefore advocate, with solid Scriptural foundation, that Christians abandon rather than attempt to reform public schools. We believe our call to Christians to leave public schools in favor of home schooling and private Christian schooling is based on Scripture, the historical American constitutional model, sound, Bible-based educational philosophy, and also free-market principles. We will not convince Congress with this argument, or even local school boards.

But we will make progress with Christians, helping them to rebuild their worldview and find their way back to Biblical and constitutional thinking which calls for them to remove their children from public schools and begin home schooling or placing them in private Christian schools.

Can we do this? It is a matter of taking the necessary steps and then trusting God.

We have a powerful precedent in Moses. Moses began his career as a man of no special importance until God spoke to him and commanded him to lead the Jewish people out of bondage in Egypt. Instead of fearing the wrath of Pharaoh, he trusted God. He went before Pharaoh and told him, "Let my people go!"

We have our modern Pharaoh: the federal government and the entire system of state-sponsored schooling. Moreover, we are at a crucial juncture in our history because the situation for Christians in public schools is getting progressively worse, and will get worse still.

I believe God is speaking to us today, just as He spoke to Moses.

The only question is, will we follow the path that Moses followed, or will we continue to follow our own paths, compartmentalize our lives, ruin the education of our children and endanger the next generation?

If we follow the lead of Moses, it means removing our children from Pharaoh's school system and taking them to the Promised Land of private home schooling and Christian schools.

SETTING FORTH A FOUNDATION

This book, then, attempts to set forth the foundation of what we hope will lead to a major paradigm shift in education in American society. Paradigm shifts, as Thomas S. Kuhn explained, are unpredictable.

We cannot claim to have addressed every problem that will come up or answered every question that can be asked.

All of us are fallible, sinful human beings. The most Christians can claim is eternal salvation and a relationship with Jesus Christ. We believe, therefore, that this is what we, as Christian citizens and parents, are commanded to do.

We know that He has spoken to us through His Word regarding the education of Christian children, and we had better listen!

The state-sponsored school system has become resolutely hostile to Christianity and to this country's founding principles. Pharaoh's school system cannot be reformed, and we should not try.

Rather, the time has come to tell our modern-day Pharoah, which is the public, state-run educational system, "Let my children go!"   ■

EXODUS MANDATE VISION STATEMENT

Exodus Mandate is a Christian ministry to encourage and assist Christian families to leave Pharaoh's school system (i.e. government schools) for the Promised Land of Christian schools or home schooling. It is our prayer and hope that a fresh obedience by Christian families in educating their children according to Biblical mandates will prove to be a key for the revival of our families, our churches and our nation.

CHAPTER ONE

THE FAMILY SCHOOL

MAY 13, 1993

HOW WE FIRST CAME TO HOME SCHOOL

**SUCCESS STORIES:
HOME SCHOOLING SPREADS**

GOALS 2000 OR EXODUS 2000?

EXODUS MANDATE: BEGINNINGS

**EXODUS MANDATE: PROSPECTS
(THE BURDEN OF DAVID AND ANNE DRYE)**

THE PATH AHEAD

The place was The Citadel, the Military College of South Carolina. The occasion was Commencement, 1993. The graduating class of that year had voted to have former President Ronald Reagan as Commencement Speaker.

The college from which I had graduated in 1965 had a grand tradition of allowing fathers who were Citadel Alumni to award their graduating sons their degrees.

Our first-born son, Ray III, or Raymond, as we called him, was to receive the medal as First Honor graduate or Valedictorian of his class. I was to award his degree, with President Reagan assisting me nearby. This was a great moment for our family, but it also was, for us, a validation of the ways of the Lord in the Christian education of our children.

We had been among the pioneering home-schooling families in the United States in this modern era, having begun in September 1977. Now it was 16 years later, and the path down which God had directed us back then had come to a dramatic fruition.

MAY 13, 1993

McAllister Field House was filled with over 6,000 family and friends of the class of 1993. At the time, I was serving as an Army Chaplain on active duty at nearby Ft. Jackson, South Carolina, and had been selected to offer the opening prayers, invocation and benediction for the graduation ceremonies.

The moment came for the procession, and we entered the large Assembly Hall. The Citadel's President, Lt. Gen. Claudius E. "Bud" Watts, USAF Ret., President Reagan, and other dignitaries were leading the procession. I was the guest chaplain that day. My wife Gail was seated in the audience with our other children.

Gail and I were the parents of the First Honor graduate, Cadet Colonel and Regimental Commander. The moment was almost surreal. We could not have dreamed of nor created such a special moment had we tried. The band played, the grand march began, and we arrived on the ceremony platform. My moment had come to offer the invocation, which came first in the ceremony.

There was silence. I stepped forward and prayed, "Lord God, our dear heavenly Father, bless this ceremony, The Citadel staff, faculty and Board during these difficult days. We are grateful for President Reagan and his service to our country these many years. Let him see the travail of his soul and be satisfied…" I concluded with "Bless the graduating class of 1993 and their families. May old men dream dreams again and young men receive vision for the road ahead. In Jesus' Holy Name. Amen."

Our experience vindicated the special form of education we had begun 16 years before. There was nothing like it! We knew that God had his hand on us. Gail and I had trusted Him, and He had brought us to this moment. On May 13, 1993, our son, who had been home schooled, graduated from The Citadel at the top of his class.

EARLY DECISION TO HOME SCHOOL
In September of 1977, my family and I embarked on what would prove to be the greatest adventure of our lives. My wife Gail and I found ourselves becoming one of the first few dozen families involved in what soon became known as home schooling.

We had just moved to West Lafayette, Indiana, to start a new campus ministry in September 1977, called Trinity Fellowship Church. Our ministry was intended to serve Purdue University and the surrounding area.

I had earned the Master of Divinity degree from Grace Theological Seminary, Winona Lake, Indiana, in 1974, and had completed all the class work for the Master Of Theology, lacking only the written thesis to finish my degree.

Raymond had reached the age when he was ready to begin the first grade. We experienced a sense of concern and even dread as we realized we had few choices in his first grade education.

When we arrived in West Lafayette, we had already decided we could not accept the local public school. We had fully expected to place Raymond in a local Christian school, but after looking at two schools, we were not satisfied with their spiritual environment or academic rigor. It was a lonely feeling to realize that of our choices, neither the public school nor the local Christian schools were acceptable.

Earlier, while I was enrolled in seminary, Gail and I had read a book entitled *Sketches of Jewish Social Life*, by the great Jewish Christian scholar Alfred Edersheim.[1] One chapter described a family-school type of education for young Israeli lads in the New Testament era, the kind of home education that our Savior, Jesus Christ, had at the hands of his parents until he attended the synagogue school at age 12. This was our only written source of encouragement, outside the Holy Scriptures themselves, offering us light to launch the new adventure.

Over a period of several days, confronted with an unexpected situation, Gail and I prayed and discussed what we should do.

I recall how my burden was lifted when Gail announced her willingness to take up the academic as well as the religious instruction of our first-born son saying, "I think I can do it."

THE FAMILY SCHOOL

We simply called our experience the *family school*, and we were careful not to tell many people except our closest friends about it. Raymond was only six years old, but he knew his parents were doing something very different in his education.

Gail and I still remember the day we announced to him he wouldn't be attending the local public school as his neighborhood playmates did, nor would he be attending the local Christian school we had discussed in family meetings. He would get his first grade schooling at home in a family school primarily from his mother, with Dad helping out in Bible and history.

As a 6-year-old he had learned to think for himself. He was pretty sure this was not a good idea and cried, "Mommy and Daddy, don't do this to me!" We promised to take it only one step at time, and we assured him this was God's will and was, therefore, best for him and our family. We assured him of our love for him and our desire to do God's will.

RAYMOND'S FAST PROGRESS
Raymond was soon doing accelerated work and reading well ahead of his age group. One day after family school had ended, I was on the porch preparing for a sermon. It was after the local public school had let out.

Raymond was playing with his neighborhood friends on the porch nearby, but also comparing his level of academic work with that of his friends. He questioned his friends carefully and was really surprised at what they were not learning at the local public school. He was doing cursive writing. They had not even heard of cursive writing.

He realized he was also reading books well ahead of his neighborhood friends. In fact, he was reading on a 4th grade level. After that experience he seemed forever satisfied that his educational experience was both religiously and academically significant.

CURRICULUM IN THE EARLY DAYS
We had some difficulty in finding a Christian curriculum in those early days but used the big red books from Foundation of America's Christian Education for history and government. We also used A Beka books from the local Christian school that sold them to us after A Beka refused us direct sales.

In those days the A Beka policy was to sell only to Christian schools. We made formal requests for three years.

Finally, in 1980, A Beka changed the policy and began to sell to home schooling families.

We pieced together a Christian curriculum, and Gail created many of her own teaching aids and materials.

ENCOURAGEMENT AND DISCOURAGEMENT
One local pastor and his wife, Ray and Alice Joseph of the local Reformed Presbyterian Church, were supportive. Ret. Gen. John and Janet Bradshaw also supported us, supplying us with good books on history and government from a traditional perspective. These two couples heard that we were home schooling, visited our home and gave us additional books and materials for our curriculum. They expressed moral support and agreement with our approach.

Other Christian friends had expressed serious doubts, and one pastor friend even implied we would harm our children if we persisted with our family school.

The Josephs were the first pastoral couple to help us, and these two Christian families validated us in this step of faith, and it encouraged us much at the time.

Home schooling was so new in those days that we were concerned about attracting negative attention and possible legal action against our family school. We were very quiet and had not informed the local public school district of our plan.

PREPARATION FOR A LEGAL CHALLENGE
Christian civil rights attorney David Gibbs of the Christian Law Association was speaking in Lafayette at a local Baptist church. We arranged a personal meeting to explain our family school and requested that he represent us if we got into legal difficulties. He agreed to help us, but we never needed to call him. But it was comforting to know he was prepared to help us if needed.

Around 1980, the Indiana Department of Public Instruction finally did contact us. They asked us what were we doing and why we were home schooling. The contact came by letter and we suspected someone had turned our name in as having truant children.

By this time we were nearly four years into the family school and knew we had discovered something wonderful. In those days we described our little home school as similar to the "…merchant seeking beautiful pearls, who, when he had found one pearl of great price, went and sold all that he had and bought it" (Matthew 13:45-46).

We were not about to give it up even under legal pressure, but the contact from Indiana's educational establishment gave us great concern. We informed them about the nature and curriculum of our home school and why we were educating our children that way. We gave them Biblical reasons that we felt this was God's will for our family.

Their next contact asked us to help them develop a "Home School Permission Form." Like most governmental agencies, they needed a bureaucratic form to cover any eventuality.

The Indiana Department said we were the first family they had known that was home schooling in Indiana, and they wanted to prepare themselves for this circumstance should other families attempt it.

We informed them that we didn't mind helping them prepare a "Home School Notification Form" but that permission to home school was not theirs to give. We informed them that it was a God-ordained right of parents to home school and they could not interfere unless they could show that we were harming the children in some fashion.

After this communication we held our breath and kept David Gibbs' telephone number at hand. But this was the last time we heard from the Indiana State Department of

Public Instruction concerning our home schooling experience. They never contacted us again.

THE GROWTH OF THE MOVEMENT
By 1983, we had influenced some friends in Indiana and around the nation to consider home schooling. We also discovered other home-schooling families in Indiana.

It was also in 1983 that the biggest breakthrough for home schooling nationally took place. That year, Dr. James Dobson interviewed noted home-school authors Raymond and Dorothy Moore on his *Focus on the Family* radio program. Gail and I listened at night to that interview and were thrilled that home schooling was getting this recognition.

After this interview came the greatest explosion in home schooling. It could be said that Dr. Dobson's interview of the Moores helped birth the modern home school movement. We later met the Moores at an early home-schooling conference in Winona Lake, Indiana. Their books on home schooling have been a tremendous help to many families.[2]

OUR HOME SCHOOL EXPERIENCE
During this period we had a temporary lapse, putting Raymond in West Lafayette Junior High school in the 7th grade. Our own convictions and theology were still in formative stages.

Like most evangelical Christians at that time, we did not understand that the public schools are an establishment of religion and are religious in nature themselves, albeit humanistic by design. Our own worldview on Christian education was incomplete. Like so many Christians who home school, we saw our decision as only a personal and family choice.

Raymond is the only one of our four children ever to attend public school, and then it was for his middle school and part of his high school years. Raymond finished his high school years at Heathwood Episcopal School, Columbia, South Carolina.

Richard, Dorothy, and Wm. Rieppe all were home schooled through 6th or 7th grades and then finished their education at Ben Lippen School, an evangelical Christian school, and a division of Columbia International University (formerly Columbia Bible College).

When we placed Raymond in the 7th grade, the local West Lafayette Junior High staff was so relieved that we had given up our home schooling that they did not even require testing to place him in an advanced class. He was placed in advanced classes with many children of Purdue University staff and faculty.

We think many in the community were also relieved, and some thought it absolutely scandalous that some Christian family would home school when West Lafayette had such a superior public school system.

Raymond excelled in this new school setting. He made all A's, and in his 8th grade year was invited to participate in the Northwestern University talent search. He was invited along with other gifted 8th graders in ten Midwestern states to take the SAT.

To our surprise he scored in the top 400 children on his SAT in his age group in the 10 states in the Midwestern region. There were forty 8th graders in the State of Indiana to make this cut.

Raymond had only 1½ years of formal schooling by this time. He was a gifted child, and even in his early youth he had a tremendous drive and a strong work ethic, but Gail and I did feel that this award was God's blessing on our obedience. At that time we were overwhelmed that we had stumbled into a forgotten Biblical pattern of education for children.

We were experiencing God's blessing that comes in obedience to His ways. Raymond and I made the trek to Northwestern University, Evanston, Illinois, on a March day when the wind blew cold off Lake Michigan. He received his award along with others from the Midwest, perhaps the only home schooler in the entire group. Driving back that afternoon was mostly quiet for me as I pondered these things in my heart.

By this time home schooling was beginning to find acceptance in the evangelical churches, and several thousand families were home schooling nationally.

EARLY HOME SCHOOL GROWTH: REASONS

The great legal battles, many fought by Michael Farris and the Home School Legal Defense Association (HSLDA), would be won in the decade of the 1980's and early 1990's. This by itself is one of the great stories of Christian heroism and leadership in our time.

I attended the Bill Gothard Pastor's Conference in the spring of 1983 held at Wheaton College Chapel. Several thousand pastors from the Midwest attended. I always found these conferences among some of the most helpful and refreshing I attended. In one of the sessions Bill Gothard discussed home schooling, which was still a new concept to most evangelical pastors.

He said he had been praying and seeking the Lord for a weapon to rebuild the Christian foundations of America. He believed home schooling to be that weapon.

In 1985, Gail and I left West Lafayette, Indiana, after eight years of campus ministry at Purdue. By now we were home schooling two other children., Richard and Dorothy. Our youngest, Wm. Rieppe, was two years old.

Home schooling had grown so well in eight years that area home schoolers held a book and curriculum fair that attracted hundreds of families from the surrounding counties in the greater Lafayette area.

We had not invented home schooling in Indiana although we were likely the first family in the modern era, according to the State Department of Public Instruction.

We had spent much of those eight years explaining our Biblical rationale and the advantages to dozens of Indiana families. Many had begun to take up the challenge.

The Holy Spirit of God, "hovering over the face of the waters," birthed the modern home-schooling movement at a moment when Christian families were seeking Him for help in raising and educating their children.

Gail and I have always had the pioneering spirit, and there is a great and inexpressible joy that comes in being one of the first families to take up this home-schooling model. We had so little light and encouragement in the early days. Home schooling did not yet exist. We only heard the still small voice of the Lord to take this step of faith and obedience, and we have learned through this that obedience to God is its own reward.

SUCCESS STORIES: HOME SCHOOLING SPREADS

We were pioneering home schoolers. It is important to realize, though, that we didn't set out to start a "movement." We made a choice to obey God's commands regarding the education of our children.

However, as we cited God's commands to others as our authority for what we were doing, our choice began to inspire others—sometimes without our awareness. Back then, almost no support for home schooling families, grass roots or otherwise, existed.

But when a practice is built on a philosophical or theological foundation, what begins as a personal choice soon develops into a movement, and the support networks begin to emerge.

In our case, God began to use us to further His will for America's children, which I am convinced is to abandon Pharaoh's school system in favor of the Promised Land of home schooling and private Christian schooling.

By the late 1980's, grass-roots support for home schooling had begun to appear, in the form of organizations such as the Christian Home Educators Network, which was started in 1986 by Paul and Karen Apple, a home schooling family based in Maryland, and now numbers some 1,500 members across that state. This is just one example.

Home schooling was starting to become a refuge from the secular humanist worldview that was taking over the public schools.

OUTPERFORMING PUBLIC SCHOOLS
Still more favorable support for home schooling existed. By the late 1990's, it was becoming clear that home schooled children vastly out-performed their counterparts in public schools. They were scoring in the highest brackets on standardized tests such as the SAT and being admitted to major universities, including Harvard, where they were flourishing at the top of their classes.

THE DOWNWARD SPIRAL IN PUBLIC SCHOOLS
Moreover, people involved in the public schools themselves were beginning to pay attention. Christians in particular who were teaching in the public schools were getting increasingly worried about the tendencies they were seeing.

One such person wrote to me back in 1998:

> I am a Christian and a teacher in the California public
> schools, and I grow more concerned daily with the insidious

and morally destructive agenda infiltrating our public schools.

I abandoned [a] Christmas program because *every* belief system is allowed *except* Christianity. We can do Hanukah, New Age, Jehovah's Witnesses, Eastern religions, etc., even Santa Claus, but *no* baby Jesus, even though at least 60-80 percent of the school goes to Christian churches!

The children in her public school were manifestly *afraid* to profess Christian commitments openly:

When I mention Jesus to the Christian children, they are shocked I would utter the very word in the classroom. They love it, of course, but are 'trained' to keep it to themselves, and there is definite fear there.

Such teachers could be a real boon to private Christian schools. Why do we need home schooling and private Christian schools? The first and major reason is that God strictly commands it, as we shall see in this book.

And even by itself, a close scrutiny of what has been going on in the secular public schools ought to persuade Christian parents of the need for alternatives to public education.

GOALS 2000? OR EXODUS 2000?

The 1990's became the decade in which one of the major education buzzword was Goals 2000. What was Goals 2000? What did it propose, and what were its assumptions?

The Goals 2000 Educate America Act (P.L. 103-227) became law with President Bill Clinton's signature on March 31, 1994. The Act provides for the distribution of federal government money to state and local school systems. Congress appropriated $105 million for the first year.

Individual states could submit grant applications describing the process they would use to implement Goals 2000 mandates. Spelled out, Goals 2000 seems innocent enough. It contains planks summarized as follows:

1. By the year 2000, all children in America will start school ready to learn.

2. The high school graduation rate will increase to 90%.

3. All students will leave grades 4, 8 and 12 having demonstrated competency over challenging subject matter including English, mathematics, science, foreign languages, civics and government, economics, the arts, and history and geography.

   Every public school in America will be expected to ensure that its students learn to use their minds well, so that they may be prepared for responsible citizenship, further learning, and productive employment in the nation's modern economy.

4. Every school in the United States will be free of drugs, violence, and the unauthorized presence of firearms and alcohol, and will offer a disciplined environment conducive to learning.

WHO COULD ARGUE WITH GOALS 2000?
At first glance, who could argue with these goals? The truth about Goals 2000 is far different from the appearances presented by such statements as those above. This can sometimes be seen by reading between the lines. What, for example, can goal #1 actually mean? How can a government program ensure that "children in America start school ready to learn"?

WHAT THE "GOALS" REALLY MEAN

The "goal" the statement really implies is the use of federal money to assume responsibility for babies as young as six weeks old while both their parents are at work, supervising them for eight or nine hours every day in government-run day-care centers.

Federal dollars mean federal control. This has always been the case, and always will be, and that lets us spell out what Goals 2000 really means: control of the education of our children by the federal government from their earliest days, eventually indoctrinating them in the latest forms of political correctness, socialism and unconditional loyalty to secular authority.

It is a vast social-engineering project. If its work is begun when the children are infants and continued on through their formative grade-school years, they will grow up never having known anything else.

THE "ENEMIES" OF GOALS 2000

Abundant evidence exists, according to Goals 2000, that *parents* are the enemy. The other enemies of the Goals 2000 effort to produce socially engineered children are pastors, Christian schools and home schoolers, along with anyone else likely to oppose this plan for our children.

Organizations such as the Christian Coalition are also targeted as enemies. This is evident from some of the cassette tapes and workbooks that have been produced by Goals 2000 bureaucrats. One of the tricks of the trade has been to try to control the language. Goals 2000 bureaucrats will portray critics of this agenda as "opposed to education."

THOSE DEEMED "AT RISK"

Goals 2000 has provisions for that special category of student determined to be "at risk."

Obviously, the more students that teachers, social workers and bureaucrats can identify as "at risk," the more federal dollars they can heroically request. We have seen, therefore, an ever-widening set of "at risk" children alongside an increase of "disorders" (e.g., Attention Deficit Disorder, and Attention Deficit Hyper-activity Disorder, never heard of before the 1990's).

"Voluntary" visits with the parents of "at risk" students are scheduled. Refusals by parents of such visits are logged, and recalcitrant parents are monitored in a computer database.

THE GOAL: GOVERNMENT INVOLVEMENT AT EVERY LEVEL

In short, Goals 2000, like its close cousin, Outcome-Based Education (OBE)—or as it is sometimes now called, Performance-Based Education—is a campaign to involve the federal government in education at every level, from the cradle through college.

Today, there are more than 750 federal education programs run by 39 agencies—costing taxpayers some $100 million a year. Since its launch in 1994, Goals 2000 has cost taxpayers more than $2.1 billion.

Education researcher and lecturer Michael J. Chapman, with American Heritage Research, gives a concise definition of Outcome-Based Education:

> OBE redefines the meaning of education in both content and structure. OBE shifts content from knowledge to attitudes, values and beliefs. In structure, OBE focuses on minimum performance instead of measuring results against a fixed "academic" body of knowledge.[3]

In a "dear colleagues" letter, Congressman Henry Hyde, a Republican from Illinois, describes Goals 2000 in very blunt terms:

> It is a concept for dumbing-down our schools and changing the character of the nation through behavior modification (a vital part of this plan).
>
> It moves away from an academically intensive curriculum to one that is integrated with vocational training, producing skilled manpower for the labor market. The economy will be controlled by the federal government by controlling our workforce and our schools.[4]

Hyde refers to the work done on Goals 2000 by Bill Clinton, Hillary Clinton, Ira Magaziner and Marc Tucker prior to Bill Clinton's election in 1992. He connects Goals 2000 to the School-to-Work Opportunities Act of 1994 (discussed in Chapter Two) and the Improving America's Schools Act, all of which were signed into law by President Clinton in 1994.

THE ABJECT FAILURE OF GOALS 2000

It is clear that, in the end, the few goals of Goals 2000 that sound laudable are actually deceptive.

Public schools are not free of firearms and violence. Events both before and after the Columbine killings show this quite clearly. Administrators in inner cities schools have not dismantled the metal detectors on their front doors because of Goals 2000. Nor are they free of alcohol and drugs.

Public schools do contain plenty of sex education, however, (often over the explicit objections of parents) helping to foster teenage pregnancy. Condoms and sometimes even abortion services have been made available to girls younger than 16.

Plentiful other trappings of secular humanism were discussed in the introduction to this book. Goals 2000 did not raise standards but lowered the bar, so more students could meet minimum standards resulting in what Congressman Henry Hyde called "dumbing America down."

What I've learned since 1977 is that Christians do not have to tolerate this.

Is reforming public schools the answer? No, it is not. Reform, in this case, means reform of a secular institution and must be carried out in terms that will satisfy the secularists. It is time for God-fearing and Bible-believing men and women to speak out against this brand of education with their feet.

In other words, I defend the idea that it is time for a mass exodus from public schools into private Christian schools and home schooling.

The reasons why Christians should abandon the public education system in this country were all present by the mid-1990's, and actually long before. What we lacked, however, was an organized movement and the inspiration and motivation to carry it forward.

EXODUS MANDATE: BEGINNINGS.

Exodus Mandate—or as I then called it, Exodus 2000—was born on February 12, 1997, the day I attended a Goals 2000 briefing in Washington presided over by Phyllis Schlafly of Eagle Forum and Congressman Henry Hyde.

This briefing was sponsored by a number of Christian groups including the Family Research Council, Concerned Women for America, the HSLDA, the Heritage Foundation, the Christian Coalition, the American Family Association, the American Association of Christian Schools, the American Conservative Union and the Traditional Values Coalition, all in addition to Eagle Forum.

These Christian groups are the main organizations responsible for maintaining a conservative Christian presence in both education and public life.

The main topic was the danger posed by Goals 2000 and the new School-to-Work agenda working to undermine Christian faith and freedom. There was a lot of "wailing and gnashing of teeth," and calls for "conservative reform of the public schools," but no real plan except to fight the Goals 2000 legislation and try to have it repealed. The problem was that Christians—even Christian leaders—were operating reactively and not proactively.

I listened to speaker after speaker all day and realized that no one had a plan to deal effectively with the problems raised.

I left that meeting intending to create a plan that would be proactive and not simply reactive. It would be called Exodus 2000—a name I chose deliberately as a counterpoint to Goals 2000. (I would change the name to Exodus Mandate in January of 2001.)

The plan would be to remove as many Christian children as possible out of public (government) schools. It already was obvious that public education, so called, could not be "reformed," and that Christians shouldn't try. It was clear from my studies of Scripture that God had intended education to be in the hands of families with assistance from the Church, and not under the control of any branch of government. This became the touchstone proposition of Exodus Mandate that distinguished it from every other Christian education movement.

SECURING THE ESCAPE OF MILLIONS OF CHRISTIAN STUDENTS

What I wanted to do was nothing less than secure the escape of millions of Christian children and youth from the yoke of government schools. Remember our Old Testament history from Exodus? "Now there arose a new king over Egypt, who did not know Joseph" (Exodus 1:8). This Pharaoh took power over the Israelites. And so it is in our own day. A secular education establishment has taken power over our children. It has the backing of legislation and the court system. This establishment barely even acknowledges the existence of our rich Christian heritage in law, government and education.

The public schools long ago abandoned many traditional practices such as teaching pure phonics and basic math, and have substituted programs such as the look-say method and the so-called "new math"—both notorious failures. Seriously flawed theories of reading, such as the look-say and whole-language methods, became standard decades ago, and have produced levels of illiteracy higher than at any time in the modern era.[5]

As a result, not only are children being harmed spiritually and morally in the government schools, they are very simply not being taught how to read, write and do basic arithmetic at the same levels of earlier generations!

The secularization of public schools has a long history, as seen in the next chapter. The U.S. Supreme Court was a primary culprit in taking this secularization into high gear during the past half century.

In 1962, with *Eagle v. Vitale*, the Court banned prayer in public schools, citing no law or precedent, under the misguided reasoning that prayer in public schools constituted an unconstitutional endorsement by government of religion.[6] (What the First Amendment actually banned was the establishment of a state church by the federal government along the lines of the Church of England.)

The next year, with *Abingdon School District v. Schempp*, the Bible was removed. The highest court in the land wrote,

If portions of the New Testament were read without explanation, they could be, and had been, psychologically harmful to the child.[7]

In 1980, the Ten Commandments followed. In this case, *Stone v. Graham*, the court opined:

> If these posted copies of the Ten Commandments are to have any effect at all, it will be to induce the school children to read, meditate upon, perhaps to venerate the Ten Commandments; this is not a permissible objective.[8]

With God almost nowhere to be found in public schools, morality was left with the false foundations of secular humanism which offers only various forms of relativism.

The primary values in public schools have become the tragically false concepts of self-esteem and tolerance, with the latter having application for every belief system except Christianity. Even witchcraft is permitted!

In this environment, youth crime is widespread at schools and in neighborhoods. With a variety of forces working against the best interests of strong families, including both parents often having to work to make ends meet, many children are growing up without the kind of moral and spiritual guidance they need.

THE REFORM EFFORT THAT FAILED:
THE GREENVILLE, S.C. STORY

But why should Christians abandon the public schools? Wouldn't that leave them entirely in the hands of secular humanists? Indeed it might. The important point is that our mission is not to throw secular humanists out of public schools. It is to remove ourselves from the public schools and our children from the influence of the secular humanists.

This removal, we shall argue throughout the book, is the only viable alternative.

"Reforming" the public schools simply will not work, and efforts at "reform" may deal the cause of Christian education tremendous setbacks with the waste of time and the waste of many young Christian children's futures.

Christians attempting to work within this system to initiate "reforms" face enormous barriers. One such example involved the school board in Greenville County, South Carolina, in November of 1996, when three Christian incumbents for the school board, Julie Hershey, Joe Dill and Bill Brooks, were defeated in their bids for re-election. This case is worthy of consideration because it points to the real direction the future of education in that state and therefore in other states, and the nation itself, is probably headed.

The Greenville County School System had maintained a statewide reputation as an island of educational and moral sanity amidst a statewide public school system characterized by education reform in the wrong direction: Outcome-Based Education, radical sex education, stagnant SAT and BSAP test scores and a general educational malaise that seemed almost irreversible.

Many Christians looked to Greenville County as a model of what could be done to correct the decades-long liberal educational misadventures and experimentation on our children by working within the system.

THE CAMPAIGN AGAINST CHRISTIAN CANDIDATES...AND KRYSTALLNACHT

In the school board election of November, 1996, an incredible campaign against Julie Hershey, Joe Dill and Bill Brooks occurred. It was unlike anything ever seen in South Carolina for normally routine school board elections. Liberals had invested huge amounts of money and of time in their effort to defeat the Christian incumbents. There was also significant coordination between media and other liberal interest groups, including even some in the business community.

These incumbents must have been either awfully bad— or awfully good. I suggest that they were doing something very right and very good, and had become a serious threat to the domain of darkness and the pall of grief that has fallen over our precious children.

Jesus said as he was being escorted to the Cross, "...Daughters of Jerusalem, do not weep for Me, but weep for yourselves and for your children. 31 For if they do these things in the green wood, what will be done in the dry?" (Luke 23:28b, 31).

If the left can do this in Greenville County, one of the most conservative and Christian counties in South Carolina, which in turn is one of the most conservative states in the nation, it can savage the Christian community with impunity anywhere. Greenville County is home to a large body of informed and courageous conservative Christians willing to lay their energy and resources on the line.

They had made progress in implementing models of conservative Christian reform capable of serving as models for school districts elsewhere. In most districts Christians are allowed to complain but not to govern; in Greenville County, voters had allowed them to govern. The results were obvious to all.

I believe this election might have been a test that was similar, on a much smaller scale, to *Krystallnacht* (Crystal Night) in Nazi Germany in 1938. Nazis and Nazi sympathizers went on a rampage throughout Germany, breaking windows in Jewish-owned shops. More than 100 Jewish German citizens were killed; thousands of others had their businesses destroyed.

It was an attempt to intimidate not just the Jews but also the entire German public. The Nazis wanted to see if there would be a public outcry—if anyone would come to the defense of the Jews. Almost no one did. A new threshold was crossed, and with this event the campaign of hatred and terror against the Jews escalated.

I might add that many Jews realized the danger they were in and emigrated to America and other secure places at that time. Others remained in denial, and eventually paid the price in the concentration camps.

Am I calling the groups allied against Christian conservatives in Greenville County "Nazis"? No. But two things should be noted. First, it is clear to me that many with a secular liberal worldview do have a similar mindset. In their own minds, they believe they know what is best for our children and our culture. They will stop at nothing to dominate both. Second, this is because they and the Nazis who came before them share the secular humanist belief that Man can be substituted for God, and a functional man-centered society can be created.

WHY PEOPLE EASILY ACCEPT LIES AND WHY PLACATING AN ENEMY NEVER WORKS

These truths about secular humanism are not easy to assimilate. *People will believe lies about good men before they will believe the truth about evil ones.* Hitler openly practiced that if someone tells a lie often enough, people will believe it. This is because man is a fallen creature with an innate tendency toward sinfulness. He does not naturally accept the truth, especially about his own nature. If we are able to see any truth it all, it is only by God's grace.

Some Christians failed their Lord in the school board races. Other Christians believed the lies and calumny spread against Hershey, Dill and Brooks.

And of course, any errors they made were magnified, while their excellent service and results were overlooked.

Others were afraid of the controversy that had arisen due to their heroic efforts to protect our children. Many decent, God-fearing people even supported their opponents, thinking that the controversy would then go away and that the attacks against Christians would cease.

Such efforts to placate the enemy always fail. The attacks on the Jews didn't cease when few protested the destruction of Krystallnacht. They only intensified—for the Nazis had further plans for the Jews.

The children of Israel faced a similar crisis in Egypt, as recounted in Exodus. Pharaoh was not willing to change. He was not going to give up his humanist agenda (It was if nothing, humanist, after all; Pharaoh had set himself up as the human equivalent of a god, and that is the starting point of humanism). Pharaoh was determined to make humanist Egyptians out of godly Israelite children. He was going to convert them even while he forced their godly parents into the bondage of becoming makers of mortar and brick for humanist sites and institutions.

Finally, the protective shield provided by the heroic leadership of Hershey, Dill and Brooks has been removed. The children of Greenville County are exposed and vulnerable again. Remember, Exodus says that God hardened Pharaoh's heart so that the Israelites would have no choice but to escape Egypt. The humanists in Greenville County showed the Christians the door, and they kicked the Christian leadership out of the public school system.

With the rejection of Christian school board members, could Christian teachers and administrators be far behind? The same God who delivered Israel from bondage to Pharaoh and set the Israelites on the path to the Promised Land has set us up in similar fashion and providentially.

The humanists have hardened their hearts; and perhaps God has hardened their hearts. Thus they cannot be placated. It is important to realize: *the secular humanists are not going to change.* They are only going to get more intolerant of Christians. Our very existence convicts them and provokes them. This should be a watershed moment when pastors and Christian leaders of our communities finally rise up and say to our modern humanist Pharaoh, *"Let my children go!"*

As I would phrase it later in the Exodus Mandate vision statement,

> Exodus Mandate is a Christian ministry to encourage and assist Christian families to leave Pharaoh's school system (i.e., government schools) for the Promised Land of Christian schools or home schooling. It is our prayer and hope that a fresh obedience by Christian families in educating their children according to Biblical mandates will prove to be a key for the revival of our families, our churches and our nation.

THE BIRTH AND GOALS OF EXODUS MANDATE

In short, the goal of Exodus Mandate is to solve the problems created by Outcome-Based Education, Goals 2000, the school-to-work movement, and other government-school initiatives, not by reforming them or trying to repeal legislation but by taking as many Christian children as possible out of their reach and placing them in the safe sanctuaries of Christian schools and home schooling.

I first announced this plan during the week the Promise Keepers met in Washington in October of 1997. Out of my list of contacts, including a number of people I met at that meeting, I started to organize a volunteer network. It was centered in South Carolina where I live (in Columbia), but soon expanded to include other states. Within a fairly short period of time, a new movement was born, and it started receiving favorable coverage.

The *Wall Street Journal*, the *Washington Times*, the *Dallas Morning News*, the *Atlanta Journal-Constitution* and *The State* based in Columbia all published stories on this movement when it was still called Exodus 2000. The Southern Baptist Convention gave it more than a passing look.

I took to the radio circuit and gave hundreds of interviews broadcast by networks on some 4,500 radio stations all across the country.

Soon, Exodus Mandate was receiving support from a number of highly visible Christian leaders, including Dr. Jerry Falwell of Liberty University and Dr. James Kennedy, president of Coral Ridge Ministries, which reaches several million people every month.

THE BURDEN OF DAVID AND ANN DRYE: AN EXODUS MANDATE

In early 1999, Exodus Mandate came to the attention of David and Ann Drye, at the time among the leading Christian educators promoting home schooling and Christian schooling in North Carolina. Based in Concord, N.C., David Drye had founded Classical Covenant School of Concord.

He was a successful Christian businessman, owner of the David Drye Company that built apartment complexes and extended-stay hotels in the Southeast. Moreover, he and his wife Ann had followed a path of home schooling similar to Gail's and mine. He was the kind of Christian who quickly acted on the truths he discovered in the Word of God and followed the paths of obedience wherever they might take him. He was also a man with a strong prayer life. I had met him years before and knew his reputation for Christian service in North Carolina.

In the spring of 1999, David heard me speak about my vision and agenda for Christian families and churches, and invited me to address the staff, faculty and upper school of his Classical Covenant School. This was the beginning of a new Christian friendship, and I grew to admire David's bold aggressive manner and financial support for projects and ministries that helped build the Kingdom of God.

One of the most important results of our friendship was David's offer to supply the funding for the Jeremiah Films video "Let My Children Go." Because of his business successes, God enabled David to give large sums of money to support Christian schools, missionary projects, home schooling, the pro-life movement and other Christian projects that built the Kingdom of God. He was obedient and generous in giving large amounts to these projects.

He financed the entire development and production of "Let My Children Go." God has used this video all over the nation in the last two years to warn Christian families of the dangers of government run schools. Without his financial support, guidance and encouragement, this video would not exist today. David himself speaks in the video several times expressing his concern about Christians allowing their children to attend state or government schools.

Because David and Ann had a great burden that Christian families become obedient to Biblical mandates in the education of their children, they thus strongly supported both Christian schools and home schooling.

David and Ann fully practiced what they preached, and home schooled or provided Christian schooling for their own children and 12 grandchildren. He was, to many, "Mr. Christian Education in North Carolina." He would promote and talk about Christian education every opportunity he got.

No one could be with him long before he would ask about that person's own family and children's education.

David and Ann Drye were also people of prayer. They were indeed intercessors. David was known to sequester himself for a day or two and fast and pray in some secluded place. How a businessman with a large company of over 300 employees could afford the time to do so causes one to wonder. But David had his personal priorities in order. He knew his tremendous success in business was due to God's blessing. So he could find time to get alone with his Lord and Savior just to talk, worship and pray.

His burdens were heavy for revival in the churches and in the entire nation. This was such a strong burden of concern that he took parts of two summers with his family and drove to each state capitol in the 48 contiguous states to beseech God for each state and its people from the state's capitol city. He asked God to bring revival in all the states, to help the churches, and turn back the forces of evil that had become so prevalent.

He was asking God for a fresh "Great Awakening" in the nation when he was suddenly taken away on June 14, 1999. The tragic loss of David and Ann Drye occurred when their plane crashed in Concord on a business trip. They were both killed along with a coworker and their pilot. It has been two and a half years since this sad moment, and the Christian community would do well to consider the lives of this notable couple again.

"BELOVED AND PLEASANT IN THEIR LIVES"

King David (2 Samuel 1:19-27) lamented the loss of his friend Jonathan. We could paraphrase this text in similar fashion about David and Ann Drye: "The beauty of Israel is slain on your high places. How the mighty have fallen. David and Ann Drye were beloved and pleasant in their lives, and in their death they were not divided; they were swifter than eagles, they were stronger than lions.... How the mighty have fallen in the midst of battle."

In one of my last visits with David Drye, he said in his characteristic fashion, "Ray, if you would pray more, more would happen." *So simple, yet so profound.* It was one of those times when I knew I had received a word from the Lord.

I have grown in my faith as a result of our short friendship and association, and I will remember them. "How the mighty have fallen in the midst of battle...."[9]

TAKING THE EXODUS MANDATE TO THE PUBLIC FORUM

The Exodus Mandate Project has continued to grow, and its mission has continued to spread. Just this past year I participated in a forum on Beacon Hill at the State Capitol in Boston, entitled "Can Christians Continue to Use the Public Schools?" Dr. Ron Crews of the Massachusetts Family Institute, who also participated in the forum, argued that each set of parents needed to answer for their particular children and their particular situation where to send them to school. He agrees that standards of decency and righteousness are under sustained attack in the public schools but believes that Christians should remain present as salt and light of the earth in whatever arena God sends them.

I see the situation very differently. I told *The Massachusetts News*, which covered the event:

> You're facing some rather serious questions here in the
> Massachusetts area with the crowding in of the homosexual
> agenda into the public schools. Society seems to be helpless
> to prevent it. The families are desperate, and they can't seem
> to forestall it. So we think that Christian people should be

looking at Christian education as the only Biblical option for educating their children at the K-12 level.[10]

The salt and light of the earth theology is laudable, but misapplied in education because small children simply don't have the experience to be evangelists for the Christian faith, given the onslaught of secular humanism, political correctness and the demand for conformity in the public schools.

Confronting these is work for adults. Christian families should not be sending in children as surrogate evangelists before they are old enough and mature enough in their own faith to handle the pressures of the hostile environment now represented by the pagan school system.

The difficult point for conservative Christians is that the choice to send their children to public schools is based on a theological mistake. It follows naturally that Christians are not going to be able to "fix" the secular public schools.

THE PATH AHEAD
It has been 25 years since Gail and I first started home schooling our first-born son in West Lafayette, Indiana, on the banks of the Wabash River when I was finishing up at Grace Theological Seminary in 1977.

We were told at that time by the State Department of Education we were the first home schooling family in Indiana in the modern era.

We describe those early experiences as taking our little first born son and placing him safely in his little home school papyrus basket down at the river.

One day some years later we came to check on him and saw thousands of little papyrus baskets floating in the river. Other families were discovering this wonderful way to care for and educate their children. Gail and I look back on our early discovery of home schooling and God's giving us the grace to carry it forward for 17 years and the subsequent provision of Christian schooling for our children in the upper years as one of the most soul-satisfying experiences we have had.

The prospects for home schooling have never been brighter in the USA than now. In some regions we are seeing 15% growth per year. Two to three percent of all children now being educated at the K-12 level are being educated at home and 70% of those are evangelical Christians. Most of the rest are traditional Catholics with whom we have many shared views. Estimates indicate that there are 1.8 to 2.0 million children now being educated in home schools at the K-12 level.

We are getting favorable articles on the front page of the *Wall Street Journal*, making Peter Jennings' *World News Tonight*, winning both the National Spelling Bee and National Geography Bee in back-to-back years, and seeing our children selected for some of the top colleges in the USA on full scholarships. Two hundred thousand former home schoolers are now enrolled in colleges or universities in the USA.

Acceptance of home schooling is increasing even among some who were previously skeptical. We have won most of the legal battles, thanks to HSLDA. Although we must be forever vigilant about our rights any time a legislative body meets anywhere, we have cause for optimism about the future of home schooling in America. We have finally come of age!

Greater opportunities for excellence and service await Christian home-schooling families. We still have the children, the teachers and the facilities to organize a bona-fide, Bible-based school system at a national level. We have the financial resources as well. In the past, we have lacked the vision—and the nerve. Many of our churches are not used five days a week. It's not too late. We can do it. The Lord will be with us as He was with the children of Israel.

THE LORD'S COMMAND

The Lord has commanded that we *"...bring them up in the training and admonition of the Lord."* (Ephesians 6:4). This means more than Sunday School. What it means is building up a new educational system consisting of networks of home-schooling parents and private, Christian schools, imparting a Christ-centered education to their children. Leaving aside the possibility of Christ's Second Coming, such an effort alone can reverse the moral and educational decline of this nation. A Christ-centered educational system will contrast markedly with the secular humanist one.

In the next chapter we will review how secular humanism came to control public schools, and why. We will also see how we were warned very shortly after the takeover began.

Then, in ensuing chapters we will develop the various aspects of our Christian alternative. We will show how home schooling or placing children in Christian schools is a Biblical and spiritual requirement.

It is still not too late to heed the warnings and reverse the threat to our children by removing our children from Pharaoh's school system! ∎

John Stuart Mill on State-Sponsored Education

"A general state education is a mere contrivance for
moulding people to be exactly like one another, and the
mould in which it casts them is that which pleases
the predominant power in government."

John Stuart Mill
19th Century Economist
Author of
On Liberty, Principles of Political Economy

CHAPTER TWO

GET BEHIND ME, HORACE MANN: THE RISE AND FALL OF STATE-SPONSORED PUBLIC EDUCATION

INTRODUCTION: HOW AMERICAN PUBLIC EDUCATION BEGAN

BRIEF HISTORY: STATE-SPONSORED EDUCATION

THE COMING OF SECULAR HUMANISM

THE EMERGENCE OF PROGRESSIVE EDUCATION

SCHOOL-TO-WORK SUPPORTS THE PURPOSE OF PUBLIC EDUCATION

FOUR PRESBYTERIAN GHOSTS OF CHRISTMAS PAST

THE ASSAULT ON THE CHRISTIAN FAMILY

INTRODUCTION: HOW AMERICAN PUBLIC EDUCATION BEGAN

Bad habits and weak theologies die hard. American evangelical Christians began to accept state-sponsored public schools as the norm for the education of their children in the mid-19th Century, and we are now paying a terrible price for this error in judgment. One of the main purposes of this book is to show the consequences of this error and provide some practical and Biblical solutions for a new and brighter future.

We believe that the wide acceptance today by the evangelical churches and individual Christian families of state-sponsored public schools has been a primary cause for the spiritual and cultural demise of the American family, churches and the nation over the last several decades. This demise is the result of the entire orientation and message of these schools, which has been secular and humanist, and they have fallen into the hands of people who don't just want to undermine the influence of Christianity, but who eventually want to put an end to individual freedom, favoring a socially engineered society.

A BIT OF HISTORY

It is important to realize that when our country began, there were no state-sponsored public schools as such.

The original colonies that preceded the new American nation started in New England with the Pilgrims and Puritans in the 1620's, products of the Protestant Reformation, who had come to the new land seeking religious freedom.

All education in America from 1620 to 1840, for 220 years, had a distinct moral character, and was almost entirely Christian with a strong Calvinistic orientation as well. Such education models existed throughout the American colonies before and after the American Revolution with the exception of the State of Maryland, which had been founded largely by Catholics.

All the early American colleges, starting with Harvard College, were founded upon Christian principles, and standard, orthodox Christian doctrine guided the faculties and curricula for many years. Harvard's original mission statement read:

> Let every student be plainly instructed and earnestly pressed to consider well the main end of his life and studies is to know God and Jesus Christ which is eternal life [John 17:3] and therefore to lay Christ in the bottom as the only foundation of all sound knowledge and learning.[1]

EARLY COLLEGES FOUNDED BY EVANGELICALS

Yale, Brown, Dartmouth and all but a few of the early colleges in America until the Civil War period were founded by evangelical Christians, and their purpose was to train clergy and other professions in the orthodox Christian Faith.

At the primary level, education was mostly pursued in home schooling, dame schools and private Christian academies. (Dame schools were small, private schools where a teacher, or dame, was entrusted with the education of a small group of children from several local families who had settled at a particular location.)

The stories of the early American founders being home schooled on their mother's knee are now making their way to the forefront, at a time when about one million American families have become involved in home schooling.

EARLY HOME SCHOOLERS WERE PRESIDENTS AND FOUNDERS OF OUR COUNTRY

George Washington, Ben Franklin and James Madison along with many other founders were home schooled in their early years. Until very recently, if public educators admitted this fact, it was usually described as an inferior model before the rise of public schools and, therefore, to be pitied.

But now, with the obvious demise of public education in America, some scholars are examining these early American and Christian educational models.

THE EXAMPLE SET BY JAMES MADISON

For example, Mary-Elaine Swanson, in her book, *The Education of James Madison: A Model for Today*[2] describes how his mother and grandmother home schooled young Madison until he was twelve. Then he was taught in a private Christian Academy by Presbyterian minister Rev. Donald Robertson.

At age 16, he entered the College of New Jersey (now Princeton University) and studied under Rev. John Witherspoon. Madison's education was completely private and Christian from childhood through college. He never attended a public school or a secular college one day in his life. His education was totally Christian!

Swanson also provides information on Madison's devotional journals and Bible study notes to show how thoroughly his Christian education impacted his worldview and spiritual life. She shows how his worldview was foundational to his drafting of the U.S. Constitution. Madison is considered the Father of the Constitution, having supplied the working document used at the constitutional Convention and having more of his ideas incorporated into the final document than any other founding father.

Is it possible that his thoroughly Christian education had no bearing on this document and that the Constitution arose from a secular or deist perspective as so many historians claim today? This is doubtful, and almost certainly a distortion of early-American history.

SCHOOLS IN EARLY AMERICA

The only exception to this completely private educational model was in New England where the Puritans did not have a concept of separation of church and state. Their local church schools were also the local community schools both church and community run. But they were distinctly

Christian in nature, and there was no state involvement or control.

Most families paid tuition, but there was a small tax subsidy for needy families who could not pay. Although given the community involvement, these schools were not entirely private, but there were no state-sponsored public schools as we know them today.

The New England Christian "common schools" weren't entirely private either. But Christian doctrine was taught and the Bible was a required textbook. They were thoroughly Christian in that Jesus Christ was taught as the only way of salvation, catechism was required, and theology and Scripture governed all subjects. These schools were sometimes referred to as "common schools."

Prior to the 1840's, many Protestant denominations maintained a vigorous Christian or parochial school system.

At one time during the Colonial period, the Lutherans had established 400 Christian schools throughout the colonies and these were strongly maintained and supported both before and after the rise of public schools in the 1840's. The Lutherans strongly opposed the emerging public schools and petitioned the State of Pennsylvania for the repeal of the free school law of 1834.[3] They intuitively understood that state-sponsored schools would threaten the existence of the private Christian schools.

OUR BIBLICAL CONTEXT AND AUTHORITY

Before going any further, a Biblical context should be established. We must assure godly generations in our families and churches, and for the renewal and rebuilding of our nation.

From the ashes of the old order dominated by humanism for the past several decades and the more recent rise of neopaganism, we can raise new generations of godly leaders. The future could belong to us if we don't stumble or lose our vision for faith and freedom, and are not spoiled or blinded by our successes.

Consider Matthew 16:21-23:

> 21 From that time Jesus began to show to His disciples that He must go to Jerusalem, and suffer many things from the elders and chief priests and scribes, and be killed, and be raised the third day.
>
> 22 Then Peter took Him aside and began to rebuke Him, saying, "Far be it from You, Lord; this shall not happen to You!"
>
> 23 But He turned and said to Peter, "Get behind Me, Satan! You are an offense to Me, for you are not mindful of the things of God, but the things of men."[4]

Let the words of Jesus Christ serve as a warning to us. Jesus knew that the crucifixion He was to suffer was essential for our redemption. No cross, no Crown for Him; no cross, no redemption for us. Our whole Christian experience of salvation by faith is dependent upon Jesus' going through a sacrificial death on our behalf.

Peter didn't have a redemption agenda at that time and didn't understand God's plan. He didn't have the big picture or a complete worldview. He even tried to correct Jesus and to stop Him from going to the Cross!

Jesus corrected Peter in a stern and direct way. Did he confuse Peter with Satan? No, he was only telling us that Peter in that moment was being used by Satan, and that Satan is ultimately behind any idea, philosophy, ideology, plan, or curriculum that rejects the Cross, ignores redemption and the place of the sacrificial death of Jesus in the total scheme of things: "But He turned and said to Peter, "Get behind Me, Satan! You are an offense to Me, for you are not mindful of the things of God, but the things of men."

THE RISE OF STATE-SPONSORED SCHOOLS
IN THE UNITED STATES OF AMERICA
(GET BEHIND ME, HORACE MANN)

Let's apply this to the Christian education of children, paying attention to the realm of curriculum, worldviews, ideologies and plans that interfere with the need to maintain a Christ-centered education in our Christian school or home schooling experience.

This chapter title is, "Get Behind Me, Horace Mann: The Rise and Fall of State-Sponsored Public Education." Who was Horace Mann? Mann is considered the father of public education in America. His role is indisputable. He organized the first state-controlled public schools in Boston around 1840 and then the State of Massachusetts.

The state simply started funding the Christian schools and shortly thereafter took over their administration as well.

Mann, however, was a Unitarian, not a Trinitarian, and a case can be made that his efforts were an indirect or oblique attack on orthodox Christianity at that time.

He was associated with a number of wealthy and influential Unitarians who had grown dissatisfied with the parent-centered, church-influenced schools that prevailed in America.

Mann went to Europe, and in Prussia (now part of Germany) where state-sponsored schools already existed, he absorbed a certain philosophy of education holding that the purpose of education is not theological instruction but the production of a certain kind of citizen, one who might retain the trappings of Christian morality but would also be loyal and obedient to secular authorities.

The term "kindergarten" is, in fact, Prussian, not English, and demonstrates the Prussian, European roots of the very idea of state-sponsored public education. Since the "K" in the phrase "K-12" derives from kindergarten, we should be able to see how deeply the Prussian model came to affect Americans' thinking about education.[5]

A THREE PART PLAN

Horace Mann's group recommended the adoption of the Prussian educational model because the state, and not the parents, would have control, and children could be enrolled at the earliest age when they were most impressionable. His group designed a three-part plan:

First, attendance would be compulsory.

Second, teachers would have to be certified, as graduates of a state teacher's college.

Third, schools would be owned and operated by the state.

Mann's group considered the second of these to be of paramount importance. They agreed that even if they could not get all three elements approved, the second was crucial, because "if we teach them what to teach, they will teach what they have been taught."[6]

At first, the Massachusetts legislature balked at the idea of creating a state teacher's college when they learned of the price tag: $50,000. But the Unitarians offered $25,000 of their own money if the state would match it. They did, and in 1837, the first state-sponsored teacher's college was established. Soon, other states followed.

Mann persuaded some of the New England churches to give up the use of distinctive doctrines like the Trinity and redemption in Jesus in the "common schools." Thus the latter would stress only the common morality of Christianity, such as the Ten Commandments, and the Lord's Prayer. Mann desired that the schools teach a generic brand of

Protestant morality. He wanted to keep the shell and husk of Christianity, but not the meat or core Christian doctrines. Horace Mann, like Peter, wanted the new state-sponsored schools to avoid the Cross; that is, he wanted to avoid Jesus Christ. He actually saw the secular model of education to which he had been exposed in Europe as the means of salvation, not the Christian Gospel.

PROTESTANT VS. CATHOLIC

One rationale why this united Protestant front was successful at that time was that they could supposedly use the public schools or common schools to convert immigrant Catholic children then entering New England in large numbers. Up to this time the U.S. had been almost entirely a Protestant nation.

The entrance of large numbers of Catholics destabilized the uneasy competition between different Protestant churches and educational institutions.

The pressure to unite and form a common front was strong. Horace Mann, though himself not an orthodox Christian, was able to show others an opportunity to bring people together to unite for the common cause of winning the Catholics to Christ and to the Protestant Christian Faith. But the Catholics did not accept this approach, and after several decades they elected to organize their own private parochial school system.

THE UNITARIAN CONNECTION

Educational scholar Samuel Blumenfeld has documented the Unitarian connection in his book *Is Public Education Necessary?* and in a July 1999 article in *Tabletalk*, the devotional and theological magazine published by Ligonier Ministries, an outreach and teaching ministry of Presbyterian scholar R.C. Sproul. Blumenfeld writes:

Unitarianism ... crossed the Atlantic and gained a foothold at Harvard College where the first liberal president was elected in 1707....

In 1785, under the ministry of Harvard-educated Unitarian James Freeman, the congregation of King's Chapel in Boston purged their Anglican liturgy of all references to the Trinity, thus establishing the first Unitarian church in America.

Twenty years later the Unitarians finally took full control of Harvard. The takeover of Harvard in 1805 by the Unitarians is probably the most important intellectual event in American history—at least from the standpoint of education....

It was, in effect, the beginning of the long journey to the secular humanist worldview that now dominates American culture.[7]

THE UNITARIAN CONNECTIONS

Theologian Rousas John Rushdoony, in his seminal work entitled *The Messianic Character of American Education*,[8] carefully chronicles the Unitarian connections to the founding and growth of the public school system in America from Horace Mann and the work of others into the early 20th Century. He traces the contribution of lesser-known, but influential, educators on the American scene in this process such as Henry Barnard, Wm. Torrey Harris, Nicholas Murray Butler, and Edward Lee Thorndike.

There were many more educational leaders who followed the early lead of Horace Mann, such as the well-known John Dewey. Clearly, American public schools were non-Christian and Unitarian, secular in trajectory, from the early days.

Rushdoony summarizes this development of several decades, starting in the 1840's, as follows:

Although other churches [non-Unitarian ones] made their contribution to the movement, and the New England "theocracy" absorbed the cause....It was Unitarianism in particular, which gave itself whole-heartedly to the cause of messianic education and statism. The influence of that church on 19th Century America is too seldom appreciated.

Unitarianism was in a sense the American establishment of its day....[9]

Rushdoony further summarized his important finding:

The [Unitarian] church thereafter became progressively irrelevant to the American scene as the [public] schools became steadily the working embodiment of the Unitarian faith in salvation by statist education. The relationship of Unitarianism, statism, and statist education in the United States is an important if neglected area of the 19th Century.[10]

Rushdoony's important book appeared on the scene in 1963 at the same time the U.S. Supreme Court handed down the *Abington v. Schempp* decision regarding Bible readings in public schools.

One would think the larger evangelical Christian community would take note, as Rushdoony had so ably diagnosed the cause of the spiritual demise of the public schools. Yet, not one Christian magazine reviewed this book; it was almost completely ignored by the larger Christian community at that time.

At the same time, secular education journals wrote numerous reviews critical of *The Messianic Character of American Education*. Christian leaders did not yet see the cause and effect relationship between the Unitarian connection and the decline of public schools. Yet the secular education establishment immediately saw the threat of

Rushdoony's research and findings. If the Christian Church at that time had awakened and seen its imminent danger and learned the true history of the formation of the public schools, the health of the nation, families and churches would be much different today. They missed their moment in 1963.

Thankfully, *The Messianic Character of American Education* and other similar works are now being read and understood by more and more evangelical Christian pastors, educators and denominational leaders.

We believe we are not too late to salvage some children and families from the ashes of the Unitarian-created public schools.

CHRISTIAN EDUCATION IN EARLY AMERICA

Until Horace Mann we could say that practically all primary education in America was Christian.

Even though the New England Puritans did not have a clear understanding of the concept of separation of church and state, their town schools were like many of our private Christian day schools today.

Large numbers of children were home schooled or educated in dame schools in colonial America. There was some tax subsidy for these schools at the town level, but most families paid for some or all of their children's education. This school system was universal if not compulsory. In Massachusetts it became compulsory in 1852.

In the South, the school system was entirely family or church run. It was similar to what is called private Christian education today. It was unlike the New England model in some respects.

James Madison was not alone in being home schooled by his mother and grandmother until he was 12 years old and was then taught in a Christian school until he entered the

College of New Jersey, today Princeton University. His entire primary education was what we would call today evangelical Christian with a Calvinistic orientation.

Dozens of other founding fathers also studied under James Madison's teacher, Rev. John Witherspoon, himself a signatory of the Declaration of Independence.

It should be clear, therefore, that our country's founding documents were implicitly Christian in formulation if not explicit. Madison's educational experiences were not atypical of the other founding fathers, after all.[11]

THE GROWTH OF HORACE MANN'S SYSTEM

The new system initiated by Horace Mann began to grow and take hold across the land until, by the end of the 19th Century, it was the dominant educational system. Many Presbyterians, Lutherans and Episcopalians continued to maintain their own school systems. We still see some facets of this today in the Dutch Reformed schools, Missouri Synod Lutheran schools, Presbyterian and Episcopal schools around the nation.

Since the public schools began to be known as the Protestant domain, the Catholics set up their own separate parochial school system. But let us be clear that these public schools were not Christian in its true parochial meaning.

Many public schools even into the modern era and as late as the 1970's were benign or even Christ-friendly in some places where the Christian community was large and dominant. But Horace Mann's Prussian-derived concept of a non-sectarian, non-doctrinal or non-confessional public school had prevailed. There was no Jesus Christ, no Gospel and no Trinity, just a generic Protestant morality and the Ten Commandments. This course toward failure was charted relatively early in our nation's history. Thus, families can surely say, "Get behind me, Horace Mann."

THE COMING OF SECULAR HUMANISM

T.C. Pinckney, Brigadier General USAF retired, and 2nd Vice President of the Southern Baptist Convention, gave an important speech to the SBC Executive Committee, the governing body of the SBC, on September 18, 2001. We have exerpted portions as follows:

> This kind of watered-down Protestantism proved to be very vulnerable to the secular humanist and materialistic philosophies beginning to emerge, especially in Europe.
>
> Just 14 years after the Massachusetts state school system was established, a French sociologist and philosopher named Auguste Comte published a massive work entitled System of Positive Polity and gave birth to the intellectual movement known as positivism, a form of humanism that substitutes science for God.
>
> The core ideas of this movement were three:
> (1) human reason is able to discern truth on its own;
>
> (2) science is reason's sole method, and therefore should replace revealed religion; and
>
> (3) society can be improved indefinitely and even perfected by the judicious application of the methods of science to society.

Comte and his followers looked forward to a world in which science had completely replaced Christian theology, and our new religion was that of humanity: the essence of secular humanism. He wrote:

"The object of our philosophy is to direct the spiritual reorganization of the civilized world.... [W]e may begin at once to construct that system of morality under which the final regeneration of Humanity will proceed."[12]

Comte did not see this plan as being completed overnight. It would probably take generations. The plan began to make progress very shortly.

When Darwin published *The Origin of Species*, the secular world at last had a fully naturalistic account of how all life on Earth—and by implication, human life—might have originated.

According to Darwin, man was not created by a specific act of God but emerged as the result of a continuous process that had been going on for hundreds of millions of years.

Darwin maintained that it was the result of natural selection: random genetic mutations, a few of which left some species better equipped to survive and breed than others, a process unguided by any supernatural hand.

One of the assumptions behind evolution is that species must constantly adapt to a changing environment or die out; as they adapt, they eventually evolve into new species. Human beings, in this view, are just one of many species of primate, and evolved from ape-like biological ancestors.

Of course, according to a consistent naturalistic or materialist worldview, there is no God for us to answer to; there are only secular authorities such as the state (i.e., government). The theory of evolution soon became one of the linchpins of the modern scientific outlook on the world and human life.

What eventually emerged was a vision of a future of Humanity without God and without individuality. The secular humanist believes we can take charge of our own evolution.

For some, however, this meant rule by the self-defined most capable over the less capable. In 1918, British author Benjamin Kidd wrote:

"Oh you blind leaders who seek to convert the world by labored disputations. Step out of the way or the world must fling you aside. GIVE US THE YOUNG. GIVE US THE

YOUNG and we will create a new mind and a new earth in a single generation."[13]

Ten years later, American sociologist Ross L. Finney wrote,

"Everything depends on passing out the expert opinions of the social scientists to the masses of the people; and the schools, particularly the high schools, are the only adequate agency available for this function."[14]

Yet another sociologist, Charles A. Ellwood, wrote that "Human institutions, sociology shows, are in every case learned adjustments. As such, they can be modified provided we can obtain control of the learning process."[15]

The American Humanist Association, finally, understood from the beginning the importance of gaining control over state-sponsored schools. One of its key statements reads:

"In order to capture this nation, one has to totally remove moral and spiritual values and absolutes from the thinking of the child. The child has to think that there is no standard of right and wrong, that truth is relative, and that diversity is the only absolute to be gained."[16]

SECULARISM GAINS THE UPPER HAND

Soon we would see Supreme Court prayer and Bible reading decisions that would indicate secularism getting control of the system. These started with the *Everson* decision in 1947 which relied on the concept of the separation of church and state; then came the *Engel v. Vitale* public school prayer case in 1962 and *Abington v. Schempp* public school Bible reading case in 1963.

There have been 12 major decisions limiting the expression of Christian faith in public schools since 1947. Starting in 1947, the Supreme Court began progressively first to limit and then eventually to expel all expressions of faith associated with Christianity from the public schools.

The Ten Commandments and a generic Christian morality, which Horace Mann could abide in public schools, were also eliminated by the *Stone v. Graham* case, from Kentucky, in 1980.

SHOULD CHRISTIANS ATTEMPT TO "TAKE BACK" THE PUBLIC SCHOOLS?

When Christian leaders and families lobby and organize today to take back the public schools, therefore, they reveal an unfortunate but serious ignorance of these schools' actual history and nature.

This history and nature includes core elements alien to our founding principles, core elements brought here from Prussia by Horace Mann and developed by a community of sociologists fully committed to the secular humanist educational model described above. And, with each passing generation, they became more and more committed to secular humanism.

In many areas, particularly outside the Northeast, churches retained much of their influence in communities and the public schools tended to reflect this. Many schools, therefore, remained benign or even Christ-friendly.

EXODUS FROM PUBLIC SCHOOLS

Public schools were, nevertheless, never in God's plan for Christian families and education, any more than was the bondage of Israelites in Egypt prior to the time of Moses.

The Christian community has been like the community of the children of Israel of old who spent 400 years enslaved under the Egyptian Pharaoh. God's will was that His people have their own land, the land of Canaan, flowing with milk and honey.

Despite the apparent Christ-friendly orientation of some state-sponsored schools, these schools have never really belonged to the Christian churches and families. We have only been away in Egypt from our rightful land for a season. Today's Pharaoh has only allowed us to work and learn in his state-sponsored public schools for a time. Starting with the *Everson* case in 1947, Pharaoh began to reclaim his state-sponsored public schools, and Jesus Christ was more and more eliminated.

Christian children and teachers have become less and less comfortable, and in some cases, openly unwelcome. Pharaoh has told the Christian Church through many Supreme Court decisions and through other means that these schools are his, and do not belong to Christians.

If the public schools today tolerate their persons and allow them to attend, there is no toleration for their Christian Faith. Other religions and leaders (Islam, Buddhism, Native American religions, etc.) can be discussed, but Our Lord and Savior Jesus Christ is persona non grata.

EMERGENCE OF PROGRESSIVE EDUCATION

If Unitarianism was the prime mover behind the rise of state-sponsored schooling during the mid-1800's, then the Progressive Education movement became its equivalent in the 1900's.

With humanist and positivist outlooks increasingly in control and ready to be applied to education, the Progressive Educators picked up where the Unitarians had left off. They finished the job of creating public schools that were bound to become hostile to Christians and a Bible-centered worldview. The major thinker behind Progressive Education was the American philosopher John Dewey.

Dewey, like Horace Mann, was steeped in the philosophies of Europe rather than those of our own founding tradition—especially, in Dewey's case, the pivotal German philosopher G.W.F. Hegel. Hegel did more than any other single thinker to create the philosophical basis for the emergence of the state as a secular entity replacing God as an object of loyalty and reverence—an idea sometimes called *statism*.

Dewey also drew on Darwinian evolution and the idea of institutions shaped and reshaped according to scientific methods. He found the idea of species needing to adapt to a constantly changing world to be a very useful tool in guiding the philosophy he wanted to see dominate state-sponsored education.

ARENAS OF SOCIAL TRANSFORMATION

Shortly after the beginning of the 20th century, he began to work out a philosophy of education that would view public schools not as places where the wisdom of tradition and the learning of ages past would be transmitted to the next generation, but rather as arenas of social transformation.

In a constantly changing world, Dewey felt, there can be no absolute rights and wrongs. There are only secular authorities and strategies for adapting—all part and parcel of taking charge of our own evolution and trying to perfect ourselves without God. This is what Progressive Educators brought into public schools.

DISMAL FAILURE OF PROGRESSIVE EDUCATION

The early efforts of the Progressive Educators, as John Stormer observed in his book *None Dare Call It Education*, were dismal failures.[17] Students didn't learn anything. Progressive Education, nonetheless, fit in with the man-centered, secular humanist/naturalist worldview, so within a generation became the dominant philosophy of major education departments and teachers colleges and, therefore, of the state-sponsored schools.

PUBLIC EDUCATION NOT IMPARTING KNOWLEDGE?

Public school philosophy began to coalesce around the idea that the purpose of education is not to impart knowledge, morals or wisdom but to "socialize" children—to enable them to fit into a society where there are no fixed moral truths, just changing conditions. Dewey's philosophy of education rejected the idea that knowledge is valuable as an end in itself; he believed that what counted was children's abilities to "solve problems," and be able to "learn by doing." By 1970, combined with more recent assertions such as Dr. Benjamin Spock's original *Baby and Child Care* and Alfred Kinsey's studies of human sexuality, the results of this kind of education started to become clear.[18]

A generation had come of age that saw, for example, sexual experimentation with multiple "lifestyles" as a kind of entitlement. Of course, if the Bible is just one of many collections of myths in a naturalistic world, then following its injunctions about sex outside of marriage is just one option of many. In the end, the only reasons for not engaging in sex out of wedlock with as many partners as possible are practical ones (avoiding pregnancy and sexually transmitted infections, for example). If there is no absolute right and wrong, then the only absolute is, *Thou shalt not get caught*!

Marriage as an institution was soon in trouble, and has continued to slip for three decades—decades that also saw the rise of herpes, AIDS, and other epidemics of sexually transmitted diseases. The public schools' solutions to these problems have been to dispense "safe sex" education to students along with condoms.

By the 1980's, it became clear that public schools were not delivering in terms of imparting cognitive ability to their graduates, whose achievements had begun to slip noticeably relative to their counterparts in other advanced nations.

In 1983, then Secretary of Education William Bennett sounded alarm bells with a major study, *A Nation at Risk*, issued by the National Commission on Excellence in Education. This study concluded in a well-known statement that our entire way of life is threatened by

> ...a rising tide of mediocrity that threatens our very future as a Nation and a people. What was unimaginable a generation ago has begun to occur—others are matching and surpassing our educational attainments.
>
> If an unfriendly foreign power had attempted to impose on America the mediocre educational performance that exists today, we might well have viewed it as an act of war. As it stands, we have allowed this to happen to ourselves.[19]

Since then, matters have only worsened, with the rise of movements centered around self-esteem and around the idea that the only purpose of education is to prepare children and young people to enter the global work force. This is, of course, just a more specific version of Progressive Education that John Dewey started.

Self-esteem is a central concept of outcome-based education, which stresses what secular philosophy education majors call the affective domain. The affective domain emphasizes expression of feelings, participation in group projects, issuing group grades, cooperation and sensitivity to others. It rejects such cognitive skills as working individually to achieve mastery over a subject, competition with other students, and so on.

Students who have been immersed in an educational system which emphasizes the affective domain at the expense of the cognitive domain will graduate as cooperative, secular-minded consumers—and supporters of socialism—without even realizing it. It goes without saying that moral beliefs rooted in our Christian heritage have no place in such schools.

CHRISTIANITY ERASED FROM SCHOOLS

While Horace Mann may have retained a place for the Ten Commandments in state-sponsored schools, clearly today even these last vestiges of Christianity have been erased.

The philosophy of state-sponsored education today is thoroughly naturalistic, socialistic and globalist. Its purpose is not to impart knowledge, Christian wisdom or cognitive ability but to prepare young people to service the secular global economy.

SCHOOL-TO-WORK SUPPORTS THE GOAL OF "PUBLIC EDUCATION"

What history we have seen of the government-school movement in this country surely supports the idea that public or government schools are fundamentally repressive and cannot be otherwise whether some or even a large percentage of those in them, administrators as well as teachers, mean well.

A study of the work of Horace Mann and John Dewey, the two main philosophers of government schooling in the United States, indicates that education in the traditional sense of that term is not what government schools have ever set out to deliver. Rather, their purpose is to turn out a certain kind of human being: fully secularized, made compliant by constant immersion in group projects, and obedient to secular authority. Although school-to-work is a new term that has swept the educational system by storm over the past several years, the idea has been germinating from the beginning of state schools. This movement culminated when President Bill Clinton signed the School-To-Work Opportunities Act of 1994.

This legislation, rather like Goals 2000 itself, allegedly sets out to be one of many "reforms" of government schools aimed at rectifying the problems of employers being unable to find employees who are qualified to do the work that is needed in an increasingly technological age. It appropriated federal funds to states, which would initiate school-to-work programs. All 50 states received planning grants, and as of 1998, 37 states had set up school-to-work programs.

The stated purpose of the school-to-work agenda was to respond to the openly acknowledged decline in educational achievement in the United States that prompted *A Nation at Risk.*

What the school-to-work agenda purports to do is to stem the "rising tide of mediocrity" by building a federally-funded, workplace-friendly, state infrastructure to integrate education reform with work force and economic development. It sets out to include all students in public schools.

It promotes career awareness and exploration in the early grades, involving comprehensive counseling intended to lead to career major selection by the 11th grade. Then it proposes to orient learning around these majors, including workplace mentoring, the teaching of "positive attitudes" about group work, certification of job skills, and efforts to link students with potential employers and community service agencies, finally assisting with job placement.

What does the school-to-work agenda actually do? Before answering this, it is helpful to realize that school-to-work follows the same premises that we have unearthed regarding secularism and the progressive education movement, and finally, outcome-based education. It was closely linked with Goals 2000.

For example, Goals 2000 created the NSSB (National Skills Standards Board) through which the "Career Clusters" of School-to-Work were birthed. What it accomplishes is to involve the federal government in education more deeply than ever before, and in a movement designed to promote the servile rather than the liberal arts.

That is to say, school-to-work views the purpose of education as almost purely vocational; it does not encourage intellectual curiosity of any sort, much less a Biblical view of the world and society.

SERVANTS OF THE GLOBAL ECONOMY

Rather than encourage individual performance, School-to-Work stifles individual initiative under an avalanche of group projects. Children are viewed not as individuals, all impressively different, but as "human capital" or future "human resources"—future servants of the global economy.

The new generation of progressive educators has invented some buzzwords for this new brand of vocationally oriented education, "career cluster," "curriculum integration" (the merger of academic subjects with vocational training), "applied learning," and so on.

Under H.R. 1, or the recently passed No Child Left Behind legislation, the "career clusters" are called "smaller learning communities." All, in one way or another, hearken back to Dewey's basic theme that the purpose of education is not to communicate knowledge, culture or morality but to adjust the individual to society.

With this emphasis, the school-to-work agenda provides seven career paths:

(1) Agricultural Science;

(2) Art, Communications and Media Technology;

(3) Business and Marketing;

(4) Health Science;

(5) Human Development, Management and Services;

(6) Industrial and Engineering Technology; and

(7) Personal and Protective Services.

One of the upshots of *A Nation at Risk* revealed how far American students had fallen behind their foreign counterparts in the sciences, mathematics and in subjects like history and geography. It is unclear where any of these subjects fit into the school-to-work agenda except, in some cases, as means to vocational ends (it is hard to imagine training computer programmers and engineers without teaching them mathematics, for example), and in others as little more than decorations.

The school-to-work agenda, in the last analysis, is using Pharaoh's school system to micromanage the lives of the nation's youth, capturing them when they are children and making participation in the system mandatory not just legally but economically.

When this system is sufficiently integrated into the business communities, it will simply be impossible for those who opt out of the system via private schools to obtain employment. Thus it is not unfair to describe the school-to-work agenda as following very closely the logic of the secular state, which is authoritarianism. This system has a utilitarian view of the masses, because people are valuable only by the work and productivity they provide the secular state or the economy.

If this system comes to fruition, the federal government will increase its power, by the transfer of enormous amounts of power into the hands of appointed bureaucrats. Parents will lose even more control over the education of their children.

Actually, the Workforce Investment Act (WIA) of 1998 has already transferred this authority to the bureaucrats. Businesses will no longer be free to hire based on traditional or free-market criteria as in the past. The Workforce Investment Act of 1998 is the third leg of the authoritarian triangle.

The WIA creates a partnership between government and the economy through a new form of governance called the Governor's Workforce Development Committee. These will manage all jobs through one-stop job centers.

Supporters of the school-to-work agenda include all the dominant political and educational organizations, tax-exempt foundations, large corporations and associations of corporations. These include the National Governor's Association, the Education Commission of the States, the National Education Association, the American Federation of Teachers, the National Parent-Teacher Association, the National Association of School Boards, the Carnegie Corporation, the De Witt Wallace-Readers' Digest Foundation, the National Association for Supervision and Curriculum Development, the National Alliance of Business, the Association of Manufacturers, the National Coalition of Advanced Manufacturing, the U.S. Chamber of Commerce, the American Business Conference and Center for Occupational Research and Development, and, finally, major employers of low-paid, "temp" workers such as Manpower, Incorporated.

WHO WILL CONTROL EDUCATION?

Critics of the school-to-work agenda all observe that it further removes control of education from both parents and local school boards answerable to parents. These critics include the Family Research Council, the Eagle Forum, the Evergreen Freedom Foundation of Washington, the Oklahoma Council of Public Affairs, the Cascade Policy Institute of Oregon, the Family Foundation of Virginia, Parents Involved in Education of California, Pennsylvania Parents' Commission, and the Kansas Education Watch.

Major think tanks such as the Heritage Foundation and the American Enterprise Institute have also joined with these critics, but one may note how many of the organizations critical of the school-to-work agenda are state-based, while also noting how many supporters are nationally-based.

THE "NO CHILD LEFT BEHIND ACT"
The school-to-work agenda may find its final culmination in the measure known as H.R. 1, also called the "No Child Left Behind Act" of 2001—recently signed by President George W. Bush, Jr. Despite the name, calculated to win support, the Minnesota-based Maple River Education Coalition has assembled documentation showing how this legislation further establishes centralized, national testing, further diminishes local control, and expands requirements for Washington-based standards that states must adopt or lose federal education funding.

While talk of "standards" looks good at first glance, many of the "standards" being discussed have almost nothing to do with academic standards traditionally understood.

For example, so-called "constructivist math, a product of the National Council of Teachers of Mathematics (NCTM), was itself a creation of Goals 2000. Maple River Education Coalition addresses this philosophy of the NCTM's in "A Brief Look at Technology in the Math Classroom":

> No longer should teachers be constrained by the artificial restriction to numbers that children know how to employ in the paper-and-pencil algorithms of arithmetic.... Because the calculator will be able to add or multiply the data even if the children have not yet learned how....
>
> Weakness in algebraic skills need no longer prevent students from understanding ideas in more advanced mathematics. Just as computerized spelling checkers permit writers to express ideas without the psychological block of terrible

> spelling, so will the new calculators enable motivated stu-
> dents who are weak in algebra or trigonometry to persevere
> in calculus or statistics.[20]

In other words, students no longer need to be able to "do math" in the traditional sense; calculators can do all the work for them. The students can go on with their group-project work. This, of course, makes them entirely dependent on the technological crutch (and on the group). The "standards" being offered here are not standards in any sense that would have been recognized even a generation ago. The decline in mathematics teaching is just one example.

Other buzzwords are "accountability and flexibility." This appeals to what much of the public already realizes, which is that public schools are not turning out educated graduates. The public wants to hold schools accountable to local voters and higher standards.

Employers lament their inability to fill job openings with employees who can read instruction manuals and do arithmetic calculations. The government reformists claim to be able to do something about this, and they speak of making schools, school districts and teachers "accountable."

But "accountability" begs the question: accountable to whom? To the public? The very words "public school" would suggest so.

But what the buzzword really means is that schools, teachers, and local and state school districts are accountable to the federal government. Supposed state standards are actually federal standards.

Thus, H.R. 1, or "No Child Left Behind" legislation, signed into law on January 8, 2002, will actually continue all the policies of Goals 2000, school-to-work, and outcome-based education in a fashion that is more centralized and dictatorial than ever.

A LOCALLY CONTROLLED PUBLIC SCHOOL?

In the final analysis, there is no longer any such thing as a freestanding, locally controlled, state-sponsored public school anywhere in the United States. The state-sponsored schools answer to bureaucrats in Washington and further an agenda that has less and less to do with genuine education with each passing year.

Christians would be advised to drop the term "public school" from their vocabulary since these schools are not run by the public and are not for the public. The nationalization of the once public-school system is now complete in content, structure and management.

One of the main issues is: Who ought to have authority over the education of children? The United States was founded under the assumption that education belongs in the hands of private citizens—usually parents themselves, but not excluding private schools. No constitutional provisions allowed for schools to be established and run by the federal government. This is prohibited by the enumerated-powers doctrine and supported by the 9th and 10th Amendments of the U.S. Constitution.

FOUR PRESBYTERIAN GHOSTS FROM CHRISTMAS' PAST

1) Dr. Archibald A. Hodge

We cannot say we weren't warned. During the period of the rise of state-sponsored public schools, many notable Christian leaders spoke out against Christians accepting a state-run school system. Dr. Archibald A. Hodge, at the time Professor of Theology at Princeton, wrote in 1887:

> **This prevalent superstition that men can be educated for good citizenship, or for any other use under heaven, with-**

**out religion, is an unscientific and unphilosophical as it is
irreligious...... I am sure as I am of the fact of Christ's
reign that a comprehensive and centralized system of
national education, separated from religion, as is now
commonly proposed, will prove the most appalling engine
for the propagation of anti-Christian and atheistic unbelief, and of anti-social nihilistic ethics, individual, social,
and political, which this sin-rent world has ever seen.[21]**

Hodge was a leading American theologian of his day, teaching young ministers and writing theology for many years
while at Princeton Theological Seminary.

2) R.L. Dabney

The South had no public schools until after the Civil War
when Reconstructionism imposed this system on Southern
states. Southern Presbyterian theologian R.L. Dabney also
spoke and wrote against this system in the 1870's and into
the 1880's. He was the South's most prominent theologian
and taught for years at Union Theological Seminary, now in
Richmond, Virginia.

Dabney questioned the ability of state schools to offer a
true education apart from ethics or religion, which they
would necessarily leave to the churches. He wrote,

> The State refuses to be understood this way. It claims to edu-
> cate. [i.e. the whole person] This can be seen in the universal
> argument of the advocates of public education. It assumes
> the state has the right and duty of providing young citizens
> shall be competent in their responsibility as citizens. But this
> responsibility is ethical in nature.[22]

Dabney argued and wrote extensively against the emergence
of state-run secular public schools in Virginia, citing the

famous Girard Will case argued by Daniel Webster before the U.S. Supreme Court.

Dabney didn't think it possible to construct an educational enterprise apart from a religious or theological foundation. Girard had instructed in his will that a college be formed using his estate that would exclude the Christian religion in all educational practice. Dabney commented on this case, comparing it to the proposals for a new state-sponsored public school system in Virginia. He did not believe such a secular education was permissible or possible saying,

> Before ours, no people of any age, religion, or civilization, has ever thought so. Against this present attempt [i.e. to set up secular public schools in Virginia]...stands the whole common sense of mankind. Pagans, Catholics, Moslems, Greeks and Protestants have all rejected any education not grounded in religion as absurd and wicked.[23]

Webster himself argued before the Supreme Court and urged them to invalidate the Girard will, saying,

> In what age, by what sect, where, when, and by whom, has religious truth been excluded from the education of youth? Nowhere. Never! Everywhere, and at all times, it has been regarded as essential. It is of the essence, the vitality of useful instruction.[24]

The Supreme Court at that time accepted the argument of Daniel Webster and invalidated the Girard will. The U.S. Supreme Court, on February 10, 1844, believed that education was not possible without a religious foundation.

Dabney lost his argument against Virginia's establishing state-run public schools. This alien educational model took hold throughout the South in the next several decades as it had in the New England starting with Horace Mann in the 1840's.

By the late 1880's, the private and Christian-based school system had faded as the dominant educational model and been replaced by a state-run public school system.

Dabney, the South's greatest theologian and thinker, had not been heeded. He died in 1898. Today many pastors, theologians and Christian educators are studying afresh Dabney's arguments against secular public schools and are amazed at his foresight into the problems that would be created if Virginia and the rest of the South accepted state-run public schools.

This venerable prophet, having been dead for a hundred years, still speaks. Will this generation heed his warning? We have been given a second chance.

3) J. Gresham Machen

More recently, J. Gresham Machen, founder and president of Westminster Theological Seminary, and in his day regarded as America's leading conservative theologian, also inveighed against state-run public schools. He wrote and lectured during the 1920's and 1930's. Some of his books are theological classics and still used in evangelical seminaries today.

But one of his lesser-known books is particularly important now: *Education, Christianity and the State.* It is a series of articles, lectures, and congressional testimony that had not been published during Machen's life. We must thank the Trinity Foundation for compiling these articles and sermons and publishing them in 1987. Machen felt the state-run public school was a threat to American liberty and said,

> But while tyranny itself is nothing new, the technique of
> tyranny has been enormously improved in our day....That

tyranny is being exercised most effectively in the fields of education. A monopolistic system of education controlled by the State is far more efficient in crushing our liberty than the cruder weapons of fire and sword.[25]

This was from a speech entitled "Forward in Faith" by Machen in 1934 given before the National Union of Christian Schools.[26]

Machen wrote and lectured in appreciation of the then small Christian-school movement. He described the Christian schools' mission:

Against this monopoly of education by the State, the Christian school brings a salutary protest; it contends for the right of parents to bring up their children in accordance with the dictates of their conscience and not in the manner pre-scribed by the State.[27]

Machen testified before Congress against an increased federal role in K-12 education. He did not know that the Lord would do something unique and beautiful in giving birth to the Christian home-school movement in the modern era.

4) Dr. Gordon Clark
Finally, Dr. Gordon Clark, who passed away in 1985, wrote on Christian education topics. Carl F.H. Henry, founding editor of *Christianity Today*, described Clark as "one of the profoundest Christian philosophers of our time."

Clark's book, *A Christian Philosophy of Education*, also published by Trinity Foundation, is essential reading for those who desire to construct Biblical convictions about education. In a chapter entitled "The Relationship of Public Education to Christianity," a speech originally delivered in 1935, Clark warned the elders of Chester, Pennsylvania, on

the dangers of public education and the need to replace that
system with Christian schools. He said in that speech,

> First of all, education is and should be regarded as the
> responsibility of the family. It is primarily to parents, not the
> state, nor even to the church, that God has trusted the chil-
> dren and their upbringing.[28]

I have selected only four prominent theologians to provide
a sense of what has been written and a brief account of the
warnings that have been ignored. These men were trained
ministers, noted in their day, but their warnings against
state-run public schools were largely ignored.

Jeremiah 2:13 says, "For My people have committed two
evils: They have forsaken Me, the fountain of living waters,
And hewn themselves cisterns—broken cisterns that can
hold no water."

AN ALIEN, RENEGADE SYSTEM OF SCHOOLING
Pointedly, state-run public schools are not the schools of
Christians. They don't belong to Christian families or
churches. "Public education" is an alien, renegade system of
schooling. That is to say, what we ordinarily call the public
school system was not the original American model. It was
never really Christian although Christian children and teachers were allowed to co-exist in it until the Supreme Court
decisions on prayer and Bible reading in public schools
starting in 1947.

Unitarians, steeped in European humanistic philosophy
and education movements, started the public schools as an
indirect attack on orthodox Christianity.

Many prominent Christian leaders and theologians
warned the churches not to adopt this system or support it,
but it happened nevertheless, and with the support, consent,

participation and blessing of much of the Christian Church of that time.

Horace Mann was successful in helping to bring about a public education system that denies God, Jesus Christ, our Lord and Savior, and now even has removed the Ten Commandments and the practice of any Christian-based morality. If we are mature in our faith, and have mustered any discernment, we can now say, "Get behind me, Horace Mann!"

We have chosen to return to Christ-centered home schooling and Christian schools for our children, and many of our fellow Christians are now wisely choosing similarly. This trend is the most hopeful sign for protection and renewal of the family, churches and nation that I see on the horizon.

These four Presbyterian ghosts of Christmas' past still speak to our generation! The question is, will we have listened in time to save the next generation?

THE ASSAULT ON THE CHRISTIAN FAMILY: RADICAL FEMINISM, THE HIGH COST OF LIVING, AND THE HOMOSEXUAL AGENDA

One of the major, long-term results of secular humanist education has been an increasingly secularized society—a society willing to forego its Christian heritage, whether in favor of any of the several versions of social experimentation or simply in making economics its highest priority.

Graduates of state-sponsored schools will eventually carry their secular humanist orientation into government, political persuasion and public opinion. A more-or-less unconscious humanism will intrude into their businesses and work lives, their personal lives, attitudes, the kinds of entertainment and recreation they prefer, and their attitudes toward the education of their children.

A Christian whose patterns of thought have been unknowingly infected by the unconscious humanism of our culture will take state-dominated education for granted.

Today, a number of current trends indicate the rise and extent of pagan and anti-Christian influences. Given birth and nurture in government schools, they created an increasingly pagan and anti-Christian culture.

A number of factors are preventing families from fulfilling their traditional responsibilities to children, leaving their children adrift. Richard Cooper, board member and former chairman of Charleston Christian School, has made critical observations on the effects of the past 40 years of radical feminism.

RADICAL FEMINISM

An increasing number of mothers in the work place, he observes, creates an obstacle to Christian education. This is because the increasing influence of radical feminism suggests that they belong in the work place.

Affirmative action efforts in both the governmental and corporate worlds often seek out women. One of the greatest achievements of feminism has been to glorify the "working woman" who believes she should be "getting ahead" just like men always have.

The position of many feminists is the obviously unbiblical one that men's and women's roles are largely interchangeable in society. This is why many radical feminists have pushed to have women in combat roles in the military.

Today, we see women in police cars and on construction jobs. Meanwhile, the stay-at-home mom has far less prestige now, and is even an object of contempt among radical feminists.[29]

This attitude surely has implications for evangelical Christianity. It is necessary that Christian women and their families think hard about the effects that radical feminism has had on this culture.

In fairness, though, feminism is not the only factor that has pushed women into the work force.

COST OF LIVING AND CONSUMERISM

The increased cost of living and consumerism has compelled many women to join their husbands as breadwinners. This is because today's tax burden is higher than ever before. Today, government spends more at all levels. It not only taxes, but regulates and micromanages.

The burdens of government regulations as well as taxes on businesses have fallen on consumers, pushing the actual tax burden on families much higher than the government's statistics indicate. In all likelihood, the average working person pays between 40 and 50 percent of his income into federal, state and local taxes.

The tax burden is not alone in driving up costs to families. Other costs are self-inflicted. As society has become increasingly secularized, it has become increasingly consumption-driven, and this influences young adults' expenditures. More and more young adults have convinced themselves that they absolutely have to have that SUV, or take that expensive vacation, gamble in Las Vegas, or obtain some other luxury.

Politicians and pundits praise their spending, as their mouthpieces in the media assert that their spending boosts the economy. But these expenditures must come from somewhere, and today's consumer debt has skyrocketed into the trillions of dollars. Millions of families have credit card debts in the thousands, because they cannot really afford luxuries.

As a result, women who climb the corporate ladder often do not make a political statement or a statement of personal identity but create a source of increased disposable income. Between the increasing tax burden and the need to have the latest luxuries in a materialistic, consumer-oriented society, generating ever more income has become more and more important to women—more important, in many cases, than raising a family.

A SERIOUS CHOICE TO MAKE
For the Exodus Mandate Project to succeed, Christian families must make a decision. Do they accept the double cost of assuming the burden of home schooling and losing mom's second income? Or do they retain this income through mom's continuing to work and use it to pay the cost of private Christian schools?

Even if Mom works, however, she needs to be at home to supervise and help educate her children, especially through the primary school years. If she works outside the home, she needs to be sure that her children are not just receiving a quality Christian education from a Biblical point of view but are being supervised in their hours outside of school.

These are not merely educational issues. They are family issues as well. What is the Biblical family, and how should it function? That is a larger question.

The Exodus Mandate Project is one component of the larger effort to restore the Biblical family. All families have the right to educate their children as they desire, but Christian families additionally have a Biblical mandate.

We can't stress the importance of this issue enough. If we lose our children, we lose most of the subsequent generation, and that means that in the future fewer Christian families will exist than now.

This could be compared to losing an entire generation of workers with a particular skill. When the workers of a given generation are gone, if they haven't trained a new generation of practitioners, the skill is gone with them. Those skills just cannot be restored from scratch.

WE HAVE ARRIVED AT A CRITICAL MOMENT IN THE HISTORY OF THE CHRISTIAN CHURCH

In the mid-1970's there was a debate fueled by *The Limits to Growth* over what would happen if we ran out of petroleum to fuel our industrial society. *The Limits to Growth* had suggested that we would run out of fuel in the early 21st century. Richard Cooper, an Exodus Mandate board member, made the suggestion, "Well, we could always go back to plowing with mules again!"

His missionary co-worker, Abel Grenier replied, "Richard, you don't understand. I was born in the time in which we still used farm animals. There were special breeds of mules for pulling plows. They are gone! People quit breeding them.

"There were people skilled in making harnesses for plow pulling. I've seen mules bleeding and getting to the point where they couldn't work because the farmer used a harness that was not properly designed. The men who made the harnesses are dead and gone! That skill has not been passed on because it was not needed.

"It would take two or three generations to build up enough breeds of mules and skilled workers to really produce enough food the old way. What would we do in the meantime?"

This is an excellent analogy for what we risk if we lose an entire generation of children to secular humanist education. When an entire generation of families fails to educate its children properly, those children will not create Christian families when and if they marry.

What does it mean for their children and grandchildren? Getting the Christian family back on track after a generation or two that has had no real Biblical knowledge will be a tough proposition. Today's pastors and Christian parents have to understand the difficulty involved.

If a Christian couple does not set up a home in a Biblical manner and take responsibility for the education of their children in the way the Bible commands, then they will lose them to the secular humanist worldview. As soon as their children get to college, they will give up whatever Biblical orientation they had gleaned from an hour a week of Sunday School.

Then the children of these parents will grow up even less Biblically oriented. The effects will accumulate. By the time the grandchildren are ready to enter college, they will have almost nothing of a Christian worldview. It will have been lost, and the people who understood it dead and gone. This is how families are lost, and this is how societies are lost.

A Nehemiah Institute study available at www.nehemiahinstitute.com, offers some good indicators of just how far down this hill we have already slid.

We can only reverse course by recovering a Biblical theology of education, and that begins with understanding the importance of Christian families and home schooling or private Christian education.

DANGER OF THE HOMOSEXUAL MOVEMENT AND THE RISE OF "TOLERANCE"

This is more important today than ever before, because during the past decade the Christian family has come under assault from a new front: the rise of an increasingly visible homosexual movement.

Numerous studies indicate that over the past decade, the public attitude toward the homosexual lifestyle has largely shifted from one of revulsion to one of tolerance and acceptance. Even certain Christian denominations have signalled approval of "gay" men and women who have even been ordained to the ministry. Homosexuals are now calling for the legalization of homosexual "marriages" (or unions), trying to gain employee benefits for "partners," as in Massachusetts, where the recognition of homosexuality has widespread support from a secularized public.[30] There are states (e.g., Vermont) in which homosexuals have been at least partially brought under the umbrella of civil rights laws.

The Henry J. Kaiser Foundation, a highly respected public-health research institute, released a study entitled "Inside-OUT," a comprehensive report on the subject. The report provides the results of two national public opinion surveys, one that examines not just the opinions of homosexuals themselves but the changing attitudes of the general public on the subject.

HOMOSEXUALITY: THE DEVASTATING IMPACT ON OUR CULTURE

These results, available on the Kaiser Foundation's website (http://www.kff.org/content/2001/3193/), provide still more evidence of the social devastation wrought by the increasingly anti-Christian orientation of secular society.

The report reveals that 76% of homosexuals themselves report increased acceptance in American society. Among the general population, 73% know somebody who is gay, lesbian or bisexual, and 62% have a homosexual friend or acquaintance.

Seventy-five percent of the general public now supports laws aimed at protecting homosexuals from prejudice and discrimination in employment (76%) and housing (74%) in a fashion analogous to the civil rights legislation of the 1960's. Large majorities also support benefits for the partners of homosexuals in the work force including inheritance rights (73%), employer-provided benefits (70%) and social security benefits (68%).

Thirty-six percent of the general public surveyed also said that their attitudes had been significantly shaped by media images—positive portrayals of homosexuals on television programs, movies, and elsewhere. A spokeswoman for the national organization Gay and Lesbian Alliance Against Defamation (GLAAD) stated,

> It's said that visibility equals power.... Inside-OUT is an important reality check, not only for gays and lesbians but also for the general public. It shows that while acceptance is increasing, there is still much work to be done to combat prejudice, discrimination and harassment. And it shows that most Americans are either squarely behind us or in the process of joining us as we move toward true equality.[31]

Most Christians are at least familiar with the passages in Leviticus, Romans and elsewhere in Scripture that condemn homosexual conduct as an abomination.

SEVERE MEDICAL CONSEQUENCES OF HOMOSEXUALITY

Many are also aware of the public health hazards of such conduct, which spreads a variety of diseases ranging from AIDS to hepatitis. Hospital emergency rooms also record a myriad of cases of rectal and other forms of physical damage caused by homosexual activity. After all, normal sexual contact between a man and another man, or between a woman and another woman, is impossible—God just didn't design the human body that way! God designed the human body and our capacity for sexual activity and enjoyment in the context of the Christian family: two loving adults, one male and one female, each with God-assigned roles.[32]

Nevertheless, homosexual activists have found sympathy for recruitment of supporters in state-sponsored schools, simply by teaching that homosexuality is a mere "alternative lifestyle," and as normal as heterosexuality.

It is ironic that schools that stress the dangers of smoking and the importance of sound nutrition and sufficient exercise totally ignore not just the Biblical injunctions but the obvious health risks and physical dangers of homosexual activity. As a class, homosexual men are the most unhealthy and youngest to die. The evidence is unequivocal.

SYMPATHETIC PORTRAYAL OF HOMOSEXUALS IN STATE-SPONSORED SCHOOLS

The homosexual movement that developed in Vermont is worth a discussion. A group of concerned parents there, at least, moved in the right direction. They had learned that state-sponsored schools there had incorporated sympathetic portrayals of the homosexual "lifestyle" into the standard curriculum.

This followed an event, held in the fall of 1999, called *The Safe Schools for the New Millennium Conference*, which openly promoted the introduction of the homosexual agenda into public classrooms, with workshops on how to incorporate homosexual issues throughout the curriculum.

Vermont had already passed "Civil Unions" legislation that amounted to a legal endorsement of "marriages" between homosexuals. Objections by parents and concerned citizens, including legislators, were denounced as "hate-mongering" or dismissed out of hand.

Finally, State Representative Nancy Sheltra, of Derby, Vermont, a spokeswoman for "Standing Together and Reclaiming the States," held a press conference and presented an "Opt-Out" form which parents could sign and present to school administrators.

The form places the administrators on notice that parents are exercising their rights under the U.S. Constitution to ensure that their children not be instructed about human sexuality of any kind without parental inspection and prior approval of the materials to be presented.

They could deny the school permission to teach certain materials to their children. The form also required schools to refrain from teaching about homosexuality and other "alternatives" to monogamous, heterosexual activity within the context of marriage in any way that suggests that the "alternatives" are normal or natural.[33]

This is a step in the right direction, but unfortunately it is not enough just to keep some children out. For the same reason, Christian or conservative efforts to "reform" or "take back" state-sponsored schools are not enough and are perpetually doomed to failure.

PROMOTION OF HOMOSEXUALITY IS NOW A METASTISIZING CANCER IN STATE SCHOOLS. WE WILL NOT TAKE THEM BACK.

Both a sizable amount of accumulated resources and an equivalent fraction of public opinion itself—the opinions, that is, of people most of whom are graduates of state-sponsored schools—has shifted in favor of homosexuals, and for treating them as just another persecuted group.

Promotion of the homosexual agenda in the state-run public schools is here to stay. From California to Massachusetts, it is a growing trend and will engulf the public schools of the nation's heartland in the future. Like cancer, it will eventually metastasize and consume the entire body. For this as well as for other reasons to be considered, there is no reason to think that any victory on the part of isolated groups of parents acting to "take back the public schools" will be lasting.

Another example of a political failure by pro-family groups to maintain control of a local school system is the Osseo School District board in St. Paul, Minnesota. The school board passed an abstinence-only curriculum.

The district's "diversity council," however, overruled the District Board based on an argument that "marriage is a hold over from an agrarian-patriarchal society that is also multicultural insensitive."[34]

Thinking parents must withdraw their children from state-sponsored schools which teach that homosexuality is normal, or should be tolerated as just an alternative form of sexuality, and either home school them or place them in private Christian schools governed by a Biblical model of education.   ■

The Priority of Christian Education of Children

"The education of children for God is the most important business done on Earth. It is the one business for which the Earth exists. To it all politics, all war, all literature, all money-making, ought to be subordinated; every parent especially ought to feel, every hour of the day, that, next to making his own calling and election sure, this is the end for which he is kept alive by God—this is his task on Earth."

Professor R.L. Dabney
Union Theological Seminary (post-Civil War era)

CHAPTER THREE

TOWARD A BIBLICAL THEOLOGY OF EDUCATION

DEVASTATION OF THE CHRISTIAN HOME

A BIBLICAL DEFENSE OF THE FAMILY SCHOOL

THE BIBLE'S GREATEST PARENT

EXPANDING THE GREAT COMMISSION TO EDUCATION

BUILDING EDUCATION-FRIENDLY CHURCHES

RESPONSIBILITY OF THE CHRISTIAN FAMILY

DEVASTATION OF THE CHRISTIAN HOME

The last chapter provided readers with an account of how state-sponsored schools came about, how they became instruments of secular humanism, and how Christian families have now come under assault from a variety of fronts ranging from the feminist and homosexual movements to matters of sheer economics.

Outlining an alternative, in the form of a Biblical theology of education that can serve as a core philosophy for Christian home schooling and private schooling must now begin. In short, we'll now argue that what is needed is a complete paradigm shift in the Christian community about how most Christians view the education of their children.

BLIND ACCEPTANCE OF PUBLIC SCHOOLS

Tragically, Christians, by and large, have come to accept government schools. They believe that while there are problems in the government schools, these problems can be solved by this or that reform. We have ample evidence to show that this is a delusion. The reforms will leave control over the education of Christian children firmly in secular-humanist hands. The only solution is to abandon Pharaoh's school system in favor of the Promised Land of home schooling and Christian schools. There is no other Biblical or logical option.

DESTRUCTIVE EFFECT OF PUBLIC SCHOOLS

First, it should be clear by this point that the dominant philosophy of government schools is not merely anti-Christian but actually destructive to children and their natural thirst for knowledge, understanding and meaning.

Understanding and meaning, of course, can only be fully realized in a personal relationship with our Lord and Savior Jesus Christ.

The purpose of such movements as school-to-work, according to the movement's own literature, is to produce not an educated citizenry but an obedient class of trained workers for the global economy.

NEW PARADIGM NEEDED

What Christians all need to experience is a paradigm shift in how they view the education of their children. Then, Christian parents, pastors and denominational leaders will clearly see why they need to abandon government schools and develop their own schools, completely independent of government agencies and secular humanism as the controlling worldview.

WHEN CHRISTIAN CHILDREN ARE SUBJECTED TO THE SECULAR HUMANIST WORLDVIEW

Nehemiah Institute President Daniel J. Smithwick's essay "Teachers, Curriculum and Control: A World of Difference in Public and Christian Schools" discusses in detail what happens when Christian parents turn their children over to education in K-12 schools dominated by secular humanism (available at http://www.nehemiahinstitute.com).

The result is that a few hours of Bible study and education per week—perhaps fewer than that, if their only real exposure to Christian education is in Sunday School—cannot possibly overcome the net effects of 30 or more hours of humanistic propaganda during the week.

Thus, too many children turn away from their Christian upbringing as soon as they get to college. They quit attending church. Often, they turn their backs on their upbringing altogether and even start engaging in such un-Christian behaviors as out-of-wedlock sex, and in many cases even living with a boyfriend or girlfriend. They may begin drinking or taking illegal drugs.

Having no actual convictions to guide their everyday conduct has made them vulnerable to losing their former faith and left them with no motivation to obey its rules.

Smithwick's strength is his awareness of worldviews and his realization that every educational system embodies a worldview that affects the way a subject matter is organized and taught.

He goes further by observing how worldviews shape students. Worldviews may enter the classroom having been brought in by the teacher; they may be incorporated into the curriculum, including which texts are selected, what kinds of assignments are made, what kinds of tests are given or they may be developed in the context of control by the federal government.

With every federal dollar, strings are attached, and these strings become instruments through which the agenda of the elites becomes the agenda of Pharaoh's school system. This agenda has promoted an exclusively secular, anti-Christian worldview.

Since Christianity may not be under attack explicitly but only implicitly and very subtly, it may not be obvious to Christian parents who are not monitoring their children's education closely. Their children are, therefore, vulnerable to what might be called creeping secularization of their overall outlook on life—the sort of disconnected values that leads them to abandon their Christian upbringing as simply irrelevant when they get to college and beyond.

HOW YOUTH ARE LOST TO HUMANISM

Smithwick observes that there are ways of determining which worldview is being promoted, such as what he calls the PEERS test (PEERS: Politics, Economics, Education, Religion, Social Issues).

This test, administered to students from Christian homes, will indicate the extent to which a worldview other than Biblical theism has permeated their education and may eventually permeate their lives, leading them to secular preoccupations and philosophies of life.

The results of the PEERS test show that youth from Christian homes who attend government schools frequently do not retain a consistent Christian worldview against the onslaught of humanistic doctrine and preoccupations.

Some teachers bring secular humanism into the classroom by virtue of their training as specialists in a technical vocation and masters of teaching methodology. In fairness to teachers, most are probably not even aware that they are doing so. That is one reason for the slow rot has occurred in much of the system.

What about teachers who are committed Christians? Even they are not immune, because most school districts require some kind of certification or other kind of credentialing. This can only be obtained from a university or some other educational entity that is part of the humanistic educational edifice that has been established everywhere, requiring a largely invisible set of litmus tests.

Christian teachers operating in Pharaoh's school system are simply not aware of the degree of secularization involved in their own education, and not aware to what extent they are aiding an anti-Christian system.

In the area of curriculum, education is dispensed to students in the form of government-approved texts, standardized lesson plans, group projects, and so on.

Largely, students are not allowed to pursue individual interests or strengths, or they are pacified with athletics and extra-curricular activities. Rewards for pursuing individual interests or strengths are scant and temporary (e.g., a prize won, or not won, at a science fair). The result is a gradual stifling of students' innate cognitive abilities as well as their faith.

They come to view school as mostly an effort to make it from test to test, and what is memorized for the test is quickly forgotten when the test is over.

For bright students in particular, this induces a cynical view of school, and since school may be their only extensive exposure to books and learning, their cynicism is transferred to the whole enterprise of education and to the use of their God-given, cognitive abilities. The secular curriculum has done its damage: By harming students' cognitive abilities and undermining their incentive to engage in independent learning, it has succeeded in preparing young people for a lifetime of drone-like behavior which services the global economy. This is the ultimate purpose of the school-to-work movement.

EFFECT OF "FREE" GOVERNMENT SERVICES

Smithwick shows that the control of Pharaoh's school system by government is the most serious problem. Students may come to realize that the government is providing them with "free" schooling. Being subsidized by taxpayers, it costs them nothing. What is "free" is never valued as much as what has to be earned, paid for if not by them, then at least by their parents.

Multiple generations, however, have grown up with free government schooling, and it is safe to say that the prevalent point of view in society is that individuals are entitled to a free education at government expense. This is a fundamentally socialist idea, as well as an anti-Biblical one.

An entitlement mentality is easily transferred to other areas of life, including a job, insurance, and health care. Today there are large numbers of people who see every one of these, and more besides, as entitlements that ought to be supplied "free" by the federal government. This is a recipe for a life of dependence on secular authority.

This combination of factors even pulls students from solidly Christian homes away from the Christian worldview and makes them vulnerable to trends such as the ones explored in the last section of the last chapter. They graduate from government high schools as what Smithwick calls "functional humanists" living lives built around humanist values.

They don't call themselves "functional humanists," of course. They may have never heard the word "humanism."

They may consider themselves Christians who would say that "One need not to go to church or engage in rituals such as daily Bible study to be a Christian," and they may not be aware that anything has changed.

In the last analysis, they have simply lost all interest in maintaining a consistently Christian way of life, centered on godly values. They are functional illiterates as far as their Christian faith is concerned.

AN IRREDEEMABLY HOSTILE SCHOOL SYSTEM

In summary: Christian parents, pastors, denominational leaders and youth counselors need to realize that Pharaoh's school system is irredeemably hostile to the Christian worldview.

This school system arguably maims their cognitive abilities and subtly undermines their faith for life. It encourages economic dependence on government and blind obedience to secular authorities. The result is that youth go astray, abandoning their Christian beliefs when they get to college, if not earlier.

In college, they are exposed to ever-larger doses of secular humanism and pagan living while living away from home and thus without the sanctifying influence of their Christian parents. They become loyal materialists and secularists—identifying themselves with their jobs and taking entanglements with government on faith without question.

Even if force of habit compels them to think of themselves as Christian or even to go to church on Sundays, Christianity has no effect on their outlook the other six days of the week.

The alternative is the Christian paradigm mentioned above, which takes the Bible as its direct guide and accepts God as the center of one's worldview and life.

In order to construct our Biblical theology of Christian education, it might be useful to begin by surveying what the Bible has to say about children that might impact on the Christian education of children. Such a survey should begin with some definitive Scriptural passages that show to whom the education of children should be entrusted according to the Christian worldview.

A BIBLICAL DEFENSE OF THE HOME SCHOOL

God's primary instructions to Christians today for the education of children can be found in both the Old and New Testaments.

In the Old Testament passage found in Deuteronomy 6:1-9, Moses stated:

> 1 Now this is the commandment, and these are the statutes and judgments which the Lord your God has commanded to teach you, that you may observe them in the land which you are crossing over to possess,
>
> 2 that you may fear the Lord your God, to keep all His statutes and His commandments which I command you, you and your son and your grandson, all the days of your life, and that your days may be prolonged.
>
> 3 Therefore hear, O Israel, and be careful to observe it, that it may be well with you, and that you may multiply greatly as the Lord God of your fathers has promised you—'a land flowing with milk and honey.'
>
> 4 Hear, O Israel: The Lord our God, the Lord is one!
>
> 5 You shall love the Lord your God with all your heart, with all your soul, and with all your strength.
>
> 6 And these words which I command you today shall be in your heart.

7 You shall teach them diligently to your children, and shall talk of them when you sit in your house, when you walk by the way, when you lie down, and when you rise up.

8 You shall bind them as a sign on your hand, and they shall be as frontlets between your eyes.

9 You shall write them on the doorposts of your house and on your gates.

Psalm 78:5 tells us:

For He established a testimony in Jacob, And appointed a law in Israel, Which He commanded our fathers, That they should make them known to their children.

Proverbs 22:6 also instructs: "Train up a child in the way he should go and, when he is old, he will not depart from it."

Joel 1:2-3 is also revealing:

2 Hear this, you elders, And give ear, all you inhabitants of the land! Has anything like this happened in your days, Or even in the days of your fathers?

3 Tell your children about it, Let your children tell their children, And their children another generation.

Consider Ephesians 6:4: "And, ye fathers, provoke not your children to wrath; but bring them up in the nurture and admonition of the Lord."

In the New Testament Gospel of Matthew, Jesus emphasized the special role children play in the Kingdom of God:

13 Then little children were brought to Him that He might put His hands on them and pray, but the disciples rebuked them.

14 But Jesus said, "Let the little children come to Me, and
do not forbid them; for of such is the kingdom of heaven."
(Matthew 19:13-14)

And again, in Mark:

14 "Let the little children come to Me, and do not forbid
them; for of such is the kingdom of God.
15 "Assuredly, I say to you, whoever does not receive the
kingdom of God as a little child will by no means enter it."
(Mark 10:14-15)

In Luke 6:40 Jesus explains, ""A disciple is not above his
teacher, but everyone who is perfectly trained will be like
his teacher."

It is interesting to observe the role the innocence of children plays in preparation for one's acceptance of the
Christian Gospel. The context is Jesus' response to his disciples' desire to know, Who is the greatest in the Kingdom
of Heaven? All had been maneuvering for the "top spot," so
to speak. In today's terms, they wanted to "be somebody."

Jesus was notoriously unimpressed by such prideful
behavior. He, nevertheless, responded to their question, but
not with the answer they expected.

His answer embodies five teachings pertaining to children that are relevant to a Biblical theology of education.

FIVE RELEVANT BIBLICAL TEACHINGS
According to Jesus, first, one must be humble and have a
child-like trust in Jesus to enter the Kingdom of Heaven.
"Then Jesus called a little child to Him, set him in the midst
of them, and said, 'Assuredly, I say to you, unless you are
converted and become as little children, you will by no
means enter the kingdom of heaven.'" (Matthew 18:2-3).

In other words, the seeking and trusting state of mind of a child is a prerequisite to anyone's salvation.

God requires a child-like mind because of the second requirement. Humility of heart and mind is the secret of greatness in the kingdom of heaven, a complete and utter dependence on God: "Therefore whoever humbles himself as this little child is the greatest in the kingdom of heaven." (Matthew 18:4).

Third, Jesus illustrates acceptance of other "childlike" believers as equivalent to acceptance of Him: "Whoever receives one little child like this in My name receives Me" (Matthew 18:5).

Christian education should focus not just on the education of adults in their theology, but on all who have a relationship to Jesus without considerations such as social status, wealth, race, or age in order to nurture as many as possible under the umbrella of Christian education.

In today's hostile culture the education of children and youth should be the highest priority of families and churches.

Fourth, Jesus gives stern warnings against offending children: "But whoever causes one of these little ones who believe in Me to sin, it would be better for him if a millstone were hung around his neck, and he were drowned in the depth of the sea" (Matthew 18:6). We believe that placing children in harm's way spiritually, morally and academically in state-run public schools is in violation of this strong command. Parents have been warned.

Fifth and finally, Jesus warns us to avoid disrespect for children because God is carefully watching them and looking out for them: "Take heed that you do not despise one of these little ones, for I say to you that in heaven their angels always see the face of My Father who is in heaven" (Matthew 18:10). This text shows the great care that parents and churches should exercise in protecting the innocence and moral formation of children.

DO NOT HARM THE CHILDREN
Some public schools have become so hostile to the Christian faith and moral order that they are disturbing this innocence and harming the moral development of children.

Two core messages emerge from Jesus' words. Do not harm the children, and become like children yourselves.

Only a few situations tested Jesus' patience, or made him angry. There were the moneychangers in the Temple, the Pharisees—and the disciples on occasions such as the above.

Jesus seemed keenly sensitive to issues that questioned His Father's honor or exploited the weak. Jesus, however, used these occasions to instruct His disciples.

His instructions contain important insights for the education of children. The exploitation or harming of children through neo-pagan or humanistic education would qualify as a concern. Do these instructions give us any specific advice regarding the foundations of a Christian curriculum to substitute for the secular-humanist one? We believe so.

THIS IS GOD'S UNIVERSE
For starters, the idea of a God-centered worldview, seeing the universe about which children are to learn as God's universe, must infuse the entire curriculum.

"In the beginning God created the heavens and the earth" (Genesis 1:1).

"…For the world is Mine, and all its fullness," says God in Psalm 50:12b.

Also in Psalms, David wrote, "When I consider Your heavens, the work of Your fingers, The moon and the stars, which You have ordained" (Psalm 8:3).

"The heavens declare the glory of God; And the firmament shows His handiwork" (Psalm 19:1).

The first question God puts to Job is "Where were you when I laid the foundations of the earth? Tell Me, if you have understanding. Who determined its measurements? Surely you know! Or who stretched the line upon it?" (Job 38:4-5).

Acts 17:24a refers to the "God, who made the world and everything in it...."

Hebrews 11:3 tells us: "By faith we understand that the worlds were framed by the word of God, so that the things which are seen were not made of things which are visible."

This is a sampling of passages from all over Scripture, penned by many different hands, but all communicating the same message: This is God's world about which we are to teach our children. Indeed, this was what the framers of the original scientific revolution assumed. Isaac Newton wrote:

> And if the fixed stars are the centers of other like systems, these, being formed by the same wise counsel, must be all subject to the dominion of One.... This Being governs all things, not as the soul of this world, but as Lord over all; and on account of his dominion he is wont to be called Lord God .... The Supreme God is a Being eternal, infinite, absolutely perfect....[1]

Thus, one of the primary architects of the modern scientific revolution worked under the assumption that the universe he studied and about which he theorized was God's handiwork, just as Scripture says.

This realization can be used to whet the natural curiosity of children when they are very young and can encourage in them a sense of wonder at God's marvelous works that will last a lifetime!

The gaining of knowledge, too, is Scriptural, provided it is carried out in a godly way and the limits imposed by human sin are recognized. "The fear of the Lord is the beginning of knowledge, But fools despise wisdom and instruction" (Proverbs 1:7).

Christians should never allow themselves to be smeared with a reputation which opposes learning, as they are sometimes labeled by secular humanists.

Hosea 4:6 offers an endorsement of the seeking of knowledge in God's Word: "My people are destroyed for lack of knowledge. Because you have rejected knowledge, I also will reject you...." Parents should pass on knowledge to the next generation; not doing so, God warns, carries a terrible price. The verse continues: "... from being priest for Me; Because you have forgotten the law of your God, *I also will forget your children*" (emphasis ours).

ENDORSEMENTS OF KNOWLEDGE SEEKING

Here is a sampling of Scriptural endorsements of the seeking of knowledge in a godly spirit:

"He who instructs the nations, shall He not correct, He who teaches man knowledge?" (Psalm 94:10).

"Teach me good judgment and knowledge, For I believe Your commandments" (Psalm 119:66).

More from Proverbs: "A wise man will hear and increase learning, And a man of understanding will attain wise counsel" (1:5).

"Wise people store up knowledge, But the mouth of the foolish is near destruction" (10:14).

"Whoever loves instruction loves knowledge..." (12:1).

"The lips of the wise disperse knowledge, But the heart of the fool does not do so" (15:7).

"The heart of the prudent acquires knowledge, And the ear of the wise seeks knowledge" (18:15).

The message here is that knowledge and instruction are profound goals, provided in a godly spirit by parents and teachers to children. Scripture even contains words easily understood by the children themselves.

The initial verse above continues, "My son, hear the instruction of your father, And do not forsake the law of your mother; For they will be a graceful ornament on your head, And chains about your neck" (Proverbs 1:8-9).

"Children, obey your parents in the Lord, for this is right. 'Honor your father and mother,' which is the first commandment with promise: 'that it may be well with you and you may live long on the earth'" (Ephesians 6:1-3).

And finally, "Children, obey your parents in all things, for this is well pleasing to the Lord" (Colossians 3:20). This could provide the framework for every subject being infused with the God-centered worldview.

ILLUSTRATING MAN'S NEED

The sciences are the objective study of God's universe, an attempt to understand the laws of the natural order God created and sustains.

The history of nations, including our own, could be governed by the realization that man is a fallen being, with historical events illustrating man's need for redemption in Jesus Christ.

History, moreover, can be presented to children as having a goal; because it is, again, the history of God's world, and in the last analysis, He is in charge despite the changes this nation is undergoing.

Secular humanism may be built up as presenting a goal for "the end of history"—that of Man becoming God. One of the earliest and best antidotes to this illusion is the story of the Tower of Babel in Genesis, when the nations of men united under the belief that they could build a tower that would reach God (Genesis 11:2-9). The effort failed, as all efforts to reach God by human means must fail. This could provide a basis for teaching children about secular humanism once they are old enough.

A sound theology of Christian education need not neglect the world that exists outside the home and Christian school; otherwise, the children might not be prepared for what they might face. But secular humanism should be portrayed to children and teenagers for what it is: a flawed system, ignoring the fact that "for all have sinned and fall short of the glory of God" (Romans 3:23) and riding on the pretense that Man can become akin to God. The Christian worldview is the basis for the paradigm shift which will transform how parents view the education of their children.

STATE-SPONSORED EDUCATION *MANDATES* THAT WHICH SCRIPTURE EXPRESSLY *FORBIDS*

In light of the possibilities of a sound theology of Christian education, do we really want our children exposed to the unlabeled, unadorned and unexamined, secular-humanist worldview that guides state-sponsored schools today?

In Colossians 2:8, the Apostle Paul warns: "Beware lest anyone cheat you through philosophy and empty deceit, according to the tradition of men, according to the basic principles of the world, and not according to Christ." This philosophy assaults our children in state-sponsored schools where secular humanism dominates.

They are being spoiled by "philosophy and empty deceit, according to the tradition of men, according to the basic principles of the world."

In 2 Corinthians 6:14 Paul says: "Do not be unequally yoked together with unbelievers. For what fellowship has righteousness with lawlessness? And what communion has light with darkness?" When we send our children to state-sponsored schools, do we not "yoke them together with unbelievers"?

In short, in the United States we have set up a government-sponsored and government-run institution—state-sponsored education—that does the very things Scripture expressly forbids! Instead of teaching our children as the Bible commands, Christians are delivering their children into a system that denies Jesus Christ—and, in particular, denies Him the very access to children that He commands!

Moreover, the daily aim of secular humanists is to tear children loose from the Christian moorings and worldview of their parents and their church.

T.C. Pinckney, Second Vice President of the Southern Baptist Convention, says:

> Moreover, many Christian denominations are failing to obey God's commands regarding the education of children. It is true that we take them to Sunday School and then to church. They may be involved in youth groups or other such programs. They may even study the Bible at home with their parents or with their peers.
>
> But the few hours represented here are hardly enough to overcome the 30 or so hours each week during which they are exposed to latent anti-Christian messages and content, not to mention the constant pagan media bombardment coming into their living rooms and sometimes bedrooms through their television sets. This may add up to ten, 20 or even more hours per week. Taken together, all this must be a great affront to a holy God!
>
> Now of course, there are schoolteachers who are Christians. Many are doing everything they can, attempting to be the salt of the earth, and with God's blessings.
>
> But they are limited by school policy, compelled to use secular humanist textbooks, involved in programs implying

the relativism inherent in tolerance of, for example, homosexuality, 'safe sex instruction' including condom availability from school nurses, and so on.

Christian teachers are simply in no position, organizationally or career-wise, to thwart an influence as large and pervasive as secular humanism.

Some Christian teachers are being forced into compromises that will make if difficult if not impossible to continue teaching in public schools in the future.

Why have we failed our God in the critically important responsibility of educating our children? For several reasons:

First, we have failed because we have been willfully, blissfully disobedient and satisfied in our ignorance. We have compartmentalized, following Scripture closely in some areas of our lives but ignoring it in others.

Thus we allow ourselves a comfort zone in which we can feel secure that the education of our children is someone else's responsibility.

Second, we have failed for the closely related reason that the great majority of us have not made the effort to inform ourselves of the facts—even though articles and books on the problems of state-sponsored schooling are readily available.

When we have informed ourselves, we have tried to rationalize away the problem, and have tried to implement 'reforms.' The reforms have been systematically blocked or have failed.

We have tried to pretend that if we tinkered with the system we could make it work; but if the system is broken at the foundations, no amount of tinkering will make it work. Secular humanist schools, by their very nature, can't be reformed by Christians. They must be abandoned completely.

Third, we have failed because even when we have known this, we have generally not had the moral courage to point it out to people. We have been unwilling to go so far as to say that the secular humanist system is broken, whether out of fear of being labeled extremists or against education or whatever. It generally takes an event such as the Columbine killings to awaken Christians to what is going on in the schools.

Fourth, we have failed because we have been afraid to offend people. So we have chosen to offend God instead.

What do we have to do? What does God command us to do?

The ideal, most Biblical solution, is for parents to home school their children, and also teach their children to become home schooling parents themselves when the time comes. All Christians should welcome and openly encourage home schoolers.

However, many parents cannot home school their children. Some are financially unable. Others are unable, for reasons having to do with the necessities of employment today.

WHAT WE MUST DO NOW

For these children we need to start up large numbers of Christian schools. These schools must be fully Christian. That is, the teachers, administrators and all staff need to be Christians. The textbooks must be Christian and not humanist in orientation. They must convey the Christian worldview in its entirety, in the spirit outlined above. They need not avoid teaching about subjects such as evolution, humanism, abortion, relativism, and so on. But this needs to be done very carefully and in a balanced way.

For example, present the evolutionist arguments fully and fairly to teenagers old enough to understand them, but also demonstrate their factual weaknesses and their usually unstated worldview-based assumptions in which the theory of evolution is most at home. Then, we should present the disastrous consequences of those assumptions when they have led entire societies, such as the communist Soviet Union and Red China, to attempt to exclude God.

Again, a sound Christian educational system will not try to isolate children from the rest of the world. Our children must be prepared to live among secular humanists, confronting them when and where necessary. They must be equipped with the information and cognitive skills necessary to triumph in debate with secular humanists.

This may seem a tall order, and it is, but God commands it, and the time has come to rise to the occasion. We should not waste any more time; the spirituality and even in some cases the very lives of our children are at stake!

What God wants should be clear from His Word. He places the onus of responsibility for educating children on the family with assistance from the Church. He does not place it on the state.

The attitude toward children embodied in Pharaoh's school system is quite different. Institutionally in the U.S., what we have done in creating a state-sponsored school system immersed in the worldview of secular humanism is just what Jesus expressly forbids!

The major error of state-sponsored schools denies Jesus access to the children by virtue of schools being set up, and their curricula designed, as if God either did not exist or was only relevant on Sundays.

Moreover, state-sponsored education embodies a worldview maintaining that we can improve ourselves indefinitely without God.

From Horace Mann through John Dewey down through the major voices in state-sponsored education today, we see individuals embodying anything but the kind of innocence and humility Jesus saw in children, much less the willingness to submit to God's will.

Secular humanism, of course, places man at the center of value, and has seen education as the primary means of indoctrinating and transforming an entire society into socialist drones serving only in state-approved functions.

THE BIBLE'S GREATEST PARENT: JEHONADAB

We have already seen how Scripture provides instructions to fathers who bear the primary burden for their children's Christian education and upbringing (Ephesians 6:4 again, for example).

It might also help if we can answer the question: In Biblical terms, who is the ideal parent?

If we can answer this question by pointing to a specific person, whom Scripture describes and whose successes are explained in Biblical terms, then we have the immediate advantage of having a role model to follow, someone Christian parents today can study and learn to emulate.

In fact, there is such a person. His name is Jehonadab, and his story can be found in the Old Testament book of Second Kings. His is hardly a household name, but by integrating a number of Biblical texts, there emerges a clear picture of why he was a successful father—in the Biblical sense of success which places God first.

WHAT CAN WE LEARN FROM JEHONADAB?

Jehonadab is important because he cracked the code, so to speak, on how to transmit faith to his children and family in such a way that his children would transmit it to their children, and so on, so that his faith would be passed down from generation to generation. He did this where much better known Biblical men and women failed. David, for example, was a successful king and military leader, but not the best father.

Men and women can be sincere Christians, but may still flounder badly as parents, unable to pass down love for and devotion to Christ to their children. What can we learn from Jehonadab?

In fact, we see four primary qualities in Jehonadab's life that made him the greatest father in the Bible.

First, Jehonadab had a great zeal for the holiness of God (2 Kings 10:15-28). In him, we see a man who was consumed by a zeal for the holiness of God in his nation and among God's people. He assisted in the great reformation started under Elijah and concluded under Jehu.

While not an absolute and pure reformation so that the proper worship of Jehovah God was completely restored, it nevertheless purged the worship of Baal from the Northern Kingdom permanently.

WHY WE SHOULDN'T TOLERATE TOLERANCE

This was a remarkable event, and we see that Jehonadab was the principal aide to Jehu in this endeavor. While their actions may seem a bit harsh by New Testament standards, the example of Jehu and Jehonadab do model the correct attitude to have toward false doctrine and religious practices that diminish and challenge the name of our Lord and Savior, Jesus Christ.

Many Christians today have become "religious inclusivists" willing to tolerate the many new gods and cults that have proliferated in America under secular humanism, so long as they themselves may worship Jesus Christ freely.

They say, "Let Jesus take His place among the gods and religions of our culture, just as long as He gets equal time and a little respect."

If Jehonadab were here today, we would be very uncomfortable with him. He would not endorse this practice of tolerance and pluralism that has become a blight to the modern church. He would not like what he sees in modern evangelical Christianity or society, or how easily we Christians put up with false gods of the New Age and other idols around us. Jehonadab was an "exclusionist," and had no use for the worship of Baal.

In a similar vein, Paul spoke of "casting down arguments and every high thing that exalts itself against the knowledge of God, bringing every thought into captivity to the obedience of Christ" (2 Corinthians 10:5).

From 2 Kings 10 we don't have much in the way of a description of Jehonadab's immediate family life. But we can surmise that he didn't have any "Baal Barbie dolls" around the house or any "Baal rock music" groups playing from the local radio station. Jehonadab and the followers of Baal just plain didn't see eye to eye, and he would have taken care of any evidence of "Baalism" creeping into his house and family life through the side door from the various cultural and media outlets of his time. His children learned that Dad didn't like Baal, that people who followed Baal were unsavory; and they learned from their earliest days to emulate these choices.

Second, Jehonadab believed the word of the Lord through the Prophets. Jehonadab would have been a good Bible student for his day. Several prophets had spoken the word of the Lord predicting the destruction of the Northern Kingdom starting with Abijah (1 Kings 14:15,16).

Then, along came Elijah a few years later and predicted the complete destruction of the family of Ahab and Jezebel (1 Kings 21:17-24). Perhaps Jehonadab had been a youth, one of many like himself, who gathered on top of Mt. Carmel that day, seeing Elijah's challenge to the prophets of Baal in direct battle and his victory.

Perhaps he saw the fire of God fall and the entire nation break before the Lord falling on their faces, crying out, "The

Lord, He is God, The Lord, He is God!" He had only to see something like that one time in his life to know that Baal was a defeated god.

He would finish the job much later that Elijah had begun that day. Also, Elijah had prophesied that Jehu would be King of Israel. Jehonadab had plenty of Scripture and many words from God. He would take steps and set standards for his family accordingly.

He was willing to risk a confrontation and battle with the family of Ahab and assist Jehu because he knew the promises of God would be fulfilled. Strikingly, he "believed the prophets," not merely had *knowledge* of the prophets. Many people believe the word of the Lord but do not live accordingly. Jehonadab knew that the Northern Kingdom would soon disappear, and he prepared his family accordingly.

TOO MUCH "AT HOME" IN THIS WORLD?

Today, too many Christians live as if this world is their final destination. I once heard an Indian evangelist say that some Christians may be disappointed in their Heavenly home as they have lived so well down here and expended so little effort for the Lord.

Let's hope not, but it sure does seem at times that we do not take seriously enough the prophets or the words of Jesus when He tells us, "Do not lay up for yourselves treasures on earth, where moth and rust destroy and where thieves break in and steal" (Matthew 6:19).

CENTERED IN THE WORD OF GOD

Third, Jehonadab ordered his family to live around the Word of God. He set the house rules, and his family obeyed him. He must have been a consistent and faithful worshipper of the God of Israel.

We know from Luke 6:40 that the faith is more caught than taught, as it tells us that a "A disciple is not above his teacher, but everyone who is perfectly trained will be like his teacher." Do you want to see how well you are really living the Christian life? If so, look at your children. Or look at your grandchildren. Your personal and direct influence can extend to the third generation.

You will be able to reach your grandchildren for Christ and influence them for God, but you would need to have a lot of "gravitates" to reach six generations with the power of your faith and testimony. Your memory and testimony would have to be strong. So it was with Jehonadab. His children were still talking about him 240 years later!

The events of 2 Kings 10 took place around 840 B.C., and finally the descendants of Jehonadab were awaiting the fall of Jerusalem around 603 B.C., some 240 years later. Six generations of obedience and faithfulness to God in this family were based on the actions and faithfulness of one man, Jehonadab, whose original house rules were still in effect.

The Prophet Jeremiah was sent to test their obedience one more time by putting wine before them, but they all refused. They were "crusty, old curmudgeons" just like their great-great-grandfather, Jehonadab. He had taught them that "just saying no" was the right decision most of the time. No is a good word. We ought to try to bring the word "no" back into the Church sometime, before we are all swept away by the next wave of modernity and compromise which will surely confront us.

Fourth, Jehonadab set standards to preserve his family spiritually. This is the hardest element of Christian parenting to implement. It is the practical applications, however, that determine success or failure as a Christian parent.

Jehonadab, back in the Old Testament, seems to have established some house rules that assured that his family would be able to survive the changes in Israel that would inevitably come due to the coming destruction of the nation that the prophets had predicted. He took measures that would permanently set his family apart. They were to be different, and to live differently from those around them. They were to maintain moral purity, hence no wine, and they were to remain a nomadic people, hence build no houses and plant no vineyards (Jeremiah 35:8-10).

We would say today of Jehonadab that he was "old fashioned" and "behind the times," but in reality he was the most contemporary man in Israel.

He was ahead of everybody else in preparing his family for what was to come. Israel was going down. Many other families didn't survive, because they had been living the good life, as if this world was their final destination. Jehonadab's clan did survive and moved on because they believed the word of the Lord through the prophets and made the necessary plans. These were practical plans and had a spiritual end.

SETTING YOUR FAMILY APART

The key point here is that Jehonadab did several things to set his family apart, spiritually and morally. He wanted them to be different, separate, and not dependent on the society around them. The lesson we can learn from him today is to be "separated Christians," in the world but not of the world.

What today's Christians must do to follow Jehonadab's example with his children is to let their own children know above all that they are not to become part of our present American culture with its secular-humanist worldview and values.

They are not to attempt to "blend in." When we simply "blend in," our testimony for Christ disappears altogether. We have been commanded to stand for what is right.

We believe home schooling and Christian schooling would fit the bill, as a fitting testimony to Jehonadab's legacy today. We believe living a pure and moral life, and demanding the same of our children, would be to live as Jehonadab did.

Teaching children to avoid the corrupting, big-city influences and nightlife, preferring instead a rural and small-town lifestyle, might be another example. Let them make their best and permanent friends among their own family and in the body of Christ. We taught our own children that "brothers and sisters are permanent friends" when they were lonely and wondered if the peer group would accept them.

Teach them a trade or profession yourself, insuring that they will be able to work and support themselves and church workers in a culture that is growing increasingly hostile toward Christians.

Teach them to stay out of debt. Teach them the necessary habits of godliness such as regular Church attendance, Bible study, personal prayer and family worship. If this culture continues to decay, it may well be they and their children, like the children and descendants of Jehonadab, will have the moral character and stamina to ride out the coming storm when others fail.

In Jeremiah 35:19, we see one of the most extraordinary promises in the entire Bible, given to a parent and his family. It is this text, and how Jehonadab responded, that earns him his title of "the greatest parent in the Bible."

The text says that the word of the Lord came to Jeremiah and rewarded the faithfulness and obedience of Jehonadab and his descendants, saying, "Jonadab the son of Rechab shall not lack a man to stand before Me forever."

The New Contemporary English Version says, "So I promise that your clan will be my servants and will never die out." This must mean that the descendants of Jehonadab still survive and serve the Lord somewhere in our world today.

Can God preserve a family like this for so long a time? Is there such a parent today? Does God bless and honor the kind of faith and obedience today that Jehonadab showed?

THE DOBSON FAMILY EXAMPLE

We may look at the example of Dr. James Dobson, the Christian family leader. His granddad, a godly man, carried an unusually heavy burden for his family and spent weeks in prayer and fasting for them. When he emerged from this time with God, he announced that God had promised him that every one of his children and grandchildren would faithfully serve the Lord in full-time Christian work. He said that God had promised this to him. Among his own children this was true. Every one of them became a pastor or missionary or married a pastor or missionary.

So it was with the dozen grandchildren of the third generation, all except one, James Dobson. Dobson did not feel led into full-time Christian work, nor did he want to become an ordained minister. He just wanted to be a child psychologist and write books on the family. But he, too, has not been able to escape from the faith and obedience of his godly grandfather.

Is it not ironic and a bit remarkable how God has used this dedicated Christian layman to minister to the families of America and the world? Dr. Dobson's grandfather had a burden for his family. God turned this into a blessing for innumerable families.

The Dobson example reminds us of this verse: "Now to Him who is able to do exceedingly abundantly above all that we ask or think, according to the power that works in us, to Him be glory in the church by Christ Jesus to all generations, forever and ever. Amen" (Ephesians 3:20-21).

THE FATE OF JEHONADAB'S DESCENDANTS

What became of the descendants of Jehonadab? We don't know a whole lot about them after the fall of Jerusalem in 586 B.C. We have only the sure promise of Jeremiah 35:19 to go on, that "Jehonadab, the son of Rechab, shall not lack a man to stand before me forever."

Since the Bible is true in this text, then I would infer that some of the sons of Jehonadab, a Rechabite, returned from Babylon with Nehemiah and rebuilt the walls of Jerusalem.

Later there was surely a son of Jehonadab on the hillside in Galilee when Jesus fed the 5,000.

Later he was gathered in the Upper Room when the Holy Spirit came in power on the Day of Pentecost. We may even wonder if a son of Jehonadab worked with St Augustine when he wrote his great works, *Confessions* and *The City of God*.

One may have trained at Geneva with Calvin or served with John Knox in Scotland during the Reformation.

Might we not see him coming ashore with the Pilgrims at Plymouth Rock in 1620 and 260 years later passing out hymnals at a D.L. Moody crusade in 1880?

We don't really know where they are today, but we know on the authority of God's Word that there are sons of Jehonadab, the "greatest father in the Bible," somewhere in the world, loving and worshipping God, and serving Jesus Christ.

EXPANDING THE GREAT COMMISSION TO EDUCATION

A Christian theology of education can be viewed as an extension of the Great Commission to the education of Christian children. Committed evangelical Christians must live and breathe the Great Commission as reflected in Matthew 28:18-20 (see also Mark 16:15; Luke 24: 46,47; Acts 1:8).

Their denominational and interdenominational structures often revolve around the cause of world evangelization, that is, seeing that the Gospel of Jesus Christ is effectively preached to every tribe, tongue and kindred on the entire planet.

Some mission groups now stress reaching the population living inside the 10/40 window where the majority live who have not yet heard a clear presentation of the Gospel message. Several of the largest overseas mission organizations in the world are run and staffed by evangelicals.

The stories of overseas missionary outreaches have thrilled the Western churches in our day from the story of the martyred missionaries in Ecuador chronicled in Betty Elliott's *Through Gates of Splendor* to the more recent book, *Eternity in Their Hearts* by Don Richardson.

Evangelists Billy Graham, Luis Palau and other international figures have carried the Gospel message into the public airways and over the entire world so that millions have heard. All these activities are based on obedience to the Great Commission.

Most of the emphasis on the Great Commission by evangelicals today seems to be on the evangelization portion only as reflected in Matthew 28:19: "Go therefore and make disciples of all the nations, baptizing them in the name of the Father and of the Son and of the Holy Spirit...."

Bound up in verse 19 is the evangelization component of the Great Commission, assumed as the first step in bringing about disciples. Sharing Jesus Christ's saving Gospel and leading men and women, boys and girls, to individual repentance and faith in Christ is absolutely the first necessary step in any effective Christian endeavor. Evangelical Christians have been faithful at this point.

Also, in Matthew 28:20 is the *teaching* portion of the Great Commission where Jesus commanded "...teaching

them to observe all things that I have commanded you...."
I believe this is neglected in many evangelical circles today, particularly in the education of children. Many Christians seem satisfied if they simply win men and women to Christ without serious consideration of the teaching part of Jesus' final command.

But can the Great Commission really be fulfilled without a complete implementation of the second step in this text, Jesus' command to teach the nations? Where is the big gap in the Great Commission today? I believe it is being truncated between verses 19 and 20.

Teaching is getting a short shrift in the American churches. Youth group and Sunday school simply do not qualify as a serious Christian education enterprise; they cannot overcome the effects of secular humanism in state-sponsored schools during the five weekdays. Our youth must be supported by a full Monday through Friday Christian education program covering all "K–12" grades.

It is not well known that Sunday school as originally envisioned by its founders was seen as an outreach to unchurched children. It was not intended to replace Christian instruction in the home.

Jesus stated in his closing command to the disciples: "All authority has been given to Me in heaven and on earth" (v.18). Then He commanded the disciples, and thereby the modern Church, to pick up the education mandate as well as the evangelization mandate.

WHO AND WHAT DID JESUS COMMISSION?

He didn't commission the state or government of that day. Nor does He commission the state or federal government to educate the population today. Jesus claims all authority for Himself and does not give it to the state. He "who is the blessed and only Potentate, the King of kings and Lord of lords" (1 Timothy 6:15) tells the Church to take up the teaching mission in the world.

If Christians are still unable to see from such a simple reading of the Matthew 28:18-20 text that the state or government has no education responsibility, surely they can see that Jesus' claim of "authority in heaven and on earth" should minimally mean the state or government has no role to educate the children of the Church.

Yet most Christians have surrendered that ground to the secular world with typically weak excuses that the Church will provide the religious instruction of their children but the public schools can provide the secular instruction.

Is there any wonder, then, that Western churches and denominations are relatively ineffective at shaping and leading this culture?

Jesus said, "You are the salt of the earth; but if the salt loses its flavor, how shall it be seasoned? It is then good for nothing but to be thrown out and trampled underfoot by men." (Matthew 5:13-14).

Conclusively, great devastation has come to the Christian home and churches by neglect in this area. Some Christians carry out the evangelism in a greater degree than earlier generations but not the teaching.

The teaching has been ceded to the government, in the form of state-sponsored schools.

We win them to Christ, if indeed we have done so, and the secular humanists are teaching the children of the Church. In this fashion, the entire culture continues to fall further under the domination of humanism and post-modernist thought.

The Church is being trampled underfoot, as we have been bamboozled by the secular humanists and have given them the tools to destroy Christianity in America in the next few generations!

BUILDING CHRISTIAN EDUCATION-FRIENDLY CHURCHES

A major place to recover some of the lost ground is in the revamping of the Christian education departments in our major Christian colleges and seminaries.

I finished my advanced degrees at Grace Theological Seminary in 1974 and 1979. There were numerous classes on Christian education as part of practical theology and these were required courses, but they did not include Christian day schools as an integral part of the necessary Christian education mission of the local church.

Home schooling was virtually non-existent at that time. In the 1970's and 1980's, almost all Christians utilized the public schools without any questions. In the late 1970's, the private Christian school movement began to grow, but most Christians still did not consider it a necessity in those days to use the local Christian schools. Most were still captive to a foolish misapplication of "salt and light" theology.

Happily, this lack of understanding about the critical importance of Christian day schools or home schooling has begun to change, but many of the seminary curricula still reflect the old Christian-education model that Sunday school, youth group and Bible study equals Christian education. Until the evangelical seminaries revise their curricula to include Christian schools and home schooling at the K-12 level as a primary means to fulfill the Christian education responsibility of the local church, the pastors will be slow to lead their congregations in that direction.

We are all products of our education, and we are taught as much as by what is neglected or not emphasized as by what is emphasized. Christian schools and home schooling must be included in the practical theology classes and Christian education classes at the seminary level if the larger Church is to wake up. They must become required courses, even including course majors in Christian education, which prepares pastors or church Christian-education directors to set up and run Christian schools.

Evangelicals have long been given to new church planting and using the outreach team concept to fulfill the Great Commission. This can now be expanded to include Christian education.

For example, when an outreach team forms a new congregation as a pioneer work, Christian education at the K-12 level should be included in the prayers, planning and preparation as it is on the foreign mission field.

This would presuppose a Christian education director as an original team member who would begin to build a new Christian school or help families to home school once a new congregation were formed.

HEADING OFF PROBLEMS AT THE START
TEACHING ABOUT CHRISTIAN EDUCATION

An emphasis must coincide with the inception of the new church that newly converted families should begin to educate their children at the K-12 level according to one of the Christian-education models. If the outreach team does not do this at the outset, it will be hard to introduce or require later.

If the team has neglected the teaching portion of the Great Commission with their new disciples, there could be resistance when the effort is made later to start a Christian school or promote home schooling.

New church plants have a real opportunity to get a fast start in the obedience of their newly won families. We have discovered in our work with the Exodus Mandate Project that when families become obedient in the Christian education of their children, many other trouble areas that need correction or Christian discipling fall into place.

Getting the families on Biblical ground with the education of their children will enable pastors to see other problems solved and sins fall away in those same families.

We believe that some non-Christian families will actually be drawn to churches that promote Christian schools or home schooling. The security that a K-12 Christian education provides for a family in this culture is a likely path toward eventually winning these families to salvation through Jesus Christ.

As government schools continue to deteriorate morally and academically, the most committed young families will insist upon local church support and help in the K-12 Christian education of their children. Local churches that allow their children to remain in government schools may lose their strongest members to other congregations that meet this need.

Having a Christian school in your church and a staff person or division helping home schooling may become a practical requirement as well as a theological one. Churches in the future will be required to assist in the K-12 education of their member families if they hope to stay abreast with current needs and build their memberships.

RESPONSIBILITY OF THE CHRISTIAN FAMILY

In attempting to move the Christian Church toward a Biblical theology of education, we must first consider how to rebuild such convictions in the individual Christian family. In particular, we should consider how to build family convictions and a fresh obedience concerning the education of children at the K-12 level.

A Biblical theology of education is built upon a proper understanding of Holy Scripture, *but understanding flows from a practical obedience and faith.* The Church in the United States has been weak in both areas.

The vast majority of evangelical Christian families utilize the state-sponsored school system for the K-12 education of their children. Most see nothing wrong, and have never considered the Biblical commands concerning the education of children. Bad habits and weak theologies die hard. It will be similar in the education of children for many Christian families and churches.

For Christian families to recover their lost sense of responsibility for the education of their own children, it will require much soul searching, serious study, strenuous effort and expense. The Christian education of children at the K-12 level is not a mere choice or option. *It is a command for the Christian family from God Himself, as revealed to Christians in His Word.*

In order to restore the responsibility of the Christian family concerning the education of children, four propositions could be suggested.

PROPOSITION 1: THERE IS NO GOVERNMENT ROLE IN EDUCATION OF CHILDREN

A major proposition of the Exodus Mandate Project is that God gave education to the family with assistance from the Church. The state has no God-ordained role in the education of children, especially at the K-12 level.

This proposition is based on such texts as Deuteronomy 6:1-9, Psalm 127:3-5, Proverbs 22:6, Matthew 28:18-20 and Ephesians 6:4. There are many applicable Biblical texts but these five are the central ones. These passages and many others are directed to the individual family, not to the state or government.

We believe that Christian people cannot delegate the education mandate concerning children to a neo-pagan or humanistic education system, which the state-run public schools are today.

All education is religious at some level since, if carried out properly and comprehensively, it deals with the full range of world, mankind and life issues: Who am I? How did I come to be? Does my life have a purpose?

These are all questions that eventually come up in any education. They are the questions to which the answers help define a person's worldview.

Perhaps unintentionally, the state-sponsored schools do this—even as they instigate school-to-work programs. Their implicit answers to the previous questions are as follows: I am a being exclusively of flesh and blood, the product (along with the rest of humanity) of a naturalistic evolutionary process, who exists in the present to service the global economy—and I have no soul with an eternal destiny. This is the secular humanist answer.

In this case, state-run schools are religious albeit not Christian. Some Christian families claim they will take care of the religious instruction at home or at their local church but believe their children's state-sponsored school should take care of their secular education. We hope it is clear by this point that this notion is categorically false. It is wrong theologically, and it is wrong from a practical standpoint.

Many school-to-work graduates are not only spiritually empty and troubled but actually unprepared for life in a technology-based society because they have not mastered basic reading and mathematics.

The problem is the assumption that government or the state ought to assume the responsibility for educating children. There are no ideal examples in the Scriptures where the government or the state educated the Christian or covenant children of the day.

Some who differ with our proposition would use the example of Moses in Exodus 2 and Hebrews 11:23-27, which recounts Moses being educated in the ways of

Pharaoh's house. They would contend that this shows how a godly, chosen child could be educated in a non-Christian environment.

Moses was raised in Pharaoh's house under peculiar circumstances, moreover, even coercive ones. His parents used this situation to save his life. When he became an adult, he made other choices to identify with the people of God. Moses is the author of Deuteronomy 6:1-9 and does not recommend his pattern of early education as the best one for covenant children.

While most believe Moses did use knowledge gained in Pharaoh's house to lead the children of Israel to the Promised Land, we could also claim that his 40 years on the backside of the desert was necessary to unlearn some of the ways of Pharaoh's house so God could use him.

In Exodus 3, when Moses was finally called to lead the children out of bondage, he was not the same self-sufficient and perhaps arrogant man who killed an Egyptian in Exodus 2:11-14. He had also been retaught of God in that time.

Others who defend sending children into secular, state-run schools cite the examples of Daniel, Shadrach, Meshach and Abed-Nego whose faith and godly Jewish heritage was preserved in the midst of a pagan Babylonian education. They, too, were taken and educated apart from their families under coercion. They were in the Babylonian school system involuntarily. Their families did not send them there.

These four young Israeli lads recognized their moral and educational danger being under the forced instruction in pagan Babylonian culture. In Daniel chapter one, they sought to develop a personal, moral and religious plan that would help separate them from some aspects of their educational experience.

Christian families today shouldn't use these few Biblical cases as an excuse for putting their own children under a pagan or non-Christian educational regimen. Rather, these passages, if properly understood, show the need for Christian families to plan carefully for the Christian education of their children.

While we believe Christian families should never delegate the education of their children to the state-run school system, we do believe some of their education can be delegated to other Christians in Christian schools. But in doing this the parent never loses the responsibility for the education of his or her own children.

Thus the Christian school or Christian tutors outside the family fulfill the commands of texts such as Deuteronomy 6:1-9 and Matthew 28:18-20. The Church can assist the Christian family in the education of children, but not entirely substitute for it.

PROPOSITION 2: CHRISTIAN EDUCATION MUST BE A CONVICTION, NOT SIMPLY A CHOICE

Christian families must build *convictions* rather than simply making choices concerning Christian education. Some Christians have no deep and abiding convictions about the necessity of a Christian education for their children. They may have abandoned state-sponsored schools for safety, moral or academic reasons. They have done the right thing in sending their children to the local Christian school, but perhaps for the wrong reasons. Thus, when social, legal, or economic pressures come, they may return to the state-sponsored schools. All of the positive and godly influence will be challenged again.

It is important that all local churches, denominations and local Christian schools teach the Biblical and theological reasons for the necessity of a Christian education. Christian families involved in one of the Christian education options need periodic reinforcement of their convictions.

There is an important reason why the proper theology must be stressed. Choice or a mere preference for Christian education may not be able to sustain Christian families if the pressure of the state becomes legally coercive and tries to limit or thwart the growing move away from public schools.

This is a possibility: In *Wisconsin v. Yoder*, a case from 1972, an Amish family said it was sinful to send their child to a government school. According to the State of Wisconsin, the family was violating the state's compulsory attendance laws.

The Supreme Court ruled in favor of the Amish family. The court based its decision partially on the fact that the Amish family had such strong moral *convictions* and that the family felt they had no other choice if they were to be faithful to their religious beliefs.[2]

According to the Yoder case, a mere preference or choice for Christian education may not be sufficient to sustain this right in the eyes of the courts.

Gail and I heard Christian civil rights lawyer David Gibbs give a lecture on the importance of the Yoder case shortly after we had begun our home-schooling experience in 1977.

On one hand, Gibbs pointed out that a preference may also be a strongly held belief, but one that could be abandoned under some circumstances. A *conviction,* on the other hand, cannot be abandoned under pressure or changed circumstances. Convictions come from taking Scriptural commands by faith and are required for Christian families.[3]

There are practical reasons supporting the need for families to build an abiding conviction concerning the Christian education of their children. If they don't, they may give it up if by some rare chance "free" state-run schools return to some moral and academic sanity. Parents must have a *conviction* before a court will recognize their legal standing to maintain that the Christian education of their children is a

God-ordained right. They must believe that it is their responsibility before the Lord and not the responsibility of the state.

PROPOSITION 3: THERE IS A COVENANT RESPONSIBILITY FOR CHRISTIAN EDUCATION

There is a dominion and covenantal aspect to the responsibility of the Christian family concerning the education of their children. Before the Fall, God instructed Adam and Eve in Genesis 1:28 to "be fruitful and multiply" and to subdue and have dominion over the creation.

This command is what some call the cultural mandate or dominion mandate and was given before the Fall. Its execution has been complicated by the Fall, but not abrogated. The bearing, raising and Christian education of children is an essential part of this command. Inherent in this command is that Adam and Eve should reproduce children after their kind.

NECESSITY OF TAKING FULL RESPONSIBILITY

Christian families, if they are to achieve some dominion over their own areas of work and their particular culture, must take full responsibility for the Christian education of their children.

For the Christian family and Church, spiritual and godly rule must be maintained in their respective spheres of influence. Christian parents are to reproduce after their kind, which means godly offspring.

Malachi 2:13-15 shows that maintenance of a godly family is required to protect godly offspring. Malachi says of God, "He seeks godly offspring" (Malachi 2:15b). These kind of themes run through both the Old and New Testaments.

Children are viewed as "a heritage from the Lord, The fruit of the womb is a reward" (Psalm 127:3). They are seen as source of strength and power; "Like arrows in the hand of a warrior, So are the children of one's youth" (Psalm 127:4). This text elaborates further upon the idea of the strength and power, hence dominion, of the Christian family which is not possible without a Christian family reproducing after its kind.

Abraham was given covenant promises about a future offspring, and if we are believers in Jesus Christ, we, too, are the children of Abraham by faith (Galatians 3:7).

In Genesis 18:18-19, God chose Abraham so that he might "...command his children and his household after him, that they keep the way of the Lord, to do righteousness and justice, that the Lord may bring to Abraham what He has spoken to him." What a tremendous promise through the generations! The successful completion of that covenantal promise is dependent upon the Christian family faithfully commanding and teaching the children to follow the ways of God.

In the New Testament we see this same pattern in the life of young Timothy where his mother and grandmother instructed him in the Word of God. This is described by the Apostle Paul who wrote, "...from childhood you have known the Holy Scriptures, which are able to make you wise for salvation through faith which is in Christ Jesus" (2 Timothy 3:15).

PROPOSITION 4: A FRESH OBEDIENCE TO GOD'S COMMAND IS NOW IMPERATIVE

A fresh obedience may be required of some Christian families to begin their responsibility to give their children a Christian education. As more Christian families grow in their Scriptural knowledge of the commands to educate their children Biblically and not in a secular humanist environment, personal convictions and some sorrow may ensue.

Recognition of past failure may be needed. Some repentance may be necessary as families come to terms with the new Christian education paradigm.

It's really the *original* and *old* paradigm being brought back to the churches, but the majority of Christian families have grown up in and with state-run schools, which are all most Christians today have ever known. We never questioned state-run schools, and they were sacrosanct in our communities, no less than Church and family.

Now, however, we must rouse ourselves to action and radical change as we awaken to the terrible tragedy that has befallen the Church and nation through the widespread acceptance and use of state-run schools as a vehicle for the de-Christianizing of the nation.

Christian families need to see God's Word again as something to be obeyed. Too many evangelical Christians today seem to parrot the lyrics of popular soul singer James Brown's hit song: "I FEEL good!"

If they get a happy or emotional feeling in church services, in Bible study or prayer groups, they are satisfied. But the Scriptures are to be studied and then obeyed. The Bible is not a guidebook only; it is the Word of God!

Many families are missing the blessing because of disobedience in this area. Too many Christian families are raising prodigal children when this was once rare. We know this is due in large part to the harm coming from pagan and humanistic instruction in state-sponsored schools, which deliberately neutralizes Christian moral conviction and implants a cancerous logic that "If it feels good, do it!"

A wholesome awe and renewed fear of God is necessary to help parents restore their Biblical obedience concerning the Christian education of children. Our growth and blessing comes from an attitude of obedience to all that God shows us.

Our fellowship and intimacy with God is also dependent upon an attitude of obedience. Jesus said, "He who has My commandments and keeps them, it is he who loves Me. And he who loves Me will be loved by My Father, and I will love him and manifest Myself to him." He said further, "If anyone loves Me, he will keep My word; and My Father will love him, and We will come to him and make Our home with him" (John 14:21, 23).

The Apostle James tells us, "But be doers of the word, and not hearers only, deceiving yourselves. But he who looks into the perfect law of liberty and continues in it, and is not a forgetful hearer but a doer of the work, this one will be blessed in what he does" (James 1:22, 25).

Pastor Paul Yonggi Cho, minister to the world's largest church in Seoul, South Korea, was once asked the secret of his ministerial success. He replied simply, "I pray and I obey." Modern American Christians might follow this same advice in the Christian education of their children with one additional caveat: "I study, I pray and I obey."

Recovering the responsibility for the Christian education of children by families and churches is no easy task given such a long history of blind acceptance of state schooling by so many Christians. Initially, to question the legitimacy of this system will offend some Christians. Others will find it a strange idea at first. But given the current emergency and failure of state-sponsored "public" schools, many have proved willing to take a second and third look at a Biblical paradigm of education.

A Biblical discernment and understanding of the critical issues we put forth in this book will place spiritual requirements upon families and churches. If individual Christian families can recover this call to responsibility for the education of their children, we will have recovered much lost ground. ∎

CHAPTER FOUR

THE BASIC ERRORS OF STATE-SPONSORED EDUCATION AND WHY REFORM WILL NOT WORK

FOUR BASIC ERRORS OF STATE-SPONSORED EDUCATION

STATE-SPONSORED EDUCATION IS NOT A PART OF THE AMERICAN CONSTITUTIONAL VISION

FREE MARKET EDUCATION VS. STATE SCHOOLS

CHRISTIAN EDUCATION IS NOT A MERE "CHOICE"

With the undergirding of a Biblical theology of Christian education, the fundamental errors of "public schooling"— constitutional errors, economic errors and Biblical errors are easily identified. They are not a problem only for various versions of state-sponsored education. They are themselves *intrinsic to all versions* of state-sponsored education itself.

An explanation of those errors will pave the way for a positive message to Christians that the time has come to abandon state-sponsored schools instead of trying to "reform" them.

The checkered history of state-sponsored education in the United States, reveals its beginnings in traditions alien to the American founding and constitutional heritage all the way to the present day.

Today we have an enterprise both fundamentally hostile to basic American principles and genuine learning as it is to Bible-based Christianity.

But we also have a sound alternative in hand, rooted in Scripture and in the Christian worldview, available for parents, their pastors and denominational leaders.

According to Marshall Fritz of *The Alliance for the Separation of School and State*, state-sponsored education involves four basic errors.

He presented them clearly in the companion video that preceded this book, "Let My Children Go" (released by Jeremiah Films, www.jeremiahfilms.com).

FOUR BASIC ERRORS OF STATE-SPONSORED EDUCATION

First is paternalism. This is the idea that the responsibility for education can be shifted from the family or parents to a governmental entity, and that this somehow improves education or society. This is now the working assumption of those in educational bureaucracies at both the federal and state levels.

In practice, it has undermined the authority of parents and the Christian family by undermining the capacity of parents to pass along their own traditions to their children. "We have to get back to the root of good education, which is parental love and responsibility, not politicians trying to acquire power," says Marshall Fritz.

Second is compartmentalism. This is the idea that life is divided up into relatively isolated separate compartments— school, home, church, etc.—so that God can be taught about on Sundays, in Sunday School and Church, but is not relevant to the activities of any other day of the week.

Compartmentalism leaves open the door for the idea that a child's home life need have nothing to do with his educational life, which has become the province of the state, and that neither one has anything to do with what goes on in Church.

Compartmentalization leads one to see such notions as Biblical-based morality having no place in state-sponsored schools.

"This is crazy," says Fritz. "We want the teachers to be instructing the children in morals. We want them saying, 'No hitting, no cheating, no lying.'"

We can look at state-sponsored schools, observe the violence, the cheating, the lack of discipline, the blatant political agendas and so on, and see textbook illustrations of the fact that no one has ever discovered a practical basis for morality outside the internal constraints created by a strong religious tradition passed down from generation to generation through strong families.

The third idea embedded in state-sponsored education is that of welfare statism. Welfare statism has a long history and essentially involves the idea that it is one of the responsibilities of government to provide "social safety nets" for everybody and ensure that "no child is left behind." Today, despite attempts at "reform" including President Bill Clinton's *Welfare Reform Act*, signed into law in 1995, many people see themselves as having a "right" to any number of government-supplied benefits, including a free public education.

Welfare statism is at the foundation of the idea that children have a "right" to an education supplied by the federal government at taxpayer expense.

Says Marshall Fritz, "We need to return to the American idea that responsibility works and get away from welfare in education."

The fourth is socialism. Some economists argue that socialism is one of the chief long-term consequences of welfare statism.

State-sponsored schools, with their European roots, embody a consistently socialist model, and it is small wonder that state-sponsored schools have more and more tended to produce graduates fit for life in a fundamentally socialist society.

Fritz describes "government ownership and administration of the means of production" as socialism that is exemplified in the state-sponsored education model.

Instead of continuing to employ this failed system, we need to return to the quintessential American ideal that freedom works. Today, that means freeing as many children as possible from the grip of Pharaoh's socialistic, state-controlled school system.

Christians, therefore, need to abandon their captivity to the notion that state-sponsored schools are compatible either with a Biblical outlook or with the original American constitutional vision.

One of the most important points to emphasize is that "public education" is not a part of the original American constitutional heritage. No state-sponsored, tax-funded public schools existed as such until Horace Mann and the

Harvard Unitarians set them up in Boston in the early 1840's.

STATE-SPONSORED EDUCATION IS FUNDAMENTALLY ALIEN TO THE ORIGINAL AMERICAN CONSTITUTIONAL VISION

State-sponsored education is actually the product of an ideology that took root in Europe and is fundamentally alien to American, constitutional, and Christian thinking.

Our Constitution was drafted by men such as James Madison who were home schooled or educated in classical Christian schools. Moreover, these men founded a constitutional republic that existed for half a century without the benefit of public schools.

The United States Constitution never mentions education as a responsibility of republican government. So it should be clear that originally, state and school were separate entities. Constitutional government—republican democracy of the sort that took root on American soil and nowhere else in the world—is simply not compatible with the idea of a government-run school system.

Moreover, the takeover of education by the Harvard Unitarians that set the stage for the rise of Progressivism and the John Dewey-led movement suggests that much of what went wrong in America during the century just concluded coincided with the mass acceptance, including by Christians, of government-run schools.

Isn't it possible that the original idea of education being in the hands of families—involving networks of home schoolers and private Christian schools—governed by free market thinking, might restore both constitutional republican values and Christian morality? It clearly worked for James Madison.[1] Why not for Christians today? If this perspective is sound, and it assuredly is, then we need to stop advocating "reform" of the public schools and scrap the idea of government schools altogether.

We should stop using the term public school—except, perhaps, to define for our audience that public schools are indeed government schools.

ANTI-CHRISTIAN, HUMANIST, SOCIALIST, SECULARIST "PUBLIC SCHOOLS"

The term "public school" is really a misnomer. It implies schools are run for the public, by the public. This is untrue and has been from the start. They were set up by a liberal-humanist elite and have become the tools of this elite.

Government schools are humanistic and socialistic not because they went off course at some point to which we can return, but by their nature. They are not, in the last analysis, about education, but power—over our children.

Their day-to-day activities may be run at the local and state levels, but ultimately they answer to the federal government and those running it. This is unconstitutional.

Again, the U.S. Constitution does not make education a federal responsibility. It does not authorize any branch of the federal government or any federal agency to set up and run schools. The most important point is that the entire system of government schooling is illegitimate at its foundation. It is unconstitutional as well as unbiblical.

Thus, when we advocate "reform," we play right into the hands of secular humanists and continue to let them set the educational agenda for the country. Efforts at reform imply the system is legitimate. It isn't. The lack of constitutional support for state-sponsored schools by the founding fathers is all the more reason we need to get out of the humanistic, government-education quicksand and advocate a new model of Bible-based education, one not associated with government at any level.

The constitutions of the various states do provide for a "system of free public schools."[2] These provisions at the state level occurred after the rise of the Unitarian-instigated state-sponsored school system.

There is a sense in which, contrary to the reformers, government schools are not "broken" at all but working well according to their design and purpose—a point argued in detail by such writers as Samuel Blumenfeld and John Taylor Gatto.[3]

This point is hard for many conservatives to grasp. Schools that are secular, humanist and socialist by design will develop in a certain direction and turn out a certain kind of graduate—and experience certain problems.

The problems do not stem from something locally amiss with this or that school or district but arise out of the government-run educational model itself.

Conservatism needs a paradigm shift in its understanding of education in the United States, realizing that "public schools" from the start have been built on a perverse, unsound and illogical educational, economic and spiritual foundation, one that has been harming children and society and can't be reformed.

There is nothing wrong, obviously, with pointing out the many failures of "public schools." But this exposure should now have the purpose of exposing the fundamental, structural errors of state-sponsored education and pointing the way to a sound alternative—not to "reform" the hopelessly corrupt status quo.

We must advance a new paradigm for Christian education in this country. We have clearly explained its theological foundation. This new paradigm looks to the Bible as its main text, obviously. This model, presently in its early stages, also maintains that the free market, and not government, best delivers an alternative to state-sponsored education.

Home schoolers have broken new ground and sown the seeds. Now we must take care to ensure the fertility of the soil and tend to a new garden. We have already reaped the tremendous benefits in the tiny home-school movement.

Now, we must turn a trickle into a flood.

FREE MARKET EDUCATION VS. STATE SCHOOLS

To deliver this Biblically-based educational paradigm to families and churches, issues of free market economics must be addressed.

It is the nature of our relationship to the world generally that the world gives us very little beyond, perhaps, the air we breathe. We are expected to produce or earn the rest.

The Bible tells us that human sin was the original cause of the need to labor to produce the means of our survival. In the following verses, God is speaking to Adam:

> 17 Then to Adam He said, "Because you have heeded the voice of your wife, and have eaten from the tree of which I commanded you, saying, 'You shall not eat of it': "Cursed is the ground for your sake; In toil you shall eat of it All the days of your life.
>
> 18 Both thorns and thistles it shall bring forth for you, And you shall eat the herb of the field.
>
> 19 In the sweat of your face you shall eat bread Till you return to the ground, For out of it you were taken; For dust you are, And to dust you shall return."
>
> 23 therefore the Lord God sent him out of the garden of Eden to till the ground from which he was taken. (Genesis 3:17-19; 23)

Economics is the study of how we "till the ground" in a broad sense to produce the means of our survival, how we have created the various trappings of civilization to satisfy human needs and wants, and how the various products that satisfy human needs and wants are distributed throughout society.

There is no reason why educating the next generation should be exempt from economic principles. If history is any indication, free economies are always more efficient at raising standards of living than command economies. They unleash the God-given, creative potential of individuals.

The American free enterprise system, to the extent it has been allowed to operate, has produced the highest standard of living in the world.

Communist systems, such as that of the now defunct Soviet Union, stagnated, having to rely on imported shipments of food and grain to prevent mass starvation.

Moreover, Communist and fascist systems have been engines of mass murder. Over 100 million people were killed by Communist and fascist dictatorships in the 20th century. Our government does not have this sort of record, of course.

Our society was founded on the ideas of liberty and of constitutionally-controlled government—and on the idea that all of us, from those with power to the most lowly servant, all answer to God, the source of a moral life as well as moral government. Throughout our history, however, government has grown and the area of freedom exercised by individuals has shrunk.

As it has grown, the tax burden has grown right along with its capacity to regulate our businesses and the other aspects of our economic lives. It should become clear that the more controls by government placed on any enterprise, including the tax burden, the less effective it becomes due to the drain on its resources and energies.

Effective, efficient businesses cannot flourish to their fullest in an economic environment characterized by a stranglehold of micromanagement from outside; and they should also resist the temptations of government largess—"corporate welfare." As we discover again and again, there are strings attached with every government dollar.

VARIOUS ECONOMIC ARGUMENTS

Sound, free-market principles are consistent with the Bible-based model presented earlier. Classical economists offer a very mixed review of the idea of state-sponsored education. Most, it is important to note, were utilitarian. That is, they believed that policies should be adopted if they helped maximize social improvements (e.g., in education) and rejected if they created a greater balance of unhappiness over happiness.

Utilitarian arguments at first glance seem to suggest that an educated public would be less apt to commit crimes and have a greater tendency toward happiness, and that a general (i.e., government-sponsored) system of education would promote economic growth.

But theirs is hardly a ringing endorsement of state-sponsored education. They observed that those nations of continental Europe that had already developed highly centralized systems of state-sponsored education were economically inferior to Great Britain, in which education was still privately supplied.[4]

Adam Smith proposed that state fees were to be limited to supplying buildings, and that education itself was to be paid for by parents' fees. Speaking of the college level, he wrote of the great disadvantage of education funded by the state:

> The endowments of schools and colleges have necessarily diminished more or less the necessity of application in the teachers. Their subsistence, so far as it arises from their

> salaries, is evidently derived from a fund altogether
> independent of their success and reputation in their
> particular professions.[5]

In other words, state support independent of parental support created a disincentive or lack of motivation on the part of teachers to do their best.

On the other hand, according to Adam Smith:

> The three most essential parts of literary education, to read,
> to write and account, it still continues to be more common to
> acquire in private than in public schools; and it very seldom
> happens that anybody fails of acquiring them to the degree in
> which it is necessary to acquire them.[6]

Thomas Malthus concurred: If persons had to pay specific fees to attend school, then "...the school master would then have a strong interest to increase the number of his pupils."[7]

John Stuart Mill was a bit more hesitant, his hesitation steeped in his basic distrust of the judgment of the public that would be deciding whether or not to send their children to a school, and if so, to which school. He says at one point: "The uncultivated cannot be competent judges of cultivation."[8] However, despite this hesitation, Mill eventually sided with private over state-sponsored education, the reason being his commitment to the principle of liberty and its capacity to produce a variety of ends that are good in themselves as well as beneficial to society: spontaneity, variety and experiment. Mill recognized that state-sponsored education would undermine these through its necessary uniformity:

> A general state education is a mere contrivance for moulding
> people to be exactly like one another: and as the mould in
> which it casts them is that which pleases the predominant

power in the government, whether this be a monarch, a priesthood, an aristocracy, or the majority of the existing generation; in proportion as is efficient and successful, it establishes a despotism over the mind, leading by natural tendency to one over the body.[9]

It is interesting that this sentiment was echoed by the Austrian-school economist Ludwig Von Mises early in the 20th century. Mises, one of the most original and prolific defenders of the free market, observed:

...the school is a political prize of the highest importance. It cannot be deprived of its political character as long as it remains a public and compulsory institution. There is, in fact, only one solution: the state, the government, the laws, must not in any way concern themselves with schooling or education. Public funds must not be used for such purposes.

The rearing and instruction of youth must be left entirely to parents and to private associations and institutions.[10]

Mill didn't go as far as Mises would later. Mill was willing to endorse compulsory education; however, he did not see the state as having a significant role beyond this. He did not believe, that is, that the state should set up and run government schools: "The instrument for enforcing the law should be no other than public examinations, extending to all children."[11]

In other words, Mill distinguished between compulsory education and compulsory schooling in government-run schools. E.G. West concludes his discussion by observing:

To see how radical such a provision would be today we have only to imagine children obtaining their knowledge by television, correspondence courses, dame schools or part-time academies or even being taught by their parents at home in the same manner that J.S. Mill himself was educated. There would even be no official pressure to supply people with teachers previously instructed in the government training colleges.[12]

In fact, the only significant political economist of the 19th century to advocate "free" state-sponsored schools was Karl Marx. To get "fully developed individuals," Marx wrote:

> One step already spontaneously taken toward effecting this revolution is the establishment of technical and agricultural schools, and of *ecoles d'enseignement professionel*, in which the children of the working men receive some instruction in technology and in the practical handling of the various implements of labor.
>
> Though the Factory Act, that first and meager concession wrung from capital, is limited to combining elementary education with work in the factory, there can be no doubt that when the working class comes into power, as inevitably it must, technical instruction, both theoretical and practical, will take its proper place in the working class schools.[13]

What Marx was advocating here rings very much like what school-to-work legislation was to become. Marx also launches into an attack on parental control over education as an instrument of "capitalist exploitation."

Throughout much of the past century, academic economics was largely statist—that is, it adopted one of two versions of the idea that government actions are integral to economic activity, or that government can effectively "manage" the economy.

In this they followed the teachings of John Maynard Keynes, who held that government and our central bank, the

Federal Reserve, could check the "excesses" in the natural tendencies of free markets and business cycles toward "booms" and "busts." This is, of course, the so-called "mixed economy."

In fascism, businesses are privately owned, nominally at least, but the major decisions are controlled by the state for the supposed benefit of the nation.

Another version of the idea of government involvement in the economy is, of course, socialism, in which the means of production are both owned and controlled by the government. This kind of economic theory, the best-known version of which is Marxism, prevailed in communist countries from 1917 down to 1989.

With the dismantling of the Berlin Wall and the collapse of the Soviet Union, Communism began to lose credibility until today, when it only controls the economies of four countries: North Korea, Vietnam, Mainland China and Cuba.

The "mixed economy" has prevailed in the United States. Thus our various endeavors are privately owned, but still answer to the government in significant ways. They are subject to regulatory oversight, told whom they may hire and in what proportions, what they must pay, and so on.

All three models—fascism, socialism and the "mixed economy"—are therefore contrary to a Biblical worldview. Philosophers such as John Locke, in his *Second Treatise on Government*, spoke of individuals having natural rights, rights derived exclusively from our having been created by God.

The French statesman and economic philosopher Frederic Bastiat concurred. Rights in this sense can be understood as moral claims to take the actions necessary for survival and for whatever improvements of life one can make. To say that any person has the right to take action to produce something is also to say that others are obligated to leave the person alone. Likewise, in this view, people may produce goods or services and then have the right to trade with others on a value-for-value basis. Each person brings his scale of economic values to the table, and trades if he can expect to benefit from the trade.

TWELVE AXIOMS OF CHRISTIAN ECONOMICS
One Christian author who explored in great detail the "axioms of economics" in a society governed according to Christian principles was Edmund A. Opitz. He summarizes them as 12 propositions:

1. Work must be performed if human life is to be sustained. (Returning to Genesis 3:17-19, 23, what we find in the world are raw materials, not usable goods. Raw materials must somehow be converted to usable goods, and this involves both information and sustained effort.)

2. Goods are scarce. The things that satisfy our needs are by their nature in short supply. Economics studies how they are produced and distributed throughout society.

3. The market is the primary labor-saving device. Because of scarcity, human beings are driven toward social arrangements making specialized production possible. This involves the division of our labors, and cooperation with others. Without division of labor and peaceful, predictable cooperation with others, no civilization could exist.

4. Goods and services are exchanged for goods and services. All use of one's abilities is provided in exchange for something one values more. All parties to such exchanges benefit from the exchange—or must believe they do so.

5. Money possesses intrinsic value. No one labors merely to receive pieces of paper. People work because they expect something of value in return.

Societies establish currency which is sound to the extent the currency can buy something its members value more. But currency is not money; gold is money. Hence currency should be solidly backed by gold.

6. Production begets production. People produce beyond their own needs under the assumption that they can exchange their surpluses for goods produced by others. If a person increases his productive output of desirable goods, others will increase their productive labors to obtain these goods.

7. Capital is the key to productivity. Economies expand with more and better equipment and more and better organization. Increasing the quantity of capital leads to more goods being produced and made available.

8. Supply and demand are alternate facets of the same thing. A given available quantity of some good, such as shoes, is simultaneously a demand for other goods which one might wish to obtain by trading shoes.

9. Customers set wages. If the economy is free, each person's economic rewards are in proportion to the economic value his peers attach to the goods or services he has to offer. If what he offers is attractive to large numbers of people, then he is rewarded greatly; if what he offers is valued only by a few, then his returns are low. This tends to guide people into lines of activity where the goods produced or services rendered are wanted.

10. Customers also determine prices. One might set a figure for one's good, but if there are no buyers the figure is not a price. The price of an item is what the item is worth to others enticed to buy it.

11. The entrepreneurial decision is the spark. The entrepreneurial decision is a creative act by a person that combines means (human beings, equipment, and resources) to achieve a given end—something to be produced.

12. Economics is only part of life. The principles of a free economy are only workable in a moral order, provided by a moral view of the universe. People must be both able and willing to trust one another.

They must also be able to defer gratification and assume responsibility. They must, finally, have a respect for what is true, and not merely what is popular—even if they have no takers.[14]

Can this be applied to education? The answer is "Yes." One study after another shows that quality education is of value in the general marketplace, that is, among ordinary people. What has been missing are the institutions that would allow free market education to flourish unhampered. In their place is the idea that dispensing education is the government's responsibility—an idea still accepted by much of the public. All of Opitz's propositions, however, tie in with Christian education.

CHRISTIAN ECONOMICS AND EDUCATION
Quality education must be created and offered to children and youth by someone. This is sufficiently clear as not to require much further elaboration.

Quality education is scarce. Government education is, in fact, a failure educationally. This explains the concern about education evident in popular surveys and opinion polls.

Both parents and would-be employers are concerned with high school graduates who emerge from state-sponsored schools unable to read simple directions or make basic arithmetic calculations.

Christian educators have a potential solution to the lack of quality education if they can pool their time, resources and expertise—dividing their labors in the creation and development of a new educational model or paradigm—that of home schooling or private Christian schools that take advantage of the resources of the local churches.

They must appeal successfully to Christian parents, who must believe that their children will benefit from the new educational model more than from state-sponsored schools if the new model is to prosper.

The new educational model must be offered as a business, offering something of value and receiving in return something of value in the form of financial compensation for those involved. It should not expect to subsist on grants from private foundations indefinitely—and it should definitely not accept money from any governmental entity!

If there is evidence that the Christian educational model is succeeding where state-sponsored schools failed, Christian parents will be motivated to do what it takes (increase their productive labors) in order to afford to send their children to private Christian schools—assuming, of course, that for some reason they cannot or do not want to home school their children.

As soon as more resources become available with an established track record of success, the Christian educational model will expand, and a new network of Christian educational institutions will emerge all across the land.

Christian parents will abandon state-sponsored education in increasing numbers.

Christian educators are supplying a service, and this is simultaneously a demand for further goods and services that Christian education can bring about in society. Graduates of Christian schools are already proving to be among the most educated of their generation as well as the most diligent and honest employees companies can hire.

With the increased demand for Christian education, financial compensation for those dispensing it will also increase, making possible still more improvements in facilities, academic development, plans for growth or expansion.

The price for Christian education will be set by the marketplace, through the beliefs and actions of its customers—Christian parents.

Christian businesses, of course, may also get involved through generous donations to Christian educational efforts and providing hands-on opportunities for students.

Having observed the successes with home schooling and private Christian schools to date, Christian educators promoting either home schooling or the creation of private Christian schools must adopt an entrepreneurial spirit.

Christian educators must be aware that the road ahead might be tough. Christian parents, many of whom are still sold on the idea of reforming state-sponsored education, will not come on board all at once.

This may mean that the rewards for adopting the new educational model are initially small, both in terms of Christian people willing to embrace the model and in terms of the ability of these institutions to sustain themselves financially.

It is, however, imperative to stand on Biblical truths as overriding whatever economic hardship that results from swimming against the popular tide.

THE PURPOSE OF EXODUS MANDATE IS TO PROVIDE SOLUTIONS

This is the purpose of the Exodus Mandate Project—to provide solutions where others have only seen problems, and to develop both an educational model for Christian parents to follow and a long-term strategy to see the educational model embodied in new Christian educational institutions.

GOVERNMENT IS NOT A PRODUCTIVE AGENCY. IT APPROPRIATES, REDISTRIBUTES

One may review Opitz's outline above and note that government is conspicuous by its absence. As all the classical economists realized, government is in fact not a productive agency. It does not create goods or services; it merely appropriates and redistributes the goods and services produced by others.

Government, by its very nature, involves the use of force or at least the threat of force. It frequently involves promoting causes that would not survive among ordinary people because there is no market-based demand for them. This, it must be said, is the primary economic objection to state-sponsored education.

With its central machinery outside the productive sector of society, well protected by teachers' unions and a huge, centralized bureaucracy, there are simply no incentives built into the government-school model to ensure a quality education.

Teachers who go into the profession because they love working with children find themselves continually hampered by the bureaucracy as well as by poorly disciplined children whose cognitive abilities and spiritual nature are being maimed by the government school environment.

Here is what the classical economist Frederic Bastiat said regarding education:

In this matter of education, the law has only two alternatives. It can permit this transaction of teaching-and-learning to operate freely, and without the use of force, or it can force human wills in this matter by taking from some of them enough to pay the teachers who are appointed by the government to instruct others, without charge. But in this second case, the law commits legal plunder by violating liberty and property.[15]

ESCAPING STATE-SPONSORED EDUCATION

This is a good starting point from which to explore the economic foundation for Bible-based education. Christians, it is essential to point out, are not advocating the use of force. Jesus says, "Behold, I stand at the door and knock: if any man hear my voice, and open the door, I will come in to him, and will sup with him, and he with me" (Revelation 3:20). Jesus does not win converts by force, but by invitation only.

When Christianity is properly interpreted in life, it does not use force; and this is why we advocate building up a system of Christian schools completely outside the state-sponsored system, as opposed to trying to reform the state-sponsored system in a more Christ-friendly direction.

What all this means is that Christian educators should become educational entrepreneurs, using Christian love and gentle persuasion with Christian parents when they encourage them to remove their children from the reach of Pharaoh's school system.

If home schooling is the ideal, but not all parents are able to home school their children, then the onus is on Christian educators to begin building up new Christian schools and networks of Christian schools. Churches may assist by making available to Christian educators facilities that are presently not in use for six days out of the week.

A private school aimed at educating a small number of children could be begun in a single home as well. (They were popular in the Colonial period, and were called "dame schools." This could be a source of income for home schooling mothers with an ability to teach more than their own children. In many states, this is illegal.)

In other words, the Biblical view agrees with the idea that Christian education should be supplied by the free market, and not by government at any level. These are, in fact, the only two alternatives.

FREE MARKET: BETTER EDUCATION, CHOICE

If history is any guide, then free markets would actually serve far better in creating the kind of conditions where quality education could be supplied to buyers. In a slim volume entitled *Education: Free and Compulsory*, Austrian-school economist Murray Rothbard (a student of Mises, whose views were noted above) developed a very common sense case for why free market education is absolutely essential, and also suggesting the real diversity that may emerge once networks of private Christian schools are built up.

We need to consider an obvious fact about children: There are no two that are exactly alike. Just as they have different appearances, they have different God-given talents and aptitudes. They have different levels of cognitive ability.

Finally, they have different levels of motivation, and are motivated by different stimuli. All this militates against the idea that children can be effectively educated by dropping them into a melting pot of 30 or so other children, to be educated by a single, standardized curriculum.

Rothbard concludes that "...The best type of instruction is individual instruction" tailored to the individual child's natural talents and abilities.[16] The ideal form of education, that is, is a kind of apprenticeship in which one pupil learns from one teacher. This contrasts with compulsory, government-run schooling that treats all students as essentially carbon copies of one another.

Classroom education involving a large number of children can only set up a system which unjustly penalizes children who are naturally gifted and, left to themselves, would tend to soar ahead of their less-gifted classmates.

Equally unjust, it either forces the less gifted to try and perform at levels beyond their capabilities; or, to keep them from falling ever further behind the rest of the class, it artificially limits everyone, further repressing the naturally gifted.

Rothbard also observes that the most natural teachers of children are the children's parents. Most parents are quite capable of teaching basic subjects like how to read, how to write, and how to do basic arithmetic. When parents for whatever reason do not have the time, they can hire tutors to do the teaching, and as their children get older will need to hire tutors anyway.

The development of small, private schools is an obvious option if tutors elect to divide their labors and work in teams, serving the needs of a number of families. In either case, effective education is going to be tailored to the needs and interests of the individual child, allowing the child to develop his natural abilities.

Thus Rothbard leaves us with a choice: Do we as a society allow the natural relationship between parents and children to include a strong educational component that provides children with the start they need, or do we allow the government to remove children forcibly from parents for eight hours out of every day and have them taught what committees of secular-humanist politicians and bureaucrats believe all children should know?

The latter explains the uniformity and the tendency to try and make everyone equal. Uniformity and coerced equality are natural outgrowths of the bureaucratic temptation. Bureaucracy must attempt to pigeonhole everyone into roughly the same set of molds.

It cannot abide much individuality, genuine diversity, or spontaneity. Such limitations are particularly damaging to extremely bright students, who may quickly come to sense a stigma associated with being ahead of the pack.

EDUCATION: FREE MARKET PRINCIPLES

Rothbard therefore also concludes that the free market and not the government should supply education. Ideally, parents should begin the education of their children at home.

Specialized education, to begin once children have mastered the basics (reading, writing, basic arithmetic, and perhaps some general science and history), can be taken over by tutors and by professionals in an apprenticeship relation.

It is perhaps worth noting that for close to a century, legal education in the country was conducted by this method. No large law schools, no LSAT tests or admission tickets to public law schools, and no credentialing of the kind that predominates today existed then. If a person wanted to become a lawyer he went to work in a law office when he was a teenager and performed a variety of "odd jobs" in the service of those from whom he was learning the profession as he went along. When he was ready, he joined the office or struck out on his own. Arguably, the legal profession had a much better reputation then than it does now.

FUNDAMENTALLY DESPOTIC AND REPRESSIVE

Compulsory, state-sponsored education in Pharaoh's school system is fundamentally despotic and repressive by its very design. Because of the clash between what children are, in all their genuine diversity, and what bureaucracy requires, "public schools" cannot be otherwise. This is another reason why we should not seek to "reform" them but rather to escape from them.

CHRISTIAN EDUCATION IS NOT A MERE "CHOICE." IT IS A NECESSITY FOR SURVIVAL

We Christians have our work cut out for us; this much is clear. Part of that work is convincing other Christians—pastors and denominational leaders, schoolteachers, and Christian parents—to make the necessary paradigm shift away from the assumption that state-sponsored education was a sound idea that went off course.

If state-sponsored education itself is the problem—and every argument we've mustered so far has clearly told us that it is—then reforming government schools is simply not a viable option.

The various reformist agendas should be abandoned. Not only are they based on unsound theology, they waste our valuable resources and will do further harm to our children, who despite the reforms will remain in the clutches of the secular humanist educational model. We have no other options besides abandoning state-sponsored education and embracing the paradigm of Christian education calling for home schooling or the creation of private, Christian schools with assistance from the Church.

IMPRACTICAL OR IMPOSSIBLE? NOT AT ALL!

If all this sounds impractical or impossible, it is because so many Christians have yet to make this paradigm shift and recognize that God commands parents to assume full responsibility for the education of their children.

However, working for public-school reform places many conservative and Christian organizations in a compromised position of being on the same side of the fence regarding some reforms with many of the groups they claim to abhor, such as the National Education Association.

This is a sad situation, and we must be as assertive as we can in winning people and organizations over to the cause of returning to Biblically and constitutionally sound education for our children. Plenty of people of goodwill in these organizations, and in Christian groups, are still involved in one way or another with state-sponsored schools. They still have to be reached and convinced through exposure to the truths we have so far unfolded. We are not faced with a "tough decision." It is obvious.

As evidence for this need to persuade Christians of the facts, consider the fact that Christian denominations, including some leaders in the Southern Baptist Convention, have embraced the idea that they can lead "reform" of state-sponsored schools by organizing and planning to out-vote, e.g., the homosexual lobby.[17]

For starters, this indicates naiveté about how the secular left works—and how extensive its control of the culture has become. The homosexuals did not get their agenda into state-sponsored schools through winning any votes, and we are not likely to get rid of this agenda at the voting booth. They were able to infiltrate state-sponsored education gradually, by exploiting the fuzzy, relativistic ethical foundation that was already there as a product of the secular humanist worldview.

Relativism, the ethical consequence of secular humanism, calls for universal tolerance of every "lifestyle choice" (except, of course, for "choices" that do not embrace the ideal of universal tolerance such as those of Biblical Christianity). Cultural relativism long ago ceased to be one of the mere "ism" words debated by academics and became a hallmark of our culture, even for those who never so much as heard the term "cultural relativism." This was the door secular humanism opened, and the homosexuals quietly slipped through it.

Following in the humanistic wake, because they no longer have the Biblical defenses against it that the Biblical worldview alone can provide, was a huge segment of the American public. The majority of the public, according to numerous polls, now favors "tolerance" toward the homosexual lifestyle. This is now the point of view of most of the school boards and the secular education establishment.

Add to this the number of people who are unconcerned and just follow the culture and do what they are told, and it is clear that a plan to "outvote" the homosexual agenda would not have a chance of succeeding.

Homosexuality is, of course, only one issue. There are plenty of others, including abortion, evolution and so on, and these are all the more reason why Christian children must be removed promptly from state-sponsored schools.

We cannot change the state-sponsored schools at the fundamental level. They are what they are: a product of a secular humanist worldview. Christian children—even those raised in homes where the Lord is loved—remaining in these schools are therefore in danger of growing up to become "functional humanists" who are vulnerable to every politically-correct, cultural fashion that comes along, no matter what the Bible says about it. Government schools will remain a product of this worldview despite all our attempts at "reforming" them. We must remove our children from them, and we must, to be obedient to God's commands.

EXODUS MANDATE IS BIBLICAL

To distinguish Exodus Mandate at the most fundamental level from various forms of "school choice" being promoted today, I will not describe what is being proposed here as a "choice" agenda. The Exodus from Pharaoh's school system to the Promised Land of private Christian schools and home schooling is more an "obedience" agenda. We are being obedient to God's commands.

We are lovingly encouraging all Christians to experience a shift in their thinking about the education of their children that could be a truly dramatic movement in our nation's history. Pastors and denominational leaders must exercise leadership in the effort to build up new Christian schools outside the corrupting reach of the secular-humanist worldview.

AN IDEA TO REMOVE FROM YOUR THINKING

In the meantime, we should not even use terminology such as "choice for educational freedom," if for no other reason than "pro-choice" is part of the sleight-of-hand language of the secular humanist establishment (usually applied to abortion). Christian education is not a mere "choice" for Christians. This is the most important point: God commands Christian education! We will never win the battle for an entire generation of Christian children until we get this right, and modify our thinking and actions accordingly.

Decades ago, I dropped the tragic notion that there is a viable "choice" between state-sponsored schools and Christian schools or home schooling. It simply has no place in genuine Christian education. Now, we must implore millions of Christian parents, pastors, teachers, and others to do the same thing.   ∎

CHAPTER FIVE

WINNING THE HEARTS AND MINDS OF THE SHEPHERDS

ESTHER AND MORAL COURAGE (FOR SUCH A TIME AS THIS)

ROLE OF PASTORS AND CHRISTIAN LEADERS

AN AMERICAN STATE OF EMERGENCY: THE CONFESSING CHURCH IN GERMANY COMPARED TO THE AMERICAN CHURCH

LET US GO UP ... AND TAKE POSSESSION (NUMBERS 13:26 – 14:10)

P astors, Christian workers and denominational leaders have a crucial role to play in preparing the way for the Exodus from Pharaoh's school system and toward the Promised Land of Christian home schooling and private Christian education. But first we have to develop the right frame of mind.

It takes more than the knowledge of the history of state-sponsored schooling and its effects on our children, and it takes more than the realization that reforming state-sponsored schools has never worked and will not work in the future. It even takes more than the correct Biblical theology.

It requires moral courage on the part of all of us to take the initiative and do what needs to be done to save our children.

STORIES OF COURAGE

When I was just a lad, my mother used to read to me the great stories of literature. I still remember vividly the story of "Horatius at the Bridge." Horatius defended Rome against the Etruscans and saved his country.

Better still was the "Song of Roland." Roland was left behind with his soldiers against the Saracen hordes who were invading France. Even now I can close my eyes and still see the childhood storybook picture of Roland, bleeding from his battle wounds, his sword broken, blowing his trumpet and calling for aid to his uncle, Charlemagne.

Then there was the story of the little Dutch boy faithfully keeping his hand in the leak in the dike, holding back the tidal sea from engulfing his country, not leaving his post, waiting for help to come.

I read and reread these same stories many times as a child and imagined what I would do in such a circumstance.

THE BIBLICAL STORY OF QUEEN ESTHER

The Scriptures, too, are filled with stories of moral courage, and they provide our most sterling examples. One such story of Queen Esther is found in Esther 4:13-16. I dedicate these remarks to Christian educators, many of whom already exemplify the principles of this passage:

> 13 And Mordecai told them to answer Esther: "Do not think in your heart that you will escape in the king's palace any more than all the other Jews.
>
> 14 "For if you remain completely silent at this time, relief and deliverance will arise for the Jews from another place, but you and your father's house will perish. Yet who knows

whether you have come to the kingdom for such a time as this?"

15 Then Esther told them to reply to Mordecai:

16 "Go, gather all the Jews who are present in Shushan, and fast for me; neither eat nor drink for three days, night or day. My maids and I will fast likewise. And so I will go to the king, which is against the law; and if I perish, I perish!"

THREE REASONS FOR MORAL COURAGE OVER COMPROMISE

In Esther 4:13-16 we see three reasons for the necessity of moral courage over compromise.

The first reason: We may suffer personal loss due to compromise. Mordecai had cautioned Esther that her security lay not with compromise and silence, but with the path of moral courage and speaking out. Moral courage is always superior to compromise.

The problem is, our minds and logic constantly tell us that our security lies with compromise. It is tempting to see self-protection and security as resulting from compromise.

Mordecai told Esther that she would not escape by doing nothing, even though it would seem that her position in the palace as the Queen would guarantee her security.

When we allow God to work in our lives, and when we overcome our fears and our temptation to stay in our comfort zones and instead take a stand on behalf of God's glory, we demonstrate moral courage.

Attempting to reform state-sponsored schools invariably involves compromise of some sort with secular humanism. But secular humanists, by the very nature of the state-sponsored system, remain in control.

Christians who continue to send their children to these schools risk the personal loss of seeing their children fall away from their faith as soon as they get old enough to leave home.

Parents must have the moral courage to do what must be done and either home school their children or place them in private Christian schools. Otherwise they may have to endure the sad realization that their children have joined the forces of the enemy.

There is an element of risk involved in this, of course. Christians who take bold steps to educate their own children may face ostracism. Worse, we may eventually face open opposition from the educational establishment, which will have the full backing of federal and state governments.

FANGS WILL BARE; THE FIGHT WILL BE ON

In the future, matters may get worse, as the owners of state-sponsored schools move to protect their territory. They're willing to let a few strays go, but when the numbers rise, the gloves will come off. The fangs will bare; the fight will be on.

I wish it were possible to promise everyone who is bold and brave that he or she would win every time and never suffer loss, but God does not promise this, and it is not the case. But we already know that we have won the final victory in Christ. It is the in-between battles along the way that give us concern.

What is clear is that when we compromise, we lose. Proverbs 29:25 tells us "The fear of man brings a snare, But whoever trusts in the Lord shall be safe."

The second reason not to compromise: We may lose our opportunity to serve the people of God. In the next verse, Mordecai told Esther that God would bring "relief and deliverance" to the Jews from another place if she failed to act. In other words, God will see to it that His work gets done. He will inevitably deliver His people. But we may fail to be the instruments of His plan.

It is important to remember that we are fighting an already-defeated foe. We are on the winning side even when we seem to be losing.

Paul told the Corinthians, "For we can do nothing against the truth, but for the truth" (2 Corinthians 13:8). This was Esther's moment, her greatest opportunity to serve the Lord. This was the reason she was where she was when she was.

In Judges 5:16 we are told that the "divisions of Reuben have great searchings of heart" because they did not join Deborah and Barak in the battle against Sisera. After the great victory they had great regrets because they had not participated when they could have enjoyed the fruit and experienced the joy of victory.

And so it will be with us. If we compromise by leaving our children in state-sponsored schools, and if pastors are unwilling to take the courageous path and make the arrangements for church-sponsored Christian schools operating on weekdays in their places of worship, all of us will look back on ensuing events and wonder if we could have done more. We will wonder if we could have been the ones who made the difference.

Great joy and satisfaction ensue when we show moral courage, trust the Lord and do our best! This we never regret!

The third reason not to compromise: We may be the ones chosen for important service for the people of God. Mordecai gave Esther some important truths: "Yet who knows whether you have come to the kingdom for such a time as this?"

Divine Providence had placed Esther in a unique place where she could affect the situation. Each of us needs to search his or her heart and consider what talents and what opportunities God has dealt him or her, and how these can be employed for His kingdom, especially in times of danger and crisis like the one in which Esther lived—and the one in which we live today. Today we live in a time of great potential for change and great opportunity.

State-sponsored schools are in serious trouble, and most people know this, whether Christian or otherwise. Christians in particular should pray for guidance, because we—our generation—may be the ones chosen for the all-important task of building up a new school system outside the reach of the secular humanists.

The graduates of such a school system could very well begin to reverse the moral decline of this nation in a few short years. Yet if we do not step outside our safety zones and assume the responsibility for home schooling our children or developing Christian schools, we will never know. Christian parents and pastors must recognize this opportunity and then trust God.

Is there anything sadder and more disappointing than to see a person who lives in the palace and either does not see the opportunity or is afraid to use his or her power for God's purposes? In other words, any of us might say, "I'm just a housewife or just a teacher, or just a factory worker—or just a parent. What can I do?" With God, one has no limits.

EXAMPLES OF GODLY COURAGE

However, God's heroes were all "simple folk." Very few, if any, would have been chosen by the crowds. Esther had been a simple Jewish girl from an ordinary family. She was perhaps today's equivalent of a beauty queen. We don't know if she was smart or bright, but she was a beauty. Our little assets, our talents and our position that we dedicate give us leverage for the kingdom of God.

We may never know what will result from any given act of moral courage. Rosa Parks had no big plans for the day when she refused to move to the back of the bus and set off the Montgomery Bus Boycott and the modern Civil Rights movement.

Can anyone really believe that Martin Luther said on October 31, 1517, "I think I will go up to the Church at Wittenburg this morning and nail up my 95 theses and kick off the Protestant Reformation and change history for the next 400 years"? I don't think so. He was exercising moral courage for the need and issue of the moment. He may have actually been the most surprised man in Europe had he known what the full impact of his actions would be.

On April 19, 1775, a few dozen farmers and merchants stood fearful and trembling with their hunting rifles on Lexington Green before the might of the British Empire.

Their commander, Captain John Parker, said, "If they mean to have a war, let it begin here." They lost that first battle, but "fired the shot heard around the world." The war for independence was underway! It would lead to the Declaration of Independence the following year, and eventually to the United States Constitution. The world would be changed forever!

We all may face choices like Queen Esther or Rosa Parks or Martin Luther or Captain Parker, dangerous ones where we face loss of prestige, status, friends, and employment or even in some cases our lives due to exercising moral courage.

In Ephesians, Paul tells how the Lord places a high premium on simply standing firm in the face of opposition. He describes a time in Ephesians 6:13 called "the evil day" when evil would seem to reign supreme. These may be times when all we seem able to do is stand. We are heading toward such a time.

We are told that the whole armor of God will protect us when we have done everything in our power, or as Paul says, "having done all" just simply to "stand." That is all that is expected. When we stand, we become part of that new "standard" raised up by the Lord against His enemies (Isaiah 59:19).

In Luke 22:53, Jesus Christ describes such moments when evil is allowed by God to hold sway in a society for a time. He speaks of such a time as His own arrest and seizure in the Garden of Gethsemane: "...But this is your [the forces of evil] hour, and the power of darkness."

During these times when secular humanism has become the dominant force in American society, our courage and loyalties are bound to be supremely tested.

Esther responded to God's challenge by promising to pray for three days and three nights, and promising to go before the king without being summoned, an offense punishable by death. She stepped out of her comfort zone and decided she was willing to risk everything. She told Mordecai, "If I perish, I perish."

Esther was successful with her intervention, and that story had a happy ending, as God's people were spared and a fresh victory was won. But what would have happened if she had not grasped the moment and heeded the question, "Who knoweth whether thou art come to the kingdom for such a time as this?"

ROLE OF PASTORS AND CHRISTIAN LEADERS

Applying this more closely to the present circumstances, Queen Esther's situation may be compared to the need for pastors and Christian leaders to show moral courage in leading their flocks into the safe sanctuary of Christian schools or home schooling.

Pastors must play a key role in the children's exodus from Pharaoh's schools if this effort is to be successful. The pastoral role in the local church is seen in multiple texts (Acts 20:17-28; 1 Timothy 3:1-7; 5:17-20; Titus 1:5-9; 1 Peter

5:1-5; Hebrews 13:17). According to the Scriptures, God has placed pastors or elders in the local church to shepherd, guard and oversee the flock under their care (Acts 20:28; 1 Peter 5:1-5).

This includes Christian families. They are responsible for these families to the Lord Jesus Christ, the Chief Shepherd of the Church. Their spiritual, moral and educational welfare is a responsibility of the local pastors even if parents in general and the fathers in particular bear primary responsibility for the Christian education of their children.

We have established previously that education is a vital responsibility of the Church and is commanded in Matthew 28:20 where Jesus gave the teaching role to the Church prior to His ascent in the heavens and return to His glory.

FIVE BASIC AREAS OF PASTORAL RESPONSIBILITY

We believe that pastoral responsibility in the K-12 Christian education of the local church falls in five basic areas.

1. The pastor or church elders have the prime responsibility to teach and preach concerning the Christian education of children. The pastor is to "preach the Word" (2 Timothy 4:2) and to "declare the whole counsel of God" (Acts 20:27).

The education of children at the K-12 level should be covered somewhere in a complete preaching calendar of the faithful pastor.

The preacher today may have a high percentage of the members of his congregation still sending their children to state-sponsored schools. What is he to do? If he is to follow the lead of Esther, appropriate care and caution should not preclude his launching a deliberate plan of action to help convince member families to use one of the Christian education options: Christian schools or home schooling.

This must begin with careful attention to Scripture. If he has not laid out the Scriptural teaching on the necessity of Christian education from such texts as Deuteronomy 6:1-9 and Matthew 28:18-20 to urge his members to pull out of state-sponsored schools, a sudden action in this regard may prove disruptive to the church. He needs to prepare his congregation *gradually* through a series of teachings and messages. He can also use the Sunday school program to provide a detailed survey of recent books developing a Christian philosophy of education.

He can hold meetings with key leaders, elders and deacons to prepare them for a policy change or alert them that he is planning to preach on the educational responsibility of both parents and the church on behalf of K-12 education.

No pastor, however, should lay these burdens on families without a subsidiary plan to provide encouragement and assistance to the families in the church. This plan should be in place before the actual preaching. In some cases a benevolence fund or a church scholarship fund could be used to assist needy families and single parents who strongly desire to send their children to a Christian school.

2. The pastor or church elders have a responsibility to pray and intercede (Hebrews 4:16) for families in the education of their children. This is as critical an element as the preaching and teaching responsibility for the pastoral staff and elders. The Apostles set the right tone in Acts 6:4 when they said, "but we will give ourselves continually to prayer and to the ministry of the word."

If preparatory prayer does not precede and accompany the preaching and teaching on the Christian education of children, the process may end up as a "sounding brass or a clanging cymbal" and have no impact.

While it's important that all preaching be preceded with prayer, the education of the congregation's children at the

K-12 level may be new to some who have depended on state-run schools. A major change in behavior or policy will require more prayer and preparation for the congregation.

The pastoral staff, elders and members could set aside times of prayer and occasional fasting about this need. In the history of the Church, when important new developments or major changes were anticipated or planned, leaders would spend seasons in prayer as part of the preparation and calling for these new developments.

Take, for example, when Paul and Barnabas were set aside and called to go on the first missionary journey. This followed a season of prayer and worship.

Acts 13:2 says, "As they ministered to the Lord and fasted, the Holy Spirit said, 'Now separate to Me Barnabas and Saul for the work to which I have called them.'"

Local church boards, sessions, ministerial fellowships or associations could follow such a pattern as described in Acts 13:2 and spend time in prayer and fasting about the educational needs of Christian children in both their local churches and in the larger community.

In some communities, Christian leaders and pastors gather regularly to pray for one another's ministries, community needs and for revival in their churches and community. Prayer for the K-12 educational needs of Christian children should become a regular part of those seasons of prayer.

3. The pastor and elders have the responsibility to counsel and encourage their families in the Christian education of their children. In most cases this will take place when advice and counsel is sought by families in the church concerning the best way to provide a Christian education for their children. The pastor needs to help them understand if home schooling could be an option for their family.

The majority of the instruction and work inevitably falls on the mother. If she is not employed outside the home, then she is in a position to home school. We believe many more such families can home school. The curricula, aids, support groups, state associations and legal assistance are now all so widespread for home schooling that few families who consider this option have a real excuse not to home school if they possess basic competencies.

The pastor himself needs to become familiar with these options so he can give good counsel. The book by Chris Klicka entitled *The Right Choice: Home Schooling* is an excellent introduction, as is Zan Peters Tyler and Dr. Terry Dorian's *Anyone Can Home School.*[1]

The pastor also needs to be familiar with the respective Christian school options in his community if his own church does not have a Christian school. He should also become familiar with some of the recent literature in support of Christian schooling and urge his members or the families he counsels about the education of their children to read several good books. Two of the best recent works are Doug Wilson's *Recovering the Lost Tools of Learning* and Glen Schultz's *Kingdom Education.*[2]

The pastor should not be reticent in pointing out the moral and spiritual danger to children left indefinitely in state-sponsored schools.

In recent decades the average Christian school has outpaced state-sponsored schools in academic performance as well as provided a morally and spiritually more wholesome environment.

With the mission of state-sponsored schools having shifted from general and academic education to work preparation under the influence of the school-to-work movement, many families may seek Christian schools just to acquire a rigorous academic education for their children.

The pastor should instruct these families on the Biblical commands for education of children. He should counsel individual families carefully to withdraw their children from state-sponsored schools and use one of the Christian education options.

4. The pastor and elders have a responsibility to warn and protect their congregations concerning the Christian education of children. This idea extends point numbers 1 and 3 above. It suggests that pastors look at specific features about government-run schools that are troublesome or dangerous from a Christian or Biblical point of view.

We recommend exploring trends—many of which we have covered—that will eventually have a negative impact on the community and the churches.

The school-to-work agenda, just mentioned, is an obvious example. Or they may look at character education.

The problem for many of today's pastors is that they just do not have time to learn what is wrong with the public schools. Much of their immediate work involves their own congregations, and matters affecting their own churches.

Some believe that since state-sponsored schools are outside the church they do not affect the church.

If the vast majority of the children whose parents attend a given church remain in these local, state-sponsored schools, their pastor has cumulatively less overall spiritual impact on them. Instead, the primary impact on the children of the church will be their government school teachers using secular-humanist textbooks and curricula.

In the case of large churches, the need for pastors to stay informed is even greater, as their time is even more limited, but it is the large churches that need to act quickly and begin setting up Christian schools. Large churches have the most to lose by doing nothing while their members' children continue in the state-sponsored schools. Moreover, large churches have staff, resources and facilities to set up well-functioning Christian schools in a short time to provide for their own families and those of the smaller churches.

One way to solve this problem would be for larger churches to appoint a Christian education pastor or staff member who would have supervisory status over K-12 Christian education of the children of the church as part of his job description.

His job would include keeping abreast of the trends in K-12 state-sponsored schools, the harm that comes to the children of the church who remain behind in these schools, and providing a morally and spiritually sound alternative.

The combination of positive teaching and preaching on the necessity of K-12 Christian education coupled with periodic warnings concerning the recent fads, political correctness and sometimes raw paganism being promoted in the state-sponsored schools will lead some parents to remove their children from that kind of environment.

The command to warn the flock of these dangers and protect them is a vital part of the pastoral role and must not be neglected (Ezekiel 33:1-6; Acts 20:27-31).

5. The pastor and elders have a responsibility to lead by example concerning the Christian education of the children. The pastor must, first of all, set the example in the Christian education of his own children. He will not be effective in promoting Christian education for his congregation if he allows his own children to attend state-sponsored schools.

Church members learn as much from example as from preaching and teaching. If the preacher does not practice what he preaches, the families in his congregation will be less inclined to home school their children or send them to a Christian school.

Luke 6:40 explains the process of the power of example for good or bad: "A disciple is not above his teacher, but everyone who is perfectly trained will be like his teacher."

A typical pastor family profile, in this case, should include the pastor's family, either home schooling or closely involved with the church's Christian school.

My own wife, Gail, began to teach in Christian schools after we had concluded the home schooling of our children. Teaching in both state-sponsored and Christian schools has been viewed as an acceptable Christian calling for hundreds of years in American churches.

I have encountered many conservative pastors whose wives teach in state-sponsored schools. Many of their families then feel secure sending their own children to state-sponsored schools since the pastor's wife is employed there.

No doubt many pastors see their wives and children as witnesses for Christ in the state-sponsored school setting, and, indeed, this is probably true in some cases. Yet we still believe this sends the wrong message to the congregation. It makes it more difficult for the pastor to urge parents to home school their children.

It is also more difficult for him to start up a Christian school in his own church while indirectly supporting state-sponsored schools by virtue of his wife's working in one, and therefore allowing his own children to attend.

Moreover, a pastor may be reluctant to expose or criticize state-sponsored public schools if his wife is teaching in one. It is very difficult to vocalize or express fault with a system from which ones derives income.

The pastor with a wife who teaches in a state-sponsored school is holding back members of his congregation from taking action on behalf of their children, whether home schooling them or helping to start a Christian school with the assistance of the local church.

Given the current educational emergency in the nation and the churches, we believe it best for pastors to wean their families from a dependency on state-sponsored schools for employment. Certainly it is not a Biblical choice for pastors to send their own children to state-sponsored schools that are humanistic and pagan in design and practice.

Many pastors today are experiencing the joy and blessing that comes from sending their children to Christian schools or in home schooling them. This sets a strong example in the church so that the pastor's preaching and teaching on the priority of Christian education has a ring of authenticity and his life message has real power.

I have noted in recent years that many more pastors are now home schooling, and more are using local Christian schools for the K-12 education of their children.

We have seen evidence of how the change from state-sponsored schools to home schooling leads to a tremendous blessing for each family making this change.

We attended an evangelical church in Columbia, South Carolina, from 1987 through 1998. The pastor's children were attending a state-sponsored school when we began. We were the only home schooling family in the congregation when we began, and only a few parents had placed their children in a local Christian school.

By 1998, that church had successfully made the transition. The pastor and his wife had withdrawn their children from the local state-sponsored school and placed them in the Christian school where the pastor's wife began to work.

Member families were either home schooling or sending their children to a Christian school. Over a ten-year period, the members of that church turned entirely to home schooling or Christian schools. This same story is going on in local congregations all over the country. If pastors themselves will home school or place their own children in the local

Christian school, they will set a powerful example and help the churches and member families make the transition over a several year process to K-12 Christian education.

REGIONAL AND NATIONAL LEADERS
While most of the work of withdrawing our Christian children from state-run schools must be done at the congregational level, assistance can be offered at the denominational level as well. Many of these same five points of pastoral responsibility apply equally to denominational leaders and major ministry leaders whose influence extends beyond local churches.

Those who have national ministries need to use portions of their time to preach and teach on the necessity of the K-12 Christian education of the next generation. These major ministries need to warn the Christian community of the dangers of leaving their children in state-sponsored schools.

To share one example, Dr. D. James Kennedy of Coral Ridge Ministries has discussed issues pertaining to Christian education versus state-sponsored schools on numerous occasions on both his television and radio ministries.

Of all the national major evangelical ministers, Dr. Kennedy has been the most forthright on why Christians need to take advantage of one of the Christian education options for their children. Dr. Kennedy has set an important example by having a church school as well. Others need to follow. There are national teaching ministries with regular access to millions of Christians by radio or television daily. They should spend much more time addressing the K-12 Christian education of the next generation.

I have personally asked two well-known Christian radio pastors with several hundred radio stations each to bring these topics to their national audience. Other Christians should request such programs.

Denominational and ministry leaders also need to use their publications to promote and explain the growing trends toward home schooling and starting up Christian schools in their churches. Southern Baptist Convention (SBC) publications such as *Home Life* and the Baptist Press have recently featured several stories on home schooling and Christian schools.

The Baptist Press has run articles, some of which have found their way into the state SBC newspapers on the problems of state-sponsored schools. Such articles will help awaken millions in the SBC churches to the need to use one of the Christian education options.

Strong hierarchical denominations can make major decisions at the superintendent, bishop or overseer, or general assembly or synod level to implement a Bible-based, Christian-education system throughout their churches.

Most Baptists, Pentecostals, and "free church" evangelical denominations, however, work with an autonomous church organizational structure and can not simply force K-12 Christian education on their member churches. These groups must work gradually and use sound and loving arguments to persuade their pastors and member churches.

It is clear that for the children's exodus from Pharaoh's schools to occur it must be pastor as well as family led. The pastors and denominational and ministry leaders are the divinely appointed shepherds of the churches.

Pastors have played an important role until now, but the children's exodus has been mostly a family affair. One by one, families have left Pharaoh's schools for the Promised Land of home schooling and Christian schooling. This has been a trickle, now a small stream, but it must become a rushing river in the next few years.

A major exodus will only happen when the pastors and national Christian leaders begin to take a major role in preaching, teaching, praying and setting the example. Pray for them "...that the word of the Lord may run swiftly and be glorified...." (2 Thessalonians 3:1).

THE CONFESSING CHURCH IN NAZI GERMANY COMPARED TO THE AMERICAN CHURCH

The American Christian community may soon be entering a state of emergency not unlike that which occurred in Nazi Germany in the early 1930's. We are woefully unprepared for this moment. Many do not yet believe that the situation in state-sponsored schools is desperate.

Pastors, if they see social issues as important, may see the gravity of the abortion issue and the growing death culture in America. But many of these same pastors do not understand how a twisted worldview made abortion an option.

They wonder why all the marching and protesting has failed to put a stop to abortions. Some others battle against gambling, and work against pornography, alcohol and drug addictions in their respective communities.

In 1975 the famous Indian evangelist, Bakht Singh, from Hyderabad, India, visited Winona Lake, Indiana, while I was attending Grace Theological Seminary.

YOUR CHURCHES HAVE GREAT TEACHING AND SINGING, BUT NO PRAYER, NO POWER

His description of the American Church was memorable and still rings in my ears: Your churches have great teaching and singing, but no prayer, no power.

The American evangelical pastors are not yet prepared to deal with the deepening crisis. Many simply do not have the moral courage, theological clarity or spiritual stamina of their forebears, men of an earlier generation such as George Truet, R.G. Lee, Francis Schaeffer, Donald Grey Barnhouse, Thomas Zimmerman or A.W. Tozer. However, the crisis is flooding our nation and it will not recede. Like Elijah of old in his moment of despair and depression after fleeing from the wrath of Jezebel, when he rested under the juniper tree, we cry out to God, "…I am no better than my fathers!" (1 Kings 19:4).

NAZI GERMANY: AN HISTORICAL METAPHOR

In 1933, a major crisis came to Germany, and the German church was not ready. Yet one of the most heroic struggles in modern times occurred between Biblical Christianity and the Fascism of Adolf Hitler between 1933 and 1945.

Only in recent years has this story been rediscovered by the evangelical church through the speaking and writing of such men as Dr. Erwin Lutzer, pastor of the famous Moody Church in Chicago. In 1993, Moody Press published Dr. Lutzer's book on this period, entitled *Hitler's Cross*.[3]

Chuck Colson has also discussed this era in many articles and speeches around the nation. The spiritual courage and lives of men like Dietrich Bonhoeffer and Martin Niemoller are now being reexamined by many pastors and Christian leaders in America.[4]

In 1934, Christians in Germany became affiliated with the movement that became known as "The Confessing Church". They set out to oppose the movement known as "The German Christians."

The Confessing Church drew up the famous *Barmen Declaration*. This document was drafted to address doctrinal issues of concern, and to reaffirm the transcendence of the triune God over culture, history and human government.

This declaration also was a statement of independence for the Church.

The *Barmen Declaration* became the primary document of The Confessing Church and it stood forthrightly for the historical creeds and confessions of the Protestant faith.

It was also co-authored and signed by the eminent, neo-orthodox, Swiss theologian Karl Barth. Specifically, it was in opposition to the growing complicity of the theologically liberal German Christian movement with the Nazi regime.[5]

In its prologue, the *Barmen Declaration* stated:

> ...The Confessional Synod calls upon the congregations to arrange themselves behind it in prayer and steadfastly to gather around those pastors and teachers who are loyal to the Confessions.
>
> If you find that we are speaking contrary to Scripture, then do not listen to us! But if you find that we are taking our stand upon Scripture, then let no fear or temptation keep you from treading with us the path of faith and obedience to the Word of God.[6]

The *Barmen Declaration* also rejected the claims of the German Christians that God reveals Himself in history. At that time their special claim was that God had revealed Himself through the German race, through the Nazi revolution, and, yes, even through Adolf Hitler.

THE ERROR OF "NATURAL THEOLOGY" AND SYNCRETISM

The Confessing Church, through the *Barmen Declaration*, completely rejected the liberal brand of natural theology and the syncretism it bred. They asserted that Christians should depend upon Christ alone, the Holy Scriptures and the historical confessions of the Church as the source of theological truth.[7]

The liberal theologians and clergy, predominant among the German Christians, relied on natural theology to provide a philosophical and ideological foundation to their movement. The result was catastrophic.

Natural theology maintains that knowledge of God can be obtained by human reason without the aid of revelation. This brand of theology bases some of its theory upon an interpretation of Romans 1:18f., which states that man can have some limited knowledge of the divine through the observation of nature.

Historic Reformation theology, however, rejected most aspects of natural theology believing that man's fallen nature did not enable him to reason properly apart from Scripture and the gracious assistance of the Holy Spirit.

Both Reformation theologians and the neo-orthodox theologians such as Karl Barth of the dialectical school rejected natural theology as it had been carried to such extremes by the German Christians.[8]

In my judgment, the tendency of some Christians today to support and even help construct a basis for character education in state-sponsored schools is a contemporary example of the *misapplication* of natural theology. The Christian community must solidly reject it.

Simultaneously, the Pastor's Emergency League formed to battle fascism, the Aryan restrictions, and the anti-Jewish pogrom [an organized massacre] that had just begun.

At one time this league included 5,000 Protestant pastors out of 18,000 active in Germany. Thus some 30% of Protestant pastors were affiliated with The Confessing Church and in sympathy with and supportive of the *Barmen Declaration.*

By 1938, however, the Gestapo had arrested 800 pastors with many being sent to concentration camps. Martin Niemoller, Chairman of the Pastor's Emergency League, was sent to Dachau.

It was not well known that there were many Christians and pastors in the death camps with Jews and other ethnic groups from 1939-45.

The story of the Corrie Ten Boom family from the book and movie *The Hiding Place* illustrates the plight of a non-Jewish, religious family during that period.

I recall Reverend Daniel Fuchs, a Hebrew Christian, recounting in 1965 how he became a Christian by watching the Lutheran pastors die for Christ in the concentration camps in the mid-1940's.

By 1938, effective opposition had begun to dissipate as so many pastors were arrested, and others began to compromise to stay alive. A few, like Dietrich Bonhoffer, went underground or participated in the plot against Hitler and his Nazi Party. Thus, organized opposition to Hitler and the Nazis came from The Confessing Church movement, but this opposition had ended by the time Germany entered what soon became World War II in 1939.[9]

EINSTEIN'S MOST IMPORTANT OBSERVATION?

These events were noted at the time by Albert Einstein, who was, of course, Jewish, and fled Germany for the United States. He described his experiences in Germany at the time of Hitler's rise to power and the lack of opposition:

> Having always been an ardent partisan of freedom, I turned to the Universities, as soon as the revolution broke out in Germany, to find that the universities took refuge in silence.
>
> I then turned to the editors of the powerful newspapers, who but lately wrote flowing articles, [and] had claimed to be the faithful champions of liberty. These men were reduced to silence in a few weeks.
>
> I then addressed myself to the authors, to those who had passed themselves off as intellectual guides of Germany, and among whom was frequently discussed the question of freedom and its place in modern life. They are, in their turn, very dumb.

Only the Church opposed the fight which Hitler was waging against liberty.

Till then I had no interest in the Church, but now I feel great admiration and am truly attracted to the Church who had the persistent courage to fight for spiritual truth and moral freedom.

I feel obliged to confess that I now admire what I used to consider of little value.[10]

It was The Confessing Church and their pastors that provided opposition to Hitler and the Nazi regime. Their pastors rose up and entered into an heroic spiritual and ideological struggle for their flocks and the soul of their nation. But they were too late. *They were too late.*

THE CHURCH AND THE GERMAN PEOPLE LET HITLER'S NAZI EVIL PREVAIL

Their nation and the world would soon be plunged into the worst and most destructive war in the history of mankind. Many of these pastors were murdered, as were Dietrich Bonhoeffer and his brother.

Others saved their lives, only by silence and acquiescence. Yet, history has not been kind to the Church of that period, while it has been kind to a few individuals such as the heroic Christian martyr, Dietrich Bonhoeffer, and the leader of The Confessing Church, Martin Niemoller.

The Catholic experience was similar to the Protestant. Initially, the Catholic hierarchy was opposed to Nazism, even more than the Protestant. But with the enactment of the Enabling Law of 1933 that gave unbridled power to Hitler, and the Catholic hierarchy signing the Concordat with Hitler, many leaders capitulated. The Catholic hierarchy was never able to rebuild its opposition to the Nazis after their hostile intentions toward the churches became known.[11]

J.S. Conway, in his definitive book, summarizes The Confessing Church opposition to Hitler:

> It found in Dietrich Bonhoeffer a martyr whose life and example have become a watchword throughout the world. The courage and energy of Martin Niemoller in the face of political persecution have redeemed some of the vacillating compromises of weaker men....
>
> If the era of Nazi persecution has revealed that man is still ready to worship the false gods of nationalism and expediency, it also produced men whose readiness to suffer for their faith saved the Church from total apostasy during the most tragic and fateful chapter of German history.[12]

Today, evidence can be marshaled that a crisis is slowly emerging in America that will be comparable to what happened in Nazi Germany.

Statism and an incipient fascism are growing in an America that no longer *understands* what the word "fascism" really means. Jesus Christ has been completely banished from state-sponsored schools and from public life generally. (Generic phrases like "God bless America" have resurfaced in the wake of the September 11, 2001 attacks, but direct references to "Jesus Christ our Savior" are still rarely heard.)

WHAT WILL HISTORY SAY ABOUT US?

What will history say about the American Church and its pastors in this period? Where are the conservative Christian clergy as we enter this most critical period of our nation's history? We have not stopped abortion or any of the other catastrophic sins gripping our nation. Children are murdering other children in state-sponsored schools where secular humanism is the reigning worldview.

A spiritual darkness has descended on this land even as many cry out for revival and deliverance. Lack of moral courage, coupled with compromise, seem to be standard fare in many Christian churches.

U.S. CHURCH COMPARED WITH SAMSON

The situation of the modern evangelical Christian Church in America also is analogous to that of Samson in Judges 16: 21-24:

> 21 Then the Philistines took him and put out his eyes, and
> brought him down to Gaza. They bound him with bronze
> fetters, and he became a grinder in the prison.

Too many Christians have consorted with this Philistine culture, as Samson did in his day, to gain some supposed "advantage" for the kingdom of God. But this has not worked, and we have become the prisoners of the Philistine culture. We have been severely weakened by this approach.

Too many lack spiritual discernment and moral courage as a result of compromise. Like Samson, this same Philistine culture has run right over the modern evangelical Christian Church and gouged its eyes out.

The modern Church, like Samson, has held her vows of holiness far too cheaply. Samson's call to holiness in the Nazarite vow as represented by his long hair made him strong. So is holiness the strength of the Church. But this has been traded off through compromise by many.

Samson came to his senses, repented and roused himself for one last effort on behalf of his people Israel. A lad led him to the support pillars of the temple of the pagan god Dagon. In Judges 16:28 he prayed, "...O Lord God, remember me, I pray! Strengthen me, I pray, just this once...." Samson pushed with all his might, and won a final victory over the Philistines as the temple of Dagon came crashing down. The evangelical Church too can realize her condition and recover her former glory through repentance and prayer. We are approaching the midnight hour, yet it is not too late.

With this new emphasis on the Christian education of our own children, repentance, prayer and revival, we may have one last chance to affect the final outcome. Spiritual victory is possible.

Let us pray like Samson, "O Lord God, strengthen us this once on behalf of the children that we may recover the glory of your church."

God is Sovereign and merciful, and He responds to repentance and obedience. If we fail now, we too may receive the judgment of history, as does the German Church even today. Even worse, we will have missed the grand opportunity to serve God and His people for which He placed us in this place and time.

THE AMERICAN CHURCH AT DUNKIRK

In terms of military strategy, the Church is at Dunkirk now. Older readers, or those familiar with U.S. history, may remember the time before America's entrance into World War II in 1940 when 340,000 English and French troops were trapped on the beaches of Dunkirk in Northern France awaiting their destruction at the hands of the German Blitz and Panzer divisions.

Suddenly, the English nation awoke to the national emergency. Suddenly every little motorboat, skiff, pleasure and sailing craft, fishing boat and the ships of the British Navy came to Dunkirk and took those soldiers off that beach while a world watched and a nation prayed. They were able to rescue all but a few thousand.

Conservative Christians and their allies are trapped on the beaches at Dunkirk now. We have been clearly defeated and outsmarted on the field of battle in the culture war by secular humanists and other enemies of the Gospel. Honesty compels us to admit this.

We must all evacuate Dunkirk by rescuing our children from that beach. We need every large church and every small church pastor, all Christian activist groups, every Christian denomination and ministry, to come to Dunkirk with us and get the children off the beach. This must be a cooperative effort involving most ministries, denominations and organizations if it is to be successful. Otherwise, the slaughter will be completed by the Panzers of humanism.

WILL THIS BE OUR FINEST HOUR?
As the Battle for Britain raged, Churchill described the moment this way: "If the British Empire were to last a thousand years, let it be said that this was their finest hour."

This too could be said of the American Christian Church, but we must first pull out of Dunkirk, all of us, and rescue our children!

We must tell pastors, ministers and denominational leaders that they must redirect significant energies to starting Christian schools and/or helping families who are able to do so to home school their children.

Conservative education reform efforts have failed completely all across the nation. God is clearly not blessing these efforts. If the "conservative educational reformers" continue with their futile efforts, they will actually short circuit the *one* cause that will work and defeat the *one* Biblical strategy that has a chance of victory. We must all work together *now*. It will take hundreds of major ministries and large denominations or church bodies to make this change.

The strategy needed is an Exodus from Pharaoh's state-sponsored school system dominated by secular humanists, toward the Promised Land of home schooling and private

Christian schools that operate according to Biblical principles. *The rising tide of Christian schools and home schooling will lift all boats.*

LET US GO UP ... AND TAKE POSSESSION:
THE CHURCH WAITING AT KADESH-BARNEA

With the Exodus Mandate analogy we have intentionally
compared the Old Testament Exodus and deliverance of the
Children of Israel from bondage of Egypt to the deliverance
of Christian children from the bondage of government
schools which we have been calling Pharaoh's school system. There are many such metaphorical examples that fit
into our overall theme of *Let My Children Go.*

One involves a largely forgotten episode in Old
Testament history at Kadesh-barnea. The account can be
found in Numbers 13:25-14:10.

It was at Kadesh-barnea that the children of Israel
camped prior to their expected entrance into the Promised
Land.

They had seen the miracles worked in Egypt to break the
will of Pharaoh to release them in order to begin their journey toward the Promised Land. They had experienced the
great deliverance at the Red Sea where the pursuing
Egyptian army had been destroyed by the floodwaters. They
had seen the fiery pillar lead them at night, and through
Moses they had been given the most marvelous Law of God.
They had seen God's glory and power as no other generation and people prior or since.

At last, they were camped at Kadesh-barnea, just outside
the Promised Land, on the banks of the Jordan River. This
was to be their grand moment of entry into all that God had
promised, reiterated many times to their forefathers
Abraham, Isaac and Jacob, since the giving of the
Abrahamic Covenant in Gen. 12:1-3; 13:14-17; 15:1-7; 17.

They had the definite commands and promises of God and had seen a full demonstration of His power to lead them to the door of the Promised Land. The hard part was done.

At that point, Moses and Aaron sent out twelve spies on a reconnaissance mission in the land they were about to possess. Some comparisons exist between Israel and the modern Christian Church, and between pastors and Christian families, as the churches stand poised to enter the Promised Land of Christian schools and home schooling.

The twelve spies, except for Joshua and Caleb, brought back a fearful report from the land. They reported that there were giants in the land and that the cities were impregnable. They reported that there were numerous tribes such as the Hittites, Jebusites and Amorites, in the Promised Land who would surely oppose Israel's attempt to possess what was theirs through the Abrahamic Covenant (Numbers 13:28, 29).

The spies did admit, however, that it was an attractive land that "flows with milk and honey" (Numbers 13:27). The ten unfaithful spies counseled against the campaign to enter the Promised Land based upon perceived difficulties and gave a bad report saying, "We are not able to go up against the people, for they are stronger than we" (Numbers 13:31).

Similarly, today many Christian leaders offer excuses for not implementing a plan for the full Christian education of their church children in Christian schools or home schooling. They see the extra financial expenses, the need to recruit and train qualified Christian teachers, the lack of facilities, and harder still, the need to win over congregational leaders and regular churchgoers in their membership to a new Bible-based education.

Many pastors see a need to teach the whole counsel of God's Word on Christian education, but the churches have sold out their children in state-sponsored, government schools for so many years that change will be hard and painful.

LET US GO UP AT ONCE AND TAKE POSSESSION

Some pastors are afraid of upsetting families who are comfortable in state-sponsored public schools. Bad habits and weak theologies die hard, but change is possible. Christians ask, "Could we have really been so wrong for living in the Egypt of public schools these past 150 years?"

If the internal tasks of setting up new Christian schools or urging home schooling on their church members is not daunting enough, the pastors and church leaders should think about the Amorites and the Jebusites in the National Education Association, the teachers' labor unions, or the public school establishment opposing such an effort.

Caleb and Joshua, however, responded courageously to the report. They urged the people on and said, "Let us go up at once and take possession, for we are well able to overcome it" (Numbers 13:30; 14:6-9).

Responsible, courageous and theologically informed Christian leaders and pastors today will stand with Caleb and Joshua and urge this fresh obedience to the Biblical commands upon the Christian church concerning the education of children.

OUR COMING FATEFUL DECISION

The Christian church, too, is poised at the edge of the Promised Land. Will we hesitate at our Kadesh-barnea like the children of Israel and miss our moment? Or will we, too, rise up and take possession? How long do churches and families have to make this decision? How long do pastors have to build up the courage to lead on this mission at today's educational Dunkirk?

FIVE QUESTIONS TO ANSWER WITH
THE PROMISED LAND IN VIEW

There are five questions the Church should ask concerning its ability to enter the Promised Land of private Christian schools and home schooling.

The first question: "Has God spoken sufficiently about the Christian education of children?" We know the answer is unequivocally "Yes!" Such texts starting with the Abrahamic Covenant in Genesis through Deuteronomy 6:1-9 and Matthew 22:36-40; 28:18-20 and Ephesians 6:4 all place the role of educating children on the family with assistance from the Church.

The state has no God-ordained role in education—it especially has no such role in educating the children of the Church. And there is certainly no mandate to place children in Pharaoh's educational system.

The second question: "Have we seen God's power to assist such a massive effort?" Again, the answer is "Yes!" The children's exodus is already underway and has been for two decades now, only at a much slower pace than is needed.

From the small beginnings of the early 1980's, home schooling has boomed. In some regions of the U.S., it is growing at a rate of 8-15% per year, mostly among committed Christians.

Private Christian schools are growing at a rate of 5-7% in some regions of the nation.

The Home School Legal Defense Association has won many legal battles and the right of home schooling has become legally established. Many individual families have had their own private Red Sea experiences. They have faced Pharaoh and have prevailed. They have already successfully evacuated their children from the beaches at Dunkirk.

The third question: "Do we have the promises of God for such an effort?" The answer again is "Yes!" What God commands, He obviously can perform.

The great lack is a vision in the churches to be acted upon in faith. Hebrews 3:19 says the children of Israel failed at Kadesh-barnea for one reason. "So we see that they could not enter in because of unbelief." Unbelief was all that stopped them, and likewise, the only thing that will keep the modern Christian church from being successful will be fear and unbelief. God's Word is clear, but needs to be acted upon in faith and with courage.

The fourth question: "Can we defeat the giants?" Currently many involved in home schooling and Christian schools are defeating the giants daily. Home schoolers are winning the national spelling bees and geography bees. Christian schools are turning out Christian citizens who excel in both the academic and work worlds. Books are being published daily which help families to educate their children Biblically. Legislative and legal victories are being won. The giants are losing, as they did in the Old Testament. The giants always lost, starting with Caleb and continuing with the youthful David against Goliath. The giants in the Bible never win when confronted by obedient believers acting in faith!

The fifth question: "Have we seen the Promised Land?" Yes, the churches and Christian families used to live in the Promised Land. We were the educators of our culture. We ran the schools and home schooled the early great leaders of our land. It was when we lived in the Promised Land of Christian education that America became great and good; however, we allowed Unitarians and humanists to take this land away from us.

This was a serious mistake, and we compounded our mistake by sending our children to their schools!

In recent years some families and churches have slowly returned to the Promised Land, one by one, at first a trickle of families, growing stronger every day, and they have indeed discovered it is a land flowing with milk and honey.

It is time we repossess the educational system that is rightly ours. These families are now beckoning to their fellow Christians, "Come over and join us in this land flowing with milk and honey."

And let our leaders also charge us as Caleb and Joshua saying, "Let us go up at once and take possession!"   ■

CHAPTER SIX

MINEFIELDS ON THE ROAD TO THE PROMISED LAND

VOUCHERING TOWARD GOMORRAH

CHARTER SCHOOLS AND THEIR DANGERS

THE CERTIFICATION/ACCREDITATION SNARE

THE CHARACTER-EDUCATION TRAP

The road to the Promised Land of private Christian schools and home schooling is fraught with danger. We could allow what successes we have achieved over the past few years go to our heads, so that we glorify ourselves and our achievements instead of allowing our achievements to glorify God. This happened to the Israelites, not just once but several times. It could happen to us.

We could, on the other hand, simply fail to see the minefields along the road, or diversions capable of distracting Christian parents and pastors.

Some of these might operate to keep Christians convinced that in one way or another, reforming state-sponsored schools is still a live option.

Others have the potential to undermine the autonomy and independence of private and Christian schools and home schooling.

VOUCHERING TOWARD GOMORRAH

One topic to consider very carefully is that of vouchers and their use in the "school choice" movement. Vouchers are "direct payments from the government to individuals, in the form of checks or redeemable coupons, to enable them to purchase education in the open market."[1]

The basic idea is to give Christian parents more resources in choosing which school to send their children, with the options including private or religious schools, which will somehow lessen the problems of state-sponsored education. All schools will be competing for both the best teachers and the best pupils. Those that cannot pass the test of this form of competition will fall by the wayside, while the "good" schools will prosper. This system provides parents with an opportunity to send their children to schools of their choice by providing them with a voucher—money from the government earmarked for school choice.

That there is a crisis in public education of gargantuan proportions and that many families would like a way out is no longer in question. Financial concerns seem to be primary reasons many Christian parents give for not sending their children to local private and Christian schools. Many of these same families would accept a tax-funded voucher if it were available, so they could send their children to a private or religious school of their choice. On the surface this seems like a good idea.

Support for the tax-funded voucher also comes from some pro-family and conservative public policy groups such as the Heritage Foundation, the Family Research Council and Focus on the Family. We have come to trust these groups as they normally favor conservative, pro-family and free-market solutions. We have trusted them to protect and represent the concerns and perspective of the Christian and pro-family communities in the public policy arena. But their support for the tax-funded voucher for private and religious schools is an unfortunate exception to an otherwise strong record protecting their constituent groups in the public policy or political arena.

My discussions with them have convinced me that they do not recognize the implications inherent in the tax-funded voucher, and so their support for it has inadvertently put us all in harm's way.

Those who support tax-funded vouchers need to consider a principle taught to every would-be physician in medical school: "Do no harm."[2] This is the Hippocratic Oath in a nutshell. This is the first principle physicians follow in the treatment of patients.

Carrying out the idea is sometimes very difficult. For example, my late father-in-law was once prescribed some blood pressure medicine that brought on a diabetic condition. Physicians are aware that it is possible that some cures they propose can actually cause new or unforeseen medical problems to develop. This must be avoided whenever possible. Accordingly, physicians routinely take enormous precautions.

Supposed cures for diseases are tested and then retested as much as possible, so that both short-term and long-term side effects can be anticipated most of the time and supposedly avoided. We need to ensure that the same precautions are taken whenever a new supposed "cure" for an educational problem is introduced.

Frequently, however, educators, politicians and activists give insufficient thought to the long-term side effects of a given recommendation. So it is with the current conservative support of vouchers or tuition tax credits for private and religious schools. The current "choice political model" being supported by many conservatives and some Christian and pro-family leaders is fundamentally flawed.

Its success is dependent on the eventual political acceptance of the tax-funded voucher or tuition tax credit as the means to achieve educational freedom for families from the public schools. This is an unwise, unbiblical, and unconstitutional approach for a number of reasons.

Strange as it may seem, the opposition of some liberal, special-interest groups to vouchers is better reasoned and more likely to assure the continued autonomy of Christian and private schools than what our allies in conservative and pro-family public policy groups are proposing.

The liberal public policy groups like the NEA and ACLU oppose tax-funded vouchers because they want to protect the state-sponsored school monopoly.

We need, however, to *oppose* vouchers because we want to protect the autonomy of private and religious schools. It's time for churches and Christian schools to remember the old adage that "In politics there are no permanent friends, only permanent interests."

The conservative approach may be flawed, but it has a superficial appeal.

Conservatives contend that vouchers will enable more parents to enroll their children in private or religious schools, and this would increase competition with the public schools. This would temporarily raise the level of instruction and quality in both private and public schools.

Monopolies breed mediocrity. Their argument is that state-sponsored education, the greatest of all American monopolies, should be broken up. This is well reasoned up to a point, and it would temporarily create the *appearance* that education was improving as more and more families would undoubtedly choose private or religious schools.

Marshall Fritz of the Alliance For the Separation of School and State, in a significant article, outlines the dangers posed by vouchers to private, Christian education.[3]

The first problem: Fritz observes that when we want something, we value it even more if we must sacrifice something (e.g., time, personal resources) to obtain it. Conversely, what is easily obtained is diminished in value. Private education is a prime example.

If parents must work extra hours, for example, to send their children to a private school, this sends the message that quality education is important to them.

Fritz goes on to argue that vouchers threaten this by replacing that sacrifice with government funding. It trivializes private education by making it easier to obtain.

The second problem: Fritz mentions that those in charge of private schools lose control of their admissions policies. They will be required to accept every student whose parents present the voucher. The result will be that the problems inherent in state-sponsored schools will come rushing into private schools.

The third problem: Vouchers will come to be seen as an entitlement, transforming good parents into poor parents who will demand more and more from the government. In the long run, then, vouchers are a form of education welfare.

Economist Llewellyn H. Rockwell argued the same point when he concluded: "Vouchers represent not a shrinkage of the welfare state but an expansion, the equivalent of food stamps for private schools."[4]

Vouchers would increase dependence upon government assistance. Once established, they would become entitlement programs: "school stamps."

Once parents come to expect them, vouchers will have created another dependent class, and every dependent class is vulnerable to both moral weakness and government control.

Some families who had been providing private education for their children at great sacrifice would weaken in the face of this new easy money. The temptations of easy money are enormous, and many would find themselves in the "school stamp" line in spite of their better judgment.

Moreover, the religious institutions themselves that accepted these new "school stamps" would find their confessions, theology, and policies in jeopardy as onerous regulations by the government threatened their freedom. This is because every government dollar comes with strings attached to it.

The corruption of private schools with government dollars would not happen immediately but gradually. Thus the concerns would not be raised right away, but maintaining the autonomy of Christian and private schools would eventually become a problem as it was whittled away a little at a time.

Small wonder that Jonathan Rauch, no friend of Christian schools, could observe back in 1997:

> I've always found it a little odd that liberals hand the voucher idea to Republicans like … Taylor and Newt Gingrich, rather than grabbing it for themselves. It is true that in many places vouchers are a solution in search of a problem: It's hard to get excited about improving rich suburban high schools that act as feeders for Ivy League colleges.
>
> However, for poor children, trapped in execrable schools, the case is moral rather than merely educational. These kids attend schools that cannot protect their physical safety, much less teach them.
>
> To require poor people to go to dangerous, dysfunctional schools that better-off people fled years ago, and that better-off people would never tolerate for their own children—all the while intoning pieties about saving public education—is

worse than unsound public policy. It is repugnant public policy.

Moreover, the arguments against school choice are as intellectually flimsy as any set of arguments in public policy today.

Will choice destroy the public school system? Competing with Toyota did not destroy GM, and it certainly did not do GM's customers any harm.[5]

Rauch goes on to make a case against liberals' resistance to vouchers, arguing that this resistance…

…reflects more poorly on liberalism than any other fact I know…. Vouchers are … a classic opportunity to equalize opportunity. Why should the poor be denied more control over their most important means of social advancement, when soccer moms and latte-drinkers take for granted that they can buy their way out of a school (or school district) that abuses or annoys them?

… By embracing school choice—if not everywhere, then at least somewhere—liberals could at one stroke emancipate the District's schoolchildren while also emancipating liberalism from that basest sort of corruption. Now is a moment, one might add, when the Democratic Party could do with looking a little less corrupt.[6]

It should be easy to see how the voucher movement is vulnerable to being co-opted by what Matthew Miller calls the "voucher left."[7]

CONFUSION OVER VOUCHERS

Among the several Christian school national associations there has not been unanimity of whether it is wise for Christian schools to accept tax-funded vouchers or not.

Some groups such, as the Association of Christian Schools International (www.acsa.org) seem willing to accept tax-funded vouchers "if no strings are attached," a popular phrase used among those Christians who would reluctantly accept the vouchers.[8] ACSI is the largest and most influential of the several evangelical Christian school associations with 4,971 member schools worldwide and 1,081,769 children.[9]

The smaller American Association of Christian Schools (www.aacs.org), with its 1,350 member schools responsible for educating an estimated 200,000 children, has taken a more cautious approach to tax-funded vouchers.

Historically, the AACS (www.accsedu.org) has opposed the voucher, and it is hoped they will remain resolute in face of growing pressure to accept vouchers, especially if vouchers do become a political reality as seems likely.

The AACS is made up of the more conservative independent Baptist and some SBC Baptist churches with a good history of limiting their entanglements with state or federal governmental agencies.

In the November 2001 CLASSIS bulletin for the Association of Classical and Christian Schools (ACCS), a rapidly growing and increasingly influential association of 150 schools, published a position paper offering reasons for strongly opposing the voucher. The ACCS is made up largely of Reformed, Presbyterian and Baptist church schools.

Moreover, the ACCS will not provide accreditation in their association for schools that accept the voucher: "ACCS will not accredit nor renew the accreditation of schools that accept government vouchers." This is not a new position for the ACCS. But the voucher movement now has sufficient momentum that their rejection of vouchers has called for more justification. The ACCS position paper explains:

Our concern over vouchers is that we do not want our schools funded by those who have shown themselves to be formally antagonistic to everything we are trying to do and teach....

In our view, the acceptance of vouchers would be a significant first step in bringing our schools under the direct control of an unbelieving magistrate.

The proverb expresses the principle well: "He who takes the king's coin becomes the king's man." If we receive money from the government, we must know that the money comes with conditions.[10]

Today, the conditions might be tolerable. But if they are not tolerable tomorrow, e.g., a new government-imposed rule orders that the school may not discriminate on the basis of sexual orientation, Christians will discover that they had gotten more intervention than they had bargained for.

Our unbelieving governmental authorities will argue (rightly) that our receipt of their money means that we must conform to the public policy they adopt.

THE LURE OF SCHOOL-STAMP WELFARE

In light of this, it is essential that Christian parents and Christian schools resist the lure of "school stamps" represented by the tax-funded voucher. Let the Lord's work be done by the Lord's people with the Lord's money. This principle used to be a guideline for many Christian ministries.

There was also a day and time in the history of the evangelical Christian Church that the very idea of Christian schools taking government aid in the form of tax-supported vouchers would have been rejected without much discussion. First, principles and convictions would have been a protective shield around the Christian schools. But this is no longer the case.

In the case of vouchers, Scriptures such as Matthew 6:1-4 should govern. Carefulness and privacy is counseled in giving and receiving of funds where Jesus says in 6:4 "...that your charitable deed may be in secret...." Such an approach to giving and receiving protects the reward of the giver and the integrity of the recipient.

If the state or government funds the religious schools or institutions even in an indirect fashion, many will almost inadvertently begin to see the state as the source of blessing and indirectly the state becomes a surrogate god, or false idol.

ACCEPTANCE OF GOVERNMENT MONEY IS MISSION SUICIDE

Moreover, the state will demand more and more influence over those schools that accept the voucher. Influence will gradually amount to control, risking the dilution of the distinct mission of private and Christian education.

Recipients of funds in the Lord's work should receive funds or private scholarships in such a way that they will see the Lord as their provider, not the state. The children of Christian families who have sacrificed or who have received private scholarships to put their children in a Christian school will always place a high value on their Christian education.

In my judgment, the tax-funded voucher is likely to diminish the spiritual value that a child and his family put on Christian education.

If private and Christian educational institutions and Christian families accept tax-funded vouchers, Christians run an all-too-real risk of becoming dependent on this easy new money.

Most will be unable to wean themselves away once the inevitable government regulations become burdensome.

The politicians who promise to protect those religious institutions will be sincere, but unless they are re-elected they might not be around a few years later.

Some Christians believe that sympathetic officeholders can craft a law that will protect private and religious schools. I doubt any legislative body today can create a law immune to being interpreted by some postmodernist federal judge in a very different way from the original intent.

A more ardent regime or faceless bureaucracy may also be in place. Those promises may be soon forgotten, the laws changed and the religious institutions they were designed to protect could end up on the chopping block.

The *Grove City College v. Bell* U.S. Supreme Court case (1984) and the follow-up *Civil Rights Restoration Act of 1987* have defined a recipient institution as one in which any student on campus receives a loan or grant from the federal government. Thus, any student or family receiving indirect aid in the form of a tax-funded voucher would make the school attended a *recipient institution*.

There is good reason to believe that a move from state-sponsored schools to the use of vouchers for private schools of whatever character would be almost immediately hijacked, as those running the state-sponsored schools moved to protect their interests.

The voucher would certainly fall under the category of provisions making private and religious schools recipient institutions, and it would probably not be long before the first court challenge erupted—possibly over Christian schools' refusal to hire a homosexual teacher (just one likely possibility). Christian supporters of tax-funded vouchers, as Cathy Duffy recently put it, could wake up to discover that they had won a battle—if vouchers become a reality—but lost the war, by having lost control of private Christian education.[11]

Already, with the growing popularity of vouchers and school choice, there is already evidence that this will happen. A case involving school choice was argued before the U.S. Supreme Court on February 20th, 2002.

The case, which could be precedent-setting, involves a constitutional challenge to the Cleveland Scholarship and Tutoring Program filed by the Ohio Education Association, the American Civil Liberties Union, People for the American Way, and other secular opponents of school choice.

The Cleveland program provides scholarships of up to $2,250 to students from low-income families enabling them to send their children to a private or religious school of their choice or to a public school in another district. If the Cleveland program is found by the Supreme Court to be constitutional, it will open the door to similar programs in developmental stages all over the country—but the basic problem created by the tax-funded voucher will not have been solved.[12]

Recently, the Wisconsin Supreme Court handed down a decision in favor of school choice advocates in Milwaukee. Some conservative and religious leaders are applauding this decision, seeing no potential for danger.[13]

The Milwaukee voucher program includes approximately 100 private schools, most of them religious. This program set by the Wisconsin Court has a requirement "allowing students to opt out of religious instruction in religious schools that accept the voucher."

In other words, the Wisconsin pro-voucher plan actually restricts religious schools from promulgating their own faith if they accept the voucher money.

A recent article from *Education Week*, September 8, 1999, describes the grief the religious schools have brought upon themselves by accepting the tax-funded voucher.[14]

The voucher idea is not new at all, but has been tried since World War II in England and France. It has also been tried recently in Canada.[15]

In all these cases, while it has taken a decade or two, the private and religious schools lost their theological and religious distinctive because of state requirements after they had accepted government aid.

In some cases, after a period, religious schools merged with the public school system. Financial aid is one technique Horace Mann, the father of public education, and his Harvard Unitarians, used beginning in the 1840's to convert the basically church-and-family-based school system then prevalent throughout America into the public school system we know today.

Government money invariably erodes the theological and spiritual essence of Christian institutions so that their "Gospel light" is extinguished, and they are merely another educational institution on the public dole.

The impact of voucher-type programs upon European and Canadian religious schools is apparent to all. Douglas D. Dewey wrote:

> The main problem with vouchers as a vehicle for reform is that it misdiagnoses the problem as overly rigid government dependency. If the clients of school welfare feel they get no respect, putting them on a longer leash and adding variety to their diet may make them more content for a time, but it does nothing to address the deeper problem of government dependency.
>
> It is well documented that every government that has subsidized private and religious schools, from Australia to France to Canada, has diminished their autonomy and blurred their distinction from state schooling. Vouchers offer private schools in America the same fate, even before the government slaps new regulations on participating schools.[16]

The issue is one of ownership. Dewey goes on to explain:

> Private schools that accept vouchers will no longer be owned by parents, but by the state.... To carry out your duty as a parent, you must own the means to produce the education for your children, by either contracting out or doing it yourself. School choice may make you a chooser but it won't make you an owner.... No government voucher frees you from dependence upon government.[17]

FUNDING STRATEGIES

The safest and most theologically sound plan is for churches or larger denominational organizations to provide scholarships and make their facilities available to their members to set up Christian schools at reasonable cost— using the Lord's money to do the Lord's work.

Older family members, grandparents, aunts and uncles, can provide scholarships to their grandchildren, nieces and nephews—thus keeping resources applied to Christian education in the family where they belong. Encourage aging family members to provide part of their inheritance early when their grandchildren need help at the K-12 level to attend a good private or religious school.

The business community can provide a private, non-governmental equivalent of a voucher to support needy parents wishing to send their children to attend private, Christian, or parochial schools.

Several million more families can home-school.

Many families can exercise self-discipline and reorient their family budgets if they see private or religious schools as necessary for their children.

These strategies will work without creating dependency and threatening the freedom of private educational institutions and home schooling.

WHY CHRISTIANS MUST "JUST SAY NO"

The futility of the many reform efforts in public schools these last 30 years has only started to become apparent to many families, politicians, and educators.

Until they see that K-12 education should operate on free-market principles like any other business and is not a government function they will struggle with many more vain and empty solutions. The tax-funded voucher is not a solution. Again, the liberal Jonathan Rauch observes:

> Conservatives want to get the state out of public education; they may succeed at getting the state into private education. Twenty years from now, they may be slapping their foreheads and saying, "What were we thinking when we crusaded to hook private schools on public money?"
>
> And the teachers' unions, which by then may have extended many of today's anticompetitive public school rules to the private realm, may be saying, "Boy, were we lucky we lost that fight. Now all schools are public."[18]

In other words, the tax-funded voucher is one of the most dangerous explosives in the minefield. We are in danger of "vouchering toward Gomorrah."

Marshall Fritz has referred to the tax-funded voucher movement as threatening to kill the goose that lays the golden egg—of independent and private enterprise. To the extent school choice by means of vouchers really is a choice, it's a "Hobson's Choice," that is, no choice at all.

Christians must "Just Say No" to tax-funded vouchers. It threatens to become another entitlement program with accompanying government encirclement that we don't want, don't need and can't afford. The real danger of the tax-funded voucher is that it will seriously erode the freedom and autonomy of our excellent private and religious school system. Recently there has been evidence that at least some conservatives have taken such arguments to heart.

SURROGATE LURE: "TUITION TAX CREDITS"

Even with some evidence that tax-funded vouchers leave students slightly better off than they were before, many private schools will not accept them out of the very fears we have been discussing: The attached strings will undermine their autonomy.

An alternative to vouchers has, therefore, been suggested: tuition tax credits. These "would provide parents with tax relief linked to expenses incurred when they select a private school or an alternative public school."[19]

Unlike vouchers, these are not transfers of wealth from the government to taxpayers, but a movement of taxation from a favored class to a less favored class. The tuition tax credit is undeniably the taxpayer's own money, only available if he pays both taxes and tuition; it "permits people to keep at least some of their own money that they would otherwise pay for the government-assigned school they are not using."[20]

Is this a viable approach? To be sure, the approach offered by advocates of vouchers and measures favoring tuition tax credits have become popular in a number of states. It retains, however, the same central drawback: government involvement with education.

The government still defines who is eligible for the tuition tax credit and as long as the government can define, it can control. It does not represent the complete paradigm shift we are seeking.

According to our Christian perspective, responsibility for education has been placed in the family with assistance from the Church—and this means a choice between home schooling and private, Church-affiliated Christian schools.

This means avoiding entanglements with government altogether.

CHARTER SCHOOLS AND THEIR DANGERS

We described tax-funded vouchers as a minefield because the funding of private and Christian schools by the state or federal government will inevitably bring about subtle control and eventual loss of their autonomy. But Christian schools are still separate from government schools. The danger to Christian education and the loss of a distinctly Christian character by the participating Christian school would be gradual, but Christian schools could elect not to participate in government voucher programs.

Charter schools are another potential minefield Christian families on the road to the Promised Land of Christian schools or home schooling must be sure to avoid. They offer an attractive option for nominal Christian families, where belief in an entirely Christ-centered and Bible-based education for their children does not run deep. Charter schools have the potential to drain off many families who would prefer a Christian school.

It is understandable that charter schools look like an improvement over standard state-sponsored schools; however, a sense of improvement can be deceptive. There is an old saying: the good can be the enemy of the best.

One of the essential points we seek to make is that Christian families and churches must insist on an exclusively Christ-centered and Bible-based education for their children in both Christian schools and home schools.

We should carefully avoid the siren calls for a secular, even conservative, education mode if they come from within the state-sponsored system. While some charter schools avoid the faddish tendencies of most modern state-sponsored education, they still do not satisfy the necessity for Christian families to provide a Christian education for their children. Some charter schools may even use a traditional education model similar to some Christian schools. But they stop short of incorporating a strong evangelical or theological component.

Charter schools are growing in popularity all across the nation. There are now over 2,000 charter schools, enrolling more than 500,000 students in 37 states, the District of Columbia and Puerto Rico.[21]

The largest teacher union, the NEA, has endorsed the charter school concept, as has the union called the American Federation of Teachers. President Clinton also endorsed charter schools as part of his education plan and urged that 3,000 charter schools be started up by 2002. Thus they necessitate a close look.[22]

ARGUMENTS AGAINST CHARTER SCHOOLS

There are, I believe, four basic arguments against charter schools from a Christian position.

First, and perhaps most obviously, charter schools, whatever their appearance, are still public or government schools and, therefore, still under state control.

They are somewhat deregulated government schools—separate from control by local school districts. They are often under teacher and parent control in some respects.

The public funds these schools through tax dollars, but there may be a fair amount of autonomy where parents and teachers are free to develop their own curriculum, hire their own teachers and operate with minimal state control.

This approach has great appeal with many conservative and traditionally minded parents who only want more discipline and phonics-based reading instruction in their public school but who are not concerned that there be religious instruction or that Scriptural and theological concepts be woven into all subjects. Committed Christian families need to be wary of this approach.

Some Christians will accept this new arrangement, as they have no serious qualms about state-sponsored schools. Their complaints are directed against particular activities and policies in state-sponsored schools, not the socialistic and humanistic government-education paradigm itself that has caused such deterioration and destruction in American education for so long. In this sense, charter schools represent the hope that state-sponsored schools can be "fixed."

A second argument against charter schools is that charter schools compete with Christian schools for students and threaten to put some Christian schools out of business.

Some Christian-controlled organizations such as the National Heritage Academies have been formed to take advantage of the public funding for charter schools.

Though based in Grand Rapids, Michigan, the National Heritage Academies system is also operating schools in North Carolina. They have hired some Christian teachers who are Bible college graduates, use a traditional curriculum and maintain a kind of Christian order and culture, but these are not explicitly Christian schools.

They offer a back-to-basics education not unlike some traditional public schools of an earlier era. The overall enterprise grew from a single school with 174 students in 1995 to 22 schools and 8,600 students by September 1999.

Since charter schools are free and some maintain a traditional curriculum, some Christian families for whom an explicit Christian education is not a requirement are transferring from the private Christian schools, where they must pay tuition, to the charter schools.

Approximately 20% of the students at National Heritage Academies are private-school transfers. This type of charter school has caused a decrease in student population in some

Christian schools and the actual closing of others.[23] This is an example in which government-run schools accommodate themselves to some of the concerns of Christian families, but not the critical one of having an explicitly Christian theological foundation.

If "traditional" charter schools grow and Christian families do not develop strong convictions about the need to provide an explicitly Christian education for their children, they may settle for less than the best. The competition from "traditional" charter schools will threaten some Christian schools, even putting some of them out of business.

A RHINESTONE CHRISTIAN EDUCATION?

To immunize their member families against joining the charter school movement, Christian pastors, denominations and education leaders must instruct Christian parents on the necessity of providing a genuine Christian education for their children. Would a man give his fiancé a rhinestone engagement ring? So why give Christian children a rhinestone Christian education?

In the past, assumptions have been made that Christian families understand the necessity of a Christian education; otherwise, they would not be in a Christian school. This is not the case with many families who place their children in Christian schools today. Sometimes parents place their children in a Christian school for peripheral reasons. They want the moral environment, the discipline and the curriculum, but they see Christian education as a non-vital choice or preference. They do not have a strong conviction that it is necessary for their children; nevertheless, we are commanded by God to provide it.

The third Christian argument against charter schools is that they exclude explicit expressions of Christianity, prayers, and the use of a Christian curriculum.

This alone should rule them out as legitimate options for Christian families who view their children's education as falling under God's commands.

EXPLICIT EXPRESSION OF THE CHRISTIAN GOSPEL IS ILLEGAL IN PUBLIC SCHOOLS

It should be obvious that given the decisions on prayer and Bible reading handed down by the Supreme Court back in 1962 and 1963, it has been impossible to express the Christian Gospel explicitly in state-sponsored schools. Charter schools, despite their relative independence from direct control by the government, are still state-sponsored schools.

To illustrate the problem, even in the case of National Heritage Academies, a case was filed in U.S. District Court by a student in one of the National Heritage schools by the American Civil Liberties Union (ACLU). The suit charged the school with a pattern of violating the separation of church and state, including the weekly prayer session held by school mothers on site.

There were claims that Bible reading occurred in class and other similar allegations of evangelism and overt religious activity taking place at school.[24]

Charter schools, then, are still no less a part of Pharaoh's school system than any other state-sponsored schools, regardless of whatever table scraps they throw at Christian parents.

This fourth objection is that because of their connection with Pharaoh's school system, however modified, charter schools eventually will lose their semi-autonomy and fall under complete domination of the teacher's unions and the public education establishment.

This is, admittedly, a prediction of sorts, but I believe it to be almost inevitable.

THE ILLUSION OF AUTONOMY: THE STRATEGY OF GOVERNMENT SCHOOL ADVOCATES

While the public education establishment loosens some restrictions and allows some families a degree of autonomy to set up traditional charter schools, they do this only out of a need for self-preservation and a desire to maintain and control education at the K-12 level.

They are quite willing to offer phyrric victories in exchange for all the real estate at the end of the battle. They are, after all, executing a long-term strategy. They recognize the unhappiness and desperation of many families to escape the foolishness and violence that has gripped the public schools.

Some government educators still reluctantly recognize the rights of parents to have at least some say on how their children are educated. But they will treat these rights as very limited, and will not allow the expression of Christian belief beyond a certain point. They have found it is wise to allow an illusion of autonomy while their cloaked hands remain firmly on the controls.

This tendency to return charter schools to complete state regulation and control means that any traditional reforms will be short-lived. *School Reform News*, a conservative publication which tracks the conservative school choice agenda and supports tax-funded vouchers and charter schools, reported on the tendency of the state-sponsored school establishment to reassert control over a semi-autonomous charter school system. It reported,

> At its annual Representative Assembly in Los Angeles in July, the National Education Association adopted a new policy on charter schools that would force charters to operate much like traditional [i.e., government] schools...without the benefit of access to tax dollars to pay for startup and construction.[25]

Furthermore, the same NEA assembly reaffirmed the teacher's union opposition to granting charters to for-profit companies. Eddie Davis, chairman of the NEA Special Committee on Charter Schools, reported to the delegates when presenting his final report: "We do not believe that charter schools ought to exist just as a choice."[26]

Eventually there will be a vicious turf battle between the NEA-controlled state-sponsored school establishment and the conservative school choice movement. I predict that the NEA public school establishment will win out in the end.

WHY CHRISTIANS SHOULD NOT WASTE TIME AND MONEY ON CHARTER SCHOOLS

We Christians really don't have a dog in that fight. Why fight for something we don't want? We hope Christians will remain on the sidelines and avoid this battle altogether by beginning to construct, staff and build an entirely new Christian school system free from state control.

This tendency to return charter schools to complete state regulation and control means that any traditional conservative reforms will be short-lived.

If Christian families invest their energies and work in building traditional charter schools the results will not be permanent. Those families will build on a house of sand, not on the rock of Christ and His Holy Word. This is not well understood right now.

Some Christian ministries need to reassess their support of the charter schools in the face of this certain scenario.

Christians are compassionate and see the immediate need to escape the worsening public-education cesspool. Charter schools, however, represent a quick fix, and quick fixes, by definition, are not permanent solutions. A recent article by Dick Carpenter, education specialist at Focus on the

Family, offers the idea that Christian families should embrace charter schools as an acceptable alternative to "regular" state-sponsored schools.[27]

If a secular K-12 education for Christian children is acceptable, then, of course, charter schools will be acceptable. It is my belief that to be obedient to God's commands in the raising and educating of their children, Christian parents must utilize a Christian alternative: home schooling or Christian schools.

Charter schools conceal the same secular-humanist approach in an even more deceptive guise. Christians must absolutely reject this bait-and-switch scheme. Certainly, we must be smarter than to accept a three-dollar bill when so much is at stake.

STATE CERTIFICATION/ACCREDITATION SNARE
A third minefield we need to avoid is the potential for state interference in the private Christian schools of the future that choose to adopt state or federal certification or accreditation requirements.

For years now, the system of state-sponsored education has required those teaching our children in this system to be certified. Certification is an indication that the certified teachers have passed through a specific regimen of training in education in addition to whatever course work they have completed in their respective fields of study.

For example, an English teacher must have completed a required number and sequence of courses in education theory and practice at an approved college or university to be able to teach English in a state-sponsored school regardless of her expertise in English or language arts.

Most Christian colleges and universities that train teachers for both the Christian and the state-sponsored school system have accommodated themselves to this requirement, and teach the required secular education courses for teacher certification.

Many evangelical colleges and universities also have attempted to integrate the Biblical worldview into this instruction, but they too must apply to the various state departments of education for approval and acceptance of their programs.

As a result, the deans of the various teacher training and departments of education in these Christian colleges are careful not to create situations in which their graduates might find themselves unable to participate in the state-sponsored school system.

So while they will integrate Biblical theology into their classroom instruction, they will stop short of questioning the right of the state to control as much of their curriculum as is necessary for certification.

If they did question the state's role they would jeopardize the employability of their graduates in state-sponsored schools.

The point is, if Christian colleges do not maintain a good working relationship with the state, they cannot teach classes or prepare Christian teachers for certification in the state-sponsored school system.

Why is this important to them? Many evangelical colleges have large departments of primary and secondary education because in some evangelical denominations, state-sponsored teaching is seen as an acceptable professional calling for Christians.

Teaching in state-sponsored schools has been viewed until recently by most Christians as an excellent means to fulfill the Christian responsibility to be "salt and light" in the culture, and as a means of fulfilling the Great Commission which is required of every believer under the Lordship of Jesus Christ.

Christian educators as well as ministerial and denominational leaders have been content to live with this questionable arrangement for decades.

Thus there has been a somewhat uneasy co-existence between Christian institutions of higher learning and state-sponsored schools and their associated state departments of education. Until recent years there have been public educators of good will who sincerely wanted to recruit evangelical Christian teachers into the state-sponsored educational system. Administrators in state-sponsored schools knew what they were getting, and they approved!

The profiles on graduates from evangelical institutions indicated aspiring professionals who were competent, dedicated and honest; and who sincerely loved children. The state-sponsored educational establishment has been willing to risk the danger of the committed and outspoken Christian teacher's occasional witness for Jesus Christ to get such committed teachers.

In certain parts of the nation, particularly in the Bible Belt areas of the Midwest and Southeast, many principals and administrators in state-sponsored schools were themselves committed members of evangelical churches or denominations. In some communities these Christian teachers and administrators were the glue that held the local state-sponsored school system together.

But there is also imminent danger when the secular state is allowed to certify Christian teachers at any level. Certification implies control, and there is no legitimate authority for that control.

As long as this procedure extended only to Christians teaching in state-sponsored schools the Christian schools' autonomy was not aggressively threatened. Graduates of Christian institutions had the option of teaching in private Christian academies, for example.

But the trend is to require Christian teachers in private Christian schools to seek some kind of state certification.

My wife has been an English and language arts teacher in an ACSI school for seven years and it was a school requirement that she be either ACSI or state certified. She elected to be ACSI certified. She recognized her need for accountability to a Christian education agency if required by her school officials, but not to a secular agency that did not acknowledge the Lordship of Jesus Christ.

WHY GOVERNMENT "CERTIFICATION" MUST BE CATEGORICALLY REJECTED

Private Christian school associations have a right to certify their member teachers, but Christian schools should very carefully reject state certification lest controls by the state ensue as well. We should not acknowledge state authority here at all.

The past co-existence between Christian institutions of higher learning and the state departments of education on the issue of certification may have seemed benign, but a growing tendency by Christian schools to accept or even require state certification of their teachers is akin to asking Pharoah's approval concerning the Hebrew religion.

This is because the worldview inherent in the philosophy of state departments of education is increasingly humanistic. It is inevitable that this will lead the uneasy "truce" between secular educational agencies and Christian institutions to be renegotiated in favor of more state control.

Their assertion is that Christian doctrine and belief has no place in any educational practice and theory. This is one of the fruits of the political correctness that has captured much of the secular educational establishment.

The philosophical orientation of post-modernism rejects the idea of transcendent moral truths in favor of relativism and cultural determinism. The movement toward building an entirely secular society that rejects the transcendent in favor of secular authority is being pursued aggressively in both elite Ivy League and state universities that also have large departments of education.

The incompatibility of such secular thought with Christian belief is easily seen, since Jesus Christ said, "I am the truth." Christian educators cannot compromise with this statement and remain Christian educators.

Moreover, in past years the states themselves were the only ones certifying teachers. With, however, the nearly completed federalization of the once local public schools, national certification has become a new measure of "skilled" teaching.

According to *Education Week*,

> ...Teachers certified by the National Board for Professional
> Teaching Standards are better teachers on a variety of
> measures than those who tried to meet the standards but
> fell short.[28]

The trend toward national certification of public school teachers is strong, and though currently voluntary, could easily become a requirement in the not too distant future. Some parts of this certification process test one's basic disposition and belief systems.

Teaching to this process in university departments of education is a potentially dangerous tool easily capable of being used to indoctrinate some aspiring teachers and eliminate others as unfit for careers in the post-modern schools of the near future.

Since certification is not permanent and must be renewed every few years with additional education courses from accredited programs, we may expect this process eventually to begin weeding out committed Christian teachers still in the public school system who are unwilling to compromise and dilute their cherished Christian beliefs.

In the past, even secular educators and legal theorists recognized the rights of parents to educate their children as they saw fit. The U.S. Supreme Court reflected this view with its 1925 decision in *Pierce v. Society of Sisters of the Holy Name.*

In a referendum, Oregon voters had previously prohibited parochial and private schools for children between the ages of eight and sixteen, requiring their attendance at public schools only. But a private academy challenged this clearly unconstitutional law. The Supreme Court ruled unanimously that the law was unconstitutional, going on to state an important principle we need to underscore:

> Children are not mere creatures of the state. A state may not attempt to standardize its children by forcing them to accept public school instruction only.[29]

This principle stood uncontested for years. No longer.

While certification looks at the rights and qualifications of the individual teacher to teach, certifying entities and accrediting agencies are more and more working to dissolve Christian schools' rights to maintain themselves as educational enterprises.

If adoption of the post-modernist philosophy sketched above is a kind of unstated litmus test, then these schools clearly face a threat the magnitude of which could not have been appreciated or anticipated by the Supreme Court in 1925.

The threat is not that private schools will be made illegal, as was the case then; it is that Christian schools could lose their distinctive Christian character by becoming only nominally private. Again, the issue is: Who can and should accredit a Christian school, the state or some private Christian educational agency or association?

We believe very strongly, on Scriptural grounds, that no governmental entity should be in the business of accrediting private Christian schools, anymore than it ought to be allowed to ordain and license Christian ministers. All Christians know that this is the sole prerogative of churches or respective denominations. This same pattern must exist for religious schools.

Douglas Wilson, a noted Christian educator, says, "A private school that is accredited by the state is, in principle, a controlled school."[30]

State and federal agencies do not, of course, recognize the authority of Scripture in educational matters—this coincided with their having adopted the secular instead of the Christian worldview. This worldview locates authority in government, not in God.

Therefore Christian schools and their allied Christian colleges and universities may soon face new pressures from the state on government-backed accreditation and other issues.

Some secular scholars such as James G. Dwyer have dissented openly from the inherent rights reaffirmed in the Pierce decision.

His book, *Religious Schools Versus Children's Rights,*[31] openly attacks private religiously affiliated education. Dwyer maintains that pedagogical practices in "fundamentalist Christian" and in Catholic schools actually *damage* children.

In line with the politically correct tendencies of our time, Dwyer contends that such education restricts children's basic liberties, stifles their intellectual development, instills dogmatic and intolerant attitudes, and inflicts psychological and emotional harm, with excessive guilt and repression.

He follows feminists in holding that girls are especially at risk for diminished self-esteem.

Dwyer openly calls for bringing private religious education under state control. His framework would result in a secular perspective reigning supreme in determining what is best for children.

Arguing on the basis of "children's rights," he believes that it is the children who have the right to state oversight of their education, and that the state must ensure that religious schools do not engage in harmful practices.

He develops the school-to-work line that religious schools be required to provide necessary instruction for a wide range of careers and full citizenship in a pluralistic and democratic society.

Dwyer's ideas have been well received by his colleagues who are flowing in the same secular humanist direction, indicating that his is not a unique perspective. This kind of neo-pagan view is starting to become dominant in increasingly secularized educational, intellectual and legal circles.

CHARACTER EDUCATION:
ANOTHER MINEFIELD TO AVOID

Education polices aimed at reforming state-sponsored schools are minefields for Christians because invariably, control over their children's education will be reasserted by the state.

Once we are outside the paradigm of education that sees education as a legitimate state function, this should become clear.

There is, however, at least one attempted reform that is more directly pedagogical, and content based. Moreover, this kind of reform may strongly suggest to Christians that some reforms of state-sponsored schools have already been effectively instituted and are working.

IDEAS LEADING TO "CHARACTER EDUCATION"

The 1960's were openly relativist and subjectivist, that is, the idea took hold that there is no objective truth.

This led to a movement in the 1970's known as "values clarification" that took hold in state-sponsored schools. Values were personal and individual, not absolute.

One of the teacher's jobs, according to the values clarification movement, was to enable children to "clarify" their personal values. This was done, of course, with no reference to God or transcendence and strongly suggesting that values were rightfully a personal choice.[32]

Accompanied by the promiscuous sexual revolution that took place during the same decade, among the fruits of the values clarification movement were skyrocketing incidences of teenage pregnancy, drug abuse, teen suicides, and eventually sexually-transmitted diseases. As those whose education in state-sponsored schools during the 1960's became adults, we saw a rise in unhealthy (and, obviously, un-Scriptural) "living together" arrangements, fractured families, rising divorce rates, absent parents, single-parent homes, abortion, drug abuse and so on.

The stage was set for the birth and growth of the next generation without the adult supervision needed for a healthy path to maturity. The results are plain, ranging from mere epidemics of cheating to acts of brutal violence such as what happened at Columbine.

Values clarification has gone out of fashion in state-sponsored schools. It was so openly relativistic, and its results so obviously damaging, that even secular humanists couldn't abide it any longer.

Only the D.A.R.E. (Drug Abuse Resistance Education) program remains, and that only because it is federally funded, not because there is the tiniest shred of evidence that it works.

But values clarification is rapidly being replaced by a new movement that began in the late 1980's and experienced a meteoric rise in popularity during the 1990's: The new buzzwords are *character education.*

Character education requires careful examination by Christians and Christian educators because its advocates claim to have discovered an objective basis for a very Christian-appearing morality that can be taught in state-sponsored schools.

Several noted Christian leaders have endorsed, participated in and promoted character education. These include former Secretary of Education William Bennett, author of *The Book of Virtues* and numerous other books, and South Carolina's Harry Dent, a lay minister and author of *Teaching Jack and Jill Right vs. Wrong in the Homes and Schools.*

More recently, John Leo, conservative columnist for *U.S. News & World Report*, penned an article praising character education as a promise of "creating a new school culture based on limits, a sense of belonging, and shared values."[33]

Important Christian organizations such as Focus on the Family have endorsed the character education movement with an article contending that "Character education programs ... offer great opportunities for Christians to get involved."[34]

For the past couple of years there has been a careful effort underway to recruit conservative clergy and leaders into supporting character education. (It is worth noting that liberal denominational leaders have already signed on board.)

Many sincere Christians are being unwittingly drawn into it due to the support and prominence of some of Christianity's most trusted public leaders—whose belief in the promise of the character education movement is entirely sincere. The leaders are giving the impression that character education solves the problems of moral instruction in state-sponsored schools, and that unlike discredited movements like values clarification, no one in the religious community ought to question it, and certainly no Christian ought to oppose it.

Christians who believe state-sponsored schools can be reformed are naturally attracted to a program like character education. Character education sounds good. It takes seriously the realization that we have a national moral crisis on our hands, and that state-sponsored schools are in trouble.

Its concern for the moral plight of children in state-sponsored schools is, of course, valid—especially in the light of our national moral decline.

However, we need to take a closer look. When we do, I believe we see that character education is not the direction consistent Christian believers ought to go in. Instead of offering the alternative to secular humanism that is really needed, character education just continues the secular-humanization of state-sponsored schools in a new and even more deceptive guise.

CHARACTER EDUCATION: DOOMED TO FAIL

Unlike values clarification, character education tries to provide a definite "right versus wrong." It tries to define and develop "goodness" in human beings without reference to God and without Biblical principles. Thus, it is doomed to failure.

Even Harry Dent admitted that the program borrows common features of the moral teachings of all the major religions—implying that "moral truth" transcends any particular religion and can be discovered by men through their own insight.

Dent named Hinduism, Islam, Buddhism and Judaism as well as the Christian faith, as offering principles consistent with character education. This makes character education uniquely suited, among recent educational trends, for inclusion in state-sponsored education. But this universalist approach ought to concern Christians.

The key spokesman for character education in the U.S. is Thomas Lickona, author of the movement's "bible," a sizable tome entitled *Educating for Character*.[35] Dr. Gerald Stiles, a former Columbia International University professor, penned a critical review of Lickona's book:

> Lickona begins with an obvious assertion: Our society, he says, is in deep moral trouble. However, Lickona advocates a new consensus in which the responsibility of moral education ought to fall to state-sponsored schools, and that they should take up the role of moral teachers of our children.
>
> Lickona professes belief in God. He is aware, however, of the debate over allowing God any role in state-sponsored schooling. He opts, therefore, for another kind of solution: Schools need to define morality not in Biblical or theological terms, he says, but in rational terms using the results of psychological research.
>
> Efforts to understand morality along these lines go back to such notions as Lawrence Kohlberg's "levels" and "stages" of moral development, which, incidentally, do not place Jesus Christ at the highest stage of moral development but only at the second highest.
>
> Lickona sides with secular humanists in holding out for a "natural moral law" which human beings can discover scientifically through the use of their reason. He believes this can provide moral content for state-sponsored educational curricula independently of Biblical principles.[36]

What does character education teach? Lickona stresses respect and responsibility.

Following this lead, an organization called the Josephson Institute of Ethics developed a program called *Character Counts!* organized around "six pillars of character" which are "trustworthiness, respect, responsibility, fairness, caring and citizenship."[37]

An Oklahoma-based group called the Character Training Institute developed *Character First!* promoting values aimed at those in the workplace: "alertness, attentiveness, self-control, kindness, forgiveness and truthfulness." School-to-work educators might find this kind of program of interest.

Other organizations devoted to developing and promoting character education include the *Character Education Partnership*, based in Washington, D.C., described by its website as "a nonpartisan coalition of organizations and individuals dedicated to developing moral character and civic virtue in our nation's youth as one means of creating a more compassionate and responsible society."

This organization developed "eleven principles of effective character education" setting out to instill in students "core ethical values such as respect, responsibility and honesty."[38]

Character education came to South Carolina with a widely publicized conference on the subject held in late September of 1995 in Myrtle Beach, sponsored by the South Carolina Department of Education.[39] Lickona was present, as were Harry Dent and then-State Superintendent of Education in South Carolina, Dr. Barbara Nielsen. Later, then-Governor David Beasley would get on board.[40]

When Jim Hodges became Governor of South Carolina in 1998, he would also endorse character education.[41] The character education movement has won the endorsement of additional prominent Christian leaders in South Carolina who followed Harry Dent's lead.

There were, however, two very significant holdouts.

Dr. Gerald Stiles, Director of Aletheia Springs Education Center, Ferrum, VA connects character education with outcome-based education and stressed the similarities between the two. Here's what he says in his review of the book by Thomas Lickona:

> What is expected to be a call to redirect schooling toward simply Judeo-Christian morality and civility, turns out to be a blueprint for the politically correct, multicultural, self esteem crowd carrying on an agenda outlined by John Dewey, who is quoted favorably throughout the book.[42]

Stiles identifies five topic-areas incorporated into the character education agenda:

1-Animal rights (with children being asked to ponder how we can treat animals as ethical subjects and still eat meat).

2-Environmentalism (having children "thinking globally and acting locally" by recycling aluminum cans and lobbying businesses about the ozone layer).

3-Cooperative learning (as opposed to competition)

4-Multiculturalism (deriving ethical positions from the ideas that all cultures are, in some sense, equal and deserve equal "respect")

5-Education for social justice (involving students in work with groups such as Amnesty International)

None of these have anything to do with the traditional role of schools in teaching literacy, mathematics, basic science and so on, and at this point we are right back to all of those things that have gone wrong with state-sponsored schooling from the outset. They are designed for social engineering and indoctrination rather than education.

Another holdout was Dr. James Carper, an evangelical Christian who was Governor Beasley's top educational advisor and one of the nation's leading authorities on the history and development of private Christian and parochial schools.

Dr. Carper raised the most important question that can be raised about character education: Is its teaching of values going to be rooted in our Judeo-Christian heritage, or in a psychological and humanistic surrogate? In other words, is the worldview of character education the God-centered one of Christianity or the man-centered one of humanism?

To the Christian mind, the foundation and reference point of any educational idea or program should be absolutely critical. None of the leading supporters of character education, whether in South Carolina or elsewhere, had answered this critical question.

Dr. Barbara Nielson was running the S.C. Department of Education at the time, and she was a solid backer of character education. Neither she nor any of character education's other backers seemed anxious to face this question.

CHARACTER EDUCATION IS SYNCRETISM: IF *ALL* ARE TRUE, THEN *NONE* ARE TRUE

Character education clearly takes an approach to teaching virtues called *syncretism*, the idea that it is possible to synthesize opposing faiths into one united doctrine based on what they all supposedly share.

A Christian cannot accept syncretism because Jesus said, "I am the way, the truth, and the life. No one comes to the Father except through Me" (John 14:6).

Moreover, syncretism's paring down the various religious traditions and treating them as more or less equal brings back relativism with a vengeance. Saying, in effect, with multiculturalists that *all* religious traditions are equally true or valid and equally capable of contributing to the teaching of virtue, is also saying that *none* of them are true.

The authors of these programs can pick and choose which components of Christianity they want to use to teach our children to be good, and which they want to discard. That is humanism. As Stiles observes, character education begs a central question: Can man be good without God? Do the virtues actually exist apart from God and Jesus Christ?

This debate over character education is not entirely new for the Christian Church. It was first debated by St. Augustine and Pelagius in the 5th century. Both were early church fathers (the former was author of the famous Christian classics *The City of God* and *Confessions*).

They had engaged in a longstanding debate over issues of faith and human nature. Augustine taught that man was born sinful and that his nature was depraved—in the sense that at our core we are fallen creatures and cannot save ourselves apart from God's grace.

Pelagius believed that man was born innocent, not with original sin, and that he could save himself by his own good efforts and deeds. This is an early form of humanism, and was condemned at the Council of Ephesus in 431 A.D. Pelagius himself, a British monk who had settled in Rome and wielded considerable influence in the Church, would not have described it as such.

The relationship between genuine Christianity and character education is similar to that between these two. Character education assumes some of the trappings of Christianity—in the syncretistic form consistent with other religions. Dr. Stiles wrote in his review of Lickona's book,

Despite his belief in God, Dr. Lickona comes down on the side of the secularist in this historical debate claiming that there is a "natural moral law" arrived at through human reason, having its own independent logic, able to give public schools "objective moral content." There is no room for Biblical revelation in the character education model; the courts would not allow it, even if Lickona himself favored this approach.[43]

Character education is a sincere attempt to respond to the dangerous nihilism that schools have been breeding which is the idea that traditional beliefs are unfounded and that man's existence is senseless. But its fundamental error is that it is a mere modification of the secular humanist world-view, not a departure.

It promises to continue the secularization of society and the leftward drift of the country, using moral language as a tool to control children and parents.

Throughout *Educating for Character* Lickona cites John Dewey as well as Lawrence Kohlberg favorably. This should not be lost on readers simply because Lickona has criticized the relativism implicit in values clarification or favors an abstinence-based approach to sex education.

Christians should not be fooled by the fact that character education has reached some conclusions that concur with Christianity. What matters, again, is one's basic world-view—one's starting point. Thus his belief system is left to rest on the shifting sands of psychological research and human reason.

Christians can find a firmer foundation than these: the bedrock of absolutes provided by God's revelation to man in the Bible.

Character education may seem to obtain some temporary results. But ultimately it will fail, because it lacks the proper foundation without which no moral education can ultimately succeed.

By embracing character education, Christians will only show their capacity to be deceived, and again outsmarted by their secular humanist enemies.

CHARACTER EDUCATION:
A WORTHLESS PLACEBO

Character education could perhaps be compared to Pharaoh offering Moses better treatment and better housing for Jewish slaves. The Jews would have had somewhat better conditions, and they might have been temporarily happier, but Pharaoh would still have been in control. In other words, character education is a worthless placebo, not a cure, for the national moral crisis.

GENUINE CHRISTIAN EDUCATION:
THE REAL CURE

The moral crisis that character education tries but will fail to address is, of course, quite real. But the solution is to leave Pharaoh's school system with its false and destructive secular humanist worldview and come to the Promised Land of alternative Bible-based Christian schools and home schooling. This is the challenge for all Christians from pastors to rank-and-file Christian parents.

In private Christian schools and in home schools, we can practice real education reform without interference, and without regulation by a bloated bureaucracy trying to foist still more nontraditional and unproven educational theories on our children. Instead, we can teach them academic disciplines based on the Word of God and America's Christian and constitutional heritage.

We can freely teach them the Gospel of Christ, as God commands us to do. If we do this, we may find many other victims of the moral and educational wasteland of state-sponsored schools coming over to join us.

I can envision millions of children drinking from the cisterns of the Living Water that only the Lord Himself can provide. It will be then, and only then, that our society may begin to turn back to the real character and moral sanity that Bible-based principles alone provide.

These are the four minefields along the road to the Promised Land of private Christian schools and home schooling:

1. Tax-funded vouchers

2. Charter schools

3. Government certification of Christian teachers in Christian schools and accreditation of Christian schools by the state or by non-Christian agencies

4. Character education

They all look reasonable and are easily made attractive to the unwary. None, however, are Scriptural. All, in one way or another, involve Christians' making compromises with the secular-humanist worldview and educational paradigm and remaining involved with state-sponsored education. ■

CHAPTER SEVEN

CIVIL DISOBEDIENCE: WE OUGHT TO OBEY GOD RATHER THAN MEN

CHRISTIANS AND GOVERNMENT AUTHORITY

BIBLE LIMITS TO GOVERNMENT AUTHORITY

BIBLICAL CIVIL DISOBEDIENCE

CHRISTIAN CIVIL DISOBEDIENCE: YESTERDAY, TODAY AND TOMORROW

Christians are expected to obey laws. But, governmental authorities are also subject to God's law. Romans 13:1-3 is the central text. The Apostle Paul tells us:

1 Let every soul be subject to the governing authorities. For there is no authority except from God, and the authorities that exist are appointed by God.

2 Therefore whoever resists the authority resists the ordinance of God, and those who resist will bring judgment on themselves.

3 For rulers are not a terror to good works, but to evil. Do you want to be unafraid of the authority? Do what is good, and you will have praise from the same.

The Apostle Peter, in 1 Peter 2:13-14, commands Christians to:

> 13 Therefore submit yourselves to every ordinance of man for the Lord's sake, whether to the king as supreme,
>
> 14 or to governors, as to those who are sent by him for the punishment of evildoers and for the praise of those who do good.

In Titus 3:1 Paul says, "Remind them to be subject to rulers and authorities, to obey, to be ready for every good work."

CHRISTIANS AND GOVERNMENT AUTHORITY

These texts, and others, command that Christians maintain a general attitude of respect for and submission to governmental authority and be law-abiding citizens.

Scripture is, as with all other things, the individual Christian's and the Church's guide for dealings with civil magistrates or governmental authority.

The Holy Scriptures, moreover, are clear that Christians are to pray for those in governmental authority with sincerity regardless of their party affiliation and political ideology.

First Timothy 2:1-2 says:

> 1 Therefore I exhort first of all that supplications, prayers, intercessions, and giving of thanks be made for all men,
>
> 2 for kings and all who are in authority, that we may lead a quiet and peaceable life in all godliness and reverence.

The Apostle Paul wrote this admonition to govern the life of the Church. He was writing at a time that would soon get extremely difficult for Christians, as the murderous Nero was Rome's Emperor. In just a few years Nero would be leading the first major persecution against the young church.

Nero went on to set the catastrophic fire at Rome that he would blame on the Christians. He would eventually be responsible for the martyrdom of both the Apostle Paul and the Apostle Peter, among many others.

The purpose is clear from this text that peace and tranquility are important objects of Church prayers for governmental leaders.

Obedient Christians in Muslim countries and Mainland China pray such prayers, as they know the daily tension when governments are hostile and threatening to the well-being of the local churches. Also, Christians are to pray that their governments do what they can to maintain justice according to the rule of law in a fallen world.

This is easy when governmental authorities respect God's law and constrain themselves under a written constitution.

When a man-centered, secular-humanist worldview comes to dominate a government, problems soon arise. Secular authority that still respects God's law is acceptable; but if governments begin to ignore or even turn against God's law, setting themselves up in God's place, godly people face a dilemma—do they obey the government's transitory edicts or God's eternal law? Of course, they need to obey God's law. But this leads to some serious practical dilemmas in a society dominated by secular humanists.

Our government was set up under the assumption that Americans were and would remain a Christian people with Christian authorities.

MISUSE OF THE ESTABLISHMENT CLAUSE

The Establishment Clause in the First Amendment was to prevent government from sponsoring a state church along the lines of the Church of England—not to authorize the systematic de-Christianizing of America we have seen over the past 50 years.

Since America was built on a Judeo-Christian heritage and until recent decades most of our laws and practices reflected this heritage, for much of American history Christians could afford to assume that their federal and state governments' laws and policies were fundamentally benevolent. But during the past half century, this has changed.

Contemporary American Christians, especially in the evangelical churches, have been entirely too compliant in terms of their loyalty to and unquestioning respect for the American governmental policies.

Because the relationship between American churches and their governments had been friendly and benign, not adversarial, Christians went on with their lives, their mission, evangelism, relief and church building projects, and largely ignored government. A few denominations even taught that participation in politics, including voting, was sinful and not a proper role for Christians in society.

During recent decades, however, the secular-humanist worldview rose and spread throughout society, including government. The will of secular humanists was imposed on society most frequently through the courts, especially the Supreme Court.

PRESERVING CHRISTIAN HERITAGE

In response, God raised up groups like the Family Research Council, Focus on the Family, Traditional Values Coalition, the Ethics and Religious Liberty Commission of the Southern Baptist Convention and numerous others to inform and work for traditional Christian values and the preservation of our rich Judeo-Christian heritage in government and the public policy arena.

These ministries and other similar ones have worked admirably and deserve our continued prayer and support. But the amount of energy devoted to policy by individual evangelical Christian and local churches is paltry when one considers the degree to which the culture and government at all levels has shifted against historic Christian beliefs and values.

BIBLICAL LIMITS TO GOVERNMENT AUTHORITY

God establishes that government authority is legitimate and that Christians are to respect it, but that governmental authority, too, is subject to God's laws. Government officials ranging from elected ones all the way down to the local police are ministers of God just like your pastors and church officers. If governmental authority begins to defy God's laws openly, it loses its legitimacy. Are there limits to government authority in church matters and with respect to the Christian family?

Until the past few decades, just to suggest opposition or rejection of some government policy or law could incur censure or disapproval in many churches.

Much of the evangelical Church community's view of government has been based on a faulty view of Romans 13:1-4 that goes something like this: "God has ordained government and police powers of the state and they must be obeyed without question and meticulously. Romans 13 was written when Nero was Emperor and the early Christians were faithful and obedient citizens. They obeyed an ungodly government and so should we."

However, the Supreme Court's 1973 decision legalizing abortion, Roe vs. Wade, and the earlier 1962 and 1963 prayer and Bible reading decisions by the same court, have done much to shake the confidence of many evangelicals in the justice and rightness of some governmental policies.

This has been one benefit of these otherwise tragic court rulings that have done a great deal of harm to the moral and spiritual welfare of the nation. Many American Christians have begun to view governmental authority in a different manner. They acknowledge governmental authority as an ordinance of God but they no longer project righteousness onto the individual office holder or governmental agent himself.

This shift of thinking is good and has opened up evangelical Christians in particular to critical, Biblical thinking and research on the limits of state power and government authority.

Further, some are raising the possibility of civil disobedience by Christians and churches when the state or government oversteps its authority and violates the Scriptures and Law of God.

THE ESTABLISHMENT CLAUSE

The Establishment Clause offers a unique arrangement between American churches and government. This is now referred to as "the separation of church and state," and has served the American church well these many years. This arrangement has protected American denominations.

Unlike many European churches, American Christians have maintained some spiritual vitality due to their having avoided being wed to, funded by, or licensed by government at any level.

It has been both prudent and Biblical for churches to maintain a strict separation from state and federal governments in their administrative and financial affairs.

In recent decades, however, federal courts and organizations such as the ACLU have interpreted the Establishment Clause improperly to allow the removal of religious values and Christianity generally from the public square. It has been a one-way street, with federal, state and local government expanding and Christianity being forced to retreat—

with the result being the practical de-Christianizing of America. The separation of church and state has been abused as a means by which federal, state and local governments have overstepped their authority.

However, it makes sense that if government continues to interfere with church affairs we can simply say, "Sorry, Mr. Government Official, your intrusion into our worship and into the educational mission of the family and church is unwelcome and unconstitutional. You must leave, as you have no authority here. We appeal to the separation of church and state." This is one of the most important constitutional limits on state control over the church and family.

THE LIMITED SPHERE OF STATE CONTROL: GOVERNMENT IS NOT UNASSAILABLE

Jesus, in Matthew 22:21, states this principle as well showing the limited sphere of state control. When asked a question about Caesar's authority to tax, He says, "Render to Caesar the things that are Caesar's and to God the things that are God's."

In this text Jesus establishes for all time the limited but legitimate role of government. He allows that within their sphere the state can demand our taxes to run their legitimate programs. These are to administer justice, provide for a police force and a national defense.

Robert Duncan Culver says of this text:

> Jesus simply recognized that, within its sphere, the state can demand what belongs to it: money, in the form of taxes. But this is not placed on the same level as God. Give God what is His! That means, give Him your life.[1]

Culver notes that Dutch theologian and Prime Minister Abraham Kuyper coined the term "sphere sovereignty" to describe the various responsibilities of church, state and family, and that these agencies were not to intrude into each other's spheres. Kuyper's idea was that each has its God-ordained role, and when one takes over another's sphere or role, disorder and confusion result.[2]

Further, Jesus uses the image of Caesar on the coin in Matthew 22:20-21 as an illustration that Caesar is entitled to receive his taxes. But whose image is stamped on men and women or children?

Genesis 1:26-27 says that God made man and woman in His own image. He has ownership of us and our tribute, our affections, lives and souls; we do not belong to the state or to government. This applies equally to the education of children, especially primary education.

LIMITS TO STATE AUTHORITY

Analyzing the Romans 13:1-4 passage is key to understanding the limits of state authority in religious matters. This text does not give a blank check to unrestrained authority by the state in all matters but specifically names areas of justice and police powers as key areas for the state or governmental control.

The text doesn't mention worship, administration of the sacraments or ordinances of the Church, evangelism, world missions or teaching and education as a responsibility of the state.

Jesus Christ in Matthew 28:18-20 delegates these responsibilities to His Church. In support of this interpretation, Francis Schaeffer wrote:

> God has ordained the state as a delegated authority; it is not autonomous. The state is to be an agent of justice, to restrain evil by punishing the wrongdoer, and to protect the good in society. When it does the reverse, it has no proper authority.

It is then a usurped authority and as such it becomes lawless and is tyranny.[3]

The authority of government over Christians is legitimate to the extent government subordinates itself to the authority of God. When it abandons this principle of delegation, it begins to lose its legitimacy.

In such cases, Christians are obligated by their own Biblical mandates to develop an appropriate response, which may include what has historically been known as civil disobedience.

BIBLICAL CIVIL DISOBEDIENCE
We can find acts of civil disobedience by believers in both the Old and New Testaments. The Old Testament offers several occasions in which governmental authorities issued orders and were refused.

In Exodus 1:15ff. Hebrew midwives Shiphrah and Puah refused to kill the newborn Hebrew boys as commanded by Pharaoh. Further, they deceived Pharaoh when he confronted them with their civil disobedience by saying, "Because the Hebrew women are not like the Egyptian women; for they are lively and give birth before the midwives come to them."

Exodus 1:20 says that God "...dealt well with the midwives...." For their act of civil disobedience, God rewarded them.

In Daniel 1, 3, and 6 we see Daniel and his friends Shadrach, Meshach and Abed-Nego in confrontation with Babylonian governmental authorities. In every case they refused to enter into pagan worship of an idol. Daniel refused to obey an edict not to pray. These are clear cases of civil disobedience, and in each case they were both rescued and rewarded by the Lord for their civil disobedience.

Prophets such as Elijah and Elisha were in regular confrontation with the ungodly kings of their day and one could describe their actions as a pattern of civil disobedience.

We can also find instances of civil disobedience in the New Testament. Usually these involve responses by the early Christians to efforts by the Roman government to thwart the Great Commission, found in Matthew 28:18-20.

The Apostles, in Acts 4:18-21 and 5:29, refused to obey the Jewish religious authority, the Sanhedrin, when they were commanded not to preach anymore in the name of Jesus. Peter answered them saying,

> 19 But Peter and John answered and said to them, "Whether it is right in the sight of God to listen to you more than to God, you judge.
>
> 20 "For we cannot but speak the things which we have seen and heard."

A second confrontation occurred with the Jewish religious authorities over the preaching of the Gospel. The High Priest of the Sanhedrin said, "Did we not strictly command you not to teach in this name? And look, you have filled Jerusalem with your doctrine, and intend to bring this Man's blood on us!" (Acts 5:28). Peter answered and said, "...We ought to obey God rather than men" (Acts 5:29).

This confrontation is the first example of Christian civil disobedience in the early Church. Thus, obedience to Jesus and consequent civil disobedience to the authorities was a result of our Lord and Savior giving them His Great Commission.

We have already established that the Great Commission gives both the preaching and world evangelization responsibility to the Church. It gives the teaching or responsibility for education to the Church as well.

Peter and the other Apostles were simply obeying Jesus' command to preach and spread the Gospel to all the nations in Acts 4 and 5. Modern Christians have attempted to carry out this part of the Great Commission but many have neglected the teaching or educational responsibility, at least at the primary level. It has not been abrogated, and if the authorities of our day attempt to prevent Christian families and churches from educating their children we should also say, "We have to obey God rather than government."

CHRISTIAN CIVIL DISOBEDIENCE: YESTERDAY, TODAY AND TOMORROW

The history of the Church provides additional examples of Christians who chose to obey God rather than their government. During the Reformation, churches frequently refused to obey authorities whose directives violated their understanding of Biblical mandates and what they had prayerfully concluded God wanted them to do.

Had William Tyndale not practiced civil disobedience he would not have given us the first English translation of the Holy Scriptures.

John Bunyan, a dissenting Baptist preacher in England, was imprisoned for 12 years for preaching without a state license. We can be thankful for Bunyan's act of civil disobedience for it was in prison he wrote the famous classic *Pilgrim's Progress*, which has blessed Christians for several hundred years.

Could grounds emerge for Christians today to practice civil disobedience? Uncomfortable though it may be, we can no longer avoid this question.

We have shown how our national government has turned away from Christianity and embraced secular humanism—particularly in (if hardly limited to) its usurpation of the education of our children.

When government begins to intrude into the affairs of the Christian family and the local church, as has become common today, grounds begin to appear for civil disobedience.

It is important to be clear: Today's government, following the secular-humanist agenda, need not refuse or deny the church, family or Christian schools certain rights; all it need do is try to impose severe regulations or controls in order to hinder or prohibit these from carrying out their God-ordained mission.

In a discussion of the limits on government implicit in Romans 13, Francis Schaeffer addressed the issue of civil disobedience:

> But what is to be done when the state does that which violates its legitimate function? The early Christians died because they would not obey the state in a civil matter.
>
> People often say that the early church did not show any civil disobedience. They do not know church history.
>
> Why were the early Christians thrown to the lions? From the Christian's viewpoint it was for a religious reason. But from the viewpoint of the Roman state they were in civil disobedience....
>
> The Christians said they would not worship Caesar, anybody or anything, but the living God.
>
> Thus to the Roman Empire they were rebels and it was civil disobedience.[4]

The only thing required of the early Christians in this area was to burn incense once per year in the town square and simply affirm that Caesar was Lord and all would be well. This was viewed as a necessary political rite that bonded the empire together.

The early Christians paid their taxes, provided acts of charity for their neighbors, prayed for the Emperor, and were loyal and law abiding citizens. They, however, did not believe they could burn incense, and say Caesar was Lord, and remain true to their Savior. Many died for this refusal.

Drs. Paul and John Feinberg, professors of Theology at Trinity Evangelical Divinity School, in their important work *Ethics for a Brave New World*, support a permissible and at times required civil disobedience. They ask:

> First, granted that disobeying a societal law when asked to break God's law leaves one open to societal punishment, does it also entail moral censure? We think not. In such cases the individual cannot obey both the human law and God's law conjointly.... The only remaining question is whether the choice made (obeying God and not man) was the correct one. We think the biblical example is helpful here. Specifically, we agree with Peter and John (Acts 5:29).[5]

LEX REX...AND A CHRISTIAN MANIFESTO

Before he died in 1984, Francis Schaeffer spoke and wrote frequently about Samuel Rutherford's *Lex Rex* (Law is King). Schaeffer was trying to prepare the Christian community in America for a time when civil disobedience might become necessary.

His seminal book, *A Christian Manifesto* was written in 1981 and well before its time. It seems very timely today considering the many encroachments of government upon responsibilities that have always been the sphere of Christian families, ministries and churches.

It would be a good Christian exercise to read or reread Schaeffer's book. It remains fresh, 20 years after its original publication.

In *Lex Rex*, Rutherford sets forth a proper Christian response to unbiblical acts by the state. He argued that the king and governmental authorities are under the law and not above it. *Lex Rex* was a challenge to the belief in the divine right of kings dominant in that day.

Today there are Christians who seem to hold to something like the "divine right of government," ascribing to civil magistrates or government generally the same kind of unquestioning obeisance that was expected by kings in the 15th and 16th centuries.

Our American constitutional experiment was based partially on *Lex Rex* indirectly through the ideas of John Locke among others in what became known as the "natural rights" tradition.

Our American founders relied much on Locke's political theory and may have studied Rutherford as well. Rev. John Witherspoon, a Presbyterian minister and President of the College of New Jersey (now Princeton University), was a Scottish immigrant and would have been familiar with Rutherford's *Lex Rex*. Witherspoon, teacher of many of the Founding Fathers, was a signer of the Declaration of Independence.[6]

The Founders of the United States of America created a constitutional republic where all are subject to the same laws under the rule of law. No one is above the law and the officials charged with upholding and maintaining the laws must not violate those laws they are sworn to uphold.[7]

WHEN IS CIVIL DISOBEDIENCE PERMISSIBLE AND NOT PERMISSIBLE?

We have established satisfactorily that civil disobedience is permissible and even required when governmental authorities attempt to interfere with the God-ordained ministries of the Church.

We have shown that this practice has both good Biblical and historical authority. American Christians, however, are not well acquainted with this approach.

The notion that civil disobedience is permissible or required will be new to many Christians. It is, therefore, crucial that we consider it with great care, using Scripture as our guide, being as clear as possible about what it authorizes versus what it forbids. For example, disobedience to governmental authorities is permissible under certain circumstances. This should be clear from the words of Jesus Christ spoken during the Sermon on the Mount:

> 38 You have heard that it was said, "An eye for an eye and a tooth for a tooth."
> 39 But I tell you not to resist an evil person. But whoever slaps you on your right cheek, turn the other to him also.
> 44 But I say to you, love your enemies, bless those who curse you, do good to those who hate you, and pray for those who spitefully use you and persecute you (Matt. 5:38-39, 44).

In a letter to Titus, Paul told Christians "to speak evil of no one, to be peaceable, gentle, showing all humility to all men" (Titus 3:2).

In the Old Testament, Jonah instructed the citizens of Nineveh to "...let every one turn from his evil way and from the violence that is in his hands" (Jonah 3:8).

Isaiah 60:18 says, "Violence shall no longer be heard in your land, Neither wasting nor destruction within your borders...."

Violence, finally, was one of the characteristics of the society that God removed from this Earth with the Genesis flood (Genesis 6:11). This message should be clear: God hates unrighteous violence. Violence is a tool of those in rebellion against God, and, therefore, not an option for God-fearing and Bible-believing Christians.

Peaceful civil disobedience, however, is an option if civil authorities have turned away from God, embraced secular humanism and compel obedience to man-centered instead of God-centered policies.

We need to outline the circumstances under which civil disobedience is both Scripturally and constitutionally permissible, and how it would need to be implemented.

Historically the Church has always said to the state or civil magistrates that areas of worship and preaching are off limits to state control or authority. These have been areas covered in the Great Commission text of Matthew 28:18-20.

EDUCATION: OFF LIMITS TO STATE CONTROL

We are putting forth the truth that teaching and education of the congregation and children at K-12 level are covered by Matthew 28:18-20 and are also off limits to state control or authority.

In the Acts 5:29 text where the Apostle Peter said, "We ought to obey God rather than men" the issue was over preaching and teaching. The early Church did not agree with the Sanhedrin and refused the Sanhedrin's commands to stop their preaching.

This book is arguing that a complete understanding of the reach and authority of Matthew 28:18-20 includes children at the K-12 level. Christians, therefore, must not give their children over to state education, which has become neo-pagan and humanistic in recent decades and appears to be never satisfied until total control over the minds of children is securely in the hands of secularists.

If the state attempts to thwart, control or regulate Christian schools or home schooling, godly pastors, church boards, Christian school and home-school associations, and individual Christian families, could safely practice a godly civil disobedience and not suffer any moral censure. They may risk, however, legal censure if the state or civil magistrates pursued a course violating their God-ordained roles.

PRACTICAL CIVIL DISOBEDIENCE

What are some practical ways modern Christians could practice civil disobedience and godly passive resistance to governmental authorities who oppress the Church?

1. A regular practice of praying for government authorities (1 Timothy 2:1-4) is the first requirement.

THE MEANING OF IMPRECATORY PRAYER

An introduction of imprecatory prayers may be appropriate where government authorities have become recalcitrant, hardened against the Lord and against constitutional law, and appeals for relief have been exhausted.

Christians should first pray for repentance and the souls of their enemies, especially those in government authority. But there are rare times when prayer of imprecation is acceptable.

Stephen, the first martyr, prayed for his enemies as they were stoning him in Acts 7:60 saying, "Lord, do not charge them with this sin." A governmental agent who was part of this event, Saul of Tarsus, who later became Paul the Apostle, was a recipient of the benefits of Stephen's prayer.

In some cases we can remind God of our enemies' threats, as did the early church in Acts 4:27-31.

Paul actually spoke and prayed against specific individuals who were harming the Church or teaching false doctrine (1 Timothy 1:20, 2 Timothy 2:17).

Our first requirement is to pray for salvation of "...those who spitefully use you and persecute you" (Matthew 5:44).

There are also Psalms of imprecation on which we could model our prayers in extreme circumstances (See Psalm 58; 68:21-23; 69:23-29; 109:5-19; 137:7-9).

These texts might apply to false religions, movements and agencies that aggressively persecute Christians and seek to destroy the Christian Faith.

SAMORA MACHEL,
"COME DOWN OUT OF THE SKY!"

In Africa in 1985, Marxist Dictator Samora Machel of Mozambique was particularly brutal to the Christian churches.

He was, furthermore, plotting a Marxist takeover in nearby Malawi which had a Christian President at that time. He had arrested many pastors in his own country.

Samora was returning from a trip to the nation of South Africa on government business at the same time a gathering of 600 African pastors and some missionaries had assembled to pray and fast for ten days about the danger to the Church in his country.

They also were praying that Mozambique would be open to the Gospel.

One night as they were praying for the deliverance of their Christian brethren, one pastor cried out in deep agony of soul under leadership of the Holy Spirit in the prayer meeting, saying, "Samora Machel, come down out of the sky! ... Come down out of the sky!"

He did not know what he was praying for, perhaps that Samora would come down from his throne of power and be humbled or perhaps for a new ruler who would give freedom to the Church.

Then hundreds of pastors began to join in with his prayer, "Samora Machel, come down out of the sky." At that very moment, hundreds of miles away on his return trip, Samora's plane encountered a severe thunderstorm, began having severe difficulty and later crashed just inside South Africa.

All on the plane were killed. When the South African authorities examined the wreckage they discovered documents that showed Samora had planned to overthrow the Christian ruler in nearby Malawi.[8]

CHRISTIAN LEGAL ACTION

2. Christian attorneys can be used to bring lawsuits or defend believers in confrontation with government authorities who overstep their bounds.

One of the best things occurring in the spiritual cultural war for the protection of the unborn and Christian children in their K-12 education is the large number of small Christian law firms which have formed in recent years.

These include new, specialty legal associations like the Home School Legal Defense Association (HSLDA), the Rutherford Institute, the Pacific Justice Institute, the Christian Law Association, and the ACLJ (American Center for Law and Justice).

Many of these Christian firms and associations have a call to defend the legal rights of believers in these special situations.

While the humanist left has captured many of our opinion shaping institutions, they have not yet been successful in replacing our basic Constitution. Legal appeals can still be made.

HSLDA has won a majority of their cases in defense of home schooling families.

Christian families and churches must develop an individual mindset, however, that they will not obey regulations that thwart or control the education of children and that all such attempts will be met with defensive legal action.

There may be cases where legal action and appeals fail. At that time civil disobedience could be considered.

NON-VIOLENT PROTEST, PICKETS, MARCHES

3. Christians can use non-violent protests, picketing and marches to express their opposition to government-

sanctioned policies and practices which are not Scriptural and anti-Christian.

Abortion is clearly not Scriptural; one of the most relevant Scriptural passages reads, "Before I formed you in the womb I knew you; Before you were born I sanctified you...." (Jeremiah 1:5).

Accordingly, defenders of the lives of unborn children have marched and demonstrated in all 50 states every year since *Roe vs. Wade.*

They have not assented to the destruction of the unborn in America. Protests, picketing and marches could be organized when the state or governmental authorities harm children at the K-12 level as well by thwarting the efforts of home-schooling families or interfering with Christian schools. We can peacefully confront governmental authorities when they are misusing their power against Christian families or otherwise behaving in an unconstitutional and not scriptural manner.

MAKING CHRISTIAN VOICES HEARD

There are options for Christians to make their voices heard. In 1988, in the early days of home schooling, I learned that a Christian home-school family was being taken before the South Carolina State Board of Education and questioned on their home-school practices.

Since it was a public meeting, I decided to go as an observer. One board member, historian and author Rod Gragg, was a committed Christian and friend. He tried to help them.

During the hearing I determined that this family had acted responsibly and were competent to home school. I could tell by the way they answered questions that they were strong Christians.

The state board, particularly the Chairman, was acting in a belligerent manner in questioning them. A main issue for the state board was that the mother did not have a college degree and was not certified. The family was using A Beka Christian curriculum and this seemed to upset some of the board members. This home-schooling Christian family was practicing civil disobedience as far as the state board was concerned.

I thought back to 1977 when Gail and I had begun to home school and wondered if I could have handled myself as well as they did in such a confrontation. My heart went out to them. Would anyone have come to my defense?

"LEAVE THIS FAMILY ALONE!"

Suddenly, and without recognition by the Chairman, I spoke up in the meeting, as he was pressing this Christian family. I just blurted out to the Chairman and entire Board, "Leave this family alone! They're doing a good job educating their children! You have no right to interfere in the Christian education in their home!"

I couldn't believe I had said it. The meeting momentarily stopped, heads turned, and everyone looked around to see who had said this. They weren't sure where this comment had come from. I didn't raise my hand, and so it was ignored. The Chairman then continued his grilling of the family. Suddenly I spoke up again and said, "You're doing a bad job in the public schools. Why don't you fix them before you harass a Christian family who only wants the best education for their children?"

By this time the Chairman had identified who had interrupted his meeting. He said to me, "If you interrupt again, I'll have to ask you to leave." I nodded but did not speak.

I continued to observe the meeting. I think they knew they were being watched.

They referred the matter to a committee, and I don't know the outcome, but that day I gave a small protest and a verbal correction to a government agency overstepping its bounds.

Christians can do this individually with elected officials and corporately in groups as well.

Protesting the state's insistence on controlling K-12 Christian education may become necessary, although Christians should only do this when the facts and issues are clear and they have prepared in advance.

4. *Church boards, church courts, and Christian denominational leaders can protest, write letters of censure and urge governmental authorities who are behaving in an unconstitutional or not scriptural manner to cease and desist.*

They can instruct the state and governmental officials in their proper roles. Some governmental officials may ignore these, but it can be attempted.

CHURCH ORGANIZATIONS MUST HAVE AUTONOMY

Church councils and denominations all have their own legal and court systems and govern their own affairs. Within their sphere they have authority. When the state intrudes itself into their affairs these church bodies can use the separation of church and state as a defense.

The Southern Baptist Convention recently passed a strong resolution concerning women in combat and put the federal government and the Department of Defense on notice that they do not agree with and will not support this approach.[9] This decision came as a resolution in the 1998 SBC Convention.

Resolutions are fine, but they do not bind either the denominations or have the same force with the government. I think the time will come when major denominations may need to instruct the state or federal government and tell them that in the future they will not cooperate with policy that violates Church doctrine or the Holy Scriptures.

For example, if the federal government were to reinstate the draft, it is very likely that out of the need to follow today's canons of political correctness the draft would have to include large numbers of females.

Christian denominations might inform the federal government that they will practice civil disobedience with regard to women being drafted and serving in combat units.

CIVIL DISOBEDIENCE IN NAZI GERMANY: THE BARMEN DECLARATION

The *Barmen Declaration* ratified by the protesting ministers of The Confessing Church in Germany in 1934 was just such a document. The Confessing Church was in an indirect fashion telling the Nazi government not to interfere in its affairs.

Martin Niemoller, who had formed the Pastors' Emergency League, helped strengthen pastors to resist the Nazi State. They made a good effort and resisted for a time until 1938 when they were ordered to swear an oath of allegiance to Hitler as Fuhrer. This was the moment when the church would decide whether to resist or to cave in.

At the June 1938 6th Synod of The Confessing Church, the synod allowed each minister to make his individual choice whether he would swear allegiance to Hitler. Dietrich Bonhoeffer strongly protested this approach, urging a united stand in accord with the synod's earlier decisions, and that no one swear allegiance.

Bonhoeffer was infuriated at the bishops' shuffling the burden of this choice to individual pastors. He said, "Will

The Confessing Church ever learn that majority decisions in matters of the conscience kill the Spirit?"

At one time there were 5,000 Protestant ministers in the Pastors' Emergency League.

When the synod voted to let each one make his own decision, it was the turning point and The Confessing Church's resistance to Hitler began to break down. This let the Nazis divide them.

Some took the oath to protect themselves and their churches.[10]

Hitler then arrested 800 of the pastors who had not taken the oath. These 800 had practiced civil disobedience and refused to swear allegiance to Hitler and the fascist state. Had all 5,000 done this, perhaps the final chapter for Germany and the world may have been different.

UNITY OF PURPOSE IN CIVIL DISOBEDIENCE WILL GIVE STRENGTH TO THE ISSUE

Church bodies, individual congregations and Christian families can practice civil disobedience in limited situations. Unity gives strength to the purpose and issue at hand. Education and protection of the children in Christian and home schools from the indoctrination of state schools should be one such cause for church bodies and Christian families to practice civil disobedience.

5. *Appeal to godly government agents or other civil magistrates for assistance is one course that needs to be considered.*

Many of our church members are policemen, judges, sheriffs and elected officials who have greater or lesser state authority. Individual Christian and church bodies do not have civil power and can't take the law into their hands.

The power of the sword in civil affairs was given to civil authorities. Many Christians serve in these roles in our communities.

Pastors should begin to instruct these members who hold civil authority that they have a Christian duty to uphold the Constitution and Law of God against the abuse of other governmental authorities that respect neither.

In Reformation times this was known as "interposition of the lesser magistrate."[11]

INTERPOSITION OF THE LESSER MAGISTRATE

In our constitutional system we have a separation of powers so that one branch of government would not gain too much power and under extreme circumstances one branch of government could check the unbridled passion and abuse of another branch. In our constitutional system it seems that the Federal Courts were to be the third or lesser branch of government.

Article 3 of the Constitution, which sets up the Supreme Court and the Federal Judiciary, is the smallest section in the Constitution.

At the founding of the Republic, the Federal courts seem to have had a smaller role than the Legislative and Executive branches.

Today, however, the Federal Judiciary has become the strongest, almost tyrannical in the minds of some. Legal scholar Raoul Berger wrote an important book on this problem entitled *Government by Judiciary: The Transformation of the Fourteenth Amendment.*[12]

Nothing, however, has changed, and the abuses of the federal and now state courts go on and on.

The Executive and Legislative branches seem impervious to the abuses or unwilling to reign in this unchecked power. We need more Chief Executives like President Andrew

Jackson in 1837 who said concerning an Indian Western resettlement case: "[Judge] John Marshall has made his decision. Let him enforce it." This story seems quaint now, but President Jackson only was applying the separation of powers doctrine in his day.

In Greenville, South Carolina, on November 8, 2001, the South Carolina Department of Social Services (DSS) seized 15 foster children from Bill Rettew and his wife Debbie without a warning.

This exemplary Christian family had a ministry of caring for children who had been forsaken by their natural families; several were children with severe handicaps. Bill and Debbie are greatly admired in the Greenville area for their loving ministry to these neglected and rejected children.

In 1999, Attorney General Charlie Condon named Bill Rettew "Father of the Year" as he and his wife had cared for as many as 24 special needs children by that time. The Rettew family was home schooling many of the children.

They are also members in good standing at Hampton Park Baptist Church of Greenville. The Rettew family has traveled to other states singing and giving testimony of God's goodness and His love for children.

The reasons given for seizing the children remain unclear since Family Court Judge Amy Sutherland has put a gag order on both the Rettews and DSS. Many Christians, however, close to the Rettews and who know the legal system in the county believe this is another case of governmental abuse against a Christian family.[13]

Greenville County, South Carolina, also has a Christian sheriff who had to execute the Family Court's warrant on behalf of DSS to seize the children. Hypothetically, if the sheriff had felt there was no probable cause of a crime for this warrant to be executed, he may have refused and said like Andrew Jackson in 1837, "Judge Sutherland has issued her warrant; let her enforce it." The Sheriff may have risked a contempt of court citation for this, but it may have been his Christian duty if this abuse by DSS and the Family Court is as egregious as some now allege.

Such situations will burden Christian office holders and civil authorities as they observe their humanist and anti-Christian colleagues exercise raw political power against the Church and their fellow Christians.

Christian office holders and civil magistrates, if they cannot interpose themselves against allowing their fellow Christians to come to harm through abuse of the law, should themselves consider the practice of civil disobedience in the performance of their duties. Interference in the family, in the Church and through attempts to thwart, control, or regulate the Christian education of the next generation should be considered as areas where godly governmental authorities should refuse to cooperate with the secular state run amuck.

WHAT IS AT STAKE? THE NEXT GENERATION!

Some Christian leaders may say civil disobedience is to be practiced only in the rarest situations dealing directly with Sunday Church worship, preaching and evangelism only. They may say that the churches should not apply such a practice to the K-12 Christian education of children.

Again, we must stand firm on Matthew 28:18-20 that it applies to the entire teaching and education mission of the Church, and this includes the defense of the rights of K-12 education in Christian schools and home schooling against unwanted and unscriptural governmental interference.

If the churches will not stand firm here we could very easily lose the next generation of Christian children to indoctrination and control in state-sponsored schools.

If the children's exodus into Christian schools and home schooling continues to grow, some government officials with the fascist mindset will certainly move to contain or restrict this through abuse of power and legal means.

Francis Schaeffer warned us with his *Christian Manifesto* in a chapter titled "The Use of Civil Disobedience."

> In the United States the materialistic, humanistic worldview is being taught exclusively in most state schools. But then, those holding the humanistic worldview will move to control through curricula and other means the Christian schools— even though these schools were set up at private cost by the parents in order to give their children an education based on the worldview of a universe created by a God who objectively exists.[14]

PREPARE NOW FOR CIVIL DISOBEDIENCE, AND STAND ON SOLID BIBLICAL GROUND

Now we must prepare ahead for this possibility that Christians will need to revive the old, neglected doctrine of civil disobedience. We will stand in good stead with the prophets, Daniel and his three friends, Stephen the first martyr, all the Apostles and the early Church.

Also, we stand with John Bunyan, William Tyndale and our Christian brothers and sisters in the Sudan, China and Muslim countries today. Schaeffer summed up the basic bottom line issue well when he said,

> If there's no final place for civil disobedience, then the government has been made autonomous, and as such, it has been put in the place of the Living God.[15]

This can't be; this won't be! Let Christian families and churches today serve our Lord and Savior, Jesus Christ, by raising up a godly generation apart from the state-sponsored schools. ■

CHAPTER EIGHT

THE NEXT GREAT AWAKENING

REMNANT OR REVIVAL?

EDUCATION: A PUBLIC PRIORITY

**THE ANTICIPATED GROWTH
OF HOME SCHOOLING**

**THE SECOND COMING OF THE
SOUTHERN BAPTIST CONVENTION**

One of the most hopeful and encouraging aspects of the American church scene today is the growing prayer and fasting movement with its hope for revival or renewal in the churches and elsewhere throughout the nation. This movement also has a focus on world evangelization.

For example, it includes the influential Concerts of Prayer movement for the least evangelized portion of the world in the 10/40 window. The 10/40 area takes in much of the Middle East and Asia.

Christians have shown renewed concern for the neglected areas of the world and missions like the *Co-Mission*, a joint venture of many Christian missions, which went into the old U.S.S.R. ten years back, and have had considerable impact in these regions. Many stayed behind to become permanent missionaries or church planters in Russia.

REMNANT OR REVIVAL?

U.S.-based missions like Concerts of Prayer have spread throughout the entire nation. Excellent books on revival like Concerts of Prayer Founder and President David Bryant's *The Hope at Hand* and Reformation and Revival Ministries President John H. Armstrong's *True Revival: What Happens When God's Spirit Moves?* have given hope to many.[1]

In some American communities pastors and Christian leaders gather regularly, sometimes daily, for long seasons of prayer. Retreats and conferences have been organized where ministers and laymen gather for periods of prayer and fasting for revival in the churches and nation.

The Southern Baptists have a program called the Prayer and Spiritual Awakening Office led by Rev. Henry Blackaby, author of *Experiencing God.*[2]

These many diverse ministries have a common burden, which is nothing less than a sweeping national revival not unlike the First Great Awakening in the 1740's that spread through the colonies with such force and power as to carry an entire nation into the Kingdom of God.

Such preachers as Jonathan Edwards, America's first great theologian, Anglican evangelist George Whitefield and the Tennent brothers, Presbyterian ministers in New Jersey, led the First Great Awakening.

The nation has had periodic awakenings such as the Second Great Awakening in 1805 and the "Layman's Prayer Revival" that began in New York City in 1858. The Pentecostal revival began in 1905, and growth in Pentecostal and charismatic churches has continued to this day. The impact of such awakenings can be felt in communities, churches and families for many years afterward.

One lesser-known Southern Baptist evangelist, Mordecai Ham, had major impact throughout the Southeast during the 1920's and 1930's. Where he preached, revival often broke out. Through his preaching, thousands of people found Jesus Christ as their Lord and Savior.

In 1930, he held a month-long crusade in Augusta, Georgia. He held children's meetings, women's meetings and men's meetings, where he would address the specific needs of each group. There's a legend that one night when Ham was preaching "the Holy Spirit was about the town" in such power and conviction that several thousand men found Christ as Lord and Savior in a single meeting.

Brethren preacher Liddon Sheridan told me a story of the time when his father was pastor of the large Curtis Baptist Church in Augusta. Liddon himself was just a little boy but saw the spiritual awakening unfold in his community. He told me, "Ray, the whole city found Christ. There was hardly one unconverted person left standing."

For months after Evangelist Mordecai Ham left town, every time a minister of any denomination gave an altar call or an invitation, dozens would come forward to give their hearts to Christ and find forgiveness.

Even today, 70 years later, some who remember this time attribute some of the decency, godly environment and dynamic churches still existing in that Southern city to the impact of this month-long crusade and the ensuing revival. Mordecai Ham has since been largely forgotten, but one of his converts, then a 16-year-old teenager from Charlotte, North Carolina, has himself carried on a career in crusade evangelism. The teenager's name is Billy Graham!

There is little doubt that America needs another Great Awakening. We have tried everything else to recover our lost moral and spiritual greatness.

Through most of the 1980-1990's evangelical Christians thought that direct political action and strong voting would help recover the lost moral and spiritual vitality of the nation. The rise of the so-called Christian Right as seen in such organizations as the Moral Majority, now defunct, and the more recent Christian Coalition, now moribund, have not been successful in rolling back the moral corruption that is growing daily in many of our communities.

THE INEFFECTIVENESS OF CHRISTIAN POLITICAL ACTION

While I do not believe Christians should eschew political action, we need to recognize how limited and often ineffective this approach is for Christians. Evangelicals have never voted more and had more participation by running for and in some cases being elected to high offices, but nothing seems to slow down the inexorable move away from our historic, Judeo-Christian values. Christians have been fighting in the right war, but often with the wrong weapons and tactics. We have been trying to jump-start a dying culture, when we need to replace whole programs and create a new parallel Christian educational system.

Paul Weyrich of the Free Congress Foundation, the dean of the Christian Right and one of America's savviest political strategists, pointed this out in an essay entitled "Conservatives, Retreat" that ran in many major dailies across the nation in February, 1999.[3] It was significant in what was said, but especially that Paul Weyrich said it.

He now believes that America won't be finally rescued by political action. The context of his essay was the failure of U.S. Senate to remove President Bill Clinton from office after his impeachment by the U.S. House due to the Monica Lewinsky affair. Weyrich wrote that the

> triumph of Clinton, and the fact that his party stood by him almost unanimously in the House and unanimously in the Senate, means that the advocates of morality have lost, and lost badly. This is just the beginning.

Weyrich drew some disturbing conclusions:

> What this means in plain English is that the efforts to return some semblance of moral order to the nation through the political process have failed. If there really were a moral majority in the country, Clinton would have been driven from office a year ago. [1998]
>
> For conservatives, the meaning of this defeat is profound. It means that we cannot depend on the political structures to protect us. Quite the contrary. The political structures, with Clinton in the captain's chair, will go to war against us....
>
> It is clear that we live in a hostile culture. Any nation that finds a Bill Clinton more popular after his trial than before, is a nation that Alexis de Tocqueville would not recognize. Consequently we are going to have to examine parallel institutions with which we can win the culture war.[4]

It is significant that Weyrich singles out *home schooling* among "parallel institutions" as one of the best hopes for the future in the United States.

His article continues:

> Conservatives have largely lost the struggle. Yet the home-school movement, now embracing a million students, gives us hope. There are some children in America who are being well educated and educated with the right values. It is upon these young people that the future of the nation must depend...
>
> It is to suggest that victory for them (i.e. political activists) and us, may no longer be possible. If that is the case, we must look to other means to survive. That effort will be an even greater challenge than fighting secular humanist liberalism. It is, though, an effort for all time.[5]

CHRISTIAN POLITICAL ACTIVISTS: STRIKING AT SYMPTOMS ONLY

Most of what we do as Christians in the culture wars and political battles is strike at symptoms. The many vices and sins that have become so strong in recent years such as the rise of abortion, gambling, and homosexuality are not causes but symptoms of a deeper problem.

Paul in Romans 1:21-24 makes it clear that the cause of homosexuality is that "they did not glorify God, nor were thankful, but became futile in their thoughts and their foolish heart was darkened" and that "He gave them over" to uncleanness, to dishonor their bodies among themselves.

The proximate cause of homosexuality may be varied, but the root cause is that the homosexual has rejected God at a profound level.

Christians won't be able to arrest or defeat such sins in our culture by voting them down. Paul tells us that "We wrestle not against flesh and blood but against principalities and power, against the rulers of the darkness of this age, against spiritual wickedness in the heavenly places" (Ephesians 6:12).

VICES...LIKE MALIGNANT CANCERS

The main cause of these problems is that our society has forgotten God, resulting in Jesus Christ's being denied access to millions of our children year after year in the K-12 government school system. We are raising generation after generation in a system called "public schools" where Jesus Christ cannot be named and where the Bible is the most censored book.

Proverbs 16:6b tells us, "By the fear of the Lord one departs from evil." We have taken the fear and knowledge of the Lord away from succeeding generations. This has taken its toll on our society in a variety of ways, ranging from the militant homosexual movement to the increased crime and behavioral vices that have fastened themselves like malignant tumors to our communities. We must stop fighting primarily against symptoms. We must stop giving secular answers to spiritual problems. "For though we walk in the flesh, we do not war according to the flesh, for the weapons of our warfare are not carnal but mighty in God for pulling down strongholds, casting down arguments and every high thing that exalts itself against the knowledge of God" (2 Corinthians 10:3-5)

THE REAL WEAPONS IN THE CULTURAL WAR

These texts remind us that our greatest weapons are still prayer, preaching, and teaching the Word of God to the next generation. We who believe in the Biblical mandate for the education of children have an historic opportunity to present before the American public, both Christian and non-Christian, the Biblical models for family, education and schooling. The rising tide of Christian schools and home schooling has the potential to lift all boats. If the Christian family and church can capture the moment to educate the next generation we may still recover some of our lost spiritual greatness.

THE EXAMPLE SET BY DR. D. JAMES KENNEDY

Marshall Fritz, President of the Alliance For the Separation of School and State, and I had an appointment in May of 1998 with Dr. D. James Kennedy of Coral Ridge Ministries to present our case for both Exodus Mandate and the separation of school and state and to ask for his endorsement.

We felt this great man of God saw the timeliness and practically of our vision.

Dr. Kennedy is among the few major national Christian leaders who consistently advocate Christian schooling as the only option for Christian families. He has been unequivocal in this call and has founded the Westminster Christian Academy for K-12 education in his community of Ft. Lauderdale, Florida.

During lunch he asked me,

> What is different now? Many of us have called for an exodus or for Christian schooling as the only choice for Christian families for years and the churches are not listening. What will change that now?

I answered, in effect:

> We hope and pray that we are on the cusp of a fullness of time moment in the history of the Church, not unlike the Reformation or other spiritual awakenings when long forgotten Biblical truths were freshly acted upon by Christians in their time. Many new ministries and organizations are being raised up now to help you and others to accomplish this.

Dr. Kennedy seemed to receive my explanation well. As we headed back to the Coral Ridge Presbyterian Church from Dr. Kennedy's favorite Chinese restaurant, Marshall Fritz began to describe for Dr. Kennedy a new America.

EXODUS MANDATE AS A PATHWAY TO THE THIRD GREAT AWAKENING

In this new America, most of the education would take place in Christian schools or through home schooling. Christian families will have rejected and abandoned state-sponsored schools.

Marshall showed how this fresh obedience by Christian families and churches could plant the seeds for the Third Great Awakening.

At this moment Dr. Kennedy seemed to grasp this possibility in a new way. We think he was animated by this vision for a fresh great awakening in our land that would be impacted by the Christian education of the next generation.

Dr. Kennedy then took us on a tour of his ministry and introduced us to the producer of *The Coral Ridge Hour* TV ministry.

As we left and he was off to another appointment, he wrapped his arms around us and prayed for our work and the success of this vision.

By September 1998, I had been a guest on both his TV and radio networks. This was a pivotal moment in the early life of the Exodus Mandate Project. For the first time we were able to reach many nationally with our message. Our discussion on the revival of the churches, families and the nation through Christian schooling and home schooling had reached deep into the heart of this great man of God who has a vision for restoring America through them.

Our meeting with Dr. Kennedy had been successful. We began to envision an America with a growing number of Christian schools and parents' home schooling their children according to the Biblical mandate, and as a result of this, America would experience a Third Great Awakening.

Yet even those of us who advocate separating school and state and promote a children's exodus from government schools still live in a world where the old government-school paradigm reigns. It is hard to see a change as large as the one we advocate, as much as we pray for and desire it.

We must be able to look over into the Promised Land from Mt. Nebo, like Moses of old (Deuteronomy 32:48-52). That day in Fort Lauderdale, Dr. Kennedy, Marshall Fritz, and I got a glimpse of the Promised Land and our hearts were renewed. Furthermore, we want to begin walking into this Promised Land now. With God, all things are possible!

What must Christians now do? If Christian families were to begin leaving Pharaoh's schools for the Promised Land of Christian schools or home schooling, it could spark the spiritual awakening for which we are all praying and longing, in order to renew our churches, our debased culture and our nation!

LOOSENING THE HUMANIST CHOKE HOLD

Such a movement could eventually loosen the choke hold secular humanism now holds over our culture by trapping children and youth as near-hostages in government schools.

The key to the spiritual renewal of the Church and of this nation may be as simple as Christians' obeying the Biblical mandate concerning the education of their children, much like the promise given the people of Israel:

"If My people who are called by My name will humble themselves, and pray and seek My face, and turn from their wicked ways, then I will hear from heaven, and will forgive their sin and heal their land" (2 Chronicles 7:14).

This will do much to inoculate them against the corruption of a secular-humanist culture. As they grow up, they will develop immunity to its temptations. This will certainly help our struggle against abortion, and homosexuality as well as lesser issues such as state-sponsored gambling.

These, again, are all symptoms. A major cause of these and other issues is that we have been raising generation after generation in government schools.

The basic Unitarian philosophy guiding these schools has been resolutely hostile to Christianity since the 1840's.

Now, it has not just banished Jesus Christ and censored the Bible, but it has become hostile to learning itself—eschewing traditional education in favor of raising and tracking youth into vocational programs to service the global economy.

The Exodus Mandate Project promises to be in the forefront of efforts to turn this culture around, not by engaging in futile acts of "reform," but by building up an entirely *new* infrastructure of "parallel institutions" of Christian schools and home schooling.

We must "pray without ceasing" (1 Thessalonians 5:17) that these "parallel institutions" will become the hope for revival of our families, our churches and our nation.

OUR AIM: A TRUE REVIVAL, AN AWAKENING

Theologians and Christian writers have carried on a lively discussion about whether a repentant and godly church can bring about revival or if revival is the gracious act of a sovereign God alone. The many books on revival seem torn between these two views.

What are the circumstances or causes of revival? If Christians really lined up firmly for God, roused themselves from their lethargy, and suddenly repentance and obedience became the norm in the churches, would revival necessarily follow? There's no harm in repentance and obedience!

The churches and Christian families must prepare themselves through repentance and godly living for such an event yet cast themselves on God alone and ask for His gracious provision of revival. It is in His mercy and sovereign grace to give what we do not deserve.[6]

Dr. John Armstrong, in *True Revival,* gives six marks of true revival as follows:

1. An awareness of God's presence
2. An uncommon readiness to hear God
3. A deep conviction over one's sin
4. A heartfelt repentance
5. An extraordinary concern for others…
6. …bringing about true change.[7]

This seems to offer the best description of true revival that I have read. Also, if these marks of true revival are correct, we are not yet seeing a revival on the scope of a great awakening at this time. His definition of true revival is as follows:

> A sovereign intervention of the Holy Spirit of God, the Spirit of Pentecost, sweeping across the visible church in blessing the normal ministry of the Word of God, and prayer, in the lives of both believers and new converts. It is best understood as an extraordinarily intense season of blessing upon normal New Testament Christianity.[8]

If this is an accurate description of true revival, and I believe it is, what circumstances may lead to this changed condition, if any?

THE GULF WAR REVIVAL

During the Gulf War, I served as an Army Chaplain and we experienced a revival throughout the theatre where thousands of American soldiers and servicemen found Christ as Savior.

One circumstance in my mind that seemed to contribute to this changed atmosphere in the U.S. Army was the anxiety and fear of the unknown. This causes many to seek the Lord for personal security and salvation who might not have otherwise done so.

We could not describe that time in the Gulf War as a great awakening in the sense of the great revivals in American and church history which brought about such long-term and permanent change, but we did experience an awakening.

In the 101st Air Assault Division, one of our elite combat divisions, there were hundreds who received water baptism after accepting Jesus Christ as personal Lord and Savior. Many others professed salvation but waited until return to the U.S. to follow up with their baptisms. Chaplain (MG) Major Matthew Zimmerman, Army Chief of Chaplains, reported that several thousand were baptized while in the Gulf War theatre.[9]

There is a saying in the Church that "man's extremity is God's opportunity." This axiom seemed to work during the Gulf War as many turned to Christ.

There were many long seasons of prayer and intense Bible study among the troops. Almost every night after work duty, I would hold a prayer meeting and Bible study in my tent for sometimes dozens of seeking soldiers.

This was not uncommon for other Chaplains. There was nothing else to do in the remote desert of Saudi Arabia. There were no bars or other places to go. The Chaplains provided some of the best entertainment and programs.

I noticed how much easier it was to carry out the Lord's work. Small efforts by the chaplains seemed to bring in bigger results and a greater harvest. Many soldiers were ready to listen and wanted prayer. Soldiers would spend their free time simply reading the Bible, for no other reason than to enjoy and learn God's Word.

MAN'S EXTREMITY

Perhaps the circumstance missing to precede revival today is "man's extremity" I have mentioned. We are just "too comfortable in Zion." John R. Price, in his book on revival, *America at the Crossroads*, points out that every revival in American history was preceded or followed by a war or depression. He observes:

> God has allowed financial collapse in America during four critical times in our history. Each panic was followed by war. These events were all followed or accompanied by national spiritual awakenings and sweeping national repentance.

God's Word tells us that He expects us to respond to His
chastening. Our failure to respond won't result in less
chastening, but more. The stage is set in America for just
that. We get to decide, will it be repentance or repression?[10]

The layman's prayer revival started in New York City in
1858 and was followed by the Depression and Civil War of
that same era. The American Revolution followed the First
Great Awakening of the 1740's.

Price goes on to note that depressions or severe economic
downturns seem to spark revivals, if indeed we are allowed
to describe the spiritual awakening by God as caused by
some human event. But the God of revival may also bring
about the economic downturn, which causes men and
women to seek Him with greater intensity than before.

World War I was preceded by the Revival of 1905 and in
Europe by the Welch Revival of 1904. These same revivals
then spiritually prepare the nation and the Church for wars
that may follow after some time.[11] This is the kind of
extremity we experienced in the Gulf War.

OUR DESPERATE NEED FOR REVIVAL IN AMERICA

The Church can't demand revival, although revival is
greatly needed. Even when such an outpouring of power and
God's Spirit does not occur, the Lord still takes great care to
preserve a faithful godly remnant of those who trust Him.

In the Old Testament Book of Malachi one text describes
this process. The Prophet Malachi writes:

Those who feared the Lord spoke to one another, and the
Lord listened and heard them; So a book of remembrance
was written before Him for those who fear the Lord and who
meditate on His name (Malachi 3:16-18).

During such times, Christians will learn that obedience and faithfulness to God is its own reward.

If and when a new great awakening occurs in American churches and families, there will be long-term blessings and residual effects that remain with churches, families and communities for years and even decades afterward.

American Christians and church historians are familiar with the impact the First and Second Great Awakenings had on our nation. I have already described the long-term impact the Mordecai Ham Crusade of 1930 and accompanying revival had on Augusta, Georgia, for years afterward.

Besides the theological improvements in the churches, thirst for an experiential knowledge of Christ by many Christians and new converts that accompanies revival, there are also social and cultural changes. Many vices and sins rampant in a community before revival, such as alcoholism, illicit drugs and prostitution, are literally swept away by the power of God's Spirit in a revival as sinners are changed overnight. Confession of sin and restitution takes place.

Historically the churches took a new interest in fulfilling the Great Commission as a result of revivals or awakenings. Foreign mission agencies grew or were started during past revivals.

Many new educational enterprises were founded as a result of the First Great Awakening such as the College of New Jersey (now Princeton University).

Christians enjoying the blessings of a great revival in our time should also see a need to fulfill the second component of the Great Commission in Matthew 28:20, which calls the Church to carry out the teaching or educational role for their members, children and converts.

In early American awakenings the emphasis was on higher or seminary education, not as much on primary education. The reason for this was that church schools and home schooling were the dominant method of education prior to the 1840's before the various state governments took over the then-existing Christian schools or sponsored state-run schools.

A NEW EMPHASIS ON CHRISTIAN EDUCATION
It is critical that Christian families and churches today begin to build a Biblical theology for home schooling and Christian schools and see the error of state-run public schools.

A revival, or indeed, a Third Great Awakening, if the Lord has mercy and grants one, will spawn a whole new emphasis upon Christian education of children as a means to fulfill the Great Commission in our time.

If this revival were to occur now with the weak or non-existent theology of education held by so many Christian leaders and pastors, there would be some danger that the Church would not respond properly and seize the moment to start up or renew Christian schools.

Home schooling might not receive the support from pastors, major ministries and denominational leaders it deserves.

Some pastors and Christian leaders would simply be strengthened in an unbalanced view of "salt and light theology." They would become even more aggressive insisting that Christian children remain in state-sponsored government schools.

Many are concerned for needy children in government schools and rightfully so. If revival were to come now and sweep through the government schools, as it has in some few cases already, some temporary good would be done.

Since many Christians today don't have a Biblical theology of education, they would think this revival represented a permanent change and that the government schools themselves would be changed.

We do not see any reversal in the many Supreme Court decisions that have excluded Christianity from these schools. We do not see any changes in funding, in curriculum or teacher training and certification. It is all in the hands of humanists who will simply step aside for a time until the revival has run its course.

Predictably, the humanists would go back to indoctrination of new converts and Christian children who stayed behind in Pharaoh's schools. This would mean that the Church would have been tricked by humanists once again.

We must insist that education and teaching is not a function of the state but belongs to the family with assistance from the Church. As long as Christians accept the state-run, "public-school" model as legitimate, any revival in these schools will be temporary and not have the kind of impact seen in the Great Awakening.

Will the pragmatic thinking that controls so many Christian leaders today control the Church during revival and bring about this weak result? If so, the results will be too short-lived to create the permanent changes we need to repair our families, revitalize our churches and turn our culture around.

WE NEED TO EMPTY PUBLIC SCHOOLS OF CHRISTIAN CHILDREN…NOW

We should pray that if a major revival should occur it would *empty* Pharaoh's schools, not simply give them a temporary reprieve. In past great awakenings new dynamic Christian educational institutions were born. It is our hope that God will prepare His Church, especially the pastors and Christian leaders, to seize the moment and institute new dynamic Christian schools, support current ones and encourage home schools that will train a stronger generation in the days of the revival to come.

The Psalmist says, "Thy people shall be willing in the day of your power" (Psalm 110:3a). When revival occurs, the people of God more easily accept pastoral leadership. Let it be done to renew the family's and Church's historic role in education.

STUDY: EDUCATION IS A PUBLIC PRIORITY

According to a recent Heritage Foundation study, education has led the polls as this country's top priority for the past four years.[12] It is a much higher priority among the general public than abortion and campaign finance reform.

Proponents of movements such as Goals 2000 and the school-to-work movement have been able to exploit the sense among a huge percentage of the public that something is seriously wrong with state-sponsored schools. Unfortunately, up until now their "solutions" to the problems have been seen in terms of reforming the schools, *always* spending more money, advocating "school choice" with or without vouchers, implementing national standards, conducting seminars on character education, and so on.

Hopefully by now the core problem with every one of these approaches has become clear. They offer a pittance of cosmetic improvements but retain both the secular-humanist worldview and institutional state sponsorship.

It is unfortunate that the vast majority of conservatives do not grasp the problem at this level. The Republican Party, to which Christians flocked a few short years ago, had the resources to become a boon to Christian schools and home schooling. But the Republican Party leadership has invariably opted for one variety or another of "school choice" or come out in support of character education, all of which are placebos offered to remedy the condition.

It is disconcerting to watch the GOP struggle with the issue of what to do about the ongoing failure of state-sponsored schools. It is a little like watching cowboys being pursued by Indians in an old Tom Mix movie. If they don't stop and rest their horses, the horses will eventually die from exhaustion, and they will be captured. But if they do stop, the Indians will catch them even sooner, and they will still be captured. So they just ride on and hope for a miracle, which, of course, happily occurs, but only in the movies.

The plan presented in this book, the Exodus Mandate, offers the cowboys a third option, letting them save their horses and still avoid capture by the Indians. This third option is to embrace a fully Christian, God-centered, world-view and use it as the basis for education in the context of home schooling and private Christian schools with assistance from the local churches.

Support for "school choice," despite our criticisms, indicates a shallow awareness of the problems. It is our hope that we will eventually be able to tap into the energy that is motivating many reforms, such as their belief that replacing values clarification with character education is sufficient. It is our hope that we can eventually *redirect* the energy that is motivating such reforms.

HOME SCHOOLING: DIAMOND IN THE ROUGH

One of the areas that makes the Exodus Mandate vision reasonable and possible is the rapid growth of home schooling in today's evangelical Christian community. Evangelical Christians make up approximately 70% of all home schoolers today, and most of those remaining are traditional Catholics. These respective religious communities have a shared Christian worldview on many issues. Presently home schooling is growing at a faster rate among Catholics as they find an alternative to state-sponsored schools and to their own historically strong parochial school system that in some cases has taken on a secular or liberal bias.

In 1993, home schooling became legal in all 50 states.

THE GROWTH OF THE HOME-SCHOOL MOVEMENT

According to current estimates, home schooling is growing from 8 to 15 percent annually, although specific rates vary from region to region.[13] In some regions, the growth rate is higher.

The Charlotte World reported that "home school enroll-ment increased by 21% in North Carolina, according to the state Division on Non-Public Education." Further they report that "home school enrollment has risen by 57% in the past two years and by 115% in the past four years" accord-ing to figures released July 27, 2001.

Religion continues to be the major reason North Carolina families choose to home school, with 70.2% listing their school as religious-based, and thus choose to avoid subjects ranging from evolution to homosexuality.[14]

Some estimates suggest that by the 2010 school year, at a modest 7% annual growth, approximately 3 million chil-dren will be home educated. This will represent six to seven percent of the total K-12 population.[15] This prediction does not consider the possibility of an acceleration of growth as the deterioration of the government schools becomes more pronounced.

Estimates of the actual numbers of home-schooled chil-dren and teenagers are hard to determine. The National Home Education Research Institute, run by Dr. Brian Ray, himself a Christian home-school parent, estimated in 2000 that "between 1.2 and 1.6 million school-age children—about 3 percent—are currently home schooled."[16]

The U.S. Department of Education estimated the number of home-schooled children at 850,000. But, most authorities in the home-school movement believe this to be well below the actual figure, because many home-schooling families do not register with their local school districts.

Now that legal rights and the freedom to home school children have been won in most court battles, many families do not even register with their local home-school private associations or support groups.

Writing in *The Atlantic Monthly*, Margaret Talbot reported:

> Patricia Lines, a former U.S. Department of Education researcher who has studied home schooling since the mid-1980's, points to evidence, such as Florida's annual survey of home schoolers, suggesting that the population of kids learning at home is growing by 15 to 20 percent a year.
>
> ...the rise of home schooling is one of the most significant social trends of the past half century.[17]

This is the quiet revolution, perhaps the forerunner of a new Christian Reformation, and over time it will inevitably effect our entire national social, moral and intellectual life.

Noted national culture and political observer David Gergen, Editor-at-large for *U.S. News & World Report*, called attention to this hidden home-school revolution.

He noted the recent contribution of Jedediah Purdy, home schooled in the foothills of West Virginia until a young man. Purdy went on to write an amazing book, *For Common Things: Irony, Trust, and Commitment in America Today*. Gergen writes:

> Critics wondered: Just who is this 24-year old kid who has given a fresh voice to the Y generation? It turns out that Purdy is a graduate of Harvard and is now studying law.... at Yale. But the twist that caught people's attention was the fact that Purdy grew up in the ragged foothills of West

Virginia and, until he became a young man, was taught at
home by his parents.[18]

Gergen also notes that pundits and scholars have largely
ignored the contributions of home schooling until now. It
was considered a fringe movement encouraged mostly by
white evangelicals who have never been accorded the
respect they deserve.

Relegating home schooling and its advocates to the
fringes of American society is no longer an option. The contribution of Purdy

forced critics to take another look at the issue. Was something going on there that they were missing? This month, the
answer came in: Yes indeed, home schooling is a phenomenon that deserves a far more serious look.[19]

Also pushing home schooling onto the national scene in a
new way was the *Scripps Howard National Spelling Bee*
won by 12-year-old George Abraham Thampy, of an
Evangelical Free Church family originally from Kerala,
India. Gergen observed that Thampy had been challenged
by *another* home schooler for first place.

The previous year the National Geography Bee was won
by David Beihl, a home-schooled 8th grader from the small
town of Saluda, S.C., also from a Christian family.

In 2001, yet another home schooled teenager, Sean
Conley, won the Spelling Bee. Three of the ten finalists
were home schooled.[20]

As home-schooled teenagers are accepted into prestigious Ivy League universities such as Harvard and Yale, the
success stories are starting to mount up. A major 1999 study
of home schooled students conducted by the Home School
Legal Defense Network but directed by an independent

researcher, Dr. Lawrence Rudner of the ERIC Clearinghouse on Assessment and Evaluation, concluded:

> Home school students do exceptionally well when compared with the nationwide average. They score significantly higher than their public and private school counterparts in every area and grade level.[21]

Educators and secular scholars are therefore no longer ignoring Christian home schooling. Home schooling families, however, have often experienced opposition from the dominant culture, and there are doubtless even more rough waters ahead.

The home-schooling movement, in the capable hands of Christian evangelical families, is slowly but steadily building up an alternative to secular-humanist culture and society. Some are willing to recognize its achievements, however begrudgingly.

Margaret Talbot observes at the conclusion of her insightful article in *The Atlantic Monthly*:

> Christian home schoolers embody a coherent, living critique of mainstream state-sponsored education and child-rearing that can be bracing, a model of carefully negotiated, mildly irritating separateness, of being *in* but not *of* modern consumer society. For the rest of us, the tensions that creates may be the most useful thing about them.[22]

This is an optimistic evaluation of the future relationship between home-school families and the dominant culture. Most home-school families educate their children for a combination of personal, religious and academic reasons. Margaret Talbot's conclusion suggests indirectly that the dominant culture produced by secularism run amuck in state-sponsored schools and the "new counterculture" being created by Christian home schooling will eventually come into direct conflict.

Home-schooled graduates, who not only reject the secular-materialist worldview but also can outperform their counterparts coming out of state-sponsored schools in every category, will set the stage.

The dominant secular culture has already become notoriously intolerant of dissenting philosophical opinions and worldviews. The intolerance of political correctness is well known. Eventually, as it becomes more and more perceived as a threat to the dominant culture, Christian home schooling will become a target.

HOME SCHOOLERS: MARINES ON THE BEACHHEAD

In my judgment, however, as a longtime participant in home schooling, many Christian families will not give up this newfound "pearl of great price." They will weather severe criticism and even harsh persecution. Talbot welcomes the critique of modern secular culture embodied in home schooling. Others doubtless will not.

It is very possible, however, that home schoolers will have awakened a hunger and even a godly jealousy among their non-Christian neighbors and family members. They will have created a healthy home environment. They will have nurtured in their maturing children the values that most families with children in state-sponsored schools can only dream about.

Moreover, home-schooled children will have proven to surpass children in state-sponsored schools academically. These, of course, are benefits of home schooling, but they are not the primary reason Christians must choose either to home school or place their children in private Christian schools. The choice of Christians to provide Christian education for their children is based on Scriptural commands. The results of this obedience to God in the matter of educating children are already in, however.

Home schooling, as well as Christian education, therefore, presents a deep and bold witness for Jesus Christ, revealing before the secular culture the superiority of God's ways for an orderly family life. Sadly, many Christians have not yet awakened to these realities.

Home-schooling Christian families need to be a witness to their fellow Christians who accept the worldly and secular model of family life and education, as shown by their willingness to keep their children in state-sponsored schools. As we have seen, there is abundant evidence available now on the destruction of the Christian home due to these unwise choices.

Christian home schooling has become a strong tangible witness for Jesus Christ both in and outside the church. Both the larger Christian community and the unbelieving secular culture are equally in need of such a Biblical witness.

HOME SCHOOLING: WHERE ARE THE CLERGY?

What is the direction of the clergy on home schooling? One small example may show a trend particularly among Southern Baptists.

At Southeastern Baptist Theological Seminary in Wake Forest, N.C., over a hundred faculty, staff and student families have chosen to home school their children.

Seminary President Dr. Paige Patterson said that if he were rearing his children today he would home school them "for the sake of relationship, academic accomplishment, safety and Christian commitment."[23] I have noted a small national trend that many evangelical pastors are becoming committed to home schooling their children, or enrolling them in private Christian schools.

These same pastors have congregations where the dominant pattern of education is still leaving children in state-sponsored schools.

What we pastors live and practice we believe, and eventually what we practice and believe we will also teach and preach.

In 1977 Gail and I started home schooling for Scriptural, personal, and academic reasons. We did not encourage others for several years to follow our leadership until we had proven God's ways and seen the blessing and benefits in our children.

Many of God's congregational shepherds are even now discovering what my wife and I discovered in the late 1970's. They will not be able to contain their newfound joy at the benefits of giving their own children a Christian education at home.

Pastors will also begin to teach and preach on God's Word concerning the education of children. When new groups of pastors begin this, the new Christian Reformation in America will have begun in earnest!

THE SECOND COMING OF THE
SOUTHERN BAPTIST CONVENTION

Historically, and tragically, Southern Baptists have been among the strongest supporters of public schools. While a national denomination, the Southern Baptist Convention (SBC) is still largely concentrated in the Southern states.

From its formation in 1845 until today, the SBC has been a virtual establishment religion in many Southern communities. In South Carolina, for example, 20% of the population are members of a SBC church. This is typical across much of the Southeast.

Even in California 1,850 SBC churches exist with a membership of 500,000. There are an estimated 16 million Southern Baptists nationally, making them America's largest Protestant denomination.

In the Southeast, members of SBC churches, especially in small towns, have staffed government schools as teachers and administrators.

Since the 1962 and 1963 Supreme Court rulings against prayer and Bible reading in state-sponsored schools, many SBC members have complained and chaffed under the growing secularism of the public schools.

Because most SBC Christians haven't had a strong theology or history of Christian education, the approach of most in the SBC has been conservative reform of state-sponsored schools or passing resolutions to put prayer back in them.

Both the Alabama and South Carolina State SBC conventions have passed resolutions to put prayer back in state-sponsored public schools. These weak approaches have failed over and over again and are largely ignored by legal and political authorities. The newspapers print the news of the resolutions, but nothing happens.

In the last 20 years, however, there has been a resurgence of conservative theology in the SBC. Southern Baptists, as a whole, had always been more conservative than their seminary faculties and administrators in the modern era.

Much of the denominational machinery and especially the seminaries had become theologically liberal starting in the 1940's and 1950's. There were some notable exceptions. The conservative theological resurgence began with the election of Dr. Adrian Rogers as President of the SBC in 1979 and had been largely completed by the late 1990's.

SBC seminaries are now thoroughly conservative, and many students and faculty are home schooling or placing their children in Christian schools.[24] The young preachers coming out of SBC seminaries are now more conservative theologically than many of their predecessors.

In the past, most evangelical higher education and seminary instruction offered classes in Christian education as Sunday school and weekend training programs. K-12 Christian schools have not been in the purview of Christian education instruction in most evangelical seminaries.

Now, some of these same seminaries have begun to offer classes with a balanced Biblical exposition of Christian education as more than Sunday school, Bible studies or youth ministry.

NEEDED: SBC COMMITMENT ON THIS ISSUE

In 1997, Southern Baptists hired an Association of Christian Schools International (ACSI) official, Dr. Glenn Schultz, as Director of Christian School Resources, Lifeway, the SBC Publishing and Education Division, Nashville, Tennessee.

Dr. Schultz published an important book for SBC Baptists in 1998 entitled *Kingdom Education*. This book deserves wide circulation, especially in SBC circles.

Dr. Schultz is developing Christian school curriculum and materials for SBC churches setting up Christian schools. He also works with the Southern Baptist Association of Christian Schools (www.sbacs.org) Executive Director John Chandler.

There are now 600 SBC churches with Christian schools, and the SBACS was adding an average of 8-10 new schools per year through the 1990's.

This growth has been slow, but according to Chandler there are plans to increase growth of Christian schools in the SBC in the next decade. But there are 42,000 individual SBC churches in the USA, and there is room for much more growth.

The SBC confession, *The Baptist Faith and Message*, was adopted on June 14, 2000, after having undergone a revision. Article XII reads:

> The cause of education in the Kingdom of Christ is co-ordinate with the causes of missions and general benevolence, and should receive along with these the liberal support of the churches. An adequate system of Christian education is necessary for a complete spiritual program for Christ's people.[25]

While not explicitly demanding a K-12 Christian school system for SBC churches, we believe *The Baptist Faith and Message* gives support for a wider and stronger emphasis on K-12 education in the SBC.

T.C. Pinckney, 2nd Vice President of SBC, reported that the revision committee discussed the issue of home schooling and Christian schooling, and it was felt that the adopted language adequately addressed this need.

National SBC leaders such as Dr. Al Mohler, past SBC presidents such Dr. Page Patterson and Dr. Jimmy Draper are supportive of increased growth of Christian schools and home schooling in SBC churches.

Dr. Jack Graham, pastor of the large Prestonwood Baptist Church in Dallas, Texas, has a large Christian school and is vocal in support of the SBC moving still more decisively into Christian schooling.

Recently elected at the June 13, 2001, SBC National Convention, Pinckney, Brig. General USAF (Ret.), spoke out in favor of Christian schools and home schooling at the September 18, 2001 meeting of the SBC Executive Committee.

Pinckney is using his tenure in this office to urge SBC churches to begin Christian schools or to home school their children.

These trends are strong, coming from the SBC seminaries, publishing houses and senior denominational leadership in the SBC. But it is still too early to tell if the majority of the SBC will abandon their longstanding support for state-sponsored public schools.

Bad habits and weak theologies die hard. The SBC is not a monolithic or hierarchical denomination. No one can command SBC churches to practice this kind of Christian education to make it uniform throughout the denomination. The local SBC churches are autonomous.

Still the direction of the SBC makes it hopeful that the majority of the SBC will gradually adopt a theology of Christian education stressing the need for private Christian schools and home schooling, and that this could become the norm for Southern Baptists sometime in this decade. This would give our movement strong credibility.

T.C. Pinckney himself thinks it will take longer than a decade for many SBC churches to transition into Christian schools or home schooling.

As the SBC grows more and more involved in developing K-12 Christian education, it will set an example and lead its smaller sister evangelical denominations in the same direction. Because of its size and influence, the SBC can provide important leadership to the entire Church in America.

As goes the Church, so goes the nation. The SBC has come to the kingdom for such a time as this. Will Southern Baptists rise to the occasion?   ∎

> *"The only thing that is going to save us from the abyss, is a God-sent, national, spiritual revival and the only way that is going to come, if it does at all, is if God is pleased enough to send it, and we cannot manipulate Him into doing so."*
>
> —Cal Thomas

CHAPTER NINE

PROSPECTS FOR THE EXODUS MANDATE PROJECT

OBJECTIONS TO EXODUS MANDATE ANSWERED

LOOKING TO THE FUTURE

The Exodus Mandate Project proposes to solve the problems created by state-sponsored education by encouraging as many Christian parents as possible to remove their children from government schools and either home school them or place them in private Christian schools.

We have argued throughout this book that "reforming" state-sponsored education is simply not an option, because the problem is not with this or that version of state-sponsored education but with the very idea of state-sponsored education itself. It is unbiblical and was not a part of this country's original constitutional vision.

It is actually an interloper, a renegade form of education that has been a major instrument in the hands of secular humanists who have almost succeeded in de-Christianizing American society.

It is now necessary, as both Marshall Fritz and Sheldon Richman have put it, to *separate state and school*. It is time for a new Exodus, a Christian Exodus out of Pharaoh's school system and into the Promised Land of home schooling and private Christian schools. I believe Christians will find it a good land, full of milk and honey.

The Exodus Mandate project, however, requires a definite change in thinking among the majority of Christians—what Thomas S. Kuhn calls a "paradigm shift." Most Christians have accepted state-sponsored education despite its many problems, and have sought to "reform" government schools.

Exodus Mandate asks Christians to "think outside the box" provided by the idea of the government school and embrace a new paradigm for Christian education which accepts our Biblical mandate to be the guide for the education of our own children.

A new paradigm for Christian education such as the Exodus Mandate Project will inevitably raise many questions both inside and outside the Church. Any new invention or mode of thought or major social reformation raises immediate objections. Doubters and nay-sayers are always present saying, "It can't be done; it's just too radical," or "It's too early," or "It's too late." They say, "Society will not accept this new idea or invention or way of thinking." Most people are normally comfortable with the status quo, good or bad.

WHEN NEW IDEAS COME ON THE SCENE

So let's begin by imagining when the first automobiles appeared on the scene. Objections were rife and even logical for that time. Some would say, "The new contraption called the automobile will never be practical for most; it will just be a toy for the wealthy few." Others would say, "We can't really get behind such a new invention because it will wreck the horse and buggy industry" or "they won't be able to locate the oil needed to run more than a few hundred such items." "They're not practical for travel because there are not roads for automobiles to travel on."

Similar objections appeared upon the advent of computers. The original computers, of course, were room-sized objects that had to be kept refrigerated. With the appearance of miniaturization technology and the idea of the personal computer, some computer leaders responded with something like, "What would an ordinary person want a computer for?" This kind of question now seems comical in this age of email and Internet activity.

We are indeed standing on the other side of a multitude of such paradigm shifts, in which new ideas, inventions or reforms had to struggle for acceptance. In *The Structure of Scientific Revolutions*, Kuhn documents a number of reasons why new ideas and paradigms are subject to resistance. In addition to its being unfamiliar, the new paradigm may seem not to solve the problems it sets out to solve. It may employ such different language and concepts—such a different foundation from the old—as to be difficult to understand for those who haven't simply grown up with it.

A new paradigm may need a certain period of time or "room to breathe," to grow and develop, before it can bear its full fruit. Kuhn's area of expertise was hard physical science and its history. He stressed that even decisions within communities of physicists to embrace a new paradigm such as that of Michael Faraday in electricity or Albert Einstein in special relativity come down to individual acts of faith that the new approach will succeed. How much more so in a "softer" field such as education?

With Kuhn's work as background, it will certainly be helpful to offer a clear account of the problems the Exodus Mandate Project faces, expressed as objections. I have encountered five basic objections to the Exodus Mandate Project, which I will try to answer briefly:

1. The theological objection
2. The financial objection
3. The educational objection
4. The socialization objection
5. The neglect of the poor objection

OBJECTIONS TO EXODUS MANDATE ANSWERED

The theological objection. Some Christian friends object that if we take our Christian children out of state-run schools we are not being good Christians by being "salt and light" in society (Matthew 5:13-16). We have addressed this topic briefly in earlier sections in this book. The need for Christians being salt and light is valid theology but is misapplied in the area of education.

State-sponsored schools are religious in nature now, but the religion is pagan and humanistic. Christian children lack the experience to be salt and light in the sense Matthew specifies. They are not equipped to recognize, much less resist, secular-humanist indoctrination and pressures at young ages.

Our argument is that Christian families who home school or send their children to Christian schools are doing a far better job of preparing their children to be salt and light, as these children are better equipped in Christian doctrine, Bible study, prayer and worldview instruction. When they reach college or young adulthood, the students of Christian education are more able to handle the pressures of higher education and serving Christ in a fallen world.

I have encountered some youth ministers who objected to the Exodus Mandate Project. Youth ministries such as Young Life, Youth for Christ and other high school outreaches to youth depend upon a few strong young men and women insiders who attend the local government school to give them access to the many non-Christian youth in these schools.

Some view the idea of a Christian children's Exodus as a threat to successful outreach and evangelism in government schools. These ministers and youth evangelists are sincere and carry out excellent ministries. Their concerns have caused me to do some soul-searching and looking for answers in prayer.

My first response is that we cannot hold an entire generation of Christian children hostage in the state-run schools in order to enable ministries to carry out youth evangelism.

Second, if the Christian children began to leave government schools in large numbers, this would not restrict the outreach to youth in those same schools and through alternative means such as clubs, sporting events and neighborhood outreaches. God is not restricted to any one method to reach children or adults for Christ.

If government schools are not a Biblical method of education for Christian children, God can still reach the non-Christian children left behind in Pharaoh's schools through prayer and various outreaches.

Child Evangelism Fellowship has used backyard Bible clubs and five-day summer clubs successfully for decades to reach younger children through neighborhood evangelism.

The Great Commission is not self-contradictory in that we must violate the teaching portion in Matthew 28:20 in order to fulfill the outreach or evangelism portion in Matthew 28:19.

God is sovereign, and He will show youth ministers and outreach ministries creative and successful techniques for reaching non-Christian youth while reducing the risk of harm to Christian youth by keeping them in Pharaoh's schools. We should not embrace a non-Scriptural approach to education in order to reach our non-Christian youth.

Also, it might prove useful to realize that one does not have to be a Christian to recognize that government schools are failing our children and our youth.

Perhaps, once the Exodus is underway, many non-Christian parents will take a second and then a third look at our Christian schools and home schooling. They will see children and youth who are academically well ahead of their government-schooled counterparts.

They will see children and youth who are motivated, well-behaved, and respectful of their teachers and their parents. The schools themselves will be free of drugs and violence, and free of the latest untested fads coming out of secular education departments.

Eventually non-Christian observers might recognize the source of these achievements and discover the true liberation that is to be found in Jesus Christ. In this way, the Exodus Mandate Project becomes a powerful witness for the Christian Gospel.

It is important that those in charge of Christian schools be alert to this and be willing to answer whatever questions come their way. In the meantime, some Christian schools may even organize as outreach schools for searching non-Christian youth.

2. The financial objection. This is the second most common objection I hear, and is very often a real need. I do believe many more Christian families would consider Christian schools if they could afford them.

Most middle class families could afford to home school if they were not dependent upon the mother's supplementary income. One helpful approach is to reorient family budgets and downsize in some areas, so that home schooling is a real possibility. Other relatives and grandparents, too, can lend financial assistance if they are able.

Many have a sound financial legacy, and could fund the education of their grandchildren at the K-12 level rather than college.

Some parents do not home school their children or send them to a Christian school because they do not see it as a command of the Lord, only an option or choice. Convictions and prayerfully seeking God for help will bring positive results for many families.

What God commands He can provide, but families may need to seek this in prayer. I have known families who sought the Lord in prayer to be able to afford a Christian school when, before prayer, it was a practical and financial impossibility. Several years later it was a reality.

Both private and business scholarships for Christian schools should be encouraged in the community and in the churches.

Pastors especially should be open to allowing the readily available facilities in many churches to be used by newly formed Christian schools or for home-school activities. By being able to use available facilities instead of going to the expense of building new ones, Christian schools should be able to keep the costs to parents down.

Businesses and corporations interested in both academically skilled and morally upright graduates should take a serious interest in investing in these schools with both scholarships and donations.

It is sad to see some businesses and corporations helping fund the failed state-run "public school" system. This is good money chasing bad, and is a poor strategy for businesses both economically and educationally. Finances are a genuine obstacle for many families but can easily be an excuse for others. It is a matter of where their priorities lie. Christian families need to search their hearts and minds to see where priorities are in their family.

3. The educational objection. This was a stronger objection in past decades but has lessened in recent years. There was time that many Christians stayed in the public schools because they thought they were academically much stronger than the private Christian schools. With the abundant evidence, however, of Christian-educated youth being far ahead of their government-schooled counterparts, this objection proves to be groundless.

Home-schooled youth have repeatedly won contests such as national spelling championships, have made some of the highest scores recorded on standardized tests such as the SAT and have been admitted to the most prestigious universities in the country, such as Harvard.

There is simply no evidence that Christian children will get an inferior education in a Christian school, or by being home schooled. All the evidence points to the contrary.

The view has changed in many communities, and Christian schools are often seen as academically superior to public schools.

With the shift in public schools, away from academic preparation to work preparation, more Christian families will gravitate to Christian schools to insure a rigorous academic experience for their children.

Along similar lines, some will object that government schools provide band and multiple athletic opportunities. Some of the larger Christian schools, however, are now providing superior sports and band.

Home-school state associations are now providing sports and even teams competing in leagues. These are trends that are bound to accelerate in coming years as the Exodus Mandate Project moves forward, and more and more children are educated in this new Christian educational environment. In the meantime, which is really more important: the bassoon or the Bible, basketball or the Bible?

4. The socialization objection. This objection used to plague home schoolers in the early years. Our case can serve as an example. The objection usually went something like this: When a family recovered from the shock of learning we were home schooling our children, they would usually ask two questions: "They let you do that?" In other words, does the state really allow us to teach our children at home?

Then they would ask, "What about socialization?" It was hard to explain that socialization was a principal reason to home school, but we tried.

One of the benefits of home schooling was that our children became self-starters and independent thinkers. All of them developed into leaders as well who could comfortably converse with adults and those outside of their age group.

There is a difference between socialization and both peer dependency and groupthink. Well socialized youth have the maturity to get along with others, and they have the educational foundation for succeeding in a market-based economy and as leaders in their communities.

Peer dependency and groupthink, on the other hand, result in youth who cannot think independently and will tend to follow the crowd, right or wrong.

Group projects, for example, are one of the educational fads emanating from secular education departments in recent years. They reduce a child's ability to think and learn on his own. Peer dependency and groupthink have not been a problem with our children. Their absence, we have discovered, has proven to be a major advantage of home schooling.

Now, when we talk to some Christian families who send their children to government schools we ask, "Aren't you worried about the socialization in the public schools?"

Most Christian families know there is crime, drug abuse, wrong sex education, subtle, humanist indoctrination and other forms of moral danger to their children in these schools. They no doubt feel some guilt about leaving them there. They are right to be worried about how their children will be socialized, with constant worries that they will "fall in with the wrong crowd."

They are also right to be worried that because of the application of faddish techniques their children will graduate with their cognitive abilities maimed for life, courtesy of the groupthink of group projects. The socialization objection is a concern now only to uninformed Christian families.

5. The neglect of the poor objection. This is the most common objection we receive when we speak of replacing the state-run public schools with private, free-market schools, Christian schools and home schools. It is similar, at first glance, to the financial objection, but cuts more deeply.

Many middle-class and wealthy families can financially afford to escape the public schools, but the poor, especially ethnic minorities, may see themselves as trapped in government schools. This is a valid question, and one with many unknowns.

When we discuss such a major educational paradigm shift as the Exodus Mandate Project proposes to inaugurate, it is inevitable that such questions will arise. We do, however, attempt a response.

First, we believe that the poor and ethnic minorities are more tragically underserved by government schools than middle class families. The schools tend to be worse, with drugs more available and violence being epidemic.

While we don't support the choice model as the best means to escape government schools, political polling for school choice shows some minorities and the poor to have a higher support for vouchers than middle-class, white America. Desire for school choice is slightly higher among some Democratic constituencies than among some Republican constituencies.[1] This is an interesting result; however, danger is lurking around the corner.

Those with fewer resources to escape government schools might be even more tempted by the minefields on the road to the Promised Land we discussed in Chapter Six.

Charter schools might prove very tempting to inner-city families. Vouchers, too, might enable poor families to send their children to a private, Christian school. The problems inherent in both vouchers and charter schools, however, vastly outweigh whatever temporary advantages they might create.

These problems might even be magnified by the fact that desperation of poor people who are serious about their children's education might lead them to overlook the likelihood that over the long run they will have even less control. The poor might be severely tested in their faith if vouchers and charter schools become widely available as options.

There are alternatives. Author Vox Day recently discussed the possibility of home-schooling families being willing to assume responsibility for the education of additional children from disadvantaged backgrounds, educating them in the same way, according to the same methods right along with their own children. This way a "home-schooling underground railroad" could be created that would enable an increasing number of poor children to obtain a Christian education their parents might not be able to pay for otherwise.

Home-schooling families should encourage such efforts, and the kinds of educational units created could well form a kind of bridge between home schooling itself and the private Christian school.[2]

Indeed, as the Exodus Mandate Project picks up momentum and the market begins to respond to a variety of demands on the part of Christian parents who want Christian education for their children and youth, a variety of different kinds of institutions is likely to emerge.

Some families will home school their children; some will send their children to Christian schools; and no doubt other kinds of small, Christian home-based schools will begin to develop as Christian people respond to the need for Christian education of children and youth.

Moreover, the idea of private Christian education is gaining support in the African-American Christian community. Christian educators Drs. James Carper and Jack Layman, in their monograph on Black Christian academies, describe the important private, Christian-school movement now growing nationally among African-American Christians.[3] New Christian school start-ups are taking place regularly in this community mostly within Black Baptist and Pentecostal Churches.[4]

In some areas demand for private Christian schools is higher in the African-American Christian community than among the white Christian community.

It is, of course, important to note that Christian education and the desire for private Christian schools is neither a white issue nor a black issue, but a Christian issue.

Some on the liberal-left have claimed for years that the move toward private Christian schools or academies was a result of racism or "white flight". The growth of black Christian academies should help put that claim to rest. Also, in many Christian schools the minority population is growing, although there is a need for continued improvement.

Some Christian schools with high white population are rightly seeking to recruit African-American Christian students. These schools, as well as the kinds of diverse institutions likely to develop as the Exodus Mandate Project develops, are capable of working wonders at healing the breaches between the two races that have badly marred the history of this nation.

Christian men's movements such as Promise Keepers are also seeking to bring about healing and reconciliation between the various ethnic and racial groups in our diverse nation and Christian population. Promise Keepers challenges Christian men to take up their God-ordained leadership roles in their families, churches and communities. Some Christian men will see the responsibility to educate their children Biblically as a result of these challenges. This new oneness and bonding is taking place among men in the Christian community and churches and finding expression in some Christian schools.

Christian churches through their various benevolence funds and programs will need to meet the needs of some of the poor who desire a Christian education or to attend a Christian school. The Catholic parochial school system has always had a rich history of benevolence for poor families who want to attend parochial schools.

Protestant Christian schools should study this history and seek to emulate the successes of the Catholic schools in providing free or subsidized education for the poor in their parishes.

LOOKING TO THE FUTURE

According to an October, 2001, survey by the South Carolina Policy Council Education Foundation, 88 percent of its members support school choice measures, and 95 percent believe that parents should have the right to transfer children from failing public schools.

Two of their top ten issues include school choice and school accountability. In light of this, what are the prospects for Exodus Mandate, and for the complete "separation of state and school" as central to a plan to build pro-family constituencies and preserve Christian civilization in America? Let's make some observations.

LACK OF POLITICAL DIRECTION IN EDUCATION

First, both major political parties, including the new Bush Administration, are locked into the hopeless reformist agenda—either liberal reforms or conservative reforms. Both want to use the government, particularly at the federal level, to fix Pharaoh's schools. This is a failed approach, and the cause of many problems in education.

It is an unconstitutional approach as well. The U.S. Constitution nowhere mentions education as a responsibility of government at any level, much less the federal level— while the Bible names parents as having responsibility for bringing up their children in the ways of the Lord.

K-12 education is one of the top two issues in most national polls, and both major parties are equally culpable for perpetuating the problems. Unfortunately, neither the Democrats nor the Republicans have a clue what to do, and this is becoming apparent to the public, especially evangelical Christians and traditional Catholics.

President George W. Bush recently signed HR 1, the No Child Left Behind Act, into law. The Republicans allowed the Democrats to make substantial changes in the bill, offending conservatives in the GOP and conservative groups including Concerned Women for America, Family Research Council, Focus on the Family and Eagle Forum.

POLLING DATA: SUPPORT FOR PRIVATIZATION

Second, Marshall Fritz's *Alliance for the Separation of School and State* (sepschool.org) ran a poll in the fall of 1998 and discovered that 27% of the public supported his two major propositions: eliminate both compulsory attendance and tax-funded government schooling at the K-12 level.[5] Fourteen percent are strong in these positions while 13 percent are moderately strong. This poll, we should note, predates the Columbine incident and some of the other school shootings of the 1990's. Currently, some 12 to 13 percent of children (or 7 out of 52 million children) attend private, parochial or Christian schools, or are home schooled.

Estimates indicate that Christian schools and home schooling are growing at a rate of 8 to 15 percent a year. This growth is primarily in the evangelical Christian community, and also among traditional Catholics. If this rate of growth holds, by 2007, three million children or 6 to 7 percent at the K-12 level will be home schooled.

Currently 2 to 3 percent of K-12 children are being home schooled. Seventy percent are evangelical Christians; most of the rest are traditional Catholics.

Phi Delta Kappa, a public school fraternity, with assistance from the Gallup Poll, ran a similar poll in the year 2000, and it found those favoring public school reform had dropped from 72 percent in 1997 to 60 percent in 2000. Those favoring a private education model grew from 24 percent in 1997 to 34 percent in 2000.[6] This poll demonstrates that much of the public is giving up on government-school reform while being willing to turn to one of the private education options.

A major GOP candidate for Governor in South Carolina completed a poll on May 12, 2001, showing that 61 percent favored reforming state-sponsored schools while 27 percent favored private, religious or home schooling. Eleven percent were undecided. The political consultant who ran the poll informed me that this 11 percent would likely tend to favor private, religious or home schooling rather than reforming the state-sponsored schools due to the wording of the question.

This recent S.C. poll agrees with both the Phi Delta Kappa poll and Opinion Research Corporation International poll run by Marshall Fritz's organization in 1998.

In other words, it appears likely that approximately one third of the American public is favorable in principle to the Exodus Mandate / Separation of School and State vision and agenda at this crucial juncture in our history.

DISILLUSIONMENT: INABILITY TO REFORM

Third, there is an internal debate going on now in the evangelical community between the conservative reformers who want to reform the public schools and those who support the basic idea behind the Exodus Mandate Project for Christian schools and home schooling. We believe that the conservative reformers are losing out.

The Christian community is gradually moving toward the Exodus Mandate / Separation of School and State position. This mood shift is being propelled by incidents such as the Columbine killings that suggest that state-sponsored schools are no longer safe places for children and more recently by the success of the homosexual lobby in getting a foothold in public schools. There is a growing sense that the political establishment, represented by the two major parties, have no solutions to the educational crisis in this country.

MEDIA EXPOSURE IS GROWING

The national mood may be shifting toward the Exodus Mandate / Separation of School and State idea, but this is still hidden from the political analysts and pollsters. We cannot count on the support of major media outlets—the majority of corporation-owned newspapers and television networks. But there are radio programs that endorse this vision of the future of education. Dr. Laura Schlesinger's radio program, which has an audience of 10 to 12 million listeners, has been preaching against state-sponsored schools on a regular basis. She boldly urges her audience to leave state-sponsored schools and put their children in religious schools. In the year 2000, she said, in effect, that the public schools were corrupting the morals of children. On April 9, 2002, she said, "I stand with Dr. James Dobson. Take your kids out of the public schools." Rush Limbaugh's radio show has discussed this topic as well.

Radio talk host Marlon Maddoux's Point of View has had programs where government schools were exposed, and the Exodus Mandate / Separation of School and State movement promoted.

This slow shift in the public mood away from automatic support for state-sponsored schools may enable Christian-based and pro-family groups to build a new separate remnant free from manipulation and control by the major political parties, the major media and related interest groups.

Fourth, Jeremiah Films has produced a video in cooperation with Exodus Mandate entitled "Let My Children Go." This video, for which I wrote the script, has been shown with moderate success around the nation. In the last year sales of the video have slowed somewhat, but it continues to be used and promoted. Jerry Falwell played the entire video on his September 3rd, 1999, national TV program.

Caryl Matrisciana, co-producer of "Let My Children Go," was on Beverly LaHaye Live, carried by approximately 200 stations, on September 9, 1999.

Rev. Joe Morecraft, III, and I were guests on Marlon Maddoux's two-hour Point of View, carried by approximately 300 stations, on September 13, 1999.

Issues in Education (issuesineducation.org), co-hosted by Bob and Geri Boyd, has invited me as a guest on occasion.

Others are promoting the idea, such as Dr. David Noebel's Summit Ministries (summit.org), which produced a great video entitled *Clergy in the Classroom* which shows conclusively that the state-sponsored public schools are humanistic in practice and design.

Some in the secular media have become curious about Exodus Mandate. I was a guest on PBS and on News Odyssey Network, available to 33 million homes via cable.

The video and the idea itself of Christian children leaving Pharaoh's school system for the Promised Land of Christian schools and home schooling is starting to capture the imagination of many Christian families in major churches.

On July 7, 1998, I was invited to serve on a panel to discuss religion in the classroom or "When Faith and the First Amendment Clash" at the prestigious First Amendment Center at Vanderbilt University, Nashville, Tennessee.

This center was funded by a $900 million grant by Gannett newspaper chain, which also owns USA TODAY.

Dr. Charles Haynes, First Amendment Center senior scholar; Hedy Weinberg, Tennessee Executive Director of the ACLU; and Dr. Jimmy Allen, former President of the Southern Baptist Convention, were among the other panelists. John Seigenthaler, First Amendment Center founder and former official with USA TODAY, was moderator.

Instead of taking an approach like other conservative education reformists advocating the takeover of the public schools and imposing a Christian agenda in the public schools, I simply conceded defeat in the cultural wars.

I then informed the panel and audience that I was leading a ministry to help Christian children and families exit the public schools. Many in the audience, consisting of university law and education professors and public school officials from the local community, expressed deep concern that I would take such an approach. My approach was unexpected, I think, and troubling to many.

I expressed my theological position: "God gave education to the family with assistance from the Church."

I explained the spiritual, moral and academic harm coming to Christian children in public schools. The panel and my participation received strong media coverage. Several public educators at the conclusion pleaded with me not to take this approach with pleas such as, "We need Christians in public schools" and "Christians are an important part of the public school scene."

EXODUS MANDATE:
A DIRECT THREAT TO HUMANIST EDUCATORS
My own conclusion is that the humanist educators who were in the audience that day recognized that the Exodus Mandate Project was a threat to their continued dominance of the children and the culture. Several tried to talk me out of continuing with Exodus Mandate. This early experience, when our Exodus Mandate vision first confronted the public education establishment, strongly confirmed to me that we offered a winning strategy and vision for the churches and families.

OUR WINDOW OF OPPORTUNITY IS OPENING
The growing interest in Exodus Mandate / Separation of School and State in the eyes of the general public, especially the Christian public, presents Christian-education activists and pro-family groups with a window of opportunity to make use of the education issue in key ways that none of the various reformist groups understand or are willing to take.

There are thousands of volunteers poised to work on behalf of Exodus Mandate / Separation of School and State in their churches, civic groups, home-based Bible studies and communities, if they have the right leadership and the proper tools.

This effort is not political, but spiritual and educational. If various Christian organizations and pro-family groups assist in this effort by showing the videos, distributing books, tapes, articles and literature–and urge others to do so–they might be able to catch the tide of this issue as it expands over the next few years. Then, the rising tide of Christian schools and home schooling will lift all boats.

This approach might guarantee the preservation of a godly remnant capable of rebuilding the present culture from the bottom up, separate from the manipulation of politics and those who believe they can rescue the education of our children by reforming state-sponsored schools.

Also, the Christian education and pro-family groups would have accomplished the purpose of driving a Biblical and constitutional approach in K-12 education toward the forefront of other national issues. This in itself could make a permanent difference in the nation.

French author Victor Hugo said, "There is nothing so powerful as an idea whose time has come." The video "Let My Children Go" is intended to begin the job of inspiring and beginning the training of this new remnant.

THE TIME HAS COME TO LEAVE PHAROAH'S SCHOOL SYSTEM...

The time has come to leave Pharaoh's school system, the godless state-sponsored schools. It is better to drain the swamp than fight the mosquitoes.

The secular humanists saw the children as their hope for conquering our civilization. Now, we are dashing their hope and rebirthing our own—a hope built on the promise of K-12 Christian education for the future.

If major ministries like the American Family Association, Focus on the Family, Concerned Women for America and others would organize and make a general call for a children's exodus from Pharaoh's schools, I believe many Christian parents are now ready to follow the lead.

Unfortunately, up until now Christians have been fighting a rear-guard action, as secular humanists slowly gained ground whether the issue was abortion, teaching children to use condoms, or advancing a pro-homosexual agenda.

CHOOSING THE EASIER PATH TO K-12 CHRISTIAN EDUCATION

Will it be easier to put the brakes on the secular humanist agenda in state-sponsored schools, or will it be easier for us to obey God and take charge of the education of our own children? Will it be easier to get humanists to give up their radical agenda or will it be easier to get pastors to start up Christian schools? These simple questions have obvious answers.

The secular humanists have been careful planners; they have slipped their worldview into every area of state-sponsored education. State-sponsored education is their territory. They have written the rules. In our judgment it would be folly to continue to fight secular humanists on their own territory. But this is exactly what reformism attempts to do.

What we must assert is that state-sponsored education was never part of the original American vision. There are no provisions for it in the U.S. Constitution. In His revelation, the Bible, God commands Christians to take charge of the education of their children, so state-sponsored education thus counters clear Biblical mandates, as well as violates the Constitution.

STATE-SPONSORED EDUCATIONAL FAILURE

Finally, and perhaps most obviously, state-sponsored education is not working. It is turning out "graduates" who know little or nothing of history or geography, science or mathematics. Because of a fear of lethal violence, some attend schools with metal detectors at every entrance, and uniformed police roaming the halls.

It is important to realize that the secular humanism that has come to dominate state-sponsored education leads to the nihilism that produces Eric Harrises and Dylan Klebolds. Nihilism can be defined as a view that the universe is without transcendent moral significance, and we are merely animals who happen, by cosmic accident, to have achieved a certain level of cognitive ability.

Secular humanists have always maintained that we can take charge of evolution. The present trajectory of this culture suggests otherwise. Man is a sinner; only Jesus Christ offers the cure for sin. Any public policy, educational or otherwise, that shuns this basic transcendent truth is doomed to fail.

Now is the time for Christian leaders, pastors, churches and parents to step up and offer Christian schools and home schooling as the road to revival for America—the Promised Land.

This is our moment to lead America into a new Great Awakening, one of those "fullness of times" moments the Bible speaks of (Galatians 4:4) when the times, the crisis of the hour and Biblical truths, empowered by the Holy Spirit, converge to carry the day—resulting in our rescuing this culture from secular humanism. This is a battle we can only fight by going before Pharaoh and telling him, "Let my children go!"   ■

LET MY CHILDREN GO

EPILOGUE

As an amateur military historian, I love to study military battles in world history that were small yet important in their time and learn how they affect history and world events.

The Holy Scriptures often compare spiritual warfare with military confrontations in this world. Paul the Apostle, recognizing that Christians are indeed engaged in spiritual warfare, exhorts us to "put on the whole armor of God" (Ephesians 6: 13).

The Old Testament describes the great campaign to conquer the land of Canaan by General Joshua and pictures the battlefield mastery of King David.

While the modern Christian Church does not engage in physical warfare, we do engage in spiritual warfare.

Even today, political and social pundits describe the cultural war as the struggle for the family, for the schools and for the soul of a nation. Yes, we are indeed engaged in a supreme spiritual and cultural war—for the future of the Church, the family and our children.

BATTLE OF RORKE'S DRIFT
In the U.S. Army Command and General Staff College, a particular battle served as a model for how a small and inferior force could be victorious over a significantly larger one, simply by using superior tactics, unity and economy of

force. The relatively small and otherwise obscure Battle of Rorke's Drift was made into a 1964 movie entitled *Zulu*, starring Michael Caine. Most Americans have never heard of the Battle of Rorke's Drift, but it is immortalized in the folklore of British military history. To British soldiers and veterans, it is equivalent to our Battle of the Alamo, which enthralls many with its story of bravery and the hope of overcoming seemingly impossible odds or the courage to die in the attempt. The Battle of Rorke's Drift took place in Natal Province of Africa on January 22 and 23, 1879, between British troops and a large Zulu army.

Prior to the Battle of Rorke's Drift, the British army under General Lord Chelmsford had invaded Zululand and provoked a major confrontation with the Zulu nation.

THE BATTLE OF ISANDHLWANA

On January 22, 1879, at the Battle of Isandhlwana, a large force of Zulu warriors defeated a regimental size force killing 1,500 of the best British troops. Only a few British soldiers were able to escape the slaughter by riding away.

The Battle of Isandhlwana is recorded as the worst defeat in military history suffered by a modern army fighting native forces. It also stands today as the most total defeat any British force has suffered in British military history.

General Lord Chelmsford had divided his force so that the regiment at Isandhlwana under command of Colonel Durnford was badly outnumbered. His regiment was simply overwhelmed and destroyed by tens of thousands of Zulu warriors.

The British were exposed in an open area on the side of a mountain and had prepared no barricades or physical defenses. They were so spread out and vulnerable that a massive Zulu army easily swarmed into their camp in close combat and killed hundreds of British soldiers before they could muster a response. Poor defenses, under-estimating their enemy and dividing their forces were all inferior tactics that guaranteed this major defeat.[1]

CUSTER'S LAST STAND: A WARNING TO US

This battle was the British version of Custer's Last Stand in America, when the U.S. Seventh Cavalry under command of Brigadier General George Armstrong Custer was wiped out by a force of the Sioux and Cheyenne Indian nations under command of Chiefs Sitting Bull and Crazy Horse.

As I study how the major evangelical denominations and Christian ministries conduct spiritual warfare, I am reminded of the Battle of Isandhlwana. I see a serious defeat looming before us if we do not seize the moment and rescue the children from the bondage of Pharaoh's schools and lead them to the Promised Land of Christian schools and home schooling. This potential defeat could be as serious and the shame as great as the British at Isandhlwana.

Church history will not be kind in the remembrance of this disaster should it happen. The defeat of the British forces at Isandhlwana helped topple the government of British Prime Minister Benjamin Disraeli. He made this statement to Queen Victoria before losing power:

> Who are these Zulus? Who are these remarkable people who defeat our generals, convert our bishops, and who on this day have put an end to a French dynasty?[2]

The Zulus in a later battle had killed the Crown Prince of France, son of Napoleon III.

Similarly, Christian families will one day ask, "Why did our pastors and Christian leaders fail to lead our families and children out of danger and into the safe pastures of Christian schools and home schooling?"

The pastors and leaders will say, "We didn't think you would follow, and we had programs and budgets to maintain. Christian schools and home schooling would have been disruptive to our plans and to some of our families."

All of us will say, "Who are these humanists that we allowed to educate our Christian children and who destroyed the legacy of our churches and Christian families?" Although this analogy breaks down in comparing humanists to the great Zulu nation, largely a Christian people today, it does demonstrate spiritual principles of war.

This carnage will have happened when we had the power of God, the power of prayer, the resources, the funds and a Scriptural model of education. We could have prevented it, but we had no vision, no plan and no courage. We thought we knew better than God; we used poor tactics, fought foolishly out in the open, and left our children to be overrun and destroyed on the mountainside of Isandhlwana by the humanists of our times. Our defeat, disgrace and regret will be as great.

OUR BATTLE: A BATTLE AT RORKE'S DRIFT
Just a few miles away from Isandhlwana, however, a small British force, part of the same army, was camped at Rorke's Drift. This location served as a supply and water point for the larger regiment. It also served as a military hospital for the soldiers too sick to join the regiment at Isandhlwana.

This force was just under 150 men, some ill and not fit for battle. When reports came to this small British contingency of the disaster that had just occurred to their comrades at Isandhlwana and that a large Zulu army of thousands was headed their way, they realized they could not escape.

They made extensive defensive preparations with barricades, organized close and tight military formations and stood their ground. Wave after wave of brave Zulu warriors hurled themselves against this tiny force, but they did not break ranks; they did not give ground.

They turned back the enemy using superior tactics of unity, defensive strategy, economy of force and superior firepower; and they won the day. This small battle has captured the imagination of Great Britain even to this day. Eleven Victoria Crosses, equivalent to our Medal of Honor, were awarded for this small engagement, an all-time high for any one battle.

OUR LESSON FROM RORKE'S DRIFT

What was the difference between the Battle of Isandhlwana and Rorke's Drift? These battles took place only a few miles apart, and the troops engaged were from the same forces. The small force at Rorke's Drift was as badly outnumbered as the soldiers who were massacred at Isandhlwana. The difference was simply the preparation and superior tactics used at Rorke's Drift.

With this historical example, the modern Church has been warned. The spiritual and moral devastation of Christian children through state-run "public schools" is apparent for all who have eyes to see and ears to hear.

Will we allow the humanists to win this battle? True shepherds of the Church should now know what must be done. We have been given the Scriptural plan and commanded to educate our children according to God's Word.

There is no Scriptural basis or allowance for Christian families to submit their children to pagan or humanistic education in state-run government schools. This is the great error and blind spot of modern Christianity.

There is one last battle to be fought for the soul of the nation, for families and for the children. It will not be fought over abortion, gambling, or decency, as important as these issues are. It will be a struggle over who will educate the current and next generation of children. Will it be Christian families with help of their churches, or will it be the state?

This situation is as if we are camped on the mountainside of Isandhlwana late at night awaiting the final battle for the children. The battle is to be fought at the first light of dawn. The churches, with their pro-family allies, are camped in the valley with campfires burning, outnumbered and dispirited.

The humanists with their allies in the government-school establishment, the media and the federal court system are camped on the mountaintop with command of the battlefield and control the high ground. They have been winning, and we have been losing the culture war.

Poor generalship, poor tactics and an incredible naivete have characterized our side. We must not fight the battle at dawn the way we have conducted spiritual warfare these past few decades. As never before we must fight smarter, not harder. We will not get another chance in this life.

We need to pick up our army in the night with the children and march to the Promised Land of Christian schools and home schooling. This will change the formulas and equations currently marshalled against us.

The children are the Achilles' heel of the humanist left and the soft underbelly of the leviathan state, but these same children are the power and strength of the Church (Psalm 8:2).

Politics has failed us, and "public education" reform has failed us. Let us go back to the Biblical command of Christian education at the primary level: and "...it may be that the Lord will work for us. For nothing restrains the Lord from saving by many or by few" (1 Samuel 14: 6b).

Which destiny will it be for the modern Church and the Christian family? Will it be Isandhlwana or Rorke's Drift? Will it be defeat or victory? Will we suffer the shame of a lost opportunity and humiliating defeat, or will we win the Victoria Cross?   ■

Dear Friends,

We need thousands of people to talk with
pastors, families, and church members, and
to share the Exodus Mandate message and
assist them to transition from government
schools to the Promised Land of Christian
schools or home schooling.

Use the coupon to order additional copies
of this book. Order the *Let My Children Go*
video from Jeremiah Films (www.jeremiahfilms.com) for $19.95. Or call toll free:
1-800-828-2290. Bulk video discount sales can be arranged: call 909-652-1006.

Share the books and videos with pastors, church leaders, denominational leaders
and church members who are candidates for home-schooling or Christian schools.
Please be prayerful and persistent. Time is short.

Exodus Mandate supporters may volunteer to form local CERTs (Christian
Education Renewal Teams) in their communities and local churches. Consult our
web page (www.Exodusmandate.org) for details on CERT and other information
on the Exodus Mandate Project.

E. Ray Moore, Jr.

Clip and mail

Make out check to: Gilead Media, P.O. Box 6646 Columbia, SC 29260

☐ Please send _____ books. (1 for $12, 3 for $30, 5 for $40)

☐ Please place me on your mailing list

Total enclosed: $_____

Name:_____

Organization:_____

Address:_____

City:_____ St:_____ Zip:_____

Phone:_____ Email:_____

SOURCE NOTES

INTRODUCTION

[1] All Bible passages are from *The Holy Bible, New King James Version,* (Nashville, Tennessee: Thomas Nelson, Inc.) 1982. Used by permission.

[2] The quote appeared in an essay written by a student named John Dunphy. "A Religion For a New Age," *The Humanist* 43 (1), Jan.- Feb. 1983, p. 26.

[3] John Taylor Gatto, *The Underground History of American Education* (New York: Oxford Village Press, 2000/2001). About this book Michael Farris, former President of the Home School Legal Defense Association, wrote, "This is the most important education book of my lifetime."

[4] This and ensuing paragraphs, excepting the discussion of Thomas S. Kuhn and paradigms, consist of a much-updated version of an article originally published in *The State* (Columbia, S.C.): E. Ray Moore Jr., "Christians Not Powerless Against the Court," August 29, 2000.

[5] Chicago: University of Chicago Press, 1962, 1970, 1996.

CHAPTER ONE—THE FAMILY SCHOOL

[1] Current edition: Peabody, Mass.: Hendrickson Publishers, 1994.

[2] See for example Dr. Raymond and Dorothy Moore, *The Successful Homeschool Family Handbook* (Current edition: Nashville, Tenn.: Thomas Nelson, 1994.)

[3] Personal interview with Michael J. Chapman, American Heritage Research, PO Box 1291, Minnetonka, MN February 24, 2002. Chapman is also an associate with the Minnesota based Maple River Education Coalition.

[4] Henry Hyde's letter is archived at http://www.eurekanet.com/~cpr/hydelett.html.

[5] See e.g. Rudolf Flesch's classic *Why Johnny Can't Read* (New York: Perennial Library Press, 1966) and the more recent *Why Johnny Still Can't Read* (New York: Harper Trade, 1983).

6 370 U.S. 421 (1962).

7 374 U.S. 203 (1963).

8 449 U.S. 1104 (1980).

9 E. Ray Moore, Jr. "A Call to Service in the Memory of David and Ann Drye," *Raleigh World*, June 8, 2001.

10 Ed Oliver, "Should Christians Stay in Public Schools? Debate on Beacon Hill Shows Differing Views." *The Massachusetts News*, June, 2001, p. 7.

CHAPTER TWO—GET BEHIND ME, HORACE MANN: THE RISE AND FALL OF STATE-SPONSORED EDUCATION

1 David Barton, *Original Intent: The Courts, the Constitution and Religion*, (Aledo, Texas: Wallbuilders Press, 1997), p. 81.

2 Mary-Elaine Swanson, *The Education of James Madison: A Model for Today*. Published by the Hoffman Education Center for the Family, Montgomery, Alabama. 1992.

3 Lloyd P. Jorgensen "The Birth Of a Tradition," Phi Delta Kappan: Journal of Phi Delta Kappa, Bloomfield, Indiana. June, 1963. p. 408.

4 All Scripture references are from the New King James Version.

5 Samuel L. Blumenfeld, *Is Public Education Necessary?* (Boise, Idaho: The Paradigm Co., 1981, 1985), ch. 3, "The Emergence of a Liberal Elite"; Sheldon Richman, *Separating School and State* (Fairfax, Va.: Future of Freedom Foundation, ch. 3, "Why Are There Public Schools?"

6 Quoted from T.C. Pinckney, "We Are Losing our Children," speech to the Southern Baptist Convention Executive Committee, Nashville, Tennessee. September 16, 2001. Cf. also Blumenfeld, *Is Public Education Necessary?*, op. cit, n. 5, pp. pp. 140-83.

7 *Is Public Education Necessary?* pp. 29-30.

8 Ross House Books, 1995 (orig. pub. 1963).

9 *The Messianic Character of American Education*, p. 333.

10 Ibid., p. 334.

[11] Stephen McDowell, "Fulfilling the Cultural Mandate," *Providential Perspective*, Vol. 17, No. 1 (Jan., 2002), p. 6.

[12] Auguste Comte, *System of Positive Polity*, Vol. I, 1851, pp. 35-36; cited in T.C. Pinckney, op. cit., n. 6.

[13] Benjamin Kidd, *The Science of Power*, p. 309; cited in Pinckney, ibid.

[14] Ross L. Finney, *A Sociological Philosophy of Education*, p. 118; cited in Pinckney, ibid.

[15] Charles A. Ellwood, *The Reconstruction of Religion*, U. of Miss. 1923, p. 177.

[16] Cited in T.C. Pinckney, ibid.

[17] Liberty Bell Press, 1998.

[18] Judith A. Reisman, *Kinsey: Crimes and Consequences: The Red Queen and the Grand Scheme* (Crestwood, Ky.: Institute for Media Education, 2001)

[19] *A Nation at Risk*, 1983, Introduction.

[20] Appendix G, Minnesota Goals 2000 Technology Plan, Sept., 1995.

[21] A.A. Hodge, "The Engine of Atheism," edited by Steven Wilkins, *Classis:* Bulletin of the Association of Classical and Christian Schools, Moscow, ID, p. 2. Republished from Hodge's *Evangelical Theology*.

[22] R.L. Dabney, *On Secular Education* (Moscow, Idaho: Canon Press, p. 13), ed. Douglas Wilson.

[23] Ibid., p. 14.

[24] Ibid.

[25] J. Gresham Machen, *Education, Christianity and the State* (Unicoi, Tennessee: The Trinity Foundation, pp. 67-68), ed. John W. Robbins.

[26] Ibid., p. 66.

[27] Ibid., p. 68.

[28] Gordon Clark, *A Christian Philosophy of Education* (Unicoi, Tennessee: The Trinity Foundation), p. 205.

[29] Perhaps the most detailed examination of radical feminism, its effects on the culture and therefore on the family is that of

Christina Hoff Sommers, *Who Stole Feminism? How Women Have Betrayed Women* (New York: Simon & Schuster, 1994).

[30] J. Edward Pawlick, "Gay Marriage Could Strike Quickly," *The Massachusetts News*, July, 2001.

[31] All available at http://www.kff.org/content/2001/3193/.

[32] See Daniel C. Palm, "Homosexuality, Public Health and Civil Rights," in *Moral Ideas for America*, eds. Larry P. Arnn and Douglas A. Jeffrey (Claremont, Calif.: The Claremont Institute, 1993), pp. 15-25. See also Harry V. Jaffa, *Homosexuality and the Natural Law* (Claremont, CA: Center for the Study of the Natural Law at the Claremont Institute, 1990). One of the best recent books on God's design for marriage is *Intimate Allies* by Dan B. Allender, and Tremper Longman, III. Tyndale House Publishers, Inc., Wheaton, IL

[33] See discussion at http://hometown.aol.com/dfjoseph/vermont-gays.html.

[34] For a definition of diversity see "Dreamers of a Godless Utopia," by Michael J. Chapman, published by American Heritage Research, Minnetonka, MN pp. 23-27

CHAPTER THREE—TOWARD A BIBLICAL THEOLOGY OF EDUCATION

[1] Isaac Newton, "God and Natural Philosophy," in *Newton's Philosophy of Nature: Selections from his Writings* ed. H.S. Thayer and John Herman Randall Jr. New York: Hafner Press, 1953, p. 42.

[2] Milton R. Konvitz, *Bill Of Rights Reader; Leading Constitutional Cases*, 5th Ed. (Ithaca, NY: Cornell University Press, 1973), pp. 96-110.

[3] Rev. Paul Jehle, "Parental Obedience in Relation to Christian Education," published by New Testament Christian School, Plymouth, Mass., 1995, pp. 3-4.

CHAPTER FOUR—THE BASIC ERRORS OF STATE-SPONSORED SCHOOLS AND WHY REFORM WILL NOT WORK

1 Mary-Elaine Swanson, *The Education of James Madison: A Model For Today* (Montgomery, Alabama: The Hoffman Center, 1992).

2 The Constitution of South Carolina, 1895, compiled by the South Carolina Legislative Council, Peden B. McLeod, Director, updated August 26, 1997, "Public Education," Article XI, section 3, p. 51

3 Samuel Blumenfeld, *Is Public Education Necessary?* (Boise, Idaho: The Paradigm Company, 1981, 1985); John Taylor Gatto's *Dumbing Us Down: The Hidden Curriculum of Compulsory Schooling* (Gabriola Island, British Columbia, Canada: 1992) and *The Underground History of American Education* (New York: Oxford Village Press, 2000/2001)

4 E.G. West, *Education and the State: A Study in Political Economy* (Indianapolis: Liberty Press, 1994), p. 148.

5 Adam Smith, *The Wealth of Nations*, p. 760; quoted in ibid., p. 149.

6 *Wealth of Nations*, p. 764; quoted in ibid. p. 151.

7 Letter by Thomas Malthus to Samuel Whitbread, quoted in ibid., p. 151.

8 John Stuart Mill, *Principles of Political Economy*, p. 953; quoted in ibid., p. 152.

9 John Stuart Mill, *On Liberty*, Fontana edition., 1962, p. 239; quoted in ibid., pp. 154-55.]

10 Ludwig Von Mises, *Liberalism in the Classical Tradition* (New York: Cobden Press, 1985 edition), p. 115.

11 John Stuart Mill, *On Liberty*, op. cit.; quoted in West, op. cit., p. 155.

12 West, ibid., p. 155.

13 Karl Marx, *The Essential Marx: The Non-Economic Writings,* Ed. Saul K. Padover (New York: Mentor Books), p. 212.

14 Edmund Opitz, *Religion and Capitalism: Allies Not Enemies* (New Rochelle, New York: Arlington House, 1970), p., 300-02.

[15] Frederic Bastiat, *The Law* (Irvington-on-Hudson, Foundation for Economic Education edition), p. 31.

[16] Murray Rothbard, *Education: Free and Compulsory* (Auburn, Alabama: The Ludwig Von Mises Institute, 1972), p. 7.

[17] Don Hinkle, "Schools in the South listed as homosexual activist group's target," Baptist Press, Nashville, Tennessee.

CHAPTER FIVE—WINNING THE HEARTS AND MINDS OF THE SHEPHERDS

[1] Lafayette, Louisiana: Huntington House Publishers, 1996; Lafayette, Louisiana: Huntington House / Vital Issues Press, 1996.

[2] Wheaton, Illinois: Crossway Books, 1991; Nashville, Tennessee. Lifeway Press, 1998.

[3] Chicago: Moody Press, 1993.

[4] Chuck Colson, *Christianity Today*, April 29, 1996, p. 64.

[5] See Geoffrey B. Kelly, "The Life and Death of a Modern Martyr," "Dietrich Bonhoeffer: A Life in Pictures," *Christian History*, Vol. 10, No. 4, published by *Christianity Today*, Coral Stream, Illinois, 1991, p. 11. Cf. also Gene E. Veith, *Modern Fascism: Liquidating the Judeo-Christian World View* (St. Louis, Missouri: Concordia Publishing House, 1993), pp. 59-62.

[6] Quotations from *The Encyclopedia of American Religions: Religious Creeds*, ed. Gordon Melton, Detroit: Gale Research Co., 1988, pp. 249-51.

[7] Kelly, op. cit, n. 5, p. 11; Veith, op. cit., n. 5, p. 60.

[8] "Natural Theology," in *The Oxford Dictionary of the Christian Church*, p. 940.

[9] Veith, pp. 56-70.

[10] Quoted in Ernst Christian Helmreich, *The German Churches Under Hitler: Background, Struggle and Epilogue* (Detroit: Wayne State University Press, 1979), p. 345. Time Magazine, Dec. 23, 1940: A quotation by Pinchus Lapide in his book, *Three Popes and the Jews*, attributes the Einstein quote as referring to the Catholic Church. Other sources attribute it to the Protestant "Confessing Church."

[11] J.S. Conway, *The Nazi Persecution of the Churches*, 1933-1945.

Reproduced by Regent College Publishing, 1997. Vancouver, B.C. 1968. Introduction.

[12] Ibid. page 338.

CHAPTER SIX—MINEFIELDS ON THE ROAD TO THE PROMISED LAND

[1] Lawrence W. Reed, "A New Direction for Education Reform," *IMPRIMIS* 30(7), July, 2001, p. 2.

[2] E. Ray Moore, Jr. "Some advice to the GOP: Do No Harm," *The State* (Columbia, S.C.), July 17, 1998.

[3] Marshall Fritz, "A Better Brand of Parent," *The Freeman*, September 1999, pp. 8-11

[4] Llewellyn H. Rockwell, "School Vouchers: Enemy of Religion," *The Wanderer*, July 9, 1998.

[5] Jonathan Rauch, "TRB From Washington: Choose Or Lose," *The New Republic*, November 10, 1997.

[6] Ibid.

[7] Matthew Miller. "A Bold Experiment To Fix City Schools" *The Atlantic Monthly* (July, 1999) p.15-18, 26-31.

[8] "Educational Savings Accounts, Tax Credits and Vouchers in the News," ACSI Legislative Update, Vol. 8, No. 4 (Summer, 1998), pp. 50-52.

[9] ACSI 2001 Directory, P.O. Box 35097, Colorado Springs, CO 80935. These figures include colleges and college student enrollment.

[10] Association of Classical and Christian Schools, "Statement on Vouchers," *Classis*, November 2001, Vol. 8, No. 6.

[11] Cathy Duffy, "Hijacking the Voucher Movement," *There's No Place Like Home*, Nov./Dec. 1998, p. 4.

[12] *The Insider* (Heritage Foundation), September 2001, p. 24.

[13] Ted C. Olsen, "Voucher Victory," *Christianity Today*, Sept. 7, 1998.

[14] Kerry A. White, "Complaint Lodged Against Private Voucher Schools in Milwaukee," *Education Week*, September 8, 1999, p.5.

15 Douglas D. Dewey, "An Echo, Not a Choice," *Policy Review* (Nov./Dec., 1996) p. 30.

16 Ibid.

17 Ibid.

18 Jonathan Rauch, *National Journal*, December 22, 2000.

19 Lawrence W. Reed, "A New Direction for Education Reform," op. cit., n. 1.

20 Ibid., p. 3.

21 Christopher J. Klicka, "Charter Schools: The Price Is Too High," *The Home School Court Report*, Home School Legal Defense Association, January-February 2002, p. 2. Information was compiled from the Center for Education Reform. Klicka's essay is one of the best recent articles opposing charter schools.

22 Thomas Dawson, *Charter Schools and the Long Road to Education Reform* (October 1999: Pacific Research Institute, p. 9).

23 Daniel Golden, "Old Time Religion Gets a Boost at a Chain of Charter Schools," *Wall Street Journal*, September 15, 1999, pp. 1, 14.

24 Ibid., p. 1.

25 *School Reform News* (Chicago: The Heartland Institute), September, 2001, p. 10.

26 Ibid.

27 Dick Carpenter, "Rebuilding Hope for Public Schools," *Focus on the Family*, August, 1999.

28 Julie Blair, "Certification Found Valid for Teachers," by Julie Blair, *Education Week*, October 25, 2000, p. 24.

29 Milton R. Konvitz, Ed. *Bill Of Rights Reader: Leading Constitutional Cases*, published by Cornell University Press (1st ed., 1954; 5th ed., 1973), p. 94.

30 Douglas Wilson, *Recovering the Lost Tools of Learning* (Wheaton, Ill.: Crossway Books, 1991, p. 30).

31 Ithaca, N.Y.: Cornell University Press, 1998.

32 Sydney B. Simon, Leland W.Howe, and Howard Kirschenbaum, *Values Clarification: A Handbook Of Practical Strategies For Teachers and Students*, New York: Hart Publishing Company, 1972.

33 John Leo, "C Is For Character," *U.S. News & World Report*, November 15, 1999.

34 Cheri Fuller, "Rebuilding Hope For Public Schools," *Focus on the Family*, August, 1999.

35 New York: Bantam Books, 1992.

36 Gerald Stiles, Review of *Educating For Character* by Thomas Lickona, *The SCEIN Report*, Dec., 1996, p. 1.

37 The Josephson Institute of Ethics web site is at http://www.josephsoninstitute.org.

38 All cited in "Legislator pushes for 'character development' in public schools," *Michigan Education Report*, Fall, 2000, p. 4.

39 Carol Farrington, "State trying to build character in classrooms," *The State* (Columbia, S.C.), September 24, 1995.

40 Paul Tosto, "Beasley calls for Character Ed," *The State* (Columbia, S.C.), September 12, 1996.

41 Chuck Carroll, "Teach character, courtesy in schools, Hodges says," *The State* (Columbia, S.C.), January 4, 2000.

42 Op. Cit. Stiles. p.1

43 Op. Cit. Stiles. p.2

CHAPTER SEVEN—CIVIL DISOBEDIENCE: WE OUGHT TO OBEY GOD RATHER THAN MEN

1 Robert D. Culver, *Towards a Biblical View of Civil Government* (Chicago: Moody Press, 1974), p. 203.

2 Ibid.

3 Francis Schaeffer, *A Christian Manifesto* (Westchester, Ill.: Crossway Books, 1981), p. 91.

4 Ibid., p. 92.

5 Paul and John Feinberg, *Ethics for a Brave New World* (Wheaton, Illinois: Crossway Books, 1993), p. 401.

6 Schaeffer, op. cit., pp. 105-06.

7 Ibid., pp. 99-102.

8 Michael Howard, *Tales of an African Intercessor* (Out of Africa Publishers, 1998), pp. 191-194.

9 Southern Baptist Convention, "Resolution #3: On Women in

Combat," Salt Lake City, Utah, June 11, 1998.

[10] See Geoffrey Kelly, op. cit., ch. 5, p. 14.

[11] Calvin, John. *Institutes Of the Christian Religion*, Volume XX. Library of Christian Classics. Edited by John T. McNeill. The Westminster Press, Philadelphia, PA 8th Printing, 1977. Pages 1517-1521.

[12] Indianapolis: Liberty Fund, 1997.

[13] Angie Vineyard, "A Christian Family Ripped Apart, *The Columbia World*," Volume 1, No 3, January 2002, published by World Newspapers, Charlotte, North Carolina, pp. 1, 3.

[14] Schaeffer, op. cit., p. 111.

[14] Ibid., p. 130.

CHAPTER EIGHT—THE NEXT GREAT AWAKENING

[1] Grand Rapids, Mich.: Baker Book House, 1995; Eugene, Ore.: Harvest House Publishers, 2001.

[2] Broadman & Holman, 1998.

[3] Paul Weyrich, "Conservatives, Retreat," *The Atlanta Constitution*, February 14, 1999.

[4] Ibid.

[5] Ibid.

[6] John H. Armstrong, *True Revival*, op. cit., n. 5, p. 181.

[7] Ibid., pp. 51-67.

[8] Ibid., p. 21.

[9] Briefing by Chaplain (Major General) Matthew Zimmerman, Army Chief of Chaplains, December, 1990.

[10] John R. Price, *America at the Crossroads* (Tyndale House, 1979), p. 137.

[11] Cf. ibid., p. 186.

[12] Kellyanne Fitzpatrick, "The 'Choice' Issue Voters Truly Care About," *The Insider* # 274 (August 2000) published by the Heritage Foundation.

[13] "N.C. Home School Enrollment Up 21 Percent over Last Year,"

The Charlotte World, August 3, 2001, p. 17.

14 *The Charlotte World*, ibid.

15 Brian D. Ray, *Home Schooling at the Threshold: A survey of Research at the Dawn of the New Millennium*, NHERI Publications, 1999, p. 4

16 Ibid.

17 Margaret Talbot, "The New Counterculture," *The Atlantic Monthly*, p. 136.

18 David Gergen, "No Place Like Home," *U.S. News & World Report*, June 19, 2000, p. 64.

19 Ibid.

20 Simon J. Dahlmon, "There's No Place Like Home," *Focus on the Family*, September, 2001, pp. 9-11.

21 Quoted in ibid., p.10.

22 Talbot, op. cit., p. 143.

23 Lee Weeks, "Homeschooling- SEBTS Style" *Southeastern Baptist Theological Seminary Outlook*, Vol. 48, p. 7.

24 ibid, p.7

25 *The Baptist Faith and Message*, adopted by the SBC, June 14, 2000, published by Lifeway Christian Resources, SBC, Nashville, Tenn., pp. 16-17.

CHAPTER NINE—PROSPECTS FOR THE EXODUS MANDATE PROJECT

1 Maggie Gallagher, "Education Establishment is Losing Black Support," *Human Events* (vol. 53, No. 33), August 29 – September 5, 1997, p. 17.

2 Vox Day, "The Home-School Underground Railroad," *WorldNetDaily.com*, January 28, 2002.

3 Dr. James C. Carper and Dr. Jack Layman, "Black-Flight Academies: The New Christian Day Schools," *The Educational Forum* 61 (1997), pp. 114-21.

4 Maggie Gallagher, op. cit., n. 1.

5 The Alliance For the Separation Of School and State @ www.sepschool.org.

6 Clownes, George, "More Parents Want to Leave Public Schools," *School Reform News*, October 2000, Vol. 4 #10.

EPILOGUE

1 Andre Maurois, *Disraeli* (Alexandria, Virginia: Time-Life Books, 1980), pp 324-326 (orig. pub. 1936).

2 Ibid., p. 325.

𝔅𝔩𝔬𝔬𝔡𝔶

𝔐𝔦𝔰𝔱

𝔓𝔯𝔢𝔰𝔰

𝔅𝔩𝔬𝔬𝔡𝔶 𝔐𝔦𝔰𝔱 𝔓𝔯𝔢𝔰𝔰

𝔏𝔞𝔰 𝔙𝔢𝔤𝔞𝔰, 𝔑𝔢𝔟𝔞𝔡𝔞

Critical Acclaim for *The Dark Side*

"The first installment of a promising new mystery series. Pull[ed] off with panache . . . a suspenseful and thoroughly enjoyable novel—the first, one hopes, in a long series."

— *Booklist*, Oct 2002

"a noir mystery in the best Raymond Chandler vein . . . a hell of a ride . . . solid characters, terse banter and page-turner storytelling"

— Carolyn Cummins, *January Magazine*

"I loved *The Dark Side*. It was full of tears, terror, laughs, comedy, and above all it kept me glued to the pages. Mr. Sherman is a natural. *The Dark Side* reads like a Raymond Chandler mystery, but with its own special flavor. *The Dark Side* is the first in Mr. Sherman's Jack Murphy books, and what a first it is. I just cannot wait for the next one to come out. Mr. Sherman has introduced some of the most intriguing and complex characters to come along in a long time. "

— 5/5 Stars, Sue Hartigan, RIO, *All About Murder*

"One aspect of novel writing which David J. Sherman has down pat is what Stephen King has called 'the gotta,' as in, 'I gotta find out what happens next.'"

— Benjamin Jones, *Mysterical-E*

"There's a new star on the horizon and his name is David J. Sherman. *The Dark Side*, Sherman's first Jack Murphy novel, is a stunning piece of contemporary noir that I simply could not put down once I started it. I took it to the dinner table with me, I took it to the bathroom with me and I took it to bed with me, finishing it up in the middle of the night because I couldn't go to sleep until I knew how it ended . . . *The Dark Side* is well worth every suspenseful minute you spend with your eyes glued to the pages!"

— Elizabeth Henze, *Murder Express*

"I enjoyed reading *The Dark Side*. Though the premise is not new, i.e. wisecracking PI with muscle sidekick, the story is intriguing, the characters believable and there is a strong sense of place. It's written in the first person and is dialogue intensive, which makes for a quick read. The child abuse issues and scenes are dealt with in a sympathetic and non-graphic manner and you can identify with Jack's responses. I'll be on the lookout for the next Jack Murphy adventure."

— Karen Meek, *Over My Dead Body*

"David J. Sherman has been touted as the next Raymond Chandler. Usually I shrug those types of statements off, not liking to compare authors. In this case, though, I found it to be true. Sherman writes with class. His violent scenes are never gratuitous and always expertly done. His characters all have morals, which I find to be a welcome change . . . His writing seemed to speak individually to me, as if Jack Murphy was whispering in my ear. I really look forward to his next novel."

— Robyn Glazer, *myshelf.com*

"[*The Dark Side* is] the start of a great series."

— Jennifer Kirchmann, *Omaha Public Library*

"*The Dark Side* marks the auspicious debut for David J. Sherman's Jack Murphy series . . . Sherman's story reads like Raymond Chandler updated for our new century. Connelly, Crais, Grafton, move over. David J. Sherman has arrived."

— Kent Braithwaite, *The Wonderland Murders*

The Dark Side

A Jack Murphy Novel

The Dark Side

A Jack Murphy Novel

David J. Sherman

Bloody Mist Press
Las Vegas, Nevada

M
c.1

Bloody Mist Press
2961 Industrial Rd #732
Las Vegas NV 89109

Author's note
Those of you familiar with Los Angeles will note that I have, on
occasion, modified the cityscape as I needed to serve a particular
purpose. I believe doing so in no way changed the overall look
and feel of the city. If you disagree, please accept my apologies.

The Dark Side is book #1 in the Jack Murphy Series

First Edition Trade Paper, December 2002

1 3 5 7 9 10 8 6 4 2

The Library of Congress has cataloged this edition as follows:
Sherman, David J., 1966-
The dark side : a Jack Murphy novel / David J. Sherman.
p. cm.
ISBN 193230651X (pbk. : alk. paper)
1. Private investigators--California--Los Angeles--Fiction.
2. Los Angeles (Calif.)--Fiction. 3. Runaway teenagers--Fiction.
I. Title.
PS3619.H464D37 2002
813'.6--dc21

2002002681

Acknowledgements

I am grateful to many people for their part in making this dream a reality. Without their help, this novel might not be.

To Robert S. Levinson (he lets me call him Bob), whose generosity was as unwarranted as it was priceless. I am proud to call you my friend.

To Lori Soard, who taught me the basics. To Darcy Vance, whose enthusiasm fueled my desire. To Karen Marquis, for her friendship. To Barb Woss, Karen Grunberg, Mik Trent, Betty Lubinski, and Raven, who helped nurture my creative self. To my dear friend Anne Gebhardt, whose support and faith in me can never be repaid.

To Jan Burke, Kent Braithwaite, and all at SoCal MWA, for their support and friendship. To Raymond Chandler, Bob Crais, Dennis Lehane, and Robert B. Parker, whose literary accomplishments drove me to follow their lead.

To Dr. Karen Baghamian, for helping me overcome my fears and move forward. To Tenzin Lhamo, Nyima, Zopa, Ilene, Ye Fawn, Geshe Samdup, Marco, and all at Land of Compassion Buddha, for being true friends and guides.

To Tami Carter, for helping me with the medical technicalities. To the Santa Monica Public Library, for providing specifics about the Santa Monica Pier. To Maria and Tino for helping with the Spanish slang.

To Allen and Val Dolling, for allowing me to commandeer a table at their coffee house for months to work on this book.

To my folks, Jim and Andrea, for providing support as I worked to get this novel off the ground.

To my dear friend Sue, you are a beacon of light in my

sometimes dim world.

To Twist Phelan, for your advice and friendship.

To everyone, named or not, who took the time to read, review, and criticize this novel. You all helped improve the prose.

To everyone whom I, by sheer ignorance, failed to personally mention. It is with a sad heart I confess my mistake.

To my readers. Without you, there would be no opportunity for another Jack Murphy novel.

Last, but certainly not least, to my wife and daughter, Bridget and Sheli. I'd be nothing without you.

A heartfelt thanks to all.

Dave

To Bridget & Sheli

ONE

"Mr. Murphy, I need you to find my little girl."

Raymond Sanders sat in one of two client chairs opposite my desk. Dark circles encompassed his eyes. He opened one of the manila files he had brought inside with him, pulled out an eight-by-ten, and set it on my desk.

I picked up the glossy photo. It was professionally shot, and depicted a blond girl in her mid-to-late teens, smiling and seducing the camera. "Missing persons is not my area of expertise."

"I understand, but due to extenuating circumstances, Mr. Lawson felt you'd be the best person for the job. A month ago, we hired an investigator to find Carrie." Raymond ran his fingers over his gray beard. "Now he's dead."

"How'd he die?"

"He was shot in the back of the head."

I made a mental note to thank Roy Lawson for the referral. "You're from Lake Point, Wisconsin, right?"

"Yes. Well, River's Edge, actually, on the north end of town."

"I know the area."

"Mr. Lawson told me you lived in Lake Point at one time."

"Many years ago."

Three years, six months and a handful of days, but who's counting?

"Not much has changed," he said.

Not much ever changes in a sleepy town like Lake Point. Eons pass and yet everything remains the same.

I lit a cigarette and leaned back in my chair. "When was Carrie last seen?"

"On Halloween."

Three weeks ago. "Did you speak with her that night?"

"No, but her mother did."

"Was Carrie upset about anything?"

"Not that I'm aware of."

I tapped my ashes into the crystal ashtray on the corner of my desk. "Tell me what you know about that night."

"Carrie was supposed to spend the night at her friend Ashley's house. She and her mother spoke briefly before she left."

"What time was that?"

"Around nine."

"How does Carrie get to Ashley's house?"

"She takes her bike or walks. Ashley lives only a mile down the road."

"Which did she do that night?"

"She must've walked. Her bike is still in the garage."

"Did anyone see her walk?"

His eyes narrowed. "Are you asking if we watched her walk away from the house?"

"Yep."

"I don't believe we did, no."

"Okay. Go on."

Raymond cleared his throat. "After Ashley called, we contacted everyone we could think of, and then drove around for hours. Nothing. At seven the next morning, I called the police and filed a missing persons report."

His eyes welled with tears. He bowed his head, pinched the bridge of his nose. "The police learned that a Greyhound employee had sold Carrie a one-way ticket to Los Angeles that night. The employee couldn't say whether Carrie had gotten on the bus, but he assumed she had."

If not for the bullets in the back of the private eye's skull, I'd have already dismissed the case. Since coming to California, I had investigated deadbeat dads, insurance claims and cheating spouses. I was bored, but every case I had worked came to a distinct conclusion. Missing persons cases were a whole new ballgame. A person who's missing more than a day or two is rarely found and, even more rarely, found alive. "What was the private eye's name?"

"Philip Jenkins."

"Did he uncover anything?"

"I don't know. He said he had some leads, but refused to comment further until he had a chance to investigate."

Maybe Jenkins was milking the cash cow. But since death probably wasn't part of his game plan, I gave him the benefit of the doubt.

"When'd he die?" I said.

"Early last Friday morning."

Three days ago. "Where are the police in all this?"

"They claim they're still actively pursuing the case, but who the hell knows?"

"You don't believe it."

"No."

"And why's that?"

He folded his hands in his lap, leaned back. "Just a feeling, Mr. Murphy." He stared at me and his jaw tightened. "Maybe they are doing all they can, but they didn't lose a little girl. I did, and I want her found."

"I understand. Have you spoken to the police since Jenkins died?"

"I called both the Lake Point Police and the Los Angeles Police this morning. Neither will discuss his death with me."

"Do you have a photo of Jenkins?"

Raymond opened a file, set a business card on my desk. I picked it up. Nice, full-color, with Jenkins' smiling mug dead center. "You know where he was staying?"

Raymond fished a piece of lined yellow paper filled with handwritten notes from the file. "Motel Six on Whitley Avenue in Hollywood."

I opened my desk drawer, took out a pen and pad of paper. My bitchy voice of reason told me to forget this case. "How old is Carrie?"

"Sixteen."

"Does she have a driver's license?"

"No."

"Social Security Number and birth date?"

He recited them—I wrote them down.

"Beside the Greyhound employee's statement, is there any reason for you to believe Carrie came to LA?"

Raymond leaned forward, rested his elbows on his knees. "Carrie's dreamed of becoming an actress since age five. She always said someday she'd live in Hollywood and be a big star. If she ran away, I know she came here."

"If?"

"Excuse me?"

"You said 'if she ran away'. Do you have some reason to believe she didn't run away?"

"No, I don't. I meant since she ran away, I know she came here."

"Does Carrie have any family here in California?"

"No."

"What about in any states along the way? Nevada, Arizona, Colorado, Utah . . ."

He held up his hand. I guess he didn't appreciate my intimate knowledge of geography.

"No, Mr. Murphy. The only living relatives we have are in the Northeast."

I thought about rattling off the New England states, but didn't want to dazzle him too much. "How does Carrie spend her time?"

"Being an honor student, most of her time is occupied with homework. But she also sings in the church choir and is part of the school drama club."

"How's Carrie's health?"

"Excellent."

"Any boyfriends?"

"No."

"What about friends that are boys?"

"I'm sure she has some, though she isn't close to any."

"Has she ever known anyone whose family relocated to California?"

"Again, it's entirely possible, though I'm not aware of any particular individual."

"What about drugs?"

His eyes widened. "Good God, no. Carrie isn't into anything like that."

"No sex and no drugs. Are you sure?"

"I find that offensive, Mr. Murphy."

"I'm sorry, but at Carrie's age, sex and drugs are two of the three major factors in MP cases."

"What's the third?"

"Abuse."

His gaze dropped to the floor. He remained quiet for a moment before looking up. "Thank you for not thinking that."

"Thinking has nothing to do with it, Mr. Sanders. My job is to gather information. My thoughts are generally kept to myself."

Tears trickled down Raymond's cheeks. He blotted them with a finger, adjusted the sleeves of his black pullover sweater, and bit his bottom lip. "Mr. Murphy, let me be very clear. Money's not an issue. I'll pay whatever it takes. I just want my little girl found."

"Let me be very clear with you, too, Mr. Sanders. MP cases are difficult to solve, nearly impossible if the person doesn't want to be found. We have no idea what, if anything, Jenkins knew, and you have no evidence Carrie's in LA, or ever was, except for your gut feeling. As I often rely on my own intuition, I don't doubt your hunch. But at the same time, I can't promise results."

"Certainly. If you tell me you'll do everything in your power to try, I can accept that."

He pulled out a checkbook, borrowed my pen and wrote a check, then proffered it. "Is this sufficient to get started?"

The voice said I'd be a fool to accept such a sure-loser case. *No, Jack, don't do it.*

I took the check, glanced at the amount: five thousand. "This'll be fine."

You idiot.

I pointed at the stack of files Raymond had set on the chair beside him. "For me?"

"Yes, that is all the information I have regarding Carrie's disappearance."

I stood. "Where're you staying?"

"The Beverly Hills Hotel, room 487."

He stood and followed me to the door. I opened it, extended my hand. "I'll be in touch."

He shook it. "Thank you."

"Don't thank me yet. As I said, I can't guarantee I'll be able to find anything. But if Jenkins' death is connected to this case, maybe we have a shot."

"I understand."

He bowed his head, walked through reception, down the hall, and out into the rain.

I closed my office door and told my voice of reason to shut the hell up.

Two

The door opened and Nadia stepped inside, strings of lights draped over her shoulders. "I thought I'd add some Christmas spirit to your office."

"By all means."

She walked to the plate glass window that exposed Wilshire Boulevard and affixed the lights to the window frame with small strips of tape. "Steven's dropping off a tree this afternoon."

"Who's Steven?"

She glanced at me, smiled. "My neighbor. You know him."

"Oh, yeah, the gay airline stewardess."

"Steward. And he's not gay."

"Uh-huh."

Nadia finished outlining the window and plugged the string into the outlet. The lights blinked, their reflection in the glass doubled their effect. I gave them maybe a day before I'd rip the plug from the wall.

She ran the last strand along the file cabinets. "There, much better."

"For who?"

She plugged the final strand into the socket, smiled when they lighted. "You're a real Grinch. You know that?"

I did. Before coming to California, I enjoyed the holiday season. I would spend hours on Thanksgiving weekend weaving assorted strings of lights through my trees, bushes, and along the roofline. Then on New Year's weekend, I'd spend twice as long taking down the lights, winding them up, repacking the huge shipping boxes labeled Christmas and stowing them in the garage until the following year.

But, I hadn't felt like doing that in a long time.

Nadia sat and crossed her legs. "You're picking up Arturo today, huh?"

"Yep."

"What's he going to do once he's back in the real world?"

"I don't know. I thought I'd offer him a job."

Nadia looked up. "Here?"

"No, at the Asian-American Pharmacy across the street."

"You're so funny."

"Of course, here."

"Doing what?"

"I don't know. I haven't gotten that far yet."

She glanced at the cobalt carpet, then back at me. "You remember I'm not coming in tomorrow, right?"

"You're not?"

"Jack, did you forget already? Sylvia's in town for the day. I told you three weeks ago."

"Sure, I remember. I was just testing you."

"Uh-huh."

"Really."

She smiled, walked to the door. "I haven't seen her in more than two years."

"What're you two gonna do?"

"Well, Dad, I'm going to take her to the County Museum of Art and then the Peterson Automotive Museum. Then, maybe we'll have dinner at the Mexican cantina on the Santa Monica pier. If it's okay with you, that is."

"Sure, but will you be up to working Wednesday?"

"Oh, yeah, like I'm some kind of party animal."

"You aren't?"

"Not. Besides, her flight leaves tomorrow night at ten."

"Good, you'll be home at a decent hour."

"That should make you happy."

I smiled. "It does. I don't want anything to happen to you."

"That's sweet."

"If it did, who would run my office?"

"That's my Jack. Say something nice and then throw it in the toilet."

The phone rang. Nadia flashed a smile, said, "It's been real fun, but I need to get back to work," and walked out of my office.

A minute later, the intercom buzzed. "Jack, it's Ellen on one."

"Great."

"You want me to give her excuse one-o-one?"

"Which one's that?"

"The 'I'm sorry, but Jack's in the bathroom' excuse."

"Nah, Ellen won't buy it. Or she'd just wait on hold."

"Do you mean you wanna talk to her?"

"Want? No. But, if I don't, I'll dread every moment until she calls back. I'll take it."

"Good luck."

"Thanks."

Even though I had decided to take the call, I had no difficulty letting the red button on line one flash for a minute. I grabbed a cigarette from the pack in my shirt pocket, dragged the crystal ashtray closer, and thought about how long I'd have her wait before I answered.

"Hello, Ellen."

"Hi ya, Jack. How's it going?"

"It's going."

"That's great, just great."

I think if I'd said I was running down the street on fire, her reaction would've been the same. "What's up?"

"Jack, listen. You're not even going to believe it. I still can't believe it myself." She giggled. "I'm getting married. Isn't that just wonderful?"

"Does this mean you'll stop calling me?"

"Oh, you're such a kidder."

Sometimes. "Who's the lucky guy?"

"His name's Randolph. He's a stockbroker in Chicago."

I knocked my cigarette against the ashtray, and then smashed the ashes with my fingertip. "That's great, Ellen."

"Isn't it? I'm telling you, I can't believe my great luck."

"I'm happy for you."

"Oh, are you? Because I can't tell you how much it means to hear you say that. I mean, I thought you might be upset because, you know, of our past."

"Why would I be upset? It's your life."

"I know, but sometimes, you know, people kinda stay attached."

"Not me."

"Well, I hope . . . Oh, never mind. I don't want to think about anything except my wedding. Of course, you'll come, won't you?"

"I don't know. I've been busy with work."

"Oh, Jack, please say you'll come."

"Why?"

"Why? Why not? Just because we couldn't live together doesn't mean you're no longer important to me."

"Oh."

"You are still upset about what happened, aren't you?"

"You mean your walking out on me? Nah, ancient history."

"Jack, I am sorry for the way things turned out."

"So am I."

"Well, I hope you can come and be a part of my special day."

Perhaps I'd rather be strung up on a spit and barbequed. "When is it?"

"Saturday, the thirtieth. Last Saturday of the millennium."

"Kind of quick, isn't it?"

"Randy and I have been going out for almost a year now."

"Oh."

"That's sweet."

"What is?"

"That you care."

I knew I should hang up the phone. Instead, I said, "I'll see if I can make it."

"Please do. Oh, and you're welcome to bring a guest, if you'd like."

"I'll keep that in mind."

"Jack, it's been wonderful to speak with you again. Now, I have to run. So many things to plan, so little time. Can you tell I'm excited?"

"Ecstatic."

"I am. I truly am."

No need to convince me. "Take care."

"You, too. Ta ta, Jack."

I hung up the phone and realized Ellen sounded a lot like a character from one of the soap operas she used to watch—Lucy something or other, I think. The *ta ta* clinched it.

And to think, I was married to her.

I thought about going outside for some fresh air when there was a knock at my door. The soft, double rap told me it was Nadia.

"Got a sec?" she said.

"Sure."

She closed the door and sat. "How'd the call with Ellen go?"

"You mean you weren't listening?"

"God, no."

"Uh-huh."

"Really. I would have, but Sylvia called." She chuckled. "So, what'd you two talk about?"

"Well, Doctor Ruth, not a whole lot. Ellen's getting married."

"Married?"

"Yep."

"And she called to tell you this?"

"Yep."

"How do you feel?"

"Like I'm being interviewed by a psychiatrist."

"Be serious."

"I am."

I pulled out a cigarette and lit it. I offered Nadia one, which she accepted, and I lit hers, too.

"Isn't it strange to call your ex and tell him you're getting married again?" she said.

"I guess."

"Maybe she wanted to see how you'd react."

"Maybe."

"Maybe she wanted you to say that you still loved her and didn't want her getting hitched."

"Maybe."

"Do you want to?"

"Stop her? Hell, no. Let her do what she wants."

"It doesn't bother you at all?"

"Nope."

"Bullshit."

Maybe Nadia was right. The day that Ellen left me, I still loved her. I told myself that my new life in LA was better for me than my old one in Lake Point, but I don't always know what's best for me. Not that Nadia knows any more than I do. "I don't know."

"Jack, you know you're still hung up on her. My God, how long are you going to stay attached to a memory?"

"What the hell does that mean?"

"You know what it means. You're still in love with her."

"I am not."

"Bullshit."

I hit my cigarette and glanced at my watch. I didn't want to get into this. "Why am I defending myself to you anyway?"

"I'm trying to help—trying to get you to see what you're doing."

"And what is that?"

"Letting Ellen win."

"Ellen isn't winning."

"Oh, no? She's succeeded in making you distrust every female you meet."

"That's not true. I trust you."

"Maybe as an employee."

"As a friend."

She glanced down, pinched a lock of her raven hair and wrapped it tightly around a finger. "That's it, though."

"What else is there?"

"Damn, Jack. I . . ." She jumped to her feet, stormed to the door, then glared back at me. "Shit."

She slammed the door on her way out.

I didn't understand these little tiffs Nadia and I had. An outsider looking in would swear we were married. Married couples are the only people I've ever seen who can do a damn fine job of fighting about nothing.

The phone buzzed and Nadia's voice came over the intercom. "Mrs. Pike's here to see you."

Professional, unemotional, post-spat Nadia.

"Okay."

"By the way, I'm going to lunch."

Click.

THREE

My ulcer flared. It always did after Nadia and I had a little moment. I reached into my desk drawer, pulled a Prevacid from its amber bottle, and washed down the pill with my remaining coffee.

I lit a fresh cigarette, walked to the reception area and ushered Mrs. Pike into my office. I offered her coffee. She declined.

She sat upright in the chair, hands clutching her purse. I removed an envelope from my desk drawer. "Are you sure you'd like to see these?"

Eyes swollen, Mrs. Pike held out her hand. "Please."

I placed the envelope in her palm. Her hands trembled. She ripped the thick brown paper, pulled out the glossy five-by-sevens. I gazed through the plate glass window at Wilshire Boulevard.

The rain still fell, heavier now. Across the street, an Asian man named Tao Lung held a folded newspaper over his head and peered at the traffic. He owned the Asian-American Pharmacy. A week ago, he'd opened for business. Now, he stood in the rain looking for his customers. He wasn't particularly interesting, but it beat the alternative—watching Mrs. Pike's heart shatter.

I never minded exposing unfaithful spouses, but when it came time to hand over the two-inch stack of 35mm shots, I sometimes wished I had gone into used car sales.

Mrs. Pike studied the photos. Tears built in a crescendo, then flowed free from her eyes. Her features grew cold, her jaw locked. She sat still, absorbing the wave of terror one frame at a time.

Several minutes later, she scooped the photos back into the envelope, stuffed the envelope in her purse and cleared her throat. "Thank you, Mr. Murphy. You mentioned something about a balance due?"

"Yes, this investigation took a day longer than anticipated."

She smirked. "You sure hit the jackpot, though."

I nodded.

She pulled a checkbook from her purse. I told her the balance on her account. She wrote out a check, set in on my desk. "Thank you. I appreciate both the urgency and confidentiality with which you handled this matter."

"You're welcome."

She moved as if she was going to get out of the chair, but stopped. "Mr. Murphy."

"Yes."

"Do you know the name of a good divorce attorney?"

I opened a drawer in my desk, pulled out a business card, and handed it to her. "Mr. Casoli's one of the best."

She stuffed the card in her purse. This time she did get up, but turned around before she reached the door. "May I ask you one more thing?"

I walked around my desk and put my hand on the doorknob. "Of course."

"Have you ever had a client come to you thinking their spouse was cheating and you discovered otherwise?"

I opened the door. "No."

She stepped into the reception area. "I figured as much. Good day, Mr. Murphy."

"Good day, Mrs. Pike."

Apparently, Tao Lung had had enough of the rain—he was gone. I lit a cigarette and propped my feet on the desk. Light traffic whizzed by the window. On occasion, a car would drive too close to the curb and send a wave of muddy water crashing on the sidewalk.

I grabbed the duplicate set of photos from my desk drawer, slipped them into Pike's folder. I wrote across the front of the manila file with a red pen, officially marking the case closed. I placed the file in one of the cabinets that lined the west wall of my office and sat back down.

Since coming to LA, I'd been a private eye. I wanted my life in Lake Point to stay in Lake Point, so I started from scratch. I apprenticed with Marshak Investigations on La Brea Avenue for 3,000 hours. Primarily, I worked cheating spouse cases. I was bored, yet thankful for the training.

When I obtained my license and opened Mid-City Confidential Investigations, I wanted to branch out, do something more exciting. Six months had passed, yet the work remained the same.

Until Carrie Sanders.

I could've spent days pondering the hidden meanings behind the Sanders case showing up when it did, my accepting it, and the plethora of possible scenarios for an ending to the case, but then I'd have been tired and ready for a nap.

I still had about thirty minutes before I needed to leave. I went online and searched the *Los Angeles Times* archive. In the first edition on Friday, November 17, I found the article: *Out of Town Private Eye Found Dead in Alley*. It said the caliber of the pistol was still undetermined, but confirmed Jenkins had been shot twice in the back of the head. Initial reports, though unconfirmed the reporter stressed, indicated that he was shot somewhere other than where his body was found-the parking lot on Selma and Morningside, two blocks from the famous Sunset and Vine. The acid in my stomach bubbled, the rank flavor crawled to my tongue. Whoever killed Jenkins not only knew what they were doing, but by dumping his body near such a busy intersection, intended on having it found quickly. To ward off future private eyes, perhaps?

The things I get myself into.

FOUR

I arrived at the California State Prison in Lancaster at one-fifty-five. I pulled my Ford F-350 into the lot, rolled near the front gates, and parked. The 72-mile drive had taken an hour and a half—possibly a record. For once, I was able to drive from my Mid-Wilshire office through Downtown LA, the Valley, Sylmar, and over the mountain on Highway 14 without running into any accidents or freeway closures. I let the truck idle and lit a cigarette.

Arturo was scheduled to be released at two. As I waited, I questioned my sanity for taking the Carrie Sanders case. Philip Jenkins, who may or may not have been experienced, was now dead, and his death was likely a direct result of his involvement with the case. What the hell made me think I could get closer, or even as close, and not wind up as he did?

I had no idea.

My mother used to tell me to be careful what I wished for—I might get it. Seems Mom was right. I'd wished for a more exciting case. I hadn't specified whether the case should be dangerous or not.

I had lit my third cigarette when noise erupted from the prison gates. Slowly, the huge sheets of steel parted. Someone yelled, "Good luck", and he appeared.

Two hundred pounds of rock hard muscle packed into a 5'11 frame walked through the gates. Fresh crew cut black hair on a head held proud as he reentered America. He carried a small black duffel bag in his right hand. When he reached the sidewalk, Arturo dropped the bag, held his arms out, and tilted his head toward the sky. He spun in a circle and screamed.

An ear-to-ear smile covered his face. He grabbed his bag and walked toward me. "Holmes, I'm free."

I stepped out of the truck. We met near the bumper. Arturo set his bag on the hood of my truck and stood in front of me. I wrapped my arms around him. "It's good to see you, buddy."

He returned the hug. "You, too. Goddamn, Jack, I'm free."

"Let's try and keep it that way, huh?"

He dropped his arms, stepped back. "I'm not out of the joint two fucking minutes and here you are jumping my shit." His monotone voice and straight face made me wonder how serious he was. He held my stare a moment, and then smiled. "Let's get out of here, eh?"

I grabbed his bag, tossed it between the bucket seats and climbed in.

"You hungry?" I said.

"For real food? Hell, yeah. I forgot what it tastes like. Almost."

"There's a Denny's in Palmdale."

"Sounds good."

I headed back on Avenue J. Arturo gazed out the window, a smile on his face.

I made my way down Highway 14 South, then west on Palmdale Blvd. I pulled into a parking space at Denny's, turned off the engine and opened the door.

"Let's eat," I said. When Arturo didn't move, I sat back in my seat and looked at him. "Everything okay?"

"Yeah, Holmes, everything's perfect."

"Let's go, then."

He stared at the dashboard a moment, said, "Thanks."

"For what?"

"For being a friend."

"You're welcome. But, if we don't get inside soon, I'm gonna die of starvation."

We got out. I set the alarm.

"Sentimental moments are rare for me, Holmes, and you took that one right in the shitter."

"Apparently, it's a gift of mine. Nadia said the same thing earlier. Not in such a poetic way, though."

"When are you two going to stop the bullshit and go out?"

"Now who's jumping whose shit?"

The restaurant was nearly empty. We grabbed two stools at the counter. A young brunette approached, popping pink gum in her mouth.

"How ya doing? You wanna start with something to drink?"

Arturo wanted a beer but settled for the kind with *root* in front of its name. I ordered a Coke. By the time the waitress brought our drinks, we had decided. She took our order, blew a bubble, and walked away.

"What's up with you today?" Arturo said.

"Nothing, why?"

"You seem down."

I moved my straw around the edges of my glass. "Nadia and I had a fight, again."

"See?"

"See what?"

"You two are destined to be a couple. You sure fight enough."

"She's a great girl."

"What the hell are you waiting for?"

"I don't know."

"Me, neither, Holmes."

I figured an answer would come when I needed it. So, as I always did when Arturo wanted to discuss Nadia, I changed the subject. "Have you decided what you're going to do now that you're out?"

"Tonight, I'm getting laid."

"Well, good for you. But, I meant about a job."

"I need one."

"Last month, you mentioned your brother-in-law's machine shop. Did you talk to him again?"

"Can't."

"Why not?"

"He got popped two weeks ago—looks like he'll be doing ten to twenty in Quentin for selling H."

The waitress set our plates on the counter. Arturo was already eating when she smiled, cracked her gum and left.

"You wanna work with me?"

Through a mouthful of eggs, he said, "You?"

"Yeah. What's wrong with that?"

"Nothing."

"You'll never find a better looking, more intelligent employer."

He nearly spit out his food laughing. "You're too much, Holmes."

"I took on a new case today."

"I don't know if my heart can handle the excitement."

"This is a real case. Missing girl."

"No shit?"

"It gets better."

"I'm listening."

"She's been missing since Halloween. Another private eye was on the case until he woke up dead Friday morning."

Arturo ate some of his hash browns. "And you need someone to cover your ass."

"Something like that."

"Let me ask you a question."

"Shoot."

"Why are you doing all this for me?"

"Hey, this is as much for me as it is for you."

Arturo set down his fork, wiped his lips and looked at me. "No, I mean everything, Holmes. What makes a successful white guy such as yourself take an interest in someone like me?"

"A Latino gangbanger."

"Yeah."

"You saved my life, Arturo. Remember?"

"Of course I remember." He paused as the waitress walked by. "I don't want you to feel like you owe me. You don't."

"You spent the last twenty-eight months in lockup for helping me."

"Oh, contraire, my good friend. I spent eight hundred thirty-eight and a third days in lockup."

"That's precise."

"Damn straight. I had nothing to do but think about it, day and night. I did my time in Lancaster because I robbed a liquor store with a forty-five. I only got caught because I saved your ass."

"Whatever."

"No, not whatever. Listen. Don't go feeling as though you owe me, Holmes. Let sleeping dogs lie." He took a drink of his root beer, held my stare. "I'm glad you're grateful, but that's behind us. Here and now, it's over."

"Hey, Arturo."

"What?"

"You want a job or not?"

"It looks like protecting you has just become my purpose in life."

"Is that a yes?"

"Sure, the detective gig should be kinda fun."

"Anyone ever tell you getting an answer from you is like pulling teeth?"

"Just you. Now, about Nadia."

I ignored him and ate my Eggs Benedict.

FIVE

I woke the next morning at seven. Arturo was asleep on the floor, smiling, so I figured last night proved successful for him. I checked the front door; it was locked. The key I had given him sat on the kitchen counter.

I lit my first cigarette of the day, walked onto the balcony, and inhaled the crisp morning air. The fourth floor view from my balcony on a clear day is soothing. Beyond the modern deco, three-story complex across Lucerne Boulevard, I can see West LA. Not that it mattered that morning; rain clouds still hung heavy and black in the sky. If the sun had risen, you couldn't tell it from here.

I went back inside and folded up my sofa bed. I stepped over Arturo on my way to the bathroom, and took a shower.

I expected Arturo to be awake by the time I finished, but he was still sound asleep. He had told me that even though he'd sleep on the floor, it would be far more comfortable than the cot he'd been provided by the State of California. I was glad to see him enjoying that comfort.

I planned on calling Nate Abbott that morning, but knowing he kept late hours, I decided to wait until nine. I grabbed a cutting board from a kitchen cabinet and took an onion, a few tomatoes, and a handful of cilantro from the refrigerator. I diced the onion and threw the squares into a mixing bowl. I ripped cilantro leaves from their stems and placed them in the bowl with the onion. I diced the tomatoes on the board and left them there—garnish for the final masterpiece.

I whipped six eggs and a healthy splash of milk into the bowl, and was melting butter in a pan when Arturo awoke.

He came into the kitchen scratching his skull and adjusting his underwear. "You know how to cook, Holmes?"

"Not half bad at it, either."

"You sure?"

"You don't trust me, you can go hungry."

"I'll take my chances."

"Good. I've got a pair of fresh towels on the sink if you wanna take a shower."

"Thanks."

I poured the omelet into the frying pan. "I also have an extra pair of jeans and a t-shirt in there if you wanna put on some clean clothes. Stuff might be a little big on you, though."

"Okay by me. Thanks."

"Make it quick. I'll have food ready in about ten minutes."

Without another word, Arturo disappeared behind the bathroom door.

I lit a cigarette and called Nate.

A voice, still thick with sleep, answered after seven rings. "Yeah."

"Nate, it's Jack."

"Jack? What time is it?"

"Nine. I need a favor."

Nate groaned. "Hang on." The receiver bounced off something hard, perhaps the floor or the dresser. "Shit. Jack?"

"I'm still here."

"Would it be possible to call me later, like in, say, six or seven hours?"

"C'mon, the morning's the best part of the day. You'll thank me for keeping you from missing it."

"Fuck you, Jack."

It sounded as if Nate was struggling to sit upright in his bed. "Christ!" The phone fell again. "Jack?"

"Still here."

"Shit. Give me ten minutes, then call me back."

"Don't be unplugging your phone or nothing."

Click.

Arturo laid on the floor, began doing sit-ups.

"Don't you need to let your stomach rest before you exercise?" I said.

"Shit, this ain't nothing, Holmes. I'm just warming up."

If this was Arturo's warm-up, I figured I'd get nauseous watching his regular routine.

Arturo pounded out sit-ups at an alarmingly fast pace for

exactly ten minutes. I smoked a cigarette and watched.

Then, I called Nate back.

He answered the phone on the first ring. "Jack."

"Hey, you must have ESP or something."

"Yeah, right. No one else is rude enough to call me at this ungodly hour."

"Sorry, buddy, but I need an answer on this one quick."

"Don't you always? What happened to your secretary?"

"Nadia has the day off."

"Lucky me. Who is it?"

"Name's Carrie Sanders. Sixteen. Last seen on Halloween in Lake Point, Wisconsin, and presumed to be in LA."

His fingers tapped on a keyboard. "Sixteen? Probably won't be much on her."

"I figured, but I have to start somewhere."

I gave him Carrie's social security number and birth date.

"No driver's license?"

"No."

"Five, five, five, six, seven, two, four. You gonna be there for a few?"

"How'd you know this number?" The moment it left my lips, I knew it was a stupid question—Nate likely had everything traced. "Never mind. Yes, I'll be here."

"I'll get back to you."

Click.

Arturo had traded sit-ups for one-armed pushups, alternating hands after every fifth one. "Well?"

"Well, nothing. He's gonna call back."

I walked back into the kitchen, washed the frying pan, cutting board and mixing bowl, and set them on a dish rack to air dry. I wiped the counters down and hung the towel over the faucet. I had just sat back on the couch when the phone rang.

"Jack, Nate. Zip on Carrie Sanders."

"Does your system check LAPD records, too?"

"Never discuss particulars, Jack."

"Oops, sorry."

"All the bases were covered."

Click.

Arturo was running in place. "Not much of a talker is he?"

"Nate feels it's professional to be quick and to the point."

"I bet his girlfriends love that."

"Speaking of girlfriends—how'd it go last night?"

"Great. I found an old home girl. We hopped in the backseat and, as they say, the rest is history."

"Good for you."

"Fucking A. I feel human again."

We drove west on Wilshire toward the office.

"What's first up today?" Arturo said.

"Raymond left me a stack of files. We'll go through it and see what we find."

"Joy."

"I hate to tell you, but real detectives aren't like the ones on TV. Most of our work is boring, with a capital B."

Arturo grunted, stared out the window.

I turned into the parking lot. "By the way, on Tuesdays I play racquetball with Tyrone, so I'll be out of the office for a few hours."

"Who's Tyrone?" Arturo said.

"Friend of mine. LAPD Vice."

"Where do you play?"

"LA Athletic Club."

"No shit? How the hell can you afford that?"

"Gift from a grateful client."

"Some client."

"Yep. The woman did everything she could to spend her husband's money before the divorce. She dropped cash for my lifetime membership."

"What'd the husband do to deserve that?"

"He was sixty-one, and banging his eighteen-year-old secretary."

"I'll bet that was fun for the secretary."

"I guess he was still an able-bodied guy. Besides, according to the wife, the girl got a good chunk of change from him."

I parked the truck, set the alarm, and we headed toward the building. The dark clouds had rolled east and the sun was breaking through the light gray ones that still lingered above our heads. I wondered whether the forecast of a clear, sunny afternoon would come true.

The elevators for my building were located in the rear, off the south parking lot. I was the only tenant on the first floor, which meant I shared the front door with only the leasing company—the employees of the law offices and accounting firms that occupied the upper three floors used the elevators.

I walked to my suite, unlocked the door and flipped on the

lights.

"Nice place," Arturo said. "This Nadia's desk?"

"Yeah. Don't touch anything."

"Jeez, Holmes. I was just asking."

"And I'm just saying. She's finicky."

"Damn, this stuff's way too organized."

I walked into my office, picked up the phone, and checked for messages. I found one—from Roy Lawson. I hit the speakerphone button and sat back in my chair. After the usual long time, no see stuff, Roy mentioned that he was now acting as official liaison for the Sanders family. He said it was better that way. He knew how I sometimes was a tad blunt when reporting my findings, he said, and he wanted to have an opportunity to soften the message on its way to the family. Funny thing was, I knew nothing, and I had no idea when, or if, I would know anything. But if Roy wanted to play middleman, fine with me.

Still.

I called the Beverly Hills Hotel, and said the desk clerk for 487.

"I'm sorry, sir, but the party has checked out."

"When?"

"I'm sorry again, sir, but I cannot divulge that information."

I hung up the phone. Arturo and I divided the pile of folders in half. I sat at my desk. He sat in a client chair opposite me. We jockeyed for the limited desk space, and began sifting.

By eleven-fifteen, I had read the two weekly reports Jenkins had filed. The first report, dated November third, covered his first two days on the job. During that time, he'd interviewed the family, Carrie's friends, and the neighbors. He'd also interviewed the Greyhound employee.

Jenkins started the next week in California. The report filed on November tenth mentioned his visiting the Greyhound bus station on 7th Street, the YWCA, the Los Angeles Mission, the Union Rescue Mission and a half dozen runaway centers or small shelters between the bus station and Hollywood. He'd also visited the morgue.

Behind the second report, Raymond had inserted a copy of a fax from Jenkins, dated Wednesday, the fifteenth. In it, Jenkins apologized for not returning Raymond's call that day. He also hinted to newly discovered information, but withheld further comment until "the facts could be ascertained."

I handed the fax to Arturo. "Jenkins was holding back."

He skimmed the document and handed it back. "Looks like it." He held up two documents. "I found the Greyhound manifest and the police report. Four females made the trip from Milwaukee to LA, though none traveled under the name Carrie Sanders, or anything close. The police report confirms that a Greyhound employee identified Carrie as having purchased a ticket. Oh, and it says the driver who drove the first leg out of Milwaukee that night died on his run back. Heart attack."

Carrie's eight-by-ten on the corner of my desk caught my eye. She was stunning. What could Jenkins have found out that had cost him his life?

I slid my chair back, stood. "I gotta go. Keep reading and see if anything else turns up."

"Okay, boss."

I left Arturo with instructions to answer the phone should it ring, and tell any prospective client that they'd have to schedule an appointment.

I walked to the front door. "After my racquetball game, I'm going to stop by Motel 6 and see what I can find."

"Can I go?"

"Where?"

"To Motel 6, Holmes."

His eyes took on puppy-dog sadness, not unlike Nadia's eyes when she wanted something.

"Sure. I'll swing by on my way."

He smiled. "Cool, thanks."

"The bathroom is at the end of the hall, on the right. The Mr. Coffee in my office works. Coffee's in a Ziploc next to the machine."

"I'm set."

"If anything urgent comes up, call my cell."

"Okay, boss."

On my way to the LA Athletic Club, I couldn't shake Carrie's image, the innocence in her smile. I hoped that innocence would still be there when I found her.

— Six —

A drenched white towel that smelled of hospital disinfectant was wrapped around my waist. The steam was so thick I couldn't see Tyrone on the bench across from me. I closed my eyes, leaned back. Layers of stress leaked from my body with the sweat that poured through my skin. I had gotten my ass kicked in three straight games, but as I relaxed in the steam room, I didn't care.

"Feel better yet?" Tyrone said, then laughed.

Tyrone was never one to let the loser down lightly. Perhaps it spawned from his usually being the loser. So, on the rare occasion that he did win, I let him gloat. "Yep. Thanks for asking."

I turned to the side, stretched my legs across the porcelain bench. I leaned against the tile wall, just below the steam head. It was nirvana—until someone turned on the valve without first looking inside.

I slid away from the wall as quickly as I could. "Shit."

Tyrone laughed. Puffs of steam rolled out as the door opened. I made out the silhouettes of two men through the white clouds.

"Whoa," one said, "guess there's enough steam."

The valve shut off. The men stepped inside. The one that sat next to me said, "Sorry."

Ten minutes later, I felt lightheaded and walked out. I grabbed a towel from the rack on the wall, leaned against the cool tile and wiped my face.

Tyrone came out of the steam room. "Hah, you couldn't even last as long in there."

"Fuck you."

"Yeah, yeah. Just remember who's da boss, baby. I whooped your little white ass."

I headed for the showers. "I let you win, Tyrone."

I jumped when a wet towel cracked against my ass.

"Keep talking, white boy."

I stood beneath ice-cold water. After my breathing slowed, I warmed up the water, soaped up and rinsed off. I was drying off in front of my locker when Tyrone came up.

I noticed a limp in his right leg. "You okay?"

He bit his lip, forced the limp gone. "Nothing wrong with me."

"You don't have to be a tough guy anymore, the game's over."

"You keep thinking that, too. You just keep thinking that."

I slipped into my Levi's. "I have a question."

"Here we go. Just cause I whooped your ass, don't think I'm extending any special favors."

"Look, you beat me good, okay?"

He looked at me, smiled. "Okay."

"You ever heard of a Carrie Sanders?"

"Nope. Should I have?"

"Probably not."

Tyrone stepped into his brown Dockers. "What about her?"

"She's a sixteen-year-old runaway."

"That really narrows it down."

He pulled a notebook from his locker, flipped it open and began writing. I repeated what little I knew and he wrote it down. He flipped his notebook shut, just like a pro.

"We're not done."

He grunted, reopened the notebook.

"I also need to find out about the death of a private eye named Jenkins."

"Now, that guy I've heard a little about."

Tyrone wrote down what I told him, then looked up. "I'm beginning to see a connection here. Isn't Sanders somehow related to Jenkins?"

"You really are a cop, aren't you?"

"Hey, I'm a little slow, but sooner or later . . ."

I turned toward my locker, slipped on my shirt. I sensed Tyrone's gaze burning holes in my back. "Yes."

"Yes, what?"

"Yes, I'm taking over Jenkins' case."

"And you hope Jenkins wasn't very good at his job."

"Why's that?"

"Cause if he was, you may wind up like he did."

Lovely thought. "Thanks for the support."

"Always happy to oblige."

I ran a brush through my hair and said goodbye to Tyrone. He was bragging of his victory to three guys sitting near him, oblivious of my departure.

I arrived back at the office at two-o-five. Arturo was reading a copy of *People*, sipping coffee. He noticed me, dropped his feet to the floor, and closed the magazine. "What's up, Holmes?"

"Looks like you've been working hard."

"I got through everything first."

I poured a cup of coffee. "And?"

"And nothing. I didn't find anything even remotely resembling a clue."

"That's usually the way it is."

The coffee was cold. I took a few quick sips, then poured it down the bar sink. "Ready to try again?"

"Sure."

"Let's go."

I hung a sign on my door—the one I always did when the office was unmanned. It gave my phone number and said that any visitors should call for an appointment.

My office didn't see many walk-ins, though. Every time I read a Spenser novel, it made me wonder if the foot traffic in Boston was so much greater than LA, if Spenser's just lucky, or both. I locked the door, and we headed for my truck.

"We did get a visitor today," Arturo said.

"Really?"

"Yeah. It was strange, though. A girl came into the office, but when she saw me, she screamed and ran."

"Sounds like a normal reaction."

"Women love me, Holmes. I ain't never scared one off."

"Sure."

I disarmed the truck and we climbed inside. I started the engine and slid into eastbound traffic on Wilshire. "So tell me about her."

"She was fine looking."

"That's a start."

"Lemme see. She was a brunette, average height, weight. She was looking at something on the desk, I think. I came out and asked if I could help her. She locked eyes with me for a second, screamed and bailed."

"Hmmm."

"What the hell is that? Hmmm."

"That's the sound us professional detectives make when we're pondering something."

I was surprised to find the exterior of the Motel 6 clean, graffiti-free. The curb directly in front of the motel was marked *Check-in Parking Only*. I pulled into the first of two spots and parked.

We climbed the steps to the front door. I stopped directly below the blue awning with *Welcome* in bold white letters across its face. "I'll do all the talking, okay?"

"Okay, boss."

I smiled. I was beginning to enjoy "okay, boss."

The lobby was small as lobbies go, but cleaner than I had expected. A sick bonsai tree sat on the far end of the counter, a single ornament weighing on its thickest branch. Propped in the dirt that probably hadn't seen water in months was a small sign: *Seasons Greetings from Motel 6*. A young Asian man, perhaps eighteen, wearing a sleeveless undershirt, black slacks and a thick gold chain around his neck, ran his hand through his gelled black hair, and set a registration card on the counter. His eyes darted from me to Arturo, then back.

"Two?" he said.

I pulled my wallet from my Levi's and flipped it open, revealing my PI license. He didn't seem impressed.

"I'm Jack Murphy. I'm here to settle up Philip Jenkins' account."

"Room number?"

"Don't know."

He stared at me a minute, his right eye twitched. "It might take me a while to find it."

I glanced at the computer on the desk, smiled. "If you don't want your money, fine by me."

I took a step toward the door.

"Wait." His fingers danced across the keyboard. In thirty seconds, he had Jenkins' account on the screen. "The room was booked November fourth, and paid through the seventeenth." He scratched at his diamond-shaped goatee with his forefinger. "You owe for four nights."

"Four?"

He pointed at a clock on the wall. "It's after twelve. You gotta pay for tonight."

"How much?"

He worked the keyboard some more. The computer beeped a couple times. "Three-hundred seven ninety-three."

"For four nights?"

He looked up, grinned. "Base rate."

He snatched the VISA from my hand, swiped it through the reader, and handed it back. The printer came to life. He tore the receipt from the printer, set it on the counter. I signed it, took my copy. "I'll need a room key."

"Extra room keys are ten bucks."

I slapped a ten on the counter. He handed me a key to room 108.

"All the way around back. You can park your car in underground valet. Entrance is on the north side of the building."

"We won't be that long."

"Doesn't matter. If you're car's still out front in ten minutes, it'll be towed."

He sat back in a wooden chair and fixed his eyes on the small black and white TV. We ceased to exist.

I read once that Motel 6 believed they had developed the perfect room. Not only did the use of every square inch make the customer feel the room was larger than it really was, its design was also easier to clean, or so they claimed. Which, of course, meant nearly every room in every Motel 6 in the world was identical. This room fit that mold to a tee.

We stepped onto the dark red, patterned carpet and I closed the door. The room was clean and comfortable, just like Tom Bodett promised it would be. "Start in the bathroom."

"What am I looking for?"

"Gather up everything."

"Everything?"

"Yep."

"Why?"

"When we're done, we'll send the stuff back to Jenkins' family."

"Okay, boss."

The top of the desk was bare. In its only drawer, I found a Gideon's bible, a few sheets of stationary and a gum wrapper. I took Jenkins' clothes from the dresser and piled them on one of the two double beds. The shelves on the nightstand were empty.

I picked up the phone and hit redial. Seven digits. Not necessarily local, but at least in the same area code. The phone rang six times, then a deep male voice answered.

"What?"

I hung up.

I was filling Jenkins' suitcase when Arturo came out of the bathroom, assorted toiletries clutched to his chest.

"Where do you want this stuff?"

"Put it in the suitcase."

"Okay. Find anything?"

"Nope."

"Me, neither."

After the suitcase was loaded, I set it on the floor and stripped the beds. I looked between the mattresses, found nothing. When we reached the front door, I said, "Hang on a sec."

I walked back to the garment valet that doubled as a TV stand, and, unlike the desk, wasn't bolted to the wall. I slid my fingers behind it. At the bottom, I felt something. "Help me here."

We slid the valet away from the wall. Lying on the floor was a notebook. I grabbed it, flipped it open. "Look what we have here."

"What?"

"Jenkins' notebook."

I opened the suitcase, set the notebook inside. "We need to stop by the front desk."

"For?"

"A copy of his bill."

"Why?"

"It'll show the calls he made."

"How do you know he made any?"

"I checked the redial on the phone."

"Wow."

"What?"

"I'm just in awe of your detective skills, that's all."

"You never know what might turn into a lead."

"No, I'm serious, Holmes. I never would've thought of that."

"I saw it in a movie once."

The clerk was annoyed that we had interrupted Rikki Lake—again—but he printed the statement and tore it from the printer. "There was a call made a few minutes ago. That'll be two bucks."

"Shit." I handed him a five.

"I don't have any change."

"You wouldn't."

He pocketed the bill. I dropped the key on the counter. We left.

SEVEN

We arrived back at the office at five-ten. Arturo went to make coffee and I removed the sign from the front door. I had just joined him in my office when I heard the front door open. I walked out to find two men standing near Nadia's desk.

"Can I help you?"

The larger of the two men, the one as solid as a redwood tree, closed the door, leaned against it and folded his arms. The skinny one removed his sunglasses, exposing an eighth-inch scar that ran from his left eyebrow across the bridge of his nose.

Skinny took a step forward. "You Murphy?"

"Yep."

"We're here about your case."

"Have a seat."

I motioned to the chair in front of Nadia's desk, but he shook his head. I smiled, folded my arms. "Okay. What case are we talking about?"

"The Sanders girl."

"What's up, Holmes?" Arturo said from over my shoulder.

Redwood straightened and dropped his arms to his side.

"These gentlemen would like to discuss Carrie," I said.

I glanced over my shoulder and saw Arturo leaning in my office doorway. A suitable offset to Redwood. I looked back at Skinny. "I'm afraid I can't discuss the case with you unless you have direct involvement. Do you have direct involvement?"

"I'm here to offer you ten-thousand dollars to walk away."

"Interesting." I kept my eyes on Skinny. "Arturo, did you hear that? These nice gentlemen wanna pay me ten grand to drop the case."

"Awful generous of them."

"Yes, it is. Why, may I ask, are you being so generous?"

"That's none of your concern."

"Sure it is. I'd like to know why it's worth so much to have me drop the case."

"The girl doesn't wanna be found."

I fished a cigarette from the pack in my shirt pocket. "She doesn't?"

"No."

I took my time lighting my cigarette, then looked up at him. "She hired you gentlemen to come and tell me that?"

"Sure."

"Makes me wonder where a sixteen-year-old girl got the kind of money to hire such well-dressed professionals."

"Wondering too much is sometimes a dangerous thing."

"Inquiring minds want to know."

Skinny looked confused. I guess he wasn't familiar with the trash magazine's slogan. He scratched his head, then reached into his jacket. My heart skipped a beat, my hand went to the small of my back, my fingers to the cold steel of my Sig Sauer 9mm. I relaxed when Skinny's hand came back with a thick manila envelope. He dropped it on Nadia's desk.

"Here, smart-ass. You're fired."

I smiled at Skinny. "Hey, Arturo, can he fire us when he didn't hire us?"

"Don't think so."

"Me, either. Thanks, but no thanks. Why don't you take your envelope and go back to wherever you came from. If Carrie wants me off the case, all she has to do is come and see me. It's my job to locate her, not return her to her parents."

"That would be a big mistake," Skinny said.

I grabbed the envelope and pushed it into his chest. Redwood took a step forward. I heard Arturo do the same. "Take the money and go."

"You're making lots of trouble for yourself."

"I've been known to do that. And tell your boss, whomever he or she is, that I don't like being visited by the help. If someone wants to get a message to me, I'd appreciate hearing it in person."

Skinny took the envelope from my hand and stuck it back in his jacket pocket. "We'll be seeing you again, real soon."

"Pleasure. And be sure and bring your mute friend again. This has been a blast."

"Fuck you," Skinny said, then turned to leave. Redwood

opened the door and they both walked out. Skinny stuck his head back in, said, "You're gonna be sorry. Real sorry."

"I already am."

After they left, I turned to Arturo, said, "Still think this detective gig is kinda fun?"

Arturo wanted to visit some friends, so I let him use my truck. I planned on being at the office a while and I could walk home from there anyway. He promised to stay out of trouble, thanked me and left.

I looked at the list I'd compiled on a yellow pad of paper. Eager to check off one right away, I called Roy.

"Jack. How the hell are you?"

"I'm doing okay. How about yourself?"

"Great. Retirement has me finally loving life."

"I hear it has a way of doing that to people."

"I'll tell you. On the green at sunrise to play eighteen holes, then lunch at the club with a couple friends. Man, it sure beats the hell out of working for a living."

"I imagine."

"How's business?"

"Can't complain. I got your message."

"Oh, good."

"Why does Sanders feel he needs a liaison?"

"Hang on a sec, Jack. Let me pick up the cordless."

The mouthpiece resonated as Roy dropped it against something hard. I waited, thankful he wasn't piping elevator music through a hold system at his home. I know the idea is to relax and soothe the waiting caller, but it had a little different effect on me—I always wanted to shoot the person who made me listen to it.

He picked up another extension, then hung up the phone. Low static hummed on the line.

"Jack?"

"Still here."

It sounded like he slid open a glass door, then shut it again. A slight breeze kissed the mouthpiece. "I don't talk business in front of my wife."

"No problem. Tell me why Sanders wants a liaison."

"I actually suggested it."

"Oh?"

"Raymond proclaims to be a realist. He says that he knows you may uncover some bad news. And he says he can handle whatever it is. But Jack, between you and me, I don't think he realizes the possibilities. Drugs, prostitution, porn. Regardless what he says, he ain't ready to hear that about his little girl."

"I didn't get that impression when he came into my office."

"Just a front, Jack. Believe me, we go back a ways."

"Do you remember Carrie's disappearance?"

"Vividly. In a town small as this, how could you not?"

"I guess."

"Carrie was well-known, well-liked, and a good looking young lady. She was, and still is, sorely missed here."

"Did you know Philip Jenkins?"

"Not really. When we spoke, it was usually by phone."

I lit a cigarette. "What can you tell me about him?"

"Not much. He was one of the best PI's in town, but mediocre nonetheless. Initially, Raymond wanted to use a local. I guess he figured a local would have a better chance finding Carrie. What Raymond didn't know was that Jenkins was never a cop and had never been to LA. He was in over his head from the start."

The rush hour traffic was building. I watched it through my window. The sun had finally begun to break through the cloud cover—just in time for it to retire for the night. "You think his death had something to do with Carrie?"

"Don't you?"

"Maybe."

"I don't know much about LA, so maybe it was just a random act of violence. But his last communication indicated something new, though he refused to speculate."

"Until the facts could be ascertained."

"You read it."

"Along with a stack of other documents Raymond left for me. Were you a liaison with Jenkins, too?"

"Near the end I was."

"Did you talk to him between the fax and his death?"

"No."

"So, you have no idea what lead was he following up?"

Roy paused, cleared his throat. "I can only guess. He and I had had some brief discussions about a rumor that Carrie had been taken first to Los Angeles, and then shipped to Mexico to work in the growing child escort trade. Maybe he was following that up."

"Have any names? Particulars?"

"Sorry, no. One thing I can tell you about Jenkins is that he was overtly cautious when it came to sharing unverified information."

"Why would someone take a girl from Lake Point, ship her to LA, and then to Mexico? Seems El Paso or Calexico would have been easier checkpoints to cross than San Diego."

"Maybe they flew her down."

"Maybe. But then why wouldn't they have just flown her out of Chicago?"

"I have no idea."

"Then again, this all assumes she didn't come to LA of her own freewill."

"True."

I leaned back in my chair. "One more thing."

"Yeah?"

"Do you have Raymond's phone number?"

"Of course. Why?"

"He hired me and I need him to tell me he wants you in the middle."

He rattled off a number. I copied it on the yellow pad.

"Thanks, Roy."

Click.

Roy had been my captain during my days with the Lake Point Police Department. As such, I had gotten to know him. I knew he was moody, and his hanging up on me was not out of the ordinary. Still, it bothered me.

I finished my cigarette and glanced down at my list. Then, I called Tyrone. He wasn't in, but the woman said she'd page him.

While I waited for his call, I fished Jenkins' notebook from his suitcase in the corner of my office, laid it on my desk and started reading.

Jenkins started this spiral five by six notebook on day one of the Sanders case. The first two weeks' worth of notes followed his reports nearly to the tee, though I didn't really expect to find any discrepancies.

The entries beginning November thirteenth were what I was looking for. The week's notes began with "Forbidden Love Productions." Though the notes said nothing of how he had ascertained this lead, they went on to mention that the company was incorporated July 2, 1990, in Nevada, and that a Jonathan K. Donovan held the offices of President, Secretary and Treasurer. The company filed for both foreign corporation status with California and a city business license in Los Angeles on July 9. The address used in both cases was in the 800 block of Seward Street in the Media District.

Forbidden Love was solely owned by Aurora Entertainment Group, and Aurora dissolved it on April 24, 1992. The only thing Jenkins had on Aurora was that it was a Cayman Islands corporation. Below that, the words "dead end."

I threw my feet on my desk, leaned back in my leather chair and stared out at Wilshire. The rush hour traffic was slowly winding down. I wanted to know how Jenkins had gotten the lead on Forbidden Love, and why he went through the trouble of digging up the legal particulars on it, and attempted to do so on its parent as well. Then again, I always was like that. I wasn't simply satisfied that something was—I wanted to know why it was. One of the stumbling blocks between God and me all these years.

Jenkins also had notes on Western Land Management, the company that leased the building on Seward to Forbidden Love. He discovered this was also a Cayman Islands corporation.

I picked up the phone.

"Talk to me."

"Nate, it's Jack."

"How lucky can I be? Twice in one day."

"Amazing, isn't it?"

"Truly."

"What can you tell me about Cayman Islands corporations?"

"Why, you looking to hide some money?"

"Don't I wish."

"What do you wanna know?"

"Can you find out anything about them?"

"Doubt it. That country's locked up tighter than a chastity belt."

"Which means?"

"Unless you're with the IRS, and have a lot of clout, you're SOL."

"Thanks, anyway."

"Hey, next time you call, make it a paying job, okay?"

Click.

I turned the page. The last page had two items that needed Jenkins' attention: "check out Seward Street" and "check out Jonathan Donovan."

And one of these two things had gotten him killed.

EIGHT

I had burned through the last of my cigarettes when Tyrone called back.

"You rang?" he said.

"Yep. Got anything for me?"

"Lemme see. It's been, what? Six hours?"

"Yeah, I know. Plenty of time."

"Right. Hang on, let me get my notebook."

I fished my pocket but came back with my empty pack of cigarettes. I balled up the pack, shot for the wastebasket. And missed. One of the reasons I never tried out for basketball.

"Okay, your Jenkins was the unfortunate victim of a mugging gone bad."

"Bullshit."

"Maybe so, but that's the official word."

"What about the execution-style killing?"

"You'd be surprised what lowlife gangbangers pick up from television these days."

"Uh-huh."

"I didn't write the report. I'm just telling you what I know."

"Okay."

"The Sanders girl is NE. Non-existent. Can't find her anywhere."

"I thought the Lake Point Police had spoken to LAPD?"

"And maybe they did. Have you ever been down to MP? There's enough paper to build a forest down there. Maybe it didn't make the computer. Maybe their conversation was no more than professional courtesy. God knows, enough locals turn up missing to keep them busy for an eternity."

"One more thing."

"Of course there is."

"This one's easy. I need info on a phone number."

I gave him the number from Jenkins' redial.

"I'll try to run it down tomorrow."

"Could you do it now?"

"Now? I'm about to eat dinner."

"C'mon, what's it gonna take, five minutes?"

Tyrone grunted and told me to hold on. I drummed my pen against my yellow pad until he returned. "Forbidden Love Productions, Seward Street, LA."

"Can't be. That company was dissolved in '92."

"You're the private detective. Figure it out."

Click.

I threw my notes and Jenkins' notebook into my briefcase and spent the next half-hour going through the stuff we took from the motel room. As I suspected, nothing turned up.

Tired and craving a smoke, I grabbed my briefcase, locked up and stopped by the 7-Eleven across the street for cigarettes before going home.

I called Raymond from my apartment at eight-o-one, and woke him up. The two-hour time difference had slipped my mind. I kept it brief, desiring only to confirm that Roy should be the liaison. Raymond confirmed. I apologized and hung up.

Arturo came back ten minutes later, and we walked down Wilshire to El Pollo Loco for dinner. We ate inside, then walked to St. Andrews Place and headed north. I needed to return a copy of the latest Jeffrey Deaver novel I had borrowed from the library. The night air was crisp, clean. This section of town didn't have any malls, or many retail properties at all, so the holiday hoopla was restricted to decorations slung in and about the high-rises, apartments and restaurants. Of course, the lack of retail also meant the holiday crowds didn't infiltrate this area much, so I couldn't complain.

St. James Church was having a get-together. Small groups of people hovered on the stairs and the sidewalk near the old, gothic building. The architecture fascinated me, and one day I had stopped by at lunchtime to have a look at the interior. Only, I couldn't—the church doors were locked. So, as we passed, I snuck a peek inside. Three boys in their Sunday best were running wild, throwing beanbags at one another. A short, fat kid nearly ran into me as we tried to maneuver by. When he realized he had been a disturbance, he looked up and, almost inaudibly, said, "Sorry, Mister." Then, he ran off.

As we rounded the corner on First Street, Arturo said, "So, do you think those guys are a real threat?"

"What do you think?"

"I think they wouldn't tie their shoes without someone's approval. But, that doesn't make them docile."

"True. What bothers me, though, is their lame reason for being there. Am I supposed to be so dumb so as not to question their working for Carrie?"

"Maybe."

I dropped the book in the night drop. Then, we continued walking west down First. I figured we could go back to Wilton, then head south back to Wilshire. Since Arturo wasn't familiar with this area, I decided to play tour guide.

Unfortunately, there wasn't much to tell of this area. Four blocks on either side of Wilshire Boulevard, the neighborhood declined. Still, for Los Angeles, this was a relatively safe area. Four or five years earlier, the Asian community had taken stock in this section of Mid-Wilshire. Along with the presence of bilingual signs, the absence of graffiti became apparent, as did the absence of Christmas decorations. This area was certainly no Beverly Hills, but it was a nice place to be.

"I got a tip for you," Arturo said as we turned on Wilton. "Don't ever take a job as a tour guide."

"Why not? You don't like my sexy voice?"

"Shit, Holmes. You're voice ain't got nothing to do with it. You just can't tell a story worth a shit."

"Thanks."

"Anytime."

This area of Wilton was dimly lit, and very quiet. Comprised of mostly apartment complexes, their white or beige walls were lined with thick shrubs, and beneath the shrubs, swaths of purple, red, and yellow plants of one variety or another blossomed.

Without warning, a small Asian boy, perhaps twelve, jumped from behind a bush, screaming in his native tongue. He held a 9mm Smith and Wesson in his hands. I had my pistol halfway out of its sheath before I realized he was pointing a water pistol at me.

"What the hell are you doing?" I said.

The boy stood there, frozen, the pistol still pointed at my chest. Another boy appeared slowly from behind the bush. He looked at me for a moment, then ran into the complex.

"Where'd he go?"

The boy shrugged his shoulders, then lowered the pistol.

"Do you realize that looks like a real gun? Do you, boy?"

"Hey," Arturo said, "lighten up."

"Fuck you, Arturo." I squatted in front of the boy. "What you did was very stupid. You could've been shot."

He blinked, tears rained on his cheeks.

"What the fuck is going on here?"

I looked up to find a heavyset Asian man rushing me. Behind him, the little boy who had run off moments earlier smiled. I straightened.

The man pushed against my chest. "I'm talking to you, motherfucker."

"Hey, lighten up, pal."

"Fuck you. This is my son."

"Well, good. Then you can tell him not to jump out of the bushes at strangers with what looks like a real gun."

"Aren't you a little old to be picking on a kid?"

"Your kid almost got himself shot."

He tried to push my chest again. This time, I anticipated it and swatted away his hands.

"Is that some kind of a threat?"

"No, it's reality, asshole. You should teach your kids better."

"You got some nerve."

I stared at him a minute longer, then walked away.

"Go ahead, walk away, you shit," he said.

I kept walking.

Arturo caught up with me in a few strides. "Hey, Holmes, what just happened there?"

"Nothing."

"Bullshit, nothing. Why did you go off on the kid like that?"

I stopped. "I don't wanna talk about it."

"That's not like you, Holmes."

I started walking again. "Fuck you."

"That's not much like you, either."

We walked to my apartment without sharing another word.

I tossed in my bed for about an hour. I went to the balcony, braved the cold breeze in a pair of shorts, and smoked a cigarette. Then I got back into bed.

I knew the dream was coming, but as so often before, I was powerless to stop it.

"YOU READY?" SERGEANT LEWIS SAID.

"YES, SIR," I SAID.

OFFICERS HILL AND MEEHAN AGREED.

"ON THREE, WE GO IN. HE'S LIKELY IN THE BEDROOM, RIGHT SIDE IN BACK. NELSON AND JONES ARE IN BACK IN CASE HE MAKES A BREAK FOR IT. LET'S MAKE IT TIGHT."

LEWIS COUNTED DOWN, THEN WE RUSHED LANCE JOHNSON'S GRAND AVENUE HOME.

I WENT THROUGH THE DOOR FIRST. THE FRONT ROOM WAS DARK. SOMEONE BEHIND ME FLICKED ON A FLASHLIGHT AND PANNED THE ROOM WITH THE STRONG BEAM.

"POLICE. WE HAVE A WARRANT," I SHOUTED.

I TOOK A STEP FORWARD.

THEN IT HAPPENED.

FROM BEHIND THE COUCH IN THE FAR CORNER OF THE ROOM, A FIGURE JUMPED UP WITH A BERETTA IN ITS HANDS. I FIRED TWICE. THE FIGURE SLAPPED AGAINST THE WALL, GRUNTED, AND FELL. SCREAMS ERUPTED FROM THE BACK OF THE HOUSE. I HEARD NELSON AND JONES BREAK THROUGH THE BACK DOOR. WE FANNED OUT AND INVADED THE HOUSE, ROOM BY ROOM. AFTER A MINUTE, NELSON YELLED, "GOT HIM."

WITH JOHNSON IN CUSTODY, WE WAITED OUTSIDE FOR THE ARRIVAL OF THE INVESTIGATIVE UNIT. A TEAM OF THREE MEN AND ONE WOMAN ENTERED THE HOUSE WHILE A FOURTH MAN STAYED OUTSIDE AND TOOK MY STATEMENT. THIRTY MINUTES LATER, I WAS INSTRUCTED TO GO INSIDE THE HOUSE.

"WE NEED YOU TO VERIFY THAT THIS WAS THE SUBJECT YOU SHOT."

"ONLY ONE PERSON WAS SHOT, AND I SHOT THEM."

"PLEASE."

I LEANED OVER THE COUCH AND EYED THE SUBJECT. A YOUNG BOY LAY MANGLED ON THE FLOOR, DRENCHED IN BLOOD. HIS EYES WERE OPEN, FIXED, AND LIFELESS.

I screamed. Soaked in sweat, I bolted upright.

"What? What is it?" Arturo said.

I rubbed my face in my palms. "Shit."

"What? You okay, Jack?"

"I'm fine."

I grabbed my cigarettes and went to the balcony. I lit a cigarette as the wind sliced through me.

"Hey, Holmes, you gonna tell me what's going on or what?"

I glanced at the white stucco building across from mine. A couple was making out on a third-floor balcony.

"Jack, what's up?"

I proffered a cigarette to Arturo. He took it, then used my lighter. "Thanks."

"I'm sorry I got bitchy with you earlier."

"No sweat, Holmes. I'm used to it."

"I'm serious. I had no right to jump your shit like that."

"Does this mean you're gonna tell me what happened?"

Since Arturo was staying with, and working for, me, I figured it would only be a matter of time before he knew. So, I told him.

Everything.

"No shit," he said.

"Yeah. And I almost did it again last night."

"Hey, you stopped yourself, long before you'd have shot that kid."

"Maybe."

"No fucking maybe about it. You reacted as anyone would have, especially considering our visit from those two goons last night."

Skinny and Redwood.

"I ain't no shrink, but it sounds to me like you're beating yourself up over something that couldn't have been avoided. It was dark, you were in a volatile situation, and you reacted to save your life and the lives of your fellow officers."

"Shit."

"What? Am I all fucked up?"

"No, you're not. That's about word for word what my psychiatrist told me."

"No shit? I have talents I never knew existed."

I finished my cigarette, threw the butt over the balcony.

"Can we go in now, Holmes? It's fucking cold out here."

NINE

Arturo and I arrived to a locked office just after nine. I opened up, started some coffee, and worked on a jelly-filled donut we'd picked up on the way.

Arturo bit into an éclair. "I thought I was gonna get to meet Nadia this morning."

"Me, too."

I checked the voicemail, but found no messages. I powered on my computer and printer, opened the shades. Though still overcast, the weatherman promised sunshine by noon. I was preparing.

After pouring a cup of coffee, I sat at my desk and called Nadia's apartment. Four rings later, her soft voice told me to leave a message. I did.

"You think that was her that came in here yesterday?" Arturo said.

I popped the last bite of the donut in my mouth. "Maybe."

"I'm sorry if I scared her or something."

"Don't worry about it. You're a scary guy on first impression."

"After which time, I become loveable. Right?"

"Uh-huh."

He smiled. "I knew it."

By ten-thirty, I began to worry about Nadia. In the three-plus years I'd known her, I never recalled her being late for work. And on the few occasions that she was sick, she always called well-ahead of her scheduled arrival time. I tried her apartment again. When her machine answered, I hung up the phone.

"I'm gonna run by Nadia's and make sure she's okay."

"You think she's home?"

"I hope so. She's never late for work."

He reached for another éclair. "Maybe she's sick."

"Maybe."

"You want me to hold down the fort?"

"Yep."

"I can do that."

"I know. That's why I'm putting you in charge."

"Really?"

"Just while I'm gone."

"Anything you want me to do?"

"Nope. Just enjoy your donuts and answer the phone if it rings."

"You don't get many phone calls, do you?"

"Nope."

"Okay, boss."

"Nadia lives in Westwood, so I may be gone for a couple of hours."

"Okay. I hope everything's alright."

"Me, too."

Arturo was devouring his third éclair when I left.

I drove west on Wilshire through Beverly Hills. I turned right on Veteran Avenue, paralleling the Los Angeles National Cemetery. At Weyburn Avenue, I hung another right, then parked in front of the garage marked #9 on the corner of Gayley Avenue.

I climbed the stairs to the third landing of the split-level, twenty-unit structure. To my left, apartment number nine. I knocked on the door, waited.

I knocked a second time before the chain slipped and the door opened.

"Jack."

"Hi, Nadia. How's it going?"

"Okay." She leaned against the door, wearing an oversized white shirt. Her tan legs and feet were bare. Her eyes spoke of sadness, her lips taut. She drummed her fingers lightly against the door. "Come on in."

"Thanks."

Nadia had lived in this same apartment since I first met her, yet this was my first time inside. The front door opened into a large living room. Straight ahead, a dining table with four chairs, and beyond it, a u-shaped kitchen. To my right, two six-foot, hunter green couches and a white-washed square end table formed an ell. A slender crystal vase with a dozen pink and white carnations sat in the center of the end table. A single matching armchair completed the conversational area.

"Have a seat. Would you like something to drink?"

"No, I'm fine."

I sat on the north-facing couch. To my left, a large sliding glass door led to a deck area and a partially blocked view of the Veterans' Cemetery. Nadia sat on the other couch, a glass of orange juice in her hand. She tucked her legs under her, peered through the glass doors.

I lit a cigarette. "I was worried about you."

Nadia picked up the ashtray from the couch and set it on the table.

I looked at her. "Everything okay?"

She looked away. "Everything's fine."

I glanced through an archway in the north wall, noticed a door due north and a window to the west. The east side of the room held no windows, probably because it faced the common walkway to the apartment behind hers, but the architect seemed to have drawn in as much glass as he or she could on the west wall. I looked at her, said, "I don't mean to be nosy, but . . ."

"But you're going to be anyway."

"Yeah. If everything's fine, how come you're not at work?"

"I just didn't feel good today."

"Why didn't you call then?"

She sipped her juice. "I didn't know what time you'd be in."

"We do have voicemail, you know."

Nadia plucked a cigarette from her pack. I leaned over with my lighter and lit it for her.

"Thanks."

"You're welcome."

She looked at me. Her eyes were puffy and pink.

"Arturo told me you stopped by the office yesterday."

"Shit. Jack, I'm sorry. I didn't think he'd recognize me."

"He didn't. But, I don't have many beautiful brunettes come into the office and go to your desk."

"You're sweet."

"He said you screamed and ran out when you saw him."

"He scared me. I guess I didn't expect to see anyone but you."

"Fair enough. But why run out?"

"I told you, I was scared."

I tapped the ashes from my cigarette in the ashtray. "They say it's supposed to be sunny by noon. You think it'll happen?"

Nadia stood, walked to the sliding glass door. Then, she began to pace. "Jack, there's something I need to tell you."

"Okay."

Nadia smoked her cigarette, her gaze moving from the carpet to the deck. Her hand grabbed the handle and slid open the door a couple inches. A cool breeze wafted into the room. "Arturo scares me."

"He's a scary guy at first glance."

"That's not it."

"What is it, then?"

She started pacing again. An inch-long ash dropped from her cigarette to the gray carpet. She either didn't see it, or chose to ignore it. "I have a problem with Latino men."

"Bad relationship?"

She chuckled, though it didn't seem to originate from a happy place. "I guess you could say that."

"You don't have to talk about it if you don't want to."

Nadia walked toward me, sat next to me on the couch. "The thing is, I think I need to talk about it."

"I'm honored you've chosen me to share it with."

Nadia smiled. This one was genuine. "You're a great guy, you know that?"

I smiled back. "Yep."

"When I was fourteen . . ." She choked on emotion, placed a hand to her mouth. "When I was fourteen, I was at a party. It was July fourth." She got up and paced again. "I was at this guy's house. His name was Jose."

I wondered if this was as painful for her as it appeared on her face. She leaned over the end table, smashed her cigarette into the ashtray. Then, she lit another and resumed her pacing.

"It was about midnight, or a little after. My friend Sonya had left already. I remember she was afraid her parents would have a fit if she stayed out any later. You see, I liked Jose—a lot. So, when he said he wanted to show me a painting in his room, I went with him." She glanced at me, then away. Tears welled in her eyes. "Once we were in his room, he locked the door. 'So we won't be disturbed', he said."

I leaned back and let her take her time getting it out.

"He raped me."

The tears broke free as she began to weep. I walked over to her, wrapped my arms lightly around her. She fell into me, cried into my chest. After a minute, she draped her arms around my back. I became aware that tears had gathered in my own eyes.

She pulled away and stabbed at her eyes and cheeks with her hands. "This is ridiculous."

"Why? Certainly it's still painful."

"Yeah, it is. But, I shouldn't be dumping this on you."

I held her chin in my hand and tilted her head until our eyes met. "What are friends for?"

She smiled, then leaned forward and kissed me. Her soft lips brushed against mine, then I tasted the sweetness of her tongue. It was our first kiss, and it was as strange as it was invigorating. I held her tight as our tongues danced. She moved her hands across my back, pressing her body tightly against mine. My hands explored the firmness of her muscles, the small of her back. I retracted my hands when they fell below her waist.

I withdrew my tongue and averted my stare, focusing it over her shoulder to a painting on the wall.

"What's the matter?" she said.

"Nothing. I was just surprised."

"Me, too. I never thought I'd have the chance to kiss you."

Me, either.

I glanced back at her. Her eyes, full of invitation, held my gaze for a moment, then she stepped around me, deposited her dying cigarette in the ashtray.

"I'm sorry Arturo brought back these memories."

"Oh, he didn't bring them back. They never left."

"Thank you for sharing."

"Thank you for listening, Jack."

She sat on the couch, then patted the space next to her. I sat down.

"About that," she said.

"What?"

"That kiss. I'm sorry."

"Why? I enjoyed it."

"Did you?"

"Why, didn't you?"

"Very much. I just wasn't sure. With your feelings for Ellen and all."

"What feelings?"

"I know you still care about her."

"I loved Ellen with all my heart and then one day, she bailed. Since I don't have any memories of long fights or wicked words, it's hard to place my anger about the whole thing. I do care about her. I always will. But, that's it."

"You do need to stop letting Ellen run your life, though."

"I'm not letting her run my life."

"Oh, no? You let her call you and gloat about her wedding. That's crazy, Jack. She's just trying to piss you off, or win you back. Either way, you're better off without her."

I knew Nadia was right. But, I knew I didn't harbor any misunderstood feelings for Ellen, either. I didn't like talking about Ellen at all. "Maybe."

"For sure."

I snuffed my cigarette in the ashtray. "About Arturo."

"Listen, I don't want you doing anything about Arturo. I know you wouldn't bring anyone into the firm that would do either of us any harm. I just need to get to know him, that's all. I'm sure he's a great guy."

"He is, actually. I hope you two can get along. He told me he was sorry for scaring you yesterday."

"It was cruel, what I did."

"Don't worry about it. Arturo understands. You're not the first person that saw him and ran. He commanded lots of respect that way in the old days."

She smiled. "I'm sure most people steered clear of him."

"They did. But, now he's on our side."

"That's good."

"I have to tell you something."

I told Nadia about Skinny and Redwood's visit. And she kissed me again.

TEN

It was one-o-three when I parked on Seward Street, half a block south of Digital Pipeline Studios. The two-story, off-white square box with a Spanish-tiled roof had blue and white striped awnings hanging above each of the four east-facing windows. A solid blue, circular awning hung above the wood door that was set three steps above the sidewalk it bordered. Bars covered the first-floor windows. An alley ran along the south side of the building. Between the upstairs windows, directly above the door, hung a black plastic cut-out of a half-moon shaped logo being held by a hand. Below it, carved from the same black plastic, *Digital Pipeline, Audio Mixing and Post-Production.*

I finished my cigarette, set the alarm, and crossed the street. As I walked atop the cracked concrete, I let my fingers slide under my jacket, to the small of my back. I had no idea what was waiting for me behind the wooden door of the building, but touching the cold steel of my Sig made me feel better.

Bells jingled as I pulled open the door. A young redhead sat behind a birch-paneled ell. Her neon pink cutoff read: *Can You Make Me Scream?*

"Can I help you?"

I pulled a small piece of folded paper from my pants pocket, leaned against the reception desk, and unfolded it. "I hope so. I'm looking for a friend of mine."

She touched her bottom lip with a fire-engine red fingernail.

I smiled, glanced at my paper. "This is Digital Pipeline, right?"

"Sure is."

I recited the address, she confirmed it.

"Then I guess I'm at the right place."

"My name is Linda."

"Hi, Linda. I'm Jack. I'm looking for Jonathan Donovan."

Linda pouted. "There's no one here by that name."

"Are you sure?"

"Honey, I know every one of the eight people that work here, and I'm sorry to say he ain't one of them."

"Only eight?"

"Only eight."

"What do you do here?"

"Just like the signs says out front. Audio mixing and post-production."

"For who?"

"Whoever needs our services. Mostly studios and indie filmmakers."

"Sounds fascinating."

She shook her head. "Not really. Sometimes we get to see a movie early, but not usually. Only Pete gets to see everything we do."

"Who's Pete?"

"He's the VP of Production."

"You guys stay busy in this line of work?"

"Sure do. We always have at least two films we're working on."

"Anything I'd recognize?"

"Depends."

"On?"

"Do you watch skin flicks?"

"You guys do pornos here?"

"Oh, yeah. All the biggies—Vivid, Four X, Gentlemen's Club. You name it, we've probably overdubbed the oohs and aahs."

I smiled and pulled Jenkins' business card from my wallet. "Johnny gave me this address and told me to stop by when I was in LA." I handed her the card. "I wonder if maybe you've seen him around."

She studied the card for a minute. "This says Philip Jenkins."

I chuckled. "Yeah, it was a gag gift at a birthday party a couple years ago. Johnny always wanted to be a private eye. But, it's the only picture I have of him."

She proffered the card. "Sorry, I've never seen him."

I pulled a picture of Carrie from my shirt pocket. What the hell, I was already here. "Have you ever seen his friend?"

Again, she took enough time to be polite before handing the picture back. "No, but isn't she kind of young for him?"

"She's a lot older than she looks."

A man who didn't look a minute older than twenty came out of a back office. He wore a white button-down shirt, silver tie and black slacks. With his spiked, dirty-blond hair, he bore a slight resemblance to Billy Idol.

"Linda, did Eric call yet?"

"No, not yet."

"When he does, be sure and get me."

"Okay."

Billy Idol started back down the hall.

"Oh, Pete," Linda said.

"Yes."

"See if you recognize the people in these pictures."

Pete came back into reception. I handed him Carrie's photo first. He let his eyes brush across the photo and handed it back.

"Sorry, never seen her."

I handed him Jenkins' card. A twitch developed beneath his left eye. He wiped at it with a finger. "Sorry."

"You don't recognize him?"

"No. Should I?"

"I don't know."

He stared at me a second. "Well, then, what exactly are you doing here?"

"Looking for my friend."

"And who is your friend?"

"Johnny Donovan."

The eye twitched again, more severe this time. "Who?"

"Johnny. He gave me this address and told me to stop by anytime."

"Linda, do we have anyone here named, what'd you say? Johnny?"

"You mean as the VP of Production you don't know all eight people that work here?" I said.

He stared for a moment, then cleared his throat and straightened his tie. "What did you say your name was?"

"I didn't, but it's Jack."

"Well, Jack. What the fuck do you want?"

"I told you . . ."

He held up his hands. "Okay, okay. I wish I could help you, but I don't know this Johnny or either person in those photographs. Are you a cop or something?"

"Or something."

He chewed his bottom lip. "I'm going to have to ask you to

leave."

I took a step forward—he took a step back.

"You sure you don't know who Johnny Donovan is?"

"Yes."

"Yes, what? Yes, you know him, or yes, you're sure you don't know him."

"I don't know him."

"Okay. Thanks for your time."

Pete whisked himself behind an office door as quickly as his legs would take him. I walked back to reception, leaned against the desk, and eyed the phone. The red button next to line four lit up.

"Pete's making a call."

She glanced at the phone. "So he is." She glanced up at me, licked her lips. "Who are you anyway?"

"I told you. Jack."

"What do you do, Jack?"

"This and that."

"You're a detective, aren't you?"

"Maybe."

"I knew it. Nothing gets by you."

"Well, thank you for saying so."

"Well, Mr. Detective, any chance I'll see you again?"

"Maybe."

She pulled a business card from a plastic holder near the phone and wrote on the back of it. She held it out to me with a smile. "My home number. In case you don't get back here, maybe you could come by there."

I slipped the card into my shirt pocket. "Maybe."

"Take care, Mr. Detective."

"See ya, Linda."

I didn't locate Johnny, but still I left with a smile. I rattled Pete's cage. He knew Johnny and recognized Jenkins, too. Just a matter of time.

And having Linda's home number in my pocket made me feel a bit studly.

"Did you find Nadia?" Arturo said as I walked into the office.

"Yep."

"And?"

"And she's okay. She'll be in tomorrow."

Arturo walked to Nadia's desk, palmed a handful of mail. "These came today."

I took the stack into my office and set them on my desk. I thumbed through the envelopes. I received a check from Simon and Haskell, attorneys I had done some work for the previous month. And there were two envelopes—one for Nadia, one for me—each claiming we were winners in a multi-million dollar sweepstakes. I threw them, along with the other junk mail, in the trash.

Arturo came into the office and sat down. "Anything you want me to do?"

I glanced at the clock. Four-thirty-seven. "Nope. Why don't you knock off early today?"

"Okay, boss."

"Do you have any plans for tonight?"

"I'm gonna hook up with some old homies. Maybe have a little fun with Maria. Or maybe Theresa."

I tossed a key across the desk. "Here's the apartment key. I'll see you tonight."

Arturo grabbed his jacket from the chair and headed for the door. "Maybe, maybe not, Holmes. Depends on how lucky I am."

"Have fun, but stay out of trouble."

He smiled. "Always, Holmes. Always."

I spent the next hour and a half compiling notes on a yellow pad of paper. The only lead, if you could call it that, was Pete Sanchez at Digital Pipeline. I knew there was a connection between Sanchez and Donovan, but in order to find it, I'd have to do one of the things I hated most about my job—a stakeout.

I figured Pete Sanchez for a daytime guy, so I'd start surveillance Friday morning. I already had plans for that night anyway.

I grabbed my briefcase, locked up and stopped by Mario's Liquor for a fifth of Seagram's and a bottle of 7-Up.

I went home and took a cold shower. I wrapped a towel around my waist and grabbed the bottles from my refrigerator. I grabbed a glass and took everything to the couch with me. I proper my feet on the coffee table and proceeded to get inebriated.

ELEVEN

In my former life, I enjoyed the holidays. Of course, back then I was a cop, had a large group of friends, and Ellen. Now, the holiday season was a time to get drunk and try to forget.

I woke sometime early Thanksgiving morning. I went to the bathroom, peed and puked, and passed back out on the couch. When I woke again, the sky had grown dark, and I had a headache that wouldn't quit. I turned on a light and checked for messages.

Arturo called to say that he'd be spending the holiday at Maria's and he'd be back sometime late.

I dialed Nadia's number and got her voicemail. I didn't leave a message.

I made another drink, grabbed my wallet and fished out the Digital Pipeline business card. I stared at the phone number on the back of the card for a minute, then dialed it. A male voice answered. I hung up.

I polished off the Seagram's and the 7-Up, and passed out.

Friday morning, I washed down four Advil with a glass of orange juice and decided the stakeout at Digital Pipeline would have to wait for a few hours. There was something else I wanted to take care of first.

I took Arturo to an Asian bakery off Wilshire that serves the best Danish in California, save Solvang. We drank coffee and ate cheese Danish for a half-hour, then headed to the office.

At ten-o-five, I parked the truck and we walked to the building. When we reached the front steps, I stopped.

"Nadia might be uneasy meeting you."

"I understand."

"No, I'm not sure you do. It has nothing to do with you

personally or the way you look. A long time ago, Nadia had a bad relationship with a Latino guy. So, don't sweat it."

"Okay."

He followed me into the office.

"Morning, Nadia."

Nadia stopped inputting into the computer, looked up. "Hi, Jack."

"Nadia, this is Arturo, the man who saved my life. Arturo, this is Nadia. My favorite secretary in the whole world."

"Your only one," she said.

"Yeah, but that doesn't mean I appreciate you any less."

"He knows how to butter people up, doesn't he?" she said to Arturo.

Arturo stepped forward and proffered his hand. "Hello, Nadia."

She smiled, but it was forced, and her hand shook as she took his. "Hello."

I watched her gaze meet his for a moment, then veer away. I walked into my office and left the door open. Arturo closed it behind him and sat down.

"Sweet girl," he said.

I started some coffee. "Yep."

Whenever I stood by the coffee machine, it took forever to brew. Still, I did it again. After two or three hours, I poured steaming coffee into two Styrofoam cups, handed one to Arturo.

"Think you can hold down the fort again?"

"Shit, Holmes. You hire me and all of a sudden I'm running your office for you."

"Is that a yes?"

"If I say no, will I be fired?"

"Yep."

"Then I say yes."

"Good. Now that that's settled, I'm taking Nadia out for coffee."

"What for?" Arturo held up his cup. "You and Mr. Coffee make the best coffee in the land."

"Yeah, but you're here."

"Ouch. Should I be offended?"

"If you want."

Arturo sipped his coffee. "Do you have anything for me to do while I wait?"

"Ever played FreeCell on the computer?"

"No."

"Good. Then it should take you a while to get bored. Besides, then you can't say I don't give you anything to do."

I powered up my computer and opened FreeCell. "See? There's even online help if you can't figure it out."

"Gee, Holmes, that's mighty kind of ya."

"Anything for a friend."

I went to the lobby. "Nadia."

She spun around in her chair.

"Would you like to go get some coffee?"

"Sure. What do you guys want?"

"No. Would you like to go out with me for some coffee?"

Her eyes darted toward my closed office door, then back at me. "Arturo's going to guard the fort."

"Okay."

She sounded unsure.

She saved her file, then grabbed her purse from under her desk. As she walked past, her shoulder brushed my chest. "Sorry."

I touched her arm. She froze solid.

"What's wrong?"

"Nothing."

"Nadia."

"You ready?"

She walked out of the office without looking back at me.

Once on Wilshire Boulevard, Nadia slowed and moved to the right. I caught up and walked beside her.

"Denny's okay?"

"Sure."

We shared no more words until we were seated inside Denny's. We ordered coffee. Thirty seconds later, the waitress was back with two steaming mugs. Nadia declined an offer to eat. So did I.

"Are you okay?" I said.

"Fine. Why?"

"You don't seem fine."

"Well, I am."

"Is this about yesterday in your apartment, Arturo, or both?"

She tucked a lock of hair behind her ear. "No."

"No, what?"

"No, nothing's wrong. I'm fine."

Her hands rested flat on the table. I placed my hand over one of hers. "Nadia, please tell me."

She stared intently into her coffee cup. "Both."

"Okay. Which one do you wanna talk about first?"

"Neither."

I squeezed her hand. "Which one?"

She looked up at me. Tears had gathered in the corners of her eyes. "Doesn't matter."

"It does to me. Let's tackle the easier one first. Arturo."

She looked back into her coffee, said nothing.

"I could tell you were uneasy when we walked in today."

"I tried to hide it."

"I know you did. I doubt Arturo picked up on it at all. But, I know you."

A half-smile graced her lips, then disappeared. "I don't know how to say this."

"Just say it."

A tear released itself from her eye. "I need to quit."

My heart dropped into my gut. "You can't quit."

"I can't work there anymore. It's too . . . difficult."

"Because of Arturo or me?"

She bit her lip. "Both."

"I can do something about Arturo. Nadia, you're the one that holds this business together. I can't lose you. Arturo won't come to work again after today."

"No," she snapped. "I don't want you to do that."

"Why not? God, Nadia, I need you."

She was quiet for a moment. A low hum emanated from an overhead ceiling fan. Dishes clanked in the kitchen to my right.

"Do you?" she said.

"Yes, I do."

She put her free hand atop mine. "My emotions are all fucked up right now."

"Mine, too."

"Yesterday was . . . weird."

"Yes, it was."

"I wanted to do that for so long, but when it happened, I wondered if it was only because of the moment."

"It was a moment. That's for sure."

She smiled—a full smile this time. Then she wiped the tears from her cheeks. "Damn, Jack. In the last couple of days, things have turned upside down. My feelings are having a hard time catching up."

"Mine, too. But one thing's for sure. Running away isn't the answer. I'm sorry for the feelings that Arturo has inadvertently conjured up. But, I'm willing to rectify that."

"No, please don't. I'm sure he's a great guy and can help out a lot."

"Okay." Now for the tougher part. "What about us?"

"Us?"

"Sounds strange, huh?"

She smiled. "Kinda."

"I can't promise things'll be smooth going, but we're still friends, right?"

"Right."

"Friends that have gotten into a sticky situation. We mounted the wave. I say we just ride it out and see where it takes us."

"No matter where that might be?"

"No matter."

She leaned forward and put a hand on my cheek. "You're a great guy, Jack Murphy."

"I know."

"Arrogant son of a bitch, too."

"Yep. So, you're working again?"

"Yes."

"Good. I need you to track someone down. His name's Johnny Donovan. And thank you."

"For what?"

"For agreeing to hang in there. You really had me worried for a minute."

I slid out of the booth and stood at the edge of the table. When she stood, she kissed me on the lips. And my heart resumed its position in the middle of my chest.

I dropped a few dollars on the table and we left.

By twelve-thirty, Nadia had dug up an address on Johnny Donovan. Arturo and I hopped into my truck and I headed west on Wilshire to Rossmore, then north through Highland Park and past the Wilshire Country Club. At Melrose, Rossmore became Vine and I continued north to Romaine, then hung a left. Just beyond Wilcox, I found the place.

The A-frame structure labeled as 6509 was a single car garage with a severely damaged rollup door. Sheets of white paint were peeling from the clapboard walls. Vines had grown up the left wall and consumed most of the front eve.

"Nice place," Arturo said.

I parked alongside a rusted chain link fence and we walked up the gravel drive. Grass had sprouted up in the middle of the drive. Near the garage door, the grass was smothered by a huge oil slick. A standard, city issue green trashcan leaned against the left front corner, overfilled and surrounded by garbage that I could smell from ten feet away. A worn pair of Dickies hung from the chain link fence.

I walked along the left side of the structure through knee-high weeds. At the rear of the building, I found a door, hanging open and loose on its hinges. The midday sun barely illuminated the inside, and I had to stand in the doorway for a minute to allow my eyes to adjust.

The inside was home to piles of garbage, broken lengths of rotting wood and a dirty mattress in the far corner. The stench of urine permeated the dust-filled air. No one had been in this place for quite some time.

As we walked back to the truck, Arturo said, "What now, boss?"

"We sit on the Seward building and see if we learn anything."

"Cool, a stakeout."

I laughed. "I can see you've never been on one before."

"What?"

We climbed into the truck and I started the engine. "Stakeouts are among the most boring things we professional detectives do."

"They don't look boring on TV."

I pulled away from the curb. "You're something else."

TWELVE

That weekend, the only person to show at Digital Pipeline was Pete Sanchez. He spent two hours in the office Saturday and a half-hour on Sunday. On Monday and Tuesday, we watched the same people come and go that had come and gone Friday. My patience was wearing thin, and Arturo was going stir crazy.

On Wednesday morning, I suggested Arturo take the day off and see some friends. I let him use my truck and called Enterprise to get an SUV. It all worked out well since I was worried about continuing my stakeout in the same vehicle anyway. He thanked me and left.

I grabbed the latest Robert Crais novel and waited on the street for the Enterprise associate to pick me up. I was given a tan Explorer and made it to Digital Pipeline by eleven-fifty.

I parked in the lot behind the building, second to last row. Fortunately, the Explorer had tinted rear windows to block me from view. I leaned back and began to read.

At twelve-o-five, the parking lot was a flurry of activity for a few minutes' while the employees of Digital Pipeline and the neighboring business rushed to their cars for lunch. Ten minutes later, all was quiet until the swarm returned at about one.

At two-ten, a black Nissan Sentra pulled into the lot and parked two spaces over. A brunette in a baby blue dress slid out of the car. Her nails were done up in a French manicure, her lips painted ruby red. The lines on her face put her at about forty, but her body looked more like thirty. Maybe she'd had a rough life.

She turned her brown eyes to me. They were warm. I smiled. She returned the smile and walked toward the building. I watched her pass the Coke machine, hang a left down the corridor and disappear. I went back to my novel and spent the next two hours reading about someone else's misfortunes.

At four-fifteen, the brunette appeared by the Coke machine, bought a soda and headed for her Sentra. She was halfway across the parking lot when Pete Sanchez came out of the building, a large box in his hands.

"Mandy," he said.

The brunette stopped and looked back. Pete Sanchez caught up to her and they walked side by side to her car.

"Give these to Johnny tonight, okay?"

"Sure, Pete."

"By the way, you were great today."

Mandy giggled. "Why, thank you, kind sir."

I wondered exactly what she was great at.

Pete Sanchez loaded the box in Mandy's trunk, then kissed her on the cheek and headed back toward the building. Mandy got in her car and pulled out of the lot. I gave her a few seconds, then followed.

Mandy took Seward north to Fountain, then east across the Hollywood Freeway and left on Mariposa. She stopped in front of a small, cape cod-style, one-story, painted light peach with blue trim. She pointed what appeared to be a garage-door opener at the wrought iron fence that surrounded the property. The gate slid open and Mandy pulled into the driveway. I went almost to Santa Monica Boulevard, then did a k-turn and parked a couple doors north of the house. Mandy went inside, and I picked up my novel.

The sky grew dark and activity picked up on the street. People coming home from work and going back out for an evening on the town. The street was made up mostly of small homes, but there were some apartment complexes thrown in for good measure. Mandy's was the nicest place on the block.

I had nearly reached the climax in the novel when Mandy came out of the house. Dressed in all black—tight miniskirt, tube top, leather jacket, and leather boots that went to the knees, she climbed in her Sentra and backed out of the drive. I leaned low in the seat as she passed me. While she waited to cross Santa Monica Boulevard, I turned around.

After several minutes of waiting to turn left, Mandy made a right. Traffic's a bitch in LA. She went to Vermont, then left to Hollywood Boulevard, then left again. She turned on Winona and parked behind a cheesy two-story motel that was in need of a paint job. I pulled to the curb in front of the motel and waited. A few minutes later, she walked onto the Boulevard and leaned against a street sign. A working girl.

I pulled up next to her, rolled down the window and smiled.

"Hey, baby," she said, "looking for a date?"

"Yep."

She came to the Explorer and leaned against the door. Her eyes canvassed the interior, no doubt looking for signs of danger. "Twenty bucks."

"How much for the night, darling?"

Her eyes widened and held my stare for a moment. "Serious?"

"Yep."

"Five hundred. And I gotta be back by midnight."

"Why? You turn into a pumpkin?"

"What?"

"Nothing. Hop in."

She opened the door but didn't climb in. She held out her hand, said, "Cash up front, baby."

I pulled five hundreds from my wallet, handed them to her. She got in, closed the door and stuffed the money in her tube top. "So, you like Robert Crais."

"Yep."

"Me, too. I haven't read that one yet, though."

I worked my way back into traffic. "Get it, it's good."

We caught a red light at Western.

"Where we going?" she said.

"How about dinner?"

"Whatever you want."

Mandy pulled an Eve cigarette from a pack in her purse, held it between her lips. "Mind if I smoke?"

I pulled my lighter from my pocket and lit her cigarette. "Not at all."

"Thanks. My name's Mandy, by the way."

"Hi Mandy, I'm Jack."

The light changed and we crawled on. A half block later, I noticed Mandy studying my face.

"Do I know you?" she said.

"Don't think so."

"You look familiar."

I smiled. "People tell me that a lot. I guess I have one of those faces."

"I guess."

I hung a left at Wilton and a right on Sunset. I craved lemon chicken and stopped at a Mandarin place near Sunset and the 101.

"You like Chinese?" I said.

"Sure."

We went inside and I ordered lemon chicken, white rice and crispy noodles. Mandy ordered some egg rolls and pork chow mein. We set the food on the hood of the Explorer, leaned against the bumper and ate.

"So what do you do, anyway?" she said.

"I'm in the movie business."

She laughed. "Darling, do you know how many times I've heard that?"

"I'll bet. But really, I am."

Her eyes narrowed and she cocked her head slightly left. "Doing what?"

"I'm a producer slash director."

"Uh-huh."

"Really."

"What have you done?"

"Oh, lots of things."

"Like?"

I took another bite of the lemon chicken. The sauce was not too lemony, more orange than yellow in color, and just the way I liked it. "I do specialized stuff."

"That's okay, baby. You've got me for the night. I'll swing from the chandelier and call you David Lynch if it'll get you off."

David Lynch. I was beginning to like Mandy.

We finished eating and I threw the garbage into a bin alongside the restaurant.

I walked to the passenger's side and opened the door. Mandy gave my arm a squeeze. "Now what, studly?"

"Now we'll have a little fun."

Traffic was thick, but we worked our way across LA in about an hour. I parked on the Santa Monica pier and we got out.

"I love this place," Mandy said.

She took my arm and we walked across the wooden planks toward the pier's entrance. The pier was crowded but not overly so. We walked past some street vendors and the arcade to the amusement park. It was closed, and Mandy expressed disappointment in not getting to ride the Ferris wheel.

We made our way to the end of the pier. A couple of Latino fishermen were packing up their gear. The waves crashed against the supports below our feet.

"It's beautiful," she said, as if it was the first time she had laid eyes on the Pacific.

A large yacht crawled along the horizon. Music from the Mexican cantina behind us spilled over the pier. In the opposite corner, two kids sat on a bench, arm in arm, staring out at the water.

After a while, Mandy said, "Tell me, Jack. Why exactly did you pick me up tonight?"

Something in my lower intestines kicked my stomach acid into overdrive. I wished I had a Prevacid. I swallowed hard, looked out over the ocean. "I was lonely."

It kicked again. The acid rose to the back of my tongue, burning my esophagus.

She leaned her head against my shoulder. "Tell me about yourself."

I stood silent for a moment.

She picked her head off my shoulder. "Sorry."

"For what?"

"I know I shouldn't ask any personal questions. I just . . ."

"Just what?"

"I just kinda like you, that's all."

Lying sucks. Unfortunately, it's a big part of being a private detective, but knowing that never made it any easier. Sometimes, you could lie to a scumbag and not lose a moment's sleep over it. Misleading nice people, though, was something entirely different. But I'd come this far, and I'd already spent five hundred of Raymond Sanders' money. I owed it to him.

"It's okay. I'm a film producer and director as I said before. You probably wouldn't recognize my name because I do specialty adult films. Fetish stuff."

"Like golden showers and bondage and stuff?"

I smiled. "Kind of."

"Oh."

She pulled a cigarette from her purse. I pulled out one of my own and lit them both.

"I'm in the adult business, too," she said.

Segue. "Really?"

"Yeah. I do some acting, but mostly voiceover stuff. Ya know, the moaning and groaning."

I hit my cigarette. "I've been away a while. Now I'm back and trying to find an old friend. Since you're in the biz, maybe you've heard of him."

"Maybe. Who is it?"

"Johnny Donovan."

"No fucking way."

"Yep. Why?"

"That's so karmic."

"Why do you say that?"

"Because I work for Johnny."

"No way."

"Yes way. In fact, I'm going to see him later tonight."

"Really?"

"Yeah."

"How cool. The number I had for him is disconnected. Of course, that was before he, you know."

"Oh," she said as she squeezed my arm, "his arrest."

"Yep."

"I know. Wasn't that terrible? I mean, the girl told Johnny she was eighteen. How was he to know she was only fourteen?"

"I know."

"Say, you wanna come with me tonight? I'll bet Johnny'd love to see an old face again."

"I'd love to, Mandy, but I can't. I've got a meeting early in the morning with some guys at Gentleman's Club. They wanna hire me to direct a new all-girl flick."

"No kidding? Hey, Johnny always said I did the best girl-girl scenes in the world. Maybe I could audition for a part?"

I turned away. The kids in the far corner had gone. A few men and women mingled near the cantina's entrance, drinks in hand. I craved a drink. "Maybe. I'll see what I can do."

Mandy took a pen and a business card from her wallet, wrote something on its back, and proffered it. "On the front is my name and number. It's a cell phone with voicemail, so call anytime. On the back is Johnny's address. I don't have a phone number for him but he's usually at that place from ten or eleven on."

"PM, right?"

"Of course, baby. Johnny still don't get up until well past noon."

"Of course."

We walked back to the car. My stomach wouldn't let up.

"Don't say anything to Johnny, okay? I want him to be surprised."

She smiled softly. "I won't." She held my gaze for a moment, then leaned forward and kissed my lips. "I really like you, Jack."

Lying sucks.

THIRTEEN

I took Vine north past Santa Monica Boulevard, turned left on La Mirada Avenue and cruised the two-block street. The north side was comprised of small homes, the south side the backs of businesses. The street was posted *No Parking*.

I made a right on Cahuenga and worked my way in a circle. Four doors east of the address was a parking lot encircled by steel fencing. No one had pulled the gate shut, so I parked there.

The two streetlamps closest to the address were burned out. I grabbed a pair of leather driving gloves from the glove box, slipped them over my hands. I hadn't gotten by the police supply store to pick up another set for Arturo, so I handed him a pair of latex gloves.

I grabbed the Bushnells from under my seat and took a closer look at the front of the house. It was a one-story, off-white box with a Spanish tile roof. Wrought-iron bars covered all the windows. The front door looked double-reinforced, and impossible to kick in.

Arturo slipped into his gloves. "What're we doing?"

"Going in."

"Cool."

We climbed from the Explorer and casually walked toward the house. Just two old friends out for an evening stroll. The street was devoid of people, and except for the residual noise from the traffic on Vine, the neighborhood was quiet. The house was surrounded by a cinderblock and wrought-iron fence whereas the lot immediately east was surrounded by cheap chain-link fence. Separating the two properties, a fifteen-foot orange tree, in full blossom, whistled in the breeze. Perfect.

"Follow me," I said.

I hopped the fence and took refuge under the orange tree. From where I was, I could see enough to notice that the house joined a six-foot-high cinderblock wall that surrounded the backyard. I walked to the wall and lifted myself up. Assorted shrubberies hid most of the yard from view.

"Well?" Arturo whispered.

I motioned with my finger and we walked back to the orange tree. "I couldn't see anyone, but I heard music and smelled dope. There's a gate off the driveway, opposite side."

We jumped the fence and walked past the house. A new Suburban was parked in the driveway. We edged between the Suburban and the house, stopping short of the gate. A detached garage, its door closed, stood at the end of the concrete drive.

From this side, the music was clearer—Nine Inch Nails. The air was pungent with the sweet aroma of marijuana. A soccer ball sat on the concrete near the garage-door. I squatted and duck-walked to it.

Arturo raised his eyebrows but said nothing. I held the ball in my left hand, withdrew my Sig with my right. I moved to within an arm's length of the gate and threw the ball against the garage door.

"What the fuck?" someone said from inside the yard.

The gate opened. I extended my right arm and placed my Sig against the round head that appeared.

"Nice and easy," I said.

The man froze. The head was attached to a six-foot-three body that weighed more than three hundred pounds. He wore Levi's, a Harley Davidson t-shirt and a leather vest with little beads attached to small strips at its bottom.

"What do you want?" he said.

"Come here."

I placed my free hand against the man's chest and pushed him against the wall of the house. I slipped my pistol from his temple to the underside of his jaw. "What's your name?"

"Fuck you."

I patted him down and found a .45 under his left arm. I took the pistol, slipped it in the waistband of my jeans. "Well, Fuck You, what's going on tonight?"

He stared cold, said nothing.

"Where's Johnny?"

"Johnny who?"

Everyone's a comedian.

"This can go two ways. Easy or difficult. Easy way, you tell me where Johnny is, I talk to him and we leave."

He sneered. "And difficult?"

"I shoot out your kneecaps and go in blind."

Fuck You seemed to ponder the choices for a minute before his gaze softened. "Okay. Johnny's inside."

"Who else's in there?"

"A couple actors and Stevie, the camera guy."

"Weapons?"

"Just the one you took."

"Am I likely to find resistance inside?"

He laughed. "From them? Don't think so."

"What's your name?"

"Mike."

"Arturo," I said, keeping my stare locked with Mike's, "watch him, okay?"

"Okay, boss."

"I'm taking my pistol away now. If you try anything, Arturo will break your legs."

I stepped to the left and Arturo took up position directly in front of Mike.

"Hello," Arturo said.

Mike wasn't going anywhere.

I slipped through the gate. The sliding glass door to the house was open. I let myself inside.

I stood in the kitchen. The interior smelled of new paint and fresh wood. Straight ahead was a family room, devoid of furniture. Ahead and to my left, a set of double-doors stood open. The music originated from inside that room.

"What the fuck's up, Stevie?" a voice shouted above the remixed version of *Happiness in Slavery*.

I stepped forward and peered inside. The walls and ceiling were entirely blue. The floor was gray and resembled a gym mat. A gray king-sized bed hugged the far wall.

The bed gleamed under the high-wattage glare of four spots. A naked girl leaned against the headboard and smoked a cigarette. A guy, also naked, sat at the edge of the bed, and smoked what appeared to be a crack pipe.

Two men stood at the foot of the bed, on opposite sides of a large camera.

The same voice said, "Jesus Christ. What am I paying you for, huh?"

"C'mon, Johnny. Just give me a sec."

Johnny walked to the CD player and hit a button. Nine Inch Nails went mute. "Aw, shit. Look at this. Monty's gonna smoke his hard-on into oblivion you don't hurry the fuck up." He peered at the girl. "Haley, honey, don't let yourself dry out too much, okay? We gotta get this fucking scene on film tonight."

"Johnny," I said.

Johnny and Stevie both jumped. Monty continued hitting his crack pipe and Haley stared at the ceiling.

He marched toward me. "Who the fuck are you? And where's Mike? Hey, Mike."

"Mike's detained."

Johnny seemed oblivious to the 9mm in my hand. He brushed past me and headed for the screen door. "What the fuck are you talking about?"

I put my hand on his shoulder, spun him around, and waved my pistol near his face.

"Is this a bust?"

"Nope."

He was five-eight, one-fifty, with beady black eyes and a triangle goatee. His thinning black hair was swept back, exposing a severely receded hairline. He stared at me a moment. "Then get the fuck out."

"I need to ask you a few questions, then I'll be on my way."

He took a swing at me. I leaned right and countered with the butt of my pistol. He grabbed his nose. Blood poured between his fingers and down his chin, dripping on his t-shirt. "You broke my nose."

"That ain't the only thing I'm gonna break if you don't settle down."

He stared at me again, but his eyes held resignation. He grabbed the bottom of his t-shirt and held it to his nostrils. He took a step toward the room, then turned to me. "May I?"

"Make it quick."

"What's going on?" Stevie said.

"Nothing. Monty's done. Get him out of here. But get Haley on tape doing herself. Jesus, I need something tonight."

"Okay," Stevie said.

I followed Johnny through the empty family room and left down a small hall to an office. A large L-shaped work area was setup in the left corner. A wet bar sat in the far right corner. An eight-foot wide window had been installed in the wall shared by the office and the blue room, and gave Johnny a bird's eye view of the action.

"Have a seat," Johnny said.

I sat opposite his desk.

He walked to the bar. "Drink?"

"Nope."

He poured himself half a highball glass of whiskey and sat behind his desk. "Haley sure is a fine young thing."

I took Carrie's picture from my jacket and set it on the desk. "I'm looking for her."

He took a drink, set down the glass, and glanced at the picture. "Never seen her."

"Look again, Johnny."

He glanced again, picked up his glass and finished the whiskey. "I've never seen the bitch. Satisfied?"

"You have papers on Haley?"

"What? What the fuck?"

"You know, the sticky little paperwork that film directors need to prove their actresses are of legal age."

Johnny walked back to the bar, refilled his glass. "Fuck you."

"Johnny, if I don't get some help from you, I'm gonna call my friend Tyrone."

"Good for you."

"Tyrone works for LAPD Vice. I bet he'd like to see Haley's papers."

"Go ahead."

I pulled my cell phone from my jacket pocket and dialed a number. "Lieutenant Williams, please. Yes, I'll hold."

Johnny tapped his foot. Small beads of sweat formed on his brow. He stabbed at them with the side of his hand.

"That's fine, I'll wait," I said.

He swallowed his drink. "Fuck. Goddamn it, hang up."

"What?"

"Hang up the fucking phone."

"Why?"

"Maybe I can help."

I hung up.

Stevie knocked on the door. "Hey, Johnny, I got it fixed."

"Well ain't that fucking grand. Then why the hell are you standing here with your dick in your hand? Get in there and get that bitch on film."

"Okay," he said, and disappeared.

Johnny refilled his glass and sat behind the desk. "Lemme see that photo again."

I pushed it toward him.

"If I help you, you go away quiet, right?"

"Right."

Johnny sipped his drink and studied the photo for a minute. Then, he downed the whiskey, set the photo on the desk next to the empty glass, and buried his face in his palms. "Maybe I've seen this girl."

"That's a great help, Johnny."

"About a month ago, four girls came over. This maybe, and I mean maybe, could have been one of the girls." He glanced up. "Maybe."

"Was it in October or November?"

"Fuck, I don't know."

"C'mon, Johnny."

"Christ, I'm trying here, okay? I think it was the first weekend in November."

"Think?"

"Okay, I'm sure. My kid sister's birthday is on November third, and it was the night before."

"So, November second."

"Yeah, the second."

"What happened to the girls?"

"How the fuck would I know? I shot a reel of each of 'em and they left. I never saw 'em again."

"You mind if I smoke?"

"Yes."

I lit a cigarette. "Where did these girls go after they left here?"

"I told you, I never saw any of them again. So, obviously I don't know where they went."

"Bullshit."

"No, really, I don't know. Girls come and go all the time."

"Who did you shoot the film for?"

Johnny walked to the bar and grabbed the fifth. Apparently, the glass was too much trouble at this stage. "I can't tell you that."

"You mean you won't."

He took a long pull from the bottle. "Whatever."

I pulled my cell phone out.

"Goddamn. What sin did I commit today that has you coming in here and busting my balls like this?"

I shrugged.

"DiMarco."

"Who?"

"Tony DiMarco."

"He brought you the girls?"

"He brings me most of my actresses."

"Where can I find DiMarco?"

Johnny wiped at the sweat on his forehead. "You gotta promise you won't tell him I told you. He'll ice me for sure."

"Where?"

"C'mon, man. You can't tell him."

I wasn't sure if I would or not, but he didn't need to be aware of my indecisiveness. "I won't say anything."

"He hangs at Club TA. I think maybe he owns a piece of it."

"Where is this club?"

"Shit, you ain't never been there? I thought everyone's been there, one time or another."

"Where?"

"On Hollywood Boulevard, over by Normandie."

I dropped a business card on his desk. "You remember anything else, I expect a call."

"Yeah, yeah."

I stood. "Johnny, you're a model citizen."

"Fuck you."

"By the way, you might wanna update your home address with the sex offenders unit. They find out your address is an abandoned garage, you'll be back playing hide the salami at the big house."

Panic crossed his eyes. The sweat poured more rapidly.

I smiled. "Have a great night, Johnny."

FOURTEEN

I figured DiMarco for a night person, so we headed to Club TA. We arrived at eleven-thirty.

The rumble of thumping metal swelled as we approached the club. I recognized the music as Pantera ten feet from the door. One very large black man, dressed in a skintight black shirt and black leather pants leaned against the doorjamb, his arms folded across his muscular chest.

He uncrossed his arms and held out a hand. "Ten bucks."

I fished a ten from my wallet and handed it to him.

"Each." I handed him another ten. "Be nice and no one gets hurt. The girls can touch you if they want. You touch them, I'll break your fingers. Have a good time."

The club was small and dark. The bar, with its dark wood top and padded red runner, extended nearly the entire right wall. To the left, a few tables, all occupied, were scattered around an entirely too large dance floor. An Asian girl was onstage, making love to a flagpole. Most of the short wooden barstools were also occupied. An ashen-skinned strawberry blond in a barely legal purple bikini and knee-high black patent leather boots balanced a drink tray on her palm as she weaved through the crowd.

"Excuse me," I said.

"Yeah. What can I get you?"

"A couple drafts."

"Sure thing."

We found an empty table near the vending machine in back and sat down. When the waitress returned, I paid for the beers.

"I'm supposed to meet Tony DiMarco here tonight. Do you know where he is?"

She gave me a look as if I had just fallen out of the sky. "Are you blind? He's right there."

She pointed over my shoulder. I turned and followed her finger to an Italian man sitting at the end of the bar, with a girl in his lap and a square-shouldered young man at his side. I dropped an extra five bucks on her tray.

"Thanks."

She smiled and blew me a kiss, then worked her way back through the crowd, passing out drinks.

I lit a cigarette and took a drink of my entirely too watered-down, too high-priced beer. I wasn't sure whether this club was in clear violation of the California Code that prohibited smoking in nearly every structure in the damn state or whether they, like some others in the city, turned their employees into owners and made good use of a loophole. Either way, I was thankful.

The music ended, the lights came back up, and the bartender announced that the next show would feature Kitten, and start in fifteen minutes. In the meantime, he suggested everyone should have another drink or two.

As my eyes adjusted to the surge of white light, Tony backed off his barstool and took the girl's hand. They disappeared down the hallway in back. The square-shouldered young man sat on the barstool and ordered a drink.

The waitress walked by. I touched her arm. "Where's that lead?"

"The head."

"Is there an exit back there?"

"Just the emergency exit."

Suddenly, I felt the urge to pee. I told Arturo to sit tight and headed down the hall. A door marked *Office* closed as I neared. Just short of the door and to my left was a set of stairs. Eight feet past the door, the hall turned ninety degrees to the right. That part of the hall boasted three doors, all on the left side, marked *Men*, *Women* and *Emergency Exit Only* respectively.

I entered the men's restroom. A single low-wattage bulb strained to illuminate three urinals and two toilet stalls. The room smelled of urine and vomit, with a hint of sex mixed in. The bathroom was empty.

I peed, then tried to wash my hands in the sink, but with both the hot and cold taps broken, I didn't get very far. On my way back, I tried the door marked *Office*. It was unlocked.

I took a deep breath and stepped inside.

Tony sat on a well-worn couch, his pants wrapped around his

ankles. The girl in his lap before now knelt in front of him. Her long raven hair flowed across his thighs.

"What the fuck?" Tony said.

I closed the door.

The girl continued to move her head up and down until Tony wrapped his thick palms around her skull and pulled her away. "Get lost."

The girl slipped into her dress and came toward me. I opened the door to let her out, then closed and locked it.

"Tony DiMarco?" I said.

"What? My big schlong give it away?"

"Jack Murphy."

"I don't know no Jack Murphy."

"Pleased to meet you."

He pulled up his pants, closed the zipper and fastened his belt. "What do you want?"

I showed him the picture of Carrie. "I want this girl."

He smiled and winked at me. "You like 'em young, huh? She's a real looker, that one."

"Where can I find her?"

"I have no idea."

"Bullshit."

"I don't care if you believe me or not. What'd you say your name was?"

"Jack Murphy."

Tony looked at me as though he were bored. "Why don't you get the fuck out of here before you piss me off, you cocksucker?"

"Tell me where I can find the girl and I will."

Tony struggled to get to his feet. I pushed him back down.

"Fuck you, asshole," he said.

"I know you had some teens filmed earlier this month, and I know Carrie was one of them."

"Oh, is that her name?"

"Where is she?"

"You know, you got some fucking nerve, Murphy. You bust in here, fuck up my blowjob and then start spouting some pretty wicked accusations. If I wasn't such a nice guy . . ."

"Then, what? You'd kill me?"

"You said it."

Someone pounded on the door. Tony sneered. I shrugged. A key went into the lock, the tumblers rolled and the door opened.

The bouncer stepped inside. "What's going on?"

"Just having a friendly chat with my good friend Tony," I said.

"The fuck we are," Tony said.

"I don't know what's going on, and frankly, I don't much care. But," the bouncer pointed at me, "you are outta here."

I smiled at Tony. "Watch yourself."

"Hey, Murphy. Fuck you." Tony spat on the ground. "You and me, we'll talk again."

I blew him a kiss. "I can't wait."

"Let's go," the bouncer said.

He grabbed my arm and manhandled me through the club. A beautiful Latino girl was on stage. Arturo was entranced.

"Arturo," I shouted.

He glanced at me, smiled, and went back to watching the girl.

When we reached the front door, the bouncer pushed me through it. Good thing it was open.

The sudden fear of an earthquake jolted me from bed Friday morning. By the time I realized it was only Arturo's morning jumping jacks, it was too late—I was already up.

"Morning," he said.

"That it is."

Arturo moved on to shadow boxing. "You're not much of a morning person, are you?"

"No."

"I wasn't either. But prison has a way of making you conform to their timetable. I hated it at first. Then, I got used to it. Now, I can't help it."

I lit my first cigarette of the day, then stumbled to the kitchen and started the Mr. Coffee. Arturo hopped into the shower. I leaned against the counter and smoked.

Startled by a knock at the door, I dropped my cigarette on the floor. I picked it up, burning my finger in the process.

"Who is it?"

"Police, open up."

I did. Two officers stood in the hall, one on each side of the doorway.

"Are you Jack Murphy?" the one to my left said.

"Yep."

"Could you step outside for a minute?"

I did. "What's up?"

"We're going to have to ask you to come down to the station with us."

"Why?"

"We need to ask you some questions."

"Can't you ask me right here?"

It was the other cop's turn to speak. "Mr. Murphy, we need you to come down to the station."

"Am I under arrest?"

"Not at this time."

"What is this in regards to?"

"A homicide."

"Who died?"

"Johnny Donovan."

"What?"

"Mr. Murphy, though you're not under arrest at this time, we do need to advise you of your rights. You have the right to remain silent . . ."

Since I was a kid who had avidly watched *Adam 12* on television, I knew my rights. The cop finished without peeking at his cheat sheet, and made no mistakes. Impressive.

"Can I grab a shirt and shoes first?"

Both cops followed me inside. I slipped into my Nikes, grabbed a t-shirt from my closet and my smokes from the coffee table. I thought about saying something to Arturo, then decided against it. "Let's go."

I was sandwiched between the cops on the walk to the elevator, and from the elevator to their cruiser I squeezed into the entirely too small backseat, deciding to stretch my legs across the seat rather than become claustrophobic by attempting to sit straight. When the door closed, I already knew the two-plus mile drive to the Wilshire station on Venice Boulevard would be a long one.

We parked behind the station and the cops escorted me to Interrogation Room A. One cop told me to have a seat. The other offered me coffee. I accepted. And I sat down.

The room was rather plain, floored in a cheap linoleum. White paint peeled from the walls. The obligatory one-way mirror hung on one wall. The remaining three walls all had large windowpanes. Cheap white blinds that had become more of a dingy gray with time draped the windows, and were turned shut. The oblong, metal table in the center of the room had a total of six metal chairs around it—one at each end, two on each side. I smiled when I saw the plastic ashtray on the table. I guess before you're under arrest, they want you to seem comfortable. That and the cops have a place to smoke inside a government building.

I lit a cigarette. The cop whom I figured would be Mr. Nice Cop today set a steaming Styrofoam cup in front of me. The other cop hadn't come back yet.

"You gonna do the questioning?"

The cop shook his head. "Detectives will be in later."

"So, you're playing babysitter until they get here?"

He glared at me, but said nothing.

"Can you tell me anything about Donovan's death?"

"No."

"Do I get to make a phone call?"

"No."

Mr. Nice Cop just ruined his image.

"Can I take a leak?"

"Leave your cigarette here."

I put it out, then followed the cop down the hall. I was supervised during my use of the bathroom, then we returned to Room A. And I relit my cigarette.

At ten-thirty, two men entered the room. The tall one was dressed in a tan sport coat, blue shirt and navy slacks. The short one was wearing a long-sleeved plaid shirt and Levi's.

The tall one nodded at the uniformed cop. "Thanks."

The cop left. The tall one sat to my left while the other remained standing.

"Mr. Murphy, I'm Detective Janklow." He pointed to the short one. "This is my partner, Detective Murdock. We need to ask you some questions."

"I've already been told that much."

"They're in regards to the death of Johnny Donovan."

"I already know that, too."

"Where were you last night between the hours of one and two?"

"AM?"

"Yes."

I lit my last cigarette. "At home. And, yes, someone can vouch for that."

Murdock parted one of the blinds with his fingers and peered out. Without looking at me, he said, "Girlfriend?"

"Just a friend who's staying at my place."

"I see."

"Do I need my lawyer here?"

Janklow cursed under his breath. "Do you, Mr. Murphy?"

"I'm asking you."

"That's certainly your right."

"Am I a suspect?"

"We just wanna ask you some questions, is all," Murdock said. He was still staring through the blinds.

"Ask."

"Do you know Johnny Donovan?" Janklow said.

"I met him last night."

"Where did you meet him?"

"At a house on La Mirada Avenue, off Vine."

"When was this?"

"About ten-fifteen. I was at the house approximately twenty minutes."

"And this is the last time you saw Mr. Donovan?"

"The one and only time."

"What did you two discuss?"

"My visit pertained to a current case on which I'm working. I'm not at liberty to discuss the details."

"Client confidentiality," Murdock said.

I wondered what was so damn interesting on the other side of those blinds. "Yep."

"We have an eyewitness that says you were pretty tough on Donovan."

I shrugged.

"Even broke his nose."

"That was in self-defense."

"Uh-huh. Did he tell you anything?"

"Nope."

"And now he can't."

"I guess he can't."

Murdock snapped the blinds shut and pulled a baggie from his jacket pocket. He set the baggie in front of me and leaned against the table. "Any idea why Donovan had this in his hand when we found him?"

The baggie contained a blood-stained business card. Mine.

"Nope." I smashed the cigarette in the overflowing ashtray and scratched my head. "Am I a suspect in this homicide?"

"Yes," Janklow said.

As much as I hated to break up the party, I was beginning to feel a bit uncomfortable. "I want my lawyer."

I spent the remainder of the day in a cell at the precinct. My lawyer called at four-thirty to say that he was out of town and couldn't possibly get to the station in time. Lucky me, I'd be a guest of the LAPD for the weekend. I asked him to contact Arturo and inform him of the situation, and try to reach Tyrone. He assured me he would.

It was after five o'clock when I was told Tyrone was gone until Monday.

I sat on the cot in this tiny white room and tried to convince myself that it wouldn't be so bad. At least I'd get plenty of sleep over the weekend.

FIFTEEN

My attorney got me released at one-o-five Monday afternoon. It happened to be the end of the 72-hour period of legal detainment anyway, so I'm not sure what he actually did for me. Still, I was happy to be out. The cops decided not to charge me, but reminded me not to leave town as I was still a suspect in the case.

"Does this mean the city of Los Angeles? Cause I like to go to Culver City for lunch sometimes."

"You're a funny guy, Murphy," the cop said.

"Thanks."

"Don't leave Southern California. If we wanna talk to you, we'd better be able to find you."

"Ten-four, good buddy."

Arturo picked me up in my truck. I drove home. I hadn't driven since early Friday morning, and I missed it. Besides, it was my truck.

When I opened the door to my apartment, I wasn't sure I was in the right place. The key worked, but the carpet was vacuumed, and the sweet smell of cleaner permeated my nostrils.

"What the hell happened here?" I said.

"I cleaned up a bit."

I closed the door and stepped into the kitchen. "Holy shit, Arturo."

There were no dirty dishes in the sink, nor any clean ones in the dishwasher. The counters sparkled and my feet didn't stick to the linoleum floor. I wouldn't regard the way I kept my apartment as a health risk, but it certainly would disappoint Martha Stewart. Not since Arturo got a hold of it, though. He would make Martha proud.

"You like?" he said.

"Like? I love. Did you do this all by yourself?"

"Yes sir, Holmes."

"Did you do well in home economics in high school?"

"I didn't do well in anything in high school. I had lots of time on my hands in prison, so I took up cleaning."

"Thank you."

"No need to thank me. You're letting me stay here. The least I can do is clean up."

I lit a cigarette and reached for the normally overflowing black, plastic ashtray on the coffee table. Not only was the ashtray empty, it was also clean.

I leaned back on the couch. "Did you see Nadia at all?"

"No, but I did leave a message at the office Friday night."

"Thanks. She didn't call here or anything?"

"Don't know. There were a couple calls, but I didn't answer them."

I picked up the phone. The dial tone stuttered. I called my voicemail access number, punched in my password, and listened to three messages. The first two were from the same computer system that said it was sorry I wasn't at home to answer the call, but wanted to tell me about an opportunity that could make me as much as $10,000 a week for doing virtually nothing. It asked me to call back. I erased the messages. The third message was from Nadia.

"Did she call?" Arturo said.

"Yep. She's gonna stop by tonight."

Arturo came in from the kitchen holding two cans of Budweiser.

"You went to the store, huh?"

"Sure did. And, I not only got beer but plenty of food, too."

"You're a lifesaver."

"I know."

He handed me a can, then sat next to me on the couch. We spent the next several minutes drinking and smoking in silence.

"Did you learn anything new?" Arturo said.

"That I hate sitting in a cell for the weekend."

"Shit, Holmes, that ain't nothing."

"Maybe not for a hardened criminal such as yourself, but for me? It was more than I cared to experience."

"Hey, I'm a reformed criminal, remember?"

"Oh, yeah. Speaking of which . . ."

"Yes, Mom. I called my parole officer this morning, like a good little boy. Can I have a cookie now?"

"No, but you can keep your ass out of prison for another week. Isn't that reward enough?"

"Fucking A."

I smashed my cigarette into the ashtray. "Okay, Q and A time. Who killed Donovan?"

"Someone who didn't like him much would be my guess."

"Arturo, you absolutely amaze me. You're a natural born detective, I swear."

He smiled. "My money's on DiMarco."

"Why?"

"Donovan gave up DiMarco. And you did bust up a blowjob for the poor bastard." He took a drink from his beer. "And, he's Italian."

"What's that got to do with it?"

"Hello? Does the name John Gotti ring a bell?"

"Point?"

"Gotti, DiMarco, Italians."

"Another fine example of your awesome powers of deduction at work."

"Italians equal Mafia. Kill the ones who talk."

"Oh."

"Finally, the *hombre* gets it. Jesus, Jack, I was beginning to worry about you."

I finished my beer then set the can in the kitchen sink. Arturo followed me into the kitchen and washed out both beer cans. He opened the cabinet under the sink and dropped the cans into a small bag-lined wastebasket.

"I started a trashcan for recyclables. You can make some good money saving cans and shit."

"Cool."

Arturo grabbed two more beers from the bottom shelf in the refrigerator, held out a can. "You getting hungry?"

I grabbed the beer, popped its lid. "Yep."

"Me, too."

"You want tacos?"

"I'm Mexican, Holmes. I'll eat tacos all day long."

I set a cutting board on the counter, then grabbed tomatoes, onion and lettuce from the refrigerator and a packet of meat from the freezer.

"Here, let me help," Arturo said.

I sent him to the stove with a frying pan and the meat. I diced the tomatoes and onion, then shredded the lettuce on the cutting board. "Setting aside your Italian theory, what've we got? We talk to Donovan, he gives us DiMarco. I talk to DiMarco, but I don't get shit. DiMarco then whacks Donovan because he talks, even though we really didn't get anything."

"Maybe we didn't, Holmes, but DiMarco did. He got the opportunity to remind his people of the price for betrayal."

I scooped the tomatoes, onions and lettuce into their own small plastic bowls. I rinsed off the cutting board and set it in the sink. "By killing Donovan."

"Exactly."

"You don't think it's any more than that?"

"Shit, Holmes. Loyalty's *numero uno*. Don't forget, DiMarco got a two-for-one out of this, too. He taught Donovan a lesson and got back at you for busting up the blowjob."

I leaned against the sink and finished my beer. "There's more to it, though. I can feel it."

"DiMarco's covering his tracks."

"That'd be my guess."

"From what, though? A child porn ring?"

"Maybe."

"Maybe DiMarco just has a thing for young girls himself."

"Maybe, but what happens to the girls?"

Arturo pushed the sizzling meat around the pan with a plastic spatula. "Dunno."

I threw in two handfuls of onion. "If you're filming little girls for your enjoyment, what do you do with them after filming? Let them go?"

"Shit, couldn't do that. One or two, maybe, but you can't have a small army of girls loose to open their mouths."

"You can't easily dispose of that many bodies, either."

"True. Maybe DiMarco ships 'em to some lowlife in Mexico like Roy said."

"Maybe. We need to do some digging on DiMarco."

"Rattle them bones and see what skeletons fall from his closet."

"Exactly. Of course, we need to be prepared for the worst."

"Which is?"

"He's good and we don't find shit."

"Such a pessimist."

"Actually, I prefer to say I'm a realist."

"Oh, that's much better."

"It is. That meat almost done? I'm starved."

I had just set the taco shells in the microwave when the phone rang. It was Roy.

"I heard you were in lockup for the weekend."

"Damn, news sure travels fast."

"I was talking to a guy in Homicide and he told me about Donovan, and you."

"How nice of him. You talk to LAPD often?"

"Just when something juicy like this comes up."

"I see."

"So, what happened? And what bearing, if any, does this have on the case?"

I lit a cigarette, sat on the couch. "I questioned Donovan about Carrie and a couple hours later, he's dead. The cops talk to Donovan's people and they say I was leaning on him hard."

"Were you?"

"Yep."

"Did you learn anything?"

"Donovan said maybe, maybe he saw Carrie November second. And, he gave me a name to follow up."

"Which is?"

"Tony DiMarco."

"Never heard of him."

"Neither had I, until Thursday night. And, no, I don't know anything about him yet, except that he hangs at a strip bar called Club TA."

"Strip bar? You think Carrie . . ."

"No, I don't. Not yet, anyway. I'm just following the breadcrumbs."

"Okay, I'll let Raymond know you're working on some leads."

"Be sure you don't let him believe I'm onto something yet, cause I'm not sure I am."

"I understand. Keep in touch, and try to stay out of jail."

"I'll try."

I meant it, too.

Arturo was sitting on the couch watching the news. I joined him. I had my hand wrapped around a taco when the doorbell rang.

"Guess it's not in the stars for you to eat dinner," Arturo said through a mouthful of his first taco.

"Guess not."

SIXTEEN

I checked the peephole. Nadia was standing in the hall, grocery bags tucked under each arm. I opened the door. "Hi."

"Hi. I thought I'd surprise you with dinner."

Nadia got as far as the kitchen. "Oh, my God."

She turned and headed for the door.

"Where you going?"

"I'm so sorry."

I held up my hands. She stopped in front of me for a moment, then leaned her shoulder forward and whisked by me.

"Nadia." She was in the hall when I caught up. "Nadia, wait."

Tears welled in her eyes. "I had no idea. I'm really sorry."

"For what? Why don't you stay and eat with us?"

She tried to wiggle away from me. I maintained a light grip on her arms. "C'mon, let me take those bags."

"No."

"I'm sorry."

"You? You didn't do anything. I'm the one that made an ass out of myself."

"No, you didn't."

"Yes," she said, held my stare. "I did."

When Nadia squirmed again, I let her go. She bolted for the elevator, then leaned into the button with her right finger. I thought she might drop one of the bags. She didn't. Not until the elevator door opened. Then she threw the bags to the ground and stepped into the car. And the doors closed.

I thought about chasing after her. But, I knew it wouldn't do any good. By the time the building's single elevator returned to my floor, she'd be long gone. I walked to the elevator, picked up the bags and went back to the apartment.

When I saw Nadia the next morning, I could tell she wasn't ready to talk about what had happened.

"Morning," I said.

"Hi."

"Good morning, Nadia," Arturo said.

"Morning."

Arturo made a beeline for my office.

"How's it going?" I said.

Nadia glanced up from the stack of papers she was filing in one of the legal-sized cabinets. "Fine. I've got coffee brewing."

"Thank you."

"You're welcome."

I stood next to her, put my hand on her shoulder. "About last night."

"Forget about it," she snapped. "I did."

I pulled my hand away and walked into my office, shutting the door behind me.

"Shit, Holmes, it's fucking cold out there."

"Yep." I walked to the side table and checked on Mr. Coffee. He had completed his brew cycle. I filled two Styrofoam cups, handed one to Arturo, then sat at my desk and put my feet up. "I didn't ask her to do a run-down on DiMarco."

"How could you? Man, she must really be pissed off."

"She'll get over it. Someday."

"Hope my balls don't freeze and fall off before then."

I finished my cup of coffee and refilled it. Then, I filled another cup and walked out to the lobby. Nadia was punching data into her computer at a furious pace.

"Want a cup of coffee?" I said.

She glanced at me, granted me a half-smile. "Thanks."

I set the cup on the corner of her desk. "Could you do a background check for me?"

Her fingers burned up the keyboard. I was amazed at how much faster she typed when she was upset. "Sure."

She stopped and spun her chair around. She grabbed a pen and scratch pad from her desktop. Her gaze focused on the paper, and remained there. "Who is it?"

"Tony DiMarco. The only thing I know is that he may own a piece of a strip club called Club TA in Hollywood. And, he had some type of relationship with Donovan."

"I'll get started right away."

"Thanks."

"You're welcome."

I was going to try the subject of last night again, but she was already attacking the keyboard. I went back to my office.

Nadia was able to come up with bank records on DiMarco in less than an hour. Back when I was apprenticing at Marshak Investigations, I learned not to ask Nadia how or where she obtained information. I didn't care so long as no one wound up in jail. I continued this tradition when she came to work for me.

Arturo and I spent the next half-hour going through the stack of papers relating to DiMarco's banking activities. Nadia not only acquired checking statements on two of DiMarco's accounts, but she also got documentation on three outstanding loans and a couple CDs.

I rubbed my eyes and leaned back in my chair. I hated researching paperwork, and doing so always made me groggy. This time proved no different.

"Well, look at this," Arturo said, studying a document on the top of his pile. "We might have something here."

"Are you trying to keep me in suspense or what?"

"I have a question for you. What kind of a security company would hire someone who has no previous experience in the field, and then pay that person twenty-five hundred a week?"

"Not a very smart one."

"Exactly."

Arturo handed me the document. It was a summary sheet of EFT transfers into what appeared to be DiMarco's main checking account. Every Friday, $2500 was wired into the account. The sender was Wells Fargo Bank, on behalf of Diamond Steel Security Services in Los Angeles. The summary sheet included only year-to-date activity for 2000. Diamond Steel was listed every week. In March and September, payments were doubled on the second and fourth Fridays in each month.

There was a knock at my office door. Nadia came in and handed me a couple more papers. "I figured you'd want this."

"And this is?"

"Prelim info on Diamond Steel."

"You're good, girl. Thanks."

On her way out, she gave up half a smile, but at least this one was a few degrees warmer.

SEVENTEEN

Diamond Steel Security was located seven blocks east of my office, in the tower known as 3333 Wilshire. This also happened to be the building's address. I knew the building well. When I opened my firm, I'd checked out the 11-story solar brown glass hi-rise. While the offices were clean and well-designed, the price was out of my ballpark. Apparently, Diamond Steel didn't have that problem.

"Are we going for a ride?" Arturo said.

"Yep."

"Oh, goodie."

"Keep your pants on, Arturo. We're just going to talk."

"Damn, I was hoping we could kick some ass."

"Not yet. But when we do, I promise you'll be there."

"I'm honored."

"You should be."

"I'm sorry, sir, but Mr. Jameson is in a meeting and I have no idea how long it will be."

The redhead behind the huge half-circle reception desk was dressed in a skintight navy dress and matching pantyhose. I imagined her feet were snuggled in tight, high-heeled pumps, but couldn't confirm it—they were nestled under the desk. She was maybe forty, but obviously worked out daily.

"That's okay, I'll wait."

She glanced at Arturo, then back at me. "Very well."

She didn't sound happy about it at all.

Perhaps the redhead's reluctance caused the wheels to spin a bit faster. We sat in the lobby less than ten minutes before she told me to go to suite 1124.

"On the eleventh floor," she added.

Really? "Thanks."

We used the elevator that the leasing company billed as "state of the art". I found it to be a rather ordinary elevator. But, I wasn't an elevator professional, and I'm sure a pro would have seen the obvious benefits. As we stepped onto the eleventh floor, the signage board indicated that Diamond Steel occupied the entire floor. Suite 1124 was labeled *Office of Personnel.* We followed the little arrows around the corner and down the hall.

The suite had a reception area, though no one was sitting at the desk. The desk was clear of all normal desktop items—phone, computer, pencils, pens, paper. I guessed it was one of those all-show reception areas. A balding man, five-eight, in his late fifties, came from behind a door. He tugged his bright red suspenders and introduced himself as Mr. Jameson.

"Please follow me."

We did. The suite had only two offices—the dummy one and Jameson's.

"Have a seat."

Jameson sat behind his desk. This desktop was cluttered with uneven stacks of documents, three coffee cups, a calculator and phone. "Excuse my mess. I'm trying to get a jump on the end of the year."

"My office looks much the same."

"Oh, no," he said, sounding shocked. "My office is rarely in this condition. I'm a very neat person."

How could I be so stupid? "Of course."

"I apologize if I'm rather quick with you gentlemen but as you can see, I'm rather swamped."

"Indeed," Arturo said.

Arturo can produce a wicked smile when he wants to. Apparently, at that moment, he wanted to.

Jameson looked at me. "Yes, well. What can I do for you?"

"We wanna ask you a few questions about one of your employees."

"Who?"

"A Tony DiMarco."

Jameson's eyes nearly bulged out of his head. I wondered if this guy went broke trying to play poker. "I, I, what about him?"

He leaned forward and shuffled some papers around his desk.

"What does Mr. DiMarco do exactly?"

"I don't know."

"That's strange. I could've sworn the suite is marked Office of Personnel. Did I mistakenly step into the wrong office?"

I started to get out of the chair. Jameson held a hand up. "You are in the right place."

"If this is the Office of Personnel, how come you don't know what DiMarco does for this company?"

Jameson glanced at the phone, then back at me. "Because I didn't oversee the hiring of Mr. DiMarco, nor do I oversee his day-to-day activities."

"Who does?"

"Someone in upper management."

"And who might that be?"

Jameson cleared his throat and fished a pen and pad of paper from the piles on his desk. "What did you say your name was again?"

"Jack Murphy."

I began spelling my last name, but Jameson held up his hand. "I know how to spell it."

He scribbled on the pad, then placed the pad and pen back in the mess. "Mr. Murphy, Diamond Steel is a nationwide security firm, and has many people in the upper echelons of management. I have no idea who was involved in the hiring of Mr. DiMarco, nor am I aware of who supervises him."

"Can't you check his file?"

"Company personnel files are confidential."

Arturo sighed.

I rubbed my temples. "Then give me a list of all the upper management people and I'll ask them, one by one."

"I can't do that."

"Why the hell not?" Arturo said.

"That, too, is confidential information."

"Okay," I said. "Let me ask you this, then. Why would a nationwide company, such as yourself, hire a man as a consultant and pay him twenty-five hundred a week when this person has no security background at all?"

James glanced at the phone again. He drummed his fingers on the arms of his chair. "I'm sorry, gentlemen, but I can't help you."

"Who do we need to speak with, then?"

"I'm not sure. Maybe you should write a letter to me and I can forward it to the appropriate people."

Arturo stood and leaned over the desk. "We ain't got time for a letter, sir."

Jameson averted [avoided] Arturo's eyes. "You men will have to leave now."

Arturo took a step to the side of the desk. "I'm sorry you can't help us, Holmes."

Jameson picked up the phone. He punched a speed dial button, then said, "I need a guard in eleven twenty-four to escort some visitors out of the building."

I held up my hands. "No need, Mr. Jameson, we're just leaving."

He held the receiver to his ear. We walked out of his office and down the hall. I looked back as we rounded the corner. Jameson had moved to the doorway, watching us leave.

"Arturo, I think we just struck a nerve."

EIGHTEEN

That afternoon, Arturo and I decided to split up. He would tail DiMarco while I worked on the Donovan homicide. I returned the SUV to Enterprise and rented a cream-colored Buick Regal from Hertz on Santa Monica Boulevard.

I handed Arturo the keys. "Stay with him all night. We'll talk again in the morning."

He climbed into the car. "I'll pick him up at Club TA."

"At midnight."

"Right."

Arturo had plans to spend the evening with Maria, and being DiMarco was a night owl, nothing much would probably happen before midnight anyway. So, he'd stay with Maria until 11:30, then head to Hollywood.

He inhaled slowly, a smile formed on his lips. "Ah, ain't nothing like the smell of new leather." He put the key in the ignition and started the engine. "Purrs like a kitten, too."

"I'm glad you like it."

We'd exhausted the information Nadia obtained on DiMarco, yielding only the connection to Diamond Steel. Since that didn't look like it would provide much help to us at this point, I decided to do what good detectives do, go back to the source.

I headed for La Mirada Avenue. I hoped someone from Donovan's crew might still be alive, and might be able to give me something on DiMarco. The parking lot I'd used last time was open, so I parked there again.

No cars were in the drive. I leaned back and grabbed the *People* magazine I had brought along to kill time.

I finished my coffee about nine. At nine-thirty, I debated whether I should pack it in when the Suburban pulled into the drive. Mike climbed from the vehicle and walked to the front door. I hopped out and caught up with him after he had the door unlocked, but before he was inside.

"Hey."

He looked at me and tried to shut the door.

I strong-armed the door, made my way inside. "What's up?"

"Get the fuck out or I'm calling the cops."

Then, he stepped outside and hurried back to his SUV.

I followed him. "Wait a minute."

He was climbing in his truck when I grabbed his arm. "I just wanna talk to you."

He reached under his seat and withdrew his .45. I grabbed the pistol, pointed it toward the windshield.

"You're not getting me, too," he said.

"What're you talking about?"

He stopped struggling and we stood frozen, our eyes locked, for a few minutes. I felt his hand relax around the gun and I took the opportunity to wrestle it from his hand. I stepped back, dropped the magazine out of the pistol, and pulled back the slide to eject the round in the chamber. The bullet hit the concrete and rolled under the vehicle. I handed the pistol back to him and put the magazine in my pocket.

"I'll give it back when we're through."

"We are through."

He fished his key ring from his pocket, fumbled to insert a key in the ignition. I swatted his hand. The keys fell to the passenger floorboard. "We haven't even started."

He sighed. His face wore a look of defeat combined with anger. "What do you want?"

"To talk to you."

"About what?"

"Donovan."

"How you killed him?"

"I didn't kill him."

He snickered. "Right."

"Why would I have killed him? He helped me. I didn't have a grudge against him. DiMarco, however, did."

"DiMarco?"

"Can we go inside? It's a little chilly out here."

I followed him inside the house. He locked the front door, then flipped some switches. The house erupted with hot-white light.

"Mind if I smoke, Mike?"

"I don't give a shit."

Mike walked into the office where I had spoken with Donovan. I paused in the hall to light my cigarette, then joined him in the office. He stood in front of the wet bar and scooped coffee into a filter. After the brew cycle had started, he turned. "I have to get the studio ready. Sit down. I'll be back in a few."

I followed him down the hall and into the blue room. He switched on the overhead fluorescents, then the floodlights beside the bed. "I said I'd be back in a minute."

"I know, but I thought we could talk while you work."

He shook his head. "Fantastic."

He went to the camera and pulled the film from it, put the film in a plastic case, then reloaded the camera.

"Where's Stevie?" I said.

"Gone."

"Gone where?"

"Just gone. Now, what's this about DiMarco?"

"After I left Donovan last Thursday, I found DiMarco at Club TA in Hollywood. I leaned on him pretty good. A couple hours later, Donovan winds up dead."

He snapped the cover shut on the camera. "So?"

"So, DiMarco got pissed off and killed Donovan for talking."

"How do you know that?"

"I don't, but it's an educated guess."

"Educated or not, it's still only a guess."

"True. Doesn't my theory sound plausible to you?"

"Maybe. But, maybe you got pissed off that Donovan didn't help you more and you whacked him."

"Not bad, except I had nothing to gain by Donovan's death. As it is, I spent the weekend in jail over it."

"No shit."

"No shit. Thanks to you, most likely."

He fished a cigarette pack from his pocket. "Me?"

"Someone told the cops I was tough with Donovan, which is why they came knocking on my door."

He put a cigarette in his mouth, lit it, and through a cloud of smoke said, "Wasn't me."

"Maybe, maybe not."

"What the hell do you want from me anyway? I don't know shit about nothing."

"Maybe you only think you don't know shit."

"You gonna start doing my thinking for me?"

"No."

"Good."

Mike stripped the bed and threw the sheets into a burlap laundry bag. He went to a dresser near the door and grabbed a fresh set of sheets. Then, with military precision, he made the bed.

"Donovan told me DiMarco brought four girls here for filming, and that my client's daughter may have been one of them."

"So?"

"What do you know about that?"

"Which time?"

"What?"

Nightstands sat on each side of the bed. Cheap ashtrays, probably stolen from hotels, sat atop each nightstand. Mike emptied the ashtrays into a trash bag. "Which time are you talking about?"

"DiMarco did this more than once?"

Mike laughed, glanced up. "You're the detective and you don't know this?"

"Enlighten me."

"DiMarco brought girls here every week."

"This was November second."

"Don't know. I was out of town that weekend."

"How long has DiMarco been bringing girls here?"

Mike walked toward a black fifty-five gallon drum in the corner that served as a trashcan. He dropped the trash bag into it, then turned. "I started working for Donovan about a year and a half ago. My first day on the job, DiMarco brought a girl over who was maybe fourteen, fifteen tops. And it's been that way ever since." His eyes suddenly grew cold. "You wearing a wire?"

"No."

"Do you realize that by saying 'no' anything recorded is inadmissible?"

"You a lawyer, Mike?"

"No."

"You sound up on the law, though."

"CYA, buddy."

I leaned over a nightstand and ground my cigarette into the MGM Grand logo in the middle of the black ashtray. "Let me be frank. I wanna find my client's daughter, Carrie. And I'll do whatever I need to make that happen. But, I'm not gunning for anyone in particular. You help me, I go away. Simple as that."

Mike glanced at his watch, then at me. "The coffee should be done, and I've got a few minutes. I'll tell you whatever I can, then you get the fuck out and leave me be."

"Deal."

I followed him into the office. He poured himself a cup of coffee and pointed at the cups, then sat behind the desk and threw his feet up on it. How quickly he seemed to feel at home in his former boss' office. I poured myself a cup and sat in a chair opposite the desk.

"Has DiMarco brought in any young girls since the second?"

"Two last weekend. I haven't seen him since."

"Do you like this kind of work?"

"What?"

"Child pornography."

"Fuck you."

"I just wonder what makes a guy do this sort of thing, that's all."

His eyes seemed to puff out and get redder than they already were. "Look, I graduated from the New York Film Institute. I'm a real producer."

"Why not get a decent job, then?"

Mike dropped his stare to the desktop. "DiMarco runs some card games around town and I got into him deep. He told me I had a choice. I could either pay off my debt, or work it off."

"I thought you worked for Donovan."

"I do, or I did, sort of. DiMarco put me here. I was to work for Donovan for four years. I would be paid a meager salary and do whatever I was asked, period. DiMarco did say, though, that if I got out of line, he'd come back to see me."

"What about now that Donovan's dead? Are you off the hook?"

"I don't know." He shot his gaze up to meet mine. "Wait a fucking minute. Don't even go there."

"Go where, Mike?"

"I know what you're thinking. You think I snuffed Donovan to get out of my contract."

"Did you?"

"No."

"Okay."

I lit a cigarette. Mike pushed an ashtray across the desk, with about enough force to send it across a football field. I held out my hand to stop it from crashing to the floor. "Thanks. Now tell me about how you guys handled the girls for DiMarco."

"What's to tell? DiMarco dropped them off. He told us to get them on tape doing themselves and each other, but to be careful of, quote, their privates. Every time DiMarco dropped off girls, he told Donovan that a broken hymen would equal a broken head."

I masked my disgust with a half-smile. "What happened to the tapes?"

"DiMarco took them when he picked up the girls."

"How long did the girls stay?"

"Exactly thirty minutes for each girl he brought. Four girls, two hours."

"He was exact."

"Fuck, man, I've never seen someone so punctual."

"Did Donovan keep copies of the tapes?"

"How? We wouldn't have had time to dupe them even if we wanted to."

I tapped the elongated ash from my cigarette into the ashtray. "You guys never used double cameras?"

"Double cameras?"

"Yeah, film the girls with two cameras so you'd be able to keep one tape."

Mike got up and refilled his coffee cup. "Good idea, but not possible."

"Why not?"

"DiMarco's an asshole, in case you haven't figured that out yet, and a mean one at that. Plus, he always went through the place to make sure no one was pulling any shit. Maybe he was thinking about the double camera thing."

"Maybe. Did Donovan work for DiMarco?"

"I don't know. DiMarco was holding something over Donovan, that's for sure, but DiMarco paid Donovan in cash when he picked up the girls."

"How much?"

"A thousand per girl."

I snuffed my cigarette in the ashtray. "So you guys were pulling down two grand an hour."

"Donovan was. I get paid ten bucks an hour in cash, plus another twenty bucks an hour against my debt."

"What did DiMarco do with the girls after you guys finished with them?"

"He took them away."

"Where'd they go?"

"Dunno." Mike glanced at his watch again. "My actors are

gonna be here any minute."

"What else do you know about DiMarco? Did he work for someone?"

"I'm sure he did."

"Why?"

"Sometimes he'd get a call on his cell phone while he was here. Usually, he became kinda quiet, but sometimes got into heated arguments with whoever it was. It sounded to me like arguing with a boss, that's all."

I stood, walked to the doorway, then turned back. "Have you ever heard of Diamond Steel?"

"The security people? Of course. Sometimes, DiMarco brought DSS guards to watch the place when we were filming."

"Why only sometimes?"

"Dunno." He met me at the door. "Sometimes they came with him, sometimes not. Look, it's been fun and all, but I really gotta get to work."

I took a few steps down the hall, then stopped. "Just one more thing."

"What?"

"Have you considered the possibility that DiMarco killed Donovan for another reason."

"Like?"

"Like, maybe DiMarco needs to cover his tracks about these young girls. Maybe he wants to kill anyone who knows anything."

"What're you saying?"

"I'm suggesting maybe you take a vacation."

"A vacation?"

I walked to the front door. "Yeah, like leave town for a month. Or more."

"You serious?"

"Yes, Mike, I'm serious. For your own sake."

Mike stepped in front of me and unlocked the front door. "I'll think about it."

I walked into the cool night air. "You do that."

NINETEEN

It had been more than a day since Nadia left my apartment in tears and yet I couldn't get myself to feel any better. Except for a few short words in passing, we hadn't spoken at all, much less about what had happened.

Knowing Nadia, she spent most of her nights at home in front of her computer or her television. So, I decided to call her. But, her machine picked up and asked me to leave a message. I didn't.

I got in my truck and drove to her apartment.

As I parked my truck in front of her garage, she came down the stairs. We stared at each other for a moment, then met at the foot of the stairwell.

"Hi," she said.

"Hi."

"I was just going to get some ice cream. Wanna take a walk?"

"Sure."

The evening air was crisp, the sky moonless and cloudy. We crossed Weyburn, then headed east. Nadia's favorite ice cream place, Juju's Java and Juice, was sandwiched between Francesca's Hair Boutique and Tower Records, just past Broxton. While her idea of ice cream might be popular with the yuppie UCLA kids that hung in Westwood Village, it wasn't what normal people called ice cream. The stuff Nadia put into her mouth looked like ice cream, but tasted like cardboard. Devil's Delight was its name. Somehow I don't think the Devil would appreciate his name associated with something so devoid of taste, fat and cholesterol.

I skipped the Devil's Delight and settled for a latte. We sat on wrought-iron barstools on either side of a small, circular table outside the cafe. While the wrought-iron look of the table and chairs was the in-thing, I found them quite uncomfortable. But I said nothing.

After a few minutes of watching the foot traffic weave its way through the overcrowded shops, I lit a cigarette. She grabbed a cigarette from her pack. I lit it for her. Then, we fell back into an unsettling silence.

I decided to break it. "How's it going?"

"Fine."

"Are you okay?"

"Of course. Why wouldn't I be?"

I took a hit from my cigarette. "Last night was a bummer."

She made a slight noise, which I took as agreement.

"I'm sorry that things turned out the way they did."

"It wasn't your fault. It was mine."

"No, it wasn't."

"I'm the one who assumed. It was ridiculous. I should've called." The tension in her voice wasn't easing any. "It won't happen again."

"Assuming, or wanting to make me dinner?"

A double-stretch black limo drove east on Weyburn, slowed as it approached us. It's not that limos are anything special in LA, but I was pretty certain this limo had circled the block three times now. For a moment, it looked as though it would park alongside the curb, then it picked up speed, turned right on Westwood.

I finished my cigarette, crushed it under the sole of my Nikes. A loud rumble of gangsta rap music drifted from Westwood. I glanced up, noticed a black Toyota Celica with a black man in shades behind its wheel, roll through the intersection. I'm no stereo expert, but I pegged it at a good hundred-plus watts to have traveled nearly a block.

Almost a full minute after he crossed the intersection, the music faded away.

Nadia said, "That was annoying."

"Yep."

Her eyes seemed bluer than normal, painted with sadness. "I'm really sorry that I barged in on you like that last night."

"Don't be. I appreciate the effort."

One of her hands was holding her wanna-be ice cream, the other rested on the table. I put my hand over her free one. "You're very good to me."

Our eyes locked. A butterfly stirred in my gut. I leaned forward.

"Hey, Murphy."

I turned toward the street. The black limo was back, stopped against the curb with its rear window down. I could see two men in the back seat—Skinny and Redwood.

"Come for a ride with us," Skinny said.

I glanced at Nadia. "Stay here. I'll be back."

I walked to the curb, leaned against the car, and peered inside. No one else was in the back. "Why?"

"We need to talk."

"Why can't we talk right here?"

Skinny brought his left hand up to the window, showed me a blued Glock, and pointed it at my chest. "C'mon, Jack, let's not make a scene, huh?"

"Jack?" Nadia said.

"Put it away. I'll go."

Skinny lowered his arm. I turned to Nadia. "I'll catch up with you later, okay?"

I opened the door and climbed in. Nadia called my name again as the limo pulled away from the curb.

I sat in the bench seat opposite the two. Redwood stared at me. He still hadn't made a sound.

"How come you didn't take our offer the other day?" Skinny said.

"If I wanted to be told which cases to work on, I would've never opened my own agency."

He smiled. "Well, we need to make you understand our position."

"You mind if I smoke?"

"Yes," Skinny said.

I lit a cigarette. "I understand your position."

"No, I don't think you do. I said I minded."

I raised my eyebrows. He pointed at my cigarette. "Oh. Did you? I'm sorry." I took another hit, let the smoke trail from my nose and mouth.

The limo veered left onto Santa Monica Boulevard.

"Where we headed?"

"You'll know soon enough."

Redwood managed a grunt that I believed was meant as a chuckle.

"Are we stopping in Beverly Hills? I need to do some shopping on Rodeo Drive. Maybe I can do it while we're here?"

"You're a real Jerry Seinfeld, Murphy."

Redwood grunted again. His burning stare never left my face.

I searched for an ashtray but couldn't find one. I knocked my ashes from my cigarette. They landed on the floor between my feet. I ground them into the navy carpet.

"Can we get something to eat? I'm starved," I said.

"Shut the fuck up."

"You're supposed to be the host of this party. You're kinda shitty at it."

Skinny stared out the window. Redwood kept his eyes on me.

We rode through the thick traffic in silence. The limo turned left on Vine.

"Hollywood," I said. "What a town. We could catch a couple drinks at Club TA. I'll buy."

"We ain't here to socialize."

"If you're not careful, you're gonna hurt my feelings."

"Fuck you."

"Okay, now I'm hurt."

The limo passed Sunset Boulevard and hung a left on Selma. A block later, it pulled into a parking lot. We cruised to the southeast end, then the limo did a one-eighty and stopped.

Skinny raised his gun. "Okay, Murphy, I'm only gonna tell you once more. Stay the fuck away from this case. The girl doesn't wanna be found."

He opened the right door. As if on cue, a white panel van pulled into the lot and stopped alongside the limo.

"You guys like this spot, don't you?"

"What?"

"This is where you dumped Jenkins."

He looked confused.

"The last PI that was on the case. You guys killed him and dumped him right here, didn't you?"

"Get the fuck out."

My heart kicked into overdrive. "Like I said before, if Carrie talks to me, I'll leave her be. But, I can't screw the people who hired me."

"It breaks my heart to hear you say that."

"I'm sure it does."

"Get out or I'll shoot you right here."

I only managed to put one foot on the pavement before hands grabbed me, yanked me to the asphalt.

"You stupid fuck. Just drop it," Skinny said.

My face was held against the pavement. I heard the limo door close, then felt a sharp blow to my lower back. Something pressed against the back of my neck, probably a knee. My hair was pulled until my head was wrenched back as far as it could go. A large man wearing a black ski mask leaned down in front of me, shoved a ski mask on my head backward. My head was released and fell to the asphalt. Suddenly, what felt like fists and boots and possibly baseball bats stuck me everywhere. I rolled to my side, tried to curl into a ball. Every inch of my body screamed in agony. The beating continued for an eternity. My lower back and legs grew numb. My heart thumped through every nerve in my body. The blows continued.

Then, they stopped. As quickly as it began, it was over. As my muscles began to relax a little, the final blow was delivered across my left cheek. I felt my head snap back against the asphalt. My body went still.

I heard at least two voices, but I couldn't understand what they were saying. The voices quieted, then a car engine came to life, then another. Doors opened and closed.

I tried to move. I couldn't. My arms and legs were numb. The metallic tang of blood grew stronger on my tongue.

The sounds of the night grew quiet. I felt nothing. I wondered if I was dead.

TWENTY

I woke to the stench of disinfectant. A soft, steady beep emitted from my left. I blinked. My vision was blurry, though slowly coming into focus.

"Well, good morning," a voice said from in front of me.

I was on my back in a bed. I looked at my left arm and, after blinking several more times, identified a clear tube stuck into my hand.

A hospital.

I glanced toward the origin of the voice. I noticed a woman's distorted face above a white blur. I concentrated and brought into focus a nurse. She wore large, round glasses above her puffy cheeks. She scribbled into a folding steel chart.

I felt a hand against my right arm. I turned and saw Nadia, an ear-to-ear smile on her face. "Hi."

"Hi."

"I'll get the doctor," the nurse said, then left the room.

"I was worried about you," I said.

"Me? You're the one that needs the worrying."

I tried to smile but the aching muscles in my face disallowed it. Little by little, pain surged through my arms, chest, back, legs, feet—each area warming as it came alive.

She leaned forward and kissed my forehead. "You had me going there for a while, you know that?"

"It's nice to know you were worried. Where am I anyway?"

"Queen of Angels."

"On Vermont?"

She smiled, nodded.

I'd never been here, but I'd driven by many times. Things seemed a little easier just knowing where I was.

The door to my room swung open and a man in his sixties entered. What was left of his hair was white. "Good morning. I'm glad you could join us today. I'm Dr. Rhodes."

The nurse handed Rhodes the chart. His eyes glossed the pages. "How are you feeling?"

"Like shit."

Rhodes' eyes met mine. He smiled for a moment, then said, "At least that's a definitive answer."

His eyes fell back on the chart. He skimmed the rest of the papers, then looked back up at me. "Can you tell me your name?"

"Don't you know it?"

"Yes, of course I do. But I want to make sure you do."

"Santa Claus."

Rhodes smiled. "Please."

"Jack Murphy."

"What year is it?"

"Are you serious?"

His smile faded. "Please."

"Two thousand."

"And who is the President?"

"Clinton. At least until January sometime."

He smiled. "Good. Mr. Murphy, you are very lucky."

"I don't feel so lucky."

"Believe me, you are. Though you sustained quite a few contusions and abrasions, nothing is broken. A few of your ribs are bruised, and you have a mild concussion. But," Rhodes said as he snapped the chart closed, "nothing a lot of rest won't cure."

"Can I go home?"

"You can, but you need to have someone monitor you for at least twenty-four hours."

I tried to straighten up. Pain bolted through my chest, forced me back down. "What the hell for?"

Rhodes tapped his finger against one machine, then looked at my IV. "Mr. Murphy . . ."

"Could you just call me Jack, please?"

"Very well. Jack, a mild concussion is basically a bruise to the brain. Usually, it's not serious, but it's impossible to tell right away. From the marks on your left temple, I'd say you were struck with a threaded object, such as a lead pipe." He stopped by my bed, rested his hand on the steel rail. "If you'd prefer, you can remain here for twenty-four hours."

Pain be damned, I forced myself into a semi-sitting position.

"Thanks, but no. I want out. Now."

"Then I'm coming home to stay with you," Nadia said.

Rhodes smiled. One smiley happy guy.

"That's a great idea," he said. "The nurse will give you a paper on what to look for, but basically if anything out of the ordinary occurs, Jack will need to be brought back immediately. Do you know him well?"

"Yes."

"Good. It is imperative that you be the judge of his condition." Rhodes glanced back at me, smiled. "I'm going to prescribe some pain medication for you."

"I don't want it."

"It is simply a precaution. If you find you don't need it, so much the better."

"I'll keep an eye on him," Nadia said. She leaned forward and kissed my forehead again. "And you, Jack Murphy, won't give me an ounce of shit about it."

Rhodes chuckled. "Somehow, I don't believe he will. The nurse will be back shortly with the paperwork."

He handed the chart to the nurse, nodded at me, smiled at Nadia, and left.

The nurse followed him out.

"Thanks," I said.

"For what?"

"For saying what the doctor wanted to hear."

"You think I'm kidding?"

"C'mon, you don't wanna be my nursemaid anymore than I want you to be."

"That sounds like you're trying to give me shit. I'm staying with you and that's that."

I sighed, but didn't push. I wasn't in any condition to argue. Yet.

With Nadia's help, I dressed, signed the necessary paperwork, and climbed into her Camry. She drove me to my apartment and helped me up the stairs.

"You sit down on the couch," she said.

"Can I pee first?"

"Make it quick. Then, right to the couch."

"Yes, ma'am."

"Are you hungry?"

"Yep."

"I'll see if I can whip up something to eat."

I used the bathroom, then sat down on the couch. Nadia came over with a glass of orange juice in her hand. She handed it to me, then grabbed the remote from on top of the television.

"Soaps are just about starting."

"Joy."

"Just find something to keep yourself entertained, okay?"

"You're gonna make one hell of a wife and mother someday. Anyone ever tell you that?"

"No."

"I just did."

"Before you."

I found a half-empty pack of cigarettes on the coffee table. I grabbed a cigarette and lit it. Blankets of tension peeled away with each hit I took, though smoking did nothing for the constant ache. The doctor had given me Darvocet for that. I hadn't taken any, nor did I want to. I hated the loss of control even more than I hated the pain.

Nadia scrambled some eggs and toasted some bread. She sat next to me and we ate and watched Maury Povich. That day his guests were a white woman and two black men. The dilemma was determining which of the men was the father of the woman's six-month-old.

After we ate, Nadia took the dishes to the kitchen.

"You can just leave those in the sink," I said.

She washed and dried them anyway. Then, she sat back down and smoked a cigarette. I smoked another.

I watched Nadia read the paper on concussions the nurse had given her.

"Wow," she said.

"What?"

"Listen to this. You need to return to the hospital immediately for any of the following—nausea, vomiting, extreme dizziness, blurred or double vision, difficulty speaking or slurred speech, ringing in the ears, loss of balance, inability to move one side of the body, suddenly more severe headache, or any other abnormal behavior."

"Damn."

"What?"

"I guess getting drunk is out of the question."

"Jack, be serious."

"I am."

"It also says I need to wake you every hour. And I have to wake you thoroughly, not just rouse you."

"That sounds like fun."

"It's not supposed to be fun, it's preventative medicine."

"Oh."

We sat in silence for a few moments, then she turned on the couch, touched my knee. "We never got to finish our talk."

"No, we didn't."

"Wanna finish it now?"

"Sure."

"Where were we?"

"I don't remember."

"Me, either."

She sat quiet for a moment, then said, "I'm sorry."

"Me, too. It was just one of those things that didn't work out right."

"I guess."

"That doesn't mean we can't make it work if we try again."

She smiled, then wrapped her arms around my torso. She hugged me lightly, as if she were hugging an egg with a cracked shell. I wrapped my arms around her, tight as I could manage.

"I'm so glad you're okay," she said. A touch of sorrow tainted her voice.

I pulled away, looked at her. Her eyes were focused on the coffee table, the tears evident. I put a finger under her chin and raised her head. She looked up at me. And I kissed her.

Her soft tongue met mine. She closed her eyes and kissed me like a long-lost lover. I ran an open palm along her lower back. She guided my hand to her breast. My fingers caressed the softness of her cotton sweater. Her nipple responded to my touch.

A knock at the door interrupted us.

Twenty One

"Hey, Nadia," Arturo said.

"Hi."

Arturo walked to the coffee table, set down a brown bag. "Hey, Holmes, heard you got a major butt whooping last night?"

"Funny, ain't it?"

Arturo sat on a folding chair near the sliding glass door. Nadia sat next to me on the couch. The air in the room seemed thick. I guess Arturo felt it, too. His gaze danced from Nadia to me.

"Hey, did I interrupt something here?"

Nadia glanced at me, then focused her stare on the brown bag Arturo had brought in with him. I shrugged.

"No, Holmes, I did, didn't I? You guys . . . Ah, man, you want me to come back later?"

"Everything's fine."

Nadia nodded but kept her eyes on the bag, her lips taut.

"Okay, then. Guess what I did for lunch."

"Eat?"

"Very funny, Holmes. No, actually I didn't eat at all. I did, however, watch two men eat."

"That's positively enticing."

"And argue, too."

"Now I'm envious."

"I bet you are. I also bet you can't guess who I saw eating and arguing."

"DiMarco?"

"That's a given. But, who did he have lunch with?"

I lit a cigarette, dragged the ashtray closer. "I give up."

Arturo looked disappointed. "You didn't even guess."

"You stumped me. I have no idea who he had lunch with."

"Neither do I."

"Great detective work there, Arturo."

Nadia tucked a lock of hair behind her ear. With an ear-to-ear grin smothering his face, Arturo got up and grabbed the bag. He unfolded the top, then scrunched down the brown paper to reveal a highball glass.

"Are you stealing glassware from restaurants now?"

"I am."

"Why?" Nadia said.

Arturo clapped his hands together. "I'm glad you asked. Lord knows, I might've waited forever for Jack to ask."

"Hey, king of suspense, spit it out already."

"On this glass," Arturo said as he pointed with his index finger, "are the fingerprints of DiMarco's luncheon date. Let me tell you what happened." He walked back to his seat, scratched his head and sat down. "It all started around eleven today."

"Do you think you could finish this story before we retire?"

"Hey, Holmes, don't fuck around. This might just be a break in this, so far, pathetic case of ours."

"By all means, go ahead."

"I followed DiMarco to The Peking Duck in Culver City. The worker dude . . ."

"*Maitre d'.*"

"Whatever. The dude sat him down with a guy in his fifties, gray hair and beard. No one brought DiMarco a menu but he got a plate of some kind of fish minutes after he sat down." Arturo paused to light a cigarette. "Anyway, these guys are talking and they start getting pissed at each other. Then, DiMarco slams down his fork and walks out. The other guy left shortly after DiMarco. He didn't finish his lunch, either."

"Then?" I said.

"Then, the busboy started cleaning off the table, so I walked over and grabbed the glass DiMarco's date was using. The dude tripped on me, but I just smiled and left."

"So, the questions are who was DiMarco arguing with, and about what."

"Exactly."

"I can answer the first one," I said.

I reached for the phone. My muscles screamed revolt. I pulled back. Nadia handed me the receiver.

"Thanks," I said, then dialed LAPD Vice.

I asked for Tyrone. He picked up three minutes later.

"Tyrone, Jack."

"What kind of trouble are you in now?"

"Jeez, lighten up a little, would you? I'm not in any trouble. Right now."

"What do you want?"

"Are we having a bad day?"

"Look, Jack, I'm in the middle of something. Can whatever it is wait?"

"No, but it's quick."

He sighed. "What is it?"

"A friend of mine's gonna come by and drop off a glass that I need dusted for prints. Once you get the prints, could you tell me who owns them?"

"This is what can't wait?"

"Time is of the essence in good detective work, you know that."

"What do I get?"

"Another notch on the Jack owes Tyrone card."

"Wonderful."

"Hey, I might just be settling up with you in the near future."

"Sure."

"Really. Who knows where this case is going."

"You still trying to find that girl?"

"I won't stop until I either find her or her parents stop footing the bill."

"Send him over."

"Thanks. How soon can I expect the results?"

"When I get them, you'll get them."

"Okay. Can you make it tonight?"

"Jesus, Jack."

"Thanks, buddy. I'll send him over."

Click.

When I told Arturo where he could find Tyrone, he seemed as thrilled about the meeting as Tyrone had. Perfect match.

"Make it quick, huh?" I said.

Arturo pulled the brown paper over the glass, then picked up the bag. "You better get over this invalid shit real quick, Holmes, cause it seems like I'm doing all the work around here."

"You are."

"Oh." He seemed baffled by my response. "I am indeed."

"Hey, that's what good bosses do—delegate the work."

"Oh, is that what you're doing?"

"You bet."

"I see."

"Tell you what, Arturo. Next time I'm gonna get the shit kicked out of me, I'll tell them to kick your ass instead. That way you can hang on the couch while I do all the work."

"Sure, Holmes, you do that."

After Arturo left, Nadia and I watched the rest of the news.

"You mind if I take a shower?" I said.

"Not at all."

"I feel like shit. Maybe it'll do some good."

"Be careful. If you need anything, just holler."

"Okay."

The hot water seemed to help as it penetrated my sore muscles. Black and blue welts had become more visible on my stomach and sides whereas my legs were marred by only a few scratches. Though it wasn't apparent at the time, except for the final blow to the head, my torso was their primary target.

It took twice as long for me to shower and dry off, but I managed to get clean and into a pair of shorts without too much discomfort.

When I came out of the bathroom, Nadia was curled up on the couch, asleep. I muted the TV, grabbed an old green afghan my grandmother had made for me years ago, and covered her. I kissed her forehead, grabbed a beer from the refrigerator and walked onto the balcony.

The afternoon air was warmer than it had been and the sun shone brightly in the azure sky. I smoked a cigarette and drank my beer, wondering who employed Skinny and Redwood. Receiving the beating bothered me, but not knowing who ordered it bothered me more.

I slipped back inside and sat next to Nadia. I finished my beer, smashed my cigarette in the ashtray and leaned back. And watched the muted television.

TWENTY TWO

Nadia and I sat on the couch while Arturo exercised. It had been less than twenty-four hours since my beating and yet I already found myself missing the everyday things I usually took for granted, like exercising, or moving without hurting. I had never been one for exercise—I did it, I just never enjoyed it. Suddenly, I was missing it. I was, however, a big fan of moving without hurting, so I missed that more.

Tyrone came by at five-thirty.

Nadia refused to let me answer the door, get an extra folding chair from the closet or get Tyrone a beer.

Once Tyrone was settled, Nadia said, "I'm gonna run home and get some clothes and stuff."

"Okay," I said.

"Promise me you won't leave."

"Yes, Mom, I promise."

"I mean it, Jack." She pointed to the spot on the couch where I sat. "I want you sitting here when I get back."

I pointed to the empty spot next to me. "What if I wanna sit here?"

She growled, then kissed my forehead. She said goodbye to Tyrone and Arturo, and left.

"Got something for us?" I said to Tyrone.

"Tell me, Jack. What exactly are you investigating here?"

"The disappearance of Carrie Sanders. Why?"

"And how did you stumble on this glass?"

"It was used by the person who had lunch with DiMarco."

"Tony DiMarco?"

"Yep."

"Are you sure?"

With tremendous effort, I grabbed the cigarette pack from the table and lit one. Arturo began doing his jumping jacks, the exercise most enjoyed by the people in the apartment below us, I'm sure.

"What's up, Tyrone?"

"These prints belong to Charles Blake."

"So?"

Tyrone ran an open palm over his bald head. "Charles Blake is a nationally renowned businessman."

"Good for him."

"He's also a major contributor to the Policemen's Benevolent Fund." Apparently, my straining to grab the ashtray caught Tyrone's eye. "What's the matter with you?"

"I'm a little sore."

"I heard about your visit to Queen of Angels last night."

"How?"

"Word gets around. A beat cop found you, or don't you remember?"

I took a hit from my cigarette. "No, I don't."

"You got yourself beat up pretty good, then."

"I'd give it an A. Nothing broken, though it feels like there should be."

"Pros."

"Yep."

"Because of this case?"

"Yep."

Tyrone took a drink from his beer, then set the can on the table. "What is it you're not telling me, Jack?"

"About what?"

"Most investigations for missing children don't involve beatings."

"Or major contributors to the Benevolent Fund."

"That, too."

Betting that my friendship with Tyrone would supersede his taking over the investigation, I decided to level with him. "Just after I took this case, I was visited by two guys. Who, I don't know. They offered to pay me to drop the case. They said they worked for Carrie."

"Right."

"That's what I said. Anyway, I told them no thanks. Last night, they caught up with me and tried a different approach."

"A more painful one."

"For me, anyway."

"What did you tell them?"

"I told them if Carrie would just contact me, I'd let her be. But, it wasn't fair to my client to just drop it."

"Noble."

"I thought so."

"Maybe stupid, too."

"Sometimes being noble is stupid."

"How does this get to Blake?"

I told him what I knew. "Now, I'm just trying to follow that trail and see if I can determine where the girls went."

"And in following DiMarco, you happened upon Blake."

"Exactly."

Tyrone stood and began to pace. "Do you think Blake is involved with DiMarco?"

"Yep."

"In what?"

"I don't know."

Tyrone stared out the sliding glass window for a moment, then spun and faced me. "You better be very careful with this, Jack. If you start to rustle Blake's feathers, he may just get your license revoked."

I smashed my dying cigarette in the ashtray. "Do you have an address on Blake?"

"Yes."

"Are you gonna share?"

"Depends."

"On?"

"Are you gonna be careful?"

"Yep."

He rattled off an address in Hollywood Hills. When I couldn't find a pen, Tyrone grabbed a spiral notebook from his breast pocket, wrote the address on a piece of paper, then tore it off. He held it out, but when I reached for it, he snapped it back. "I mean it when I say be careful."

He held it out again, let me take it this time.

"I will. If it makes you feel any better, I promise you the collar."

"What collar?"

"The one I'm gonna give you."

"If you find something."

"If."

"How sweet of you."

"Hey, who knows? A child porn bust surely spells promotion."

"I gotta tell you, Jack, I'm not sure if I can help you out anymore. You got shit. I mean, really. Maybe this, maybe that. I could never get an investigation into Blake opened with this."

Good. "Well, when I have something substantial, I'll let you know."

"You do that. By the way, I got my ass chewed for running Blake's prints."

"Oh, yeah, that 'word gets around' thing."

Tyrone walked toward the door. "Yeah."

"Thanks," I said.

"Oh, one more thing," Tyrone said. He turned back to face me. "Wilshire Division got a call about you today."

"Another citizen proclaiming how great it is that I'm keeping the city safe, no doubt."

"That's funny, Jack. Really, that is. This guy works at Diamond Steel Security. You've heard of it, I suppose."

"Yep. Let me guess, the personnel manager called to complain about my tactics."

"Something like that."

"I found out DiMarco's getting twenty-five hundred a week from that place as a security consultant."

"So?"

"DiMarco hasn't had a day of security experience in his life."

"And how did you come up with all this information?"

"Don't know."

"Won't tell me."

"Really, I don't know. Someone gave it to me."

"A little birdie?"

"A hard working detective, a little hacking . . ."

He held up his hand. "I don't wanna hear it."

"I figured. But, you pushed."

"I want you to contact me before you make any moves on Blake."

"I'll try."

"No, you'll do it."

"Thanks again for the help."

Tyrone's eyes narrowed and I was sure he would say something. But, he only locked his jaw. And left.

TWENTY THREE

"Well, what now, boss?" Arturo said.

I channel-surfed until I found a soccer game on one of the ESPN channels. I left the sound low and set down the remote. "We dig deeper into DiMarco's affairs."

"How?"

"Bug him."

I quickly tired of the soccer game. I picked up the remote and flipped through the channels again. A beautiful redhead in a tiny two-piece black bikini was introducing something on another channel. I didn't know what, but she caused me to set down the remote anyway.

"I can get a bug from Eddie the Ears," Arturo said.

"Eddie the Ears?"

"Yeah."

"Cute."

"Eddie's the best bugger in the business. And, if you piss him off, he'll cut off one of your ears. He's got a dozen or so in a freezer behind his office."

"What, ears?"

"Yeah. It's easy to spot the ones who've crossed him."

I lit a cigarette and discovered that the redhead was trying to sell car wax. A man had joined her on-screen and claimed his wax was the best thing since sliced bread. I had no interest in the car wax, but the redhead was leaning over the car applying the wax to the hood, and the camera angle was pleasing.

"We'll plant it at Club TA," I said.

"Didn't Mike the Biker say DiMarco talked a lot on his cell?"

"Yep."

"Got a plan for that, too?"

"Nope."

"Swell."

"Maybe he'll be nice enough to give us something."

"Maybe. You want me to get a guy from Eddie to plant it?"

"He has men, too?"

"Sure, lots."

"Would he be controllable, though?"

"Controllable?"

I tapped ashes from my cigarette into the ashtray. "I don't want a loose cannon."

"I'm sure Eddie'll give us a pro."

"But why would DiMarco let him in the office?"

"He can get in himself."

"I don't want any B and E. It'll tip him off."

Arturo looked shocked. "So, you want someone to just waltz through the front door, into the office, and casually slip the bug under the desk?"

"Something like that."

"Where's the head smashing come in?"

"You do have violent tendencies, don't you? I thought you were reformed."

"I am. But if this guy's preying on little girls."

"If. I know how you feel, but imagine how you'd feel if you rousted the wrong guy."

Arturo nodded slightly, then focused on the TV. The redhead finished wiping off the hood, then the camera panned to a workbench conveniently lined with several containers of the wax. The man had walked behind the bench and was explaining his money-back guarantee. The redhead disappeared and I lost interest fast. Remote securely in hand, I searched for something else.

"What about Nadia?" Arturo said.

"Are you nuts? I'm not putting her in the middle of this."

"She could be applying for a job down there or something."

I smashed my cigarette in the ashtray and found myself quite upset that Arturo would even suggest such a ludicrous idea. "And have her strip? I don't think so."

"You guys married yet?"

"What?"

"You're already jealous of someone else seeing her naked."

"That's not it."

"Sure."

I punched the channel up button, repeatedly. "We're not using her."

The apartment door creaked open, then shut.

"It'll be okay, Holmes. I'll find someone to escort her in and watch her back."

"No."

Nadia stepped into the room, a blue gym bag in hand. "What's up?"

"Nothing," I said.

"Nadia?" Arturo said.

"Forget it."

Nadia set the bag on the floor. "What?"

"How would you feel . . ."

"I said forget it."

" . . . about doing a little fieldwork?"

"Goddamn it, Arturo, I said forget it."

Nadia sat on the couch, put a hand on my knee. "It's okay, Jack. What're you guys thinking about?"

"We need to plant a bug in the strip joint where DiMarco hangs out."

I channel-surfed again at a furious pace.

"What do I have to do?"

"Just get into the office and plant a little bug under the desk."

"I can do that."

"No, you can't," I said.

She tapped her palm on my knee. "It's sweet that you worry about me, Jack, but c'mon. I wanna help. Besides, what could go wrong?"

"They could kill you."

"I'll get a guy to go in with you and watch your back."

"You're starting to piss me off, Arturo."

"You'll get over it."

"Fuck you."

I dropped the remote against the coffee table, grabbed a cigarette from my pack. "You're not doing it, Nadia."

"Why not? Don't you think I can handle it?"

"That's not the point. It's too dangerous."

She pulled her hand away from my knee, folded her arms across her chest. "So, only the guys get to do the real work, is that it?"

"What is this, kick the boss' ass day?"

Through an immense grin, Arturo said, "Maybe we could start

that. Guaranteed it'd go over big with the workers of the world."

"Do you have an alternate plan?" Nadia said.

I picked up the remote.

Apparently, Arturo felt qualified to answer for me. "No, he doesn't."

"If you do, we'll listen to it. Otherwise . . . By the way, what'd Tyrone want?" Nadia said.

"He found out who owned the fingerprints," I said.

"Who?"

"Charles Blake."

"You're kidding."

"No, why?"

"That name came up when I was researching Diamond Steel. Isn't he the guy who owns Blake Enterprises?"

"Could be. I guess he's rich and famous."

"I'll check my notes in the morning." Nadia grabbed the remote from my hand. "If you don't stop that, you'll burn out your TV."

She set down the remote. We sat in silence watching the Food Network.

Joy.

Twenty Four

It had been less than an hour since Arturo and Nadia left. Already, I was letting my imagination get the better of me. Most likely, they were barely getting to Eddie's house before heading over to Club TA. But, I'd never been very good at sitting on the sidelines, watching and waiting. This time would be no different.

Minutes passed like hours. I found myself chain-smoking and drumming my fingers on the couch. I couldn't concentrate on the television. I kept glancing at the phone, though I had no one to call.

And my muscles were taut, sore.

I tried to think about Blake and how he fit into the picture. But, with no data on him yet, it was a futile effort. I finished my cigarette and hobbled to the kitchen. I opened a can of chicken noodle soup, warmed it in a pot on the stove to just above room temperature, then stood in front of the sink, ate it from a large green latte mug. Every couple of minutes, I shifted my weight from one foot to the other. Then, I grabbed another Budweiser and sat back down on the couch.

Roy had said that Jenkins thought the girls were being shipped to Mexico. It seemed to me either the men in charge had total control of the girls and simply drove across the border with them or, more likely, they smuggled them across. But how? Possibly cargo ships, but it would be difficult to keep their presence on board from the horny crewmen. They could fly them down, but unless they were able to avert the customs authorities, they'd have trouble. Then again, maybe the girls didn't go to Mexico at all.

I thought about places where child pornography flourished. The obvious biggie was The Netherlands, but since it was legal for 12-year-olds to consent to sex there, who would smuggle children in? I heard South America was also big. But pedophiles seemed to be, for the most part, homegrown in the good ole US of A. Of course, it was entirely possible that Carrie was not among the group DiMarco funneled through Donovan, so I could be grasping at straws—the wrong straws at that.

One thing was for sure. If DiMarco was involved in child porn, he wouldn't let that fact surface without a fight. Probably more than any other illicit business, child pornographers couldn't afford to be found. Besides the obvious public ridicule, the Draconian laws would certainly drive one to great lengths to keep his business a secret, which could explain Jenkins' death.

Of course, it didn't help to know what DiMarco was doing, or Blake, if Carrie wasn't involved . . .

A sudden bolt of pain surged through my chest, maybe a simple reminder that I was graciously given a beating to draw me away from this case. And that meant I must be onto something.

At ten, the news on channel 11 started. I half-expected their lead story to be breaking news about a shooting at Club TA. Instead, they led with a story about a woman who called 911 after her pet monkey had attacked her.

I heard a key in the door a few minutes later. They were back.

"It's about time," I said.

"Hello to you, too," Nadia said.

Both Arturo and Nadia had wide smiles that reminded me of kids standing in front of an overflowing pile of presents under a Christmas tree.

"How'd it go?"

"Perfect, Holmes, just perfect."

"The bug's in the office?"

Nadia sat on the couch next to me. "Yes, sir. And, I'm still in one piece."

"I can see that."

"And she didn't have to show any skin, either."

"No, I sure didn't."

I muted the television. "Okay, let's have it."

I thought Nadia might burst from excitement as she told me the story. "I went into the club with one of Arturo's friends. Arturo waited outside. We walked up to the bar and I asked to speak with DiMarco in private. The bartender asked me what I wanted to talk about. I told him it was none of his business."

"A pretty girl with an attitude," I said. "So, you played yourself."

"Funny. Some guy let me in the office and told me to wait. While I was waiting, I put the bug under the desk. Five minutes later, DiMarco still hadn't come in, so I went back to the bartender and told him I was tired of waiting. Then, we left."

"That's it?"

"That's it."

"And, Holmes, a van's on the street, recording everything on reel-to-reel tape."

I hated to admit that the two of them had pulled off the job without a hitch, and without me, but they had. And, I wasn't about to let myself look like a sore loser. "Good job, you two."

"Great job," Nadia corrected. That silly smile still covered her face.

"Okay, great job."

"Thank you for noticing."

"Damn straight, Holmes. This girl's a natural. I'm gonna take a shower."

"Make it quick," I said, "we're going out."

"What?" Nadia and Arturo said in unison, as if they had planned their response.

"We're gonna stick to DiMarco until something breaks."

"Okay, boss," Arturo said.

Nadia didn't say anything until after Arturo had disappeared in the bathroom. "What do you mean you guys are going out?"

"Just that. No one's handing us any clues, so we gotta go get 'em. You know, be assertive."

The child-like smile had faded from her lips. "Not in your condition."

"What condition, Nadia? Jesus, I can sit in a car as well as I can sit on a couch."

"That's not the point."

"What is the point?"

She turned away. "Nothing."

"C'mon, why do you think I shouldn't be working?"

"You're in pain."

"That's true. But, I'll be in pain whether I go out or stay at home."

"You can take your pills at home."

"I could, but I don't want to. I wanna find Carrie."

"What about the bastard who had your ass kicked?"

"Him, too."

I thought I noticed a tear fall on Nadia's cheek, but she

suddenly stood up and walked in the kitchen, so I couldn't be sure. She turned on the faucet. The running water drowned out any sounds she may have been making. I hit the mute button to get the audio back. The sportscaster was explaining how the Kings came from behind to tie it after three periods and still went on to lose the game.

When Arturo finished, Nadia said she was taking a shower and disappeared into the bathroom. Popular place.

Arturo and I left.

TWENTY FIVE

That evening, we followed DiMarco to Club TA, then to a pawnshop, an apartment and two different restaurants. DiMarco ate full meals at both. Then, he went home. After he'd been home for an hour, we decided to call it a night.

I drove back to my apartment.

Nadia was sleeping on the sofa bed. I grabbed two cans of Bud from the refrigerator, then motioned to Arturo as I walked out to the balcony. He followed.

I handed him a can, leaned against the railing and lit my last cigarette of the night. I glanced north. The nearly deserted Wilshire Boulevard had an eerie aura about it. Within the half-hour, traffic would pile up, jamming every intersection from downtown to Santa Monica. But at that moment, Los Angeles seemed more of a ghost town than the overcrowded metropolis that was its true identity.

"Ya know, Holmes, we're damn lucky we got a hold of Jenkins' notebook."

"Yep."

Arturo took a long drink from his beer. "DiMarco's dirty."

"No doubt. And I'm willing to bet he's dealing underage girls, too. But, we're still a long way from finding Carrie."

"How long does her father want us to keep looking?"

"Till we find her or his money runs out, I guess."

"Good for us."

"But maybe not so good for him."

"Why not? You're certainly good at what you do."

I flicked the ashes from my cigarette over the railing, watched them dissipate in the slight breeze. "That's not it. He may be getting his money's worth, but Carrie could be long gone by now."

"Or six feet under."

"Yep."

The possibility that Carrie was dead was strong. The possibility she was dead and her body would never be recovered was also strong. If she were seven or eight when she disappeared, I wouldn't have taken the case. But, at sixteen, she might have instilled in her the will to survive, even against the treacherous conditions someone like DiMarco would have placed her under. I hoped I was right.

I finished my cigarette and ground the butt into the pot of the fern that was attempting to overtake my balcony. Though much of the time I was wrong, I still had faith in my intuition. I had to. Intuition was a private eye's most valuable possession. And my gut told me she was still alive, and still in Los Angeles, and Jenkins wound up dead because he was on the right track. I'd never been much in the religious department, but as I leaned over the balcony, I prayed. I prayed that I would find Carrie before I wound up like Jenkins did.

Nadia had written *Wake me up as soon as you get home* on a note and propped it on the pillow nearest the sliding glass door. Arturo tapped my shoulder, then I followed him into the kitchen.

He took my can, washed them both out in the sink and deposited them in the recycle bin. "I'm gonna stay awake tonight."

"What for?"

"To wake you up every hour."

"Don't be ridiculous."

Arturo turned, narrowed his eyes. "No, Holmes, don't you be. This is nothing to fuck around with."

"You sound like my mom."

"Fuck you," Arturo snapped. He lowered his voice a couple notches before he continued. "I don't want you to wake Nadia up. And she'll kill both of us if you don't wake up. And . . ." He turned toward the refrigerator. "I don't want nothing to happen to you."

"Okay."

"Okay?"

"Yeah, you know. Okay, yes, alright, I agree."

He held his hand up. "I get it."

I laid down beside Nadia, kissed her softly on the side of her head, then went to sleep—on top of the covers with my clothes on.

* * *

I was irritable, tired and basically felt like shit when the ringing of the phone jarred me awake. I blinked my eyes, focused on the clock—10:28. The phone rang again. Where the hell was Arturo? Twenty-eight lousy minutes since he'd last woken me. My head throbbed, my torso ached and he left me to answer the phone. Again, it rang. I growled, then leaned over to pick up the receiver. A bolt of lightning surged from my lower back through my shoulders and down my arm to my fingers as they extended to meet the cold plastic.

"What?"

"Arturo."

"Hang on."

I called Arturo's name four times, each louder than the previous. Then, the toilet flushed, the sink ran for a moment, and he stepped out of the bathroom.

"You calling me, Holmes?"

I thrust the receiver toward him. "It's for you."

Arturo took it from my hand. I climbed out of bed as quickly as my sore body would allow. Nadia wasn't here. I figured she headed over to the office.

I thought about going back to sleep, but the anger in my gut had risen to a point that made me want to simply stay awake rather then suffer another rude awakening from Arturo. He was a good friend and all, but the way he grabbed my shoulders and violently shook me awake indicated he had no future in a profession that required a bedside manner.

I climbed in the shower. The hot water worked like a masseuse as it beat against my chest and back. After my skin numbed from the pounding, I let it work on my stress level another ten minutes. Then, I washed, shampooed, rinsed, climbed out and dried off. I wrapped a towel around my waist and walked to the kitchen.

Arturo was dicing onion on a plastic cutting board; scrambled eggs cooked in a skillet atop a gas burner.

"Smells good," I said.

"Thought I'd take a shot at this breakfast-making thing. How hard can it be, right?"

"Right."

"Besides, I figured you wouldn't be in the mood."

"I was bitchy, huh?"

"That's putting it mildly."

I knew how I got when I suffered from lack of sleep. And being woken up every hour only intensified that mood. I certainly wouldn't want to be subjected to that, so it bothered me when I subjected others to it. "I'm sorry."

Arturo finished the onion. "Hey, don't worry about it, Holmes."

"I do. I'm sure I was an asshole."

"Yes, you were."

"Thanks for making me feel better."

"Anytime, Holmes, anytime."

With the edge of the knife, Arturo brushed the onion across the eggs, then used the spatula to fold the semi-solid omelet in half. "By the way, that was Eddie on the phone."

A plastic dish next to the cutting board held diced tomatoes. I pinched a few, threw them in my mouth. "And?"

"And the bug's dead."

"Fuck."

"Eddie said a low hum appeared on the tape at about four-thirty. It lasted a few minutes, and was followed by a loud pop. Then, dead air."

"A sweeper."

"Probably."

"Did he manage to catch anything useful before it went dead?"

"No. A guy and a girl came in the office, talked a little. Then, he thinks the guy got a blowjob before ordering a pizza and popping in a Frank Sinatra CD."

"Good stuff."

"Win some, lose some."

"Thanks for your efforts, anyway."

"No problem, Holmes."

I helped Arturo finish breakfast. Then, we stood in the kitchen and ate from paper plates.

"Did you see Nadia this morning?" I said.

"She left about nine, right after you went back to sleep."

"Did she say anything?"

"That someone needed to run the office."

"Was that it?"

"And she bitched about your not waking her up. But, when she realized I dutifully woke you every hour, she relaxed a bit."

"Nothing else?"

Arturo rinsed the plates, then threw them in the trash. "What else did you want her to say?"

"I don't know. She did get the opportunity to sleep with me last night."

"Oh, yeah, she did say something about limp dick syndrome."

He laughed. I didn't.

I called the office. Nadia answered on the first ring.

"Mid-City Confidential."

"Morning."

"Good morning, sleepyhead. How're you feeling?"

"I'm still sore, but it's a little better than yesterday."

"That's good."

"Yep. By the way, thanks for keeping an eye on the office."

"Someone has to."

"I know. And I appreciate it."

"While you were dreaming about whatever you were dreaming about, I was hard at work."

"Hey, I already said thank you. Don't tell me you're looking for a raise, too."

"From you? Hah. It'll never happen."

"What's that supposed to mean?"

"Nothing."

"I'm not a cheapskate, you know."

"Uh-huh."

I chose not to pursue that further. "While you were slaving away, did you happen to come up with anything useful?"

I lit a cigarette as Nadia told me the Blake that popped up in her search of Diamond Steel Security was Charles Blake of Hollywood Hills. And, BEI, Blake Enterprises, Inc., wholly owned DSS.

"He's got a thing for acronyms, doesn't he?"

"Looks like it. I also found out something else."

"Pray tell."

"Good ole Charlie is having lunch at one o'clock today."

"Yippee."

"By himself."

"And would you happen to know where?"

"Vinnie's Ristorante on Melrose and Wilcox."

"You're a peach."

"How about a sweetheart?"

"That, too."

"How about the best office assistant you've ever known?"

"Don't push it."

"Can't blame a girl for trying."

"You know you are."

"It's still nice to hear."

"You're the best office assistant I've ever known."

"Thank you."

"You're welcome."

"By the way, Lena from Marino and Silverman called. Twice. She has another claim she needs investigated."

I took a hit from my cigarette, then set it in the ashtray. "What'd you tell her?"

"I told her you were moving up in the world and so busy now that you couldn't possibly take on another case."

"What'd you really tell her?"

"That we'd get back to her this afternoon."

Nadia told me the case involved a guy who claimed injury at work and was suing for twenty million. But, rumor had it that he spent his days retiling his roof. Lena wanted pictures to "nail his fucking ass to the wall." The pay was good, so I asked Nadia to see if she could get ahold of Larry Adams, a private eye in downtown that we used on occasion when our workload was too much. She said she would.

"One more thing. Call Spies R Us in West Hollywood and see if they have the Trakker 750 in stock."

"The GPS transmitter?"

"Yep. If they do, put one on hold for me."

"Okay."

"Thanks."

"You're welcome. By the way, how'd it feel to sleep with me last night?"

"It was fabulous, baby. Don't you remember?"

"Remember what?"

"I'm shocked."

"What?"

"You don't remember."

"Jack, what're you talking about?"

"Hey, if you don't remember, I'm not telling you."

"I'll ask Arturo. He was awake all night."

"He was, but for a while he was in the shower."

"Jack."

"Take care."

"Jack."

I hung up the phone with a smile on my face. In my mind's eye, I saw her face. And found no smile.

TWENTY SIX

Before I had left the apartment, I searched the *LA Times* online archive. I found seven articles on Charles Blake in recent history. The last was dated mid-October and explained that Blake had donated half a mil to the Daughters Against Abuse Foundation. Dead center on page one of the business section was a photo of Blake shaking hands with a Latino woman in her early thirties. The caption identified her as Lydia Marks, the CEO of the organization.

I printed the page on my HP Inkjet. Though the quality didn't do the handsome man justice, it would do for a positive identification.

I headed north on Wilcox and was stopped at the light on Melrose. Vinnie's Ristorante sat on the northwest corner of Melrose and Wilcox, at the edge of the Media District. Small bungalows neighbored the restaurant on its west and north sides.

Melrose offered no parking and the spaces that I could see along Wilcox were filled. I turned left on Melrose and passed the restaurant. A small sign indicated the restaurant had valet parking, and one was to turn down a small alleyway next to the building to utilize the service.

"You know this restaurant is famous?" I said.

"For what, Holmes?"

"The interior's been used in lots of TV shows and movies."

"No shit? Does this mean we'll see movie stars inside?"

"You never know. It is an industry hangout."

"Cool, Holmes, but all this talk about food's making me hungry."

I looked at him, unsure at that moment if we occupied space on the same planet. "Hey, *hombre*, we're not talking about food."

"We're talking about Vinnie's, an Italian restaurant. A restaurant, by the way, serves food. Get it?"

"Isn't that a bit of a stretch?"

"I don't care what you call it, Holmes. I'm starving."

I rounded the block and pulled down the alley. Two men, both early twenties with cropped black hair, wearing identical black vests over white button-down shirts, black bowties and green aprons over black slacks appeared on either side of the truck, opened the doors.

"Good afternoon," the one on my side said.

I stepped out of the truck and fished a twenty out of my wallet. I slapped it in his palm, said, "Keep it close."

"Yes sir."

From the outside, Vinnie's resembled many of the other buildings in the neighborhood. It was old yet clean. The building sported a fresh coat of cream-colored paint. A large awning hung from the front side of the building, done up in standard Italian colors—red, white, and green. The awning extended away from the building above the front door to cover the walk. This part had a red strip along the bottom that appropriately displayed *Vinnie's Ristorante* in white block lettering. The front door and frame were black, the doorknob gold.

"Looks like a classy place," Arturo said.

On either side of the front door were five-foot square planters, bordered in red brick. In each planter, orange and white chrysanthemums paid homage to large birds of paradise propped dead center. The planters provided a nice barrier between the restaurant and the street.

Vinnie's had a small bar area to the left of the front door. I smiled at the *maitre d'* and slipped into the bar.

The restaurant looked busy but the bar was nearly empty. I walked to the end of the bar and sat at the corner stool. Arturo sat next to me. A lanky man in his thirties, five-six, seven tops, maybe a hundred-fifty, washed glasses in a sink brimming with soapsuds. He looked up and nodded. He finished washing the glass in his hand and wiped his palms on his white apron. "What can I get you gentlemen?"

"Got Bud on tap?"

"Yes sir."

I ordered two. The bartender, whose nametag introduced him as Phil, walked to the tap, pulled two beers, set them in front of us. "Four fifty."

I handed him a five and a one. "Thanks."

Two televisions were mounted from the ceiling, one above each corner of the bar. One was tuned to CNN, the other to ESPN. Both sets were muted. Arturo seemed interested in the television showing CNN.

From my seat, I had a partially obstructed view of the alley alongside the restaurant. Shortly after one, a white Lexus pulled in. A man I pegged for fifty-three or four, wearing an Armani suit hugging a body that could only have been attained, then maintained, with rigorous, five-day-a-week exercising, stepped from the vehicle. A Vinnie's employee appeared with a smile on his face and climbed in the Lexus.

The man came through the front door and stopped at the podium. He was greeted warmly by the *maitre d'*. I pulled the printout from my jacket pocket, glanced at the face. I looked up at the man again and back at the printout. "It's him."

Arturo glanced at the man, then at the printout. "You sure, Holmes?"

"You don't think so?"

Arturo looked back at him. "No way."

"Then maybe you need some glasses. It's definitely him."

"I'm telling you, Holmes, it ain't the guy."

I finished my beer, then set the glass on the table. The man had been ushered into the restaurant and out of my view. "Let's go find out."

An Italian man in his forties stood behind the podium. "Good afternoon, gentlemen. Two for lunch?"

"I'm here to meet Charles Blake," I said.

Arturo stood behind me and to my right.

The man stared at Arturo. After a moment, he looked back at me. "Mr. Blake is expecting you, I suppose?"

"Of course."

The man ran his hairy finger down the reservation list. I leaned against the podium. His finger stopped at Blake. Next to the name was the number one.

"I'm sorry, but Mr. Blake made reservations for one."

I leaned closer to the man. "What's your name?"

He cleared his throat. "Mario."

"Look, Mario, Mr. Blake's been waiting a long time to hear what I have to tell him. If you wanna dick me around here, fine. I'll just let him know he has Mario to thank."

His eyes darted from me to Arturo and back. "Him, too?"

"Of course."

The man grabbed two menus from a holder attached to the side of the podium.

"We won't be staying for lunch."

As the man dropped the menus into their cubby, I thought I heard him sigh. Relief perhaps.

"Right this way."

Mario led us through the dining room and into the kitchen. Arturo raised his eyebrows. I shrugged.

At the opposite side of the kitchen was a set of double doors. We walked through them and found ourselves in a dimly lit, walnut-paneled room. The room appeared empty. Each of its corners held half-circle booths, elevated a step above the floor. White-lace curtains hung at each entranceway. We walked to the farthest corner. The curtains were drawn shut.

Mario pulled back the curtains, cleared his throat. "Sir, your guests have arrived."

"What?" Blake said.

I walked up next to Mario, slipped him a twenty and waved him away. "That's all, Mario."

I sat to Blake's right, Arturo to his left. I drew the curtains closed.

A magnum of wine sat dead center on the table. I turned the bottle and read the label. *1997 Fontodi Flaccianello, Tuscan, Italy.* "Good taste."

He nodded.

The curtains parted. A waiter set a plate before Blake, said, "Your *Risotto alle Salsiccia e Formaggio* sir."

"Thank you, Piedro."

The waiter nodded and closed the curtains.

Blake tucked a white napkin in his shirt collar. "What do you want?"

"Charles Blake, right?"

"So what?"

"Charlie, I'm Jack Murphy."

"Don't call me, Charlie. I'm Mr. Blake to you."

"Charlie, I need to ask you some questions."

"What the fuck? You a reporter or something?"

"Something."

"Jesus H. Christ. You guys can't even leave me alone while I'm eating. Don't you have any respect?"

"Apparently not."

Blake dropped his fork against his plate, poured more wine in his glass. "What do you want?"

I righted an empty wine glass. I grabbed the magnum, filled the glass and sipped the wine. "Lots of things. But let's start with why you employ Tony DiMarco."

Blake's eyes grew cold. "Who is this Tony whatever? And what makes you think I employ him?"

"Don't you own BEI?"

"Of course."

"And BEI wholly owns Diamond Steel Security."

"What did you do, spend fifteen minutes in the corporate section of the library?"

"DSS employs Tony DiMarco for twenty-five hundred a week as a security consultant."

Blake resumed eating. "You interrupt my lunch for this?"

"I'm wondering why DSS pays DiMarco such a large salary as a consultant when he has no previous experience in security. A little odd, don't you think?"

"First of all, Mr. . . ."

"Murphy."

"Murphy. Why the hell are you bothering my lunch for this petty bullshit? And second, what do you care who DSS pays anyway?"

"To be honest, I don't give a shit that I'm bothering your lunch. And second, I don't care who DSS pays." I paused to sip more wine. "I do, however, care about DiMarco. Where you aware that he's a criminal?"

"I wasn't even aware this DiMarco existed until you mentioned him, so how would I know he's a criminal?"

"That's funny," Arturo said, "because about this time yesterday, you were seated in the Peking Duck Restaurant with DiMarco. And you two were getting into it about something."

"What was that about, Charlie?"

"You guys following me? I should sue you."

"Go ahead," I said.

"Fuck you," he said to me. To Arturo, "And fuck you, too."

"Aren't you going to tell me why you two were arguing?"

Blake picked up a phone on the wall and told someone to come over right away. "You dirt bags are about to be thrown out of this fine establishment."

I held Carrie's picture in front of his face. "Where can I find Carrie Sanders?"

Blake continued eating, ignoring my question.

Mario pulled back the curtains. "Gentlemen, you are going to have to leave."

"Yeah, okay." I finished my wine, then turned back to Blake. "Let me say this, Charlie. I'm going to find Carrie Sanders. And if I find you had anything to do with her disappearance, I'm gonna hang you up by your balls."

"Fuck you."

I wiggled out of the booth, tapping the bottle on the way out. The red wine poured across the tablecloth and onto Blake. He jumped up, smacked his legs against the tabletop. "You fuck." He grabbed two fistfuls of his shirt, stared at the stains. "Goddamn it."

"Have a nice day, Charlie."

"Please, gentlemen. You must leave," Mario said.

I held up my hand and we walked out.

As we waited for the valet to bring my truck, my cell phone rang. "Hello?"

"Hi," Nadia said.

"Hi."

"I wanted to let you know that the Trakker 750 is in stock at Spies R Us."

"Great, thanks."

"It's five-hundred-fifty for the remote transmitter. But if you want to follow the signal, you'll need the base unit as well. It's nine-hundred-fifty."

"Do they have the base unit in stock?"

"Sure do. I've put both on hold for you, just in case."

"You're a sweetheart."

"I know."

"Thanks."

My truck pulled up and we climbed in. I turned onto Melrose and headed for Spies R Us.

TWENTY SEVEN

Arturo spent Saturday with Maria. I had convinced Nadia that I no longer needed a mother hen, so she reluctantly went back home. I spent a few hours going through the manual for the Trakker 750. When I was sure I understood the system, I found myself with nothing to do until Arturo and I went back out after DiMarco later that evening. So, I decided to see how much trouble I might be in.

I went to see Cueball.

Terence "Cueball" Greene owned Silverlake Billiards in Silverlake. We'd met a few years earlier when I was hired to locate a bail-jumper named Jerry Jones. He was known to frequent Silverlake Billiards before his arrest. I had a talk with Cueball and offered five grand for Jones. He was in my custody within twenty-four hours.

I learned that Cue had one ear on his business and the other on the street. If there was something to know, he probably knew it.

Business had treated him well in Silverlake so he'd recently signed a three-year lease on a two-floor unit at Sunset and the 101, sharing the complex with the Metropolitan Hotel, my favorite Chinese restaurant, a liquor store and a few small offices.

The lot was filled except for a lone handicapped spot. I parked in it. The double doors to Cue's suite stood wide, shipping boxes at the foot of each to keep them open.

The place exuded the aroma of fresh paint. I stepped on the plush navy carpet. A dining table for eight was in the middle of the room. Behind it, a bar with a dozen black oak barstools. To my left, a staircase. To my right, an elevated, marble floor with another dining table, an L-shaped counter in the corner with pool cues, chalk and a small sink, and nine pool tables—seven broken-down and two assembled. The tables were carved from black oak. The assembled tables sported thick red felt. Cueball ran his finger slowly across the felt. "Why is this taking so long, Mr. Ritchie?"

"Sorry, Cue. We're short some bolts. Andy's gone back to get replacements." Ritchie stood, wiped the sweat from his brow with the sleeve of his filthy t-shirt. "We should still be done today."

"I hope so."

Cueball inspected both assembled tables, then looked in my direction. I waved. The heels of his shiny loafers cracked on the fresh black marble as he walked toward me. "Jack."

"Hey, Cue, this place's looking sharp."

"Thank you."

"What's with the dining tables?"

"I'm expanding."

"Oh?"

"C'mon, I'll show you."

The staircase led to a second floor dining room. This room had the same blue-gray walls and navy carpet. The wall to my right supported two huge plate-glass windows that afforded a chosen few diners a view of the pool tables below.

"I've signed a deal to get some tournament play here."

"You're moving up in the world."

"Yes sir, I am."

We walked through double-doors at the far end of the room. We hung a right and passed through another set of double-doors into an enormous kitchen.

"Damn, Cue, you need this kind of kitchen to feed nine tables?"

"Hell, no. But, I do need it to supply the seventeen corporations that inked deals with me for daily delivery service."

"Impressive."

"I also received verbal confirmation from Capitol Records that I'll be their first choice for catering their little shindigs."

"Good for you."

"C'mon, my office is downstairs."

A freight elevator occupied space in the near corner of the room. We took it to the first floor, turned left through a large reception area and into an office. Cue sat behind the black oak desk. I sat in one of the two side chairs.

Cue took half a stogie from his ashtray and put it between his lips. He held a lighter to it until the cherry glowed orange. "So tell me, Jack, to what do I owe the pleasure of this visit?"

"I wanted to get your opinion on something."

Cue opened a ledger book, grabbed a pen and began writing. "Shoot."

"Charles Blake."

"What about him?"

"Exactly."

"He's a big time business man and good friend of the police."

"That, I know."

"He owns a large corporation named after him."

"I know that, too."

Cue stopped writing, looked up. "You know about the porn, too?"

"Nope."

"A film company, distribution house and a theatre."

"Didn't see that on the list of assets for BEI."

"Cause it ain't there. He has an off-shore outfit that controls them."

"Let me guess. Cayman Islands."

"Yes, sir. The good ole Caymans." Cue went back to his work. "Man's got lots of muscle, too."

"You mean the hunks at Diamond Steel?"

Cue laughed. "Man's a riot. I'm not talking bout no pansy security outfit, Jack."

"Why does he need real muscle?"

Cue's face drew up in solemnity. "That's a good question."

"Porn's not that dangerous, is it?"

"Depends."

"On?"

"What you're pushing."

I pulled an ashtray close and lit a cigarette. "What's Blake pushing?"

"Dunno. Man's a cool cat."

"Guesses?"

"Too many possibilities."

"What about kiddy porn?"

"That's one possibility, sure."

"You don't sound convinced."

Cue shrugged.

"You don't know, or you ain't saying?"

He looked out the window, shrugged again.

"What's the deal here, Cue? You know everything, so why are

you so tight-lipped about this?"

Cue ran a hand across his shiny bald head. "Jack, lemme tell you a story." He puffed his cigar, creating a veil of smoke that hung above his head like a rain cloud. "I had a daughter."

He paused. I knew this wasn't going to be comfortable. I never knew he was a father. And he said "had." I leaned back and let him get it out.

"Wahine. It's Maori for beautiful woman. She was beautiful, too. Then one day, some motherfucker come by the house and kidnapped my baby. She was fifteen." He smashed his cigar in the ashtray. "They found her a month later in a goddamned alley in Lennox, naked with a hunting knife still inside her."

I straightened up, fought to keep my lunch down. "I'm sorry."

"I know some motherfucker put my little girl on film before he tortured her. I seen the fucking tape." He stopped and a tear rolled down his ebony cheek. "Since that day, I've stayed up on the business, if you know what I mean. I could tell you where to get little girls that give blowjobs like seasoned veterans, little boys who'll let you do anything to them, any sick shit you could think of. But in all this time, I've never heard Blake's name mentioned. So you see, I ain't saying cause I just don't know." He looked up at me. "Now, that don't mean he ain't connected to something somewhere. But, if he is, it sure as fuck is covered by some deep shit."

We sat for several minutes. I chain-smoked, Cue stared out the window. Then, he said, "You the first person I told that story to."

"I'm so sorry, Cue."

"That's fucking life. I do want something, though."

"Name it."

"If you find out anything, I wanna hear about it."

"Okay."

"What else you wanna know?"

"How's Blake connected to Tony DiMarco?"

He'd apparently submerged the hurt deep within. He smiled. "I see the detective's been clocking some hours on this case."

"You bet. I've almost earned my gold star."

"Good for you. What do you know about DiMarco?"

Cue buried his head back in the ledger, but I knew he was listening intently just the same.

"I know DiMarco brought young girls to Donovan's place for filming. I know, in all likelihood, that DiMarco killed Donovan because he talked to me. And I know DiMarco's doing something

1

with the girls after filming them, but I'm not sure what."

"Not bad. And how did you get turned on to Blake?"

"DiMarco and Blake got into an argument while eating lunch at the Peking Duck Restaurant."

"And being the good detective you are, you started sniffing around Blake."

"Exactly."

Cue stopped writing again, leaned back in his chair. "And you wanna know if Blake might retaliate."

"Not so bad as a detective yourself there, Cue."

He nodded.

"I'm particularly interested in the likelihood of Blake trying to rub me out."

Cue chuckled. "Rub you out?"

"You know, kill me."

"Oh, I know what it means. You've been watching too many movies, my boy. Rub you out." He chucked again. I'm glad he found me so amusing.

"Well?"

The laugh disappeared, the smile followed. "Easily, my boy, very easily. But, Blake's not stupid. He's a businessman. He'll check you out and then weigh the risk against the reward." Cue fished a fresh cigar from the humidor and clipped its ends. "You got anything else that ties Blake to DiMarco?"

"Gee, Cue, I came to you for information. I'm beginning to think you're squeezing me."

"What's good for the goose . . ."

Good point. "I know Blake owns Diamond Steel, and Diamond Steel pays DiMarco twenty-five hundred a week as a security consultant. And, I know DiMarco ain't no expert in security—at least not the kind DSS claims to employ."

Cue puffed hard on the cigar but eventually got it going. He leaned his head back, exhaled a large puff of smoke toward the ceiling. "Tell me. What do you think is going on here?"

"I think Blake's not what he appears to be. And I'm sure DiMarco is into way more than little girls, so I'm not ready to make the leap and say Blake's involved in that."

"DiMarco is, yes sir. He's a loan shark, muscle man, and a partner in a couple local businesses. Rumor says he's connected, but I'm not so sure."

"To the mob?"

"So they say. But, just because the man's last name ends with a vowel don't mean he's connected. And, he's a small time player. If I was you, and at this moment I'm not sure I'd wanna be, I'd spend my time watching DiMarco and worrying about Blake."

I found a small yellow slip of paper tucked beneath my wiper. A ticket. Across the parking lot, a female cop leaned against her cruiser, watching me. She stared for a moment, then pinched the brim of her hat and nodded. I yanked the ticket from the windshield and climbed in the truck.

Rookie.

My pain had eased greatly. But, when I found myself under stress, the soreness reared its ugly head in my lower back and temples. My drive home from Cue's was one of those times.

When I got home, I found a message from Nadia on my machine. She asked that I call her back ASAP. I did.

"Hi," she said. "How're you feeling?"

"Well, Dr. Belisi, I'm doing okay."

"Seriously, are you?"

"Yep."

"You need a night off."

"I do?"

"Yes, and I've got the perfect solution."

From time to time, Nadia offered one of her solutions. Most of them, I found, were spur of the moment and a bit shaky, but I figured this couldn't be any worse, so I took the bait. "What's that?"

"Get ready. I'm going to pick you up at seven-thirty."

"For?"

"It's a surprise."

I don't like surprises at all. Nadia knew it, but still I reminded her.

"You're no fun," she said.

"Sorry."

"I wanna take you out."

"What do you mean out?"

"You know, out."

"Like a date?"

"Okay."

"I'm asking."

"Whatever you wanna call it, just get ready."

"Where're we going?"

"I have two tickets for the Kings game tonight."

I wondered how best to answer this. Apparently, I waited too long.

"Jack? You still there?"

"I'm here. Did you buy the tickets yet?"

"Yes," she whispered.

"Oh."

"You don't wanna go."

"No, it's not that."

"What is it?"

"I just . . ."

"You just what? Don't wanna go with me."

"Nadia, you know that's not true. It's just this case."

"What will it hurt taking a night off? You deserve it."

"Whether I do or don't, I've got to equip DiMarco's car with the Trakker. Who knows what he's going to do."

"Probably nothing."

A sharp pain bolted through my spine. Damn stress, again. I paced my living room. "Probably, but still."

"I understand."

It didn't sound like she did.

"I appreciate the thought. I really do. And I don't want you to be out the money. How much were the tickets?"

She hung up.

I called back. Her line was busy.

I was startled by a voice behind me. Instinctively, I grabbed my Sig, spun around and pointed it in the direction of the voice.

Arturo held his hands up. "Fuck, Holmes. It's just me."

I relaxed my arm, dangled the pistol at my side. "You scared the hell out of me."

"I guess so."

I put the pistol away, scratched my head. "What'd you say?"

"I asked if there was trouble in paradise."

"What?"

"The phone call, Holmes. You were talking to Nadia, weren't you?"

I don't know why, but I glanced down at the phone. "Ah, yeah."

"And you two weren't expressing your love for one another, so there must be trouble."

"Fuck you."

"I knew it."

Arturo smiled. And walked to the bathroom.

TWENTY EIGHT

While Arturo was in the shower, I called Roy.

"Anything new to report?" he said.

I lit a cigarette and told him about DiMarco's generous salary from Diamond Steel, my being roughed up, and DiMarco's meeting with Blake.

"Sounds like you're pissing some people off."

"Maybe."

"Maybe? Christ, Jack, do you have blinders on? Maybe getting you involved in this case wasn't such a good idea."

More stress-related pain in my back. "What the hell's that supposed to mean?"

"I just don't wanna see you hurt."

"Don't worry about me."

"Ah, my Jack. Always thinking that he's an iron man or something."

"I prefer Superman."

"You would."

Roy asked if Raymond was keeping his retainer sufficient. I said yes. He then asked what I was going to do from here.

"Stay on DiMarco."

"You be careful."

"Always."

I hung up.

"Are you two speaking again?" Arturo said as he stepped from the bathroom, a pale yellow bath towel wrapped around his waist.

"You're dripping on the carpet."

Arturo looked at his feet, lifted them one by one from the carpet, and shrugged. "Sorry."

He went back into the bathroom, closed the door.

I didn't feel much like cooking, so Arturo and I grabbed some tacos at El Taco Grande on Melrose. Next to mine, they were the best in town.

Melrose Avenue invites a slightly different crowd than does the Strip and other sections of the city. Home to numerous adult apparel stores and bondage houses, Saturday nights brought out lots of men and women wrapped in cowhide. I watched a couple parade down the street. He was a good fifty-five, tall, well-built, maybe a stockbroker or lawyer. He looked old in skintight leather pants and pointed black boots. His thick, peppered chest hair protruded from under a leather vest draped over his bare torso. His female companion looked to be in her mid-twenties, with flowing blond hair and wearing a black evening gown that ended just above ankles wrapped in six-inch spiked heels. I was surprised she didn't have a dog collar tied to a leash in his hand. Maybe they'd get into that later.

He nodded, she smiled.

Arturo stuffed the last of his taco in his mouth, then said, "Embarcadero clients?"

Embarcadero is a bondage house one block west of El Taco Grande. "Maybe."

"She looked pretty good."

"He looked pretty stupid."

"Maybe she should ride with us a while."

"Whoa, big doggy. We got work to do."

"I can still dream."

I had parked my truck four blocks from the taco stand, and considered myself lucky to have gotten that close. I lit a cigarette, then dumped our trash in the garbage can.

After we began the walk back to the truck, Arturo said, "You think we'll get lucky tonight?"

"Probably not."

"Such a pessimist."

"Realist."

I stopped alongside a Lincoln Towncar parked on the street. "This is a beauty."

"You want a Lincoln?"

"It'd be nice."

Arturo leaned forward, peered through the passenger window. "All leather, CD player. Yeah, it's fine."

Loud rap music poured from somewhere to my left. I looked

up and found a black BMW to be its source. Four black men sat in the car. The car slowed as it neared us.

Arturo noticed the car, straightened up. "Shit."

The two men on the passenger side of the car leaned out their windows, Uzis in hand. I was pushed to the ground as bullets ripped through the Lincoln. The car's alarm went off. I felt Arturo's weight on top of me, pinning me to the concrete. Small shards of glass rained from the sky. Screams echoed down the street. A car engine raced, tires squealed, then deft silence.

"Fuck," Arturo said.

He pushed himself off me, extended his hand to help me up. I took it. We stared at each other for a moment. Uneasiness pumped through his eyes. I'm sure it did through mine as well.

Then, Arturo smiled. "And you said we probably wouldn't get lucky."

"Lucky? You call that fucking lucky?"

"Damn straight, Holmes."

I brushed bits of glass from my hair and shoulders. The Lincoln's alarm had gone quiet at some point during the attack. Maybe the bullets ripped it to shreds as they had the rest of the car. I looked up at Arturo, pointed at what was left of the Lincoln. "How the hell can you call that lucky?"

"Easy, Holmes. You just experienced a staged drive-by."

"Staged?"

"How many bullets you think were fired at us?"

"A lot."

"And how many times were we hit?"

I looked Arturo up and down. No blood. I checked myself. "Looks like none."

"Shit yeah, none. That's because it was staged. It's a warning, Holmes. They didn't want us dead. They wanted us scared."

"It fucking worked."

The police showed up several minutes later. Arturo and I both gave statements to the officers, then headed for my truck.

"You wanted excitement," Arturo said. "You got it."

TWENTY NINE

Day six. Arturo and I sat in my parked truck, around the corner from Club TA. I checked my watch: ten-thirty. I hadn't spoken more than a few words to Nadia since last Saturday's blowout, DiMarco hadn't been nice enough to do anything more incriminating than slapping a pimp, collecting from a bookie and sleeping with a couple of his whores, and I was hungry.

As if Arturo had read my mind, he said, "This is the shits, Holmes. And I'm starving."

DiMarco's pattern of the past five nights had been to stay at Club TA until around eleven, then go out on his rounds. I figured we had time to grab some food, so I started the engine and pulled out onto Hollywood Boulevard.

We ordered tacos and sodas from El Taco Grande. As we waited for our food, my pocket beeped. I reached inside and pulled out the Trakker. "He's moving."

"Shit," Arturo said. He leaned through the little window. "Hey, *esse, hora le puez.*"

"We gotta go," I said, heading for my truck.

"No way I'm leaving without food, Holmes."

I turned on the map overlay and watched the little green dot make its way down Hollywood Boulevard and onto the 101. Arturo shouted at the guys inside the kitchen. I opened my door. The little green dot moved further away.

I climbed inside and started the engine. Arturo jogged up a minute later. I was rolling before he had the door shut. I spun an illegal u-turn on Melrose and headed toward the freeway.

I tried to watch the screen and the road at the same time. After two near-accidents, I handed the Trakker to Arturo. In front of Paramount Studios, traffic ground to a halt.

Up ahead at Western, I saw flashing red and blue lights. I was trapped in the right lane, between side streets. Nowhere to go.

A half-eaten taco in one hand, the Trakker in the other, Arturo said, "He's heading into downtown now."

I slapped my palms against the steering wheel, nudged the truck forward an inch. When I was fifty feet from the next side street, I contemplated hopping the curb. Unfortunately, the telephone pole, mailbox and manicured lawn kept me from doing it.

"Looks like he's getting off the freeway."

"Shit."

I was still ten feet away, but I was clear of the mailbox and telephone pole, so I jumped the curb and made a right. I doubled the speed limit as I worked my way south on Wilton, then east on Beverly. Five minutes later, I entered the 101 at Silverlake Boulevard.

DiMarco's Jaguar had left the freeway at East First Street, and made its way to the 3000 block of Boyd Street. I barreled toward the First Street exit at 95.

Since installing the Trakker, I hadn't lost visual contact with DiMarco's Jag for more than a minute or two. I prayed that the mapping feature was accurate as I headed south on Mission into the Industrial Belt, the overcrowded section of warehouses between downtown Los Angeles and Boyle Heights.

We turned left on Boyd. Like most streets in the Industrial Belt, Boyd was a narrow one-lane road with dirt shoulders that doubled as trailer parking for the dock doors facing the street. If a forty-five-foot trailer was backed into a dock door, the entire street would be blocked.

I glanced at the Trakker. According to the map, we were less than three blocks from DiMarco's Jag. I scanned the dark street and found nothing but a blue twenty-seven-foot trailer backed to a dock door on the left, and two purple twenty-seven-footers parked at doors on the right.

The area was desolate, so I decided it was better to cruise with the headlights off. The second to last warehouse on the right emitted light from its windows. As we approached, the Trakker beeped. We were within fifty feet of the Jag. I stopped. Two tractors parked near the end of the street, but no Jag.

As I passed the last trailer, a small alley came into view on the right. The maroon Jag was backed against the far wall, next to a pile of 55-gallon drums, pallets and the shell of an old hotrod. There was a rollup door on the right wall. I drove to the end of the street, did a k-turn and parked behind the tractors.

All the warehouses on the street were early 1900s brick buildings with windows twenty feet off the ground. Better to let daylight in, but hell if you're trying to spy.

I left the keys in the ignition and switched the dome light to the always-off position. I slipped into a pair of skintight leather gloves. Arturo did the same.

"Let's take a look," I said.

We crossed the street and stayed close to the wall. When we reached the alley, I paused. The two purple trailers were backed to doors that looked like they belonged to the lighted warehouse. I could climb atop a trailer and try to peer through the window. Or, I could climb atop the pallets and drums in the far corner of the alley. I wasn't keen on either option.

I leaned against the wall and lit a cigarette. The roar of a modified engine broke the silence. Shards of light appeared on the street, growing brighter. Someone was coming.

The trek back to the truck was too far, and I saw no easy way to climb atop the trailer, so I bolted for the far corner. Arturo followed. We crouched behind the rusted shell of a car and waited.

Moments later, the lights turned into the alley, stopping in front of the rollup door. The car was a gray Ford Explorer, lowered, its windows blacked out. I pulled a small notebook and a pen from my jacket pocket and jotted down the license plate.

The car horn blasted twice. The rollup door clanked as it opened. As soon as the door was high enough to admit the Explorer, it crawled inside and the door came down.

We sat for a minute, listening. The engine died, feet shuffled against the concrete floor, then nothing.

"Holmes, I gotta pee," Arturo said.

"Great timing."

"Hey, when nature calls."

"Make it quick. I'm gonna climb on top of those drums, see if I can see anything."

"Be careful."

He walked past the rollup door and turned toward the parked trailer. I pushed against the pallet. It was firm. I hoisted myself atop one drum and tried the next. Soon, I was standing on top of the pile and, craning my neck, got a partially obstructed view of the warehouse's interior.

Pallets of assorted drums and boxes lined the walls, but the heart of the warehouse was empty. DiMarco stood face-to-face with a black man that had a good six inches on him. The black man held a chain in his hand. My gaze followed the chain. Attached to it by handcuffs were three girls that couldn't be a moment more than sixteen. Two wore short black mini-skirts, black heels and lacy blue shirts. The third wore black stretch pants, running shoes and a pink shirt. They all looked stoned and dismal.

DiMarco paced circles around the black man. He stopped in front of the girls for a moment, then resumed his pacing. A crick suddenly appeared in my neck. I straightened, took a last hit from my cigarette and threw it to the ground.

"Hey, motherfucker," a voice said.

I looked down and found a thick Italian man pointing a Beretta at me. "Come down from there now."

I held my hands out for a moment, then slowly made my way to the ground. Once there, he grabbed my shoulder and threw me up against the rusted car.

"Nice and easy," he said.

I relaxed against the hood, spread my arms out. "That's my middle name."

His hand molested my torso, stopped on my pistol, and withdrew it from my pants. Then, the hand continued down one leg and up the other, firmly grabbing my crotch before ceasing its assault.

"Be careful, I might get aroused."

"Shut up." He seized my shoulder, straightened me up. "Now walk, very slowly, to the door."

He ground the barrel of his pistol into my neck, led me toward the mouth of the alley.

A few steps away from the door, the cold steel backed away from my neck. From behind, a grunt, then a thud. I turned and found Arturo wielding a strip of rebar in his hands, hovering over the Italian who was out cold, if not dead. The pistol lay on the ground a few feet to his right.

I leaned down and took back my Sig. Then I grabbed his Beretta from the dirt, dropped the magazine, and pulled the slide. The bullet flew from the chamber, bounced off the ground. I stuffed the pistol in the Italian's coat pocket and tossed the magazine under the trailer. "Thanks."

Arturo nodded, and pointed to the Italian with the rebar. "Let's go. Probably more of these hanging around."

I held a finger to my lips, listened. Footsteps. Then the rollup door creaked on its way up. We stayed near the front door, my pistol at the ready.

"So, what's up, Tony?"

"We're gonna be taking a few weeks off. Holiday and all."

The voices grew louder. We backed under the trailer and waited.

"Okay. You got something for me?"

DiMarco appeared at the mouth of the alley, smoking a cigar. The black man walked beside him.

"I've got some China White coming in day after tomorrow. I need it driven from Long Beach to San Francisco."

"I can do that."

"Of course, you can. I'll pay ten large."

"Count me in."

Tony wrapped his arm around the black man's shoulders, pulled him close. "Good boy, Jimmy."

They stood silent for a minute, then Tony reached into his coat pocket and came back with a thick white envelope. He handed it to Jimmy. "Nice work. Stay by your cell. I'll call you tomorrow night with the details."

"Will do," Jimmy said, and walked away.

DiMarco stared at the dark sky and puffed on his cigar. The Explorer's engine came to life, and slowly crept out of the alley and down the street. DiMarco disappeared a moment later, but he didn't close the rollup door.

"I'm gonna kick the shit out of that guy," I said.

Arturo touched my arm. "No, Holmes."

I knew he was right. The idea was to follow DiMarco and find out where the girls went, but I was boiling with anger and felt like ripping DiMarco a new asshole. Then, the moment passed and I relaxed. A little.

Footsteps made their way across the concrete and into the alley.

The unmistakable crack of open palm meeting cheek fired through the air. My muscles flinched.

"Stop fighting, you little bitch." The Jag's alarm beeped and a door opened. "Get the fuck in."

The door closed. Footsteps crossed the alley and the rollup door creaked down. We inched toward the back of the trailer, hidden by the stairwell. The front door opened, then closed, and DiMarco walked down the steps and into the alley.

The Jag came to life. DiMarco eased his car out of the alley and down Boyd Street. We waited ten seconds, then ran for my truck.

THIRTY

DiMarco led us to Donovan's former house-turned-studio on La Mirada Avenue. He backed into the driveway, honked his horn twice, and climbed out of the Jaguar. Two men came outside to meet him.

Mike the biker was not one of them. I wondered whether he had taken my advice and skipped town. The two men unloaded the girls while DiMarco used his bulk to shield their activity from eyes on the street. When the girls were safely in the backyard, DiMarco closed the door and followed.

"You gonna follow DiMarco when he leaves?" Arturo said.

"That was my plan."

"You want me to hang out here and see if anything happens?"

"Sounds like a good idea."

"Just don't forget about me."

"I could never forget about you."

He puckered up, blew me a kiss. "I love you, too, Holmes."

Several minutes later, DiMarco came out of the building and hopped into his Jag.

Arturo opened the door. "Be careful, Holmes."

"You, too."

Arturo stepped onto the asphalt and closed the door. He went behind the truck. In my rearview mirror, I saw him crouch down behind a large shrub. DiMarco pulled onto the street. Traffic was light on La Mirada Avenue, so I gave him thirty seconds before going after him.

DiMarco headed out to Melrose and west to Robertson. I dialed Tyrone's number and was a bit surprised I actually got him.

"Ain't I the lucky one? What's up, Jack?"

"I have a tip for you. It'll make you an instant god with the boys in Narco."

"Pray tell."

He didn't sound enthused, but I gave him the info on DiMarco's heroin shipment anyway. I waited for him to dig up a pen, then gave him the Explorer's license plate. "I don't know if you'll be able to get Jimmy's cell phone number that quick, but at least you can watch Long Beach. Ten to one Jimmy will be driving that extremely inconspicuous Explorer."

"How much product is involved?"

"Dunno, but DiMarco's paying ten grand to have it moved to Frisco, so I imagine quite a bit."

"Thanks, Jack."

"Don't say I never did nothing for you."

He started to say something, but I hung up. DiMarco turned on Burton Way and stopped at the Four Seasons Hotel.

A young, clean-cut man in a cobalt jacket, navy tie and white shirt greeted him. DiMarco held out the keys, then handed him a couple bills and pointed to a spot very near the front doors. As soon as DiMarco vanished into the hotel, I pulled up and tried the same thing.

The young man frowned at me when I handed him two twenties and asked him to keep my truck close. He didn't frown at DiMarco. Still, I gave him a wide smile and bolted inside.

I entered a plush, entirely overdone lobby. The black and white checkered marble floor seemed designed specifically for this layout. Dead center in the room, the checkered pattern gave way to a black circle drawn around a black diamond. On top of the diamond sat a large sandstone table. The table held a single flower arrangement, approximately six feet tall. Above that, a white chandelier hung from the vaulted ceiling, lighting the lobby. Live ferns grew from oversized white planters in each corner. Four blue velvet chairs with gold trim were strategically placed near each towering fern. In my white button-down shirt and jeans, I felt like a homeless man in a room full of celebrities.

To my left, the checkered marble melted into what could have been white or pale yellow marble as it flowed from the lobby into the reception area. With the floor's remarkable sheen and the bright lights in the reception area, the actual color was difficult to discern. A square archway that looked to me as if it was of Roman design separated the two areas.

DiMarco stood at the counter. He pulled a large envelope from his jacket pocket, and handed it to a blond man who nodded and smiled. DiMarco turned left, walked away. I moved forward in time to see him enter the men's room.

I walked to the counter.

"May I help you?" Blondie said.

I rested my forearms on the counter, leaned forward slightly. Inches from his keyboard, I saw the envelope. Only trouble was that it was turned upside-down and nothing was written on the back.

Ever the quick thinker, I smiled and said, "I'd like to apply for a job."

Blondie's eyes narrowed, his faced donned a look of disapproval. "Excuse me?"

"I'd like to fill out an application."

He stood for a minute longer, then reached under the counter. His hand blindly fished. His eyes never left mine. His hand came back empty. "I'm sorry, but we're out of applications."

"Isn't this establishment an Equal Opportunity Employer?"

"Of course, sir." His mouth curled on the word sir, as if he'd just swallowed a glass of limejuice.

"Don't you have any more apps in back or something? I'd really hate to have to make a trip to the ACLU office."

He sighed. "One moment, I'll check."

Blondie walked through a door to his left. I leaned over the counter and pinched the envelope, flipped it over. Scrawled in black ink across the envelope's front: "RL - Room 419".

DiMarco came out of the bathroom. I kept my head forward, tried to trail him with my peripheral vision. He seemed to be heading straight for the reception desk. My heartbeat kicked up a few notches. This whole damn place was so large, yet barren. No place to hide. I was about to make a beeline for the doors when DiMarco veered away from the desk, toward the foyer. I was half-turned to follow him when Blondie came back.

"I was able to locate one."

That's what he brought with him, too—a single copy of an application.

"I suppose you'll need a pen?" He held a Four Seasons pen between his fingers. "We will need it back, of course."

I snatched the app from his hand but left the pen. "I'll fill it out and bring it back later."

"Very well."

I smiled, then sprinted through the foyer and outside. DiMarco's Jaguar was gone.

I glanced at the Trakker. The dot hadn't moved from the corner of Doheny and Burton-where I stood. I punched a few buttons and realized the batteries had gone too low. "Shit."

I grabbed the closest valet worker and shoved a twenty in his palm along with the ticket. "I need the keys to my truck now." He stared at the twenty. "Now."

I followed him to the key box. He pulled my keys from a peg, then took a step toward my truck. I stopped him. "No need. I'll get it."

I took the keys and left. I figured DiMarco would take the same way back to the house on La Mirada. Provided, of course, he was going back there. His Jag was nowhere in sight, so I had to gamble. I worked my way east on Burton and north on Robertson.

Luck was with me. I caught up to him as he turned right on Melrose.

THIRTY ONE

DiMarco was already inside the house when Arturo climbed into the truck. "It's about time."

"Blame DiMarco, not me."

He closed the door, leaned back in the seat. "What happened?"

"DiMarco stopped by Four Seasons."

"No one ever said he ain't got good taste."

"He left an envelope for room 419. Someone with the initials RL."

"What was inside it?"

"It was sealed."

We sat for a moment, then Arturo tapped my shoulder. "Hey, Holmes, isn't this where you prove what kind of detective you are?"

"What?"

"You're gonna tell me who RL is, why DiMarco left him an envelope, and what was inside the envelope."

"Right." I fished a cigarette from the pack in my shirt pocket. "The envelope was a cash payoff. No theories yet on who RL might be."

Arturo lit a cigarette. He rolled down the window an inch and blew his hit through the gap. "Since I'm the one who's learning here, tell me. What makes you think that?"

"Instinct."

"Really?"

"Yep."

"Where can I pick up some of that?"

"What?"

"Instinct. I want some, too."

I found myself at a loss for a great comeback. Fortunately, DiMarco came out of the house—saved by the bell, more or less.

The two men who had unloaded the girls earlier now loaded them into the Jag. DiMarco carried a banker's box, it's lid taped shut.

"According to Mike the biker," Arturo said, "the box DiMarco's carrying is full of videotapes."

"You do listen to me."

"Of course."

"I'm touched."

"Hey, Holmes, my hands are clear over here."

DiMarco waved at the two men and they disappeared into the backyard. He climbed in his Jag, started the engine and pulled out of the driveway.

He took Fountain to Western and headed north. The American Film Institute sits on the west side of Western where the street makes a forty-five degree turn. He slowed his Jaguar so much that, for a moment, I thought he might turn into the Institute. Instead, he continued on what had become Los Feliz Boulevard, then turned left on Fern Dell Drive.

"Money land," Arturo said.

We continued north into Griffith Park. DiMarco turned left on Red Oak, then left again at Live Oak. By now, we were in a very pricey neighborhood. Homes got larger, as did the lots. Trees were older, the stench of wealth stronger.

Near the intersection of Mountain Oak, DiMarco made a sharp left into a steep driveway, complete with gates and a callbox. I continued on, parking a block away. The gates swung open and DiMarco drove up the hill. The house that he parked in front of was more a castle than a single-family dwelling. I counted four floors and two separate garages, a three-car and a two-car. The driveway poured into a concrete slab that could easily hold a dozen more cars.

I grabbed a pair of binoculars, pointed them at the house. DiMarco got out of the Jag, the girls remained inside. A man appropriately dressed as a butler met him on the grand staircase that led from the parking area to the doublewide front doors. The butler pointed down the hill. DiMarco threw his hands in the air, then turned around and headed back down the drive. The gates remained open.

The house's two-car garage was atop the hill to the right of the staircase. The three-car garage had direct access from Live Oak.

DiMarco turned right on Live Oak and pulled into an open door.

"You see anything?" Arturo said.

"DiMarco just pulled into the garage."

In the hour that we waited outside the house, I moved my truck three times. With the price tags on the houses in this neighborhood, I was worried someone might mistake us for burglars.

Arturo sat slouched in the passenger seat, his eyes closed. I peered through my binoculars, switching my gaze to different areas of the home. To me, it displayed a European medieval flair. The house had more windows than I thought possible, yet I was unable to see something through any one of them.

Ten minutes later, the garage door opened.

"He's leaving."

The Jag backed onto Live Oak. The streetlamp on the corner provided just enough light to see inside the car. "And he's alone."

"Great. Now what?"

"We stay with the girls."

"That's just dandy, Jack, but how long do you think we can hang in this neighborhood before Johnny Law comes calling?"

"We may get to find out."

"I love detective work."

"It does have its finer moments."

Half an hour and four cigarettes later, a limo pulled up to the house. The gates swung open and the limo drove to the top of the hill. A man had already made his way down the stairs and into the limo before I could get a look at his face. The butler followed the girls to the car. Their handcuffs were gone, and they were obedient. Once they had climbed into the back seat, he closed the door and headed back to the house. Then, the limo descended the drive.

We followed the limo back down Fern Dell Drive, Los Feliz, and Western, then west on Franklin to the 101 North. The limo merged north on the 405 to Sherman Way, under the tunnel beneath the Van Nuys Airport, then made a right on Balboa Boulevard.

I reached for my cell phone. "I've got a bad feeling here."

The limo made a right on Stagg Street and parked in front of an old National Guard building.

I called Tyrone, left a message with someone to have him call me immediately.

The man got out of the limo first. This time, I had my binoculars poised. And I saw his face.

"Holy shit."

"What?"

"The guy."

"What guy?"

"The guy in the limo. You'll never guess who it is."

"No, I won't. So tell me, Holmes."

"Charles Blake."

The girls climbed out of the limo and Blake led them to a Gulfstream G-IV. Blake gave a cursory look around the grounds, then got into the jet.

A man who I assumed was the pilot was circling the jet when my cell rang.

"Shut down Van Nuys Airport right now," I said.

"What?"

"You heard me. If you want Charles Blake red-handed, get this fucking airport shut down now."

"You gotta give me more than that, Jack."

"Look, he just boarded his jet with three girls that were delivered to his house by DiMarco. Keep the jet on the ground and you've got him."

"Hold on."

The pilot finished his pre-flight inspection and climbed into the jet. The hatch closed.

I set the binoculars in my lap. "Fuck."

The jet taxied down the runway and did its u-turn in preparation for takeoff.

"Can't do it, Jack. Sorry."

"What do you mean, sorry? Goddamn, Tyrone, three innocent girls are on that plane, on their way to God knows where, and all you can say is sorry?"

"Christ, Jack. Gimme a break. I'm not God, you know."

I hung up the phone. The jet raced down the runway and took flight.

I sat silent for several minutes. I couldn't believe what had just happened, what I had just let happen. I was responsible, at least in part, to three girls' lives being destroyed by maggots like DiMarco and Blake. Arturo sat quiet with me. When I was ready to go, I turned the truck around and headed back to the freeway.

That night, I spent hours sitting on my balcony, smoking and drinking. Sometime after the morning light engulfed the blackness, I went to bed.

THIRTY TWO

The rain was merely a drizzle when I parked my truck in the office lot around one on Friday afternoon. Before I had left the apartment, Arturo told me he needed to run some personal errands, which meant he was going to see Maria. I reminded him that I wanted to exchange the Regal for a van at Hertz. He assured me he'd be available when needed.

Nadia was at her desk, her fingers dancing across the keyboard. I hung my jacket on the coat rack and kicked the water from my shoes. "Hi."

"Hi. You have a couple messages." She stopped typing and pointed to three foot-high piles on the corner of her desk. "This is stuff for you to go through."

She spun her chair back toward the computer and resumed whatever it was she was doing.

I walked to the edge of the desk and leafed through the first stack. "What's happening with the Marino case? Did you get ahold of Larry?"

"Yes. Larry gathered enough evidence in a day and a half to 'crucify the bastard', as Lena put it."

"That's great. Thank you."

"You're welcome."

I hated when Nadia proved she could carry on a conversation while staying engrossed in her typing. I felt like she was using it as a way to avoid more than passing conversation with me. Maybe she was.

I opened my office door and transferred the first two piles from her desk to mine. I had the third stack in my arms when I stopped in front of her desk. "Nadia."

"Yeah."

"I'm sorry about Saturday."

"Water under the bridge."

"Maybe, but I'm still sorry."

"Don't worry about it."

"Could you stop typing for one second?"

Her fingers froze, hovered over the keyboard. "What?"

"We need to talk."

Her eyes remained glued to the screen. "About?"

"About whatever. We just need to talk."

"If you say so."

"Don't you?"

"No."

"This afternoon, we're going to talk, like it or not."

"Can I go back to typing now?"

As I walked toward my office, I caught a glimpse of the side of Nadia's face, and thought the corner of her mouth was crooked in a smile. I stepped into my office and, with my heel, kicked the door shut.

I spent a good thirty minutes reading the same set of documents from the first pile. The words just didn't register. I made a pot of coffee, propped my feet on my desk and smoked a cigarette. When Mr. Coffee finished his brew cycle, I poured myself a cup and smoked another cigarette.

I called Hertz and asked whether a van was available. The bubbly girl said yes. I told her I'd be exchanging the Regal for the van later that afternoon. She assured me everything would be ready.

I spent two more hours mulling the paperwork, trying to absorb what I could. The only problem I had was seeing the word *asshole* in every paragraph. Of course, I knew it was referring to me. Following DiMarco instead of going to the Kings game with Nadia on Saturday had proved worthless. Which meant she was right. Again.

I suppose I didn't want to confront my feelings. I didn't want to get involved in an office relationship. My only experience with one was actually watching my old partner, Rick Nelson. His relationship with Jill Monroe, a beat cop, began with infatuation, ended with divorce. The bitter stare Jill burned in Rick's eyes still haunts me. And it's enough to make me leery of having a go at it myself.

I knew I was distancing myself from Nadia, but not without good reason. This case was quickly becoming dangerous, and I

didn't want to have to worry about her. I hated the fact Nadia
helped Arturo plant the bug at Club TA, and if I had anything to
say about it, she would do nothing more for this case. Nothing, that
is, that involved leaving the office.

Even with all my distractions, I managed to decipher some
information. I learned Blake was a jack-of-all-trades. His empire,
BEI, included a hotel, three restaurants, a casino in Jean, Nevada,
part ownership of another in Primm, a Lexus dealership, and
Diamond Steel Security.

The last stack of documents included the financial status of
Blake. He was sole owner of the nine-million dollar estate on Live
Oak Drive. He also owned a condo in Hawaii, a home in Cape Cod
and a villa in Paris. BEI owned the multi-million dollar G-IV, but
since Blake was sole owner of BEI's stock, it was just semantics.
He had five million in two investment accounts with Smith-Barney,
another half-million with Strong Funds, and nine-hundred
thousand with Fidelity Investments. On top of that, he had another
half-million or so spread across a dozen checking, savings and
money market accounts.

I love reading so long as it's neither legal nor dull. Most of this
stuff was both. Still, I forced myself to be the consummate
professional and worked my way through it all. And, the one thing
that became clearer as I muddled through the paperwork was that
both Cue and Tyrone were right about one thing—Blake was a
major player.

At ten past four, I left the mounds of paper and walked into the
reception area. Nadia was on the phone. I walked to the window
and looked out on Wilshire Boulevard. The evening traffic was
mounting, the black sky promised more rain.

Nadia had placed the incoming mail on the corner of her desk.
I grabbed the stack, thumbed through the envelopes. Nadia
appeared to be on a business call, and appeared to be taking her
time.

Among the ten envelopes were my rent, electric and telephone
bills. Six were junk mail. As such, they made it to the trashcan
unopened. The last envelope was a check from a San Francisco
firm that had hired me last October to look into an accident that
occurred in downtown LA.

Nadia finished her phone call. Before she could put those
delicate fingers back on her keyboard, I dropped the mail on her
desk. "Ready?"

"For what?"

"To talk."

She stared at me a moment, then grabbed a manila file folder from her desk. "I'm not finished yet."

"So?"

"So? I've got to finish this stuff tonight."

I set my open palms on the desk, leaned toward her. "Or what?"

"Or . . ."

"Or it won't get done until tomorrow. C'mon, I'll buy you some of that slop you call ice cream."

I followed Nadia to her apartment, waited while she parked her car in the garage, then pulled into the short, concrete drive. I hugged the garage door, yet most of my truck remained in the street.

"It'll be fine," Nadia said, then took off down the sidewalk. I set the truck's alarm and followed—jogging until I caught up to her. Nadia tucked a lock of hair behind her ear, flashed me half a smile. And we walked to Juju's in silence.

Nadia ordered her laboratory manufactured ice cream. I had a latte. We found a table outside and sat down.

"This is the same table we had last time, isn't it?"

"Uh-huh," Nadia said, through a mouthful of whatever it was.

I sipped my steaming latte and concentrated on the traffic. I wasn't sure how to start.

She apparently was. "What's been going on with the case?"

"It's getting kinda messy."

"How so?"

I lit a cigarette and told Nadia about the events between DiMarco and Blake.

"What did he do with the girls?"

"I have no idea." I took a hit from my cigarette, a sip from my latte, and cleared my throat. "Nadia, there's something I need to say."

"If it's about Saturday . . ."

"No, it's not about Saturday."

She stuck her spoon into her ice cream stuff, rested her chin in her hands, and looked up at me. "What?"

"It's about this case."

"Okay."

"Things are getting dangerous. I've been told Blake's not the kind of guy you want pissed off at you. And, he's pissed at me."

Nadia smiled—a warm, genuine smile. "You do have a way

with people."

"I'm serious. I don't want you getting hurt."

Her eyes grew dark, her face taut. "What the hell are you saying?"

I averted my stare. A taxi pulled to the corner and two twenty-something girls hopped out of the backseat. The first girl out dropped some money through the passenger window, waved at the driver, then they both went into Juju's, laughing hysterically, looking very stoned.

"I'm saying I don't want you to do any more field work."

"You're still pissed about my helping Arturo plant that bug."

"No. Maybe. It doesn't matter. I don't wanna spend my days worrying about you instead of trying to find Carrie."

"You don't think I can handle it."

"No, that's not it."

"Then you don't wanna be around me."

"That's ridiculous."

"Is it? Ever since we first kissed, you've been distant. Like maybe you're afraid of what might happen."

"I am afraid of what might happen, sort of. But, that's not the point. I just want you to be safe."

Nadia spooned a couple bites into her mouth, then replaced the spoon in the bowl. "What about you?"

"What about me?"

"Who's gonna keep you safe?"

"Arturo."

"Who's gonna keep him safe?"

"Me."

"Then why can't you keep me safe, too?"

"You don't understand."

"Sure, I do. You and Arturo can handle it, but I can't."

"I didn't say that."

"You didn't have to."

Her words hung in the thick air between us for several minutes. I finished my latte and my fourth cigarette. Nadia finished her fake ice cream. Then, we sat and stared at one another for a moment. I broke the stare and watched the two stoned girls stumble from Juju's in a fit of laughter.

"You don't have to do this," she said.

"Do what?"

"Try to distance yourself from me. If you don't want to go any further, just tell me."

"Nadia."

"No, Jack, wait. What am I to you?"

"What kind of a question is that?"

"One I'd like an answer to."

"You're a very sweet person."

"Am I desperate?"

"I don't think so, but only you can answer that."

"No, I'm not. I like you. You know that. I think I might even be able to love you. If you'd let me, that is. But, if you don't want me trying, just tell me. Just fucking tell me."

"Nadia, that's not it at all."

She slammed her palms against the table, drawing the attention of a couple sitting at a table behind us. "Then what the hell is it?"

"This case and all. I just need time to think."

"You go ahead and take all the time you need."

"Don't be like that."

"Like what, Jack?"

"Like that. All shitty."

"I'm not being shitty."

"Yes, you are."

"I just want you to . . ."

She stopped talking when my cell phone rang. My stomach ached with the inopportuneness of the call. I answered it.

"Jack, Arturo."

"What's up?"

"I'm down at Hertz. The lady's giving me shit about exchanging the car."

"Why? What'd she say?"

"She said since it's your credit card, you have to sign for the van."

"What time do they close?"

I heard Arturo repeat the question to someone. Then, he said, "Six."

I glanced at my watch. "Hang tight. I'll be there in a few."

I killed the call and looked up at Nadia. She was already on her feet.

"I have to go."

"Figures."

"What figures?"

She took a deep breath, released it slowly. "Nothing."

"C'mon, please."

"Please what? I'm just . . . No, forget it. Go do whatever you need to do."

"Arturo can't pick up the van. I need to go over there."

"Are you . . . You know what? I don't even want to know." She turned and took a few steps, then stopped and glanced back at me. "Just be careful."

I watched her walk to the corner, then across the street to her apartment complex. I followed. With determination, she marched straight up the stairs, unlocked her apartment door and disappeared inside. All without looking back once.

THIRTY THREE

The van we rented was a Chevy Astrovan—not precisely what I had in mind, but it would work. I pictured a full-size conversion van with drapes covering its windows and an extended roof. Not only would that have better blended into DiMarco's upper-middle-class neighborhood, it would have made it easier for us to remain incognito.

One of the fundamental rules of good detective work is to always inform the police when working a stakeout. This, of course, eliminates the chance a patrol car will stumble upon you and ruin your surveillance. But, I didn't know many cops, and the few I had met didn't seem to like me much. So, I decided to take my chances.

As we neared DiMarco's, I scouted the available parking spaces. This neighborhood couldn't have had a home in it worth less than half a mil. Above that, the offerings were mixed. The west side contained mostly one-story homes in the bottom range whereas the right side had two and three-story ones, some pushing a good five mil. I noticed one or two that could pass in my book for mansions, or estates, or whatever the hell the rich called them—maybe humble little abodes. DiMarco's home was unique to the area in that the left front corner of his house resembled a two-story octagonal bell tower, though the rest of the house was single-story.

The larger homes not only boasted more living space, but more yard space, and by default, more security and privacy. I parked in front of a two-story Mediterranean with eight-foot block wall running its perimeter. The house was dark, the wall high, and two enormous weeping willow trees separated the wall from the road, providing an extra measure of anonymity. In lieu of curtains and an extended roof in the van, we needed all the help we could get.

I climbed in the middle bench seat, grabbed my Marlboro

duffel bag from the floor, set it next to me. I unzipped the bag, removed a pair of binoculars, my 35mm Nikon camera with telescopic lens, and a fresh pack of cigarettes. I pulled the cellophane and tin foil from the pack, discarded them on the floor. I placed a cigarette between my lips, pulled a lighter from my pocket, and ignited the cigarette with the yellow-blue flame from the Bic.

"You think we'll discover anything tonight?" Arturo said.

"I have no idea. But, since we're now officially on stakeout, I'm prepared."

"You got a Porta-Potty back there?"

"Nope."

"Then you ain't fully prepared."

Arturo unlocked the door.

"Hang on, there, big fella. You can't go pissing in the yards of these homes."

"Watch me."

"We're not even here ten minutes and already you're putting the operation in jeopardy."

"Fuck you, I gotta pee."

"Try not to attract any attention. Okay?"

Arturo didn't smile, but he did step out of the van.

Shortly after nine o'clock, a black Lexus crawled down the street. The car paused as it came alongside the van, then continued on. By the time the car pulled behind DiMarco's Jaguar, I had my Nikon in focus and snapped a picture. I was sure I got the license plate in focus, but I took two more, just in case. Arturo held a pair of binoculars to his eyes. Two men stepped from the Lexus.

"They're wearing uniforms," he said.

I pressed my Nikon against my eye and focused on the men. I snapped a few more shots as they made their way to DiMarco's front door.

"I'll be damned," I said.

"You saw that, too, huh?"

"Yep. DSS uniforms."

DiMarco came to the door and let the two men inside.

"Wish we had a bug in there," Arturo said.

"That'd be nice."

The bell tower had windows on each side that I could see, but only on the first floor. Light basked the windowpanes. I focused my Nikon. From our vantage point, I had an almost straight shot through one of the windows. And through it, I saw DiMarco.

He walked to what appeared to be a wet bar and poured a drink. He turned and leaned against the counter, sipping from the glass in his hand. The larger of the two men walked to DiMarco's right. The other one hadn't come into view yet.

From his body language, I could tell DiMarco was upset. He waved his arms, pointed his finger, and threw his glass to the floor.

The larger man grabbed DiMarco by the nape of the neck, dragged him to the desk and forced him to sit down. I snapped some pictures. When DiMarco tried to turn his head, the larger man straightened it back out and held him still.

In the far right corner, the smaller man screwed a silencer on his pistol, 9mm I guessed. I snapped more pictures. He walked beside DiMarco and pushed the barrel against his temple. A small flash erupted in the room. Twice. Blood splattered on the windowpane, then DiMarco's body slumped forward. The smaller man unscrewed the silencer, put it in his jacket pocket. He slipped the pistol in its holster and closed his jacket.

Thirty seconds later, they walked out the front door. I took two more shots, which would clearly depict at least one of their faces, I was sure. They hopped into the Lexus, backed out of the drive, and headed back to wherever they came from.

"You think anyone else saw or heard that?" Arturo said.

"Probably not, but we'll give the cops thirty minutes to show anyway."

"We're going in?"

"Yep."

"Oh."

I checked my watched every couple of minutes. When thirty had passed, I said, "Okay, let's go."

I grabbed a wrench and two pairs of gloves from my bag, slipped them in my pocket. We climbed out of the van and walked the block to DiMarco's house.

The house was set back from the street just enough to allow an old acacia tree room to grow. The only light came from an overhead porch lamp, and through the first-floor windows of the tower.

The porch creaked under my Nikes as I stepped to the front door. The door was ajar. "How nice of DiMarco's visitors to leave the front door open."

"Doesn't that mean we can go inside?"

"Yep. It's not B and E if the door's open."

I handed Arturo one pair of gloves. I put on the other pair. I grabbed my Sig from its holster against the small of my back, pulled the slide. I held the pistol close to my leg and knocked on the door. "Hello. DiMarco?"

No answer. I knew DiMarco couldn't answer, but I wasn't sure if anyone else was inside the house.

"Ready?"

Arturo took a deep breath, exhaled slowly. "Let's do it."

I pushed the front door open, stepped inside. A few recessed, high-wattage bulbs burned from the ceiling above the entryway. There was a door to my left and another to my right, both closed. I held a finger to my lips until I was sure Arturo saw me, then I pointed at the door on the right. Arturo walked to it, swung it open. He shook his head when he found a closet. The opposite door was a bathroom.

The entry gave way to a large living room. We began on the right side and worked each room—a bedroom, laundry, family room, another bedroom and an outside deck. All were clear. More than that, they looked unused. They were clean, just not lived-in. I knew DiMarco was living alone. Maybe after his last divorce he decided to stay in this place even though it was entirely too big for him.

Along the back of the house, next to the deck, were the kitchen and the dining room. An espresso machine on the granite countertop held a couple shots, still warm. The dining room also boasted the unused look.

We crossed back through the living room. We had two doors left. One I knew led to the office. The other I figured was his bedroom. I was right. Knowing we were alone, I decided to poke around a bit.

Sparsely furnished, the room had only a chest of drawers and a bed. Arturo went into the master bath. I searched the chest of drawers. DiMarco only used two of the four drawers, which made my job easier. I looked under the bed, then said, "I'm going in the office."

"Okay. I'll be there in a minute."

The office door was open. In direct view was DiMarco's high-back executive chair, and his body slumped over the desk. And blood, lots of blood. It dripped from the windowpanes, the desk. Pools had formed on either side of the chair. The stench of urine and feces permeated the air.

The office, an otherwise square room, gave up its left corner to the bell tower, and all the mess was neatly contained there. Searching the desk was out of the question, but the four file cabinets and the wet bar were fair game.

Arturo came in as I finished the cabinets in the bar.

"Shit, Holmes, what a mess."

"Yep. Left or right."

"Left."

"Okay, you start with that cabinet."

He pulled the first drawer. It was filled with manila files. My first drawer was the same.

"We're going through everything?"

"Everything."

"I hated reading in school. I'm glad I get to do it again."

"It's good for you."

"Shit."

"Makes you smarter."

All the drawers were equally stuffed with documents. DiMarco liked to keep his corporate records at home, it seemed. He had records for all of the businesses I knew he owned, and a dry cleaner, Laundromat, and a liquor store I didn't. But, in the two hours we spent rifling the papers, we found nothing with so much as Blake's name on it.

I pulled the bottom drawers from each cabinet and stacked them on the floor.

"What're you doing?" Arturo said.

"Checking the bottom."

"What?"

"There's a ton of room below the bottom drawer. Great for hiding shit."

"See that in a movie, too?"

"Yep."

The first three cabinets housed only spider webs and dust. The fourth, though, was a different story.

"Pay dirt."

"DiMarco must've watched the same movie you did."

A gallon-sized Ziploc bag was stuffed against the kick plate. Inside, a small spiral notepad and a folded piece of paper. I unfolded the paper. It was a receipt for a safe deposit box rental at a Bank of America in the 5600 block of North Figueroa, near Mount Washington. Taped to the paper, a key.

Arturo replaced the drawers. I flipped open the notebook. It appeared to be a ledger of some sort. Initials were in the left column, dollar amounts in the right. The two sets of initials that appeared most often: RL and CB.

Arturo slammed the last drawer into place. "What is that?"

"A ledger."

"Oh."

"And a safe deposit box key."

"Does it help?"

"If we can get in the box, it does."

"So, it doesn't."

I closed the notebook. "I'm not saying that. We just need to figure out how to get inside it."

"I see."

"I better call this in."

Arturo looked at me as if my hair had just started on fire. "To who?"

"The cops."

"You're nuts."

"I have to. Someone might've seen us here anyway. I'd rather be the one to call it in than have to explain later that I really didn't kill him, but I was here and left without calling."

"I guess that's a good point."

"It's a great point."

I slipped underneath DiMarco's Jag, pulled the wrench from my pocket, and removed the Trakker.

We walked back to the van. I put the wrench, Trakker, ledger, receipt and key, my 9mm and its holster inside my duffel bag, and pulled my gloves from my hands. I took Arturo's gloves and put both pairs in the bag. I pulled the film from the camera, put the roll in my pocket and the camera in the bag. "Take the van and go to my place. I'll be by later."

"You want me to leave you here?"

"Yep."

"I don't know."

"It'll be much easier talking my way out of this if you're not here."

"What if they arrest you?"

"Then I call and you can bail me out."

"Again."

I grabbed my cell phone, then closed the van door. "Yep." I held the keys out with my fingertips. Arturo grabbed them. "See ya."

I dialed 911 and explained the situation as I walked back to the house. Then, I stood on the front porch and smoked a cigarette.

And waited for the arrival of homicide.

THIRTY FOUR

A black and white screeched into the driveway just before two AM, and parked directly behind DiMarco's Jag. I stood on the front porch, leaned against the stucco wall, and watched two uniformed cops jump from the car, pistols in hand.

"Against the wall," the driver shouted. "Now."

I took a last hit from my cigarette, flicked the butt into the yard, and turned to face the wall. I extended my arms away from my body, palms against the stucco. Then, I spread my feet, leaned into the wall.

"Done this before, huh?" the driver said as his hand pressed against my back. "Do you have any weapons, needles, sharp objects or the like on you tonight?"

"Nope. No weapons, needles, sharp objects or the like."

His hands roamed every inch of my body, squeezing, probing. Then, he said, "Okay, turn around very slowly."

I did. The driver was about a foot in front of me, his pistol holstered. The nametag pinned above his breast pocket read "K. Malone". Over his left shoulder, the other cop stood, five yards back, his pistol aimed at my heart.

"You Jack Murphy?"

"Yep."

"You reported finding a dead body?"

"Yep."

As the other cop stepped onto the porch, the overhead light illuminated the eighth-inch scar that ran from his left temple to the corner of his mouth, cutting a valley through his thick, brown moustache. He stayed a few feet back, lowered his pistol. But, he kept it firm in his grip as it dangled by his side.

"How did you ascertain that he was dead?" Malone said.

"It's kinda hard to miss."

"Where is he?"

"In the study. Go through the entry and turn left. It's the door on the far left."

I turned to follow Malone when the other cop said, "This is a crime scene. You'll wait out here with me."

Yippee.

The cop backed down the steps, onto the grass. He instructed me to sit on the stairs. I did.

He holstered his pistol and withdrew a small, blue notebook and pen from his breast pocket. He flipped open the notebook, glared at me. "Your full name."

"Jack Murphy. What's yours?"

"Officer Hector Lopez, badge number 97359."

"Nice to meet you Officer Hector Lopez."

"Address."

I gave it to him, followed by my phone number, date of birth, and driver's license number. A brown Chevrolet Caprice rolled into the driveway, stopping just behind the patrol car.

"Stay right here," Lopez said, and walked to the car.

A man in his mid-fifties, nearly bald, complete with a salt and pepper five o'clock shadow and belly that hid his belt, puffed on a cigar. Lopez approached him as he stepped from the driver's seat. They spoke for a moment, then Lopez returned his notebook and pen to his pocket, and greeted the other detective—a six-foot chunk of steel that was well under thirty. Lopez stood near the trunk of the patrol car as the two detectives approached me.

Baldy said, "You're Murphy."

"Yep."

"I'm Detective Schuster." He pointed his thumb over his shoulder. "That is Detective Rock."

How appropriate.

With a gleam in his eye, Rock said, "You found a DB."

"DB?"

"Dead body."

"Oh, sorry. I'm just getting used to all these technical terms. Yes, I did."

Schuster walked past me, into the house. Rock stood a few feet in front of me. He pulled out a notebook similar to Lopez', except the cover of his was red. Maybe notebook color distinguished the detectives from the beat cops.

He gathered the same information Lopez had, then said, "Tell me, Mr. Murphy, why were you here?"

"I was staking out DiMarco."

"Staking out?"

"Yep."

"You have a license to play private dick?"

I grabbed my wallet, flipped it open. He stared at my license for a moment, then copied the number into his notebook.

"Did you inform the police about your stakeout?"

"No."

He glanced up from his notebook, raised his eyebrows. "No? Isn't it customary to inform us when you're playing detective?"

I bit my lower lip. I quickly tired of his cheap shots, but I kept my mouth shut. "Yes, sir, it is. But, I just started the stakeout tonight. I planned on informing the police in the morning if the stakeout was going to continue."

"I guess it won't now."

"Nope."

"Okay," Rock said, flipping his notebook closed, "I'll need you to wait in the car."

"Am I going to the station?"

Rock ignored me, walked to his car, held open the back door. I sat inside.

"Can I play the radio?"

"Just sit here and don't fuck with anything."

He closed the door and walked into the house. I took my cell phone from my pocket and called Tyrone. He wasn't in the office. I explained the situation to the desk sergeant. She said she'd page him.

I lit a cigarette and leaned back in the seat. I knew it was going to be a long night.

I didn't see anyone again until the coroner showed up forty-five minutes later. The crime scene photographer, a black and white, and another car with two poorly-dressed men immediately followed. Maybe they caravanned. I'm sure the neighbors would've gotten a kick out of that.

Shortly after the motley crew disappeared into the house, Schuster came outside, lit the cigar stub hanging from his lips, and opened the car door.

"What a mess," he said.

I got out, stretched my legs. "Yep."

Schuster leaned against the rear quarter-panel, pulled a spiral notebook and pen from his jacket pocket. The cover of this notebook was green. So much for my theory about notebook covers distinguishing job descriptions. Maybe the department was simply being fashionable by offering notebooks in various colors.

"For the record Mr. Murphy . . ."

"Jack."

"Of course, Jack. I should bring you down to the station to take your statement."

"I've always rather enjoyed hot white lights and rubber hoses."

His stare burned into my eyes.

"Sorry, poor shot at humor."

"As I was saying, I should take you to the station, but I'm tired, and if you level with me, we'll talk here and then maybe you can go home."

"Fine with me."

He readied his pen, said, "When did you discover the body?"

"About nine-thirty, give or take a few minutes."

"Give or take." Schuster scribbled in his notebook. "And you called nine-one-one at," he said, pausing to review the notes on a previous page. "Yes, one-thirty."

"Give or take."

"Of course, give or take." He looked over his notebook, caught me square in the eyes. "I wonder, Jack. What did you do for four hours? Give or take."

"I was staking out the place."

"Staking out?"

Not again. "Yep. I'm a private investigator. Your partner already copied down my license number."

"Did you happen to see anything during your stakeout?"

"Yep."

"Care to tell me?"

"Around nine, a black Lexus pulled into the driveway. Two men went inside, stayed a short time. They argued with DiMarco, then shot him and left."

Schuster crooked his eyebrows. "Really?"

"Really."

"I don't suppose you got a license number?"

I thought for a moment about holding back the film until Tyrone showed up. Then again, maybe he wouldn't show up. And I needed some brownie points.

I pulled the roll from my pocket. "Better than that, Detective. I've got a picture of the license plate, along with some of the action inside, and at least one of their faces."

He snatched the roll from my fingers. "What luck."

"Yep. You can thank me for doing your job later."

He smiled. "Now, this thing about you witnessing a murder."

This wasn't going well. I witnessed a crime and didn't report it immediately. I entered the house of the deceased and spent four hours inside before calling the police. I knew what that sounded like. But, when in doubt, the truth is the best policy—especially when you don't know enough about the extenuating circumstances to lie.

"I saw it, yes."

"You called us from a cell phone, right?"

I held up my phone. "Right."

"So, why didn't you call us right away?"

"I knew DiMarco wasn't going anywhere. I had a look around."

His eyebrows went up again. "You what?"

"The two guys left the front door open. I simply walked in."

"The front door was open?"

"Yes, sir."

"And you just walked on in."

"Yep."

Schuster had me repeat my story four more times. He was trying for a fifth, but was interrupted when Tyrone pulled up. He met him halfway to his car. They shook hands.

"Tyrone Williams. How the hell are you?"

"Not bad. You?"

"Hanging in there. I got four years left till thirty. Then, I'm off to Jamaica, man."

His pronunciation of *man* did a Jamaican no justice.

"Ah, de islands, man."

Tyrone was only marginally better.

"What brings Vice's finest over here?"

"We had a sting running on DiMarco. He was knee-deep in shit over some hookers he ran on the boulevard."

"No shit? I thought DiMarco had wiped his ass clean of Vice years ago. Shows you what I know."

"You haven't been in Vice for, like, four years now."

"It shows, too, don't it?"

Schuster gave Tyrone an encapsulated version of the events, then they walked back over to me.

"Hello, Jack."

"Hey, Tyrone."

"You two know each other?"

"Yep."

Schuster looked at Tyrone, narrowed his eyes. "Did you know he was working on DiMarco?"

"We spoke briefly about it."

"He didn't know I was here tonight."

"Thank you, Mr. Murphy." To Tyrone, he said, "A word."

I lit a cigarette. They walked to the front porch. Tyrone had his back to me. I couldn't hear their voices or see Tyrone's expression, but Schuster looked up at me a few times, pointing his finger. When they finished, Tyrone walked back to me alone.

"What's up?" I said.

"How come everyone's dying around you lately, Jack?"

"Luck, I guess."

"Some luck." He leaned against the car. "Until they can verify your photos, you are suspect number one."

"I figured."

"Why did you wait four hours to call it in?"

"I had a look around."

"You broke . . ."

I held up my hands. "Wait a sec, Tyrone. The front door was open. I just walked in to say hi to my good friend."

"DiMarco."

"He let me call him Tony."

"Sure he did." Tyrone glanced at the porch. "They're thinking about taking you in."

"Why?"

"Right place, right time. And, of course, this is murder number two for you."

Schuster had walked up behind Tyrone. He smiled, leaned close, said, "Give or take."

"Fred."

"Sorry, couldn't resist."

Schuster tapped me on the shoulder, walked back to the house.

"You know I didn't do it," I said.

"Do I?"

"What the hell does that mean?"

"Jack, I used to know you. You used to be a nice, quiet private eye chasing bail jumpers, shithead dads and insurance fraud. You remember him? Cause that's the Jack I know. This new you is—what's the word—dangerous."

"Dangerous. Little ole me?"

"Keep being a funny guy. You'll wind up in the slammer for sure."

"C'mon, that's bullshit and you know it."

"You've admitted to being here around nine-thirty. You claim you witnessed his murder, but all you have is a roll of film which may or may not contain anything."

"I know I got the license plate and at least one face."

Tyrone held up a hand. "Prelim coroner reports will place the time of death near enough to your admitted time of arrival that it can't be overlooked."

"I'm the one who called it in, remember?"

"So? It's not unheard of for the murderer to call in the crime, or even to hang out at the scene. They think it makes them look innocent."

I flicked my cigarette into the yard, lit another. "I know that."

He leaned in close, whispered, "Then act like it, goddamn it."

"What do you want me to do?"

Tyrone glanced over my shoulder, then back at me. "I'll talk Schuster out of taking you in tonight. Then, you and I are going to Denny's to have a chat."

"I'm hungry anyway."

Tyrone raised a finger, but before he could say anything, I added, "Sorry. Thank you."

I finished my cigarette as Tyrone went over and spoke with Schuster. I couldn't hear what they were saying, but Schuster was definitely upset. He did appear to respect Tyrone, though.

In the end, Tyrone and I left together.

THIRTY FIVE

"Follow me," Tyrone said as we walked down the drive.

"Sure." With my next step, I remembered Arturo took the van with him. "We could go together, too."

We reached the street. I turned my head to the right and, about a block down, a white Chevy Astrovan.

"As much as I like you, Jack, I want to get home to my wife sometime. I don't need to take you back here after we talk."

"I thought we were going to eat."

Tyrone unlocked the driver's door of his navy Crown Victoria, then climbed in without another word. I jogged back to the Astrovan. Arturo was asleep in the middle bench seat.

"I thought I told you to go home."

Arturo blinked his eyes several times, ran his palms across his face. "What?"

I sat in the driver's seat, closed the door. "I told you to go home."

"Oh, yeah."

I started the engine. "Well, why didn't you?"

"I couldn't leave you hanging, Holmes." He climbed in the passenger seat. "You mighta needed me."

"I wanted you gone for a reason."

I pulled away from the curb. Tyrone was a good two blocks ahead, and the way he was heading was not the way I entered this subdivision, so I didn't want to get lost. Doing forty-five in a twenty-five, I was able to catch up to him as he pulled into southbound traffic on Cahuenga Boulevard.

"Which is?" Arturo said.

Traffic was heavier then normal for this time of morning. I waited for the moment when I could punch the accelerator and zip into a lane. I inched forward with each opportunity gone awry. "Which is what?"

"The reason, Holmes. Why did you want me gone?"

"Look at you."

"Look at me?"

I readied myself as a BMW moved from the right lane to the middle. As I released the brake, a Toyota cut from the middle lane to the right, flipping off the BMW's driver as it passed. I kicked the brake. The van jolted to a sudden stop. I turned to face Arturo. "Yeah, look at you."

"Am I too brown for the job?"

"Fuck you."

"Fuck me? Fuck you."

"Tattooed convicts on parole have no place in a murder investigation. That's all I'm saying."

He looked down at his arms as if admiring them for the first time. "My tats are sweet, though, ain't they, Holmes?"

"They're fucking gorgeous."

"Thank you."

We drove on Cahuenga for about a mile. Tyrone turned into Denny's parking lot. I followed.

"Cool, we're eating," Arturo said, licking his lips.

"Just keep your mouth shut and a smile on your face. Okay? I haven't told Tyrone you were with me yet."

"Feed me and I'll be the happy smiling Mexican."

"Wait in the car a sec."

I parked to the right of Tyrone's car and got out. Tyrone looked me square in the eyes, then past me, then back. His eyes were narrower, darker. "What the fuck, Jack."

"Nothing. Arturo was asleep in the van."

Tyrone walked over to me, set his boot on the van's bumper. "Now I suppose you're going to tell me he wasn't in the house with you."

"No."

"No, what? That's not what you're going to tell me, or he wasn't in the house with you?"

I pulled a cigarette from a pack in my shirt pocket, then a lighter. I held the cigarette between my lips. "No, I won't tell you he wasn't." I lit my cigarette. "It's not a big deal, Tyrone. Arturo's been helping me on this case all along."

Tyrone leaned into me until our noses were almost touching. His gaze jumped from one eye to the other. "We're sitting down inside and you're telling me everything, every fucking thing. Or I'll let homicide have their way with you."

"Don't do that," I said in a falsetto. "I only want you to have your way with me."

He dropped his boot to the asphalt. "Fuck you."

I waved to Arturo. He stepped out of the van. "Everything cool?"

"Just peachy."

We went inside. Tyrone didn't acknowledge us until we'd been seated at a booth in the very back of the restaurant, next to the payphones and restrooms. A good eight tables separated us from any other patrons. Tyrone sat on the far side, strategically placing himself in the exact middle of the cushion. Arturo climbed in opposite Tyrone. I nudged Arturo, sat next to him.

Tyrone buried his head in a menu until the waitress came over. He ordered a coffee and a Grand Slam breakfast. I ordered a Coke. Arturo had ham and eggs, orange juice and coffee. The waitress smiled at us, took the menus and left.

"Well," Tyrone said.

"Well what?" I said.

Arturo was reading an ad card stuck into a clear plastic base. Each side held an advertisement for a different Denny's dessert.

"Well, start at the top and don't leave anything out."

"Even what you already know?"

"Don't leave anything out."

"I was hired to find Carrie Sanders. She disappeared on Halloween and there's reason to believe she came to LA. The PI who was originally on the case, Phillip Jenkins, was killed in Hollywood."

Tyrone's eyes burned intently on my own. "Go on."

"I did some checking on the street and came up with the name Donovan. I found him in a house on La Mirada Avenue off Vine. He gave up DiMarco."

The waitress came back with our drinks. We all smiled at her. When she left, I continued.

"DiMarco basically told me to go fuck myself. I found out he was being paid twenty-five hundred a week from Diamond Steel Security, even though he has no prior security experience. I thought that was strange, so I checked into DSS. That's when you ran Blake's prints for me. Turns out that DSS is owned by BEI, Blake Enterprises Incorporated, which is wholly owned by Charles Blake. I went to question Blake. He wanted me to fuck myself, too."

"Becoming a common theme with you, ain't it?"

A small smile formed on Arturo's lips, but his eyes remained focused on the dessert ad. I made a mental note to tell Denny's the trance this advertisement inflicted on my friend.

When I didn't continue again, Tyrone said, "Well, I'm waiting."

"Are we off the record here?"

"Off the record? Why? What the hell's going on?"

"Look, my job is to find Carrie. Nothing else. I told you already I'd give you any busts that come up, but I can't have this thing get way out of hand until I find her."

"What thing? What's getting out of hand are all the dead bodies showing up around you."

"Are we off the record?"

"Fuck," Tyrone said. "Yes."

"A couple guys showed up at my office shortly after I took the case. They offered to pay me off. I refused. So, they grabbed me off the street and tried a different approach."

"They kicked your ass," Tyrone said through a small smile.

"Yep."

"This is what you want to be off the record about?"

"You said mention everything."

"Right."

I reached for a cigarette, but left it there. I couldn't smoke inside the restaurant anyway. "We were following DiMarco. We saw him pick up three girls in a downtown warehouse. He took them to Donovan's old place on La Mirada Avenue, where I believe they were filmed. In the meantime, DiMarco goes to the Four Seasons and drops off an envelope for someone with the initials RL."

"What was in the envelope?"

"Cash is my guess."

Tyrone nodded. I continued. "DiMarco goes back to the house, picks up the girls, and take them to Blake."

"How old were these girls?"

"You know how old."

"Tell me again, damn it." ·

"Sixteen, tops. They stay at Blake's a while, then Blake takes them to Van Nuys Airport. I call you to shut down the airport, but you fail. And he flies away with them."

"You could've given me more notice."

"And you could've worked harder at it."

The veins in Tyrone's temples swelled. He started to say something, but stopped.

"I'm sorry," I said. "I know you did what you could."

"So did you, Jack."

We sat in silence a moment, then Tyrone said, "I can get a copy of the flight plan they filed."

"But what good would it do? If he's smart, and I'm sure he is, he would've filed double, or even triple plans so no one could easily track him."

The waitress delivered the food. Tyrone and Arturo both ate without taking their eyes off their plates. I received two half-hearted grunts when I told them I'd be outside having a cigarette.

When I returned, they were both finished eating.

"So," Tyrone said, "you think Blake killed DiMarco?"

"Maybe, though I'm not sure of motive. DiMarco wasn't about to tell us anything."

"But Blake's working for DiMarco in some kind of kiddie ring."

"Or DiMarco's working for Blake. Or they're working together. But, something was definitely going on."

"What did you find in DiMarco's place?"

Another moment of truth. I didn't want to give up what I rightfully found, albeit illegally. But I didn't want to impede an official investigation, either. "A ledger."

"Where is it?"

"In the van."

"Go get it."

"Hang on a sec, Tyrone. I'll give it to you, but I want copies of it, all of it, today. Agreed?"

"Look, Jack. You're in no position to bargain here. If it wasn't for my sweet black ass, you'd be getting puked on by drunks in the holding cell by now."

"Okay, but it ties together some leads I have. There are primarily two sets of initials in it—RL and CB."

"So?"

"RL. Same as the envelope DiMarco dropped off. And CB. Charles Blake."

"That's a long shot."

"Maybe, but it's all we got. And it fits with what we know so far."

"What else do you have?"

"Nothing."

"I don't believe you."

"I told you I'd give you any busts that come up. Believe me, I want these bastards nailed to the wall. I just want Carrie first."

"So what're you holding back?"

"Nothing you could use."

"I'll be the judge of that."

"A key."

"To what?"

"Dunno."

"Bullshit."

"A safe deposit box key."

"I want it."

I leaned forward. "Look. I believe I can use it to further my investigation. And what I find might help you as well. I'm asking for three days. Then, I'll give you the key and whatever I find out."

The waitress came around and offered coffee. Everyone declined. When she was out of earshot, Tyrone said, "How do you know Carrie wasn't flown to wherever like the other girls?"

"I don't."

"How do you know Blake or DiMarco are even involved in Carrie's disappearance?"

"Except for Donovan's shaky testimony, I don't."

"What the hell do you know?"

I thought for a minute before responding. What did I know? "Pretty much nothing."

"Yet you've gotten yourself in deep shit with two, count them two, separate murder investigations. You're quite a piece of work, Jack."

"Thanks."

Tyrone paid the check and we walked to the parking lot. Arturo got inside the van. I walked Tyrone to his car.

"What do you know?" I said. "Off the record."

Tyrone unlocked his car, opened the door, and leaned against it. "I don't know shit. DiMarco's a pimp. That much we know, but not underage shit. Blake's clean as a fucking whistle."

"Apparently."

"It remains that way until we can prove something."

"We?"

Tyrone looked up at me. "What?"

"You said 'we'. You gonna work with me on this?"

"There's no working with you. I'm a cop, you're not."

"Thanks for clearing that up."

"Christ, this is fucked up."

I lit a cigarette. "Yep."

"No one's gonna want to pursue this, you know."

"I do?"

"I told you about Blake—largest single contributor to the Benevolent Fund."

"That's right. Cops don't want to shake their money tree."

"Fuck you."

"Isn't that what you're saying?"

"I'm saying he's clean. Or at least appears to be. So, nothing happens until there's concrete proof."

"These are underage girls."

"I know. That's fucked up, too. Just like this whole goddamn City of Angels. One big, fucked up, black hole of shit."

"Very poetic."

He glanced at the sky. "It's gonna be light soon. You might consider some sleep."

"I might. You, too."

"Where do you think I'm going? Home to my wife, and my bed."

"By the way, did you get anything on Jimmy?"

"I don't know. I gave what I had to Narco. I'll hear something in a few days, probably."

Tyrone got in his car, closed the door and rolled down the window. "I want that key Tuesday at racquetball."

"Okay."

"When I whoop your sorry white ass."

I walked around the hood as he started the engine and backed out. By the time I got in the van, he was deep into traffic on Cahuenga.

"Well?" Arturo said.

"Well, nothing. No one knows shit."

"At least we ain't alone in the boat."

I backed out of the parking space, turned on Cahuenga, and headed for my apartment.

THIRTY SIX

I fell asleep at about six to the ethereal sounds of Enigma. Next thing I knew I was sitting upright in bed, heart pounding, sweat wetting my brow. I stood next to the bed, searched the room with blurry vision. Something snapped me awake, and made me panic. Then, I realized the phone was ringing.

"Yeah?"

"Jack, it's Tyrone."

"What time is it?"

"About quarter to eight. You were sleeping, I suppose."

I scratched my head. "I was."

"You're too fucking lucky. Soon as I got home, they called me again. Now I'm at the Santa Monica Pier."

"Okay."

"Are you awake?"

"I am now."

"Are you sure?"

"Of course, I'm sure."

"Good. Then get down here now."

"Are you serious?"

I heard a scurry of muffled voices in the background. Tyrone said, "Hang on a sec."

I did.

"Jack, you're interested in closing your case, right?"

"Of course."

"Then get your ass down here."

He didn't elaborate. He hung up.

"What's up, Holmes?" Arturo said.

"Tyrone wants me down at Santa Monica Pier."

"Now?"

"Now."

Arturo jumped to his feet, slipped one leg in his Levi's, then the other. "Let's rock."

The haze in my brain slowly lifted. I found my pants, slid into them. I went to my closet and grabbed a fresh shirt, then went to the bathroom and splashed cold water on my face. I was almost awake. A latte and a cigarette or two and I'd be fine, more or less.

I wiped my eyes, yawned, and grabbed my keys from the counter in the kitchen. I lit a cigarette and enjoyed the first, crisp hit of the day. The smoke whirled round my lungs. I grabbed my Sig, a jacket, and said, "Okay, let's go."

Morning traffic on the freeway is not something I often subject myself to. Today was no different. I drove Wilshire Boulevard west, through the Miracle Mile, past the La Brea Tar Pits, through Beverly Hills, Westwood. The traffic thickened around the UCLA campus and well beyond the 405 freeway.

After what seemed like hours, but was about forty minutes, I turned left on Ocean Boulevard. Crowds of people had gathered in Palisades Park, and traffic stood still. I rolled down my window, listened to the morning waves crash against the beach.

The police had cordoned off the Pier. The stoplights were flashing red while policemen stood in the middle of intersections, pleaded with the traffic to cooperate. I spotted Tyrone's Crown Victoria just to the left of the Pier entrance. I pulled behind it, flipped on my hazard lights. I barely had one foot on the asphalt when a cop rushed me.

"Hey, you can't park there."

"I'm here to see Tyrone Williams."

The cop stood in front of me, breathing hard. "I don't give a shit who you're here to see, you can't park there."

"Where am I supposed to park, then?"

"Not my problem. Just not there."

I looked beyond the cop, tried to peer through the crowds of people and police vehicles, hoping to spot Tyrone. No luck.

"Jack," Arturo said, "I'll drive around while you talk to Tyrone."

The cop stared at Arturo as if unsure whether to thank him or tell him to shut up. He looked back at me. "Leave the car there and it will be towed."

He held my stare for a moment, then walked back to the Pier's entrance. Waiting for me to try and get beyond the barrier, I was sure.

Arturo walked to the driver's side. I handed him the keys. "I'm not sure how you're going to drive around in this shit."

"You want me to wait somewhere?"

"Why don't you park over in the Third Street Promenade? Go back down Ocean to Wilshire and turn right. Parking is between second and fourth. Park anywhere. I'll come over and find you."

"Okay, boss."

He smiled, then hopped in the truck.

"Hey."

He closed the door, looked at me through the open window. "Yeah?"

"Don't fuck up my truck."

"Ye of little faith."

"Whatever. Just be careful with her."

"Her?"

"My truck."

His mouth formed an O, his eyes bright, wide. "Okay."

As I walked up to the Pier, I noticed the only person who seemed to be having a good day was a hot dog vendor that had set up his cart on the edge of Palisades Park. He smiled, served the growing line of angry people complaining about the nerve of the police to shut down the Pier. I heard one especially loud woman swear she'd write her councilman about this grave injustice. She was in her late forties, her weight being highlighted by her entirely too small Playland Arcade t-shirt and jeans. Her age and attitude told me she was likely an owner.

The happy-go-lucky cop on parking detail met me at the barricade. In case he'd forgotten, I said, "I'm here to see Detective Tyrone Williams."

"I'll need to see some ID."

I pulled out my wallet, flipped it open. On the left side, my driver's license. On the right, my PI license. I kept my gun permit behind the PI license. I found displaying it to scare more than impress, so I only showed it when specifically asked for it.

This guy wasn't impressed by my PI license, either.

"Wait here." Just to be sure I understood, he pointed to the ground where my feet stood. "And I mean here."

The cop took a few steps. He leaned over to another cop, whispered something, then both of them looked at me, and smiled. I smiled back. What fun it is to deal with cops.

I looked back toward the street and found Arturo inching his way onto Ocean Boulevard. I didn't think it possible, but it looked as though the traffic worsened in the few minutes I was here.

I smoked two cigarettes during the fifteen minutes that I waited for Mr. Happy-Go-Lucky to return. His face bore a frown, and his tight lip and locked jawbone made it clear that he was not happy about my interrupting his Hilterian parking patrol. I'm sure his eyes bore similar hatred, but they were buried so deep beneath blackened glasses I couldn't be sure.

We walked down the pier. I took a deep breath of salty sea air, savored the scent as it filled my nostrils. I always admired the hypnotic draw of the ocean. It lured millions to its shorelines. These millions then put up with horrendous traffic, crime, drugs, prostitution, and gangs, just to be near her. If she left, so too would most, if not all, of the population. Or, at least I would.

A makeshift command post was set up along the wall of Sinbad's. Tyrone was talking with two other men and a woman, none of whom I recognized. Tyrone pointed to a large, crude schematic of the pier with a pen.

As I approached, they stared at me. And stopped talking.

"Hey, Tyrone."

"Jack." He took a step toward me. "Let's take a walk."

We walked down the pier. Ten-foot lengths of yellow caution tape were strung along the end of the pier. Two men and a woman, all in Coast Guard uniforms, stood near the tape, watched a crane in the water.

"What happened?" I said.

Tyrone leaned against the railing. "A car went off the pier."

He held his Bic to a cigar, puffed furiously. Once the stogie was lit, he drew a big hit, let it float around in his mouth, and blew it above his head. The smoke dissipated into the cool breeze that floated off the ocean. "Seems a guy and a girl got drunk, then drove straight into the water."

"Why are you here?"

"One Jorge Marcia, big time pimp and card shark. Witnesses gave a description of the guy that pretty much matches Jorge. Someone got the license plate from the car. It's his."

"Why am I here?"

"The girl he was with is a dead ringer for your Carrie Sanders. In fact," he said, pulled a baggie from his jacket pocket, "we found this."

I took the baggie. Inside was a gold bracelet. The engraving on the front said *Carrie Sanders*. I turned the baggie over and looked at the back. *Our angel, all our love.*

"We found it right about where the car went over the side."

"Really."

"Kinda interesting that it happened to fall out of the car just before it plunged into the ocean."

I handed the baggie back. "Yep."

The Santa Monica Pier was quite a tourist attraction as well as a hang out for fishermen, artists, street vendors and the homeless. And, being open late every night, I was sure the pier was crowded when the incident occurred. "Did the car take anybody out?"

"Surprisingly, no. I guess they raced around a little bit first, so everyone was clinging to the railings by the time they made the final run."

I looked back down the pier. The majority of it was off limits to vehicles, except for the occasional maintenance truck. With a police substation at the foot of the pier, I wondered where the cops were during all this.

I leaned over the railing, noticed metal plates jetting out from under the pier. "Lucky he cleared the plates."

"A diver was down earlier, says he found no scratch marks on any of the plates, like the driver knew how fast he'd have to travel to clear them."

"Interesting."

"There's another piece to this puzzle."

"Which is?"

"No bodies."

"What?"

"The Coast Guard found the car in minutes, but no bodies."

"Which means?"

He turned and stared into my eyes. "Which means, nothing really. The ME said the tides could have easily washed the bodies out to . . ." He pointed out, across the water. "To there, somewhere."

"Are they going to search for the bodies?"

"Oh, yeah, they'll start as soon as the car's up. They won't find shit, though. They've already said that. It's simply a gesture of goodwill on behalf of the victims' families."

"Convenient that the bracelet was left behind."

"Fuck yes, it is." Tyrone dangled the baggie between his fingers. "Even without bodies, though, this'll seal the coffin on Carrie, so to speak."

"It smells of setup."

"Maybe, maybe not."

"Bullshit. For sure."

"Truth is, Jack, no one will care. Carrie's name will go on the report, and you'd be wise to close your case."

"Why?"

"Because you won't find a cop in this whole fucking shithole who'll give you an inch. Everyone's going to believe the girl's dead, and you're a nutcase for continuing to search."

"Nice to know."

"Hey, I felt you were straight with me last night, and I'm returning the favor."

"I appreciate that."

We watched the Coast Guard work for several minutes. Tyrone puffed his cigar. I smoked a cigarette.

"It's not over," he said.

"What's that?"

"This shit with DiMarco and Blake. If there's something there, I'm going to find it."

"There is something there. I saw it."

"I'll take boatloads of shit for it, but I'll drive Blake into the ground if it's the last thing I do."

"I hope you do."

"I will. No one's gonna sell young girls in my neck of the woods."

"I'm glad to hear it."

"But you. That's a different story."

"What about me?"

"I don't want no more dead bodies turning up around you. Got it?"

"What can I do about it?"

"Back the fuck off."

"That depends."

Tyrone clenched his cigar between his teeth, stared at me. "On?"

"On if my client wants me to continue."

"Jesus, Jack, the girl's dead."

"Maybe."

"Maybe nothing."

"What's the chance of that bracelet falling out like that?"

"Slim to none. But, did you ever think that maybe Carrie threw it on the pier so her parents could stop worrying?"

"Nope."

"Maybe you should. It's possible she had a heart."

"Sure it is."

"You don't buy it."

"Nope. But, it's not up to me."

"It's up to your client."

"Exactly."

"Don't fuck around here, Jack. I can't keep bailing your ass out. You're number one on the hit list for two separate murders. Jesus, how much shit do you want to get yourself in, anyway?"

"Less than I'm already in, so what's another couple feet?"

"Suffocation, my friend. Keep going at this pace, you'll be out of air by the end of the month."

I crushed my cigarette under my shoe. "Thanks for letting me know about this."

"Our deal still stands, right?"

"What's that?"

"You give me everything you get, I take down whoever needs to be taken down."

"Sure, Tyrone, sure."

THIRTY SEVEN

I caught up with Arturo in the Promenade after half an hour of walking aimlessly amongst the multitude of cars. He was speaking Spanish to a girl, early twenties, with brunette hair, straight as an arrow, down to her waist. She smiled, laughed. As I approached, she turned to me. Her blue eyes dazzled in the sunlight.

"Hey, Holmes," Arturo said. "Meet Michelle. Michelle, this is *me hombre* Jack."

"Hello, Jack."

"Hi."

Her voice was soft, deep, sexy. She extended a long, slender hand. I shook it. She held my gaze for a few moments, then said, "Nice to meet you."

I smiled. Arturo handed me the keys. I waited in the truck while he spoke with Michelle for a few minutes longer. Then, she leaned forward, looked up at me, kissed his cheek. She smiled at him, then me. And disappeared back into the crowd.

"Sweet girl," I said as Arturo climbed into the truck.

"Damn right, Holmes, but enough about her. What's up with the *policia*?"

"A car went off the pier last night. Cops are pretty sure Carrie was inside."

"Pretty sure," he said. He closed the door and I started the engine. "What about you, Holmes? You pretty sure, too?"

I pulled out of the parking space and maneuvered my way to Wilshire. "I don't know." I waited for a clearing in the traffic, then jetted into the near lane. "A bit too contrived."

"Are you gonna tell me or do I have to guess?"

I changed lanes. "It might be fun watching you try."

"Yeah, yeah. So?"

"So, a girl matching Carrie's description was seen last night getting drunk with some pimp named Jorge. Jorge and the girl are in the car, then suddenly drive into the ocean."

"They were wasted."

"They were, supposedly. The kicker is that they found an ID bracelet almost exactly where the car went over the side."

"Carrie's bracelet."

"It said Carrie Sanders, yes."

"What's the big mystery, though? Is it her, or ain't it?"

"Don't know."

"Why not?"

"The Coast Guard can't find either body. Just the car."

"No shit? I see what you mean."

Arturo spent the remainder of the drive back to the office staring out the window. I thought about what I knew, and what I didn't know. And how this whole case seemed a bit easy from the start. And how things have been easy and yet so baffling. I was thinking so much my head hurt. I turned up the CD player. James McMurtry sang about life in the plains. I tried to bury myself in his misery, even if only for the ride back to the office.

I parked the truck and we walked inside. Nadia was typing on her keyboard, phone perched on her shoulder. She glanced at us and smiled, not cold yet not warm either. Her typing was even and quick.

I walked into my office, dumped the old coffee out of Mr. Coffee, and brewed a fresh pot. I lit a cigarette and sat at my desk. A small pile of mail had gathered on my otherwise clean desktop. I knew Nadia had been in here, cleaning, filing, tidying up. She must have been upset. She always cleans when she's upset, rarely when she's not.

Arturo sat in a side chair, crossed his legs at the ankles, and stretched out. For a minute, I thought he might grab a *siesta*, but his eyes remained open, focused on Mr. Coffee as it brewed a new batch of energy.

As always, most of the mail was junk. Letters telling me I'd won a million dollars, or offering me an exclusive membership that only preferred individuals receive, an urgent telegram from a book club stating I hadn't paid for my last book of the month—the same club that six months ago refused to acknowledge my request for cancellation. I grabbed a black Sharpie from my top drawer, scratched out the address and marked it *Return to Sender*. After three phone calls, four letters, and a whole lot of frustration, I had invested enough time into this issue. I dropped the envelope in the wire basket on the corner of my desk—outgoing mail.

The last envelope, opened and attached to a photocopy, was from Raymond Sanders. Nadia copied the check, attached the envelope to it, and left it for me to see. Normally, she would file these, but this had a personal note from Raymond, and I suppose she thought I should read it.

Mr. Murphy, enclosed please find a check to replenish my retainer with your firm. I am grateful for all the work you've done to date, and sincerely hope you are able to end this case successfully. Yours, Raymond Sanders.

Me, too, Raymond.

Mr. Coffee finished its work. Arturo poured two cups, handed one to me.

"Figure we'll need a lot of this today," he said.

I raised my Styrofoam cup in a toast, then sipped the steaming coffee. I set the cup on my desk and took a hit from my cigarette.

"I guess I should call Roy, let him know what happened."

"You want me to wait outside?"

"Either way."

I picked up the phone and dialed Roy's home number. He answered on the second ring.

"Hey, Jack, I was beginning to worry."

"Why?"

"I hadn't heard from you in a while. You have some news, I presume."

"It's not good."

Roy was silent for a moment, then said, "What?"

I told him of the incident at the Santa Monica Pier and the bracelet. I kept my personal thoughts to myself.

"So that's it. All this work and she drives herself off the pier."

"He was driving. But, yeah, that's what it looks like."

"I'll call Raymond. Damn, he's gonna be heartbroken."

"I'm sure."

"Let me ask you, Jack," he said. I heard a door close in the background. "What's the chance it wasn't her?"

"Hard to say. The police are naming her in the report. They do have the bracelet."

"Right, right. Damn shame. I always pegged the kid as being smarter than that."

"Even smart people do stupid things."

"Do you think she was using drugs?"

"I have no idea. I didn't get that far."

"What was this guy's name?"

"Jorge Marcia."

"Hmm," he said, paused for so long I thought maybe he'd hung up. "Don't recognize that name."

"Why would you?"

"Oh, no reason. Just my old cop mind at work. Jack?"

"Yeah."

"Fax over your final bill tonight. I'll see that Raymond pays it promptly."

"No worries. He just sent me another retainer check. I'll owe him some money."

"Okay. Listen, I'm sorry things didn't turn out better, but at least it's over. Take care."

Click.

I sat back, put my legs atop my desk. I wasn't sure how I felt. Weird, that's the best way to describe it. I had never had a case end so abruptly. I was baffled that a case could screech to a halt with so many unanswered questions, so many vile people and vile activities, and a dead girl. Girls died every day in the streets and, as most of America, I watched it with a pitying eye, then switched to *Late Night with Bill Maher*. Though I'd never met Carrie, I'd become emotionally attached somehow. I wanted to find her. And I had. But, I wanted to find her alive. And I hadn't.

Everything about the pier smelled of setup. The why was a given. Someone wanted me off the case. Probably wanted Raymond to stop hiring PIs altogether. What better way to stop us all from digging than to stage the girl's death? It certainly would explain the lack of bodies. But, it would take pros, not only to plan the incident, but to pull it off as well. Tyrone seemed pretty sure the pimp Jorge went down in the car. Could he have been good enough to pull off a stunt like this? Again, the why was easy— money. I could even see Carrie agreeing with this plan, for money, loyalty, or just because she was scared of whoever asked this of her. But could a sixteen-year-old girl have the wherewithal to do it? To agree to plunge into the cold ocean in a speeding car, then try and swim to safety? No one mentioned either of them wearing wetsuits, so they'd have had to put them on while underwater or risk hypothermia. Then, they'd have to grab scuba gear from the car and swim away. All while the car was plunging to the ocean floor. Risky. And doubtful. And if they did, where the hell would they go now that they were supposedly dead?

Then again, maybe I was manufacturing things that just weren't there. The ME seemed ready to buy the fact that the tide pulled the bodies out of the car, deeper into the ocean. Why couldn't I buy it as easily? Why couldn't I buy it at all?

"You're thinking again," Arturo said.

He came back in the office. I hadn't realized he'd left.

"Yep."

"From the look on your face, I'd say you're having trouble swallowing this shit."

"Yep."

"So, what are we gonna do about it?"

"I don't know."

He sat down. "Why not?"

I set my feet back on the floor, sipped my coffee. "It's one thing to chase pipedreams when someone else is footing the bill. But, without Raymond's *carte blanche*, how far can we pursue this?"

"We're not chasing a pipedream. I've had some of those and I know one when I see it. This is real shit."

"We don't even know if those girls were underage. For all we know, they were young hookers on a daytrip to Vegas with Blake."

"I see your point."

"I wish I had some bucks tucked away so I could bring this to a close on my own, but I don't. And we all need to eat."

Arturo slapped his belly. "We sure do. Speaking of which . . ."

"Yeah, yeah. You want me to order pizza?"

"Anything, Holmes. Just get some food in me before I pass out."

I walked into the reception area. Nadia had stopped typing. She doodled on a notepad and talked in a low voice on the phone. In front of her face, locks of wavy brunette hair dangled. I don't know why I so seldom noticed it, but she was a beautiful girl. She saw me, straightened, and ended her call.

"You didn't have to do that."

"I know," she said. "It was just Sylvia. Guy problems."

"You feel like eating some pizza?"

"Sure."

Her voice was non-combatant, unemotional, just one coworker speaking with another. I wished she was angry, emotional, something. I was fighting with everything inside me to remain calm. Seeing her like that made me want to scream. Instead, I went back into my office and ordered a large pizza and a six-pack of Coke.

When the driver showed, I handed him a twenty, told him to keep the change. Then, Nadia followed me into my office. I set the pizza on my desk. Nadia sat in the side chair next to Arturo. They exchanged smiles. I grabbed three paper plates from the cabinet under the coffee machine, set them next to the pizza box. Arturo already had the lid flipped and his hand on a piece. He threw three pieces on his plate, sat down. I put two on a plate and handed it to Nadia. She dispensed a quick thanks. Her gaze remained on the floor. I grabbed two pieces for myself and sat back in my chair.

We ate in silence. Arturo and I both had seconds. Nadia ate only two pieces. She always eats only two pieces. I finished my Coke, threw the can and my plate in the wastebasket.

"So, where to go from here," I said. Nadia got up to leave. "Don't you want in on this conversation?"

She walked to the door. With her hand on the knob, she turned to me. "I'm staying out of it."

"Wait."

She walked out, closed the door.

"You really pissed her off, Holmes."

"Yep."

"What did you say?"

"I thought this case was getting too dangerous and I asked her to confine her activities to the office."

"Ouch."

I lit a cigarette and wondered how much I could actually accomplish with the rest of the day. Eating always makes me sleepy, and I pondered going home to catch some zees. I told Arturo. He thought it was a great idea.

We ate the last two slices of pizza, then I threw the box away, brushed the crumbs from my desk.

"You ready?" I said.

"Of course."

Then, the phone rang. Nadia picked it up after only one ring. I stood there, stared at the phone. Line one flashed, the intercom beeped, then Nadia said, "Raymond Sanders is on one."

"Thank—"

She hung up.

I sat down, picked up the line.

"Hello, Mr. Sanders."

"Mr. Murphy, I'm glad I caught you."

"What's up?"

Raymond spoke slowly, quietly. "Roy called me."

"I'm sorry to be the bearer of such bad news."

"From what I understand, facts are vague."

"To some degree, yes."

"I'd like to hear the whole story from you, if you don't mind."

"Not at all."

I recounted everything about the pier incident. As with Roy, I left out my personal thoughts. He did a lot of "uh-huh", and "I see", but offered no commentary of his own, until I was finished.

"It's simply not possible," he said.

"What's not?"

"It wasn't Carrie."

"What about the bracelet?"

"Oh, I have no doubt the bracelet is hers. That is exactly the way we had it engraved. But, it wasn't Carrie."

"I understand your frustration."

"Frustration, nothing. Carrie would never do something like that."

"Sometimes people do strange things for reasons apparent only to themselves."

"Not Carrie. Not this. She was scared to death of water. Not just oceans, mind you, water of any kind. We had a hell of a time getting her into the tub when she was little. Although she eventually got to the point where she'd bathe or shower on her own, she never liked one minute of it. No, sir, she would much rather have gone dirty than had to get near water."

"Why is that?"

"When she was two, she fell into a pool and nearly drowned."

That blew my theory of Carrie staging the incident. "I see."

"Mr. Murphy, do you still work for me?"

"If you want me to, yes."

"I do. Yes, sir, I do. Until the police can come up with Carrie's body, you are to proceed under the assumption that my little girl is still alive. And, don't you worry about the expense. As before, you do what you need to do and I'll see to it you're compensated." He paused, then added, "Please, don't give up."

I hated the idea of taking someone's money when I knew it would lead nowhere, but this little twang in my gut told me it might lead somewhere. At least I'd be able to put to rest all the other issues that had arisen. And even if I couldn't find Carrie, I might be able to take down some pedophiles, if that's what they were. I felt lightheaded, sick to my stomach.

"I will, Mr. Sanders. I will."

"One other thing. Effective immediately, I am offering a three-million-dollar reward for the return of Carrie." He stopped, then added in a whisper, "Dead or alive."

"That's not necessary, Mr. Sanders."

"Don't tell me what's necessary, goddamn it."

I lit a cigarette, let things cool a second.

"I'm sorry. I'm just wound up pretty tight these days."

"I understand."

"The money's yours, if you can bring me Carrie."

"I'll do my best."

"Thank you. And God bless."

He hung up. I held the phone to my ear for a while, listened to dead air.

"So," Arturo said, "what now?"

"We're still on the case. And now there's a reward."

"Cool. What's next?"

"We still have the ledger and the safe deposit box key."

"I've been thinking about that."

"Watch out."

"Hey, fuck you, Holmes. I'm getting pretty good at this thinking thing."

"Uh-huh."

He ignored me. "We can get into the bank."

"We ain't going in with AK-47s."

"Hell, no, Holmes. I got a plan."

Great. More than I had, but still.

THIRTY EIGHT

I drove east on Wilshire Boulevard downtown, past the Good Samaritan Hospital, the 110, and the Omni Hotel. At Figueroa, I turned left to 6th Street, then right. Figueroa marked the start of the one-way streets that cut through downtown Los Angeles, streets I hated. I sat at the light at Grand Avenue, peered at the black IMM building. Nearly every window glowed from the overhead fluorescents in the offices. Coupled with its dark exterior and the almost black night, the windows appeared to be floating in the air.

We were about to embark on Arturo's plan—find the Evergreen forger, Eddie, then use him to somehow get into DiMarco's safe deposit box. He told me his plan in my office. I wasn't impressed. Nor, however, could I offer an alternative. Reluctantly, I agreed to take the first step, only the first step, and see where it led, if anywhere. I had no doubt Arturo could locate Eddie "the Hand", nor did I doubt he'd think Arturo *loco* for asking him to try and pull this off.

The light changed. I continued on 6th through downtown. At the Los Angeles River, 6th became Whittier Boulevard. I continued past the interchange of freeways 101, 5, 10, and 60, commonly referred to as the East LA Interchange, though East LA is much closer to the 710 than this interchange.

I was halfway into the intersection at Soto Street when Arturo said, "Left, Holmes, left."

Fortunately, oncoming traffic was light. I pulled hard to the left, my tires squealed.

"Pay attention, Holmes."

"Me? You're the one that knows where we're going." I glanced at him. "Next time, tell me before I enter the intersection, okay?"

We hadn't yet passed the Lincoln Hospital Medical Center when Arturo pointed through the front window, said, "See the light up there. That's fourth, make a right."

I did.

He told me to turn left on Evergreen, just past the Evergreen Recreation Center. The city's face had grown wearier, older, dirtier. Arturo had me pull to the curb in front of La Cabaña Restaurant. I waited in the red zone as he sprinted inside. A couple minutes later, he jumped back in the car.

"Okay, Holmes, straight ahead."

When we crossed First Street, the streets turned violent, ugly. Most of the street lights were burned out, or shot out. Some of the homes and businesses had installed flood lights near their property, so most of the tattoos on the walls were apparent—black spray paint displaying the insignia of a particular gang. Many insignias had been desecrated by a large X, another one of different shape and size near it. Rivals or competing artists, I couldn't be sure.

Two blocks down, and on the left, were the Evergreen Apartments. A tattered 18-unit, two-story structure that fifty years ago may have been pristine white. Gang insignias not only covered nearly every inch of block-wall around the building, but more than half of the doors to the apartments as well. A group of young Latino men smoked a joint as they leaned against the block-wall, stared me down. Again, Arturo left me to wait. Like a bright light in an otherwise dim hallway, my whiteness glowed in this neighborhood.

Arturo knocked on the door to unit 17, spoke to an attractive young lady for a minute, then came back to the car. Directly behind him, a 300-pound bald and shirtless Latino. Tattoos ran from his neck down his chest and back, and bounced as his muscles flexed.

"Park here, Holmes."

"What?"

"Park here. We gotta walk."

"Are you nuts?" I realized my voice was loud—the wall-of-a-man picked up on it. I lowered it a notch. "I'm not leaving my fucking truck here."

"Don't worry about it, Holmes. Popeye's gonna sit with it."

"That makes me feel much better."

"Nothing's gonna happen."

"Easy for you to say. It's not your truck."

"Would I fuck with you, Holmes?"

I knew he wouldn't, but a sharp pain poked at my gut telling me Arturo wasn't who I needed to worry about. I rolled up the windows, stepped from the truck, and set the alarm. My hand went to the small of my back. I relaxed a little as my fingers caressed my Sig.

After a few steps, I turned to look back at my truck. Popeye leaned against the hood, a foot on the bumper, his back to us. Across the top third of his skin, shoulder-to-shoulder, a tattoo spelled "Evergreen". The tattoo of a lifer. If Arturo trusted him, so did I.

Across the street stood the ornate, gothic gates to the Evergreen Cemetery. The concrete on either side of the main gate sported carved gargoyles. Stretched between the beasts were two four-foot wide wrought iron gates, clasped together by half-inch chain and a huge padlock. On either side of the main gate stood smaller, matching walk-through gates. We crossed the street, and a sign hanging from the main gate came into focus. In red block letters on white metal: *Police Patrolled. Cemetery Closes at 4:30 p.m. sharp.*

Arturo stopped in front of one of the walk-through gates. He pulled a key from his pocket, unlocked the padlock. He swung open the gate, stepped aside. "After you."

"Gee, thanks."

I stepped into the cemetery and immediately felt as though I was trespassing. Which, of course, I was. I had not been inside a cemetery at night since I was seventeen and very drunk. That night, a group of us swore we saw the ghost of the Scarlet Woman, a ninety-year-old lady said to haunt a cemetery back in Lake Point. I wondered what I'd see that night.

The mortuary-slash-funeral home sat just inside the gate. Just past the building, the street split, allowing traffic to head either to the left or right. Arturo relocked the padlock, and we headed right.

"Why do you walk around with a key to a cemetery?"

"It ain't mine."

"Sounds like something you'd say to the cops."

"Maybe. But, really it ain't. Gabriela gave it to me."

"The girl at the apartment?"

"Cute, ain't she? But her boyfriend is mucho grande, so don't get no ideas."

"You saying that for my benefit? Or yours?"

The freshly-topped asphalt snaked through well-manicured grass. Many of the headstones were upright, some standing twenty, thirty feet in the air. A few low-wattage lights were scattered about, and I caught the dates on some of the headstones. Most dated back to the 20s and 30s. Trees were in abundance—acacias, poplars, oaks, palms. A few of the gravesites were monuments, complete with tombs and small fences cordoning off the parcels. Some even had walk-in structures.

In the center of the cemetery stood a single-story building. It reminded me of the two-bedroom homes that were common to this area, except for the wrought iron gates at the top of the concrete steps.

"It's a chapel," Arturo said.

"We're going inside?"

"Of course."

We walked up the steps, stopped at the entrance to the chapel. In the front pew sat three men, two women and a little boy. Arturo pointed to the man on the left.

"That's Sniper," he whispered. "The one next to him is Elbow. Then, it's Hand, his wife, her sister and his son."

"Where do these guys get these names?"

"Popeye liked the cartoon. Sniper is just that, a sniper. Elbow can get an elbow of marijuana, quarter pound, in ten minutes flat." He touched my shoulder. "It all makes perfect sense, really."

"Yep."

Elbow glanced up at us, then tapped Hand's arm. They both sprinted toward us, each throwing their arms around Arturo. They spoke in Spanish, hugging, not yet realizing Arturo was for real, not yet realizing a white man stood in their presence.

I stepped back and lit a cigarette. When their reunion was complete, Elbow pointed at me, said; "Who's he, *esse?*"

"*Me hombre* Jack."

Elbow and Hand eyed me a full minute. I nodded, smoked my cigarette.

"Hand," Arturo said, "we need you."

"We?"

"We, I. I'm doing the asking, okay?"

"*Sí,*" Hand said.

Elbow just stared.

Hand said something in Spanish to Arturo. Arturo nodded, then turned to me. "Give us a sec, Holmes."

I walked down the steps and paced the asphalt. Through the cemetery's dim light, I saw no one else. I saw no trash on the ground, no graffiti, no defacing of any headstone. And no legitimate reason for the cops to patrol. I saw respect—respect for the dead, for the cemetery itself—a deep respect that outsiders could probably never understand. I felt a smile of admiration crook my lips.

Ten minutes later, Arturo walked over to me, Hand behind him. Elbow had gone back inside the chapel.

"He's in, Holmes. You got DiMarco's signature with you?"

I tapped the front pocket that held the rental receipt. "Yep."

"Okay, we'll go to Hand's and he'll practice on it."

"Okay."

We headed for the exit. Arturo said, "We need to figure out how to get inside the bank."

"Yep."

"Any ideas?"

"Nope."

"It's a damn good thing I'm around then, ain't it? Shit, Holmes, pretty soon I'll be doing all the work around here."

"That's my goal."

I smiled. Arturo didn't.

We followed Hand across the street, back to apartment 17. The dope-smoking trio had vanished from the block-wall.

"I need a favor," Arturo said.

He stopped walking. So did I. Hand hiked the stairs. He left the front door open, the screen ajar.

"Anything."

"When we leave here, I want to go by my old pad."

"Okay."

"I just need to see it, you know. I need to see."

I knew. Closure. That's what the therapists would call it. Arturo was incarcerated when his son fell victim to a drive-by. In the front room of the home where Arturo lived with his wife and son, his boy bled to death on the carpet from a 7.62 mm round to his forehead. A bullet fired in retaliation, anger, or just plain stupidity. Also, a bullet likely aimed at his girlfriend, the boy's mother, Juanita.

Arturo hadn't spoken much about the incident, except to acknowledge that it had happened, and that Juanita left two weeks later to live with a relative in New York. He told me the story with a soft voice, crouched shoulders, his face scrunched in a look of defeat. No tears, though, those weren't for Arturo to shed. He did tell me that much.

Hand's apartment was a small two-bedroom. Years of leaky windows and neglect caused the stucco beneath each windowsill to wear to its mesh core. As we stepped into the tiny entryway, there was a closed door on the left, a living/front room on the right. In this room, a woman in her late teens sat on a yellow couch nursing a baby. Her slim frame sunk into the worn cushions, her arm leaned on an armrest that was split open and leaked its stuffing onto the dirty brown carpet below. Her eyes remained fixed on the TV. A show starring all Latinos was on, dialog in Spanish. I could tell it was a sitcom, but no more.

We walked down the hall. Behind the front room was the kitchen. A woman in her fifties stirred something in a pot on the electric stovetop. A young girl, perhaps fifteen, sat at the scarred wooden table reading a paperback. We passed another closed door on the left. Judging from the distance, I guessed the first door to be a bedroom, the second a bathroom. The last door on the left was ajar. Arturo stepped into the room. I followed.

I was surprised to find a good-sized bedroom, maybe thirteen by fifteen. A queen-sized bed was against the far wall, under the only window in the room. The right wall held a dresser and mirror, the left wall two straight-back chairs, a good fifty years old. Next to the chairs was a humidifier on a stand. Two bean bag chairs sat in a pile in front of a small walk-in closet in the near corner.

Hand laid on his stomach on the bed, a clipboard in front of him, the receipt to his right. He held a cheap Papermate pen in his left hand, his eyes focused on the receipt. The paper on the clipboard was blank.

Arturo sat in one of the high-back chairs, pointed to the other. I sat down. We watched Hand concentrate for a few minutes. Then, Hand looked up at Arturo, then me, then back at Arturo.

"Shit, you dudes can talk. I ain't gonna be bothered."

His eyes went back to the receipt.

"Okay if I smoke?" I said.

"Sure," Hand said without looking up. "Got an extra one?"

I leaned forward and held out my pack. He grabbed a cigarette. "Thanks."

He fished a lighter out of his pocket, lit the cigarette, and held it between his lips, his eyes still studying the receipt.

I lit a cigarette, then said, "So, what's your plan?"

Arturo's eyes widened, like a kid about to tell his parents he scored an A on an especially hard test. He leaned forward, his elbows rested on his knees. "Hand is gonna be blind."

Hand glanced up. "*¿Qué el infierno eres hablando, esse?*"

"You and Jack go inside the bank. You sign the card, but since you're blind, Jack's gotta go in with you. How could the bank people turn down the request of a blind guy?"

"*¡Eres un loco mejicano! Loco en la cabeza, esse!*" Hand dropped his pen. "You didn't say nothing about going in no fucking bank."

"How else are we gonna get that signature on the card?"

Hand looked down at the blank paper a moment. "I didn't think about that." He looked up. "But, no fucking way, esse. *¡No es mi problema!* I ain't going inside."

Arturo turned toward Hand, leaned a bit farther forward. "Listen, motherfucker, what if I had told you no when Spiderman wanted to cap your ass? You fucking owe me."

"Owe you or not, I ain't going in the bank."

"The fuck you ain't."

Arturo and Hand engaged in a staring contest. Arturo won.

"Five g's, *esse*," Hand said.

"Two-five."

"Five."

"Fuck you, Hand. I'll find someone else."

Arturo stood, headed for the door. For a minute, I thought Hand would let him go. Arturo had one foot in the doorway when Hand said, "Wait, esse. Fuck it, two-five it is. And the debt is repaid in full. *La deuda se compensa en por completo. ¿Entienda, esse?*"

Arturo spun around, stayed in the doorway. "Agreed. Now, you better get cracking. I'll call you in the morning." He stepped into the hall. "Oh, one more thing. You better have that signature wired, *esse*, fucking wired."

"What do you think I am, *esse?*" Hand held an open palm across his chest. "I'm a fucking professional."

"Thanks," I said to Hand.

"*Adiós.*"

I followed Arturo down the hall. The girl had finished nursing the baby, but still had her eyes glued to the TV. Must've been one hell of a show.

THIRTY NINE

Arturo walked out of Hand's first. I followed him to the street. He turned left, and remained two steps ahead of me. We didn't speak.

At Cesar Chavez Avenue, he turned right, walked about halfway down the long side of the cemetery, then crossed the street and headed up the east side of Ezra Street. The homes that lined this street seemed to have come from the same cookie cutter mold—small shacks, freestanding apartments, really. In the lawn of the corner house, two men formed a semi-circle around a young girl who was maybe fourteen. She wore a white shirt that bore the insignia of the late Los Angeles Raiders. The shirt, cut short, revealed all of her flat, brown stomach. She held her arms above her head and danced, hypnotically, in a circle, laughing, smiling. The men shared a joint. Each working on their own can of Budweiser. Arturo nodded at the group, walked beyond the house. He stopped in front of the second house, a pale blue one-story, its front door and three street-side windows boarded. Someone had strung yellow caution tape across the porch.

"This is it," he said.

One of the few street lights that worked on this block hung between the second and third houses. Its light radiated to the small yard that stretched the length of the property. What may have, at one time, been grass was now mounds of dirt, weeds three feet high, beer bottles, fast food·trash, an old truck tire, a rusted refrigerator who's door hung open, a burgundy couch with nearly all its stuffing missing. The concrete path was cracked, uneven. The concrete drive had large squares missing, sickly crab grass grew wild in their places. The front door sat crooked in the frame, a sign that the house likely shifted from its foundation. A city sign hung on the front door: *Condemned.*

"Shit," Arturo said.

He wrapped his hand around the caution tape, ripped it away. The wood of the porch creaked under the weight of his foot. Two 2x4s crossed the door in an X. He grabbed one in his hands, tugged at it. I looked to my right. Amongst the trash, I noticed a length of metal, from a car's frame, I think. I picked it up, handed it to him.

"Thanks."

He wedged the metal behind the first 2x4 and broke it free. The second board proved much more willing to cooperate. He threw the metal into the yard, opened the door. He stood in the doorway for a minutes, staring into the darkness.

"Can't see shit in here," Arturo said. "I'll be right back."

He walked to the house on the corner, spoke briefly with one of the guys in the yard. He returned with a flashlight in his hand.

I followed Arturo into the house, feeling like an intruder into someone else's nightmare. He took a few steps in the hall and turned right, faced the room where his son died. With the boarded windows, the darkness in the house was absolute. I took a few steps forward, peered into the front room.

Arturo stood, statue straight, his eyes shifting from the carpet to the front window and back. It seemed his mind was a million miles away. I shifted my weight from one foot to another, lit a cigarette.

"You want me to wait outside?" It came out harsher than I had wanted.

He shook his head. "No."

He handed me the flashlight, took a step forward. I kept the circle of light around him.

A tear slid down his cheek and he fell to his knees. His hand touched the dark black clots of blood in the worn carpet. And he cried.

I thought about Leroy's parents. How they must feel every time they think of Leroy. Different time, place, circumstances, yet the same result. Another boy who never got a chance to grow up. I brushed a tear from my cheek.

After I'd shot Leroy, people told me I was being too hard on myself, that I was just doing my job. For everyone, it boiled down to the fucking job. Never mind the fact that a couple had lost their son, a boy had lost his future. Sweep it under the rug since the father was a lowlife scum anyway. He was shit. His kid would've been shit, too.

The cops on the scene started it. Ellen all too happily picked up the torch and ran with it from there. The department psychologist, my friends, family—no matter the source, the bullshit was the same. In some ways, I wish I could've bought into it, just swept the incident under the rug, continued with the force, and continued with Ellen. But, as shitty as I felt thinking about Leroy and his family, I was glad I wasn't living a skewed, perverted lie. Goddamn it, it did matter.

Arturo drew imaginary circles in the bloodstains. His cries went mute, though tears still trickled down his cheeks.

I knelt beside him and put a hand on his shoulder. "I'm sorry."

"My little boy."

The drips of tears turned into rivers. He chewed his bottom lip. I kept my hand on his shoulder.

"Right here, you know. He was standing right here and those motherfuckers shot the window out. He was probably fucking playing."

He pointed to the back wall of the room. I swung the light around to illuminate a broken rocking chair looming in one corner. "Juanita was sitting in that chair. They had no idea it was coming."

"Neither did you."

He glared at me. "So fucking what? I should've known. *La vida loca*, Holmes. Live by it. Die by it."

He pushed against the floor, hopped to his feet. He stared at the window. The plywood that covered the window from the outside seemed to accentuate the bullet holes. In the portions of the glass that hadn't fallen out, or been shot out, I counted seventeen holes.

"AK forty-seven. Look at this."

I knew Arturo was no stranger to drive-bys. But doing it and having it done to you are in two opposite universes.

I wanted to tell him it wasn't his fault. Only it was. He knew it. I knew it.

I stood up. "There is something positive out of this whole fucking mess."

"What? What positive came out of this whole fucking mess?"

"You're living life straight."

"At the expense of my child, Holmes." He spun toward me. "You wanna live with that kind of guilt?"

I didn't answer. He stared for a moment, then his face softened, his eyelids sagged. "I'm sorry, Holmes. That was a fucked up thing to say. I know you're living with that kind of guilt, too. You and me, one fucked up pair, huh?"

I wrapped my arms around his torso, hugged him. "Hang in there."

He hugged me for a minute, then pushed away. "Shit, Holmes, someone's gonna see us. I can't have my homies thinking I'm a limp-wrist."

"That would be devastating."

"Fucking A, it would." When he looked up at me, his eyes were soft, resigned. "Wanna get drunk?"

"I'd love to."

"We can put all this shit behind a bottle of JD, at least for a while." Arturo grabbed the flashlight. "Wait outside, okay Holmes? I'll be out in a minute."

"You sure?"

"I'm sure."

I walked into the front yard, stopped near the street. A minute later, Arturo came outside, flipped off the flashlight. "Ready?"

We walked to the house on the corner and returned the flashlight. Halfway to my truck, he said, "Thanks, Holmes."

On the drive home, Arturo said nothing about his moments alone in the house. And I didn't ask. We stopped by a liquor store near my apartment and bought a fifth of Jack Daniels. When we got home, we watched CNN.

And got plastered.

— Forty —

I woke Monday morning with a splitting headache. I stumbled to the bathroom, downed three Advil and took a hot shower. Wrapped in my towel, I walked to the kitchen, poured myself a glass of orange juice, and drank it while leaning against the counter.

I glanced at the clock: seven-fifty. "Hey, Arturo, get up."

It amazed me at how light a sleeper Arturo was. He rolled from his bundle of covers, hopped to his feet.

"It's almost eight. We gotta get going."

Arturo nodded and walked to the phone.

"Who're you calling?"

"Eddie. I'll need to wake his ass up."

Arturo disappeared in the bathroom and I grabbed my only suit from the closet, a simple black two-piece that I'd purchased years ago for a fellow officer's funeral.

Before I had left Lake Point, I owned seven or eight suits. Ellen wanted me to wear suits when we went out, and tired quickly of my black JC Penney special. I was happier in Levi's, but went with her to a tailor on the waterfront anyway. She decided on everything.

When I packed up for California, I decided that my simple black suit would work for any occasion and donated the others. Fresh from the dry cleaners, I laid the suits across the Formica countertop at Goodwill. The clerk's eyes bulged as if he'd gone a week without eating and I had just dropped a twenty-ounce steak in front of him. He thanked me seven times before I stopped counting. He continued to thank me as I walked out.

My time in California added a few pounds to my once firm, lean frame. As I buttoned the pants, my suit reminded me all the pounds traveled to my waist. My stomach was still flat to the eye, more or less, but the suit had been closely tailored to the old me. The new me was not liking it one bit.

I was applying fresh polish to my black loafers when Arturo came out of the bathroom, a towel tied around his waist.

"I'm glad I don't have to dress up for the occasion," he said.

I set the first shoe on sheets of newspaper that I'd spread across the coffee table, put my hand in the other shoe. "Yeah, so I don't wanna hear no more bitching about you doing all the work."

"You are getting the short end this morning."

He laughed. I applied more shoe polish.

Arturo picked up the phone, dialed a number. He spoke Spanish for a minute, then covered the mouthpiece. "Hand's mom. She can't get him out of bed." He spoke some more, then hung up. "Well, he's up now. He swears he'll be there at nine."

I set the other shoe on the newspaper. "Did you give him the directions?"

Arturo slapped his forehead with an open palm. He could've had a V-8.

He picked up the phone and called again. I had scribbled the directions on a notepad by the phone. Arturo picked it up and read them off, slowly, repeating several of the turns. "Don't be late, *esse*," he said, and hung up. "He'll be late."

We left the apartment at twenty after eight. By then, Arturo had made another call to Eddie's, reminding him to get his ass moving. He called again from my cell phone as we crawled down Wilshire toward downtown.

"Shit," he said, punched End.

"What?"

"His phone's busy."

"See, now you went and pissed him off."

"Yeah, well."

I switched on KFWB just in time to catch a traffic report—major injury accident southbound 110 at the transition with the 101. I turned on Figueroa and took it north. I wasn't the only one with the idea to use Figueroa to avoid fighting northbound looky-loo traffic. Still, it seemed a better idea than taking the freeway. Once we merged with 110 north, the accident was behind us, the traffic a bit better than normal. We exited at Avenue 52 toward Mount Washington. At Figueroa, I turned right. A block past Avenue 54, on the right-hand side, I spotted the Bank of America.

"I don't believe it," Arturo said.

I slowed, turned into the parking lot. "What?"

"Hand. That's his black Mercedes over there." He pointed it out to me. "Son of a bitch, I don't believe it."

Hand must have recognized the truck. He stepped from his car as I parked in a stall three spots away. Unlike the previous evening, Hand looked sharp. He wore a gray pinstriped three-piece suit, snakeskin shoes, and a black tie over a charcoal shirt. He had slicked his hair straight back against his head, the still-wet look from handfuls of gel. Ebony-framed Ray Bans with glass tinted to limo black shrouded his eyes. I wondered whether the pinstripe suit was an effort to look more Italian. If so, it worked.

I climbed out of the truck. I pulled my suit coat from a hanger behind my seat, slipped into it. I lit a cigarette, then came around to the passenger side. Arturo had already walked to Hand. They spoke in Spanish as I approached.

"Morning," I said.

Hand flashed a minute smile, said, "*Hola.*"

"Hey, *esse*, you ready to look blind?"

Hand pinched his Ray Bans, smiled. His head swayed, slightly high and to the right. Maybe Eddie had watched a Stevie Wonder interview. "I am."

"Very good," I said.

"Think so? I'm really an actor, you know. This other bullshit just pays the rent until I can get on NYPD Blue."

I nodded.

"I guess my acting abilities are being put to the test today."

"Mine, too."

Hand leaned his head forward, peered at me above the sunglasses. "You ain't done shit like this before?"

"Nope."

"*Madre del dios.*" Hand paused, made the sign of the cross with his right hand. I thought he might break down into prayer chants. "Are you shitting me?" To Arturo, "Hey, *esse*." He jabbed Arturo's chest with his forefinger. "I go to the big house, I'll be thinking about you every day. *¿Eres escuchando mí, esse?*"

"Relax, Hand. As long as your signature is right on, you got nothing to worry about."

Eddie dropped his finger. "I'll be dreaming about you, too."

I leaned against the truck and finished my cigarette. A small crowd had gathered near the front doors by the time a woman in her forties, shoulder-length straight auburn hair, designer-cut beige mini-skirt and matching blouse, unlocked the double doors, pushed one open. She smiled at the Asian man who squeezed past her, but she looked like a nervous security guard at a general admission concert.

I dropped my cigarette to the asphalt, crushed it with my shoe. "Ready?"

Hand ran his hand down his tie. "As I'll ever be."

"Let's go win us an Oscar."

Neither Hand nor Arturo smiled.

I took Hand's arm. He sidestepped. "What the fuck?"

"You're blind, remember."

"Oh, yeah."

"Try not to forget that little fact."

He tilted his head high and to the right. "Okay."

He held out his arm. I grabbed it. And we walked to the front door.

From the outside, the bank looked architecturally pleasing and promised more by stepping through its doors. Inside, it was a letdown. The interior could've been any Bank of America in California, at least any one I'd ever seen. Drab orange and brown color scheme. The double doors led to a small entryway, modular desks lined along the left wall, a small waiting area with a couch and a kid's play area, crayons strewn about, a young boy and girl drawing on the carpet rather than the paper in front of them. The right side was a long counter, broken twice. The first area was for merchant customers. Next, twelve teller stalls. The line had nine customers in it, two stalls had tellers in them.

In the far right corner, a sign hung on gold chain from the ceiling announcing *Safe Deposit/Special Services*. I was impressed with the way Hand carried himself. During the walk across the linoleum bank floor, he banged into a small customer counter stuffed with deposit tickets, withdrawal slips, and a discarded Del Taco soda cup. Reflexively, or so it seemed, he muttered "Excuse me." I felt a small smile purse my lips.

At the counter, a woman in her fifties stood erect in a baby blue blouse, her gray hair crunched into a perfectly circular bun, stapled to the back of her head with a large, black clip of some kind. Her large breasts bulged from the shirt, forming a small gap between the buttons, exposing the white of her bra.

"May I help you?" she said.

I leaned against the counter, still holding Hand's elbow. The woman wore a black mini-skirt, probably pilfered from her daughter's closet. A large, single diamond, encased in thick gold prongs, sat atop her ring finger.

"I need to get into my box," Hand said.

My admiration increased a notch. I thought I heard an Italian accent in his voice. He held his head high and to the right, swaying slightly.

"Certainly, sir."

She grabbed a 3x5 signature card from beneath the counter, laid it in front of Hand. She held out a pen. He didn't move, smiled. I took the pen and placed it between Hand's fingers.

"He's blind," I said.

"Oh," she said, held a hand to her mouth as if she'd just uttered an obscene word.

Hand wrapped his fingers around the pen. I guided it to the paper. He scrawled his signature across it. He missed the line by a good half an inch. Nice touch, and damn fine signature, too.

He thrust the pen in front of him. The woman started, then grabbed the pen and the card.

She studied the signature for a moment, then looked up. "I'm sorry. Your name, sir?"

"DiMarco. Tony DiMarco. Box number 117."

She went to a file cabinet, pulled open the top drawer, fished through the cards inside. After a minute, she pulled a card from the cabinet, shifted her eyes from one card to the other, and walked back to us with a frown.

"May I see your ID, sir?"

"ID?" Hand said.

My heart skipped a beat. I coughed into my hand to displace any surprise that may have made its way to my face.

"Yes, sir. Your signature card requires that proper identification be displayed."

"I know what it says," Hand snapped. "Sorry, bad morning."

"May I see your driver's license, sir?"

I started to suggest he left his wallet in the car, but Hand's laughter kept my mouth shut.

"My what?" he said.

"Your driver's license, sir."

Hand had gotten the attention of a few customers in the teller line. I felt beads of sweat push through the pores in my forehead.

"Ma'am, I'm sorry to laugh, but I'm blind. Even the State of California, such as it is, refuses to allow me to drive."

The woman's features scrunched up into embarrassment, then confusion. She looked back at the signature card, confirmed her facts, no doubt, and looked back up.

"I'm sorry, sir, but your card clearly says driver's license."

Hand stopped laughing. His features grew stern. "Ma'am, when I rented the box, I had a license. You see, I've not always been blind."

"Oh." She didn't put her hand over her mouth this time. I guess she was getting used to the word.

"No, industrial accident. I was working with some hydrochloric acid, splashed it in my eyes. Poof, my sight was gone."

Her face showed genuine concern. "I'm sorry."

"But, not to fear," Hand said. He reached into his back pocket.

I thought coronary failure was imminent. I saw Hand grab the butt of a pistol, saw an army of police gun us down as we walked into the parking lot. I blinked my eyes. Then, I saw a wallet in Hand's palm.

He flipped it open, removed a California ID card, and handed it to her. "The State would give me this, though."

She looked it over, smiled, handed it back. I grabbed it from her, put it into Hand's palm. He stuffed it in the wallet and returned the wallet to his pocket.

"Right this way," she said, blushing. "Sir, will you be accompanying Mr. DiMarco today?"

"Yes," Hand said.

Authoritative, to the point. I was beginning to really like Hand.

I led Hand by the elbow to a swinging door in the counter. We followed the woman into the vault. She stopped in front of 117.

"Your key?" she said.

Hand held the key in front of him, to no one in particular. I took it, put it in the lock. The woman inserted a key, pulled open the door. I pinched the handle on the long, cold metal box, withdrew it.

"You may use this room here," she said, pointed with her finger.

"Thank you," Hand said. I opened the door and we walked into the small, windowless room. The room was all white, with a small counter and two straight-back brown chairs with orange cushions, identical twins to the chairs in the waiting area.

I closed the door.

"Hard work being blind," Hand said.

"You're a natural born actor."

"You think? Bitchin', man. Thanks."

I opened the lid. A small stack of papers were inside, fastened with a large paperclip. Beneath it, a stack of Polaroid photos, banded together by a thick rubber band.

"Find something?" he said.

"Maybe."

The first photo showed a man in his forties sliding his tongue across the cheek of a girl who couldn't be a day over fourteen. I pocketed the photos, flipped through the papers. DiMarco's will, the deed to his house, pink slip to his car, a living will and a stock certificate from Club TA. DiMarco held 10,001 shares. I wondered how that converted to percent of ownership. I replaced the papers in the box.

"Time for act two," I said, and opened the door.

The woman met us in front of 117. I replaced the box in its drawer. She closed the door, turned and removed both keys, handed one back to me. I placed it in Hand's palm. He smiled, put the key in his pocket.

"Thank you," he said.

"You're welcome, Mr. DiMarco."

She walked with us until we reached the swinging door, then smiled and walked back to her post. We turned and headed for the glass doors.

I held Hand's elbow until we got to my truck. He leaned against the hood, next to Arturo. I stood facing them, lit a cigarette.

"Well?" Arturo said.

"Oscar fucking-winning performance," Hand said.

I took a hit from my cigarette, blew it into the headwind. "He's one hell of an actor."

"I'm gonna take my act to fucking Broadway, *esse*. But first," Hand said, held out his palm.

Arturo took a wad of bills from his front pocket, counted off twenty-five hundreds, put them in Hand's palm.

Hand curled his thumb over the bills to fight off the wind, but kept his palm open. "I had to pay an extra grand for the ID on short notice."

"What ID?" Arturo said.

"A genuine false State ID card."

"It would've been a problem without it," I said.

Arturo peeled off another ten hundreds, set them atop the others. Hand curled his palm around the money, stuffed it in his pants pocket. He handed the key and the receipt back to me. "It's been real, dudes."

He stepped to his Mercedes, unarmed it, then opened the door and looked back at us. "Thanks, *esse*. This was actually kind of fun. Call me next time you need a man of my talents."

He sat in his car, closed the door and disappeared behind the limo-tinted glass.

Arturo and I climbed into my truck.

"So," he said.

"So what?"

"So, what was it you said about my plan again? Refresh my memory."

I started the engine. "Yeah, yeah. It was a good plan. Okay?"

"That's better. Did we get lucky?"

I backed out of the parking space. "Maybe." I tossed him the stack of photos.

Arturo thumbed through them. "Did you see this shit, Holmes?"

"Just the top one."

"This is some fucked up shit."

I pulled out the driveway, waited for traffic at Figueroa. "I owe you, what? Thirty-five hundred?"

"On the house, Holmes."

"I'm not having you pay for this."

"Don't worry about it."

"Where'd you get that kind of cash anyway?"

"The house."

"What house?"

"My house, in the bedroom. I had some emergency cash stashed in a floor safe in the closet."

I found an opening in traffic and pulled out. "Still."

"Still, nothing, Holmes. I hired Hand. I paid him. Simple as that."

I was forced to go east on Figueroa, and it wasn't until Avenue 60 that I could maneuver to the left lane and make a u-turn.

"It's not my money you're saving, you know."

Arturo smoked a cigarette, his gaze fixed somewhere beyond the window, beyond the cab of the truck.

He didn't respond. I let it go.

FORTY ONE

When Arturo and I got to the office, I found a note from Nadia. Tyrone had called and the copies of the ledger were ready. Finally. She went to his office to pick them up.

We sat in my office and I spread the photos across my desk. Forty-two in all. Every photo contained the face of a young girl and a man. In each case, the man could have passed as the father of the girl. Each also contained some incriminating form of contact.

Blake was in twenty-one of the photos. In twenty of them, he was with girls whose identity was as much of a mystery to me as anyone. In the twenty-first, he had his tongue pressed against the tightly closed lips of Carrie Sanders.

I wondered where Carrie was, and what some sick man, or men, had forced her to do. Did she like it? Was she doped enough not to mind it? Or, was she waiting for the day she could close her hand around a butcher knife, plant it into some asshole's stomach, or use it to whack off his penis?

I had no idea what she was doing, or with whom she was doing it. Nor did I really have any idea where she was. But, I did know that Blake knew much more than he'd shared. And I intended on rattling his cage.

I picked up the photo of Blake and Carrie. "I'm gonna go see Blake."

"You remember I have to see my PO at two today, right?"

"Yep."

"So?"

"So, I hope you have fun."

"Gee, thanks. But I thought it might be wise if I came along for the ride to Blake's."

I lit a cigarette. "You can't. You've got your meeting."

"Give this man a medal."

"What?"

"What? I can't miss my meeting."

"Exactly."

"So, postpone the meeting with Blake until later."

"Gee, let me think." I paused the obligatory two seconds. "Nope."

"Aw, c'mon, Holmes. I wanna go."

"Look, I'm sorry you won't be there for the fun, but I'm tired of all the bullshit. And I don't want Carrie waiting a moment longer than necessary."

Arturo held my stare. "You need backup."

"I appreciate the thought, but I'm a big boy. I can take care of myself."

"The hell you can. How many times I got to save your ass before you realize that?"

"What the hell's going on, Arturo?"

"Nothing," he said, turned away. "It's just . . ."

"Just what?"

"Just a fucking dream, that's all."

I leaned back in my chair. "Okay, tell me about it."

He sat down, lit a cigarette. "Well, Dr. Murphy, it all started on the moon."

I laughed. I couldn't help it.

"Some fucking doctor you are."

"I'm sorry. I know psychologists are trained not to laugh at their patients, but Christ, Arturo. The moon?"

He ignored me. He explained that he and I had gone on a mission to the moon. We collected samples and searched for life. We found some clues, but in the end, we wound up back at our ship with nothing but pocketfuls of dirt.

"Pocketfuls?"

"Yeah, we lost the containers or something, had nowhere else to put the shit."

"I don't think the moon's made of dirt."

"Whatever, Holmes. It was my dream and I can have dirt on the moon if I want."

I held up my hands. "By all means. Please, continue."

He glared at me, kept talking. We got back in our spacecraft and phoned home. Phoned? Yes, phoned, he said. Then, he told me to stop interrupting. Our leaders told us we now had to travel to Mars, continue our search there. We did. We landed on Mars and took more samples, probed, investigated. But, in the end, we just had more pocketfuls of dirt. And we were tired. That's when I told Arturo I was going back out there. He didn't like the idea, he wanted to go but he was too tired. Wait, he said. I told him I had to go now, before it was too late. He complained, but I left anyway. He tried to follow but his legs wouldn't cooperate. I walked a couple hundred feet, then an asteroid crashed into Mars and turned me into space toast.

"Space toast, huh? What did you do, spread jelly across me?"

"Fuck you."

"I'm sorry. You do have one hell of an imagination. I'll give you that."

He looked at me, fear in his eyes. "Don't you get it?"

"Of course. Your dream is simple to interpret, up until the space toast anyway. This case has been like our trip to outer space. We were led somewhere, got some clues, but didn't find Carrie, or in terms of your dream, life. So, we went somewhere else to look, but again, no life. Now, about the space toast."

"Blake's going to kill you."

"No, he isn't."

"Don't prove me right." He turned his head, gazed through the window at Wilshire Boulevard. "It's a warning, Holmes."

"Arturo, I appreciate your concern. But, Blake's too smart to have me whacked. He knows I've been digging, and he's gotta figure I've been talking. All fingers would point to him, especially now that DiMarco's pushing up daises."

"Maybe he'll react emotionally, not think about what he's doing."

"Do you think a man could build a fortune like his by acting emotionally? This guy's a rationalist."

He looked back at me. "I don't have dreams like that very often."

"This is getting kind of scary here. Are you really this freaked about it?"

"Fucking A."

I lit a cigarette. "Look, I'm going to go by his house in broad daylight. I'll ruffle his feathers a little, try to make him talk. He won't. But, I have to try. Maybe I'll pick up something."

"You do what you have to." He glared at me, intensity brushed across his eyes. "But, be careful."

An hour later, I had convinced Arturo to stop by Maria's after the meeting with his parole officer. He needed some stress relief.

He was still freaked about his dream when he left.

And, he freaked me out, too. Not the fact his dream was as it was, but that he felt so strongly about it. I never knew Arturo to believe in ghosts, spirits, premonitions, or tarot cards. He was a straight-laced Catholic. Or, at least he tried to be. But, after all, it was just a dream.

What the hell was space toast, anyway? That part bugged me as much as any of it. If I was going to turn into it, I sure as hell wanted to know what it was.

FORTY TWO

I thought about Arturo's dream more on the way over to Blake's house. Or would his structure more properly be referred to as an estate? Huge is what it was. An enormous multi-story home on at least a full acre of land. His backyard gave way to a wooded area that may well have been part of the Angeles National Forest. I had no idea how far back the natural wilderness extended, but if I had to guess, I'd say he had more than a half-acre of forest. But, what differentiated a house from an estate? I didn't know, and didn't much care. I was just killing time in heavy traffic.

I decided to drive around Blake's place to see just how big it was. I turned on Live Oak, followed the windy road uphill. I saw where Blake's parcel ended and the high block-wall fence pivoted ninety degrees. Only problem was that the road didn't turn along with it. Another parcel began, the road continued more or less straight. After about a half-mile, passing nothing as large as Blake's, I turned around. It was nothing but idle curiosity, so I didn't pay it too much attention. I parked in the same spot I had when I followed DiMarco here before. And waited.

No cars were in front of the house. None of the five garage doors was open. I lit a cigarette and pulled out a Lawrence Block novel.

I had about ten pages read when a blue Cadillac pulled to Blake's gate. A blond woman leaned out of the car. She wore a white halter-top, her exposed skin well-tanned. She put a card into the slot near the speaker, the gates swung open. She leaned back into the car and drove up the steep drive.

She parked near the stairs and got out of her car. Dark sunglasses covered her eyes, a green mini-skirt covered everything from her stomach to just an inch above her knees. The rest of her legs were firm, tanned. They ended in a pair of six-inch black stilettos.

I wasn't sure whether Blake was home, but guessed he was at his office, or at some fancy restaurant stuffing his face. I drove to the gate, pressed the button, waited. A gentleman's voice, thick with British accent, came across the speaker.

"May I help you?"

"I need to speak with the lady driving the Cadillac."

"Miss Jenn—"

He cut it short, knowing he was giving out information-something I'm sure he was trained not to do. "One moment please."

I wondered what Jenn ended in. Was it her first name or last? Jennings, Jennifer, Jenkowski? Shit, it could be anything. The voice didn't return to the box but the gates opened. I parked next to the Cadillac. The woman was standing behind my truck before I got out.

"May I help you?" she said.

Curt, bold, kind of bitchy.

"I need to ask you a few questions."

I met her near the truck's tailgate. Her breasts pushed the limits of the halter-top. From up close, the green mini-skirt hugged her shapely thighs tighter than I thought. It was almost too tight, yet not quite. And it was very sexy.

Her face showed lines despite her efforts to cover them up with far too much makeup, downplaying her cute, perky nose, thin lips, chiseled cheekbones. I thought the makeup actually served to draw attention to the lines it tried so hard to conceal.

"May I see some ID?"

I pulled out my wallet, flipped it open to expose my driver's license and PI license.

"Private investigator? I thought you were LAPD."

"Why would you think that?"

"I don't know. What you said, I guess."

"I didn't say I was a cop."

"What do you want?"

I pulled the photo of Carrie from my jacket pocket, held it in front of her. "Have you ever seen this girl?"

Her lips tightened, her muscles drew taut against her sculpted cheekbones, then relaxed. It all happened so quickly, I wondered whether I saw it, or just imagined it. After all, her recognition would make my life easier. As much as I hoped for that, I didn't expect it. If she didn't have the shades on, her eyes would've told me what I wanted to know. But, behind the sunglasses, I couldn't hear what they were saying.

"Who is this girl, and why would I have seen her?"

"Her name is Carrie Sanders. As to why, I'm just asking."

"I don't know her."

"What about Mr. Blake? Do you think he might know her?"

Her foot tapped the concrete, but the rest of her shapely body seemed relaxed. "I don't know why he would. He's not in the habit of conversing with runaway children."

"I didn't say she'd run away."

"You implied it. Are you private dicks all so technical?"

"Yep. At least us good dicks are."

"A good dick. Hmmm."

"What's your connection to Mr. Blake?"

"That's none of your business."

"Do you live here?"

"That's none of your business, either."

"Look, I'm just trying to get a handle on the situation."

"What situation?"

"With Carrie."

"What are you talking about?"

I lit a cigarette, leaned against my truck. "My client hired me to find Carrie."

The gates rattled open. A white double-stretch Lincoln crawled up the drive, parked directly behind the Cadillac and my truck. The driver got out, opened a rear door, and out stepped Charles Blake.

"What the hell's going on here?" He looked at me, then the woman. "Jenny?"

Ah, Jenny. I felt so much better knowing.

She looked at him, spun on her stilettos and marched up the steps, into the house.

He focused his glare on me. "What are you doing here, Mr. Murphy?"

"You remembered my name. I'm flattered."

"Don't be. I've been checking you out."

"Really?" I puffed up my hair with a palm. "You wanna ask me out on a date?"

"You're a real funny guy, you asshole."

"Thanks."

The driver closed the rear door, sat back in the driver's seat. He kept his door open, pretended to have his eyes focused on a newspaper.

"You haven't answered me," Blake said.

I took a hit on my cigarette, blew the smoke above my head. "I'm here to ask you a few questions."

He walked up to me, got his face so close to mine that our noses nearly kissed. "Are you looking to lose your private dick license?"

I could almost taste the alcohol that smothered his breath. "Nope."

"I can arrange that, you know."

"I'm sure you could, Charlie. You're quite good at arranging things, aren't you?"

"I told you not to call me Charlie. And what the hell do you want?"

I looked at the driver, then back at Blake. "Do you really want to have this conversation here?"

He looked over his shoulder, said, "You can wait here or in the servant's wing."

The driver glanced at Blake, nodded.

"Follow me," Blake said.

He walked up the staircase. I realized that the double French doors at the end of the stairs were actually on the third floor of the house. The doors gave way to a foyer large enough to hold my entire apartment. Correction, this foyer could hold nearly two of my apartments. A stairway was to the left, archways straight ahead and to the right. The ceiling-less foyer provided a glimpse of a hallway above.

"Quite a place you have here."

"I know."

"Are you going to give me the grand tour?"

Blake started up the stairs. "Hardly."

I followed him up the stairs. The hallway I noticed from below was about three apartment's worth. So much space, so bare, like a museum with no sculptures, no paintings, no life at all. At the top of the stairs, just to the left, were a bay window, two recliners, and a circle coffee table. He sat in one chair. I sat in the other.

The three huge, single pane windows provided a complete view of the parking lot in front, the drive, and part of the street below. Blake pulled a cigar from his breast pocket, unwrapped it. I lit a cigarette. The crystal ashtray on the coffee table was immaculate until I tapped my ashes in it.

Blake pulled a cutter from his pocket, clipped the ends of the cigar, and rolled one end around in his mouth. He exchanged the cutter for a Cartier lighter, lit it and held the blue-yellow flame to the cigar. His cheeks puffed fat, smoke trickled from his lips, his nostrils. Satisfied he had the cigar going, he doused the flame, put the lighter in his pocket, and stared out the window, puffed his cigar.

"Who's Jenny?" I said.

"None of your business."

"Maybe not. Just trying to make conversation."

"I'm not interested in conversing with you."

I hit my cigarette. "Why'd you tell me that you didn't know Carrie Sanders?"

His eyes remained forward, poker-faced. "Because I don't."

"Are you in the habit of trying to stick your tongue into the mouths of young girls that you don't know?"

My peripheral vision indicated a slight twinge in his face. Or maybe it was nothing.

"What're you blabbering about?"

"I have twenty-one photos of you with kids."

He puffed his cigar, waited a minute to answer. "Really?"

"Really."

"I suppose next you'll tell me that the girl you're looking for is one of them."

"Yep."

"Bullshit."

The limo driver opted to stay with the vehicle, though now he leaned against the bumper, smoked a cigarette. I pulled the Polaroid from my pocket, held it between my fingers. I said nothing. He focused on the photo for a moment. Another twinge—this time there was no question.

"Where'd you get that?"

"Where I got it isn't important." I put the photo away. "What is important is that you know her, and I want her."

"I didn't even know her name. I saw her once."

"Only once."

"That's it."

"What about the other girls? You see them only once as well?"

"Indeed."

"What exactly do you do with twenty-one underage girls that you see only once?"

"None of your business."

"For twenty of them, I agree. They're not my concern. But Carrie's another story. I'm gonna find her, I promise you that. And, if you don't cooperate with me now, I'm going to make your life a living hell."

He leaned toward me, stared through cold eyes. "Is that some kind of threat?"

"No, it's a promise."

"You have some nerve, coming into my house and speaking to me that way."

"I just call it as I see it."

"Maybe you should have your eyes checked, then."

I could see this game going on for quite a while. Time to change gears a bit. "Why'd you have DiMarco killed?"

"I didn't."

"Really?"

"Really."

"Okay. Where did you fly to on Monday night?"

"Nowhere."

"Yes, you did. DiMarco dropped off three cute, young girls here. You took them to the Van Nuys Airport and boarded your Gulfstream. That's a beautiful plane, by the way."

"Thank you."

"Where'd you take those girls?"

"My turn to ask you a question. What drugs are you on?"

"Why, you got some?"

He laughed—a cold, bitter laugh.

"Why'd you kill DiMarco?"

"I didn't do any such thing."

"You had him killed."

He didn't respond.

"One thing puzzles me, though."

"Only one?"

"How exactly did you pull off that stunt at the Santa Monica pier?"

He looked at me, bewilderment in his eyes. "What?"

"You know. The guy and girl going off the pier. Carrie's bracelet conveniently left nearby. That was pure genius, Charlie. Really, I was impressed."

"I have no idea what you're talking about."

First time he said that. "You can tell me." I patted my chest. "No wire, nothing. Just two guys shooting the shit."

"Indeed."

"So, did you think of that, or was it someone else?"

He puffed his cigar, his stare focused on something outside.

"Charlie, let me say this. I came into this case wanting only to find Carrie. But, I've found a messy can of worms here, haven't I? I should tell you that if you try to take me out, all of my evidence goes directly to Tyrone Williams, LAPD Vice squad."

"I hope you enjoyed your days as a private dick, because they'll soon be over."

I stood, crushed my cigarette in the ashtray. "I'm gonna see to it you go down hard."

"In five minutes, I'll have my lawyers on the phone. You're through, Mr. Murphy."

Lawyers. I pictured a pack of wolves drooling around a conference table in Blake's building. And it wasn't a pretty picture.

"Good. You're gonna need them. No, don't get up. I know the way out."

I walked down the stairs and outside. I felt his stare burn against my back as I headed to my truck. The chauffer reluctantly moved the limo. I glanced at the window before heading down the drive. Trained on me, Blake's eyes, like the red dot from a laser sight.

I shuddered. The gates were open by the time I reached the bottom of the drive, and closed as soon as I was back in the real world.

FORTY THREE

I spent most of the night thinking about Blake. Most of what he said was a lie, that much I knew. But, his surprise about the Santa Monica Pier bothered me. Why would he have acted surprised only about that? Maybe he didn't stage the accident. But, if not, who did?

I went over what I really knew. I knew DiMarco brought girls to Blake's house, and Blake flew those girls to parts unknown. I knew Blake was in a Polaroid with Carrie, and the photo was in the possession of DiMarco. And, I knew DiMarco was being paid twenty-five hundred a week as a security consultant for a company owned by Blake.

Beyond that, I surmised. I surmised that DiMarco worked for Blake in some capacity other than "security consultant" as was indicated by DSS, that DiMarco and Blake were in some sort of child porn ring, and that between the two Carrie had passed.

It depressed me to spell it out. I knew very little and could prove even less. Some detective.

I drifted off to sleep before Arturo returned.

Arturo woke up about nine, did his morning exercises. I cooked *huevos rancheros*. We ate in the company of the Ricki Lake show.

After we finished, I lit a cigarette. Arturo said he wanted to do the dishes this time, so I let him. Ricki was arguing with a pregnant teenage girl about why it would be better to keep the child and live with her mom than have an abortion and go off with her boyfriend, a twenty-seven year old Hell's Angel who also happened to be a convicted pedophile. I turned off the TV and joined Arturo in the kitchen.

"So," he said as he washed the plates in the sink, "what happened with Blake yesterday?"

"Not much."

"Did you piss him off?"

"Yep."

"Then we know how it went."

"But, I didn't go expecting otherwise."

"You know, Holmes, maybe you should take a human relations class at UCLA."

"I relate just fine. I piss people off, then I leave."

My mom used to tell me that I could catch more flies with honey than vinegar. The only problem had been finding the honey to use. I always managed to find plenty of vinegar.

Arturo hopped in the shower. I called Nadia.

"Hello, Jack," she said.

I found no combativeness in her voice. Nor did I find affection. I found professionalism. And I hated it.

"Hi. How's it going?"

"Fine."

"Anything happening?"

"Not really."

"Did you get the ledger from Tyrone?"

"Yes."

"And?"

"And what?"

She was making me earn every word. "Did you find anything?"

"You mean you wanted me to go through it?"

"I thought you might."

She paused. "I did. DiMarco took money from CB and paid money to RL, and a few others. So far this year, he's collected four-point-two million from CB. He's paid out a total of three million seven-hundred thousand. Two-point-one million of that went to RL."

"Good work."

"Thanks."

"How're you doing?"

"Fine."

"I'd like to sit down and talk after this case is closed, if that's okay."

"Fine."

I rubbed my temples. "Any messages for me?"

"One, from a Lawrence Greensboro." She said Lawrence

seemed upset when he called. He mumbled something about my meeting his wife the previous day, something about Carrie, and said it was extremely important that I phoned him at once.

"I checked the phone number after he called and it's registered to L. Greensboro of Los Angeles."

"Thank you."

"For what?"

"For being there for me. I can always count on you."

"You're welcome."

I wondered if the warm, tender smile that usually accompanied those words was there this time. "I met with Blake yesterday."

I told her briefly about my meeting.

"Are you going to call this guy back?" she said.

"Yep."

"Let me know what happens, okay?"

A tinge of rejection in her voice, the feeling of being left out of the loop. And not liking it.

"Sure."

I hung up saddened. I hoped for a quick resolution to this case so we could make things right between us. Of course, that meant I'd actually have to confront the feelings I had for Nadia. And that scared the hell out of me.

Arturo got out of the shower. I got in, hoping to wash away the last few minutes.

A panicked male voice answered the phone. "Yeah."

"This is Jack Murphy. You called my office."

"Jack, yes. Thank you for calling back." He confirmed that the girl I met yesterday at Blake's was his wife, Jenny. Jenny had gone home and told him about our conversation. "She was scared."

"Of Blake?"

"Yes. She recognized the girl in the photo. She'd seen her with Blake."

"Lawrence."

"Larry, please."

"Larry, what did your wife do for Blake?"

"Do?"

"Yeah, did she work for Blake?"

He paused. "Yes."

"Doing what?"

"This and that."

I grabbed my cigarettes from the table, lit one. "Go on, Larry."

He said Jenny didn't like some of the things Blake did, and wanted to break away from him. But, she feared him, feared retaliation. She knew too much, she was sure of that. And someone like Blake was bound to have her killed.

"What kinds of things?"

"With Carrie."

"Is Blake a pedophile?"

"She thought so." He stopped, cried. "She's dead."

"Who?"

"Jenny."

"Did you tell the police any of this?"

"No." Quick, short.

"Why not?"

"I can't . . ."

"Can't what, Larry?"

"I can't tell the cops anything."

"Because you're afraid of Blake?"

"Fuck yes. Wouldn't you be?"

I couldn't make any sense out of Blake's killing Jenny over what she might have said to me. But, nothing else made sense, so what was one more?

"What do you want me to do, Larry?"

"Get him."

He said Jenny was called out of the house about ten o'clock last night. An emergency is what Blake said to her. Jenny promised to be back by midnight, but didn't show. The cops called Larry around three. Her body was dumped in the same place as Jenkins'. Popular place. Ladies and gentlemen, come to Hollywood, meet the stars, get an eyeful of death as an added bonus.

"I know about Carrie," he said.

"What do you know?"

"I know Blake's keeping her around because he's grown fond of her. He usually ships the girls overseas, but he hung on to Carrie. But he's freaking out. He's moving her around today. He'll fly her out of the country tomorrow."

He recited the address of a motel in the Valley. "She'll be there by ten tonight. From there, they'll move her to the airport. Go get her, would you? Maybe she'll be able to put this bastard away."

"How do you know all this?"

"I spoke to a few people this morning."

"How do you know this information is reliable?"

"It just is. Okay? I can't tell you any more than that. But, if you don't get her tonight, she'll be gone."

Larry pleaded with me for another five minutes, then hung up. He sounded genuine enough, but the whole thing smelled of a setup. On the other hand, Larry did give up quite a bit of information on Blake, information that may or may not prove true. But, a simple setup wouldn't have required divulging any of it. Maybe Larry was for real. Maybe Jenny was dead. On the other hand . . .

I switched on the TV, glanced at the clock: eleven-fifty-four. I turned to Channel 11 and waited for the noon news.

"Good afternoon, I'm Cynthia Lopez and this is news at noon. We have a breaking story for you on this Friday. Early this morning, police discovered the nude body of forty-four year old sex therapist Jennifer Greensboro in a parking lot in Hollywood. Early reports indicate she had been stabbed more than thirty times in the chest and abdomen. For more on this late breaking story, we turn to our own Jeff Simpson, live at the scene. Jeff."

Jeff was a man in his late twenties, crew cut blond hair, pale features, beige suit coat, white shirt, and blue tie. Jeff repeated everything Cynthia had already said, added that new developments would be forthcoming following a police statement, and said Jennifer's husband, Lawrence, was unavailable for comment.

Finally, one sure thing—Jenny was dead. It was interesting that a sex therapist consoled Blake, more interesting still that the sex therapist was discussing Blake's pedophilic tendencies with her husband at night. And that she perhaps witnessed it, or suspected it, and didn't discuss it with the police. I was beginning to feel the ominous power of Charles Blake.

Arturo came into the room. I pointed at the TV. "I met that girl yesterday."

"No shit? Should I be worried?"

"About what?"

"Everyone around you seems to meet with an untimely death. Like you got the Midas touch or something."

"Midas turned everything to gold."

"He turned it to gold, you turn it to shit. Six of one."

"Now who's trying to be comedic?"

"Your comedy is contagious, Holmes."

Arturo left to buy some flowers for Maria. I got ready for my racquetball game with Tyrone and had one foot out the door when the phone rang. It was Nadia.

"Did you call him?"

"Yep."

The wounded puppy voice again. "You said you'd let me know."

"I'm sorry. I had to confirm something on the news."

"That sex therapist? Who is she?"

"A woman I met yesterday at Blake's house."

I told her about the motel. I told her I would go.

"It's a setup."

"Probably."

"Is Arturo going?"

No, he wasn't. But, if I said that, I'd never hear the end of it. Nadia would be sure I needed him. Arturo could have his date any time, she'd say. Technically, Arturo was going, just not to the same place I was going. "Yep."

"You be careful."

"I will."

I hung up the phone feeling like a kid who told his parents he was going to a friend's house for a sleepover but really was going to spend the night with a girl, and his parents blindly said okay.

I had planned to ask Arturo to come along. Under other circumstances, I would have. But, after spending nearly three years in prison, and finally hooking up with a girl that seemed good for him, he was having his first official date. He was taking the lady to a concert. I wasn't about to stand in the way of that, nor was I going to let the job stand in the way of that.

The motel incident could've been a setup. Also, it could've been a husband's last chance at revenge against the savage who murdered his wife. Either way, I knew I'd find out if I showed up. And I wouldn't if I didn't.

I headed to the LA Athletic Club before Arturo got back from the florist, and when I returned, he was gone. Tyrone was so happy I'd given him the key that he kicked my ass three straight. I was exhausted and still had some time, so I stretched out on the couch and caught a nap.

When I woke, I was in the dark. The sun had disappeared for the night and Arturo didn't leave any lights on in the apartment. I tripped over the coffee table on my way to the switch.

I grabbed the half-gallon of orange juice from the kitchen. It was nearly empty, so I opted not to dirty a glass, drank directly from the cardboard carton. I found a note from him on the kitchen counter. *Call me if you need anything.* He underlined *anything* twice.

Apparently, he'd picked up a pager on his way to the florist. He had jotted its number on the note.

The clock above the kitchen sink told me it was eight-thirty—ninety minutes until show time. I sat on the couch, turned on the TV. I caught the entertainment half of the news on an independent station.

The phone rang while I was in the bathroom washing my face. I reached it after four rings, but found only dead air when I picked up.

I dressed in a pair of sweats, a large t-shirt, my Nikes, and a thin windbreaker. Loose fitting clothes. I wasn't sure how much mobility I needed, but wanted to be prepared. Since my sweats didn't hold up my belt holster well, I opted for my shoulder holster, and secured my Sig under my left arm.

I pulled the pistol out, dropped the magazine, and verified it was full of hollow-points. I popped the magazine in and replaced the pistol in the holster. I grabbed two backup magazines, loaded with like bullets, from a drawer in the kitchen. I set them in my jacket pocket, and felt ready. If whatever I encountered couldn't be stopped with 45 hollow-point 9mm rounds, then it would be time to raise the white flag.

I climbed into my truck and headed for the motel.

FORTY FOUR

I exited the 101 freeway at Reseda, turned right on Sherman Way, found the motel two blocks up on the right. I passed the building once, slowing to catch a glimpse of the layout. Room 211 faced the street, second level, last room on the right. A metal stairway was only feet from the door, parking spaces were available near the stairs. A light hung above the open staircase, its bulb burned out. I went around the block and pulled into the lot.

I sat in my truck, smoked a cigarette. I wondered if Arturo should be there. I thought about calling it off, just waiting. Throwing the dice and seeing if tomorrow would bring Lucky 7, or craps. Then I thought about Raymond Sanders, his wife, and Carrie. If Carrie was in there, how could I allow someone to inflict even one more moment of terror on her? I felt like a Good Samaritan. I felt like a fool. I stopped thinking before I felt any more. I reassured myself by touching the cold steel of my Sig, and stepped from the truck.

I did have the element of surprise on my side, maybe. If it was a setup, it didn't really matter one way or another. But if not, it's possible they didn't expect me. I could have an edge. I stuck with that theory. Good thing—the alternative would've made me get back in my truck and go home.

I took the steps two at a time. When I got to the second floor, I held my 9mm firm in my right hand, close to my leg. The pride of the Lone Ranger overcame me as I stood in front of the door, ready to knock. The pride quickly turned sour at the thought of being the stupid Lone Ranger.

I knocked. Three times. I took a step to the right, held my pistol loosely at my side, waited. Someone said something from behind the door. I couldn't make out the words. The chain slid, the door opened. An Arab stuck his head out. He turned to look at me. I set the barrel of my Sig against his forehead.

"Come on outside, hands first. Nice and slow."

His right hand was already in plain view, his left concealed behind the door. He blinked. We took a step. His hand was still behind the door.

"Your left hand. Show it to me."

He did. It was empty. We continued, I backward, he forward, until we both stood on the catwalk that encircled the building.

"Who else is inside?"

"Just a girl," he said with a heavy Mediterranean accent.

"Turn around."

He did. He was shorter than I was, maybe five-eight, a hundred and fifty pounds. His black hair cropped short to his head, Marine-style, his shoulders wide from pumping iron. I put my left hand against his neck, the pistol against the back of his head. "In we go."

He pushed the door wide open with his palm, then we stepped inside. Long blond hair flowed across one of the pillows on the bed and the thin white sheet. Someone was sleeping. The sheet hugged the definitively female body. I saw no one else. We took a few more steps until we were clear of the front door.

"Stay there," I said, released my hand from his neck, reached behind me to close the door.

My body went weak, my vision starry. I fell to my knees. My Sig fell from my hand. I felt dizzy, warm. Another sharp blow to my shoulder blade and my face met the musty brown carpet.

Tightly gripped hands pulled me by the arms, turned me on my back. A shadow was at my feet, tying my legs together. My arms were pulled above my head, then banded together at the wrists with rope. Bile rose in my throat, my stomach flipped like a fish out of water. I was in deep shit.

They sat me in a straight-back chair facing the bed. The Arab whom I met at the door touched the girl's shoulder and she sat straight. He handed her some cash. She stood and turned toward me. It wasn't Carrie. Except for the hair, she wasn't even a close match. This girl's face pegged her closer to thirty.

She said, "Anytime you need me, Reza, just call."

Reza flashed what may have been a smile in his native country, but seemed more like a condescending grin here. The girl left and Reza locked the door behind her.

"So, Mr. Murphy," Reza said. "It seems you took the bait."

"Yep."

The two men laughed. My vision came back to me, but my shoulder felt like it had just met a semi-truck, head on at seventy. The man that hit me stepped into my view. He was also an Arab, but older, perhaps forty. He wore his hair in the same Marine-style. His pudgy cheeks ended in a thick chin clothed by a small goatee. His thick belly hid a good two inches of his belt. There was no smile on his face. A thick joint smoldered between his lips.

The fat Arab sat on the edge of the bed, leaned against his knees, stared into my eyes. "Mr. Murphy, why did you push Mr. Blake?"

"My job."

"Your job." He puffed on the joint, let the smoke trickle from his lips and nostrils. He held my stare. "I hope your job is worth dying for."

"Why, is that what I'm going to do?"

I didn't see his hand until its palm connected with my cheek, snapped my head to the left. The metallic tang of blood filled my mouth. I spit on the floor. Geniuses that these men were, they tied my wrists together but forgot to tie my hands to anything else. I raised my fists from my lap, delivered a crushing uppercut to the fat Arab's jaw. He fell back onto the bed, held his chin, blood poured from his mouth. Reza picked up the joint that had broken free from the fat Arab's lips and dropped it in an ashtray.

"Now, we're even," I said.

The fat Arab lay back on the bed, holding his jaw. Reza now had my pistol in his hand. He placed the barrel against my forehead.

"How does it feel, Mr. Murphy?"

"It's cold, yet inviting, I'd say."

"What?" He seemed to ponder that a moment, then said, "How does it feel to know you're going to die?"

"Everyone's going to die, even you two losers. Thing is, I wonder whether you realize how soon it will be."

I was not feeling particularly invincible. My natural defenses led me to take an adversarial position when confronted by fear. Sweat flowed from my armpits, my brow. My palms were moist, and I wondered just how I'd manage to get out of this alive. But, damn it, I was going to give these two a run for their money.

The fat Arab sat up straight, clutching his jaw. The rage boiled in his eyes. I knew he wanted to beat that rage into me, but Reza said something to him in Arabic, and he remained seated.

I figured that if they were going to kill me in the motel room, they'd have done it already. The fact that I was still breathing gave me hope.

The fat Arab and I sat locked in a stare-fest. Reza stood with my 9mm to my head. We stayed in that pose for a minute.

Reza said something else to the fat Arab, then he walked to the phone and dialed a number, my pistol still aimed more or less at my head. I had no idea how good of a shot he was, but I wasn't feeling particularly lucky and had no desire to find out.

Reza spoke softly into the receiver, his eyes moving from me to the fat Arab, to some spot on the ceiling. I glanced at the alarm clock on the nightstand: ten-forty-eight. Reza spoke a little more, then replaced the receiver.

"We go."

"Where're we going, Reza?"

Neither man spoke. The fat Arab untied my feet, Reza kept the pistol aimed at my head. The fat Arab pulled me to my feet and walked me to the door. Reza got behind me, held my neck as I had his, my pistol firm against the base of my skull.

"Try anything and I shoot you."

"Where're we going?"

The fat Arab opened the door and walked onto the catwalk. He looked left, then right, then left again. He nodded at Reza and we followed him outside. The fat Arab started down the steps first. As I took the first step, I felt the barrel of my 9mm slip away from my head. I heard choking sounds from behind me. The fat Arab turned around, started to get past me. I kicked him in the groin, sent him reeling backward, holding his crotch. I turned and found Arturo standing over Reza, my pistol pointed between Reza's eyes.

Arturo looked at me, smiled. "Hello, you stupid shit."

FORTY FIVE

Arturo had applied a chokehold to Reza that rendered him unconscious. Arturo untied my hands, then we dragged Reza back into the motel room. We secured his hands and feet, then went out for the fat Arab.

"How is he?" Arturo said.

I knelt down beside the fat Arab. He'd fallen down half a flight of stairs and smacked the back of his head against the concrete landing. A small pool of blood had formed under his head, but I had no idea how serious the injury might be. We picked him up and brought him to the motel room. There was no need to secure him.

Reza started coming around. I knelt beside the fat Arab. The blood draining from his head had already wet the carpet. I grabbed some towels from the bathroom, stuck them between the wound and the carpet. "This guy needs a doctor, but we need them to stay on ice."

Arturo hovered over me. "Are we playing possum?"

"Yep."

Arturo paced the room for a few minutes. He looked deep in thought. Then, he snapped his fingers. "I got it, Holmes."

"Good for you, but don't give it to me."

"I can get a doctor to look at his head. Maybe he'll even keep them for us."

Arturo picked up the phone, dialed a number, and waited. Reza was back in the land of the living, and not looking any too happy about it. Arturo spoke in Spanish for a minute, then hung up. "Okay, Doc will be here in twenty minutes."

I stood up and walked toward Reza. "Now it's time to get some answers."

My shoulder blade still throbbed, my cheek stung, and I was generally pissed off. Reza was sitting on the floor, his back against the foot of the bed. I sat next to him, put my arm around him. "Reza, how does it feel to have the tables turned?"

Reza stared straight ahead, said nothing.

"Let me tell you what's going to happen."

I held out my hand, palm up. Arturo placed my Sig in my palm like a surgical nurse handing the doctor a scalpel. I looked at the side of the pistol. "You didn't even disengage the safety. You haven't worked many Sig Sauers in your time, have you?"

Arturo laughed, Reza stared at the wall.

"See Arturo there? In case you can't see it, he's what white collar people call a gangbanger. He's got lots of friends who are also gangbangers. As much as you and Fat Boy wanna think of yourself as thugs, you're really nothing. You're pieces of shit that work for a pedophile. Arturo eats wanna-bes like you for breakfast, and still has an appetite when he's through. You getting my drift?"

I tightened my grip around his neck. "Wanna meet some of his friends?"

Reza kept his stare on the grimy white, textured walls.

"I didn't think so. So, you're going to answer my questions. I'll give you three strikes before you're out, just like baseball. You do know what baseball is, don't you? Little white ball, bunch of guys looking stupid in uniforms, hitting and catching the ball."

"I know what it is, you idiot."

"Good, good. Now we're getting somewhere. If you strike out, Arturo will introduce you to his friends. You'll really like Sniper, he's a barrel of laughs, hangs out at the graveyard and shit."

A thin line of sweat formed at his brow. His eyes softened. "What do you want to know?"

I held my 9mm against my left leg, tapped it lightly against my jeans. Subtle, yet noticeable. "Where's Carrie Sanders?"

"Who?"

"Carrie Sanders."

"I do not know her."

I set my pistol on my leg, fished a cigarette from my pack. I held the cigarette between my lips while I grabbed my lighter. "Strike one."

"It is the truth."

I lit my cigarette, blew my hit toward the ceiling. "Okay, we'll keep that strike at bay for the moment. Tell me who sent you and what your instructions were."

Reza inhaled, looked as though he was going to say something. Then, he pinched his lips together, exhaled slowly through his nostrils.

"I should warn you that failure to answer would constitute a strike."

"Fuck you."

"Being discourteous also constitutes a strike."

Reza looked at Arturo. Arturo held his stare. Reza's eyes strayed to Arturo's neck and the head of the snake tattooed on it. He looked at Arturo's arms below the sleeves of his shirt. Tattoos covered nearly all the visible skin. Something flickered in Reza's eyes—perhaps fear. He looked back at the wall, chewed on his bottom lip.

I repositioned myself until I was directly between Reza and whatever the hell he was staring at on the wall. He glared into my eyes for a moment, then away. I handed the pistol to Arturo, held Reza's cheeks in my hands, forced his head straight.

"Look at me."

Our eyes met. His focus danced from my left eye to my right and back. When I was certain I had his attention, I continued.

"Did you know your boss likes little girls? That son of a bitch molests them before they're old enough to drive. Did you know that?"

His blank stare told me he either didn't know, or didn't care.

"I care," I said. "I care a whole lot."

I released his cheeks. He stayed focused on me. "I'm taking him down. If you help me, I'll make sure that I mention it to the cops. If you don't, I'll mention that, too. See, I have a friend at Vice. He really hates pedophiles. One time, when he found a pedophile in a bathroom playing with some little boy's weenie, he took the guy outside, tied him to his bumper and dragged him around a gravel parking lot. Can you imagine? Fucking gravel."

From the look in his eyes, I saw that he could.

"Who sent you over here tonight?"

"Is that not obvious?"

"Blake."

He nodded.

"What'd he tell you to do?"

"He said if you show up, we should call."

"And that's the call you made earlier?"

He nodded.

"Did you talk to Blake?"

"No, Akmad."

"Who's Akmad?"

"Our boss. He works with Blake."

There was a knock at the door. I took my 9mm from Arturo, my thumb on the safety.

"Who is it?" I said.

"Quincy, ME."

Arturo said, "He was a big fan of the TV show."

Arturo got up, glanced through the peephole, and opened the door. A Latino man in his late forties with raven hair slicked back from his forehead, spots of gray at his temples, came into the room. He carried a little black bag that went well with his designer beige blazer and matching slacks. His navy shirt was unbuttoned at the collar. Arturo closed and relocked the door.

Quincy knelt down next to the fat Arab and began doing whatever it is doctors do.

I continued to question Reza while Quincy examined the fat Arab. Reza said they were supposed to take me to the warehouse on Boyd Street. Men would be waiting there to take me off their hands. "He wants you dead."

He went on to say that he knew nothing of Blake's sexual desires or any girls he may or may not be keeping on the side. He worked for Diamond Steel Security and valued his job. "So I never ask questions."

"After you dropped us off, what then?"

"Nothing until tomorrow."

"What's tomorrow?"

"Blake's party. I am working security."

"Where?"

"At his house."

"Who's going to be there?"

He reminded me of his never asking questions.

"What happens if you don't show?"

"I will be fired."

"Sorry to say it, my friend, but you're unemployed, then."

"Why keep me? I told you what I know."

"Because I can't have you talking to Blake, that's why. Looks like you're going to get to meet Arturo's friends after all."

"You fucking son bitch."

"If you don't pull any shit, you'll be released in a few days unharmed."

"Fuck, fuck. Son bitches you all."

Quincy stood, packed his things back into his bag. "This one should be okay. I'll need pictures of his skull to be sure, but I don't think it's serious. You want these guys on ice, right?"

"Frozen solid, *esse*," Arturo said.

Arturo opened the door. Quincy stepped outside. He said something, then came back in. Two large Latino bodybuilder-types appeared. They hauled the fat Arab's body downstairs, then returned for Reza. One of the men held a roll of duct tape in his hand. He ripped off an eight-inch piece, smiled at Reza. Then he taped Reza's mouth shut.

"I'll be in touch," Arturo told Quincy.

Quincy nodded at Arturo, then me. He followed the two outside. Arturo closed the door.

He smirked. I held up my hands. "Don't even start."

"I told you . . ."

"I said, don't."

FORTY SIX

We entered the lot from the back. With me were Arturo, Popeye, Sniper, Elbow, Hand and a lean, young man who was introduced as Cheetah (being given that name after successfully outrunning police officers on four separate occasions). Elbow and Hand each carried a duffel bag full of our night's equipment—two pairs of binoculars, a length of rope, seven pairs of gloves, three flashlights, two automated lock pick drivers, a Beretta 9mm, two Smith and Wesson .45s, two Glock 9mms, three HK-94 assault rifles and a Remington 30-30 rifle with a sniper scope.

During the previous evening's reconnaissance, Arturo and I found Blake's estate to be on a lot that was about twice as long as it was wide, consuming at least an acre of land. The majority of the lot had been elevated twelve feet. The home was four stories, and except for the three-car garage that faced Live Oak, the ground floor was buried. In front of the house, the lot sloped downward to accommodate the driveway. In back, beyond the caged tennis courts, a kidney-shaped pool, and changing shed, the lot sloped down to meet a river. Whether the river was man made or not, I hadn't been able to tell from the street, but what I saw with binoculars looked natural. Behind the river was a deeply wooded area, obviously natural. Unusually high block wall surrounded the property, giving way only to the garage facing Live Oak and the wrought iron entry.

We determined that we couldn't enter from the front and go unnoticed. With the lot's extreme elevation, windows, patio doors, and balconies were out. The garage facing Live Oak was a possibility, but upon closer examination, I found electronic eyes protecting each door. That left the back.

The back had its definite advantages. It was probable one could camp out for days by the river without ever being seen by anyone at the house. It seemed to me Blake had painstakingly recreated, or preserved, a natural habitat in his backyard, so the chance of gardeners coming down to this area was nil. In addition, just opposite the perimeter wall in back was a nature trail for residents of the area to escape the concrete jungle for a while. This put the nearest house to Blake's lot a good half-mile behind. Except for the occasional jogger or woman walking her dog, the area was deserted. During recon, we saw no one use this trail after nine, and we'd made the decision to enter from the back.

The wall proved difficult to scale only for me. I was by no means a workout junkie, but I didn't let myself balloon up, either. But, standing at the base of the wall, I felt like an out of shape ball of adipose tissue.

Popeye and Sniper had strung a rope over a thick poplar branch that extended beyond the block wall. Making a noose-like knot, they secured the rope to the branch. One by one, the Evergreeners took the rope in hand, swung their feet against the wall and proceeded to walk up the cinderblock. My feelings of inadequacy multiplied with each man that made it over the wall.

Ready to climb, Arturo hesitated, looked at me. "You sure you can do this?"

"Piece of cake."

He smiled, then walked the wall. He sat atop the wall, one leg dangling over each side, peered down at me. "Okay, Holmes, let's do it."

After three false starts, I began my climb. Instantly, the muscles in my arms burned. I placed hand over hand on the rope, hoisted myself a little further. About seven feet up, my arms gave out. I was able to grab the rope halfway down, break my fall somewhat. Still, my ass hit the dirt like a rock.

Arturo erupted in laughter. Someone from the other side kept asking what was so funny. Arturo waved at them, looked back at me. "Take it easy, Holmes, you'll get it."

Two more false starts, then I was sitting atop the wall. Embarrassment more than strength got me up the wall, I'm sure. I followed Arturo onto a limb of the poplar tree, then down to the ground.

"Ready to call it a night yet?" Arturo said.

I glared at him. "Fuck you."

The wooded area was even denser that it looked from the street. Crickets chirped, frogs sang. It was like a Twilight Zone episode. Before we crossed the wall, we were in Hollywood Hills. Now, it seemed more Montana than California.

From the outside, I estimated this area to be between fifty and seventy-five feet deep. The fractions of light that seeped through the brush from a streetlamp ended ten feet in. Beyond the woods was the river, then a slope up to the inhabited backyard space. I'd estimated the incline was a hundred feet from the back wall, far too long a distance to travel without light.

Arturo agreed. Popeye dug two flashlights from the duffel. He handed one to Arturo, kept the other. Popeye flipped on the flashlight, began shining its beam in front of him, overhead, like a kid with a new toy. Arturo charged him, planted his shoulder in Popeye's gut, and took him to the ground. He grabbed the flashlight from Popeye's hand, flicked it off.

"What the fuck are you doing, *esse?* You wanna get caught?"

Arturo said a few more things in Spanish, then climbed off him. Popeye leaned back on his elbows, looked stunned. Arturo handed Popeye's flashlight to me, then said, "Lead the way."

I pointed the flashlight to the ground, cupped my hand over it, and turned it on. Slowly, I peeled my hand away from the bulb. Once my eyes had acclimated themselves, I began walking. Popeye got to his feet, and we formed a single line. Arturo brought up the rear. When we reached the river, I paused.

The riverbed was reminiscent of the drought-like conditions Los Angeles often experienced. With its low water levels, the river was more like stagnant pools of water with patches of moss-covered mud separating them. The beam of light reflected off the black water. Carefully, I raised the beam to illuminate a portion of the opposite side. Mud draped the incline on the far bank, stopping at a deliberate line of maples displaying burnt orange, red and brown leaves. I knew what climbing that mud would be like. I could almost hear my Nikes cry in protest.

What I found when reaching the other side was that the mud was actually much drier and sturdier than the riverbed itself. Good thing, too, since we had to lie down against it. Arturo and I took up positions at the edge of the maple trees, binoculars in hand. The others stayed at the riverbed, smoking cigarettes. I wanted a cigarette, too, but wasn't sure if it would be spotted, so I held an unlit Marlboro between my lips, peered through my Bushnells.

I started at the left side and worked my way across the yard. Three couples and two single men sat in chairs by the pool, drinks in hand, smiles on their faces. Blake was walking with a Hispanic woman in her fifties, dressed as a French maid, and a young girl, maybe fifteen, dressed in a short black mini-skirt and a blue blouse. Her blond hair bounced against her shoulders as she walked. She seemed happy until I focused in on her face. Her eyes admitted that she was high.

"See that?" Arturo said.

"The girl."

"Yeah. What's up?"

"I have an idea and I don't like it."

As I suspected, the girl was brought to the edge of the pool. The maid stayed with her, Blake walked nearer his guests. He spoke to them, then pointed at the girl. One of the women stood, walked over to the girl. She stood next to the girl, ran her hand through the blond hair, rested it on her shoulder. She looked into the girl's eyes and smiled. Then, she ran her hand across the girl's breast, let it hover for a moment, and walked back to her male companion. They spoke for a minute, then the man stood and took Blake aside. He produced a large stack of bills from his pocket, handed them to Blake. Blake smiled, nodded at the maid. The maid led the girl to the woman who'd touched her. The woman took her hand, then met her companion in the grass. The three headed up to the house.

"They just bought that little girl," Arturo said.

"Yep."

"Fuck, we gotta stop this."

"We will. One way or another, we will."

Sniper crawled up the incline, came to rest on his belly between Arturo and I. He held the 30-30 in his hand. "Anyone to shoot yet?"

Arturo said, "Not yet, but hopefully soon."

"Cool."

He sounded thrilled.

Blake spoke to the maid for a moment and then she took off toward the house. Blake rejoined his guests. I took a moment to scan the remaining portion of the yard. The tennis courts were on the right, but the lights were out. The cage for the courts fastened to the block wall, so the only chance we had to make it to the house was along the left side. Unless, of course, we barreled down the path. I hadn't seen any security yet, but knew they were lurking somewhere. Reza didn't know how many were working the party, but I was sure that even though Reza and the fat Arab were tied up, literally or otherwise, Blake had a full staff on hand. I just didn't know how many a full staff consisted of.

"Check out the guy standing by the pool," Arturo said to Sniper. Sniper leveled his rifle, peered through the scope. "That's Blake."

"Take him out?"

"No," Arturo snapped. "Not yet, I'm just telling you."

"Oh."

I started to wonder how many people Sniper had taken out with his 30-30, then decided I really didn't want to know.

During the next half-hour, the maid brought up two more girls. The first girl, an Asian with jet-black hair, apparently was good enough for one of the single men. The second girl, a brunette who didn't look a day over twelve, went inside with one of the other couples.

"These people are some sick motherfuckers," Sniper said.

Blake stayed poolside with the single man and the last couple. They had formed a semi-circle around one of the glass tables, drinking, talking. Twenty minutes passed. I began to wonder whether the parade of underage girls was over.

"Maybe we should go up," I said to Arturo.

"Anytime you're ready."

I spent a few minutes explaining the plan to Sniper. He was to fire no shots unless our lives were clearly in danger. Otherwise, his finger stayed off the trigger.

"Clearly," I repeated. "You have to see the gun pointed at our heads before you fire."

"Jesus, white boy, I hear you."

"Sorry, but you seem a bit itchy."

"Probable kill, that's what Arturo promised." He glanced at Arturo, said no more.

Arturo and I left Sniper with his 30-30, climbed back down to the riverbed. I lit my cigarette and enjoyed my smoke. Arturo took a Glock .45 from a bag, held it out to me.

"Thanks, but I've got my Sig."

I touched the butt of the pistol against the small of my back for reassurance. Arturo stuffed the Glock in the waist of his jeans.

"I'm not one to mother," I said, "but are you sure you wanna be packing? I mean, with your parole and everything."

Arturo gave me a stern look that told me not to push, so I backed off, went back to my smoke.

Arturo grabbed two pairs of gloves, handed one pair to me. I pulled a lock pick driver from the other duffel, put it in my pocket.

Arturo handed Elbow and Hand our flashlights and told everyone to wait, and take instructions from Sniper.

We walked to the far end, up the incline, stopping behind a large cypress tree just in front of the wall of maples. I ground my cigarette into the dirt, leaned over to pick up the butt, and put it in my pocket.

The changing-room shed blocked our view of Blake and his guests. But, if we couldn't see them, they couldn't see us either.

Our inability to spot any security made me nervous. Maybe Blake forbade them to come out back for fear they'd bother the guests, which meant they were all inside or out front. I expected a couple might be hanging out front, but not many. This was a quiet street and I'm sure Blake didn't want to attract the attention of any neighbors.

Reza and the fat Arab both were to work the party, so at the very least, they'd be two guards, but I suspected a man like Blake would feel inadequate with only two men guarding this acre-plus lot. I put the number at four to six.

"What now?" Arturo whispered.

I motioned, then skipped from tree to tree until I was leaning against the back of the shed, which was more like a small stand-alone apartment than a shed. I held a finger to my lips, inched along the wall. Blake's laughter caught me by surprise. I hadn't realized we were so close to him until that moment. It sounded as though he was just on the other side of the wall.

Other voices joined in his merriment. The laugh of drunken pedophiles. I wanted to grab my Sig, jump out, and give each one of them two rounds in the chest and one in the forehead. I exhaled slowly, let my murderous intentions pass, thought about the mission at hand.

I'd only been inside the house once, and then it was only a quick trip up a flight of stairs to a nook for a not-so-memorable few minutes with Blake. One thing I had noticed, though, was that Blake was not a fan of clutter. His hallways and enormous foyer were a testament to that, providing precious little in the way of refuge should one need to hide.

A high-wattage lamp hung above the end of the pool closest to us. Fortunately, the light was angled to illuminate the water and not the trees separating it from the perimeter wall, so we had a good chance of passing unseen.

In a loud roar, Blake offered to refresh his guests' drinks. Glasses clanked, and a female voice with a Hispanic accent spoke with Blake. Then, the clanking stopped, as did the conversation. The maid must have returned to fetch the glasses, then went back to the house for new drinks. I took the opportunity to lunge for a large maple beyond the shed. I crouched down, turned slightly, peered across the pool. Blake and his guests were facing me, but if they saw me, they didn't give it away. I stayed there for a full minute, then motioned for Arturo to follow. He joined me at the tree. No one seemed to notice him, either.

I felt lucky and ran behind the maples that lined the pool, and stopped at a weeping willow near the edge of the house. My heart beat out of control, but slowed some once I realized I hadn't been seen. Arturo joined me a moment later. "Where to now?"

Suddenly, I was lightheaded. I leaned against the tree, closed my eyes.

"What is it?" he said.

"Nothing, I'm just not sure where to enter the house, that's all."

"Christ, Holmes. You didn't think about that until now?"

"Nope."

"That's great. You're gonna get us killed."

"I hope not."

"Me, too."

I spent all my time worrying about how to get to the house, not how to enter it. I guess I was doubtful we'd get this far. Now that we had, I saw only one option. "There's a door halfway down this side of the house, off that terrace. We go in there."

"Where does that put us?"

"I have no idea."

"Perfect."

Forty Seven

Several windows lined the walls near the door. None elicited light. The next floor had even more windows along this side. Those, too, were dark.

I crouched, leaned against the willow and smoked a cigarette, careful to cup the cherry with my hand. I calculated the distance between the willow and the door. The yard on this side of the house was dark, but I knew if Blake happened to turn our way, he'd certainly spot us. With the auto-driver, I estimated ten seconds tops to get the door unlocked, but it was sure to be one of the longest ten-second stretches of my life.

"We're gonna have to make a break for it," I said, craning my neck to glance at Blake and his guests. "Hopefully, they're drunk enough not to notice."

"If they do?"

"We're in deep shit."

"No, Einstein, what's the backup plan if they spot us?"

"How the hell should I know? I came up with plan A. The least you can do is come up with the backup plan."

"I always gotta save your ass."

I ground my cigarette butt under my Nike, then placed the butt in my pocket. "There's nowhere to go, so let's not be seen, okay?"

If we ran toward the front of the house, the gate, if not a security guard or two, would stop us. Blake would be behind us, and going to the river could mean trouble if he was armed, or if he could get security in the back quickly. Behind us was block wall, and considering the ease with which I climbed the last wall, I wasn't looking to that as an option, either. We had only one option—get through the door unnoticed.

The maid had returned with new drinks, and Blake toasted

with his guests.

"I'll go first."

I took a deep breath, hopped to my feet and sprinted for the door. A railing lined the patio. As I approached, I wasn't sure if I could clear it with a running jump. If I missed, my body crashing against the wood deck would be about as subtle as screaming at Blake, so I had no choice. Two steps away from the railing, I exerted a bit more in my run, launched myself off the ground. My first leg cleared, then my second. My Nikes landed hard against the deck. I flattened myself against the door, using the couple of inches provided by the doorjamb to the best of my ability.

I stood frozen, pressed against the cool wood door. My chest heaved, my heart raced. I heard no sounds from either side of me, or from the other side of the door. After a minute, I forced myself to turn toward Blake. He seemed oblivious to my presence. Thank God for alcohol.

I squatted in front of the door, put on the gloves, grabbed the auto-driver from my pocket and attached a pick. I drove the pick into the lock, pulled the trigger. The first pick wasn't right, so I exchanged it, tried again. After five seconds of jabbing, the bolt opened. I replaced the driver in my pocket, motioned to Arturo.

He ran across the lawn, looked like Michael Jordan as he cleared the railing with ease. I noticed his feet landed softer, too. So much for my gracefulness. A nearly combustible mix of envy and anger boiled in my stomach when, while my breathing still hadn't returned to normal, he didn't even appear winded. I wanted to say something, but was at a loss for words, so I held my breath, opened the door.

As I suspected, the room was dark. We stepped inside far enough for Arturo to close the door. I withdrew a pen light from my pocket, held it in my left hand. Then, I filled my right with my Sig.

I put the butt end of the small flashlight between my teeth, used my fingers to rotate its head. A small beam of light broke the blackness. I continued to turn the head until the beam was narrow, focused, then took the flashlight from my teeth, and held it in my hand.

The light illuminated a dining table. I moved the beam to the wall. A small curio cabinet, filled with dishes that, to me, seemed exquisite, but were probably hand-me-downs from the man upstairs. I scanned the room, found a small island, an L-shaped kitchen area. Again, a very nice kitchen, but not the kind a house of this size would have for its residents.

"Servants' quarters," I said.

We walked deeper into the room. To our left, a grandfather clock silently swung its pendulum. Next to it, a closed door. We had to start somewhere, so we started there.

The door creaked as I opened it. My finger circled the trigger of my 9mm. My heart beat so fiercely that I wondered if Arturo could hear it. So far, this case had taken me from computer work and surveillance of low-level scum to breaking and entering the house of a prominent, wealthy pedophile, so I figured it would take my heart a while to get used to the tension. I stepped inside the room.

A maple dresser sat on the right wall. Beyond the dresser was another door. The room was an ell, and once I took a few more steps, I noticed a queen-sized bed to my left. The sheets looked so taut you could bounce a quarter off them. Small nightstands stood on either side of the bed. I walked to the other door, pulled it open. Gasoline and oil fumes met my nose. A cursory look confirmed it was the garage accessible from the front parking area. I closed the door.

As the beam made its way across the room, I noticed Arturo's hands.

"Hey, put your gloves on."

His right hand was wrapped around the butt of his Glock. He held his left hand in front of him, palm up, stared at it. He turned it over, glanced at the back of his hand.

"Oh, yeah," he said. "Shine the light here."

He pointed to the bed. I maneuvered the light to the corner of the green comforter. He set the Glock down, slipped on the gloves, and picked up the pistol.

We walked back into the kitchen, through an archway that led to a sitting room. The left wall was angled forty-five degrees. A set of double doors was dead center. On one side of the doorway, a Kenwood component stereo system. On the other, a large screen television. The right corner of the room held a sofa and coffee table.

Besides the double doors, two other doors led from this room, both on the right side. I peered inside both rooms. They appeared to be a bathroom and bedroom respectively, though neither contained any fixtures or windows, as if they were abandoned somewhere during the construction process. That seemed strange, especially in a house of this caliber.

Arturo pointed at the double doors. "What do those lead to?"

"How do I know?"

"That's right, Mr. Prepared."

"Let's find out."

We stood behind the doors. Both of us had an ear pressed against wood. Soft classical music played. It sounded like a full orchestra playing Mozart, so I was sure it wasn't live. I heard no voices or other sounds. I put my hand around one knob and pulled the door ajar.

The light that met my eyes temporarily blinded me. I blinked them into focus. The area was a large hall of sorts. Recessed fluorescent fixtures lined the ceiling. The mahogany parquet floor reflected the light well, adding to the degree of illumination. To the left, two couches sat against a wall with four armchairs in front of them, coffee tables in between. What looked like a bar sat next to the far couch. In the middle of the room was a staircase leading up. Next to that, two archways, one leading to another hall area, one to what looked like a dining room.

Suddenly, I heard footsteps. They were faint, but growing louder. My eyes scanned the room and came to focus on a pair of legs descending the stairs.

"Shit," I whispered. "Someone's coming."

"Now what?"

The legs were that of a woman wearing low-heeled black shoes and a black dress over bare, brown legs. My guess was the maid, but I couldn't be sure. I closed the door, sprinted across the sitting room, and went into what I had deemed the unfinished bathroom. Arturo slipped in behind me. I closed the door, leaving just enough room to peer through. A moment later, one of the double doors opened.

I saw the black silhouette pause in the doorway. The silhouette moved a little and the room was flooded with light. The deer in the headlights feeling came over me. I wanted to shut the door. Here I was staring at the Mexican woman in the French maid outfit who'd brought the girls to Blake. Unsure of how much noise the door might make upon closing, I opted to leave it as it was. The woman headed for the kitchen, unaware. She whistled a tune I didn't recognize.

Cupboard doors opened, closed. Water ran, then stopped. A door opened and closed. Hoping she went into her bedroom, we snuck back into the sitting area.

"Let's try this again," I said.

From the doorway, I hadn't noticed the baby grand piano on an elevated stage in the right corner of the room. A music room, and only about triple the size of my apartment. I really liked my place, but after seeing how many of my little cubicles could be stuffed into a single room of Blake's house, I found a tinge of jealousy in my gut. And I didn't like it.

I put the penlight in my pocket and made a quick check of the dining room. A set of saloon doors separated the dining room from the kitchen. The kitchen led to the hall I'd seen earlier, but rather than re-enter the music room, we opened a set of double doors to our right.

"Holy shit," Arturo said. "This is outrageous."

A sign of wealth is more what it was. Four eight-foot couches were set up, two on each side, in front of a 100-plus inch television monitor. We stood in Blake's private screening room. Another door led to a bonus room that contained two corner showcases filled with awards of some type. The controls for the monitor, a wet bar and a small bathroom completed this area.

As we passed, I snuck a peak up the stairs but saw nothing. Next to the sitting area was another archway, which exposed two more doors. The first one led to a narrow hallway and another door to the garage. The other led to the laundry room. In there, we found an industrial washer and dryer, folding tables, coat racks, cabinets filled with laundry supplies, and a door leading to a flight of stairs down.

"Well, up or down?" Arturo said.

Down would put us on the first floor. My guess was that up would lead to the main entrance of the house.

"I wish I knew where the guards were," I said.

"You and me, both."

"You have a preference?"

"No."

"Me, either. Let's go up."

No sooner had we left the laundry room and the door to the servants' quarters opened. The maid stepped into the music room holding a tray of cookies in one hand, pulling the door shut with the other. She headed toward us, eyes on the tray.

I pushed Arturo back into the laundry room. He was about to say something. I raised a finger to my lips, stopped him. I pointed to the stairwell, then followed him to the door. He opened it, and we stood on the stairs, door cracked.

The laundry room door opened, the maid appeared. I left the door ajar and motioned for Arturo to descend the stairwell. I followed.

The bottom of the stairs held another door. Arturo opened it and we scurried through. I barely got the door closed when I heard the door at the top of the stairs creak.

We were in an empty room. Beside the door to the stairs, there were three other doors—one in the far left corner, two in the far right corner. I ran to the right corner first.

Both doors were gray. One was locked, the other open. The open door led to a wine cellar. We stepped inside, but before I closed the door, I examined the locked door. This door was steel, I was sure of that. And, an electronic keypad was just to its right. The door at the foot of the stairs opened. I left the wine cellar door ajar, held my Sig tightly in my grip.

The maid approached our corner. She still held the silver tray of cookies in her upward-facing left palm. She balanced the tray with the expertise of a waitress. Closer, she came.

I took a step back from the door, motioned Arturo to the side. I held my pistol out, waited. I heard her heels click against the concrete floor. A few more steps, then the clicking stopped.

I pointed my pistol at the back of her head. She keyed numbers into the keypad and stood still, facing the door. The door lock snapped, then the steel pulled itself back, slowly.

"Don't move," I said.

I tried to keep my voice low as not to frighten her more than necessary. Still, she jumped. The tray of cookies, though, stayed firm in her palm. She turned to me with a hand over her heart.

Her features were dark. Crow's feet at the corner of her round, brown eyes, black-blue half-moons below them, lines etched on her cheeks and around her thin, pale lips. Estimating that a good number of her years were difficult ones, I put her at fifty-five.

"Come in here," I said.

I walked backward a few steps into the cellar. She obeyed. When she was inside the room, I told her to close the door. She did.

"What's going on?" she said. Her accent was definitively Hispanic, though I couldn't pinpoint a specific region.

"What's behind that steel door?"

She gazed over her shoulder, then back at me, said nothing.

I repeated my question.

"I . . ."

I pulled the photo of Carrie from my inner jacket pocket and held it toward her. "Where is she?"

The woman stared at the photo. Her eyes gave her away—instant recognition. Her lips squeezed together, her eyes narrowed. "What do you want with her?" She glared at me. "You are not a customer."

"No, I'm not. I'm a private investigator hired to find Carrie." The name didn't appear to ring any bells. "The girl in the photo."

"Oh."

"The girls are behind the steel door, aren't they?"

She didn't answer. Before this case, I had never found much use for intimidation, though I was acutely aware of its power of persuasion. I pulled the slide back on my pistol. Her waitress skills failed her—the tray of cookies clanged against the concrete. "I want some answers."

"*Sí,*" she whispered.

Arturo stood, arms crossed over his chest. Had I thought of it, Arturo's advancing toward her a step would probably have done as much good as my readying my pistol. He was a scary sight when his face went stone cold, as it was at that moment.

The woman's features took on a shade of fright. Her mouth hung slightly open, jaw loose on its hinges. She held her eyes narrow, not from contempt, but from fear. She probably thought she was going to be shot. Guilt pulled at my stomach, but I couldn't give up the instant power my pistol had afforded me.

"What were you doing?" I said.

"I was bringing the girls cookies."

"Is it your job to take care of the girls?"

"*Sí.*"

"How many girls are in there?"

"Three. The others are upstairs with customers."

"Are they buying the girls?"

"*Sí.*"

"How long do you keep the girls down here?"

"A week maybe. Not long. *Señor* Blake moves them out quickly."

"Sells them you mean."

She glanced at the floor. "*Sí.*"

Disgust for this woman mounted inside my chest cavity. For a moment, I saw the darkest side of myself come alive. My trigger finger itched to contract, depositing a bullet in this woman's skull. Not only was she aware of Blake's atrocities, she was a participant.

The burning rage behind my eyes must have become apparent in my stare. Arturo tapped my shoulder, said, "Ease up, Holmes."

I took a deep breath, let the fury secrete through my skin, evaporate in the dank air of the wine cellar. He pulled his hand away, my finger relaxed.

"Why?" I said.

"*Qué?*"

"Why do you do it? Why do you help a sick man like Blake?"

"I must."

"Bullshit." My remark came out harsher, louder than I had anticipated. I let it hang in the air a moment. "No one must participate in exploitation."

Tears welled in her eyes, dotted her cheeks. "I am illegal. *Señor* Blake knows this. He promised to have me sent back to Panama if I didn't help him."

"So you did."

Her eyes remained focused on the pristine concrete beneath our feet. "*Sí.*"

"And you're okay with that?"

"No," she snapped. She looked up at me and for the first time I saw a fierceness appear within her pupils. "I am not okay with it."

"Were you supposed to bring Blake any more girls?"

Confusion spread across her face.

I said, "We saw you bring the girls out to the pool."

"No more tonight."

"Is Carrie back there?"

"*Sí.*"

"Besides the girls, who else is in there?"

"Franco."

"Is he a guard?"

"*Sí.*"

"Does he have a gun?"

"No."

"Here's what we're gonna do."

FORTY EIGHT

I dictated the plan. Up until that point, I hadn't had one, and was surprised how easily it came to me. The maid, who told me her name was Isabella, agreed to help us. It became apparent to me that Isabella liked Blake's activities no more than I did.

"When I was in Panama," she said, "my family was killed. I hid in the bushes and watched the soldiers walk up and gun down my husband and my children. A friend of mine got me into Mexico, and I found someone to take me here."

She'd been in Los Angeles only three weeks when Blake found her. No doubt, Blake wanted someone with a big secret, and finding an illegal saved him the trouble of digging up something on someone.

The adrenaline that pumped through my veins made my urge for a cigarette irresistible. I had lowered my pistol as I spoke with Isabella, but kept it firmly at my side. She showed no signs of contemplating escape, so I holstered my pistol and lit a cigarette.

Isabella told us there were five security guards in the house. Two out front watching the limos, she was certain of that. Blake never left the front of his house unmanned, especially during these parties—parties that generally occurred once a month, though had occurred as often as four times a month when demand required it.

Besides the two in front, there was one guard on the third floor. He manned his station just outside the bedrooms where the customers test drove the girls. Another guarded the fourth floor, Blake's private floor, with his bedroom, game room and private balcony. She was unsure of the fifth guard's location—his job was to roam. Last she'd seen, he was with the guard on the third floor.

Something Isabella had said bothered me. If the girl's spent only a week with Blake, why was Carrie still there? I asked her.

"*Señor* Blake likes her. He might keep her for himself."

Lucky for me, and I guess it may have been better for Carrie, too. Who knows what kind of shithole the girls would be subjected to once out of this country. For Carrie, I don't suspect it mattered much. She was already in hell.

The first thing we had to do was get Carrie. Overpowering one unarmed man seemed almost effortless. The second thing, though, was to get out alive. And I wasn't sure how we'd do that yet. But, I decided not to waste time. I'd figure it out soon enough, I hoped.

I held my Sig at my side and we walked to the steel door, which was closed. Apparently, it stayed open only so long. Isabella punched her code on the keypad again and the door crept open. I stepped in front of her, pointed my pistol down a long narrow hallway, but I found no one to aim at. Isabella said there were two more doors to go through before we were actually inside. We walked to the end of the hall where she punched a code on another keypad. The second steel door opened and the first closed.

Walking inside, I found another door, another keypad. Blake cut no corners down here. Without Isabella, we'd never have gotten in. I looked around the room and found that this last door attached to walls built within the walls of the outer room. The inner walls were a good foot thick, and except for the small entryway where we stood, only eighteen inches separated the two sets of walls, and that was packed with soundproofing material.

Isabella held her hand in front of the keypad.

"Wait," I said. "Where is Franco?"

"Probably watching TV with the girls."

"Will they see us as soon as we walk in?"

"No, there is a hallway. At the end, we turn left."

"Okay."

She punched in the code, the door slid open. I held my pistol in front of me, walked down the hall. I heard voices from the TV and a guy and two girls talking. The male voice was slurred, likely by alcohol.

I stood one step from the end of the hall, exhaled slowly. Arturo stood next to me, Isabella behind. I took the last step.

A dark-haired, balding man sat on the couch, a girl on either side of him. They seemed oblivious to our entrance. I walked toward the couch, pistol firmly in my grasp, aimed at the bald spot on Franco's head.

When I was ten feet away, I said, "Don't move."

He turned to me, his face skewed in disarray. "What the fuck?"

"Stay where you are."

I stepped to my left, noticed Franco's hand buried in the panties of one of the girls. He withdrew it slowly, his eyes locked onto mine.

"Get Carrie," I said to Arturo. Isabella led him through another door, out of my sight. To Franco, I said, "Stand up slowly, motherfucker." To the girls, "Stay on the couch, okay?"

He stood, they didn't. "Take a step toward me." He did. "On your knees."

He knelt down, interlocked his fingers and set his hands on his head. And without my having to ask. With all the rage inside me, I landed my Nike under his chin. His head snapped back, his body fell against the carpet. He was out cold. I smiled. That felt so good.

Arturo held Carrie's arm as they stepped into the living room. She glanced at Franco, then up at me. "Are you buying me?"

"No, Carrie, I'm getting you the hell out of here."

A small smile crept onto her lips, but was quickly extinguished. She eyed me suspiciously, chewed her bottom lip.

"Your parents hired me to bring you home."

The smile tried to force its way back, but she fought it. I'm sure the weeks of hell taught her not to hope. The crack in my heart widened a little more.

"Let's get out of here," I said.

I led the way down the hall. The steel doors were only key padded on one side. This side held a small green button. I pushed it and the door swung open.

I stepped through the third door to find an AK-47 pointed at my forehead.

"Far enough," the voice said.

Behind the machine gun, I saw an Arab, late thirties, two-fifty. A veritable sheet of rock.

I stopped. Thought I wasn't certain, I assumed Carrie, Isabella and I were visible to the guard, but Arturo may still have been in the hall. A scurry of voices, footsteps, and two more bodies appeared from the stairwell, neither of whom I recognized.

The barrel of the AK-47 came to rest against my skin. "Drop your weapon."

I did. The clank of metal against the concrete echoed in this large hall. We stood silent for a minute, then more footsteps. And Blake walked into the room.

"Goddamn it, Murphy. You're a real pain in the ass, you know that?"

"I try."

He walked up, sucker-punched me. My head twisted right, blood drained over my lips, my cheek burned as the blood rose to the surface.

Isabella ran to Blake, threw her arms around him. "*Señor* Blake, thank God. They were going to kill me."

Blake wrapped his arm around her, patted her shoulder. "Don't worry, darling, no one's going to hurt you."

So much for loyalty. So much for the plan.

The guard backed the AK-47 away from my skin. Another guard walked past me. I turned my head. Arturo was hidden in the hallway, but without knowing the keypad code, he couldn't go anywhere. The second guard came back with his AK-47 pressed into the small of Arturo's back. Carrie stood between us, chewing the quick of her thumb, glancing at the floor.

"Carrie, my dear," Blake said, "would you like to go back to bed now?"

She nodded.

Blake told a guard to put Carrie away. The guard grabbed her arm.

"Be careful with her," Blake warned.

The two disappeared down the hall. Only once Carrie was gone did Blake turn back to me.

"You stupid son of a bitch. Why couldn't you just leave well enough alone?"

"It's not my nature. I'm like a pit bull . . ."

"Oh, shut the fuck up." He turned to the guard with his AK focused on me. "Take them to my office."

The two AK-47s led Arturo and I toward the stairs.

"Isabella," Blake said, "fix me a double scotch, would you, darling?"

She nodded at him, preceded Arturo, me and the two guards up the stairs.

— Forty Nine —

The guards took us to an office on the third floor, directly below the nook where Blake and I had our earlier conversation. One of the guards produced two sets of handcuffs. He applied a set to Arturo's wrists, then mine. We sat in sitting chairs on the visitor side of an oversize mahogany desk. Behind the desk was a high-back maroon leather chair. Three large single-pane windows lined each wall of the alcove, just like the nook above. But, these windows had blinds, pulled tight.

The guards stepped out of the office. Before closing the door, one said, "We'll be right outside. Please give us a reason to shoot."

The two laughed and the door closed. Fortunately, they handcuffed us with our hands in our laps, which made it relatively easy for me to fish cigarettes from my pack. I grabbed two, set them in my mouth, grabbed my lighter and ignited it. I handed one cigarette to Arturo.

"Thanks, Holmes."

I searched Blake's desktop for an ashtray. Unable to find one, I used the parquet floor. Arturo did the same.

"Is it time for a plan B yet?" Arturo said.

"Yep."

"Well, what is it?"

"That was your department."

"We're in deep shit."

"What's the chance of Sniper and the boys coming to our rescue?"

"You were quite explicit with your instructions, Holmes. I doubt they'd want to risk being ridiculed by you again."

"Such wimps."

Arturo took a hit from his cigarette. "We're on our own."

Yippee.

Fifteen minutes later, the door to the office opened and Blake walked in. He held a highball glass, nearly empty, in his hand. He went directly to his chair and sat down.

"There's no smoking in here," Blake said.

I took a long, slow drag from my cigarette, savored the smoke as it trailed through my nostrils, over my lips. "Oops, sorry."

Blake sneered. "Laugh it up, Murphy. You're in deep water now and I'll be damned if I'm going to give you a life raft."

"Figures."

"Oh, shut up, would you? You're goddamned annoying."

"Thanks."

Blake leaned back in his chair. The anger sat heavy on his brow. "Why couldn't you leave well enough alone?"

"Because you're fucking scum."

"Fuck you, Murphy. You have no idea."

"Yes, I do. You get off on little girls. And you supply girls to other rich pedophiles like yourself."

He grinned. "Do you realize how much of a nothing you are?"

"If you compare wealth, you're right. I'm nothing. But at least I don't go around fucking babies."

"Shut up."

"What's the matter? Don't like to talk about your fetish?"

He slammed his fists on the mahogany, so hard the paperclips jumped from the dish on the corner of his desk. The highball glass crashed to the floor. "I was hoping Reza had taken care of you at the motel. Of course, now I will have the pleasure of watching you die."

"Getting your hands dirty ain't your style, Blake. You watch your goons kill us, you'll be covered in dirt that'll haunt you forever."

His response was to turn his chair toward the window, twist open the blind. He stared out the window for a good five minutes before closing the blind and facing us again. When he spoke, his voice was quiet, controlled.

"I wish you would've left this alone, but you've backed me into a corner, so to speak, and I am going to fight back."

"Like a cornered rat. You're a miserable fuck, Blake, and it'll be a pleasure watching you get shipped off to San Quentin. Did you know the inmates in San Quentin especially like to fuck child molesters up the ass? You should get fucked three, four times a day."

Blake came around the desk, landed his fist against my left cheek. Blood returned to my palate. At least it was the other cheek this time. My right one was still sore from the last hit.

"Enjoy your last moments on earth," Blake said.

He stood, peered down at me for a moment, and stormed from the room.

"Why'd you have to go and piss him off?" Arturo said.

"It's my nature."

"Some fucking nature you got, Holmes. You'll have Blake laughing all the way to our graves."

"You're such a pessimist."

"Realist, isn't that what you call it? And reality says we're fucked."

A short burst of machinegun fire erupted, voices shouted. A woman screamed, then another. Glass shattered, wood splintered.

One of two things had just happened. Either the guards had freaked out, or the Evergreeners had shown up.

"Then again," I said, "maybe not."

The commotion continued. Arturo and I sat quiet. The more I heard, the more I was sure the house was under siege. Whether it was the Evergreeners or not, I didn't know. But, I was pretty sure it wasn't the cops—no one yelled *police*.

I walked to the door, opened it a little, and peered out. No guards. I flung the door open and told Arturo to follow me.

I stood in the entryway. The front doors were closed. One of the bedroom doors opened and a woman in her forties glanced out. She eyed me for only a second, then disappeared back into the room. The lock on the door then snapped. I peeked into the living room and found it empty.

"Guard the bedrooms," I said. "Don't let anyone out."

"With what, Holmes? They took my Glock."

"Then use your charm to persuade them."

He smiled. "Okay, boss."

I stood at the stairwell for a moment. All the noise seemed to be coming from the second floor, so I headed there. Halfway down the stairs, I was met by the barrel of an HK-94. Fortunately, Sniper was on the other end. He lowered the machinegun.

"I'm sure glad to see you," I said.

A single shot rang out. I guessed it was one of the Glocks. Then, a second, and a third. A man screamed for a moment, then went silent.

"Fucking guards," Sniper said, "they're giving us a hassle. We had to shoot one already. That was probably a second."

"There's five total."

"Good, then that means we have them all. We've got control of the first two floors. I was just working my way up." He glanced down at my wrists. "Let's get that taken care of."

We walked down the stairs. Hand and Elbow had an HK each, standing between the small crowd in the music room and the sliding glass doors leading to the backyard.

"There's a big living room on the next floor. From that floor, you need to either go down the stairs or out the window."

Sniper stopped, smiled. "Sounds good."

He shouted something in Spanish. Hand and Elbow both nodded, then explained to the crowd they were going upstairs. I scanned the people. The couple and the single man from outside were amongst the crowd. Also, three guards, a cook and a young girl were there. Blake and Isabella were both missing.

"Where's Blake?" I said.

"I haven't seen him yet. But, don't worry. Cheetah's covering the back and Popeye's in front. No one's going anywhere."

"Good."

I glanced through the glass doors and saw a man crumpled on the ground. A pool of blood had formed on the grass near his chest.

"That son of a bitch wouldn't get inside the house," Sniper said. "He was caught in the first spray of bullets."

The guard who'd handcuffed us was leaning up against the wall near the doors to the servants' quarters.

"He," Sniper said, "is a loud-mouth fuck. Looks like he caught a couple in his tits."

"He's the one."

We walked over to him. He breathed slowly, his eyes clouded. He held a hand to his chest weakly, as if it would help stop the stream of blood filling his shirt and the floor around him. Sniper crouched over, searched the guard's pockets. His fingers came back with a handcuff key. He unlocked my cuffs, handed me the key. I leaned down and relieved the guard of my Sig and Arturo's Glock.

Confident the guard wasn't going anywhere, Sniper helped Hand and Elbow get the people upstairs. I followed.

Arturo saw us coming. A smile crept over his lips.

"*Esses*, you made it."

I unlocked Arturo's cuffs, handed him his pistol. He put the Glock against the small of his back, then rubbed his wrists. "Damn, they had those on tight."

"Anybody move?"

"Not an inch."

The living room was furnished with three large couches and four armchairs. Elbow told everyone to find a seat. He and Hand stood guard near the alcove. Enough light seeped through the archway to allow sufficient vision. Still, the cook flipped on the lights. Elbow went berserk.

"Turn off the goddamn light. Now!"

The cook flicked the switch.

"Now sit the fuck down and don't move. Don't none of you move a fucking muscle."

"Let's clean out the rooms," I said to Arturo.

The rear wing of the third floor had four doors. The first room was empty. The second was the room from which the woman appeared. Arturo tried the door. It was locked.

"Open the door and come out," he said.

I heard no sounds from the room. Arturo glanced at me. I shrugged. He pulled his pistol.

"Stand away from the door. I'm gonna shoot out the lock on the count of three. One. Two. Three."

He fired twice. The handle blew into pieces, dangled from the wood. Using his right foot, he kicked open the door.

The man, woman and little girl sat on the bed. Only the little girl was naked.

Arturo held his Glock in front of him, pointed it at the man's forehead. "Get the fuck up and out into the living room."

The woman looked at the man. The man stood up and the woman followed.

"Not you, sweetie," I said to the girl. "Put your clothes on."

She grabbed her underwear, shirt and dress from a chair in the corner then ran into the bathroom, slammed the door.

The rage that had spiked in me in the wine cellar reappeared as the man came closer. I stood just outside the door. Our eyes met, and he froze in his tracks. I rested the barrel of my pistol against his forehead.

For the little girl in the bathroom violated by this sick motherfucker, for all the little girls he had had his hands on during his life. My hand shook as I glared at him. The woman shrieked, held a hand to her mouth.

"No, don't shoot him," the woman screamed.

I balanced on my left foot, swung my right back. Then, with all the force in me, I landed my Nike against his groin. He grunted. His legs went rubbery. His hands clutched his balls. He fell to his knees. I kicked again. My foot connected with his nose. Blood poured from his nostrils as he fell on his back. I glared at the woman. "Better?"

"You maniac," the woman said.

I trained my pistol on her.

"Hail Mary, full of grace. The Lord is with thee."

"Shut up. Do you think God's gonna listen to you after what you've done? I should . . ."

The corners of my vision blackened. My heart grew cold. My soul was inundated with hatred. I could taste the sweetness of the kill on my tongue.

"Please," she whispered.

"Is that what the little girl said to you? Did she beg for you to stop?"

"No, she was willing."

The darkness in me swelled, the demon inside took over. I relaxed my pistol, shifted it to my left hand. Then, I landed an uppercut to this woman's jaw. She was out cold before her body hit the floor.

FIFTY

"Goddamn it," I said.

I said it for everything—the situation, the girls, the pedophiles, myself. This whole thing was just one large pit of shit, feeding on itself, growing blacker by the minute. And now I was a party to it as well.

I looked at Arturo. He stared at me for a moment but said nothing. He crouched over and picked up the man. "Let's get them into the living room."

I put an arm under the woman's neck and another under her knees. As I lifted her, I noticed her lip had split, spewed blood across her face. A knot had formed where my fist connected with her jawbone. A bruise had appeared around the knot, slowly turning a deep shade of purple.

All eyes were on us as we entered the living room. Arturo set the man in the middle of the floor. I laid the woman next to him. We walked back into the entry.

When we stood in front of the third door, Arturo said, "Take it easy this time, Holmes. I understand your frustration, but you need to watch out or you're gonna kill somebody."

The third room was empty. The fourth door was locked. Arturo knocked.

"Yes?" a feeble male voice answered.

"Open the fucking door."

"Why?"

"Open the door or I shoot my way in."

"Oh, Christ, don't do that. I can't believe this shit." The sound of wood furniture scraping a wooden floor seeped through the door. "Hold on a second. I'm coming."

The man continued to mumble. A few thumps, more

scratching, then the lock popped, the knob turned. Arturo stepped back and nailed the door with the sole of his foot. The door snapped open, the man cursed. The door bounced off the man and almost closed again. Arturo stopped it with his hand, pushed it wide open.

The man was lying on the floor, holding his nose. Blood spurted through his fingers.

"See, calm, rational. Like that," Arturo said.

Arturo grabbed the man's arms, hoisted him to his feet, and dragged him into the living room. I walked to the bathroom, knocked lightly on the door, and opened it. The Asian girl sat near the toilet, sobbing.

"C'mon, honey, it's okay."

When her gaze met mine, I felt sick. Fear spewed from her big, brown eyes, her body shook. She clutched her knees to her chest. Her clothes, torn, lie next to her.

I took a step in the bathroom and held out my jacket. "Here, put this on."

Her eyes widened. Her stare went from my eyes to my jacket to her scraped knees. She was obviously confused. One minute, a man is ripping her clothes off, molesting her, and the next, a different man is handing her his jacket to cover her naked body.

I took another cautious step to her. She didn't recoil, but she didn't become any more receptive either. "Tell you what. How about if I leave the jacket on the floor and go outside. Then you can put it on and come out when you feel like it. Would that be okay?"

She nodded.

"Okay." I set my jacket on the linoleum, and smiled at her. "Don't worry, honey, no one's going to hurt you again. You'll be with your family soon."

At the word *family*, she smiled. Something, I'm sure, she never thought she'd see again.

I closed the bathroom door on my way out.

Arturo stood in the hallway. I approached him. "I'm going to get Blake."

"Where is he?"

"Probably the fourth floor. That's his private suite or something. Wait for the two girls, then take them downstairs. Have them wait in the music room while you find Isabella. We need her to get back inside the dungeon."

"Where is she?"

"I don't know but she's in this house somewhere."

He slapped my shoulder. "Hang in there, Holmes. Blake's gonna fry for this."

I headed for the stairs.

Sig firmly in hand, I climbed the stairwell. I turned in full circles as I walked. The foyer had no ceiling and the entire hall area from the fourth floor looked down on it. My eyes danced around the railing as I took another step, then another. When I reached the top flight of stairs, I found no one.

Along the back wall, near each corner, were double doors. I assumed that was Blake's master suite. I tried the ones in the left corner. The doors swung inward, creaking slightly. Directly in front of the doors was a sectional couch facing a large, single pane window. Blake sat near the window, his gaze fixed on something beyond the glass.

I took a couple of steps, then leveled my pistol with his head. Without looking at me, he said, "We meet again."

"So we do."

He raised his right hand. It held a pistol. "Please don't come any closer. I don't want to shoot you."

"What do you want?"

"I just want this nightmare to go away."

"It won't."

"I know that. I just wanted a few minutes alone."

Save the missing wife, Blake reminded me of Adolf Hitler in the cellar as he waited for the enemy, gun in hand.

I lowered my pistol but kept it in my grip. "I need some answers."

"Don't we all." He sat silent for a moment. "Go ahead, ask me."

"This operation is all about underage girls, right? You and DiMarco round them up and sell them off."

He broke into laughter, held his belly with his free hand. "Yes, it's all about the girls. Sorry, I know it wasn't funny. I can't help it."

I waited for him to stop before I continued.

"In the time I watched you, it seemed you did most of the work. What exactly did DiMarco do for you?"

"For me? He did nothing. DiMarco didn't work for me."

"Whom did he work for?"

"That I don't know."

"So, DiMarco sold the girls to you and you, in turn, sold them to others."

"Exactly."

"Why not Carrie?"

He turned to me, his eyes swollen, red. "Because I love her."

I had a few things to say to that, but I let them go. He looked back out the window. "I know you can't understand that, but it doesn't matter."

I glanced to my left. Through another archway, the bedroom. The only furniture in it was a king-sized bed. No nightstands, dressers, chest of drawers. The domicile of a sick, lonely man. To my right, a huge walk-in closet, complete with a vanity, two chest of drawers and nearly two hundred square feet of space. Not a single piece of clothing in it.

I took another step toward the sectional. Blake raised his pistol again. "Please. Don't make me use this."

I guessed he hadn't seen my pistol or regarded it as futile.

"Why did you have DiMarco killed?"

"He double-crossed me."

"How?"

"He was supposed to give me only clean girls. Which meant no drugs, no sluts, and no girls that had ever appeared on film."

"He didn't do that?"

Blake turned to face me. "The funny thing is, the girls were clean until DiMarco got ahold of them. Him and that sleaze ball Donovan put the girls on film before they brought them to me. Then, DiMarco sold the films on the black market."

"How did you find out about it?"

"Last time I was in Argentina, a client said he had just gotten ahold of a great film. 'Beautiful girl,' he said. 'You'll love her.'" He chuckled. "Turns out I did love her. It was Carrie."

"So you killed him."

"Something like that, yes."

"What about the pier?"

"What?"

"The staged accident at the pier. How did you pull that off?"

"I have no idea what you're talking about. Now if you'll excuse me, I'd like to be alone."

I knew what was going to happen. I found myself with mixed feelings about it. On the one hand, it was quick, final. On the other, it was freedom. But, I was still four feet from the sectional and I wasn't about to take a bullet over it. I turned and walked out, closed the door. The gun went off before I reached the stairs.

FIFTY ONE

From the phone in Blake's office, I called Tyrone. He wasn't home but his wife said she'd reach him, tell him to call right away. Then, I called Nadia. She answered after three rings. Her voice was groggy.

"Hi," she said.

"Hi. Listen, I need a favor."

"What is it?"

"Remember you told me you had a friend at American?"

"Yes, Betty. Why?"

"I need three tickets on a flight to Chicago or Milwaukee. It's an emergency."

"Did you find Carrie?"

"Yep."

"What happened?"

"I promise to fill you in later. Do you think you could call her now?"

"Now?"

"Is it too late?"

"What time is it? Eleven-thirty. No, I'll give it a shot."

I thanked her and told her to call me back at Blake's house. I hung up the phone, but before I could stand up, it rang.

"Hello?"

"Jack, Tyrone. What the hell's going on? Patty said it was an emergency."

"It is."

"Well?"

"You need to come over to Blake's place."

"Oh, shit. What did you do this time, Jack?"

"I got you the case you've dreamt of."

"What?"

"Just come over here now. And alone."

"Give me twenty minutes."

Arturo located Isabella and had already cleared out the dungeon. The girls were with her in the kitchen. She was making brownies.

"So, boss, how does it feel?" he said.

I fished a cigarette from my pocket, lit it.

"I don't know how I feel. I'm numb. I am glad we found Carrie, though."

"Me, too. How do you think she is?"

"Fucked up. All these girls are, I'm sure." I lit a cigarette. "I wish I could've stopped Blake from killing himself."

"What for? He was a douche bag and now he's dead."

"He got off too easy."

"Maybe, maybe not. You believe in God?"

"I try."

"Then, don't forget. He's speaking to the Big Guy now. No worse punishment for his shit than that."

"I guess you're right."

"Fucking A, I'm right."

"Still, I would've liked to see him spend a few miserable years in prison. God would've waited."

Arturo took a hit from his cigarette, said, "I've got a question."

"Shoot."

"What the hell's gonna happen here?"

"I imagine the foreigners will go to prison, the girls will go home, if they remember where home is. And the servants will probably be let go."

"What about us?"

"You and me?"

"And my posse."

"We'll leave."

"But, this mess."

"Tyrone's coming over, alone. I'll explain it to him and let him deal with it. Why don't you tell everyone to gather up all our shit and wait for us in the van."

"You sure?"

"Yep. Keep an HK, though. Everyone's scared, but I don't trust any of these sick fucks."

I walked into the kitchen. Carrie was staring out the bay window behind the sink. The other girls were huddled around

Isabella, who was pulling fresh brownies from the oven. The chocolate smell awoke my stomach. I was hungry but I bypassed Isabella and her brownies, stood next to Carrie.

"Hi," I said.

She looked up at me, then back out the window. "Hi."

"How're you doing?"

"Okay."

"Really?"

She looked back at me, pinched her lips together, and nodded. "Yeah, I'm okay."

"Are you looking forward to going home?"

"Are you going to take me home?"

"Yep."

"Why? Don't you like me?"

"Sure, I like you, but not in the way these sick men said they liked you. But, that's over now. Soon you'll be back in Wisconsin with your family."

"Will I?"

"Yep."

"Promise?"

"I promise."

She turned her body to face mine, looked up at me. "Can I ask you a favor?"

"Sure, honey, anything."

"Can I have a hug?"

"This is a fine pile of shit here, Jack."

"I executed it as neatly as I could."

"I'm sure you did. Did Blake decorate the wall himself or did he have help?"

I stood behind the sectional in the master suite. Tyrone crouched in front of Blake's lifeless body.

"That was all his own doing."

"Boy, the media is going to have a fucking field day with this story."

"Yep, but you get to return those girls to their families. That won't go unnoticed."

He smiled. "That's true. One of the finer points of my job."

"We need to work out the logistics with Carrie."

"I have a feeling I'm not going to like this."

"Arturo and I need to leave with Carrie now. Maybe we can get the Lake Point police to take her statement after she's had a few days to rest."

"What the hell is Lake Point?"

"The town she's from in Wisconsin."

"Oh."

"I wanna get her back to her family before Christmas, and if we stay and fuck around with this, we'll be tied up for days."

"Maybe more."

"Exactly, so I need you to let us leave before calling it in."

"How the hell am I gonna explain this to homicide? Fuck, forget them, what about the Chief? He was a friend of Blake's."

"I don't know, Tyrone. But, I can't hang around. If I do, Carrie won't get back."

He stood straight, walked out of the bedroom. I followed.

"Shit, Jack, you're asking me to not only stand by and watch a cover up, but to initiate it." He stopped near the nook, peered out the bay window. "You and Arturo had help here."

"Yep."

"Who?"

"Some nameless friends."

"Nameless, huh? You've really got my balls in a vice on this one."

"Won't the collar be worth it? C'mon, Tyrone, the cops would never have suspected this fucker. You said as much yourself."

"Can you and Arturo keep your mouths shut about what happened here?"

I fished a cigarette from my pocket. "Yep."

"Give me one, would you?"

"I thought you quit."

"I just started again."

I lit two cigarettes, handed one to him.

"What about your friends with no names. Can they keep their mouths shut, too?"

"They already forgot they were here tonight."

"Good, good. If this turns to shit, Jack, I'm not the only one gonna drown."

"Fair enough. Once I get Carrie home, I'll do whatever's necessary."

He stared out the window, smoked his cigarette. "What did Blake do exactly?"

"He brokered girls. Bought them from DiMarco and sold them to foreigners."

"Like the ones in the living room?"

"Yep."

"I should just shoot them, put them out of their misery."

"I know how you feel."

He glanced at me, a smile in his eyes. "You do, huh?"

"I almost took out a few tonight myself."

"So the guy with his balls in his stomach and the girl with the broken jawbone are both courtesy of you?"

"Yep."

"Good job."

The only problem was I couldn't believe it was a good job. I'd let my emotions get the better of me, I lashed out. Yes, they were scum. Yes, they deserved it. But, I did something I promised myself I'd never do—I hit a woman.

We walked downstairs, headed for the living room. The phone rang. I sprinted toward the office.

"You Blake's secretary now?" Tyrone said.

"Nadia's supposed to call me back."

I slipped into the office, answered the phone on the sixth ring.

"I was about to hang up," Nadia said.

"Sorry, I was out in the hall with Tyrone."

"Are you in trouble?"

I sat in Blake's chair, threw my feet up on the desk. "No more than usual."

"That's reassuring."

"Yep."

"I talked to Betty, everything's set. You guys leave tomorrow morning at twelve-thirty. Non-stop LAX to O'Hare."

"You're a god-send."

"I know."

"Thank you."

"You're welcome."

"And I promise . . ."

"Hold up, big boy. Don't make a promise you're not sure you can keep."

"I can keep this one."

"Just hold off. Okay?"

Her voice was strong, her comments firm. I knew better than to push. "Okay."

"And, please be careful."

"Always."

I hung up wondering whether I had done anything careful since I took this case.

"Nadia arranged everything. We leave tomorrow night," I said.

"Great, but what do we do until then?" Arturo said.

"Sleep sounds pretty good."

"Amen, Holmes. Amen."

I went back to the kitchen. Isabella and the other girls had moved to the dining room and were working to consume the entire plate of brownies. Carrie was still staring out the bay window. She had a brownie in her hand but it was untouched.

"Hi," I said.

"Hi."

"Are you ready to go?"

"Where?"

"We have a flight back to Chicago tomorrow night. Tonight, we'll sleep at my apartment."

She furrowed her eyebrows, scrunched her nose. Doubt had crept into her features. "What?"

"You can sleep on my couch. Arturo and I'll sleep on the floor."

"Arturo?"

"He's a friend who helped me out tonight."

"Okay."

We walked into the hall.

"What's your name?" she said.

"Jack."

"Thanks, Jack."

"You're welcome."

Tyrone had relieved Arturo of his HK. I introduced Arturo, and asked that the two of them wait for me while I spoke to Tyrone.

"You're not gone yet?" he said.

"Just about. Listen, one more thing."

"Jesus, Jack. Is this the last one?"

"Yep, and it's an easy one, too."

"What is it?"

"Isabella, the maid. She helped me a lot tonight. In fact, without her, Arturo and I'd probably have bullets in our heads by now."

"Do you want me to give her a medal or something? You know, she might've saved me future headaches if she had just minded her own business."

I said nothing.

"What about her?"

"She's an illegal."

"Big surprise."

"I want you to fix it for her."

"What?"

"Get her a green card so she's not deported."

"Covering up your involvement here tonight ain't enough, huh? God almighty, Jack, I swear you're out to ruin me."

"Isn't this bust worth it? Cause I could call up someone else and hand it to him."

"Fuck you."

"Thanks. I really appreciate it."

"Now, get the fuck out of here. Or I might just change my mind about this whole thing."

"No, you wouldn't."

He stared at me, chewed his bottom lip. "No? And why's that?"

"Because we're doing the right thing. These girls will forever be in our debt."

"Oh, goodie. Now go."

I smiled at him, then joined Arturo and Carrie.

And we left.

FIFTY TWO

I woke up at nine-thirty Thursday morning. Carrie was still asleep on the couch. Arturo was on the balcony doing his morning exercises. I grabbed the cordless phone, walked onto the balcony.

"Morning," Arturo said.

"Morning."

"Who you calling?"

"Raymond Sanders."

Arturo was doing sit-ups. I let the phone ring ten times before hanging up. Then, I dialed Roy's number. His wife answered on the second ring. After exchanging pleasantries, I asked to speak with Roy.

"Jack, how's it going?"

"Are you ready for some good news for a change?"

"Always."

"I have Carrie." Roy didn't answer. For a moment, I thought I lost the connection. "Roy, you there?"

"Sweet Jesus, how? Where?"

"It's a long story."

"It's unbelievable, that's what it is. How is she?"

"Physically, she seems okay. Mentally is another story. I'm sure she's gonna need counseling."

"That's to be expected."

I lit my first cigarette of the day. Arturo had moved on to jumping jacks. "I tried to call Raymond, but no one's home."

"He's probably at work. Are you bringing Carrie here yourself?"

"Yep. We've got a flight out tonight. We should be in Chicago around six AM local time."

"That's wonderful. Is Carrie with you now?"

"Yep. And I won't let her out of my sight for even one minute."

"Good, fantastic. Listen, Jack, I knew if anyone could find her, you could."

"Thanks."

"So what are you two going to do today?"

"I don't know. Why?"

"No reason, just curious. I thought maybe Carrie might want to do something fun on her last day in California."

"Last night she said she wanted to see Beverly Hills before we leave. When she decided to come to California, that's where she wanted to go. But, she never made it there."

"That should be fun. You gonna show her Rodeo Drive and all that rich people's shit?"

"Maybe. Rodeo Drive is something all tourists want to see, isn't it?"

"My wife made a big to-do last time we were there."

"I guess we'll go by there."

"Good. I would hate to think Carrie didn't get to do anything fun in LA."

"Me, too."

"I gotta go, Lisa's calling me to lunch."

"Okay. Are you gonna be at Raymond's tomorrow?"

"I wouldn't miss the big homecoming for anything."

"Good. See you then."

When I went back inside, I heard the water running in the bathroom. At that moment, I realized Carrie didn't have any clean clothes to wear. While I had a closet full, I was sure she wouldn't want to wear anything I had to offer.

I called Nadia and asked if Carrie could borrow something comfortable. She told me she'd be right over. And, fifteen minutes later, she was.

"Hi, come on in."

"No," Nadia said, "I better not."

"Why not? C'mon."

"No, I've got a ton of things to do today."

"That's too bad. I was gonna invite you to Beverly Hills. Carrie's never been there and asked if we could go before we leave."

"That sounds like fun, but I can't."

"Okay."

Nadia handed me a pair of sweats and a white t-shirt with *Foxy Lady* across its front. "All I could do on short notice."

"I'm sure it'll be fine. I forgot to grab her clothes from Blake's last night."

"Have a nice flight, and be careful."

I missed our friendship, I missed what I thought was starting between us. I wanted to lean in and give her a kiss. Instead, I leaned against the doorjamb. "Always. You, too."

"I will. Bye, Jack."

I told Arturo we needed some food for breakfast. He offered to make a run to the store. I jotted down a few things—milk, eggs, cheese, cilantro, tomatoes, green chili. I gave him the list, a twenty, and the keys to my truck.

After Arturo left, I had enough time to smoke two cigarettes and drink a bottle of Palomar Springs before the shower water stopped. I glanced at my watch. Carrie had spent nearly an hour in the bathroom, but I didn't mind. I figured she was trying to rid herself of the stench left from Blake and who knows what else.

I turned on the TV and found nothing of interest. I stopped on a rerun of a boxing match between two unknowns in Las Vegas some time last year.

"Good morning. You got an extra one of those?" Carrie said.

I turned to lay my eyes on one of the most beautiful girls I had ever seen. A good night's sleep and a shower easily shaved five years from her face. Her baby skin sported a dark, even tan, her eyes sparkled. Wrapped in a large yellow bath towel, tied just above her breasts, she resembled the Carrie I saw in the picture her father had given me.

"Morning. An extra one of what?"

"Cigarette."

I opened my mouth ready to spew a lecture on how underage kids shouldn't smoke. Fortunately, I snapped it shut before any words slipped. I handed her a cigarette and, when she pursed the smoke between her lips, lit it.

"Thanks."

I've never been one to contribute to juvenile delinquency, at least not since I became an adult. But in this case, smoking a cigarette was the least of Carrie's worries.

"Nadia, a friend of mine, brought some clean clothes you can wear." I pointed to the sweats and t-shirt in the chair. "I hope they'll be okay."

She smiled, tilted her head when she looked at me. "Why are you so nice?"

I wasn't sure how to answer that. Nice is not a word I would've used to describe myself. Apparently, I waited too long to answer.

"Anyway, thanks a lot."

Carrie sat on the couch next to me, crossed her legs and then adjusted the towel. I smiled at the modesty still inside this girl's heart.

"What?" she said. "What's so funny?"

"Nothing, I just . . . It's nothing."

"Tell me, please."

The transformation in Carrie struck me as somewhat of a miracle. Last night, her aura exuded a slave. Now, it hinted to young lady.

"I think you're a sweet girl, and I'm glad we found you."

"Me, too. Thank you."

"You're welcome."

She leaned forward, tapped her ashes in the ashtray while she held the towel to her breasts with her free hand. "What did my parents say when you told them that you found me?"

"I couldn't speak with them. I called Roy and let him know."

"Roy?"

"He's the person who put me in touch with your parents. I used to work with him at Lake Point PD."

We watched a round of boxing in silence. Arturo came back with two bags of groceries. He unloaded the bags, put everything in the refrigerator. Carrie glanced at him, then ground her cigarette in the ashtray, picked up the clothes from the chair and disappeared into the bathroom.

"Did I scare her off?"

"Probably."

Arturo did his best to imitate a lion's roar. The ensuing sound resembled more a punk rock band than a fierce animal. I laughed.

He repeated the sound, accompanied this time with erratic arm movements and a hunched back.

"That don't look like any lion I've ever seen."

"That's cause it ain't a lion."

"What the hell is it, then?"

"An ape."

"Apes don't roar."

"In my world they do."

Seeing the impossibility of arguing with such a statement, I lit a cigarette. "I didn't get a chance to properly thank you for last night."

"No need."

"Yes, there is. You saved my ass. Without your friends, I'd be breathing dirt right about now."

"Me, too, Holmes."

"Yeah, but it was because of you they were there in the first place. I would've done something stupid like tried to do it alone."

"Sounds like you."

"Shut up. The point is that I owe you, and the Evergreeners."

"Okay, I'll chalk it up in the Jack owes me column."

He reached over, grabbed my pack of cigarettes from the table. He put a smoke between his lips, exchanged the pack for the lighter, and lit the cigarette. "They were glad to help. It's not often people like us get to do something that's good."

Of all the possibilities for Arturo's friends to help us, that thought had never crossed my mind. I figured Arturo called in some markers, but maybe all he did was tell them they had a chance to do the right thing for a young girl who was in trouble. And that seemed the best possible reason of all.

Carrie came out of the bathroom. Dressed in the sweats and t-shirt, she looked a healthy sixteen years old.

"Are you hungry?" I said.

"Yes."

I walked to the kitchen and started cooking omelets.

FIFTY THREE

We watched the rest of the boxing match and the first part of a B movie. Carrie insisted on cleaning up the dishes after brunch. Arturo seemed to enjoy the movie, his eyes remained fixed on the TV while I sat at my desk and added notes to Carrie's file.

I wrote in the file for two hours, replayed the case in my head as I went along. The objective had been realized, the missing girl found. Yet, uneasiness swept through me as my pen recorded the end of the case. The ending still felt contrived. All the dominos lined up neatly according to someone else's plan, then crashed down when and as they saw fit. I did all I could to simply avoid the little black plastic chips, lest one might crush me.

I glanced at my watch: three-fifteen. I wanted Carrie to see all of Rodeo Drive, and as little of the rush-hour traffic as possible. "Let's go."

"Where?" Arturo said.

"Rodeo Drive."

Carrie turned to me, her eyes wide, bright. "Really?"

"Yep. I said we'd go."

"Yeah," she said, glanced at the carpet, "but . . ."

"But, nothing. C'mon, Arturo, move your lazy ass." I grabbed my keys from the countertop, jangled them. "Hurry up."

Arturo's middle finger got up before he did. But, his body eventually followed and we left.

I had been to Rodeo Drive once previously. I'm sure that in the 20s and 30s, it was great. But, unless you were rich, a tourist, or a rich tourist, Rodeo really held little value. It was overcrowded, filled with stuff you'd have to mortgage a home to buy, and a general stench of wealth permeated from the walls as well as from its regulars. Sure, you might spot a movie star buying a new pair of earrings or new clothes, but so?

I reminded myself that Carrie was a tourist and she wanted to see Rodeo. I had to remind myself again as I fought the gridlock to the parking structure off Dayton Way. Rodeo Drive had two parking structures. One offered two free hours of parking while the other did not. Subsequently, the lot I tried first, the one with the free parking, was filled. I followed the street to Beverly Drive, turned right and found the lot that was advertised at a bargain—a mere eight bucks an hour. But it, too, was full.

Fortunately, I know the guy who runs an office plaza in the 9400 block of Wilshire. When the spots aren't filled by tenants, he rents them out. He had one spot available. I took it.

We started at Via Rodeo, a block-long stretch of cobblestone walks. Carrie stopped at Cartier and again at Tiffany, stared in the window. She didn't say anything, but I could hear her mind as it tried to fathom actually making a purchase. Anytime I saw merchandise without a price tag, I knew it meant I couldn't afford it and, therefore, didn't want to know its cost. Most of the stuff I saw fit into that category.

We spent an hour window-shopping. By then, I was in serious need of a caffeine rush. I spotted a coffee house at the northeast end of the drive.

"You guys want a coffee?"

"No, thank you," Carrie said.

"Sure."

We walked to Java City. Arturo waited with Carrie at a table outside while I went in and ordered. They were sitting down when I returned. I gave Arturo his coffee. "What do you think so far?"

An ear-to-ear smile formed on Carrie's lips. "It's exactly what I thought it would be. Fantastic."

"I'm glad."

We sat for half an hour, filling the time with cigarettes and small talk. We threw our trash and walked toward my truck.

As we walked down Wilshire, I noticed a black Mercedes with jet-black windows stopped at the light. It had driven by while we were in front of Cartier and again while we were at the coffee house. I touched Arturo's arm, nodded in the direction of the street. "Black Mercedes stopped at the light."

The light turned green, the traffic rolled forward. The Mercedes took off much slower than the rest of the traffic. As it approached us, both the windows on its right side slipped down, exposing two angry black men and two assault rifles.

"Down," Arturo said.

I grabbed Carrie's arm, pulled her to the concrete, then laid on top of her. She didn't move, didn't make a sound.

The gunfire splintered the early evening air. People screamed, ran, glass shattered. The bullets continued for what seemed like forever. Then, the Mercedes' motor revved, and disappeared into the traffic on Wilshire.

I waited another ten seconds before lifting myself off Carrie. She didn't move.

"Are you okay?"

"Yes," she said, barely above a whisper.

"Arturo? You okay?"

I turned to where I last saw Arturo. No longer next to me, he was facedown on the concrete. It took a few moments longer before I noticed the pool of blood expanding from beneath him.

I crawled to him, called his name again. He didn't respond. I put my hand under his shoulder, rolled him on his back. His shirt was drenched in blood. I tore it away from his chest and found at least two bullet holes.

"Fuck. Somebody call an ambulance."

Carrie stood over us. Tears filled the corners of her eyes. "Is he okay?"

"I don't know. Go to the parking garage and make sure someone called nine-one-one, okay?"

She nodded and ran.

It took the ambulance nine minutes to arrive. A man and a woman rushed over.

The woman knelt to Arturo's left side, said, "Please, sir, give us some room."

A hand rested on my shoulder. A male voice from above me said, "Please, sir."

I stood up, took a step back.

"Is he okay?" Carrie said again.

I gave her the same answer—I just didn't know.

Two black and whites were on the scene before the paramedics had Arturo on the stretcher. One of the cops told Carrie and me to sit on the curb. By the looks on the cops' faces, I could tell this sort of thing just didn't happen in their neck of the woods. I also assumed they would blame me for bringing it to their town. I snuck out my cell phone and called Tyrone.

After a few minutes of complaining, Tyrone agreed to come down. I emphasized the urgency, he told me to fuck off and hung up.

I sat beside Carrie. Because of a parked car and the way we hit the ground, Carrie and I were shielded from the bullets. Arturo, however, was wide open.

And he took at least two in the chest.

FIFTY FOUR

"Let's go over it one more time, shall we?"

The cop who interviewed us was the epitome of an asshole. Five-seven, two-fifty, beer belly that he wore poorly, gray hair that covered only half his head. He spoke in a deep monotone, glared at us through beady, brown eyes. His nametag read *Stevens*.

"How many times do you want to hear it?" I said.

This was the fourth time.

He stared at me. "Mr. Murphy, we will go over it until I am satisfied. Understand? If you prefer, we can do this at the station."

A rebuttal formed on my tongue, ready to be fired. But, my eyes caught sight of Tyrone and I held back.

Tyrone walked up to us, nodded at me, said to the cop, "A word."

The cop said, "Don't move," and followed Tyrone.

"What's happening?" Carrie said.

"Tyrone's gonna explain the situation."

"Oh."

"Are you okay?"

Carrie's tears had dried, but she had become withdrawn, quiet. "Yes."

"I'm sorry about this."

"It's okay."

"No, it's not. Obviously, someone's still upset with me. I should've anticipated that."

She rested her delicate palm on my forearm. "It's not your fault."

At that moment, a sixteen-year-old girl made me believe everything would be okay. I found myself lost in that moment. I blinked, and was thrust back into reality. "Thanks."

Tyrone sat next to me. The Beverly Hills cop had vanished. He rubbed his temples. "Jack, this really has to stop."

"I agree. I'm tired of being shot at."

"And I'm tired of covering your ass. You've managed to piss off cops in Beverly Hills, too."

"I didn't bring this here, you know."

"Yes, in a way you did." He glanced at Carrie, then back at me. "Who do you think was behind this?"

"It must be the person DiMarco worked for. It was a black Mercedes, four black men. The two shooters wore red bandannas."

"Bloods."

"That'd be my guess."

"You better lay low, my friend. Soon as word gets back that you're still breathing, they're gonna visit you again."

"I know."

He glanced at Carrie. She sat stiff, staring at the traffic. He nodded.

"We'll be right back," I told Carrie.

"Okay."

Tyrone walked ahead of me, leaned against the wall of the office plaza.

I joined him. "What's up?"

"What's the chance the shooter's target was Carrie and not you?"

"Possible."

"Not probable?"

"Maybe. Maybe they were aiming for a two-for-one deal."

"When's your flight?"

"Twelve-thirty tonight."

"Make damn sure your ass is on the plane. And, once you've delivered Carrie home, make sure you call me before coming back. Got it?"

"Yep."

"Good, now make sure you do it."

"Where'd they take Arturo?"

"I don't know, but I'll find out. You have your cell?"

I tapped my pocket. "Yep."

"Keep it on. I'll call you."

"Okay."

"Go home right now, get your shit and leave. And don't go back."

Tyrone left. I got Carrie and we walked back to the parking

structure.

"I hope Arturo's okay."

I slammed my door, started the engine. "Me, too."

I paid for the parking and headed straight home.

FIFTY FIVE

Carrie and I stayed at my place just long enough to pack some things. Then, I headed to Nadia's apartment, parked in her driveway. My mind raced as we walked up the steps to her apartment.

Carrie had barely spoken since the shooting. I didn't blame her. After being dragged out of one hell, she found herself smack dab in the middle of another. What was there to say?

I knocked on the door to apartment 9. Nadia opened the door almost immediately. "Hi."

"Hi. Can we come in?"

She peered past me for a moment, closed the door. The chain jangled as it came free from its slider bar, and the door opened wide. Nadia took a step back.

I still hadn't come up with a suitable way to tell Nadia. So, in my usual way, I just blurted it out. "Arturo's been shot."

Nadia's face went pale. Her eyes bulged, her lips fell open. "What?"

I took the doorknob from her hand, closed it. I threw the deadbolt and replaced the chain. "We went for a walk on Rodeo Drive. A Mercedes came by and decided to turn us into hamburger meat. Arturo took at least two bullets in the chest."

"My God. Are you okay?"

"Shaken, but not stirred." She didn't laugh, so I added, "We're okay."

Nadia and Carrie sat on the couch. I recapped the evening's events from a side chair to Nadia's left.

"Do you guys want something to drink?" Nadia said.

"Water, please," Carrie said.

"Jack?"

"A beer, if you've got one."

Nadia went into the kitchen and came back a moment later with a clear glass filled with ice water and a bottle of Miller Lite. I twisted the cap on the beer, took a drink.

Nadia sat back on the couch. Dressed in gray sweat pants and a pink t-shirt, bare feet, and mussed hair, she looked stunning. I realized she was one of the few women I'd known that could manage to remain beautiful in any setting. I repositioned myself in the chair, hoping to ease the sharp pain that suddenly gnawed at my gut. "I need a favor."

Carrie sipped her water, her eyes focused on something in the kitchen, or something a million miles away, I wasn't quite sure. Nadia rested her elbows on her knees, glanced up at me. "What?"

"Actually, I need your help."

"Really?"

"Will you fly back to Wisconsin with us tonight?"

Her eyes chilled, narrowed. "Are you serious?"

"Yep."

She bolted to her feet, walked to the edge of the kitchen, and spun to face me. "A few days ago, you said you didn't want me anywhere near this case because it was too dangerous. Remember that?"

"Yep."

"Now, after Arturo's been shot, you want me to jump in with both feet. Am I correct so far?"

I lit a cigarette. I knew this would be a difficult discussion. The grinding pain in my gut made me nauseous. "I suppose you could put it that way."

"You suppose? Jesus, Jack, I don't understand you."

"May I use the restroom?" Carrie said.

Her voice was quiet, as though she hated to ask.

"Sure. Let me show you where it is."

Nadia took Carrie down the hall. I smoked my cigarette, tried to anticipate what might come next. Nadia was back in less than a minute.

She sat on the couch, grabbed her pack of cigarettes from the table and lit one. She took two hits before she turned to me. "You're a very frustrating person, Jack. When I do help, you get pissed off and tell me not to do anything more. Then, when a man goes down in the line of duty, you come running back to me, begging for help."

"It's not just a man that went down. It's Arturo. And I'm not begging."

"Begging, asking, whatever you're doing, it's frustrating. And I know it was Arturo. I didn't mean it the way it sounded."

"I'm sorry."

"No, you're not. And don't pretend you are."

I tipped my ashes in the ashtray, sat back in the chair. Her words hung in the air like dense fog.

"I'm sorry I asked. I'll go alone."

I didn't realize she still had her lighter in her hand until she threw it against the coffee table. It bounced off the glass, fell to the carpet. "Goddamn it, Jack."

"What? I understand if you don't want to get involved. It's a stupid idea, anyway. It's my job, I'll do it alone."

"If you felt you could do it alone, why did you come here in the first place?"

"Tyrone said I should stay away from my apartment. It looks like Bloods were behind the drive-by tonight."

"So, you figured you could use my apartment for a couple hours to hide out?"

"No."

"You're not making any sense, Jack."

I knew I wasn't, too. If I had any control over the words that appeared on my tongue, I would have cut them short. But, I didn't. "Look, either you want to help or you don't. Simple as that."

"Shit. Why do you have to do this?"

"Do what?"

"Be an asshole."

"I don't know."

She dragged an open palm down her face and shook her head. "Why do I bother?"

I assumed her question was rhetorical so I didn't answer.

"I need to ask you something," she said.

"What?"

I looked up as Carrie came down the hall. She sat on the couch. "Thank you."

"You're welcome," Nadia said.

"What?" I said.

"Nothing. Let me get some stuff together."

Nadia left the room. Carrie asked for another cigarette. I lit one, handed it to her, and turned on the TV. Carrie kept her eyes focused on the early edition of the news, yet I don't think she watched it. I did the same—saw it without watching it. Nadia came back twenty minutes later with two bulging suitcases, a carryon and a makeup bag.

"I wasn't sure how much I needed to pack."

I glanced at the suitcases, smiled. "I think you're covered."

She set the bags in the entryway. "You guys want anything to eat?"

Both Carrie and I declined. I added that we'd get food on the plane. Maybe it was because of what I said that Nadia went to the kitchen and made herself a sandwich.

Nadia ate her sandwich as we watched the rest of the nine o'clock news and the first half of the ten o'clock news. At ten-thirty, I suggested we leave. Carrie thanked Nadia again for the water, set the empty glass on the coffee table. Nadia grabbed my empty beer bottle and the glass, set them in the kitchen, then we met in the entry. I grabbed the bags.

"I can get those," Nadia said.

"I'd like to help."

She shrugged. And we left.

The departure terminal at LAX was busy. I parked in the drop-off area. A white man in his fifties, dressed in a blue uniform with American's logo on his left breast, smiled as I approached. I gave him the luggage and told him which flight we were taking. He assured me the luggage would make the flight without any problem. Every time someone makes such an assurance, I worry. Obviously, one would assume that the luggage would make the flight. Otherwise, why bother packing it in the first place?

I spent the next thirty minutes locating a parking space in the multi-story garages. I wrote down the section number on my cigarette pack, then rewrote it on a gasoline receipt in my wallet. With only five cigarettes left, I knew the pack would never leave the airport, and I hated having to hunt for my truck.

"Are you excited about going home?" Nadia asked Carrie as we crossed the street.

"I guess."

"You're looking forward to seeing your parents, aren't you?"

"Yes."

"Don't worry," I said, "I'm sure you'll feel better once we get you home."

"I guess."

Carrie must have felt as though she were living in a dream, and any moment she would wake up back at Blake's house, a slave to his sexual fetishes. I wrapped my arm around her shoulder, squeezed.

Once inside the terminal, we paused in the lobby. In all the planning for this flight, I had forgotten to store my pistol inside my suitcase. My eyes were scanning the lobby for the storage lockers when I felt a hand on my shoulder.

"Hello, Jack."

I didn't recognize the voice. It was deep, hoarse, definitely a black man's intonation. I looked over my shoulder and felt something hard, circular, poke my lower back.

"Easy, partner. We don't want anyone getting hurt."

Another black man dressed in a black leather jacket, white t-shirt and black Levi's walked around, stood in front of us.

"We're going to take Carrie and be on our way. Then, you and the lady here can go wherever it is you're going."

I fished my keys from my front pocket, suddenly very grateful that I had forgotten to check my pistol. "And what if I say no?"

My keys were in my palm by the time he said, "I shoot you right here."

I glanced around the lobby. While filled with people, no one seemed to pay us any attention. "With all these people around?"

"Dirty job, I know. But, it's not like anyone will step forward to identify us. I'm sure they realize what would happen if they did."

I looked into Nadia's eyes, held my keys out. "Take them." She did. "Now, take Carrie to the truck and leave."

The man behind me chuckled. "I don't think so."

I leaned into Nadia, put my hand on her neck, kissed her cheek and whispered, "Tower atop Transamerica, one o'clock."

She kissed my cheek, whispered, "Be careful."

Grabbing my Sig, I spun to face the man. I placed the pistol's barrel against his forehead and screamed, "What the fuck did you say?"

A group of Asians near us stopped in their tracks. The woman and child screamed in unison, the man's face drew up in a blank stare. I turned and found Nadia and Carrie already gone. I grabbed the man's pistol, stuffed it in my jeans.

FIFTY SIX

Within one minute, I was surrounded by LAPD cops, guns drawn. The man's partner had disappeared in the ensuing chaos. I hadn't moved my pistol from the man's forehead. He hadn't moved his stare from my face.

"Sir," one of the cops said, "put your weapon down."

"Get Tyrone Williams on the phone."

"What?"

"Get Tyrone Williams from Vice on the phone right now. I wanna talk to him before I do anything."

I took a step to my left, got around the back of the man who had a good four inches on me, wrapped his neck with my arm. The barrel of my 9mm slid to the man's right temple.

"What's your name?" I said.

When he didn't respond, I pressed the barrel harder against his skin, and repeated the question.

"Omar."

"Well, Omar, I bet you didn't plan on this little chain of events, did you?"

"You will die," he whispered.

"We all will, sooner or later. For both of us, let's hope that's later."

The cop who had spoken to me was on his radio. I couldn't make out most of what he said, but I did hear the part where he claimed he had a hostage situation and needed a negotiator. And that's when I wondered what I had gotten myself into this time.

When the cop finished talking to his radio, he replaced it in his belt, took a step toward me. "Sir, Tyrone Williams is on his way."

"Good, then we wait."

I had inched backward so I had my back against the glass

windows. I didn't want someone to come up from behind again.

"Sir, you can't possibly escape."

"I know that. Do I look stupid to you?"

"No."

That's good. Keep the suspect at ease as much as possible. This guy looked like he had been on the force one, two years tops. The look in his eyes told me this was his first hostage situation. Mine, too. I just happened to be on the wrong end.

After what Tyrone had said to me, I wasn't sure he could, or even would, do anything about this sudden turn of events. But, he was on his way, or so the cop said, so I had to hope for the best.

In the fifty minutes we held a Mexican standoff in the lobby, the terminals had been cleared. Traffic outside was non-existent. I imagined what it looked like on Century Boulevard with all traffic for the departure level kept at bay. I thought about the options that may have been available to me. And I couldn't come up with an alternative that would've kept Carrie safe, so I reminded myself I did the right thing by protecting her—at any price. I tried not to think about how high a price that might be.

Tyrone came through the double doors in a t-shirt and jeans. He was with a young white man dressed in a three-piece suit, carrying a clipboard. The young man joined the lead cop. Tyrone stood a foot from me. His anger radiated like an aura circle around his bulk, his stare burned like lasers against my eyes. I expected a barrage of profanities, screams, utter disgust to flow from him. I was surprised when he spoke and his voice was calm, quiet. Very unlike Tyrone.

"What are you doing?"

"This guy wanted Carrie. I had no choice."

"So you decided to pull a gun in the airport?"

"I had no choice."

"You always have a choice, Jack."

Omar stood still as a statue.

Tyrone glared at Omar, then back at me. "Son of a bitch. Do you know who you have here?"

"Omar."

"Yeah," he said, laughed. "Fucking Omar Donaldson, a Lieutenant for the MOB Bloods."

Omar turned his head toward Tyrone but said nothing.

"He's a class A asshole," Tyrone said. "There's been a warrant out for him for almost six months. Someone must've wanted that girl real bad to bring Omar out of hiding."

I wondered if suddenly Tyrone thought what I did was a good thing, and whether the LAPD cops who were pointing their pistols at me would feel the same way.

"You're one fucking surprise after another, Jack."

"Thanks."

"Shut up," Tyrone snapped. "That doesn't change the fact that you brandished a weapon inside the airport and held a man hostage, even if the man is little more than fucking scum." He turned to Omar, said, "It's been a long time, Omar. I'm looking forward to catching up in the interrogation room."

"Fuck you," Omar said.

"Yeah, fuck me. But, at least I'll get to go home tonight."

Tyrone laughed again, then walked to the young man in the suit and the lead cop. They spoke for a few minutes, though I couldn't make out anything they said.

"No shit, huh Omar? I can't believe I snagged a big fish."

"You will die."

"Can't you say anything else to me?"

"Fuck you."

"At least that's different."

"Your day will come."

I swallowed hard. Through all my smart-ass comments, I knew Omar wouldn't just forgive and forget.

Despite all Tyrone's pleading, both Omar and I were escorted in handcuffs to the station. We were brought into booking together, had our photos and fingerprints recorded. Then, we were ushered back upstairs. He was placed in Interrogation Room 3, I in Room 5. I sat in a metal chair at the head of the metal conference table and lit a cigarette. I glanced at my watch: twelve-twenty-three. Nadia was probably at the Tower already. I wanted to talk to Tyrone, figure out what was going on. But, I couldn't leave the room.

I was smoking my last cigarette when he did come in. He sat in a chair at the opposite head of the table, stared at me a minute before he spoke.

"This is one hell of a mess, my friend."

I was glad that he started with *my friend* rather than asshole, or something similar.

"I had to think fast."

"And that's what your mind came up with, huh? Not smart."

"What else could I do? I wasn't about to let them have Carrie."

He put is face in his hands. "Is this nightmare ever going to end?"

"I hope so."

"When?" He dropped his hands, glared at me. "When, goddamn it? You're up to two fuck-ups in one night now."

"I didn't plan for any of this to happen."

"That girl is sin."

"Fuck you. None of this is Carrie's fault."

He paused, exhaled loudly. "Christ, I know that. But, when she's around, shit hits the fan. Where is she, by the way?"

"With Nadia."

"Nadia was with you? I thought you wanted her out of it."

"I did, but I wanted someone else along, just in case."

"At least she was able to get Carrie out of there."

"Omar had a partner. He slipped away, too."

"Figures."

He paused a moment, then laughed hysterically.

"I'm glad you find this funny," I said.

"In a way, it is. We figured that warrant on Omar would never materialize into anything. It was something we did just to make the paperwork look good. And here you go, in the middle of one of your fuck-ups, and hand him to us on a silver platter."

"When you put it that way, I guess it is funny. Does everyone see it that way?"

He stopped laughing. "No, they don't."

"Nadia and Carrie are gonna be at the Tower at one."

"Downtown?"

"Yep."

"That's a half-hour from now."

"I know, which is why I have to get out of here."

"You're gonna cost me my badge. Do you know that?"

"I hope not."

"Yeah, me too."

"I need a ride."

"Of course. Would you like your shoes shined, too?"

"No, thanks, I'm wearing Nikes. But next time I have dress shoes on, I'll let you know."

"Fuck you, Jack."

Tyrone assured me he would get me out as soon as possible. It was eight minutes to one when we left the station.

"I hope you can drive fast," I said as we climbed into his Caprice.

"Not that fast, I can't."

Using my cell, I dialed information and got the number to the Tower. While waiting, I said, "Thanks."

"Yeah."

"No, I mean it. You've saved my ass more times than I can count."

"I can, and it's a lot."

"I know. So, thanks a dozen times."

"That's a start."

I called the restaurant as Tyrone raced up the onramp to the 405.

FIFTY SEVEN

Nadia was at the Tower when I called. I told her to sit tight, I'd be there soon.

"What did you find out about Arturo?" I said.

"Shit, nothing. Course, when have I had the time? You've kept me busy all fucking night."

"Sorry," I said, held the cell phone out. "Could you call now, please?"

He grabbed the phone and punched a number. I lit a cigarette and waited.

He spoke for a few minutes, then ended the call, set the phone on the bench seat. "He's still in surgery at Cedars-Sinai, will be for a while yet."

"Thanks."

I wanted to be at the hospital. My best friend was in surgery from gunshot wounds that he incurred because of me, yet I couldn't be there. No one had to tell me that once the Bloods figured out what happened, they'd put someone on the hospital to see if I'd show. Nausea crept into my stomach—I swallowed the bile that rose in my throat. Tyrone headed east on 10. The traffic was light at this time of the morning. He set the cruise at 85.

I didn't have any prior experience with the Bloods, but I knew from the media that the gang's influence reached far beyond Los Angeles. Bloods had turned up in Santa Fe, New Mexico selling crack. So, it was fair to assume that they might be in places like Oklahoma, Missouri and any of the other states we needed to drive through to get to Wisconsin. And, it wasn't beyond the realm of reason to think they'd know what kind of car I drove. My Ford F-350 dually wasn't exactly a car you saw all the time. I grabbed the cell phone, dialed Cue.

"It's Jack."

"How's it going?"

"Good. I need a car."

"I'm not in the used car business."

"I know that. I need a loaner."

I told him about my impromptu 2000-mile drive. He told me to come by in half an hour. I pressed END.

"Change of plans."

"Fuck. What now?"

"I need to go to Cue's on Sunset."

"What for?"

"You heard me. I'm picking up a car."

"Jesus, Jack, I'm telling you. It's getting to be a full-time job dealing with you."

"It'll be over soon."

"Uh-huh."

"Really. Tonight, I'm getting the hell out of California."

"What about this Mr. X who still wants you and or the girl dead?"

"About that. I need a favor."

Tyrone sighed, wiped his palm across his face. "What now?"

I told him.

With traffic as light as it was, Tyrone made it to Cue's in less than fifteen minutes.

"Thanks, Tyrone. I appreciate all your help."

"Don't get used to it. It ain't gonna continue."

"Still, I appreciate what you've done."

Tyrone half-smiled, then pulled it back. "Go on, get the hell out of here."

I closed the door.

"Hey," Tyrone said through the cracked window. I turned, faced him. "Be careful, Jack."

"Always."

"No, I mean it. Starting now, you be careful."

"I will."

I walked to the alley. A gray Lincoln Towncar sat near the rollup door to Cue's. I knocked on the door. It opened.

"Hey, Cue. Is this it?"

"Yes, this is it."

"She's beautiful," I said.

"Yes, she is. And take a real good look at it, Jack. It's fucking immaculate. Bring it back that way or I'm gonna have a problem. And, if I have a problem, you'll have a problem, too."

"Got it."

He held out a set of keys. I grabbed them. He yanked back on them before releasing them. "Take care of my baby."

"It's yours?"

"Got it last week."

I opened the door. The smell of new leather filled my nostrils. "Thanks."

"You're welcome. Good luck with your drive."

I sat down, sank into the seat. The engine fired right up, purred like the powerful eight-cylinder beast that it was. I smiled. It would be a comfortable trip.

I watched Cue in the rear view mirror watching me until I turned out of the alley and onto Sunset Boulevard. I checked my watch: one-twenty. I stepped on the accelerator, the engine responded. I leaned back in the seat, a smile on my face.

I was downtown in less than twenty minutes. A young man in a black vest met me as I pulled in front of the Transamerica building.

"Good evening, sir."

I stepped out of the car, handed him the keys. "Keep it close, I won't be long."

He snatched the twenty I dangled from my fingertips, and thrust it into his pocket. "Yes, sir."

I walked through the double glass doors, took the elevator to the thirty-first floor. The doors opened and I stepped into the bar of the Tower restaurant. Nadia and Carrie sat at a table near the window. Only three other couples sat at tables, two guys sat on opposite ends of the bar. I asked the bartender for a double JD, and paid Nadia's tab.

Nadia smiled as I approached the table. I slid into a chair, set my drink on the wood tabletop.

"Hi," Nadia said.

Carrie looked at me, smiled, and then resumed her gaze out the window. I glanced out the window and realized that from thirty-one floors up, the city looked serene. She hid her dark side well.

I swallowed my alcohol in two drinks, then said, "We're gonna drive." *gulps*

"Why?" Carrie said.

"Because whoever shot at us will be watching the airport."

"Won't they be watching for your car, too?" Nadia said.

"Probably. That's why I borrowed a car from Cue."

"You thought of everything, didn't you?"

I smiled. "Where'd you park the truck?"

"The valet has it."

"Okay, let's go."

We walked downstairs. The young valet saw me, ran to the Lincoln. I waited at the curb less than fifteen seconds before the car was in front of me, driver's door open.

I grabbed my cell, called Cue. I asked him to send someone to Transamerica and pick up my truck and bring it back to my apartment. He said he'd take care of it.

"I owe you another one."

"You owe me more than that. But, don't worry about it."

"Thanks."

I explained to the valet that someone else would pick up my truck, and handed him two more twenties.

"Yes, sir. I'll take care of it."

With our luggage on the plane that we weren't on, we had a 2000-mile drive to do in the clothes on our backs. I figured we'd find a mall somewhere along the way and pick up a new outfit for each of us. But, I'd worry about that when the time came.

Nadia agreed to alternate driving with me. We'd each take six hour shifts, stopping for ten minutes during each break. At that rate, I hoped we'd be in Lake Point Christmas morning.

I took the 10 East out of downtown, then grabbed the 15 North in Ontario. By the time we passed through Rancho Cucamonga, Nadia and Carrie were both asleep.

Fifty Eight

We checked into the hotel suite in Lake Point at 4AM Christmas Day. We had found a mall in Iowa and picked up a new set of clothes, but decided not to wear them until we arrived in Wisconsin. We needed something clean to wear when we met the Sanders.

During the many hours of driving, I went over the case in my head. Fifty, sixty times, I went over everything. And each time I came up with the same answer. Whoever Mr. X was, he had access to my conversations. How, I wasn't sure, but Tyrone's results of my last request would either confirm or denounce what had begun to brew deep in my gut.

"Why don't you guys rest for a couple hours?"

"What're you going to do?" Nadia said.

"Tie up loose ends."

"What?"

"Don't worry. If and when anything materializes, I'll let you know."

Apparently, she was too tired to argue. "Be careful."

The room had two king-sized beds. Nadia and Carrie were going to share one bed, but I insisted that they each use a separate bed. I didn't plan on getting any sleep until after Carrie was home with her parents anyway. I jumped in the shower. By the time I dialed Tyrone's number, Nadia and Carrie were both asleep.

"What?" Tyrone said, groggy and irritated.

"It's Jack. Merry Christmas."

"Son of a bitch. Do you know what time it is?"

"About five."

"Not here it ain't. It's three in the fucking morning."

"Sorry, I forgot."

"Yeah, yeah. Merry fucking Christmas, Jack. What do you want?"

"What'd you find out?"

"Both your apartment and office are clean."

"You're sure?"

"Sure? You're fucking unbelievable. I'm a cop, for Christ's sake."

"Right, sorry."

"Anything else?"

"No, that's it."

"Good."

"Sorry to wake you up. Have a good night."

Tyrone hung up. And the pit in my stomach grew larger. With the results of Tyrone's investigation in, I was left with only one possibility.

And it made me want to throw up.

I knocked on the door just after six AM. I wondered whether he would be awake. When no one answered the door, I knocked again, louder.

"Who is it?" a sleepy female voice said.

"It's Jack Murphy."

"Jack?" She opened the door, her eyes widened. "Well, it's been a long time."

"Yes, it has."

She hugged me. "It's good to see you."

"You, too. Is he up?"

"He's on the back porch. C'mon in."

She led me through the house, opened the sliding glass door. He was sitting in a white plastic chair, sipping a cup of steaming coffee. The cold air slipped into the house. She shivered.

"Thanks," I said, walked out onto the concrete.

"Hello, Jack. I didn't expect you here."

"Why not?"

"I don't know. It's just a surprise."

"Oh."

He finished his coffee, stood up. "Let's go inside. It's cold out here."

I followed him back into the house. He refilled his cup in the kitchen. "Want a cup?"

"No, thanks."

He led me down the hall to a bedroom-turned-office. He

closed the door and sat behind a metal desk. I stood opposite the desk.

"Sit down," he said.

"No, thanks."

"Okay." He sipped his fresh coffee. "What's up?"

"I have a couple loose ends. I wanna pick your brain a little."

"Sure."

I told him about Blake, DiMarco and what I knew about the case.

"One of the problems, though," I said, "is this thing at the Santa Monica Pier. Mind if I smoke?"

"No, go ahead."

I lit a cigarette, leaned against his desk. He grabbed a glass ashtray from a drawer in his credenza, set it on the desktop.

"Thanks. When Blake knew I knew, he didn't hold back anything. But he claimed to know nothing about the incident at the pier. He also said DiMarco didn't work for him, just sold him the girls. And DiMarco sure wasn't smart enough to run that operation alone. So, the assumption is that whoever DiMarco worked for was responsible for the car going off the pier."

"Sounds reasonable."

"There're a few other things, too." I sat in a side chair across the desk, tapped my ashes into the ashtray. "I found a ledger at DiMarco's that listed payments from CB, Charles Blake. But, it also listed making payments to someone with the initials RL."

Blood rushed to his cheeks, he turned away from me. "Interesting."

"Yep."

I sat quiet for a few minutes, finished my cigarette. I smashed the dying butt into the ashtray, then stared at him. "One more thing. Only one person knew I was going to Rodeo Drive the other day, when a carload of Bloods tried to take me out."

"What're you saying? You don't think. Son of a bitch, you do. Have you ever thought that maybe someone bugged you? It's certainly possible considering the power of the players in your case."

"That's a good point. But, I had my apartment and office swept. And they came up clean."

"This is bullshit, Jack. We've known each other forever."

"There's no other explanation."

He sat for a moment, stared at me. Then, he opened his desk drawer. I had my Sig in hand by the time he came back with a cigar.

I dangled the pistol alongside the chair. Bile rose in my throat.

Roy took his time lighting the cigar. Thick puffs of smoke circled his head. "As a former police officer, you know that you haven't got a pot to piss in. And," he paused to take a hit from his cigar, "if you go blabbing this bullshit, I've got your ass on slander."

I wanted to reach across the desk and pistol whip him. Instead, I said, "Why do it, Roy? They're little kids."

"What're you now? A crusader for teenage girls?"

"No."

"You talk like these girls were innocent. They ran away from home. No happy kids were taken from their parents."

"That doesn't give you the right to exploit them just because they had problems."

"We all have problems."

"We do."

"And yours, my friend, is getting the fuck out of this house before I shoot you."

I laughed. Not because he was funny, but as a reaction to the whole situation. Everything I knew about this man whirl-pooled down the gutter. So much for my instinct. And to think, I became a PI.

"You'd better leave," he said, standing.

I straightened my arm, pointed the Sig at his chest. "Sit down, Roy."

"Fuck you."

I stood. "Sit the fuck down. Now."

He held his hands up, sat in his chair. "What?"

"Where's the money, Roy?"

"What money?"

"Stop playing games."

Roy smiled, perhaps in spite of himself. "Put the gun away."

"We're not through."

"Yes, Jack, we are. You know and I know you won't shoot me. I'm going to get up from this chair and walk out of this room. And you don't have the balls to do a goddamn thing about it."

He stayed seated.

"I want the money."

"Ooh, you're dangerously close to crossing the line, my friend."

I pulled the slide. "I know which side of the line I'm standing on. And you're no longer my friend."

"You think I'm just gonna give up what I worked years to

acquire?"

"If you wanna live, you will."

"Empty threats."

I went around the desk and pressed my pistol against his kneecap. "Are you gonna give me the money?"

"No fucking way."

I fired.

His kneecap went to bloody mush. He screamed, grabbed his leg. "You motherfucker."

"I want the money."

His expression melted from stone-cold to fearful.

"Roy? Jack?" Lisa said, knocking on the door. She tried the handle. It was locked. "Roy?"

"Answer her," I said.

"Yeah, honey, we're fine. Just a minor mishap."

"Open the door," she said.

"Ah, we're in the middle of something. I'll see you in a bit."

Lisa said something, but I didn't understand.

"I said I'll see you in a bit," Roy said.

After a moment, silence blanketed the room. "Roy, either I get the money or you lose both kneecaps."

"This is crazy, Jack."

I rammed the pistol into his still-good knee.

"Christ, Jack, don't. Son of a bitch. Okay, okay. Just put that fucking thing away."

I leaned against the desk, kept my pistol in sight. With my free hand, I flipped open my cell phone and called my friend Susan. She runs a 24-hour rehab clinic in North Hollywood, and chooses to work graveyard. I wrote down her bank information and thanked her. I set the paper on the desk. "Wire everything to this account."

Roy kept one hand clasped to his knee, picked up the phone with the other. He recited a string of numbers and his password, *chica bonita*. How fitting.

"I'd like to wire everything. Yes, I'm closing the account." He gave the person on the phone Susan's routing and account number. "Thank you. Goodbye." He glanced up. "It'll be there by tomorrow evening."

"How much?"

"Twelve million five."

"Susan'll be pleased."

"Fuck you."

"You should be pleased, too, Roy. You're dirty money is gonna help people. And you saved your other kneecap."

Roy stared.

"This is how it's gonna go."

"Oh, you're giving me orders now, Jack?"

"Damn straight, so shut the fuck up. You tell anyone what happened here today and I go public with what I know. Fuck the prosecutor, I'll go to Barbara Walters. I'll assassinate you in the media." I lit a cigarette. "In other words, you're fucked if you open your mouth."

"I get the picture."

"Good. Now, I suggest you go to the hospital and tell them what a dumb shit you are for trying to clean your loaded pistol."

I walked to the door. "Oh, and if I ever see you again, I will kill you."

On my way out, I told Lisa about Roy's unfortunate accident and that he didn't want to go to the hospital. She ran to his side, oblivious to the kind of monster she was about to help.

FIFTY NINE

I got back to the suite around ten. Carrie was in the shower. Nadia was watching TV.

"What happened?" she said.

I sat next to her on the couch, lit a cigarette. "It's a long story."

"I've got time."

"Can I have a hug?"

She wrapped her arms around me. Though I fought them, tears made their way through my tired eyes, down my face. I got lost in the moment, in her love. She didn't say anything, didn't push. She just held me.

After a few minutes, I broke the hug, kissed her cheek. "Thanks."

Her lips met mine. I tasted the sweetness of her tongue. Her arms went around my neck. And a little bit of my pain dissipated.

The door opened and Carrie stepped out of the bathroom in her new outfit. "Oops, I'm sorry."

"No, it's okay. You look béautiful," I said.

"Thank you."

Nadia wiped the tears from my cheek with an open palm, then said to Carrie, "Are you ready to see your folks?"

Carrie nodded.

"I'll call them," I said.

Carrie joined Nadia on the couch and they spoke softly. I dialed Raymond's number. He answered on the first ring.

"Hi, Raymond. It's Jack Murphy."

"What is it?" he said, his voice filled with fear.

"I have some good news."

"You found her body."

My heart sank into my gut. He had been anticipating that

Carrie's body would eventually be found. And he sounded resolved that at least he would find closure.

"She's alive."

He gasped, then cried. "Oh, my God. She is?"

"Alive and physically okay."

"Oh, my God." He shouted away from the phone. "Honey, come here. Jack found Carrie." To me, "I can't believe it. Where was she? No, it doesn't even matter. She's alive and well, that's what matters." He paused for a moment. "Does she want to see us?"

"Yes, she does."

"When's she coming home?"

"How about now?"

"Now? Where are you?"

I told him the name of the hotel.

"That's just down the street."

"Why don't you come by in half an hour? I'll meet you in the restaurant. I wanna speak to you for a moment before bringing Carrie down."

"We're on our way."

Carrie and Nadia were both hungry, so I ordered them room service. I could've used some food, too, but I didn't want to make Raymond wait another minute. I could eat after parents and daughter were reunited.

"Stay up here until I call you, okay?"

"Okay," Nadia said. "We'll eat and talk."

"Good." I leaned over, kissed Nadia's cheek. "Thank you."

She smiled. "No problem. Carrie's lots of fun to talk to."

"Thanks. I really appreciate everything you guys did."

I leaned forward, kissed Carrie's cheek. "You're welcome."

The room service was delivered as I was walking out of the room. I grabbed a piece of Nadia's bacon, shoved it in my mouth. "I owe you."

"Yes, you do. I'll collect later."

I wondered how much I'd have to pay for that piece of bacon as I walked down to meet Raymond.

Raymond and his wife were already seated when I walked into the restaurant.

"Good morning," I said, sat down.

"Yes it is," Raymond said.

His wife smiled, sipped her orange juice.

"I still can't believe you've found her."

I explained the story in wide brush strokes. I figured Carrie could fill in any details if she chose to do so.

"My God, that's horrible," he said.

"She'll need to see a psychiatrist for a while."

"Of course, but only when she's ready."

"I think she's ready now. She's been through a lot, but she's an amazing girl."

Raymond's eyes brimmed with fatherly pride. "Thank you."

"Are you ready to see her?"

"Yes, of course. But, first, this is for you."

He set a check on the table in front of me. I glanced at the amount: three million dollars.

I slid the check toward him. "Thank you, but I can't."

He pushed the check back toward me. "Yes, you can. I insist. You did what the cops and the other detective were unable to do. You brought me back my child."

I folded the check in half, put it in my shirt pocket. "Thank you."

I excused myself, called the room. Nadia said they had finished eating and were ready to come down. "I'll see you in a minute."

I sat back down. Nadia and Carrie came into the restaurant a few minutes later. Raymond jumped to his feet, met Carrie halfway across the floor. He wrapped his arms around his little girl, lifted her off the ground, and swung in a circle. His wife turned toward them but waited until they returned before wrapping her arms around her little girl. All three were crying tears of joy by the time I stood up.

"It's so good to see you," Raymond said.

"I'm sorry," Carrie said.

"For what, honey?"

"For running away."

"Now, you just forget about that. The important thing is that you're back here with us."

Nadia and I walked away.

"Oh, Jack?" Raymond said.

I turned back to face him. "Yes?"

"Merry Christmas."

"Merry Christmas, Raymond."

"You've given me the best Christmas present possible. I'll never forget that."

I had a smile on my face as Nadia and I slipped away.

"So, how does it feel to be a hero?" she said after we got to the room.

"I'm no hero."

"According to Raymond, you are."

"I'm just glad we were successful."

We sat on the couch.

"Thanks," she said.

"For what?"

"You said 'we'."

"Yeah, so?"

"So, it's nice to be included."

"You played an important part, you know."

"I'm glad you noticed."

I kissed her on the cheek. "I've got a call to make."

I called Cedars-Sinai. After telling the woman on the other end of the phone that I was Arturo's brother, she told me he had been moved into his own room. He answered the phone, sounded like he was high on morphine. Which, he told me, he was.

"Shit's great, man. I can't feel anything."

"That's good, I guess."

"Have you ever been shot?"

"Nope."

"Then you have no idea. I was shot before, but never with an AK, and never in the chest. It hurts like a motherfucker."

"I'll bet it does."

"Did you get Carrie home?"

"Yep. We met her parents a little while ago."

"I bet they were glad to see her."

"Yep. How are you doing, really?"

"I'm okay. Doctor says I'll be released in a couple days. I hope he gives me some painkillers, though. He says I'll be hurting a while."

"Just relax. I'm going to change the message on our machine. Tell them we're closed for the holidays. Nadia and I'll be back in a couple weeks."

Nadia raised her eyebrows and smiled.

"A couple weeks?" Arturo said.

"We're gonna stay here for a few days, then drive back. But, the drive back won't be as quick as the one out here."

"How long did it take you anyway?"

"We got her at four this morning, left a couple hours after the shooting."

"Good time, then."

"Great time. Cue let me borrow his Towncar so we made the trip in style, too."

"Lucky man."

"Yep."

"Now, tell me. Is Nadia going to get lucky, too?"

"We'll see."

"She better, Holmes. That's all I gotta say."

"Merry Christmas, Arturo."

"Merry Christmas. Now, give Nadia the present she's been looking forward to for so long."

"What's that?"

"Holmes, if I gotta spell it out for you, you got a serious problem."

I smiled, hung up.

I grabbed my cigarettes from the coffee table, lit one.

"So, what's this about staying for a few days?" she said.

"Feel like a vacation?"

"Sure do."

"We earned it, that's for sure. But, I have to tell you that I have an ulterior motive."

Her eyes narrowed. "You do, huh?"

"Yep."

"And that is?"

"You'll find out."

"When?"

"Soon."

She wrapped her arms around my neck, kissed me. "Does it include more of that?"

"It just might."

I joined Nadia on the couch. She was watching the Macy's Christmas Day Parade. Oh, joy.

"How's Arturo?"

"He's doped up, but sounds good. He says he'll be released in a couple days."

"That's great."

"Yep."

"What else did he say?"

"You two in cahoots or something?"

She smiled, turned to the TV. "Whatever gave you that idea?"

"Nothing. I have a plan."

"Uh-oh."

"Hey, that's the response to your plans, not mine."

She growled.

"Why don't we get some sleep, then have a nice candlelight dinner at the restaurant?"

"Okay."

I called the restaurant, made reservations for nine-fifteen at a table by the window overlooking the hotel's beautiful courtyard. The girl who made the reservation assured me it would be quiet and romantic. I thanked her, hung up.

"I have a question before we get some rest," I said.

She turned off the TV. "Yes?"

A wave of panic swept through me. Suddenly, I felt like a boy on his first date, standing at the porch with a girl, debating whether he should try to kiss her goodnight. Then, as the scared little boy, I turned and walked away. "Nothing."

"C'mon, Jack, what?"

"I'll ask you later."

"Promise?"

"I promise, after dinner."

"Okay."

She crawled onto the bed where she had slept earlier. "Join me, I won't bite."

"You won't?"

"Not unless you want me to, that is."

I smiled. "Oh, okay."

I joined her, rolled onto my back. Nadia rested her head on my chest. I wrapped my arm around her and we fell asleep.

SIXTY

The restaurant in the hotel had a distinctive Italian flair. The pale white walls glowed with a hint of orange from the overhead lights. Thin, white-lace curtains, drawn back with black velvet rope, caressed the windows. The curtain rods were forged from carved wood, stained black to match the window frames.

An overweight man in his thirties, dressed in a sleeveless black vest over a white button-down shirt, a thick bowtie, black slacks and freshly polished black Italian loafers, greeted us. "Good evening, sir, madam. Two for dinner?"

"We have reservations. Jack Murphy."

He glanced at a computer printout on the podium, nodded and smiled. "Ah, yes, sir. Right this way, please."

He grabbed two menus and a wine list from the side of the podium before directing us to a table in the corner. Each wall had a large single-pane window overlooking different sections of the courtyard. When checking in, I had gotten a glimpse of its beauty, but found it didn't compare with the evening view from the restaurant.

The *maitre d'* held out a chair for Nadia. I sat next to her. The table was strategically placed diagonal in the corner of the room so both of us had equally pristine views from our seats.

The man propped the wine list on the table, handed Nadia a menu, then me.

"Our specials tonight are Filet of Bass, freshly caught in our own Lake Michigan just this morning. It's served with potato medallions or rice pilaf, salad and garlic bread for only twenty-two ninety-five."

He rattled off four more specials before asking us whether we'd enjoy a drink before dinner. Nadia ordered a glass of champagne and I ordered a double JD on the rocks with a twist of lemon. This was how I preferred to drink JD, though I usually settled for JD straight.

He smiled and promised to return shortly. I noticed that our table was one of only a half-dozen tables that had been set up for a candlelight dinner. Two large, white candles stood on either side of a single, long-stem red rose in a clear glass vase. The lights in our corner of the room seemed to burn dimmer than the rest. Maybe it was just my imagination, but I didn't care. This was perfect.

"This sure is beautiful," Nadia said.

"Yep. I couldn't think of another place I'd rather be."

"Really?"

"Really. Or someone else I'd rather be with."

"That's so sweet."

"Maybe, but it's the truth. How's the champagne?"

"Great. And you even got your JD served as you like it."

"Yep. Are you hungry?"

Nadia smiled. "I'm famished."

"Me, too."

One of the things I most enjoy about eating dinner out is attentive, patient service. This place had it down to an art form. We didn't see the waiter again until we had decided on food. He was at our table less than a minute after the menus hit the white linen tablecloth.

Nadia ordered lasagna and I asked for cheese manicotti.

"Would you care for a bottle of wine this evening?"

I looked at Nadia. She nodded.

"What do you recommend?"

"Personally, I have to recommend *1995 Pieve di Santa Restituta Brunello Di Montalcino*. We just received a limited shipment of this extraordinary red wine. *Brunello di Montalcino* is an excellent red wine made from the *Brunello* clone of *Sangiovese* and grown around the Tuscan hillside town of Montalcino."

I held up my hand gently. "We'll take it."

He leaned toward me, softly said, "Sir, it is one-hundred seventy-five dollars for a magnum."

At that moment, I was glad I wasn't eating or I might have needed CPR. Then, I thought about the beautiful woman at my side, the perfect setting, and the check in my pocket. "Very well."

And it felt damn good to splurge, too.

I'm no expert, but at first taste, I knew this wine was something fabulous. We each drank a glass with dinner.

The waiter was careful to stay away until we needed something. The room had thinned and only a few tables were occupied, though none were within earshot.

"I want to thank you again," I said.

I motioned to Nadia with the bottle; she nodded. I refilled her glass, then refilled my own.

"You're welcome."

"And I wanted to apologize."

"You don't need to apologize."

I touched her arm, looked into her eyes. "Yes, I do. I was an asshole and you didn't deserve to be treated like that."

Her soft eyes stared into mine, not a drop of anger in them. "I understand. I was pushy. I don't know why, Jack, but I'm nuts for you."

She quickly averted her stare as if something had escaped that wasn't meant to. I kept my hand on her arm, waited for her to look back at me.

The last time I tried, fear forced me to back off. But, with the wine on top of a double JD, I found the courage to step into the territory I had avoided for so long. I assumed I knew the answer to my question, and if I was right, both Nadia and I would pass through a door that would forever close behind us.

"What were you gonna ask me before Carrie walked in on us?"

She glanced at me, then out the window. "Do you really want to know?"

"Yes, I do."

"You don't want to go there."

"I don't want to keep avoiding it, either."

She looked back at me. Her eyes filled with water. She blinked. A single tear ran down her cheek.

I brushed it away with a finger. "What's the matter?"

She fought back more tears, and succeeded. She cleared her throat. "It's just that I wanted to know how you really feel about me."

"I cherish your friendship. You mean the world to me."

"What are we, Jack?"

"What do you mean?"

"Are we friends?"

"Of course."

"Is that all we are?"

I pulled the ashtray near and lit two cigarettes, handed one to Nadia. This conversation was going exactly where I thought it would. I wasn't sure whether I wanted to bring it to its natural end, or not. Actually, I knew that I did, but I was scared to. My last relationship was with Ellen and it broke my heart. As much as I cared about Nadia, I wasn't sure I was ready to open up again.

"It doesn't have to be."

My words beat my fear, and suddenly it was there, out in the open, dangling in the air between us. In the moments while I waited for Nadia's response, I held my breath, thought I felt my heart stop.

"Do you mean that?" she said.

"Yes, I do."

She leaned forward, kissed me. "Can I tell you something?"

"Anything."

As soon as I said it, I wondered whether I really meant it. I anticipated what she'd say just before I heard the words.

"I love you, Jack."

The moment of truth. The half-second when one must make a sudden decision. Do you say the words? And, if you do, do you mean them? In that moment, I realized that I made that decision long ago. But, it wasn't until that moment that I admitted it to myself, or to her. "I love you, too."

As if I'd held up a flag, the waiter reappeared. Our glasses were empty, but we still had a couple glasses' worth left in the magnum. The waiter offered to have it brought to our room. I thanked him and signed for the check.

We walked to our room, arm in arm, Nadia's head resting lightly against my shoulder.

I closed the door to the room and we began undressing each other, locked in a kiss, inching toward the bed. By the time we reached the mattress, we were both naked, our clothes a trail of breadcrumbs to the front door.

I laid down on my right side, facing Nadia. I kissed her neck, ran my hand along her firm stomach, across her thighs. The scent of her skin flowed into me, our souls melded. I reached between her legs, touched her. She moaned softly, her legs spread further. Her hand moved to me, hardened me in an instant. Our tongues encircled one another and I rolled on top of her.

My mind drew black as I entered her. The wave deep inside me roared, crested. I fought to keep it at bay. Nadia whimpered in delight, called my name. So long had I anticipated this moment, and yet it was well beyond my dreams. I felt our souls leave us, dance their way to the heavens, play amongst the clouds in a clear blue sky.

The relentless wave approached again. Stars flashed across the landscape of my mind. Again, it roared. I reached for the roaring whitecap of the wave. Then, as a surfer who's conquered the biggest wave of his life, I rolled over it, tumbled head first into complete serenity. My mind went blank, my muscles melted into a pool of jelly on top of Nadia. She wrapped her arms around me, hugged me tight.

"I love you," she whispered.

SIXTY ONE

Tuesday morning, Nadia and I went to the airline to retrieve our luggage, and then spent the next four days touring Lake Point. It snowed every day. Nadia loved it. Snow was one thing I'd never missed.

Though I had lived in Lake Point most of my life, I hadn't realized until then how many things there were to see. We made love every day, sometimes twice, held hands everywhere we went. I was in love again. And that both thrilled and terrified me.

On Friday, the twenty-ninth, Nadia asked to visit a special site.

"Sure, anywhere."

"Anywhere?"

"Where do you wanna go?"

"To Leroy's house."

Nadia couldn't have put it any more delicately. "To Leroy's house", rather than "where Leroy was shot" or "where you shot Leroy". Still, I was taken aback, frightened at the idea. "Why?"

"Closure."

"For me?"

She walked to me, wrapped her arms around my neck. "Yes, for you."

And she kissed me.

This was not an event I had prepared for. I understood what Nadia meant by trying to bring myself closure. I had to see if the family was getting along. Actually, the father was probably still in prison doing the balance of his fifteen-year sentence, so I guess it was all about the mother. How she was coping with the loss of her child.

It was selfish, I thought, though I didn't mention it to Nadia. She seemed set on confronting this issue, or rather forcing me to confront it, and I was in no emotional position to argue. Leroy's death had haunted me since it'd happened. The feeling in the pit of my stomach when I had had to look at Leroy's bloody body behind the couch reappeared with a vengeance.

We drove to the house. I pulled to the curb. "That's it."

Dead shrubs and weeds poked through the snow-covered planters. Small patches of sickly brown grass snuck out from under the blanket of white that had enveloped the yard. Two front windows had been busted out—one was boarded, the other draped with a blue tarp. A *For Sale* sign, faded by the elements, stood at an angle near the street. No one had occupied this house in quite some time.

Nadia touched my arm. "I'm sorry."

I nodded. My stomach tightened, and I was strangely saddened that Mrs. Johnson was no longer there. After all Nadia's prodding, I was looking forward to burying this demon.

We drove back to the hotel in silence.

We decided to head back late on the thirtieth. I had motels lined up for us along the way. As comfortable as the Lincoln was, I had no interest in sleeping in it any more. We woke up on Saturday about nine, stayed in bed until two. Finally, I rolled over and order us room service.

"What do you want to do on your last day in Lake Point?" Nadia said.

"I have something in mind."

"Well, are you going to share?"

"In due time."

"I hate surprises."

"Me, too, but you'll like this one, I'm sure."

"That makes me feel much better."

"Wear your best outfit."

She set down her fork, wiped her lips on a linen napkin. "Now you have me intrigued."

"Good."

I put our dishes back on the tray and set the tray outside the door. Then, we showered together and dressed.

Though I was from Lake Point, the Kiwanis Club was somewhere I had never visited. So, I got directions from the concierge before we left. It turned out to be on the lakefront. Having time to kill, I took Nadia for a scenic cruise along

Lakeshore Drive.

From the invitation, I knew the party started at six and the bride and groom were scheduled to make an appearance about seven. Fortunately, while the Club was decorated for a party, it was not immediately apparent what type of party it had been readied for. We arrived shortly after seven.

"What are we doing here?"

"More of that closure stuff."

I parked the car, and we walked hand in hand to the entrance.

"Is this what I think it is?" she said.

"That depends on what you think it is."

I pulled the invitation from my jacket pocket.

Nadia smiled. "I thought so."

She kissed me on the cheek, and we walked inside.

It took less than thirty seconds for me to spot her. "Hello, Ellen."

"Oh, my God. Jack. I can't believe it. You came."

Ellen introduced her new husband. I introduced Nadia. We exchanged hugs, then the groom stepped off to mingle with other guests.

"I'm so happy you made it," Ellen said.

"I was on the fence for a while."

"I pushed him over," Nadia said with a smile.

"Why, thank you, my dear. I don't want any bad blood between Jack and me."

"And neither do I. Congratulations, Ellen."

"Thank you, Jack."

A slow-dance song I didn't recognize came over the speaker system. Ellen touched my arm, said, "Dance with me?"

Nadia kissed my cheek and pushed me toward the dance floor. I danced with Ellen, her head on my shoulder. And I knew at that moment things had worked out for the best. She was happy.

And as I glanced at Nadia, I realized so was I.

.

About the Author

David J. Sherman has been writing for more than twenty years. He has had short stories and poetry published, both in America and abroad. *The Dark Side* is his first mystery novel.

David has held a variety of jobs, including computer programmer, warehouse manager, truck driver, dispatcher, safety consultant, and record store owner. He has been writing fulltime since October 1998, and is an active member of Mystery Writers of America, National Writers Union, Sisters in Crime, Private Eye Writers of America, and the American Crime Writers League. He also serves on The Board of Directors for Sisters in Crime, Los Angeles Chapter.

When not writing or promoting, David spends his time at home with his family. He loves to cook, read mysteries and question life itself by contemplating the works of master lyricist Greg Graffin (Bad Religion), Nietzsche, Descartes, the Buddha, and Steven Hawking.

David was born in Racine, Wisconsin, and currently lives in Southern California with his wife, daughter and a black Labrador named Emily.

http://www.davidjsherman.com

COMING AUGUST 2003

from
Bloody Mist Press

Clouded Judgment

A Jack Murphy Novel

David J. Sherman

ISBN #1-932-30660-9

http://www.davidjsherman.com